Everyday Ideas

EVERYDAY IDEAS

Socioliterary Experience

among Antebellum

New Englanders

Ronald J. Zboray ✦ Mary Saracino Zboray

The University of Tennessee Press ✦ Knoxville

First Edition.

Ronald J. Zboray and Mary Saracino Zboray, "Cannonballs and Books: Reading and the Disruption of Social Ties on the New England Home Front," in *The War Was You and Me: Civilians in the American Civil War*, ed. Joan E. Cashin (Princeton, N.J.: Princeton University Press, 2002): 237–61.

Ronald J. Zboray and Mary Saracino Zboray, "Home Libraries and the Institutionalization of Everyday Practices Among Antebellum New Englanders," *American Studies* 42, no. 3 (Fall 2001): 63–86.

This book is printed on acid-free paper.

Zboray, Ronald J.
Everyday ideas: socioliterary experience among antebellum New Englanders/ Ronald J. Zboray and Mary Saracino Zboray. — 1st ed.
p. cm.
Includes bibliographical references and index.

ISBN 1-57233-471-1 (acid-free paper)

1. Books and reading—New England—History—19th century.
2. Literature—Appreciation—New England—History—19th century.
3. Authorship—Social aspects—New England.
4. American diaries—New England.
5. American letters—New England.
6. Literature and society—New England—History—19th century.
7. Popular culture—New England—History—19th century.
8. New England—Intellectual life—19th century.
I. Zboray, Mary Saracino, 1953– .
II. Title.

Z1003.3.N4Z36 2006
028'.9'097409034—dc22 2005019802

Contents

Part III ✦ Reception

149

Illustrations

Acknowledgments

Since we began this project in May 1992, we have accumulated many debts to people and institutions. We must first acknowledge generous support provided by the National Endowment for the Humanities at two crucial times in this book's development. In 1992, we were benefited by an NEH–American Antiquarian Society six-month resident fellowship awarded to Ronald J. Zboray that allowed us to embark upon this undertaking. Six years later, NEH once again came to our aid with a 1998–99 Fellowship for University Teachers for Ronald J. Zboray's year-long leave from teaching for writing.

We also must acknowledge the Schlesinger Library at Radcliffe College (now a unit of Harvard University), which provided a Study Grant in 1993 and, in 1998–99, dual Honorary Visiting Fellowships. During our fellowship year, the Schlesinger afforded office space and gave us a colloquium for delivering a slice of the book. We must therefore thank then–acting head Mary Maples Dunn and her staff, especially Anne Englehart, Marie Hélène Gold, Jane Knowles, Sylvia McDowell, Deirdre O'Neill, and Ellen M. Shea. We also thank Jacalyn R. Blume, with whom we recently worked.

The Massachusetts Historical Society has played an important role in our research since 1994, when it awarded the Benjamin F. Stevens Fellowship to Ronald J. Zboray. Members of the staff were then (and during our many return visits) always generous with their time and help. We are especially grateful to Peter Drummey and Brenda Lawson, who remain there, Ed Hanson, Virginia Smith, Chris Steele, and Len Travers, who have moved on, and more recent staff members Nicholas Graham and Kimberly Nusco. The director of the Center for New England Studies there and Ford Editor, Conrad Edick Wright, has enlightened our research in many ways beyond editing our essays published in volumes resulting from two MHS-sponsored conferences, one on the Boston business community (1993) and the other on Transcendentalism (1997). He also invited us to present our research at the Boston Seminar on Early American History in January 1999. Our commentators at these sessions, Robert F. Dalzell, Leo Marx, Glenn Porter, Kathryn M. Tomasek, and Alan Trachtenberg, offered invaluable insights, as did other participants, especially John L. Brooke, Dean Grodzins, Philip F. Gura, Mary Kelley, Joel Myerson, and David S. Reynolds.

The American Antiquarian Society, besides providing the NEH-funded six-month fellowship in 1992 (for which we are particularly grateful to that year's fellowship committee chair, Marcus McCorison), has also given us numerous other reasons to be thankful. During the six months we spent at the society in Worcester, Massachusetts, in 1992, we shared many illuminating conversations with readers and scholars in residence, including Victor Berch, Richard D. Brown, Daniel A. Cohen, Patricia Crain, Linda Frost, Sally Griffiths, Karen Halttunen, Bruce Laurie, Ken Moynihan, David Paul Nord, Stephen Nissenbaum, and Jane Pomeroy. We presented some of our research before them informally and at two AAS-sponsored seminars. We also wish to thank the society's entire staff, but especially Susan M. Anderson, Georgia Barnhill, Nancy Burkett, Joanne Chaison, John Hench, Thomas Knoles, Marie Lamoureux, Dennis Laurie, Joyce Tracey, Laura Wasowicz, and Sue Wolfe. More recently, Terri Tremblay has assisted us in finding illustrations. On return visits, we benefited from insights by Kathleen M. Brown, Lawrence Buell, Scott E. Casper, Harvey Green, William Gilmore, Charles Monaghan, John C. Nerone, Edward A. Pearson, David Rawson, Scott A. Sandage, Erik Seeman, and Emily B. Todd.

To the staff of the many archives we visited, we owe inexpressible thanks for graciously accommodating us when they were short of space, time, and funding. Never were any of these kind folk short of patience. Some have since left the places we first met them, but they will long be remembered by us. Others have entered our lives only within the past few years as we have followed up our research with queries and requests. Thanks go to Ellen Smith (American Jewish Historical Society), Anne M. Cadrette (American Textile History Museum), Barbara Brown and Peg Hughes (Andover Historical Society), Robert Johnson-Lally (Archdiocese of Boston), Darren J. Brown, Robert W. Lovett, and Lorraine Muise (Beverly Historical Society), David E. Horn and Ronald D. Patkus (Boston College, Department of Archives and Manuscripts), Giuseppe Bisaccia, Eugene Zepp, and Roberta Zonghi (Boston Public Library, Rare Books Department), Mary Ann Gray (Chatham Historical Society), Robin D. Wear (Clifton Waller Barrett Library, University of Virginia), Lois Hamill, Rev. Paul J. Nelligan, S.J., and Mark W. Savolis (College of the Holy Cross), Nancy Milnor and Martha Smart (Connecticut Historical Society), Mark H. Jones (Connecticut State Library), Edward Galloway (Digital Research Library, University of Pittsburgh), Leslie A. Morris and Jennie Rathbun (Houghton Library, Harvard University), Alison Dinicola (Huntington Library), Barbara Anderson and George Comtois (Lexington Historical Society), Diane Shephard (Lynn Historical Society), Christine Albert, William David Barry, Nicholas Noyes, and Elizabeth Oatley (Maine Historical Society), Karen MacInnis (Marblehead Historical Society), Judy Huenneke and Sally A. Ulrich (Mary Baker Eddy Library), Marylène Altieri (Monroe C. Gutman Library, Harvard University), Joellen El Bashir (Moorland-Springarn Research Center at Howard University), Jerry Anderson and Timothy Salls (New England

Historic Genealogical Society), Bill Copley, Betsey Hamlin Morin, and David Smolen (New Hampshire Historical Society), Andrew Boisvert, Lisa Compton, Jane M. Hennedy, and Greta Smith (Old Colony Historical Society), Daniel B. Doucette (Peabody Historical Society), Irene V. Axelrod, Lyles Forbes, Christine Michelini, and Jane Ward (Phillips Library, Peabody Essex Museum), Philip J. Weimerskirch (Providence Public Library), Dana Signe K. Munroe, Meredith Paine Sorozan, and Rick Stattler (Rhode Island Historical Society), Susan Boone, Amy Hague, and Margaret R. Jessup (Sophia Smith Collection, Smith College), W. Eric Emerson (South Carolina Historical Society) and Paul Carnahan (Vermont Historical Society). Finally, we are grateful to the staffs at the Beinecke and Sterling Libraries at Yale University, and the manuscript room at the Library of Congress.

All of this archive hopping would have been impossible without substantial intramural support from Georgia State University. First and foremost, that institution cost shared the 1998–99 NEH year, which turned what might have been a half-year release from teaching into fifteen months. Research Initiation Grants in 1994 and 1997 provided needed funds for, in the first case, graduate research assistants, and, in the second, travel through New England archives. A Quality Improvement Fund Award in 1994 funded the project's computerization. A Summer Faculty Research Grant along with a College of Arts and Sciences Outstanding Junior Faculty Award supported a long summer of travel in 1996, while another summer grant in 2000 was used to put finishing touches on the book's first draft. The History Department's 2001 Dale Alan Somers Memorial Award provided funds for last-minute quote checking in New England. It granted research leave in fall 1997 to tie up loose research ends in New England. It also provided a string of dedicated graduate research assistants: Steve Blankenship, Drew Brandon, Daniel Bronstein, R. Michael Brubaker, Robb Haberman, Christopher Hawkins-Long, William Simson, and Dale Vanderhorst.

Although recent arrivals in Pittsburgh, we have already accumulated debts. The Hillman Library's remarkable PALCI and interlibrary loan staff worked miracles. The faculty and students of the Department of Communication at the University of Pittsburgh deserve our warm thanks, for they have encouraged our work in many ways.

Throughout the years we have benefited from our various presentation commentators' advice: Norma Basch, Janet L. Coryell, Hazel Dicken Garcia, Robert A. Gross, E. Jennifer Monaghan, Marilyn Ferris Motz, Tamara Plakins Thornton, Alison Scott, Barbara Sicherman, and Deborah van Broekhoven. Finally, we wish to thank several scholars who do not fit into any of the above categories but have assisted us in numerous different ways. These include Thomas Augst, Charles Capper, Ken Carpenter, Joan E. Cashin, Barbara Cloud, John Y. Cole, Phyllis Cole, Cathy N. Davidson, Donald G. Davis Jr., Ellen Gruber Garvey, Karen V. Hansen,

Leon Jackson, David Jaffee, Greg Kucich, Thomas C. Leonard, Lucy Maddox, Ann Smart Martin, James L. Machor, Michael D. Pierson, Jonathan Rose, Eleanor Shevlin, Lydia Shurman, Wayne Wiegand, and Thomas Wortham. David Katzman and Norman Yetman have permitted us to use pieces of our "Home Libraries" in chapters 2, 5, 6, and 11. Princeton University Press granted us use of our "Cannonballs and Books" essay in the epilogue. Finally, Kenneth Silverman, a graduate advisor to one of us but a model scholar to both, has given generously of his time in support of us over the years, but he has been even more generous than he could ever realize with his faith in us, for which we are forever appreciative.

Our experiences with the University of Tennessee Press have been only the most pleasurable. We owe our deepest thanks to Joyce Harrison, former acquisitions editor, who, from our manuscript's earliest inception to its passage through the specialist reader review process, took an enthusiastic interest in publishing it. Her successor, Scot Danforth, caught that enthusiasm and in numerous ways helped us bring the revised version through to its copyediting phase. Our very able copyeditor, Karin Kaufman, made just the right changes in wording, ferreted out elusive inconsistencies, and helped us authorize a complex set of proper names and references. Stan Ivester, our managing editor, always kept our book on target and promptly answered our queries. Finally, we wish to thank our two anonymous specialist readers for their thoughtful insights and helpful criticism.

Introduction

On 12 September 1853, Charles M. Cobb, the seventeen-year-old son of a Woodstock, Vermont, hardscrabble farmer, got up early as usual, breakfasted on "potatoes, butter, sweet-cake, & half a water-melon," complained about the cold weather, condemned an antisocial neighbor's gossip, and, sometime before eight o'clock in the morning, read "The Tree of Knowledge" in a borrowed *Harper's Magazine*. The tragic story concerned a brilliant German metaphysicist so obsessed with understanding life's essence that he sequestered himself from loved ones to experiment in his laboratory with electrically produced organisms. After toxic fruit from a tree he created from these charges killed his young wife, he was left alone to contemplate man's hubris. Affected, Cobb wrote a lengthy philosophical response to the story that morning in his diary:

> I read in Harper's Magazine about a man's studying intensely, and finally by means of galvanism, making a plant grow without any seed—('twas fiction of course, but *might* be true I think). He transplanted it into his garden & it grew, but bore fruit which were deadly poison, and which poisoned his family to death & nearly did the same for him. Well if that story might be true, then men might have grown out of the earth without being created, and would do so again if every living thing were now destroyed, both animal and vegetable. But they wouldn't grow at first, no[r] would animals, and 'twould be almost an eternity before the earth would be as well peopled again as it is now. This is Atheism—holding that the principles of nature have been creating and perfecting systems and planets forever, & will be forever. [E]very man has a little of that principle in him and it *doesn't die with him either*—it only assumes another form, and presently perhaps another man gets the use of some of the same share. But I can see again that a man gets the use of two different kinds of that principle—1st what he eats, lives on, & has in his body, which I spoke of above, and 2dly what he knows, i.e., his mind, which I hardly believe can be produced from the first. At least I've never read of a philosopher's producing mind from cabbages, tho' perhaps it is REALLY done in the human system, and Daniel Webster['s] mind has now assumed the vegetable form. But this doesn't seem agreeable. I know that a full grown

man knows more than an infant, and I don't know why his extra portion of intellect isn't produced from what he eats, smells and breathes, & how if it is admitted to be so, then it must be admitted that that intellect must lose its identity when his body does, & return with it to the dust, to be used by something else. That is—a man's intellect strengthens with his body, decays with his body, dies with his body, and both assume another form. No particle of matter can be destroyed or lost—it may assume another form, and so it is with a particle of LIFE. Life is the same whether animal o[r] vegetable, though vegetable life is the most alloyed with matter, but vegetable life produces animal life as every one that eats knows, and let animal life decay & 'twill produce vegetable life. And life exists in all matter in a latent or inactive state,—at least I BELIEVE it does and the principle of life which a man may have in him sometime now carries the earth round the sun, or helps do so, and that if all animal or vegetable life were destroyed from off the earth—as it can't be—but say if it were chaos again, and no life existed, life would spring up again. Life at work made this system in space. It then made vegetables, animals, finally man, and no one knows what 'twill be engaged in making during *the remainder* of all eternity, nor what it's making now, though I know what a small portion of it is making. But all this don't account for the creation of life itself, and space for it to work in. That subject men might as well let alone. We know nothing of living before we came here, and why can we expect to preserve our identity hereafter. [T]here is nothing created when a man or a dog is born, for what little intellect he then has is nothing but matter in a fine state. When a chicken is hatched out it has intellect, but let a person eat the egg beforehand and he guzzles that intellect entire, and finds it nourishing. In order to make it reasonable to suppose that a man lives after death, it has to be assumed that he has something in him altogether different from mind, called soul, which is created when he is born and which isn't matter in any way—has no form, weight or location of course—is nowhere of course—must be somewhere, and so on. At first I didn't think that mind was matter, but soon saw that it was, for it is produced from it, and produces it. But that doesn't prove but what a man has a soul that isn't mind, —nor can it be proved that he has, only by *faith*. A man certainly knows more than a dog, but that doesn't prove that his mind isn't matter, while it is admitted that a dog[']s is, but on the contrary, phrenology shows that a man ought to know more [than] a dog, horse or elephant, without saying that he has a soul. SO ends the fracas, no

> one can reason farther, backward or forward, and folks have the acknowledged right to believe what they have a mind to about it. —the Bible, Koran, book of Mormon Swedenborg & the spirits, or Thomas Paine.[1]

In his complex reaction, one can almost see Cobb puzzling through the implications of what was, for him, a disturbing scenario laid out in the story, even though he strayed far from the text. If life could indeed spring from virtually nothing, then perhaps there was no divine creator. Furthermore, he reasoned, if nature sustains itself without a divine force, then particles of living things, including humans, never truly die; they are merely recycled in new strains of life. But, he reminded himself, life itself is the body *and* mind; is the mind therefore created out of material particles and recycled too? As unsatisfactory as that seemed, he eventually concludes that, yes, the mind and its accumulated storehouse of knowledge was material because it is dependent upon the body's health and dies with the body. However, that mind-body synthesis cannot explain the origins of life itself, which the *Harper's* story hypothesized began in electrically charged gas. Nor, Cobb argues, does the fact that material regenerates itself ensure that any living being will have an eternal identity. If one is to believe in immortality, there must be something else, something nonmaterial, at work beyond the life principal. That is the soul, but, he maintains, its existence is a matter of faith. All the knowledge in the world will never prove what the heart believes.

Sophisticated for their sly humor, metaphysical complexity, philosophical relativism, and humanistic understanding, Cobb's ideas crystallized in a very small world. He only infrequently attended the town's inferior local school. The general store offered a very limited selection of books and newspapers, if he could afford them, and the neighbors from which he borrowed had even fewer. He seldom ventured outside of Woodstock, a town of but 3,041 people in 1850; the very notion of traveling to Boston, a city with a population forty-five times larger, terrified him. Yet his perception of himself within a larger universe shines through his words. The "principle of life which a man may have in him," he believed of himself and all other human beings, is one with the principle that "now carries the earth round the sun." He knew he did not think in a vacuum but as part of humanity, for he ventured that "every man has a little of that principle in him and it *doesn't die with him either*—it only assumes another form, and presently perhaps another man gets the use of some of the same share." Cobb put his belief into practice by sharing his thoughts with posterity through a diary. Upon his death, a part of his mind would remain if only his daily records survived. Fortunately, they did. He did not think his scrawl, especially what he wrote about the stories and books he read, worth much to anyone.[2] Yet however small his world might have been, he had a desire to communicate his ideas about literature.

Ideas generated from literature were central to other antebellum New Englanders, too. Because these folks so commonly put ideas to work in their everyday lives, as Cobb did to puzzle through his doubts over humanity's divine origins, they could hardly subscribe to an easy division between mind and matter. Ideas simply seemed too real, too present in day-to-day social existence for that. They were viewed as material, somewhat like the minds born of cabbages that horrified Cobb. Like matter, thoughts and ideas had structure, substance, and animation. One could "catch" ideas or lose them. They could be "flying around" or they could "run through" the mind. A schoolboy joked he would "keep on my boots so the ideas could not get through my thick soles." As material, ideas could also grow and reproduce, for "'[t]hought engender[s] thoughts,'" and in multiplying, "each new idea serves to strengthen the superstructure" of the mind "little by little," just "[a]s the coral reef grows atom by atom." But ideas, like a misplaced set of keys, might "seem to have vanished" altogether only to reappear when least expected. Because ideas were pliable and malleable, they could be harnessed, but to do so was often difficult. "[Th]oughts will wonder of[f]," one young woman complained. "I try to keep them together, but they will not stay." "My thoughts are the most rambling, chaotic things imaginable," another New Englander claimed. "How shall I learn to control them . . . [?]" As independent as they seemed, ideas were hardly disembodied from their creators or receivers. A "fanciful idea" had an "authoress," for example. Ideas could be transmitted from writers' minds in several ways. A person could read prodigiously and have a "head full of literature & overflowing" or could "transfer . . . the ideas of authors" to paper by excerpting in letters to friends and family or paraphrasing in diaries. Authors not only contributed new thoughts but also expressed other people's ideas for them. "I wish I had the power to clothe my thoughts in language," one woman reflected, "but it is only in others' writings that I find my meaning adequately expressed." Likewise, "New ideas in abundance" might be hatched by listening to public lecturers. Everyday ideas, those of common thinkers, seemed so real because they arose from one's own experience and from learning that of other people. As one father wrote to his daughter, "[S]oon you will be drinking-in beautiful experiences, giving you ideas which will doubly interest me." These people thus were aware that ideas resulted from giving and getting, seeing and hearing, reading and listening, doing and watching—in short, action and experience.[3]

With ideas materially meaning so much to them, little wonder that antebellum New Englanders achieved one of history's most literate—and literary—societies, from its wealthiest to its poorest members.[4] Few populations have made literature and the ideas they got from it as much a part of their everyday lives. These folks did not just consume reading matter or attend lectures to kill time, but, rather, reflected deeply about their literary experiences and applied the results of their thinking to their social world. Luckily, they did not leave these experiences unrecorded. Indeed, perhaps no other people left as many emotionally and intellectually rich diaries and letters concerning their encounters with literature. Many of them did all this with little formal education and often in the face of sunrise-to-sundown workdays for little gain. The literary encounters that nearly a thousand men, women, and children discuss in four thousand or so of their diaries, letters, and other manuscripts form the basis of this book.[5] Its pages resound with the voices of seamstresses, housewives, domestics, mill workers, farmers, seamen, businessmen, lawyers, doctors, ministers, students, clerks, and even California-bound Forty-niners. Protestant, Catholic, and Jew, the churched and the unchurched alike, testify here, as do African Americans, Native Americans, and Irish immigrants. Testimony comes from all over the region, but also from New Englanders traveling across the United States and abroad, and from those at sea. Together, they report numberless encounters with literature and do so often eloquently and revealingly, indeed, at times with almost shocking candor.

They speak here directly in their own words to the hearts of current-day readers. We hear a preliterate toddler's first words as he opens a book to imitate his parents reading aloud. Neighbors knowing the value an elderly man placed upon his library risk their lives to save it from a devastating fire. A young woman mourning the loss of a literary confidante inscribes ghostly verses from her via a spiritual medium. A lonely seaman writing to his wife on a still, clear night supposes he could read by moonlight reflected in schools of shiny fish swarming around his ship. Hearty mariners gather around a ladies' magazine fashion plate to debate the proper name for a cut of sleeve. After hearing Ralph Waldo Emerson lecture on walking in nature, a black schoolteacher fancies strolling with him. Characters from a novel by James Fenimore Cooper enter the dreams of a homesick Salem woman in China. A law student muses over poetry to leaven long study hours. Poorly paid mill workers create a mutual lending society so they can share various volumes, including John Milton's *Paradise Lost*, James Philip Bailey's *Festus*, and Sir Walter Scott's *Lady of the Lake*—poetry they could not afford on their own. A recent widow taking up a novel for solace describes it as "mental Chloroform." A Maine frontier woman on her deathbed solemnly summons neighbors to give them the first and last books she owned.[6] From birth to death, these people course down the river of life in boats ladened with literature. In deteriorating diaries and fading letters scattered among nearly three dozen libraries and local historical societies we visited over the last twelve years, these people testify to their literary life journeys and bear witness to the journeys of others.

These readers refashioned ideas gleaned from literature into webs of local knowledge that were spun out through social ties. Insofar as ideas themselves became everyday, common social experience became literary as genre conventions structured thinking and interpersonal expression. Literary experience unfolded in often dense networks of kin, friends, and neighbors, deeply imbuing it with social relations and implicating it in them. Most basically, literature supported family life and socializing. This was especially true when people read materials out loud to others—the most common type of reading practice. As one New Englander explained, "[W]here we all hear the same we are more apt to converse about the subject, & thus its most prominent features are fixed in the mind, & new ideas elicited upon it."[7] People talked so much about literature that authors became like old friends, a part of the daily social fabric. Literature thus became familiar or neighborly, simply a part of living. Being so fundamental, socioliterary experience seeped into every nook and cranny of life. Beyond the printed page, it also trickled into lecture halls, schools, theaters, commemorations, commencements, and churches, where composed texts were read or declaimed for public scrutiny. Literary allusions flitted through popular songs, and fictional characters appeared on bed hangings, wallpapers, and other consumer goods throughout the home. On a deeper level, literature filtered into the very hearts of people struggling to maintain social relations threatened by rapid economic change, ever-distant residential moves, and the hazards of childbirth, accidents, and disease. Shared ideas from reading, letter writing, diary keeping, and discussion helped keep loved ones close and social ties intact.[8]

Everyday Ideas provides a comprehensive picture of how the social and literary dimensions of human existence related in antebellum New England. We concentrate less on who responded to what, when, where, and how (we discuss this generally below, while specifics are apparent in the ensuing chapters) and more on what literary encounters meant to readers and listeners in the social contexts of their lives as they went about producing, disseminating, and receiving literature. To each of these activities, we devote a separate part. In Part I, "Production," we consider these folk as diarists and letter writers, then, in turn, as compilers of authors' words and writers of private literature. Part II, "Dissemination," follows literature as it courses through letters, is presented as gifts, is lent and borrowed, and is broadcast orally. Part III, "Reception," considers literary socialization, constraints upon reading, various modes of reading, group engagements with spoken literature, encounters with books' and periodicals' physical properties, and, finally, reactions to words on the page. The "Epilogue" traces the fate of antebellum socioliterary experience into the Civil War era, when it becomes both less social and less literary.

Mode of Presentation

In presenting this material, we chose to emphasize our informants' voices rather than spotlighting our own interpretive performance. Since our research design was inductive (accumulating material, structuring and engaging it, and developing generalizations from it), our mode of presentation reflects the same spirit. Throughout the book, we offer generalizations derived from our grasp of the full documentary base, and then we supply specific evidence, via quotes or paraphrases, from a few illustrative cases cited in the notes. We otherwise minimized our interjections in the name of permitting our informants to speak for themselves directly to readers and, indeed, to one another, as if all were sitting around the same table. After all, we could never match the nuanced and varied ways they describe their own experience. Moreover, their life writings are so infused with literary sensibilities and social consideration that they provide prima facie evidence in support of our main point. A book about past experience should more demonstrate it in its original context than discuss it in today's academic idioms.

To be sure, this is a book about collective experience, as several voices speak, not always in unison, to support our generalizations. Our use of multiple perspectives upon common practices meant treating the time period as a single cultural moment, a standard practice among cultural historians. Such a synchronic approach to presenting collective lived experience has a distinct advantage: it allows us to represent the broad richness of the socioliterary experiences our informants report. For, as we will see, literary engagements were deeply social not in just a few areas of everyday life but also across a wide cultural terrain. We present our informants' recorded experiences as evidence of a way of life that persisted in the region during the antebellum years, much as archaeologists reconstruct cultures from assemblages of surviving objects. Like these investigators, we are more concerned with understanding larger persisting patterns than tracing minute changes in patterns over time. Since we aim to establish what literature meant to antebellum New Englanders, we also make no claims that any one (or clusters) of the practices and observations are unique to this group; precedents for many could be found far back in early modern Western Europe. We claim, modestly, however, to have captured the pattern's particularity—the way the various elements were put together. The result, we hope, offers to readers the essence of competency, the basic knowledge required to engage socioliterary life then as a virtual insider, to experience it vicariously through our informants' eyes and ears. A key demand of experiential history is to remain as true as possible to the unpolished language of diarists and correspondents speaking from the heart. In this vein, one of them once wondered "if the world would not think the better of us if our entire hearts could be laid open to its view." We have allowed this New Englander and hundreds of her contemporaries to lay their hearts open to readers who otherwise would never have heard their beatings.[9] And we believe that the world will think better of them.

Who Engaged What Text, When, and Where

Who are these people?[10] Two main groups appear in these pages: diarists and letter writers who provide the main evidence for this book (our informants) and the people whose socioliterary experiences they describe (their subjects). In practice, the boundary between the two blurs because, on the one hand, some writers' best reporting is about their own experiences; on the other hand, the experiences of those upon whom writers report are often conveyed verbatim or through paraphrase, so they, too, can "speak" in their own voices, albeit mediated by the reporters.

Despite the overlap, this book summons much testimony from avid readers or lecture goers who kept extensive diaries or sustained intensive literary correspondence over years and consequently have the most articulate insights into cultural practices surrounding literary experience. Anthropologists have traditionally consulted such key informants among living subjects to study cultures. Historians, in pursuit of verisimilitude, however, must instead call upon "dead informants" by carefully and faithfully reconstituting their ideas and habits through the written words they left and using that as evidence of the group's everyday life.[11] A disadvantage, of course, is that historians cannot interview the dead informant, while an advantage is that their presence cannot affect the testimony's quality. Also, like some anthropologists, historians pursuing literary experience through personal documents become "participant observers" insofar as their understanding emerges via deliberate suppression of their cultural identity through close, disciplined engagement with the full text—not just the relevant parts—left by the dead informant. Historians must live vicariously yet observantly through the key informant's textual representation of everyday life.

In selecting informants, key and otherwise, we avoided people regarded by contemporaries as notable intellectuals whose thought and writings had directly impacted the superstructure, that part of society most formally devoted to making, propagating, and evaluating ideas. Most of our diarists and correspondents probably never published more than a letter in a newspaper, if anything at all, nor did most speak formally before the public. Even the small proportion who would lecture or see some of their essays, poems, pamphlets, and books in print before 1861 did not earn their living in this manner.[12] The vast majority of diarists and letter writers were ordinary in the conventional sense of simply being unremarkable socially; they were people who were commonly encountered among the masses. However, in a complex society like antebellum New England, with its myriad social types, using only a few key informants (anthropologists' common practice) cannot do. Yet how many informants must be summoned before social and personal differences cease to distort the bigger picture of shared patterns?

The answer to that question came largely through our archival fieldwork. The study group of informants emerged from several visits beginning in May 1992 to dozens of New England archives (and a few from outside the region), where finding aids led to the local cache of diaries and family correspondence. We selected documents to achieve the widest social and geographical representation possible and examined them to see if they contained any reference to literature. If so, we next engaged the evidence in the field. If time permitted (as it did in almost all instances), we read the entire document and transcribed word for word every literary encounter that appeared in it which seemed relevant (we noted pertinent biographical details, too). We kept going from archive to archive, transcribing until sufficient repetitions of practices or responses were occurring to justify an end to our collecting. That point of redundancy eventually occurred more than five and a half years after archival work began.[13] By this point, too, the general outlines of the study had come into focus.

The result was that 931 informants, most of whom left diaries or letters, contributed material in which they describe the socioliterary experiences of themselves and at least five thousand subjects they observed.[14] Including these subjects means that we can gain insight into not only informants' reading but also that of the people around them, many of whose own records did not survive or were never kept to begin with. So people who neither kept diaries nor wrote letters are well represented. Our informants provide insight even into literary experiences of nonreading listeners of texts read aloud—often children yet learning to read or adults with failing eyesight. The informants seldom distinguish themselves from these subjects as somehow different in their literary practices from people who keep diaries or are avid correspondents.[15] In short, our informants represent broad numbers in more ways than one.

Yet the word "representative" takes on another dimension when used to describe evidence for experiential history. The key question becomes: Is the testimony provided by the informants representative of their and other people's overall literary experiences? A sociologically representative sample of the population would by no means guarantee a yes to this question, yet we did try to include as many types of people as possible in order to reduce whatever biases might have inhered in the sources themselves. Since we did not keep running tabs on types of people, one rough indication that we achieved some randomness in our selection is that it resulted in roughly equal numbers of men and women.[16] Just about every major occupational endeavor appears, too.[17] The simplest breakdown, perhaps, reflects the ten categories used by the 1850 census compendium. The defects of the census categories are immediately obvious because they cannot be made to accord with our modern notions of class, but still they provide a rough way of establishing that we covered the full ground of occupational types.[18] When occupational groupings of our adult male informants—the census left women's occupations virtually uncounted—are compared with those for all New England, the top three categories, Commerce, Agriculture, and Labor, remained in the same ranked order but with somewhat smaller percentages. The category "Sea and river navigation" was only two percentage points higher among our informants than in the census.[19] The relative percentage of our informants departs most dramatically from the census in three professional categories: "Law, medicine, and divinity," "Other pursuits requiring education," and "Government Civil Service."[20] Of course, the overrepresentation of these three categories among our selection of diarists and correspondents is due to the simple fact that these occupations required a good deal of reading and writing, so those engaged in them left more of a "paper trail" for modern historians. After we had reached the representative proportion, we could have simply closed ourselves off from further information from these three categories. We persisted in including them, however, because these occupations play such an important role in the overall story of literary experience, which underscores the point we made above that the quality of testimony is more important than quantitative adherence to sociological representation.[21] In any case, because we usually use occupational descriptions to refer to informants unnamed in the book's chapters, it will be clear when any members of these or any other occupational groups speak.

Attributes other than occupations are even harder to discern and thus to measure. Religion is a case in point; apart from the usually obvious identities of Catholics and Jews, the most common type of Protestant affiliation stopped short of full church membership and can only be described as a tenuous persuasion. Yet based on internal evidence of affiliation in the documents we consulted, this is much more than a study of Congregationalists and Unitarians who usually dominate histories of this time and place: there are also agnostics and atheists, Baptists, Episcopalians, Methodists, Millerites, Quakers, Spiritualists, and Swedenborgians, to name a few. Similarly, we have testimony from adherents of all major parties and most partisan factions, such as Democrats, Anti-Masons, Whigs, Free-Soilers, Republicans, and Constitutional Unionists. Leading activists, rank-and-filers, and closet sympathizers on all sides of the temperance and slavery issues are here, too. Along with dominant white ethnic groups, Irish (Catholic and Protestant), French, Native Americans, and African Americans are included among our informants and subjects. Indeed, we include a greater proportion of the latter group in our informant base than was present in the region in 1850.[22] Age was easier to ascertain but more difficult to quantify, since most informants wrote over several years and some over many. In any case, on the basis of year of birth, all age groups are included in the informant pool, even some octogenarians and nonagenarians.[23]

This varied informant pool, which we assembled from thirty-five archives, contributed 3,799 documents to our study.[24] These documents were virtually all in manuscript form, and few had been used by previous researchers. Hence the bulk of material we quote is appearing in print here for the first time.[25] About three-quarters of the items used were letters. Diaries, though a fifth of the whole, yielded more information, however, because each volume of many pages counted as one document, while letters were usually much shorter. The remaining documents are a miscellaneous lot, ranging from postmasters' records and library charge ledgers to personal account books and handwritten amateur newspapers.[26] The breakdown of numbers of items cannot begin to get across the extent of the testimony they contain, for our final transcriptions totaled about two million words. After we accumulated this information in the field, we systematically reread the transcribed material in order to devise analytical categories based on what readers themselves were saying, in view of structuring the eventual book manuscript. We created about nine hundred categories, arranged hierarchically leading up to the three major aspects of literary experience reflected in the material: production, dissemination, and reception, our book's three parts.[27]

As we plugged passages of text into the categories, we were surprised that there were few recurring titles of books or periodicals, but this simply reflects the nature of the material and the practices it represents.[28] Though we did not undertake a systematic overall count of titles of imprints and specific lectures or other oral performances, we did so for about a third of our textual material. This alone resulted in 3,401 titles, with no increase in repetitions to suggest that the number would soon level off. We estimate that our informants and subjects reported they encountered at least seven thousand, but perhaps as many as ten thousand, separate titles—a fair proportion of everything published in the United States and probably well beyond half the number produced in New England.[29] Such proliferation of titles, however, cannot be easily boiled down to meaningful numbers in relation to numbers of readers.[30]

The overwhelming number of titles our informants and subjects read grew from the peculiar and transitory nature of the contemporary book trade, which had yet to undergo full industrial consolidation, under a regime of a relatively few heavily marketed "best sellers" (there were some before the Civil War, of course). This alone marks the antebellum years as deserving of special focus in the nation's literary history, something not lost on generations of scholars studying the so-called American Renaissance, lasting from the 1830s into the 1850s. During these years, the region's literature has been seen as reaching "its peak of distinction." It was a time of literary development in other publishing areas, too, ranging from a cheap-fiction paperback revolution beginning in the mid-1840s to the foundation of the first successful "ladies magazines." The lyceum and public lecture blossomed and spread, giving local speakers a forum and national figures a circuit from which they could make a living, if they chose. With this dramatic regional surge in literary development coinciding with the huge documentary base of letters and diaries bequeathed by ordinary New Englanders, it is clear why we chose this site and time for study. We examine the very soil from which the "flowering of New England," one of the most significant and creative periods in the cultural history of the United States, bloomed.[31]

Our book, as its subtitle indicates, covers the antebellum period, which by definition ends with the start of the Civil War, the firing on Fort Sumter in April 1861, but which traditionally has had a very vague onset. We go along with the terminus and limit our informants' reports to the end of the month the war started.[32] Our epilogue, however, traces the experiences of twenty-seven of our informants (and their families and correspondents) into the Civil War. The terminal point at first glance may seem somewhat arbitrary for an overview of popular intellectual history; nevertheless, it reflects, as we will see, the material's changing nature, which suggests the war opened a new chapter in experiential life.[33] After all, during wartime, it is not unusual that social relations become strained or in other ways altered, but the Civil War disrupted them with unusual force and permanency in the region. The starting point for our study follows tradition and "peters in" during the late 1820s and increases thereafter. A common beginning point for historians has been Andrew Jackson's 1828 election as president, won against New Englander John Quincy Adams. In the ensuing years, the region's political influence waned while its cultural influence gained—again, as seen in the American Renaissance, dominated by Yankees, as well as in abolitionism, reform, and evangelicalism. Our account, we believe, helps to explain why this was so, but it also recognizes the peculiar economic undergirding of the move from colonial scarcity to antebellum abundance in regional literary culture. For the 1830s saw the rapid development of a regional rail network aided by increasingly regular coastal transportation, which together helped to play down urban-rural divergences evident since the colonial era due to the geography of inland areas. The transportation development allowed people (including public lecturers and itinerant book agents) to get around, or circulate on a predictable schedule through the mail and parcel post, all matter of manuscript and printed material. The industrially inspired business boom of the early nineteenth century affected the printing trades as well, bringing with it a good deal of elasticity to meet market demand. The cheap blank books and ever cheaper stationery that our informants scratched their life writings upon were only one product of book-trade development. Finally, the destabilizations due to economic development had scattered people around the region and nation, indeed, around the world in search of making a living or simply trying to keep families together; this created a powerful incentive to keep in touch with distant loved ones, even if they were as close as the next town. Letter writing and sending print matter was one way to do this, short of visiting.[34] In brief, the raw materials, the motives, the means, and the methods were all in place to encourage a rich local literary culture, which naturally registered in diaries, letters, and other personal writing by our informants. The distribution of these writings over time reflects these developmental considerations, for they increase in bounds, by decade, beginning with nearly eight hundred in the thirties and more than double that in the fifties. This growth mirrors, more or less, increases in the region's general population and upticks in its economy.[35]

Where did these people reside? While about 85 percent of our informants were strewn throughout the region's six states at the time they wrote, the remainder could be found in all the nation's other regions, sailing the high seas, or in other countries, ranging from Canada to China. Travelers afforded particularly rich insights, for people away from home tended to be more aware of habitual practices they missed while roaming.[36] Within New England, the greater Boston region (the eastern third of Massachusetts and southeastern New Hampshire) dominates in terms of the number of documents originating there. The reason for the disbalance is clear: within the emerging greater urban systems, correspondence boomed, largely because of infrastructural links but also because of services (like express companies) that utilized those links to maximum efficiency. The point has been made regarding the enormous upsurge in city-to-country business correspondence, but our findings suggest that family letter writing was also stimulated within this system.[37] In any case, our close reading of the letters has revealed few town-country distinctions in socioliterary experience, apart from obvious differences in rural opportunities, such as a more limited selection of lectures to attend or fewer local libraries or book retailers. Nor were there many distinctions in socioliterary experience between different types of cities and towns (such as market centers or factory villages).[38] Nevertheless, such intensive geographical coverage was necessary to establish that the cultural patterns we unearthed were expressed throughout the region.

Still, we must stop short from calling what we have done definitive; there simply are too many more diaries and letters yet to be analyzed. As new information is brought to light, new patterns may emerge, but we strongly suspect that they will not deviate too much from what we have described in this book. We hope that the book may act as a baseline for future research, especially of the in-depth sort on the literary experiences of specific people, families, and communities in this time and place. Only then may we more fully understand how the everyday interacts with both subjectivity and literary engagement. Only then, too, may antebellum New Englanders' "entire hearts . . . be laid open," as the informant we mentioned earlier would have it, for the world to "view."

Part I

Production

Antebellum New Englanders not only consumed published material but also produced their own "literature" and disseminated it among family members, neighbors, and friends. Although their end product was sometimes amateurish, everyday writers showed by spontaneously imitating genres that they could not help but think in a literary manner. Literature was embedded deeply enough in their consciousness as to structure it.[1]

The most pervasive everyday literary creations were personal diaries and letters. These "texts of life" detailed, explained, and often embellished the events of a life. By the antebellum years, diaries, kept by literate people of all classes, were generally (but by no means always) becoming longer, more complex, varied, secular, and bellestristic than their more religiously focused spiritual antecedents, which were largely kept by the upper crust. Personal letter writing, too, had become democratized and more stylistically expressive as increasing numbers of migrants struggled to communicate across distances. As one's own story, letters and diaries, however, challenged writers to represent themselves accurately. To do this meant accounting for the literature passing through their hands and recruiting it to tell their tales. Little wonder so many of these diaries and letters are literary. These documents provided outlets not only for prose writing but also for versification, fine penmanship, and illustrating. They also served greater social purposes. People filled diaries with accounts of social activities in the name of loved ones or wrote their diaries collaboratively. Even "secret" journals fell into other people's hands. Personal letters, of course, were almost always social in that they maintained relations and discussed shared literary experiences.[2]

These creators also produced new works, editions, or anthologies out of existing ones.[3] *With printed materials ever more cheaply available, people were inspired to refashion already published materials, even if it meant mutilation, into new formats. Such "texts from texts" included scrapbooks of periodical clippings and commonplace books loaded with literary excerpts. By assembling these materials, compilers subtly transformed them, the whole exceeding the sum of the parts, but literature could be altered in other ways as well. Readers who scratched marginalia in books concocted a unique edition, as did spiritualists who supposedly transcribed messages from the Great Beyond. People who ill committed favorite lines to memory created variant "mental editions," while those with foreign-language skills improvised loose translations. Like texts of life, texts from texts were social productions. They were usually collaboratively contrived for the pleasure of others' eyes.*

Ordinary folk produced original literature, too. Although "social authorship," or writing without printing as an end, predates this era, it now implicated a wider range of people trying their hand at something literary. They tackled the full range of genres, including poetry, humorous pieces, cartoons, speeches, manuscript newspaper copy, genealogies, histories, and fiction. Most effusions intentionally remained unpublished, yet they had an audience: they were often requested by other people, read in social settings, or given away as literary gifts. Because literary dabblers shared with prominent authors similar joys and anguish of coming before a public, their affinity and appreciation for their renowned counterparts only deepened.[4]

Part I unfolds from private expressions of letters and diaries to writings employing more formalized literary conventions. We thus consider, in turn, writing "texts of life," creating "texts from texts," and devising original pieces for local social networks. Throughout, we emphasize the remarkable depth of these writers' commitment to weaving literature through their social lives.

Chapter 1

Creating the Text of Life: Motives and Practices of Diarists and Correspondents

Twelve-year-old Charles Cobb began a memoranda book in October 1848 with a simple entry, a stark chronicle of his everyday life: "James Cobb came up to get some apples of Father but did not. Jeremy Cox threshed oats for Father in the afternoon. Fair." Less than a year later, the farm boy had become a diligent diarist who concocted a mock "newspaper" called "The Vermont Collection," filled with songs, original comical stories, and puzzles—a rich record of his everyday ideas. In "No. 4 Extra," he set a new direction, resolving to merge his older biographical and recent literary approaches. "Friends, This little nothing is to inform you," he announced to an imaginary reading public, "that afters [*sic*] this our Collection will not be all trash, and foolery." He would now present his very life in literary terms: "We will have a Memorandum and a History of the great Author's life in it, instead of a few good-for nothing stories or rather, scraps." Yet he immediately vowed to cast his autobiography in a social light, as he promised it would be "a history of the World." In this "Extra," he thus mentally fused his two prior identities as a writer: the faithful scribe of mundane events and the imaginative scribbler. For potential "readers" within his social world, he had refashioned himself as an "Author" of a unique work, his own "text of life." He would continue writing until November 1862, by which time he had produced thirty-two volumes, brimming not only with daily entries but also with copies of letters, other people's memoranda (with his own commentary), original essays, lectures, and comic sketches, as well as tables and charts of presidential elections. No mere literary consumer, he self-consciously and prodigiously produced literature every day he wrote (fig. 1.1).[1]

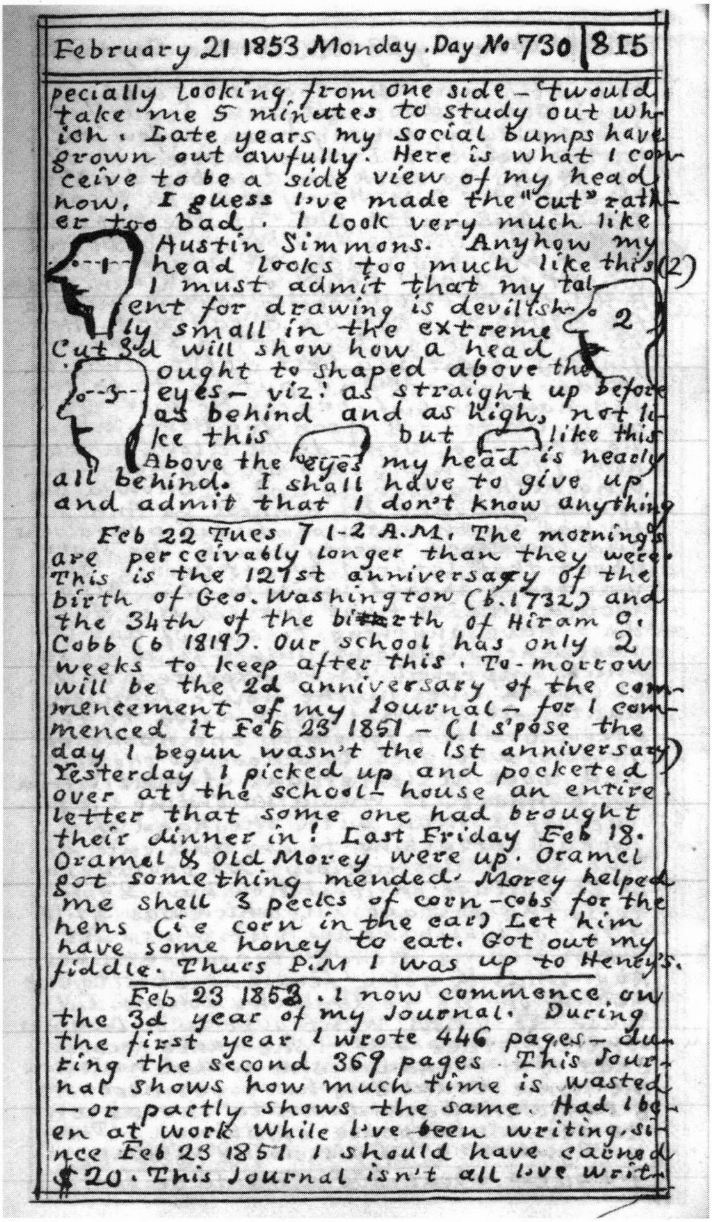

February 21 1853 Monday . Day No 730 | 815

pecially looking from one side — t'would take me 5 minutes to study out which. Late years my social bumps have grown out awfully. Here is what I conceive to be a side view of my head now, I guess I've made the "cut" rather too bad. I look very much like Austin Simmons. Anyhow my head looks too much like this (2) I must admit that my talent for drawing is devilishly small in the extreme Cut 3d will show how a head ought to shaped above the eyes — viz: as straight up before as behind and as high, not like this but like this Above the eyes my head is nearly all behind. I shall have to give up and admit that I don't know anything

Feb 22 Tues 7 1-2 A.M. The mornings are perceivably longer than they were. This is the 121st anniversary of the birth of Geo. Washington (b.1732) and the 34th of the birth of Hiram O. Cobb (b 1819). Our school has only 2 weeks to keep after this. To-morrow will be the 2d anniversary of the commencement of my Journal — for I commenced it Feb 23 1851 — (I s'pose the day I begun wasn't the 1st anniversary) Yesterday I picked up and pocketed over at the school-house an entire letter that some one had brought their dinner in! Last Friday Feb 18. Oramel & Old Morey were up. Oramel got something mended. Morey helped me shell 3 pecks of corn-cobs for the hens (i e corn in the ear) Let him have some honey to eat. Got out my fiddle. Thurs P.M I was up to Henry's.

Feb 23 1853. I now commence on the 3d year of my Journal. During the first year I wrote 446 pages — during the second 369 pages. This Journal shows how much time is wasted — or partly shows the same. Had I been at work while I've been writing since Feb 23 1851 I should have earned $20. This Journal isn't all I've writ-

Fig. 1.1 ✦ Charles M. Cobb drew his profile in his diary to keep account of phrenological changes and noted that his "social bumps have grown out awfully." Page 815 of the Charles M. Cobb Journal, 21 Feb. 1853. Courtesy of the Vermont Historical Society.

Most of Cobb's contemporaries lacked his scribbling stamina, but they nonetheless told their own life stories in diaries and letters and so must be seen as agents within the larger system of literary production. As writers, they looked upon their reading with a producer mentality, for "social authors" such as Cobb shared with their published counterparts similar expressive compositional challenges. Indeed, insofar as diaries were more than mere memoranda and letters more than simple vehicles of personal news, such "life writings" frequently stand as pieces of literature themselves.[2] In constant conversation with both literature and their social circles, diarists and correspondents self-consciously produced a text of life as they coursed through their journals or down stationery pages.

Though both diaries and letters could be equally literary, their differences merit separate treatment here. We begin with diaries because to twenty-first-century eyes they seem unlikely candidates for social expression. As we will see, however, most diaries then were hardly private, and they employed forms of address—like in Cobb's when he summoned "Friends"—in which the reader is clearly not assumed to be the writer.[3] We conclude with letters, more obviously social than diaries but not so narrowly interpersonal as might be expected today. After all, either by being read aloud or passed on, a letter then was often disseminated far beyond its intended initial recipient. More than merely transmitting messages, letters had to entertain and edify unknown readers while demonstrating the writer's character. Thus, many letters, like diaries, were surprisingly literary by modern standards. As we discuss both types of documents, we first examine the purposes for writing them before considering the practices surrounding their creation.

Diaries

People of all sorts tucked away details about their literary experience inside their diaries. They reveal there what literature they engaged, why they did so, and what they thought about it. They might record receiving a newspaper, buying a new book for a gift, reading a story to a sick child, or letting a neighbor borrow some old magazines. But diaries indicate more than such activity: by their very nature they situate literary encounters amid other daily events, such as meeting business clients, cleaning, traveling, teaching, sewing, churchgoing, gardening, or resting. Diarists also tell us how such everyday experiences related to literature, what it meant to them overall, and why it was so important to them. Yet diaries themselves do not make people turn to literature. Then as now, they were essentially compendiums of daily events written on blank sheets, usually stitched together and bound at home or by commercial binders or on lined, predated manufactured books. Some epistolary diaries were written in letter form.[4] The 798 diaries used here vary in size, appearance, contents, continuity, and purpose, but they all have something to say about literature's place in everyday social life.[5]

Purposes for keeping diaries often centered on recording life experiences for future reference. One diarist, Frances Merritt Quick, a twenty-three-year-old school teacher, explained her motive by alluding to the title character of Walter Scott's popular novel *Old Mortality:*

> I think I must make my journal a wardrobe where I may put my new acquired clothing of mind or soul, not only that I may now and then open its doors and view my possessions, that I may more correctly judge whether I am growing rich or poor, but also that I may protect them [from] the dust of care and preserve them from the grasp of Old Oblivion. Perhaps these records will act the part of Old Mortality when old age throws its rubbish of humanity around the soul, by clearing away the debris of Time and deciphering the characters that tell the history of my youth.

She first likens her diary to an unmarried young woman's most vital furnishing, a wardrobe to store and protect her clothes, then effortlessly layers upon this intimate metaphor another well-known literary one. She casts her diary as Old Mortality, an eighteenth-century cemetery caretaker who painstakingly swept clean the gravestones of Presbyterian heroes fallen during the previous century's wars between Scottish Covenanters and Cavaliers. Just as that custodian safeguarded monuments to past lives by removing deteriorating dirt, molds, and lichen, her diary would preserve her memory, "the history of my youth," unsullied by time's ravaging of pristine experiences: visiting, attending school, shopping, and sewing, but also reading, borrowing books, spending evenings at a Shakespeare club, versifying, and writing imaginative prose. With the long-term prospect of writing for their future, older selves, little wonder many diarists, like Quick, pursued worthwhile, not frivolous or egocentric, ends.[6]

Thus there often was a shorter term purpose for diary keeping: self-improvement. Many diarists hoped that writing something down every day, no matter how inconsequential, would develop desirable attributes, such as patience, persistence, and mental discipline. "My object is improvement," a weaving room clerk declared, "for this reason I will study neatness, method and punctuality in recording my observations." Beyond better habits, some diarists sought improved self-awareness, as did one who in her "life diary" vouched to write "the expression of my daily thought, to obtain self-knowledge, and secure self-improvement." Not only thoughts but also the diarist's emotions could be registered. "A journal! what a source of amusement and improvement," a ship carpenter's daughter observed, adding, "We may there make a record of our lives, our minds and our hearts." Self-improvement could also encompass, in so-called spiritual diaries, assaying one's religious growth. One Methodist divinity student found keeping a diary "teaches me more effectually than in any other manner Christian experience. For I sit in judgement upon my own life and regard the exercises of my own mind." Harsh self-scrutiny could accompany awe for tender mercies, as in the case of one Vermont farmwife who saw her diary as a "record, though it be smal[l], of that Goodness which has sustained me in every trial, given me unmerited every blessing, and often made light to shine out of the darkness." If diaries like these were stepping stones to heaven, others tracked scholastic progress. James Healy, an African American Catholic seminary student and child of a slave-master union, started his in December 1848 and fulfilled his promise "to continue it until the end of the scholastic year." After many entries recording his daily struggles and triumphs, he reached his goal upon his graduation. "Today 5 yrs ago I entered this college. What a change!" he exulted, painfully aware of his humble origins. "I was nothing now I am a Catholic."[7] Diaries could be testaments of self-transformation.

Some diaries were launched without the overt justifications ventured by these writers. Being given a pocket diary with its convenient chronological entry headings, might be reason enough. One nonagenarian, for example, having been presented with a diary in December 1844, dutifully began writing that January and continued through the year, only to die shortly after completing it the next New Year's Eve. Sometimes only circumstantial evidence hints at diarists' motives. A disabled plat maker commenced writing a journal after first copying excerpts from Ralph Waldo Emerson's *Essays* in a large blank ledger. The line he misquoted there—"Each young and ardent person writes a diary upon which when the hour of prayer arrives he inscribes his soul"—may or may not have inspired him. Special events or landmark eras coinciding with diary keeping's onset more certainly prompted other writers. A Taunton law student began his volume, perhaps eyeing his own mortality, after being struck by "*lightning* coming down the chimney, passing through my body and thence through the window." Loved ones' deaths occasioned diaries, as well. New Haven's four Jocelyn sisters all started theirs just after their five-year-old brother died. Of course, joyous or propitious moments led to diaries, too: Daniel and Mary Child's 1839 wedding sparked a twenty-two-year-long one, while Jewish peddler Abraham Kohn's began with his immigration from Germany.[8]

Though many diaries, like the Childs' or Kohn's, track literary experience as only one thread among many, so-called reading diaries, filled with references to books engaged and extensive reflections upon them, provide the best insight into it. Such diaries proliferated in Boston and its immediate region or in industrial towns, where a flourishing publication industry, abundant bookstores and libraries, and a lively lecture circuit encouraged literary encounters. Salem, Massachusetts, was one such site, where sixteen-year-old African American student Charlotte Forten, a native Philadelphian, kept one of the richest reading diaries we found. Alongside keeping alive "thoughts of much-loved friends from whom I may then be separated, with whom I now pass many happy hours, in taking delightful walks, and holding 'sweet converse,'" she vowed at the outset to discuss "the interesting books that I read." Harriett Low's diary, begun on a voyage from Salem to Macao for a four-year stay, shows that she lived up to her aim to "write every day and put some ideas or extracts of what I have been reading in the course of the day." She, too, like Forten, had a social purpose: to ship off each completed volume of her diary to her sister back home. Some reading diaries, like the one academy teacher John Park resumed upon his retirement, filled expanses of time. Acidly taking stock of his initial year of diary keeping, he mentioned reading first: "Now, I read my books—go to the Post Office—attend Church on Sundays—work a little in the garden in Summer—talk with my family—eat, drink and sleep, and am thus wending my way quietly to my grave." Still, his diary reveals an active social life shot-filled with literary experiences, from attending lectures to bookish chats with friends. Maintaining reading diaries required as much time as diarists could draw from other activities and, indeed, from reading itself. One Dartmouth College student keeping a reading diary pondered, after an evening's work on it, whether he should continue: "If I do, I shall not read more than half as much as I otherwise should, but shall reap, I do not doubt, five times the advantage from my reading."[9] Writing about reading leveraged comprehension, allowing reading diarists to squeeze more everyday ideas from the literature they engaged.

As producers of their texts of life to which they added a "chapter" a day, all diarists could claim the title of "author." Indeed, as life narratives between covers, diaries beg comparison to published works. The similarity struck a few diarists, including John Park, who, while reading Lockhart's *Life of Walter Scott,* noted the obvious affinity between his diary, recommenced at age sixty-two, and that of the famed writer, who, "at the age of 54, prepared himself a blank book with a lock and key, and began a regular Diary." Charles Cobb compared his diary's humorous tone to a novel he had just finished, "Zuleika or the Castilian captive." He saw echoes in "a place or two where I give the Truth a gentle twinge, to make something funny, or something of the sort."[10] Literature supplied models for enhancing records of everyday experience.

Like many published authors, diarists obsessed over not just writing but also tools of the trade. They usually attended to their blank books with loving care, painstakingly noting the date, cost, and place of purchase. One domestic in a wealthy Boston household recorded that she went into town to buy a "velvet Bonnet" and her pocket diary for twenty-five cents, for example, while a rural itinerant leatherworker jotted down his purchase of a handsome pocket memorandum. So customary was marking a diary's acquisition that James Healy recorded his neglect to do so. "I forgot to mention that I bought this book of Mr. O'Callaghan," he disclosed, referring to one of his teachers, weeks after he first began writing; two days later still, he added that the blank ledger cost forty cents. The outlay signaled the start of a long-term commitment, so it could not go unheeded. Diarists carefully weighed cost against the quality of paper and binding, as did Charles Cobb when he criticized his father for buying his mother but a "sheep-skin covered thing . . . [that] cost only 12 cents." A journeyman printer justified paying a steep $1.50 for a diary of "good paper" on the grounds it "will last me much longer" than a cheaper one, besides being conducive to "more interesting and better kept" entries.[11] Diaries were clearly meant to be permanent records.

High-quality blank books made ideal, lasting gifts, much esteemed by their recipients. They usually were given by family members, friends, or lovers, as in the case of Frances Jocelyn, who received her diary as a "Gift from Mr Peck," the Yale Divinity School student she would later marry. Special occasions, too, like New Year's, saw blank books presented. Grateful diarists could become sentimentally attached to receiving this kind of gift annually. "Do thank . . . dear John *too,* for his little Diary," one Boston abolitionist remarked of her present. "I enjoy this steady little . . . attention very much. It makes me feel trustful, in spite of all the changes of men & women, when my little book comes just as certainly, as the New Years day."[12] What better way to be remembered than through a gift that would become so much part of the recipient's life?

Instead of awaiting diaries as gifts or purchasing them, some writers fashioned their own. Diarists without easy access to stationery shops or bookstores, or lacking disposable cash, sewed together pages of paper into books. One Vermont Congregationalist minister made his own by stitching through pieces of paper that were sometimes already used and covered them with heavy sheets that might be engraved with illustrations—one of them of a paper factory. Threading pages together kept them in proper order, but it took time and patience. An accountant noted that he "worked nearly one hour in making this book. [I]f it takes me as long in proportion to the labor to fill it as it has to make it I shall be grey before I get through." Charles Cobb explained why it consumed so much time: "Th[er]e being 78 leaves to sew through it was a mighty job—i.e. to keep 'em all even, draw tight &c." To avoid the burden of accurately cutting, pasting, and stitching through sheets of paper, some wealthier diarists called upon binders to custom make their diaries for the new year, with the occasional risk that they might not arrive in time to record holiday events.[13]

Diarists demanded proper writing accessories, especially quality paper for adding new leaves to used-up books, along with good ink and pens. Handsome handwriting depended on fine paper that absorbed ink evenly, allowing an easier flow of script. "[My] writing looks as bad as ever," one elderly inveterate diarist admonished herself, "and there is no help for it. . . . [T]his paper is hard to write on." "I would delight to begin to write Journal again," Cobb griped when stalled one Christmas. "But all the paper I have had lately was either greasy (like this) or scratchy or blotty." Cheap paper irritated writers more than poor-quality ink, the effects of which only registered in years to come. A whaler regretted using low-grade ink for his letterbook, which he found thirteen years later to be "rendered by time & badness of ink, nearly illegible." More than bad ink, poor pens could mar writing or even bring it to a halt. The traditional quill, still then in broad use, required skill in cutting the nib and frequent "mending" or sharpening. "What a miserable pen I've got! I will mend it, ere I write another word," a farmer vowed in the middle of an entry. "There, now let me try it." Writers unable to fix a worn pen suffered the embarrassment of sloppy inscription. Reviewing her recent poor penmanship in her diary, one schoolgirl conceded, "Some of it [I] ascribe to carelessness and, some to my pens, as I never before tried to mend my own." The problems with quills led diarists to experiment with different implements, such as a newfangled "India-rubber pen," a more conventional steel one, and, for Charles Cobb, a precious gold one. He noted the difference between an old diary written with it and one produced with a quill: "When I look in the last mentioned book, I observe that its print and appearance is much better than this. The reason is . . . Father bought me a gold pen March 1849 and I have used it ever since."[14] Authorial pride rested upon a well-crafted writing instrument.

Adequate lighting helped writing, too. Since many diarists chose evenings to write, they needed artificial illumination. Candlelight was cheap but not very strong, unless a way was found to radiate the light. One inventive diarist discovered that "by placing a candle in a drawer" she could make her bedroom "so light" that she could easily write. "I have not, however, set the drawer on fire, it was lucky that I did not," she mused. Gaslight, at first used for industrial lighting and only gradually available in cities, was potentially brighter than candles. "We had over thirty jets of gas in the window," one boarder exclaimed when his landlord installed gas pipes in 1856, "& one jet gives a more brilliant light than three candles." Most homeowners did not install these exorbitant pipes; by one account, the fixtures for one room alone cost ten dollars in 1853, never mind trench-digging expenses, installation fees, and quarterly bills. People preferred lamplight, which could be directed and placed near or on a writing surface, rather than firelight, which was seasonal, diffuse, and far away from most furniture. Lamps, however, acted up from time to time. Long wicks sent nasty fumes into the air when lit, as one female academy pupil found: "I think if the person who invented oil-lamps could have foreseen the trials which they must impose upon the human race, that person would have committed suicide! Especially if he could also have foreseen that their wicks wd. be picked up a mile, to set them vomiting carbon, like a volcano." Winter exacerbated problems for diarists who could ill afford artificial illumination. "The days are so short that I can do but little, unless I write evenings, or mornings, by Lamp-Light," one clerk wrote, shivering in his fireless boardinghouse room during a cold December.[15]

Bright light, a sturdy pen, and a well-bound book of fine paper could not alleviate writer's block, though—a characteristic social authors shared with their professional brethren. The resulting exasperation spilled onto one farmer's diary pages: "Your quill may be perfect as any that the featherd tribe can produce; your ink may be all that you would wish or devise; Your book may be spread out before you with the kindest look inviting your stray thoughts & yet one does well if he makes out to catch a single idea." Other befuddled diarists expressed similar frustrations. After seeing "Bayne's Panorama," a student exclaimed, "[m]y pen is not adequate to describe it," and she wondered "why do I write[?] 'tis vain to endeavor to convey my impressions to paper, and write out the feeling that pervade[s] my soul." "I have put by my [sewing] work to write," a spinster began, but soon admitted that the "thoughts . . . seem to have gone with it by some species of Galvanism I suppose." A shoe binder fretting over her lover's return from sea attempted to corral ideas with a mind of their own: "[W]hen I sit down to write, my t[h]oughts will wonder of[f]. I try to keep them together, but they will not stay."[16] Articulation was a hurdle even the most heartfelt thoughts faced.

Advice books and other testimony from seasoned writers seldom salved sluggish diarists. A customs officer tried one suggestion. "I read this morning that 'Thought engender[s] thoughts. Place one idea upon paper; another will follow'," he wrote. "'Still another, till you have written a page.'—but I have been trying to think and have made but poor progress." The works of Jacob Abbott, who advocated certain writing regimens, appealed to some journalists. One diarist "determined to adopt the plan of keeping my Journal as recommended by Abbot in his 'Young Christian.'" He quoted the writer's nostrum, which declared that "'the style should be a simple narration of facts, chiefly descriptions of scenes through which you have passed, & memoranda in regard to important points of your history. Every thing relating to your progress in knowledge, your plans for your own improvement, the books you read, & the degree of interest which they exerted, should be noticed down.'" Yet even the wisest instruction could not dissolve stubborn mental blocks. A farmer who remembered reading countless advice books by "Writers for youth" still found, as an adult, "for my part I am so habitually & irretri[e]vably given to *laziness* & procrastination that I never could keep a journal more than a week: after that time I was tired; my ideas were faint, my pen lame or wornout and finally I would give up the attempt."[17] Lack of fortitude may have been writers' worst enemy, but that so many sought advice suggests how deeply ingrained diary keeping was as a social value.

Not surprisingly, when diary keeping lapsed, writers castigated themselves severely. Charlotte Forten, burdened with studying for school examinations, noticed that "[a] month has elapsed since last I wrote in thee—my Journal; and conscience has busily whispered 'What! has thy *daily* diary become a *monthly?*'" One negligent young women even imagined "my poor Journal actually reproaches me with its *blank* countenance." Some accepted the penalty of "bringing up" by summarizing days or weeks of events or by copying parts of other, more fastidious family members' memoranda. Lapses, however, provided respite from an exacting persistence that inevitably became tedious. One spinster wondered how often diary keeping "becomes merely a mechanical action & one writes to fill up for who would be willing to call *life* a blank?"[18] A life worth writing about was a life worth living, hence generic or formulaic entries were to be avoided.

Despite blockages, less-than-ideal materials, and unfavorable conditions, writers developed methods to help them persist against the odds. Many tenacious scribblers would agree with one diarist who announced, "Let my motto be slow & sure," while others subscribed to Charles Cobb's rule, "Little and often is the best way." Sometimes writing daily at a set time seemed to start thoughts flowing; this could be anytime, but for most diarists it was bedtime. "It has now become my habit to close my days duties with my pen and journal," a printer realized after eight consecutive years of success, "so that 'Have you written?' is generally the question asked me when bed time comes." For one mechanic's son, "10 minutes every night" did the trick. But persistence could mean writing anywhere at anytime available. One second mate under sail took to "writing on my [sea] chest and sitting on the floor . . . the steadiest place I can find." Other diarists placed their blank books "on the hen house" or "on my knee" when no other surfaces were available; some thought a scrivener's standing position conducive to writing. "Linked up a hanging shelf for my portable desk, where I may write standing," a student remarked one evening in his college dormitory. "Am using it now and pride myself on its ingenuity."[19] Whatever ensured the habit's maintenance was acceptable.

As self-conscious authors of their own life stories, diarists naturally and sometimes playfully alluded to publishing conventions. Harriett Low prefaced the sixth volume of her journal with a novel-like title: "The *Lights* and *Shadows* of a Macao Life by A *Travelling Spinster* / Dedicated to her beloved Sister." Moreover, she conceived her diary's very content in terms of entertaining fiction. "Oh! what a book I should have—to note all the funny things said in this house—the inconsistencies of *men!*" she remarked. "It would be as good as a play." Some diarists appropriated the form of newspapers. A rural New Hampshire family contrived a diary (dubbed the "Home Journal") to look like a newspaper, complete with a hand-drawn masthead and vertical columns of writing. Other diarists designed whimsical frontispieces decorated with elaborate cartouches featuring their name or hand-painted self-portraits, or aped printed books' initial epigrams. The title page of a California-bound man bore a bon mot from a beloved Scottish poet which threatened to expose nosy shipmates: "'A chiel's among ye takin' notes, / And, faith, he'll prent em!'—Burns." Ironically, many diarists undermined published forms like pocket memoranda with preprinted blanks under standard headings. One housewife parsimoniously listed the letters she sent to people under "cash accounts," a clever, almost impish subversion of these volumes' dollars-and-cents purpose.[20]

Although diarists emulated published forms, they seldom produced a smooth narrative or achieved a single literary effect, but life seldom proceeded smoothly, either. Illness, tragedy, or lack of time caused blank spaces in the account. Respites from writing meant beginning the story again, often in completely different parts of the diary. Verses or even stories could intervene between entries. Today's readers must invent strategies to fill in blanks mentally, move backward and forward chronologically, and stop in the middle occasionally to turn the book over and upside down before resuming reading, back to front. In the course of life, too, diarists found material mementoes more eloquent than words, and so they inserted flowers gathered on a romantic day with a lover, locks of hair left by the deceased, recipes made and enjoyed with family, and newsclippings sent by distant loved ones or saved by oneself. Such potpourri interleaved in texts of life remain difficult to interpret and insist that readers now pause to open up clippings, touch mysterious ringlets in tiny envelopes, or lift up pieces of dried fern and violets to see what is written underneath. Even as they slow down or interrupt the narrative, these breaks from the simple daily succession of entries underscore how creative keeping diaries could be.[21]

As highly unpredictable, haphazardly compiled, and almost indecipherable as they sometimes are, diaries seldom escaped the scrutiny of other people. In this sense, diaries were generally conceived of as public forms of literature; their creators knew full well that someone would probably scan them then, if not in the future. The likelihood of this potential readership contributed to diarists' vision of themselves as authors in their own right. As Harriett Low prophetically wrote of her own literary production, "What an authoress I am, my 5th book. Fancy them given to the *public. Oh tempora. O Mores.* What an *amalgamation."* By contrast, one Massachusetts farmer saw practical use, rather than entertainment, in his mundane diary, as, he noted, "it may fall in some hands that may just look it over if their cattle should be sick or to see . . . at what time we got certain pieces of grass and [completed] other work such as planting, [or] ploughing." Sometimes diarists authored their texts with specific contemporary readers in mind, as did Rhode Island seaman John R. Congdon, who kept a journal written "solely for the Amusement and instruction of his beloved . . . wife Cynthia A. Congdon" and was presented on his return with her own. But he conceded, and rightly so, that a larger crowd—Cynthia's friends, her mother, or his own shipmates—might sneak a peek from time to time. "Should others peruse any of these pages let them understand they were written by a Husband to, or for, his wife, their earthly existence being so nearly united they look upon each other as one and the same being," he warned trespassers. "The writer of this as a *man,* is not ashamed of the above remarks." Among the many other diarists writing for only one set of eyes was Harriett Low, who, like Congdon, envisioned outside spying. "[F]or you, my Dear Sister," she inscribed on the first page, "shall this journal be kept," but later added a cautionary note: "I am afraid to write anything of *consequence,* thinking that it may be left to the mercy of the rude elements, and may be exposed to the satire of an uninterested person."[22] Diarists, like published authors, obsessed about their public.

A few people who attempted to maintain private journals realized they could not secure total confidentiality, but they tried anyway. While most diarists wrote at night in the privacy of their chambers, some who rented rooms took advantage of lighting in public parlors where snooping inevitably became a pastime. One boardinghouse resident joked of another, "I wonder how long it will take Frances to finish her stocking if she watches over my shoulders all the time I am writing. I shall have to put a pair of leather spectacles over her eyes, for she is such a hand for telling over what she reads and hears, that my private journal will be made public, I fear." Resourceful interlopers found ways to steal away a secret diary. "The cook has now[,] which is the 2nd time[,] asked me very authoritatively what it is I am writing in this book," a seaman complained. "I have already lost . . . some scraps which I suspect him to have stolen and shall [not] be surprised if this book is stolen also." There was, it seems, always a public ready to receive the diarist's production. One solution to breaches of privacy was to destroy pages or the entire volume. "This was my dear mothers journal," a bereaved daughter added in her own hand to the precious document. "A short time before she died, she cut out some of the leaves, which are gone, probably not wanting anyone to see them." Confidentiality could be ensured by other, less drastic means. Because diaries then were almost always without locks and keys, they remained vulnerable to curious readers. Pocket diaries offered the most security, for they could find a safeguarded place—a person's pocket—but remembering to carry a diary everywhere was a burden. Some diarists locked their larger journals in desks but risked losing keys. "I have really been very neglectful of you my dear journal, & the reason is this I lost the key of my writing-desk, & have only just found it," one teenager apologized to her diary. The chance of misplacing keys and the nuisance of having them always at hand prior to writing inspired alternative strategies, as one young man pointed out: "Owing to this my book has always been kept under lock & key wh. perhaps may be the cause of its being so much neglected, . . . I adopt[ed] the method of writing nothing but what I am willing to [have] seen by any one of my family, that I may not have the trouble of locking and unlocking my desk whenever I have a moment."[23] Thus could a diary's content by necessity come to address a wider audience.

Lack of privacy certainly inhibited diarists and made their record at times less than candid, but some actually hoped others might steal glances. "It is refreshing and conciliating, to have the assurance that Mother has seen & read what I wrote last night," Charles Cobb admitted after writing a scathing account of a family "jaw"; "for by my mistake my box has been right before her ever since, and judging by myself I am sure that she hasn't let the opportunity pass unimproved." A businessman's wife barely concealed a desire to have her husband learn how much she detested his profligacy: "God knows I state facts & nothing else & he, the cruel one, these lines may meet his eye when the hand that guided the pen may be cold in death, driven to the grave by his injustice & oppression," she bitterly scratched. "But now, if now he should by any chance look over this page, how [he] would scorn & curse me, for daring to place pen to paper in expression of my feelings, & never before, have I done it."[24] The very limited access of such diaries ironically made them a forceful medium of communication.

More commonly, diarists openly welcomed family members and acquaintances reading their volumes. One traveling businessman who maintained a diary for his wife told her he "anticipate[d] much happiness the coming winter when we can read it together." A Saco, Maine, mill worker recorded that his brother "read some and wrote in my *journal*" during a visit. At times only a portion of the diary was open to other eyes. Charlotte Forten explained that her teacher "Miss Shepard allowed Lizzie . . . and me to read a few pages of her journal which interested us very much," though she graciously declined to see more, as "we dared not appropriate any more of its precious contents." One way diarists could regulate access was by reading aloud select portions. "Before retiring Bessie read me some extracts from her journal when abroad which was very interesting," one woman told her diary. As finished diaries circulated to novice writers eager for elegant models, journalizing perpetuated itself. One housekeeper voicing diarists' constant lament, "[I] wish I could write my *thoughts,* but I don't seem to know how," determined, "I must read some journal."[25] Little wonder that among groups of friends or family their diaries came to resemble one another.

Occasionally, two or several hands contributed to the same diary. In that of Bangor's Williamson family, no less than five family members signed their initials after various entries. Not all collective diaries, however, received equal input from writers. For over two decades Daniel Child wrote nearly all entries in the one he and his wife Mary began together, but he honored their shared authorship by referring to himself as "husband" and to her as "wife." Only after she died in 1861 did he use the first person "I" in the lonely diary he continued until his death in 1876. Other co-writers joined in for the first time after spouses died. Sarah Greene tried to carry on her husband Christopher's diary after consumption claimed his young life, but picking it up for the first and last time after the tragedy, she emphasized the unwritten pages that would remain: "Christopher left this world, a *blank* it seems to me now. What shall I do—where go—every place so lonely. As I look back upon the pages of this book—most of which he penned—and see how insidious has been the disease which conquered him, yet how determined, I feel all in a dream. Can it be, my husband, who has walked with me so many years, is silent, still—gone! . . . Sacred little Book! The last writing of my Beloved." Unable to persevere, she bid "Farewell to writing in this. I cannot again. Often shall I look over these pages, but they are sanctified now, and naught common must be put down here." One widower attempted to continue his late wife's diary by writing in it on anniversaries of her death. "Ten years have passed since my dear Sarah's Death," he sadly chronicled. "I believe I have observed every anniversary, except the last when I lived in Cambridge, and had not her mementoes. O God! kill the earth in me, and make him the spirit!"[26] Thus, a record of a life became a monument to it.

Even lacking such commemorative intentions, nearly all diaries invoked memories of loved ones. These texts of life were richly peopled and, at the same time, literarily wrought yet not self-absorbed. How one felt in a world of one's own mattered less than what happened in social relations. In fact, journalizing expressed these relations, even in the absence of the loved one, kin, friend, or neighbor, who remained present in spirit, anyway. In short, when diarists wrote, other people looked over their shoulders figuratively, if not, as we have seen, literally. In this sense, keeping a diary was—almost as much as letter writing—an act of social communication.

Letters

New Englanders produced letters as devotedly as they kept diaries. Travel, hospitalization, or schooling pulled people away from their friends and relatives for short amounts of time. Rapid economic development across the nation and overseas beckoned people to leave their homes and resettle in search of betterment, in some cases forever. For them, letters became the only reliable link to distant loved ones and thus often brim with urgency as they crammed essential news into a few pages. Even so, correspondents usually described literary experiences such as their children's progress with reading and composition, the newspapers they exchanged, the books read aloud, and the public lecturers they heard. After all, how could they convey themselves to distant intimates without sending along their everyday literary ideas?[27]

These social needs fulfilled by letters underscore how letters differed from diaries. Letters usually bespoke ongoing communication with specific people, whereas diaries maintained the illusion of privacy. Letters expecting an answer read like one side of a discussion, yet they usually contain responses to a previous letter received, along with, perhaps, echoes of several earlier exchanges. Letters were thus interpersonally, not individually, determined. And more than recipients and addressees peopled the page; other correspondents might be quoted or paraphrased, while whomever might have been in the room chimed in, perhaps scratching a postscript. Letters, in this way, were open windows onto a social universe of conversations that continued according to the varied needs of correspondents.

Chief among those needs was that of maintaining ties. This can be seen in the copious letters Mary Pierce Poor wrote as she moved throughout the Northeast. Born in Brookline, Massachusetts, in 1820 to John and Lucy Pierce, she attended school in Northampton between 1836 and 1837, migrated to Bangor with her husband Henry Poor in 1841, where the couple lived near her sister Lucy, and then settled in New York in 1849, only to return to Brookline after the Civil War. Her wanderings gave her ample reason to write to her cherished family (fig. 1.2). In one of these letters, she revealed various manifestations of everyday life, including the place of literature in it:

> . . . a day . . . might be described thus—rose so-so early—breakfasted on buckwheat cakes—swept parlour carpet & dusted said parlour, watered plants, looked over basket of clean clothes and found a hole in one of Henry's stockings and a button missing from one of his shirt wristbands. Repaired the before mentioned articles & put away all the clothes in their places—made bed—ran over to Lucy's—kissed all the children—back to dinner, had roast pork and apple pie. P.M. Played one game of chess with Henry before he went to his office—sewed till nearly dark, then took a book and knit & read—Tea—toasted bread—butter—and rest of the pie we had for dinner. Eve. Henry down in Town, Mahala [their domestic] over at Lucy's, sat alone in the house, sewing and hearing Mr Abbe's cow stamp in his barn & imagining it was somebody breaking into my kitchen. Between nine and ten Henry comes home, reads aloud or talks, go to bed a little after eleven.

Amid the small events she and many of her contemporaries capture in correspondence, reading assumes a strikingly prominent place, punctuating the day. Literature infiltrated even the most routine life.[28]

Poor's letter was typical of those routinely written to keep in touch, yet accounts of literary experience coincidentally shine through even letters bearing special tidings. Christmas season missives usually acknowledged gratitude for presents, especially literary ones, along with best wishes for the new year, and they might nonchalantly drop a few unrelated lines about everyday reading habits, too. One bank teller sending a holiday note to his brother back home queried about another of his sibling's appetite for light reading matter: "I wonder if he devours the newspapers as he used to!" More than Christmas greetings, condolence letters evoked literary expression. One woman writing to her sister and brother-in-law of the death of their daughter, a overworked mill girl, summoned the lyric of a traditional song: "Abigail your dear Abigail is no more. [W]e shall see her face no more you will . . . hear her cheering voice no more." She signed off with 'So fades the lovely blooming flower.'"[29] A literary fragment could so frame a life.

Fig. 1.2 ✦ It is not surprising that avid correspondent Mary Pierce Poor would have her image taken reading a letter, perhaps one from her family. Portrait of Mary Pierce Poor, c. 1860. Photo by John A. Whipple, Boston, Mass. (A132-2-2a). Photo courtesy of the Schlesinger Library, Radcliffe Institute, Harvard University.

Some correspondents related to one another mainly through literary matters, as they filled their letters with commentary on books, authors, lyceums, and lecturers. This kind of exchange depended upon mutual enjoyment of both reading literature and writing about it, so correspondents took pains to keep common sentiments aligned. One fifteen-year-old sought such affirmation from her equally bookish cousin: "I should be afraid of wearing out anyone's patience but yours, dear Lizzie, by such a dissertation upon books, but I believe you like to hear about them as well as I do." As part of these delicate negotiations, some writers headed off the charge of literary self-absorption, as did one rural down-easter whose account of her reading began self-deprecatingly, "Oh, I forgot I intended egotising a little—well I have been reading the Court and Camp of Bounoparte, it is extremely interesting, but *such* ministers & Generals preserve me from. Most of them were utterly corrupt. Bernadotte is a noble exception." She then added, "Am reading in French with a little assistance Corinne—Kenilworth for the first time & Dix's Christian Philosophy—quite a *melee* is it not?" Such hesitations as they gave way to mutual literary relationships could garner comment. "By sharing in this way the studies in which you employ your leisure time," a brother in Europe disclosed to his sister back home in Boston after a stream of literary correspondence, "we are brought as it were into a kind of intellectual community much more close and interesting than that of the two lovers who when separated agreed to look at the moon the same hour."[30] Attaining such "intellectual community" was one of the highest purposes of correspondence between like-minded literati.

Correspondents shared a concern for economy in writing. Instead of dispensing bits of literary activity throughout their letters, many referred to books and reading only if they had extra space after communicating more pressing matters. One correspondent described her reading in the top margin of a page, marked with a dingbat to signal it: "It is a pity to waste this great piece So I will tell you that I have read 'five years of youth.'" Bits of literary information were nudged into postscripts. "P.S. . . . My Birth Day Present from Father was the Young Ladies Friend," one young woman added after signing off to a cousin. "I think [it] is very interesting and instructive."[31] "Crosshatch" lines also caught last-minute literary thoughts. These sentences penned perpendicularly over the original message made for hard-to-read checkerboard pages, but they squeezed in twice the amount of writing, affording space for literary matters.

Correspondents practiced such economy because letters were relatively expensive to write and send. Paper costs ranged between one and seven cents per sheet, and ink prices varied even more: a bottle might run from four to twelve cents, and if of quality ink, from twenty-five cents to thirty-seven and a half cents. Inkstands and wells, depending upon their materials of construction (for example, freestone or glass), were priced at between ten and thirty-five cents, but cost even more when made of brass or highly ornamented. Quills might be had at four for a penny, steel pens cost about one cent each, and gold pens could fetch two dollars. Envelopes, which could be obviated by skillful folding, averaged about a cent and a half each, and sealing wax (lick-and-stick items lay in the future) cost about fifty cents a bottle, with a pack of the wafers that added color and further adhesiveness to the seal at about twelve cents. Seals that were impressed into the wax as it cooled bore specific designs to ensure that letters remained unopened in transit; because they could be made from anything from gemstones down to base metal and could be quite elaborately or simply engraved, seals ranged in cost dramatically. Postage rates, too, were not uniform; the rate was figured, at various times by distance, number of sheets, or weight—and whether prepaid or by the receiver—plus an added fee for city deliveries, but the rate for a single-sheet item was never less than three cents. So, in a time when skilled white, male workers made about a dollar in a twelve-hour day, and most other laborers considerably less, the expenses of a single letter could equal several hours' wages. No wonder one freshman congressman was pleasantly surprised to find that his room in Washington was equipped with "an inkstand a bundle of pens a box of *sand* and a *sand box* two pieces of tape two boxes of sealing wax—a pencil—several pieces of paper—a bottle of ink," all "at the charge and expense of uncle Sam."[32] Taking advantage of the situation, he wrote home about every other day.

The expenses letter writers incurred were matched if not exceeded by the amount of special effort and painstaking care they put into their letters. A few correspondents even hammered out verses, as one mill worker did, making light of his friend's all-too-long lapses: "Irving dear, why dont you write / Write to me, and let me know / Whats well or ill whats wrong or right / When you come or when you go." Other correspondents graced their texts with quotes from published authors or embellished their notes with visual images: fanciful borders, sketches of themselves, or representations of their schools. Some writers expressed their regard for their letters by modeling them after books. In fact, the most common form of letter then was an oblong sheet folded midway across the longer side so that, with the fold on the left, the sheet became a four-page pamphlet. With similar sheets added, an ersatz volume could be created, as can be seen in the instructions one seaman gave his wife: "take say 3 sheets and form them the same as a Book. Write your pages in Book form when the[y] are full take others." Some sets of letters became epistolary diaries; Mary Pierce Poor often referred to her own letters—continuous streams of daily entries written on large sheets sent home periodically—as her "regular journal."[33]

Of all enhancements to letters, the most prized for lending refinement was elegant penmanship. Pride in good handwriting was instilled in children when they first learned to write and receive letters. A mother enjoined her children to "learn to do them up neatly and properly, for the *appearance of* a letter is of some consequence, as well as its composition." Relatives boasting of children's progress pointed to penmanship. "I think Charlotte will write as handsome a hand as her mother, she prints beautiful letters to her little friends," one proud aunt ventured. Reinforced by such attention, learning to write with a fine hand became a rite of passage, as is suggested in one rural widow's entry: "[T]hursday was Henry's birth day, just seven years old, he commenced writing with ink to day at school for the first time." She rewarded such achievement in a way to foster further development: "I bought him a nice writing book & pen . . . [;] his sister gave him a slate pencil for a birth days present."[34] Writing with ink, insofar as it symbolized the child could be trusted not to tip over the bottle or drink its contents, was a milestone on the way to adulthood.

In producing a handsome letter, the quality of script mattered. Letter writers took more care than diarists to exhibit fine penmanship so as to avoid the criticism of illegibility, carelessness, or haste. Even the "hurried scrawl" required to finish letters in time for the next mailing called for an apology. Pencils might be acceptable, but only if both parties agreed about the degree of legibility. "[P]erhaps it would make your eyes ache to read pencil does it?" a store clerk seeking his fortune in Illinois asked his Vermont spouse. Pens rather than pencils predominated as writing tools because ink contrasted more sharply with white paper and made for easier reading. Pens caused problems, too, though; Charles Lenox Remond, a Salem black abolitionist, jested in a postscript, "Some distinguished author says public men should never apologize for poor writing pens or paper." Public men and private writers nevertheless discovered many ways to ask pardon for bad pens and paper despite other legitimate excuses. "I cannot write any more to night," a worker wrote to her mother in Maine after a hard day in the Andover mills. "[Y]ou will think by the looks of what I have wrote that I had better stopt before but my . . . pen & ink are both poor & my hand trembles afte[r] working in the Factory all day." Like diarists, letter writers substituted a variety of surfaces for tables and desks, many of which could result in bad penmanship. "Excuse this frightful letter," a woman pleaded to her husband. "I am obliged to write at Mary's *ironing table,* so I cannot help the tremendous joggles." Correspondents wrote on top of books, by the kitchen stove, on the floor with "a lamp upon a chair," "on a low stool, at a doll's table," or with a "babe in my arms." "I am writing upon my Astronomy book, I hope you will not detect any moonshine about this," an academy student joked to her mother.[35]

Occurring just about anywhere, letter writing did not banish sociability, for it was acceptable and often necessary to write while among people who were doing other things (fig. 1.3). In factory boardinghouses, writers found it impossible to escape the din: "I am once more a factory girl! . . . seated in the short attic of a

Lowell boarding house with a half a dozen girls seated around me talking and reading and myself in the midst of trying to write to you," a correspondent scrawled to her friend who only years later would escape life in the mills. "With the thoughts of so many persons flying around me . . . [,] I can hardly tell which are my own." Babel could affect the hand that wrote. Lecturer Charles Lenox Remond, staying at a friend's home, confessed, "I write while in conversation with the Young ladies, and one at the Piano[;] you will pardon imperfections & scribbling." In home parlors, reading aloud (a common form of social entertainment) could compete with concentration. "I have written this evening while Father has been Reading aloud some *slavery* articles," a woman explained one frigid Vermont night; "such a *fiery* subject that you will I trust be ready to excuse my mistakes and bad penmanship." Writing in such social settings may reflect peculiar New England customs, for when one Salemite visited the watering holes in Saratoga Springs, New York, she found she had to sequester away her letter writing: "The only reason I dislike to write home is, that it is an unsocial occupation to those here, & yet I find I never can write a short letter to one of the family."[36] Present company would not abide the maintenance of distant ties through the sustained public letter writing so acceptable at home.

If letter writers struggled to create beautiful script, they more easily attained "'facillity in epistolary composition,'" for heartfelt sentiments flowed more freely in letters than diaries. Though letters expressed spontaneous personal thoughts, they drew upon a long tradition of epistolary novels and abundant examples of letters in print. A collegian emulated letters in Thomas Gray's *Works* as "models of a flowing, easy, epistolary style" that he believed "tends to make an interesting, an appropriate letter." Not everyone with writing "facility" recognized it in themselves. Mary Pierce Poor's letters flowed as elegantly as anyone's, but she diffidently perceived in them only "awkwardly turned sentences & incoherent stringing of ideas," perhaps in deference to proscriptions against women taking too much pride in their intellects. She explained, "I have so much to say that I cannot stop for rhetorical graces." She felt a published author looking over her shoulder: "The author of 'hodge podge' would be shocked indeed if he perused one of my rambling sheets, viewing it in the light of a theme to be corrected." She continued: "I fear he would draw his pen over the whole in dispair—but I am nothing daunted, I do not write letters to be printed in books but only to tell you how much I love you all & to run on about things which interest me just as they come into my head, so here goes."[37]

Yet not all women felt so reticent, least of all Persis Sibley Andrews, a sometime-schoolteacher in rural Maine. After reading "Mrs. President John Adams' letters" in 1842, she deemed them "very commonplace & wo'd never have been published if written by an individual less exalted by honors." She boasted that her "letter trunk

Fig. 1.3 ✦ In this engraving, writing and reading are but two types of social activity within a large fireside gathering. "A New England Fireside," *Ballou's Pictorial Drawing-Room Companion* 8 (10 Mar. 1855): 145. Courtesy of the American Antiquarian Society.

would afford matter for a vol. a thousand times more talented than this first." On reflection, she painfully realized that her own words, if they survived, might be subject, like Abigail Adams's, to the whims of posterity: "And will a few years render all this world of *feeling* of *mine* insipid? The dearest, most sacred & tenderest emotions of my heart only subjects to be laughed by a future generation[?]" Her concerns for the publicity of her private sentiments proved prophetic, for after she married a Democratic assemblyman a few months later and became herself a public figure and his political confidante, the couple's correspondence was subject to the sticky fingers and hungry eyes of adversaries.[38]

Other political wives faced the same dilemma of writing private letters with an awareness of their potential public value—or damage. Worcester's Eliza Davis learned that an 1840 letter about local politics sent to her absent husband John, a U.S. senator, was read by none other than his distinguished colleague, Daniel Webster. She confessed that "it was all without an idea of its falling into M[r] Webster's hands, or I should have taken more pains with the penmanship at least; for I even doubted if you could spell it out." She concluded with reference to a local writing master, "Its of no use to be sorry about it now; and as for penmanship my days of writing are so nearly ended it matters little for the future whether I am a pupil of Bristow or not." To her chagrin, the political opposition got wind of the story and, in its newspapers, viciously mocked the letter, the couple, and Webster.[39]

Most correspondents, politically prominent or not, understood that their private letters might be seen lying about or even torn open "by mistake" and then read anyway. After all, one downside of these candid, well-crafted letters was that they could potentially entertain anyone into whose hands they fell. "I know darn'd well that I should do so, i[f] similarly placed," Charles Cobb admitted upon discovering a stranger had taken his letter at the post office and "broke it open." More commonly, letters provided matter for sociable reading when they were recited aloud for family or company or passed on to other people. "Martha had written a number of letters and sent them home by her father; the family were reading them when we arrived and were much surprised at our visit," a young man explained while at his fiancée's home.[40] Given the potential public forum for "private" letters, writers delicately balanced discretion with disclosure.

Fearing publicity or snooping, some people burned their letters, though, to be sure, not without some deliberation. After all, their texts, like diaries, chronicled a life and thus held special meaning. "All the afternoon looking over & burning old letters & wondering at the changes," a melancholy but scrupulous woman recorded. Destroying letters of the deceased especially tormented those facing the task. With his own death approaching, John Park at age seventy-six took a match to his first wife's precious letters: "Doubting the propriety of leaving the affectionate letters of my wife, Louisa, for the perusal of strangers, & finding a considerable number remaining . . . , I concluded, today, to go through the painful operation of committing those still in my keeping to the flames. I glanced over several of these interesting pages *for the last time,* then with tears flowing I consumed them in the fire. Did the dear spirit of the departed witness how much it cost me? I know not."[41] Thus wary correspondents consigned the precious text of life to ashes.

Conclusion

Many life stories fortunately survived conflagration or the mosses, molds, and dust of time, as if Old Mortality himself, that gravestone cleaner earlier likened to a diary, were overseeing their care. Thus everyday ideas that could take flight within a day's time or fade from memory after a lifetime found enduring substance in these texts of life, where pen, ink, and paper, posterity, and a large measure of good luck ensured their preservation. With "ideas to record" pressing so much upon them, these writers employed their literary experience and skills to capture them articulately in diaries and letters.[42] Grasping for proper words, striving for aesthetic unity, comparing themselves to published authors, squeezing their words into confined space, ornamenting their pages, suffering creative blockage, addressing their public, and seeking after new ideas from reading and lectures, these everyday writers shared with professionals the trials and rewards of producing literature. And even if some of these personal testaments only list books read or lyceum lectures attended, something literary remains.

But something of the social life surrounding these creations lingers, as well. As we have seen, diaries and letters could be collaborative endeavors. Even if composed by one person, they were usually intended for at least a limited readership. Both correspondence and diaries were read aloud or otherwise shared with family and friends and so found even wider audiences. Furthermore, both texts of life were always susceptible to the prying eyes of interlopers. The materials for writing these texts, too, were imbued with social meaning. After all, blank books, pocket memoranda, pens, and inkstands were purchased as much for reading audiences as for writers of diaries and letters. And as a token of social relations, writing paraphernalia was ideal gift-giving material. As historical documents of unique lives lived, diaries and letters still promise to share themselves eloquently with readers today, risking the indifference of—or, worse, ridicule by—"a future generation." As only Persis Sibley Andrews could understand, however, in her inimitable defiance of hierarchical constraints, the literary experiences of everyday writers like her, living ordinary lives, could indeed make "matter for a volume."[43] Indeed, this volume in your hands would not be possible without their everyday ideas to fill it.

Chapter 2

Creating Texts from Other Texts: Deploying Preexisting Literature

As December 1849 drew to a close, Enoch Hale inventoried his literary possessions. Having left a "very poorly paid" job as an editor of the *New York Express,* he had returned home to Newburyport, Massachusetts, to work in his father's fish yard before venturing out again. "For several days past," he explained in his journal, "I have been engaged in arranging my papers, books, &c. preparatory to a journey to some place,—*where* I have not definitely settled, as yet." He recorded a wide range of books he himself had produced over the past decade, mostly compilations of published literature—texts created from other texts. He had assembled a catalogue of his personal library with a *"General Index"* registering "the more valuable portions of the contents of the Books, Pamphlets, &c"; two *"Piece Books,"* or "matter collected from Newspapers, and other sources" pasted in; a volume of poetry extracts; a book of transcriptions from "books or papers which may not be mutilated"; and, finally, a letterbook containing copies of correspondence "worthy of preservation."[1] Hale's collection was unusually extensive, for most compilers made only one or two volumes of the types he mentioned: book lists, indexes, scrapbooks, commonplace books, and letterbooks. While Hale may have been obsessed with assembling pieces of preexisting literature into books of his own fashioning, those books represented hours of intellectually creative work and a deep engagement with literature. No mere literary scavenger, he was producing meaning as he organized the seeming chaos of literary fragments passing through his hands.

As Hale's collection shows, literary creativity was not restricted to devising original texts of life such as diaries and letters; one-of-a-kind texts could be fashioned from parts of preexisting ones in myriad ways. Beyond compilations made up of clippings or inscriptions of printed texts, however, were a host of other kinds of texts from texts. Unique, variant editions of books were created when readers annotated, defaced, or marked them. Original English-language texts were devised from published foreign literature when ordinary people translated that literature, especially when they strayed far from the literal. Not all texts from texts began with printed words, however. Some had their genesis in orally delivered manuscripts. Lectures and sermons, for example, were transcribed or paraphrased in writing by auditors. Nor did all texts from texts become finalized in writing. "Mental editions" came into being when readers memorized, often imperfectly, favorite pieces of literature. Finally, texts from texts could encompass even those created by mediums who believed they merely channeled composed texts, such as poetry, from "the world of spirits." All of these refashioned and reworked texts were stamped by human creativity.

There was, besides individual creativity, often a social motivation behind deploying preexisting literature. Scrapbooks were commonly collaborative productions shared with many readers. Commonplace books provided quotable material to enlist in conversation or correspondence. People used texts they marked (or defaced) as vehicles of communication, often to amuse readers. Literature was memorized in order to provide tip-of-the-tongue bon mots to facilitate social interaction. Groups of spiritualists together listened to "knockings" and verbalized or transcribed messages from the Great Beyond. When texts heard at lectures or as sermons were later captured in writing, their social origins in audiences were remembered as well. Finally, translations of sometimes rare foreign-language texts into English were often undertaken as a service to those who otherwise might not have read them.

The creativity and sociability people experienced as they made new texts out of old ones is the focus of this chapter. It moves from those forms that permitted little deviation from original wording, such as scrapbooks, and ends with translations, which demanded a total substitution of words while preserving the original text's essence. The prodigious exertion of weaving published words into new combinations testifies to the important role literature played in these people's lives.

Scrapbooks

"[T]his sort of mania has seized me—a scrapbook mania," Charles Cobb once confessed to his diary. To fuel his obsession, he vowed to "use just about every [news] paper" he could lay his hands on, "leaving nothing behind." This fixation upon making scrapbooks, into which newspaper clippings, short articles, engravings, and other items were arranged and pasted, was one of the most popular pastimes for clippers of all ages. Insofar as it demanded few skills beyond knowing how to cut paper and apply paste, it was an ideal exercise for children developing their manual dexterity. One mother reported that her toddler has "been employed this afternoon in paisting on pictures he lately learnt to cut." By age seven he was handy enough to help his five-year-old sister in making "quite a pretty scrap book." Teenagers with more discerning eyes aspired to cleaner and more exact cutting. "I find it rather difficult to cut out the pictures," a fifteen-year-old averred, "but not so much so as I expected I should[;] I am far from being discouraged." Older clippers might spend the better part of a night shearing snippets to perfection; one scrapbook aficionada set upon the *New York Mirror* for her evening's task. Helpers could transform the lonely tedium of snipping into a sociable occasion, as happened to a thirteen-year-old printer's daughter, whose callers "came here and cut pictures out of old books and papers." It was a sociable world of cut-and-paste in an era of abundant, inexpensive, and expendable printed material.[2]

Prior to gluing sessions, scraps had to be collected and stored. During assembly, friends and family might donate pieces, as in the case of one Orange, Massachusetts, woman who got "a letter from Lib. with 3 pieces of poetry for my 'Scrap Book.'" Thoughtful donors anticipated recipients' special interests. "The scrap about the Irish is delightful & shall be carefully preserved in the scrap-book," a minister's daughter promised her sister. "I have ever felt lively interest in the Irish," she explained. Senders of scraps thus participated as silent collaborators with these books' compilers, whose outside help continued during storage. An eighteen-year-old who had just moved away from home involved several family members in retrieving his old scraps: "Don't make a mistake and send me the scrapbook that is filled," he instructed his mother in a postscript to a sister's letter asking her brother to climb up into the attic for them—"but the big one—blue covered. I had a budget of pieces cut out." Careful compilers kept "scrap boxes" for amassing, ordering, and preserving material, but occasionally even these contained a messy heap. "I was at Eliza's again pasting in J. M.'s scrap-book[;] H. A. & T A T came in with his box," a teenager noted. "Hohohokumm! What a sigh[t]!"[3]

Once collectors assembled scraps, they arranged and glued them into books that would preserve them and make them easily accessible. Some compilers reserved blank books for the purpose, but clippings found their way into diaries, commonplace books, and other personal writings. A few diaries became virtual scrapbooks when scribbling ended and cutting and pasting took over. Thrifty compilers recycled books; over pages in an old penmanship "copy book," one woman superimposed a variety of recipes and newsclippings, including poems from the *Ladies' Magazine* and political articles from the *Independent Chronicle and Boston Patriot.* On another occasion, she used a Maine annual state register as a base. So, too, a frugal Charles Cobb resolved to "get some old Legers . . . if possible and convert them into scrapbooks." Virtually any bound or stitched printed material could be sacrificed for the purpose. Once pasting the clippings on pages began, it could easily devolve into a tiresome and messy chore. "Have been pasting in my scrap book. . . . O, how I wish it was done!" a stable keeper's wife moaned. A week later she congratulated herself: "Finished my scrap book to day of which I am *very* glad." Pasting rarely inspired mirthful accounts in diaries, except when other diversions attracted attention: "In the evening I pasted in my Scrap-book," an engraver's daughter wrote, "and meanwhile we were all very much amused by the antics of a little mouse, which had found its way into the chamber." Sociable efforts, too, could spur solitary scrapbook makers on. "Mrs. Susan, Luthard, & Phebe Young visited us. We girls are making [a] scrap book," one young Vermonter told her diary. The next day, she added, "I shall finish mine tomorrow."[4] There was nothing like the inspiration of friendly competition.

Scrapbook makers said little about arranging their material, but the final product told the story. They tended to crowd their clippings without overlapping. Scraps formed pieces of a jigsaw that, when properly laid out, filled up the entire page. One compiler learned from a friend how to economize space: "Spent a very pleasant evening, and learnt a new way to patch difficult pieces in my scrap-book." Fancy layout was a secondary goal; after all, scrapbooks showcased reading matter, not the maker's flair for design. Some compilers, like one Beverly shoe binder, however, viewed their scraps with an artistic eye. In one well-balanced collage combining word and imagery, she surrounded an engraving of a bark with newsprint clippings, including verses from "The Bridal of Vidoque," cut from a popular magazine. The arrangement's sum was greater than its parts, for it expressed a tragic incident in her life, the recent death of her seafaring lover. The ship may represent the one on which he died, while the poem reflects the despair she voiced in her scrapbook-journal: "[H]ow vain were my hopes. . . . Now who would wish to live."[5] In this way, scrapbook makers left a series of clues, some mute, others indicative, yet others eloquent.

What happened to scrapbooks once they were finished? They entered into social circulation as they played roles in friendship, courtship, and family life. One thirteen-year-old, for instance, borrowed a friend's and inscribed into her diary an anecdote she found amusing; eleven years later, her betrothed came to call one night "& brought his Scrap Book," perhaps to demonstrate his literary character. Scrapbooks might be presented as gifts to loved ones relishing quotable lines. After sending a scrapbook to a family member in Maine, a Bostonian penned a follow-up: "I suppose you have got that trifle of a book the contents of which I scraped together in my leisure." He offered, "[Y]ou [might] possibly find among its contents a motto for some of your momentary cogitations for the newspapers."[6] These personalized anthologies that sometimes inspired literary production also represented compilers who wished to be remembered through their selective reading tastes.

Commonplace Books

Rather than scissoring passages and thereby leaving gaping holes on book or periodical pages, some people transcribed parts of novels, essays, and biographies or captured entire short works such as poems. Volumes devoted to these selections from printed works were called commonplace books or extract books; they differed from scrapbooks in that they were handwritten, and yet they were like them in sometimes circulating to borrowers who could contribute to them. The main object of commonplace books, like scrapbooks, was having a ready storehouse of miscellaneous reading matter. "I suppose you . . . no doubt have filled your Extract books—and added a great deal to your stock of 'General Reading,'" a friend posited to a convalescing former classmate. These assemblages of quotes provided a resource for people authoring compositions, public addresses, and, most commonly, private letters. But there were other reasons for commonplacing. One farmer keeping a book in which "All that is written in . . . has been written before" believed he was providing a service for his children in that they would not have to read the same material: "Few can read much—No one can read every author—Hence the necessity of this essence of Writing." He extracted novels such as Bulwer-Lytton's *Devereux* and *Rienzi,* but also religious works such as the *Book of Martyrs* and the *Life of John Summerfield.* Extracting consumed hours; as even one resolute commonplacer remarked, "I should like to extract a great deal, but time would fail me."[7] Still, it saved time in rereading books to find that one dimly remembered uncommon passage.

Commonplace books ideally contained only the most select extracts, so compilers actively applied their aesthetic judgment to seek out worthy passages. Enoch Hale, who opened this chapter, resolved that only "the more elegant pieces of a brief nature, such as may answer well for *quotation,* in the course of *Writing* or *Speaking,"* would find their way into his extract book of poetry. Lecturers exhorted keepers of commonplace books to be discriminating. A well-read bonnet factory worker took such advice to heart when she paraphrased one Lyceum speaker's counsel "to read with a pen in our hands, so that we might note the beauties or striking truths of authors. . . . [He] discoursed at some length on the choice of reading—the cultivation of a fine taste—enumerate[d] several authors. [He] seemed to think *Milton* the *highest* and sweetest of the English bards, even ranked him before Shakespeare. [S]aid Gray, Thompson [*sic*], Cowper, Hemans, Wordsworth and others are classic." Some extractors were generally guided by the kind of selectivity this lecturer advocated. One, for example, excerpted from European authors such as Samuel Taylor Coleridge, William Wordsworth, Friedrich Schiller, Percy Bysshe Shelley, and a few Americans such as James Russell Lowell and Lydia Sigourney. Of course, personal taste could be at odds with what connoisseurs deemed the "best." A Westering schoolmaster transcribed some cherished songs and ballads titled "The Old Arm Chair" and "The Carrier Dove" in his extract book, while an elderly Hartford woman sprinkled in, among quotes from Whittier and Walter Scott, a "Valuable Remedy for Sailors, by Capt. S. J. Gerry." Even in sophisticated commonplace books excerpting classic works, news items with personal import frequently appear. Some commonplace books contained not only quotes from less-than-renowned authors but also original verse, personal commentary, and copies of letters, not to mention drawings, newsclippings, and other items, all scattered among the words of literary luminaries. A few people even composed critical responses, as did one woman who, after years of transcribing fragments, "determine[d] from this time to write reflections upon every book I read." In this way, texts from other texts could encourage original composition. When passed on to others, these books became a form of social capital.[8]

Just as commonplace books could give way to original material, so could diaries, through extensive deployment of quotes, come to resemble commonplace books. For some diarists, quotes occasionally began to outnumber daily entries. "But I must stop or I might transcribe till my little book were filled," a bonnet-factory worker exclaimed after copying seven verses of poetry in her journal, "but this is not the purpose of my *Diary.*" If these urges to excerpt in diaries troubled them, why did they persist? Some habitual quoters did so because they needed to record something on the spur of the moment with no blank sheet available other than the diary page; the temporary exigency spawned a permanent practice. For many readers, excerpting in diaries, as in commonplace books, was a way to hold onto a small portion of a borrowed book. After charging out *Memoirs of Wordsworth,* the aforementioned factory hand exclaimed, "Oh! this is one of the deprivations of poverty, not being able to buy books. Am tempted to transcribe the little poem, ['I Wandered Lonely as a Cloud'] here it is so exquisite." Extracting also preserved a poem from her "much worn copy" of Longfellow's work *The Seaside and the Fireside.* Whether scribblers excerpted in diaries or extract books seemed arbitrary; storing quotes in one seemed as tenable as garnering them in the other. The diary, though, encouraged writers to use quotes to lend special meaning to the life story. "I think it well that these beautiful things be interwoven into the texture of our daily lives," the bonnet maker wrote.[9]

Quotations could be deployed in diaries to enrich and savor everyday experience. After catching "a sweet little bird in the schoolhouse this noon," a New Haven schoolteacher transcribed a stanza from Felicia Hemans's "Bird at Sea": "Bird of the greenwood! / Oh! why art thou here? / Leaves dance not o'er thee, / Flowers bloom not near. . . ." Something as unremarkable as contentment could call for a quote. By quoting, a farmer's daughter favorably assayed her mundane life in light of a ball she had just attended. "We are apt to think that another state is a greater good until we have tried it," she wrote, after which she applied lines from Cowper: "'It is content of heart gives nature power to please / The mind that feels no smart enlivens all it sees / Can make a wintry sky seem bright as smiling May / And evening's closing eye as peep of early day'." Many diarists wound down their nightly diary entry with a well-chosen quote about slumber, especially after a tiring day. An exhausted traveler signed off, "'To bed, to bed, ye sleepy head.'—*Mother Goose,"* while a journeyman printer, having strenuously pulled a hand press over a thousand times the previous afternoon, closed with a quote from Edward Young's *Night Thoughts:* "I must seek 'Tired nature's sweet restorer, balmy sleep.'" At day's end, quotes might express feelings, even sexual ones, otherwise unutterable, as when a newlywed summoned the "Light of the Harem" from Thomas Moore's poem "Lalla Rookh": "There's a bliss beyond all [that] the minstrel hath told, / When two, that are linking in one heavenly tie."[10] Because transcriptions inserted between daily entries in diaries could be associated with contemporaneous circumstances, they held more social significance than ones left typically undated in commonplace books.

Diarists deployed quotations on rarer, upsetting occasions, too. Offenses against one's heartfelt social commitments could summon an author's well-chosen words. Charlotte Forten declared her indignation over Bostonian Anthony Burns's May 1854 arrest under the hated Fugitive Slave Act by quoting from William Cowper's poem *The Task:* "The weather is gloomy and my feelings correspond with it, how applicable now are the words of the immortal Cowper,—'My ear is pained, / My soul is sick with every day's report / Of wrong and outrage, with which earth is filled.'" It was as if the poet had sympathized with her innermost feelings. Verses could comfort when inscribed alongside painful reflections. A recently migrated German Jewish peddler invoked an "old maxim" as he pined for his home while selling wares in Massachusetts. "I long for the beautiful days in my beloved homeland. Will they ever return?" he wondered. "Yes," he replied, "a secret voice tells me that all of us will again find happiness. . . . When you go the way of duty / God is ever at your side / Even though new dangers threaten / Courage in your heart shall bide." Quotes could also give succor in times of illness. One Lowell weaver complained, "This week my health very poor. I feel often to express myself in the language of a poet 'Sorrow and pain attend us to the tomb.'" Of course, when a loved one's death left diarists speechless, transcriptions filled the void. While sacred words often held the most meaning, mourners also cited secular writers' inspirational works, such as Felicia Hemans's poetry, Alfred Lord Tennyson's *In Memoriam,* and Henry Wadsworth Longfellow's prose poem *Hyperion.* Universalizing the ever-potential singularity of distraught emotional states, literary quotes were deployed as therapy.[11]

When mourners, however, turned from diaries to consolation letters, quotes negotiated the delicate social intrusion upon private periods of grief. More than other types of correspondence, condolence letters contained poetry. Mere conversational words truly could not console the inconsolably grieved, so verse especially suggested sympathizers' respectful awareness of the futility of the situation—and the supportive distancing it required. Most complied with a line from a clipping that Mary Baker Eddy inserted in her scrapbook: "Step not within the shrine where sitteth sacred grief." Consequently, only very close friends or family members properly extended written sympathies. "[M]any times I have earnestly wished to essay with my pen a word of sympathy, but I feined to intrude, for in the season of severe affliction the language of sympathy seems to belong only to our intimate personal friends," one woman wrote to an acquaintance who had lost a brother. "And even they are poor comfisters." The writer then sought shelter beneath Elizabeth Barrett Browning's "Substitution": "'When some beloved voice that was to you / Both sound and sweetness, faileth suddenly; / And silence against which you dare not cry / Aches round you like a strong disease and new.'" Condolence letter writers sometimes quoted the deceased's favorite poems to demonstrate former bonds of intimacy within a dense social network. "A year or two since Mr Paine repeated to me a verse of poetry that he said your brother was in the habit of repeating very often to him," a rural widow explained to the grieving sister before quoting Horatius Bonar's "Resurrection": "'Here in the body pent / Absent from heaven I roam / I nightly pitch my moving tent / A days march nearer home.'"[12] Departed loved ones could yet exist, embodied in shared poetic lines.

Correspondents who summoned favorite authors to help them express themselves, had to ensure that the recipient would get the allusion, especially if it was ironic. They did this by quoting more familiar sources such as the Bible, Shakespeare, Tennyson, and then-well-known writers such as Hannah Flagg Gould and Felicia Hemans. But such familiarity varied. A rural Vermonter worried that she would be left in the dark by references to the Bard's works: "I shall go to reading Shakespeare as fast as is possible. For I find I am getting quite behind in the times, as everybody old and young is quoting the great dramatic poet and to me poor thing it is all *'Heathen Greek.'*" Writers took precautions in quoting possible unknown sources; in humorously referring to *Hamlet,* a country schoolteacher made sure that he cited the author. "'What was I about to say?'" he opened his letter. "'By the mass, I was about to say something.' *Shakesr.*"[13]

Letter writers sometimes emphasized a specific message with appropriate quotations. When Prudence Crandall, principal of the Canterbury Female Boarding School in Connecticut, was faced in 1833 with the white community's bigotry because she wanted to admit black students, she quoted the Bible in such a way as to tell her correspondent, abolitionist leader William Lloyd Garrison, to moderate his wrath. "Permit me to intreat you to handle the prejudices of the people of Canterbury with all the mildness possible as every thing severe tends merely to heighten the flame of malignity amongst them," she pleaded, enlisting Proverbs 15:1: "Soft words turn away wrath but grievous words stir up anger.'" An elderly farm woman invoked Isaac Watts in writing about the birth of a nephew she feared would be spoiled, or worse, taken by death, from doting parents: "I think a son there will be a great pet I hope they will not make it too much an idol and that he may be spared to them for a comfort and consolation in the journey of life[.] 'Children and friends are blessings too[,] / If God our Father makes the[m] so.'"[14] Quoters thus summoned the authority of published words to footnote their point.

Quoting could be overdone, however. Overquoting without close integration into the information and observations being conveyed could seem a waste of good paper at the expense of sociable exchange. A mill worker feeling economically thwarted quoted two lines of a thematically related Mother Goose poem—"'When I was a little boy and lived by myself / All the bread & cheese I had' &c"—before stopping herself. "You probably know the rest and can sympathize with me," she assumed of her friend. Some people even apologized beforehand for excess. After using one extensive reference in a letter to her storekeeper husband, one Vermonter begged forgiveness for the second. "Excuse my quoting poetry," she implored, "and allow me to write one verse more." "Having resorted to quotations," a land speculator apologized to his sister, "I will [sign?] . . . out this letter, which I feel is becoming tedious."[15] Writers wanted to inject their letters with a literary sensibility but had to do so without seeming pedantic or showy. Not surprisingly, indiscriminate or prodigious citation was universally disparaged by correspondents.

One way to avoid overquoting was to personalize excerpts by adding something of one's own. For example, one of the condolence letter writers we discussed earlier appended to her lines from Browning's "Substitution" a stanza by her own hand aimed at the immediate situation: "Our sufficient help then cometh / from another source than even / the closest earthly friendships / And I know *that help* is yours / that it never faileth you." Thus, quoting could be a springboard for literary creativity within the social needs of the moment. So, too, could the many slight, perhaps intentional variations in transcription. Such emendations and alterations of published texts were not confined to correspondents, of course, but appear in commonplace books and quote-filled diaries.[16] In all, the creative impulse was satisfied, ironically, through acts of preservation and transcription of preexisting texts.

Annotation and Defacement

Readers' marks upon printed texts provide firmer evidence of deliberate alterations of the original. They often emended books by writing in them, either on endpapers or flyleaves, in the margins, or on the print itself. Besides serious commentary ("annotations"), there were irreverent or irrelevant inscriptions—defacements in the eyes of some or playful notations in those of others. Regardless of their purpose, these scribblings created a unique, variant "edition," yet another kind of text from text.[17]

Markings on printed passages ranged from simple symbols to full sentences. Although many annotators evidently devised their own systems, some followed published advice. "To day I learned in my [Isaac] Watts a very useful way of marking my books," one careful reader explained in her diary. "When I differ from the author I shall mark it with a + when I doubt any thing with an interrogation? When any thing is good with a marginal line, & when it is *very, very* good with two marginal lines." If overly ambitious, markers' methods could break down. One Dartmouth College student targeting passages for extracting sighed in defeat that he "found the margin one continuous mark, before I finished." Marks of this sort usually had a designated purpose in mind, if only to help readers retrieve specific passages. To contemplate the text more fully, annotators used extensive commentary, which might potentially reach out to future readers, too. "All along are little notes of her pencilling," a schoolteacher observed after examining a poetry anthology left by a late friend. "How they carry me back to the days when she was reading it," she concluded. "And the many times we shared our intellectual pursuits."[18] Annotations enhanced a book's value when they became a record of social relations.

Annotations that challenged institutional authority might have in their time been deemed defacements, but they nonetheless allowed markers to vent frustrations, dissatisfaction, and boredom cleverly. School books, tracts, and music books seemed the most susceptible to these mischievous notes in which annotators spoke to peers. New texts from older, drier texts could result from wordplays of omission as much as from marginalia. Charles Cobb and his district school classmates collectively corrupted a copy of Noah Webster's spelling book to amuse themselves. "[T]he boys got a notion of marking out phrases in it with a lead-pencil," he recounted of a classroom day. "We would enclose certain words in different lines, but near each other in marks, of which I will give two modest specimens. 1 The beams of a wood-house are upheld by God. 2 Our friends send forth an agreeable smell." In order to contrive the joke, the students struck the line in Webster's text which intervened between "by" and "God," as well as the remainder of the line beginning with that latter word: "The beams of a wood-house are held up by ~~post and joists; these are parts of the frame.~~ God ~~makes the ground bring forth fruit for man and beast.~~" The other original text, with appropriate strikeouts, went: "~~Grave stones are placed by graves, as memorials of the dead. They call to our remembrance~~ our friends ~~who are buried under them or near them The blossoms of spring~~ send forth an agreeable smell." The surreptitious antics ended when Cobb "put it in the stove, for fear the School-master would get hold of it." While Cobb and his friends contrived their scheme for a moment's laughter, one college student, bored while listening to a long-winded professor's recitations, addressed generations of abused students, past and future. He recounted that he "was very amused on looking over a classmate's book, to find an entry, made by some individual who had before owned it, in the margin . . . several passages of the story the professor had told in illustration (and finding with what critical regularity the old man brought up the same never failing never forgotten anecdotes)." As a warning to future victims of the professor's blustering, he determined "to make similar notes in my own book, for the benefit of my successors." One of the most creative challenges to textual authority was undertaken by a West Point cadet from Rhode Island who mocked the title page of his school book for "all persons into whose wretched hands it may fall." He transformed "Theory and Practice | of | Gunnery. | Translated from the "Cours de Balistique" of | Profr. Percy of Metz; | For the use of the | Department of Artillery, | U.S. Military Academy. | West Point, | May 1833" into "Theory and Practice | of | DISGUSTING. | Translated from the French Curse | de Ballassticks | By | Professor N. Persy—Principal Longearred | Professor at Metz | For the use of the Foolish | and the ridicule of the Sensible | Cadets | of the US Mil^{y} Acd^{y} | By Zeb Kinsley | Professor of Artillery | and | Furnisher of Provender." Not content to corrupt the title page alone, he caricatured the "Genius of Artillery," complete with a cannonball shot from the substantial nose of his professor (fig. 2.1).[19]

For some defacers, the substance of the text little mattered, for social situations alone determined the content of the annotation. One traveling schoolteacher amused herself by using her sister's religious pamphlet as a journal. "I had a tract which I had purloined from E.'s library," she explained, adding that "after perusing it, all at once I found myself scribbling all over the margin." After reporting at length fellow travelers' eccentricities, she observed, "I can gossip a little longer if my margin holds out. 'Oh how I dread going back to the city again' says a lady behind me. So do I, too, but I have come to the last leaf of my tract, and shall be obliged to wait till I can obtain a sheet of paper to finish." An irreverent Vermont bachelor used hymnal marginalia to flirt during Methodist services. "In front of us was a slip full of Ladies, with one of whom I kept up quite an animated conversation." The deed scrivener continued: "We used up all the spare leaves in two hymn book[s] to carry our communications, after which we resorted to the *Deaf* and *Dumb* alphibet." Surrounded by boys during a rehearsal for an amateur theatrical production, seventeen-year-old Calista Billings, a financially strapped shopkeeper's daughter, also flirted, by "writing in William[']s singing book" before he arrived and circulating it. When "William came," however, she "rubbed it all out" before he could spy her suggestive pencilings.[20] Subjected to the eraser, they remain forever Calista's secret.

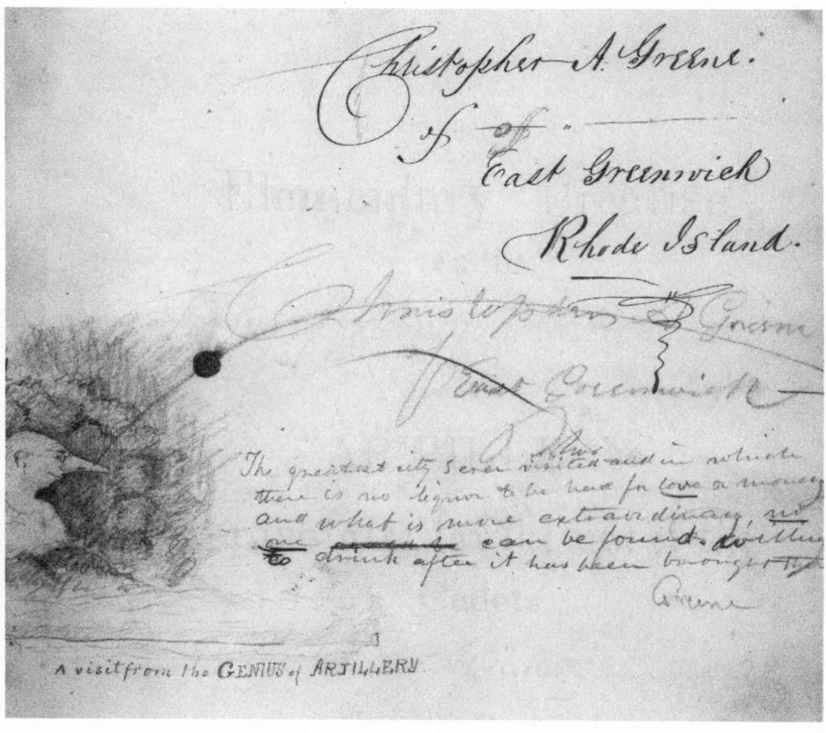

Fig. 2.1 ✦ In his doodlings in a ballistics textbook, Christopher A. Greene, a West Point cadet from Rhode Island, caricatures his professor and enters some humorous original lines. "A Visit from the Genius of Artillery" and inscription, 1833, in the student's copy of Persy de Metz, *Elementary Treatise.* RHix 37716. Ink on paper. Manuscript MSS 1003, Folder 2, Christopher A. Greene Papers. Courtesy of the Rhode Island Historical Society.

Mental Editions

Some editions produced without the aid of pen or pencil were those stored away in the minds of their creators who memorized texts "fit to be hung up in the antechamber of every body's heart." Not only verses but also excerpts, prayers, and hymns were committed to memory by old and young alike. Memorization was practiced both in the classroom and beyond. As an educational skill, it impressed various pieces of literature, rules of grammar, and other facts and figures upon the mind for dissemination through recitation, declamation, or examination. But beyond the schoolroom, when it was practiced voluntarily, it promoted self-cultivation. An Irish Catholic immigrant businessman told his son, a student at Harvard, that memorization "for a scholar or gentleman is indispensible." He advised him "to commit to memory several choice pieces or extracts from elegant Authors and Orators making yourself well acquainted with their *sentiment—imagery—argument*—and their other leading *properties* and *proportions* so you may at all times be able to draw from them ideas strengthening your assertions." Although elite folk practiced memorization to maintain status, farm boys such as Charles Cobb might do so for a sense of empowerment, as when he wanted to predict the outcome of the 1852 presidential campaign based upon his mental version of state electoral tables.[21] Memory plays tricks, however, and memorizers inevitably created "flawed" editions that varied slightly from the original. These imperfect editions also bore the stamp of extraneous ideas and associations filling the head while one memorized and the circumstances under which such activity was undertaken. But because of the varied contexts of memorizing, even perfectly committed texts would differ in personal meaning from the original.

Memorization started early in life, when family members read aloud to children from the Bible, poetry, and simple stories. One rural Maine mother gauging her four-year-old's progress noted that she delighted in memorizing; "she laughed & said a little black grasshopper flew by her & [']He looked in my face with his little round eye / I was sorry for that for I was afraid he would fly.['] These lines she has heard me read, or rather almost exactly like them, she has slightly altered them." Children naturally conflated memorization with reading; being yet illiterate, they could only recite back what they heard read to them from books, as if an open volume somehow induced words to flow from page to mouth. In this sense, children's memorization often mimicked reading, as a Maine farmwife observed of her nephew, "little John," who would "sit down and open a book and read off gravely as if the lines were indeed before him—'The *dods* delight to bark and bite.'" However imperfect, these precocious mental editions could linger over the years, as one Rhode Islander testified at age twenty-seven: "There are two lines of one of the first hymns my mother taught me when a little child, that has haunted my mind ever since." The lines were "'What more than others I deserve? Yet God has given me more.'" The reason for their impact, she ventured, was that it "is a sort of peaceful wondering at the goodness of God, that pervades my mind" upon remembering them.[22]

Aware of the high social capital flowing from memorizing literature, adults demanded more of themselves, such as longer, more intricate, and nearly exact mental editions. After all, they were subject to others' scrutiny as they deployed them in conversation and letters. "My dear father you speak of Pollok's 'course of time,'" a minister's daughter wrote in her diary kept for her parent. "I intend to attempt to comply with your request *in part* by committing the finest extracts to memory." However, she feared not being able "to grasp & retain the whole of such a prize." Others worried, too, that low memorization skills would limit their capacity to perform before audiences. A sickly farmer, subdued by the "Canadian Boat Song," complained, "I have been trying hard to learn it, so that I may have the opportunity to sing it to my companions, if they wish, without the aid of the book. It is extremely difficult for me to remember the words of any thing." Mental distraction could vex memorizers hoping to acquire language skills for reading continental literature. Wanting to impress the rich mercantile circles in which she moved with her French yet unable to memorize grammar, Harriett Low harshly chastised herself : "I got sad and *triste;* perfectly dissatisfied with myself and my capability. . . . [A] sensible man would soon be sick of me."[23] In tying her frustration in memorizing to mental dullness, she worried that she could never attract an intellectual spouse.

There were many other, no less challenging reasons for memorizing literature. At school, the pressure was to get good grades. "Milton is the hardest of all—I can write two compositions, in the time it takes me to get 30 lines of Milton by heart," an academy student grumbled, observing, "Shak.[espeare] is much easier." Regular classroom drilling promised to remedy fragile memory. Beyond schoolrooms, people who designed courses of study for themselves also memorized to sharpen the mind. "I think if I read poetry, and attend to its beauties and commit to memory," a woman explained to her friend, "I can cultivate my memory in that way." The devout practiced daily memorization of passages in the Bible, sometimes as parts of nonliterary routines. A believer resolved at the start of her journal that along with daily bed making before breakfast, saving "two cents a week for benevolent purposes" and giving up butter for the year, she would "learn a verse of Scripture every morning." When recalled, memorized material could provide uplift. "If heeded they would charm away evil spirits quicker than any amulet," Frances Merritt Quick remarked of some verses she learned to ward off despondency. Lawyers in particular honed their memory by recalling poetry, adding literary spice to a steady diet of jurisprudence. One attorney who held that a "little poetry now & then is beneficial" memorized, after office hours during a single month, Thomas Moore's "Sacred Songs" and Byron's "Know Ye the Land." During another week he learned all of Thomas Gray's "Elegy Written in a Country Churchyard" and "Progress of Poesy." Some women committed poetry to memory while sewing to relieve the tedium. Such endeavors required considerable self-discipline, but pleasurable rereading of messages from loved ones could impress words effortlessly. On receiving a letter from his spouse back home, one Illinois shop clerk "put up the blinds and lit the lamp and cut the envelope and then I read the dear words over four times so I knew it by heart own." Mental etchings of this sort could long endure, as one whaler realized in summoning a clipping of poetry given him by his first love in 1820. After transcribing it into his commonplace book fifteen years later, he remembered, "I need not say that every line was quickly engraved on my memory as I thought how fondly! they were Eliza's actual sentiments."[24] The distance from memorization to memorialization was often small indeed.

Texts from the World of Spirits

Another kind of text from other texts was produced by "spiritualists" who believed gifted mediums could communicate with the dead. Although some adherents, and not a few charlatans, turned table rappings and séances into spectacles, others simply professed a deep religious faith in the intercourse of earthly and spiritual worlds. Whatever the case, mediums attempted to receive and transmit, often in writing, those "texts" delivered to the living from the "world of spirits." Skeptics, of course, saw much to ridicule in such communications. For them, spiritualist transcription was but a figment of the medium's imagination, not an edition of a text conceived in the afterlife. Yet few scoffers could deny at least the possibility. "These so-called Spiritual communications are singular and some of them are rather striking to an unbeliever," an editor's wife concluded after watching a friend channel messages from a deceased relative.[25]

According to believers, spirits delivered messages that could be clearly received, spoken, and transcribed by the living. A mediumistic neighbor asked Charles Cobb to record a séance. "He wanted I should write off his revelation while he read it," Cobb began. "Having armed myself he dictated as follows viz—Communication from Samual C. Wood, deceased to" three members of the spiritualist circle. "Wood" rhetorically asked and answered his own questions at length, which when transcribed read in part, "'How are the spirits permitted and enabled at this time and in this manner, to communicate to us' Answer 'In the year 1843 a change was made in the world of spirits.'" For some mediums, words flowed directly into the pen. Black abolitionist William Cooper Nell once "attended a meeting for Spiritual reading and conversation—several articles were submitted—the readers declaring them to have been written by their hands controlled by an invisible agency." Such abilities were not to be taken lightly and usually believers deferred to others with a true calling. Mary Pierce Poor felt she could achieve contact with her deceased father, but only through talented mediums. "I have had some beautiful communications purporting to be from father & I cannot help believing in them," she revealed to a sister. But when a message came down that she herself should channel with a pen and ink, she demurred: "'The spirits' tell me I am a 'writing medium':—they must be mistaken." One could not even trust oneself where spirit matters were concerned. One channeling seeker who worried, "[I]t seemed my writing must be the result of my own will," transcribed in her diary verses addressed to her from a deceased friend: "Meet me in the silent evening / Where the busy day is done, / Then I'll tell you of our being / In the bright and beautiful home."[26] These earthly editions of heavenly messages offered solace to this schoolteacher who missed the only friend who could understand her literary sensibilities. More than an undisciplined flow of words, channeling was an outlet for structured poetical inspiration on the part of mediums who thought themselves merely scribes.

In some cases, the spirits supposedly delivered their messages via knocks, tips of the table, or other bumps and noises. These raps that seemingly came out of nowhere first resounded in Rochester, New York, in 1848 but quickly spread throughout New England. By the winter of 1852, even Charles Cobb was hearing them. "I am going to be a Rochester Knocker sometime," he predicted. "I had a host of raps up back of me on the door last night—no mistake—and was kept up half the night in a sweat." Sounds needed an interpreter, however, someone who would assign the knocks to letters of the alphabet and thus transcribe them, otherwise the clamor might resemble rough music. "There are nocking[s] up to Mr George Westgates," one shoemaker recorded; "the 'spirits' if they are spirits nocked out pop goes the Weazel." One method of interpreting raps was to write the alphabet on a sheet of paper and have the human hand guided by the spirits point to successive letters until they formed words and sentences. Charles Cobb reported of one medium that a spirit "rapped at the letters while he run a pencil down the alphabet—No one saw the alphabet, not even himself sometimes—he didn't know anything about what was coming." Ingenuity extended beyond the written word. To aid the spirits, that same medium invented a "Rapping Machine" with "36 keys like a Piano, 26 letters & 10 figures, so that the Spirits could communicate" without human interpretation. The spirits, vexed at the unreliability of mortals as transcribers, were foreshadowing the modern typewriter. Whether delivered through machine or human hand, some knocks performed "line editing" upon transcribed messages, as Mary Pierce Poor reported of a medium receiving otherworldly editorial advice. "[A]fter he has written," she explained to her sister, "he reads it over & Spirits rap (through a medium) corrections. I will send you a session he wrote in this way."[27]

These texts, supposedly authored by spirits and transcribed under their guidance by the living, possessed a strange power when granted the authority of publication and dissemination to a wider audience. For believers, they represented a viable link between mortality and the afterlife—and the continuation of literary communications with loved ones, even after death. But it took the agency of human hands to render these invisible texts visible through transcription. And it took the faith that such human intervention was sanctified.

Texts from Oral Texts

A more down-to-earth rendering of "invisible" texts was practiced by listeners attempting to capture spoken words in writing. Texts delivered orally, such as lyceum lectures, speeches, and sermons, inspired some auditors to paraphrase or even transcribe bits and pieces in notebooks, diaries, and letters. Some scribes took notes while listening, others recapitulated the performance at home, but both tried to capture the fleeting moment, even if only a fading echo of what they heard.[28] How much remained depended upon note-taking methods, strength of recall, and the listener's proclivity to interject both new words and meaning.

Given that memorizing spoken words was hard, some listeners attended sermons and lectures with notebooks in hand. A Congregationalist reported she "took notes this morning from Mr Duttons sermon" as well as at secular lectures at the local institute. Forgetting paper and pencil (pen and ink was impractical) was a chance lost. "I did not take any minutes of his Sermon," a member of the Boston Baptist Tract Society explained, "as I left my book at home." Whether or not he would have used shorthand is uncertain, but it would be necessary to keep up with orators, as a wheelwright's daughter saw when she thought of taking a course in it: "I should like to learn the system if for nothing more only the convenience of being able to write down the words of interesting speakers, &c." Although most of those knowledgeable of the system used shorthand for encoding secret diary entries, not for attending lectures, nearly all devised abbreviations to accelerate their script. Whatever the method, accurate transcription could not redeem a garbled, incomprehensible, or unworthy speech. One academy student who "attended a lecture delivered . . . by Hon. George Bancroft . . . [,] was able to take only a few scattered notes of the lecture" and complained that "it was beautifully written but poorly delivered."[29] Word and performance could deviate drastically.

Most listeners awaited their return home to write down what they had heard. That this was a prodigious exercise of memory can be seen in one listener's account of a lecture by Richard Henry Dana Jr.:

> . . . He said that Lecture going might be rendered a species of dissipation as well as frequenting the theatre, & that there was a fear of there becoming a new amusement; instead of subjects being treated in a solid manner to promote reflection. He remarked that Literature should be made more practical; brought into daily use; & that poetry which even Coleridge observed is "to please.["] Mr D. did not view in that light; it was for meditation & thought, our reading was too miscellaneous, & we read too much & the mind instead of receiving food for reflection was hurried to this & that; & presented but a confused mass. That it was a defect in the education of the children of the present day there was no doubt. He spoke of the Excursion of Wordsworth in his estimation as the greatest poem that had been written since [Milton's] "Paradise Lost." He endeavored to impress the idea that literature was adapted to the wants of man, whether incidental to his constitution or to his mere condition. . . .

In recording such detailed albeit hardly verbatim accounts, time was of the essence, as one lecture-goer found when she noted, "I ought to have written from memory copiously—but it is now too late." To drive home the lesson, she slightly misquoted Edward Young's *Night Thoughts:* "Too often with me is 'procrastination the thief of time.'" Weariness might also prevent listeners from making timely records of lectures. "Have been to my work as usual," a machine shop worker chronicled on Christmas Day 1855. "This evening here attended the Peabody Institute Lecture. . . . Subject 'The Puritan Fathers'—interesting," she recorded, but admitted, "I am weary and sleepy, too sleepy to write." Yet even good intentions and a fine memory, as Charlotte Forten possessed, could not revive a singularly stunning oral text. At times she simply gave up, thinking it vain to transcribe such special passages. "In the afternoon went to Lynn to hear a lecture from Wendell Phillips . . . [who] spoke eloquently and beautifully, as he always does," Forten entered in her diary. "I wish I could transfer a few of those glowing words and noble sentiments to paper; but that is quite impossible." Conversely, nothing could salvage a bad performance. "[His] Sermons are generally common place-noncommital sort of productions . . . —forgotten as soon as heard," a country lawyer's wife criticized a local minister. "I am never impressed with a remark or expression to transmit to my book."[30]

Despite such impediments, many listeners managed to capture something, from highly detailed narratives to sketchy impressions. The notes might be passed on to friends and kin who missed a lecture or read "aloud to the family."[31] In this way, texts created from oral texts not only immortalized ephemeral words for posterity but also coursed through social networks, bearing the listeners' unique stamps. If seen as simple transcriptions of speech, these notes fall short, in that listeners' own words instead of those of the speakers predominate. If seen as products of active minds engaging speakers and transforming evanescent words into subjective but concrete literary artifacts, then these texts speak with eloquence as well as verisimilitude.

Translations

Like recording oral performances, translating foreign-language works required that writers use their own words. Novices might translate literally as an academic exercise, but they still had to choose words from a range of possible replacements. An exact and literal transposition of words was not desirable, anyway, for the end product would be a wooden, awkward version of the original. Because of this, skilled translators tried to retain as much substance and meaning as possible. If not always reaching that, most foreign-language speakers enjoyed transforming one text into another composed solely of their own words. With even intermediate translators eschewing literalness, loose interpretation licensed a creative, challenging form of writing. Translators acquired the ability to do this in two basic ways: in academies and colleges, where students translated assignments in Latin, Greek, French, and German, and outside classrooms, where students did so for their own pleasure or as favors to friends and relatives. The many private study groups offered participants, some of whom had never studied a modern language in school, the skills and incentives to style English language versions of Western European literature.[32]

Although formal educational opportunities often eluded women, private lessons were available. One farm woman, for example, learned Latin in 1782 from a minister and as a girl studied French with her father. Having taken on Italian in the mid-1820s possibly with a tutor and having translated in midlife Tasso and other books that were loaned to her, she maintained her desire to polish her skills at age eighty. As girls attended school in ever greater numbers throughout the nineteenth century, they studied languages more commonly. Latin translation often overwhelmed Mary Pierce Poor at Northampton's Gothic Seminary during the late 1830s: "Oh dear me! what a Virgil lesson! How can my poor brain bear the exertion of translating such a long one!" At Cambridge's Agassiz School in the late 1850s, one student translated Friedrich Schiller's *Song of the Bell,* Heinrich Zschokke's *Broken Pitcher,* and Friedrich H. K. La Motte-Foque's *Undine.* A typical day in 1860 at Miss Porter's brimmed with foreign-language study:

> From nine to 9½ is my Nat. Phil. class, from 9½ to ten my Latin in which I study Cicero from ten to 10½ I study. From 10½ to 11 is recess when we generally walk & have our luncheon (generally crackers six apiece). From 11 to 12 I study my German from 12 to 12½ recite it & from 12½ to 1 when school is done I recite French in which I study Fasquelle & Noel et Chapsal & translate "Le Philosophe sous les Toits." In German I study Douai's Grammar & translate Wallenstein. At 1½ we have dinner, then we walk & at 4½ we have Study Hour, at 6½ we have supper. Then about 7½ or eight Miss Porter reads aloud to us while we work. Unless Madame comes when one class goes into the parlor to talk French. . . . C. Porter sat in my room till Study Hour learning German with me. Finished my French composition in Study Hour.

Charlotte Forten, who began learning Latin and French while at normal school, felt so passionately about the former that she gushed in 1856, "Now to my Latin which I like better than anything else; and which will, I know be still more *interesting* to me when I commence to translate." Latin was not everyone's amusement, though. In January 1861, a Lenox schoolgirl griped, "I'm half dead, going to church, learning my Milton, translating stubborn latin—& freezing—Thermo. 13° bel. zero!"[33]

Translation was the lot of most college students. One student who entered Dartmouth knowing Greek and Latin taught himself French there and translated works in that and other languages; these included Goethe's *Faust* and Madame de Staël's *Corinne,* along with Latin and Greek classics. Voicing a strong "objection applying to all literal translations," he savored stylistic subtleties between the same text rendered in different languages. Holy Cross seminarians were assigned translations of "Fr Sacchi's fables from the Spanish" and the "'edifying letters' of the Jesuits of S. America," some of which were published in a Boston Catholic paper. Translation assignments were not always so coveted, for they could be punishment for incompetence. "Devlin got 40 lines in Horace for asking Jo Callanen where the 'De profundis' was in the prayer book," seminarian James Healy reported. He later quoted *Hamlet,* when yet another lazy student received some "Italian Sermons" as a penalty: "'There is something rotten in Denmark.'" Regarding the pile of fresh translations, he quipped that "[a]t least we shall have no cause to forget many of the Jesuits."[34]

Although men joined extracurricular language courses, women especially applied translation skills they acquired outside schools in private classes or on their own. Mary Pierce Poor, long after she graduated and had children of her own, joined a French class in which she translated Latin into French. "I take my time to prepare," she admitted. One Bostonian recently out of school prepared translations of "tales & fragments from different authors" for her German class, which met locally. Harriett Low having time on her hands as she nursed her ailing aunt whose husband conducted trade, studied both French and Spanish. With a rudimentary knowledge of French when she began study in August 1829, she could fluently translate passages by March 1831. Spanish, which she learned from private tutors starting in March 1830, came somewhat easier. She soon tackled the three-volume *Los Comedias de Moratin* and the two-volume historical novel *Las Ruinas de Santa Engracia* effortlessly. Low prided herself on her accomplishments. "I get great praise for my translations," she could say after only three years of study. After a morning spent translating, she defended herself: "You may think I spend a great deal of time learning languages and so I do, but I do not feel that I waste the time." She argued that "independently of the pleasure and benefit of learning the language, or rather of knowing it, I think it is of advantage having some fixed occupation. It fixes the attention too." Other women translated simply because they enjoyed the language. After graduating from normal school, Charlotte Forten continued with French and Latin, as she took up Gustave de Beaumont's *Marie,* Julius Caesar's *Commentaries,* and Madame de Staël's *Corinne.* After she completed Aesop's Fables, Forten exulted, "How much I love the beautiful Latin language! It always *rests* me, however weary and dispirited I may feel."[35] Facility with a foreign language afforded empowerment and uplift.

Amateur translators often introduced foreign works to friends and families who did not know the language. Harriett Low translated plays and opera librettos for her English-speaking friends and family. German translations were especially welcome since so few people knew the language. In Bangor, some literary neighbors shared their "fine translations of German poetry into English" with seventeen-year-old Mary Pierce. Even John Park, who abhorred German romantic literature, appreciated a friend's offer to read "a manuscript translation of Schiller's review" of Goethe's *Egmont.*[36] Amateurs usually found creative satisfaction in both their personal accomplishment and in providing a literary service to their communities.

Conclusion

Texts created from other texts here testify to immense literary productivity in an everyday social setting. The irrepressible impulse to create by transforming printed materials at hand spawned endless variety. Scrapbooks and commonplace books were literary collages in which snippers and excerpters constructed new meanings through selection and arrangement, often with other people at hand and in mind. To manipulate literature in this way was to make it one's own, but that so many loved ones donated material and helped out in pasting made it their own, too. The memory of this collaboration was as much glued to the page as the scraps. Of course, when diarists and correspondents artfully deployed quotations, published authors turned from contributors to commentators upon texts of life who supplied the right word at the right moment. That so many people could summon the proper quote so easily suggests how much literature lived at their fingertips, but it also hints at their faith that it would touch diary readers and letter recipients. Those same fingers, though, might try to grab a published text away from its writer by correcting, amending, or defacing it—a quite different way of adding one's imprint to the page, while providing a service to subsequent readers. Texts could be also completely reformatted into mental editions through memorization, thereby storing them in the "antechamber" of the "heart," where they could be recalled and freely voiced in social conversations.[37] Such matter-to-mind transformation was reversed for spiritualist mediums and lecture-goers creatively recapitulating on paper texts they imagined or had heard. Finally, translators had to invent ways to describe in their own words foreign expressions, often to appreciative audiences. Everywhere texts were refashioned, literary ingenuity abounded amid sociability.

Such creativity was not always enough, however. Several days after Enoch Hale looked over his impressive 1849 list of texts from texts he had produced, he claimed at his eleven-year journal's close, "I can do better than that." With a long felt "desire . . . very strong for writing," his dissatisfaction was as much social as creative, for he saw little use in "spending time on a book nobody may look at but myself." Charles Cobb, by contrast, hoped to put his scribbling, copying, and extracting to higher social use: "I must be an editor or a clerk." As soon as he penned this, he worried that it was a pipe dream: "[B]ut oh God!—I believe after all unless I do something nice, I shall be a miserable cuss forever." Then, like so many of his contemporaries, he tempered a grim thought by deploying and personalizing an apt quote: "However in any case I'll do the best I can.—'Whatever my hand findeth to do.'"[38]

Chapter 3

Everyday Literature: Writing within Genre Conventions

On the last day of September 1858, Frances Merritt Quick attempted a verse about a celestial event. "Our comet visitor is still more bright and beautiful to-night," she told her diary after a long day of teaching and an evening's walk in the woods. "The length of the tail has increased about four-fold during the last fortnight," she continued before abandoning empirical description for poetic effusion:

> O wonderful wisp of vapor light,
> Why turnest thou earthward thy spatial flight?
> Why spreadest thou out before every star's face
> So proudly, so vainly thy luminous grace.
>
> No doubt our meek stars think that one of their train
> Has travelled abroad and not travelled in vain
> But brought back in place of its own native grace
> A robe from the glittering treasures of space.

She stopped abruptly; helplessly she watched the inspiration drain from her hand. "Poor unfinished poem—," she lamented, "the comet is not very suggestive, notwithstanding I thought I had become quite poetical from having reclined on a rustic bridge in the quiet woods, and looked down into the clear shallows of a little brook, with its sandy floor and its waving weeds and grasses and its autumn leaves." Having struggled but failed to retain the writing impulse, she concluded, "A poet must be a born poet."[1]

Quick was not unusual in trying her hand at original literature, nor was she alone in her frustration. Most of her contemporaries scribbled verse, prose pieces, or other literature—in short, everything literary outside of texts of life and texts from texts.[2] Written for self-edification or friends and relatives, these usually did not result in publication; nor did their writers harbor illusions, for very long at least, that their writings would ever appear in print. So why did they write these unpublished pieces? This chapter's two parts, writing for one's self and for a social purpose, answer this question and discusses conditions and circumstances surrounding composition as well as what these writers felt and thought about their creations. Throughout, we see these unremarkable yet earnest writers channel their "everyday ideas" into everyday literature and so demonstrate how much they imbibed genre conventions.

Writing for One's Self

Much everyday literature was written for the sake of writing itself, not for any special occasion, and neither to meet a certain request nor execute a specific assignment. While many youths picked up the pen in search of a creative outlet, with no need for explanation, older folks at least tried to rationalize any impetuous drive. Inspired by their reading, some emulated celebrated authors, however futile the result. Still others looked to nature, while several wrote for therapy, at times taming overwhelming thoughts with tempered words. Notable, amusing, or memorable events might ignite the creative spark, as might religious awe. Whatever the cause, such impulses summoned spontaneous self-expression.

Some young literary enthusiasts with little training or practice felt they possessed natural writing talent. The resulting squall of pages brim with the pleasure that comes absent self-criticism and aesthetic discrimination. Often those outpourings met a terminal fate, as they did for one down-easter who had prodigiously poetasted during his early whaling years. He recalled, "I was addicted to the habit of writing stuff, that *I* called *'poetry'*" and admitted that "at the time, I thought I succeded very well, but an *improved taste* has since told me that it was such trash, that it is well, it is all lost." Bouts of writing fever became part of the local conversational fabric. Charles Cobb once told his diary a story about a neighbor who got "a notion he could write Poetry and when he tryed (tried) it, he became fully convinced that such was the case." The lad later "examined a few of his former pieces, when to his amazement he found them as he said, enough to make a dog vomit. That night he ended his poetry, by committing about half a bushel of it to the flames." Cobb reflected that one day a shift in artistic self-perception might send his diary up in smoke: "May not this be similar to the end of these VERMONT COLLECTIONS?"[3]

Although self-motivated writing seemingly sprang from an obsession, it more likely emerged from emulating published authors. After reading "quite a pretty thing" by poet John Wesley Hanson, Martha Osborne Barrett, a working-class schoolteacher, fancied, "I shall try and see what I can write out in the form of poetry." Fated to leave teaching for factory work, she envisioned for herself, beyond her humdrum existence, a poet's life like that of French writer Alphonse de Lamartine, "spent with Nature, and amid the happiest influence to cultivate his mind and soul." Against the odds, though, she scribbled. Motivated on one occasion by "a little light reading" squeezed into "a moment or two," she revealed the social ends often lurking beneath the personal creative urge. Referring to a literary friend, she recorded, "[H]ave written some lines to Lucy . . . composed while I was busy at my ironing board." As people read literature that moved them, it naturally brought to mind distant loved ones with whom they wanted to share the moment; any versifying that emerged after shutting the book might address them. First Mate John R. Congdon noted that some lines to his wife were "[w]ritten at sea upon reading and reflection" during a voyage from New York to West Africa. While settled in his cabin with book in hand, he thought of his spouse and daughter: "A mother by the fireside I fancy I see / With laughing prattlers around her knee / The long winter hours beguiling / With this sweet and playful smiling / Provoking many a fond caress / Of ever yearning tenderness / From that delighted Mother." For sojourning Harriett Low, romantic poetry inspired writing, under her aunt's scrutiny, for her sister back home. "Forgot to tell you," she exclaimed, "after reading Lord Byron last night . . . I filled the paper with *poetry* which has just afforded Aunt Low a good laugh." Her aunt's clever gibes only spurred her on. "[S]he has given me the name of *Byrona,"* Low disclosed before picking up her quill again to fashion "some more poetry, I think of a *higher order."* It led her to "think in the course of time I may be a *POETESS."* While celebrated poets lit the way for some writers, fear of mediocrity haunted others who might confess they "had no *genius* that way" after poorly imitating popular authors.[4]

Like the romantics, everyday writers sought literary inspiration from nature. As a Gothic Seminary student, Mary Pierce Poor wrote home about a classmate groping for poetic sensibilities while staging an outdoor commune: "[I] found her with a handkerchief before her face. Upon asking her the cause of her grief, she replied that nothing troubled her, but that she was *trying* to weep in sympathy with all nature around her, the sky was weeping & water was incessantly dropping from the trees, and she did not see why she should not join in the universal mourning. Quite a fanciful idea, though & its authoress confessed that she was not quite as sentimental as she should be, since do what she would not a single tear could she succeed in shedding." Romantic literary inspiration might be confused with its sentimental accouterments, but, just as frequently, dramatic scenery occasioned writing. Upon ascending "Poet's Seat" overlooking "beautiful" Greenfield, Massachusetts, one traveler "felt the only poetical inspiration which ever dansed upon me, & *'impromptued'* in my sketch-book two verses to my home friends." While shipboard during a White Mountains hunting excursion, a Boston Irishman versified in the vessel's guest book, "Think not that it was for mine own self's sake / I traversed the mountains or moved on the Lake, / The Beauties of Nature indeed are all fine / Giving precept on precept and line upon line." The moment became one of infectious literary sociability, as his usually taciturn sporting companion "himself could not help on such a muse inspiring place to honor this Genius of the Lake with a few picturesque lines." Natural settings close to home could also summon verses. Frances Merritt Quick looked to her hometown to create "a Virgilian Eclogue": "In all the varying phase of day / In every season's happy round / What-e'er nature sad or gay / Some gleam of beauty may be found." Then, as with the aforementioned comet, her muse dried up: "To be continued," she resolved, "revised and corrected,—perhaps never." A singularly gloomy dawn of a winter's day by the sea gave a fisherman his topic. Looking out from his cottage window, he noted that "[t]his morning it looked very much like rain . . . it rains very fast and is quite lonesome." The observation resulted in some meditative lines. The first he borrowed from a famous Cowper poem of the same title, but the rest he devised to suit his immediate situation: "God moves in a mysterious way / Strange things he does perform / He makes it ra[i]n when clouds arise / And from rain snow does form."[5] Unlike the renowned nature poet discerning the divine in the sublime, this mariner found it in the mundane, somber veil of rain-filled skies.

Besides capturing natural settings, verse writing offered an emotional outlet that conventional journalizing often could not. Everyday scribblers took up their pens when they needed to confront and stabilize agitated feelings that could not be reckoned within mere diary keeping or letter writing, the conventions of which limited full self-disclosure. Lacking this confessional outlet but still needing to emote without opening themselves to the charge of self-absorption, they veiled the self beneath literary genres. By patiently conforming to the structured framework of poetic forms or literary prose, they tempered the free flow of strong emotions. Such writing allowed people to draw upon internal wells of sentiment connected to cataclysmic life incidents and became a way of controlling internal emotional pressure. This was never truer than in cases of bereavement. The shoe binder who left a scrapbook of verse written upon her lover's death, helped ease grief by bidding farewell: "Adieu—adieu—and once again / I say farewell to thee, kind heart; / When Memory dies and only then / Thine image from my soul shall part, / Our friendship was A summer's day. / Which Death['s] cold hand has chilled away." Like her, the young African American seminarian James Healy poetically grappled with death, that of Roman Catholic bishop Benedict Joseph Fenwick. A tribute to a distinguished public figure "whom thousands loved so well," Healy's poem also reflected his own faith in heaven's rewards: "The smiling flowers are blooming round, / Though no proud columns of him tell. / But there behold the simple cross, / The sign of hope to man below, / So that while we bewail his loss, / We still may hope he is happier now." In his pious and surprisingly optimistic poem, he restrained his sorrow while reaffirming his belief that redemption is within everyone's reach. Beyond evoking such immediate poetic reactions, bereavement could usher in a period of sustained literary production. One student began writing literary prose and verse in her diary about three months after her parents died in a horse-and-carriage accident. Once she expressed the pangs of loss that attend living in a house that no longer feels like home:

> My home has changed, & other things
> Each youthful thought beguiles;
> I love the spot—but oh, those scenes
> Appear not now in smiles.
> 'Tis as some desolating blast
> Had swept o'er every thing
> And left nought in its desert track
> To lure me there again.[6]

Writing her poem may have been a way for her to move from shock to resignation.

Other draining emotions elicited therapeutic writing. A Vermont schoolteacher vented her sorrow in verse, while leaving the reader guessing the cause of her woe: "I sometimes feel a weariness / A sense of present pain. / When the aching mind turns gladly back / To childhoods scenes again. / Fond recolections even yet, / Those spells of memory raise, / And fill the bosom with regret, / For life's young careless day." For some writers, like Charlotte Forten, who never hid her hatred toward the racism she experienced, the reasons for writing are clearer if yet still circumstantial. "Commenced writing a story—subject 'prejudice against color,'" she told her diary, ". . . on the impulse of the moment. 'Tis not possible that it will ever be finished." If anguish demanded treatment through verse, so did love, for passions could be mastered by writing about them, or so it was thought. One betrothed schoolteacher had to somehow ward off her "Cousin Bill" seeking to steal her heart away from her fiancé. The tempter tried everything, from arming himself with presents and making nightly calls to sweeping her off on a romantic ride around a lake one beautiful October day. After this soiree, she turned to her pen and paper for counsel: "As on we went o'er hill and dell / He talked so fast I ne'er can tell / One half the pretty things he said, / I do believe they turned my head." By the end of her poem, she determined never to date the man again, and her marriage took place as scheduled. Like her, a college student wrote to reign in an obsession, this with a young woman, in a strikingly free style: "Julia Victoria Beers / Julia Maria Beers / Jule Beers / bow. wow. wow. hydrophobia." He quickly remarked, as if waking from a trance, "What a page this is! Equal to a page in an *'Omnibus,'*" or literary miscellany.[7]

Not all literary writing healed the lovesick soul or wounded heart, for sometimes literary ideas grew from unusual, unprecedented, or amusing life episodes. Writers away from home and familiar faces might elevate everyday circumstances in new surroundings, as did a Forty-niner who versified during his outbound voyage. He produced one poem, "Spare the Albatross," after the ship's fastidious Captain Whiting sentenced a captured bird to death. "Whiting! Spare that bird / Touch not its downy wing," he scribbled, parodying the popular song "Woodman! Spare that Tree!" Startling events close to home could inspire sociable versifying, as when teenager Calista Billings, turning in for the night, reported that "an Irishman fired off 2 guns & This eve Uncle A & I made poetry on it." Even grooming, if associated with fun, called for a poem. "[W]e had quite a time combing hair," a fisherman wrote during a visit to a neighbor's farm. "Emily combed mine and curled it. She is a first rate Girl. I must make some poetry about her." Frances Jocelyn also found comic relief in everyday events when she composed a mock eulogy: "'Poor Piggie' was slaughtered this morning—shocking to relate. Oh let the Muses mourn and weep for one of their fairest noblest sons thus called down from active busy life to an untimely grave. Grave did I say—ah no not a grave—his enemies would scorn to give him a grave but like the voracious cannibals on foreign coasts they devour the body of Poor Pig. His death is lamented by all his fellow citizins and his memory will ever be cherished with deep regard by all who knew and loved him." She thus squeezed a vignette from life into literary form while satirizing bombastic contemporary orators. When life lent nothing notable for the writer's pen, bemoaning that very lack could prompt a poem. One African American clerk's daughter immortalized time's passing in her poem "I've Lost a Day": "The day how neglected it has been, / The hours how swift they've fled, / The moments, Oh, where are they? / The seconds they too, have gone; / The sound echoes in my ear / I've lost, I've lost a day."[8]

Everyday religious impulses also spawned literature. Of course, much secular writing, whether about love, death, or nature, alluded to religion, if only in a passing biblical reference, but some writing was entirely inspired by religion. A fisherman discovered divine grace's enlightening effects in two sets of poems, "Lines written by me while in Darkness" and "Lines written after darkness has fled away, and God's marvelous light has appeared." One Transcendentalist expressed pantheistic beliefs in his "impromptu lines" derived from intuition rather than prayer or meditation: "I can do naught but be all passion then, / And suffer the deep mingling of my soul / With that in which it would be interfered / Until I feel myself at one again / With the great soul of all from whence I came / A bubble sparkling for a moment's space / Upon the bosom of the boundless sea— / To which with gladness I return again." More conventional religious lines echoed biblical archaisms, like those one Vermonter employed: "Lord in humble reverence now / At thy gracious throne we bow."[9] That this appeared in a family cookbook suggests that some pious verse, though sparked by personal impulse, might also have a social purpose.

Religious meditations, like romantic verse written to enhance everyday observations or prose penned for therapeutic ends, naturally flowed from inspirational source, to author's mind, to blank page. These writings emerged from direct engagement with the font of literary invention: a demon obsession, good book, sylvan setting, life tragedy, romantic attachment, common event, or sacred moment. Because writers' relationship with the creative catalyst was subjective, the resulting piece was primarily self-expressive. Only secondarily might it have social uses, as it circulated to friends and family and beyond.

Writing by Social Invitation

Quite different was everyday literature composed with specific audiences in mind. These pieces, including birthday greetings, valentines, mourning verse, farewell tidings, amateur newspaper contributions, and album poetry, all answered a call from other people to "write something for me." Writers did this under two sets of circumstances: involuntarily as part of their education and voluntarily outside the classroom. Compositional exercises and, indeed, children's first creative efforts, reflected literary socialization: writing in a manner that could be clearly understood, evaluated, and appreciated by other people. However, not all or even most writing naturally resulted from formal training, because far too many of these writers of everyday literature spent far too few days going to schools to explain the facility and creativity—and knowledge of literary conventions—these compositions demonstrate.

Children first attempted literary pieces at home. As they listened and memorized stories, poems, hymns, and biblical verses that adults read out loud, they saw little dividing reading from reciting original compositions. Mary Pierce Poor reported that her precocious though as-yet-illiterate daughter "gets a book & says 'now mother I am going to read a story' & sits down & makes little poems." She worried, though, that her baby's literary and social development suffered by her preoccupation with her imaginative world. "[W]hile she is reading this way," Poor confided to her parents, "she never hears or sees anything that is going on around her—I have been anxious about her brain this winter." If satisfied with their child's budding social sense, parents actively encouraged original, imaginative ideas by simply recording amusing or touching sayings. Daniel Child, for one, jotted down his children's effusions in his diary, an act that helped them understand that words could be made palpable through writing. He once recorded an evening of star gazing with his preliterate four-and-a-half-year-old son: "Evening—an eclipse of the moon; during which, George, who had been watching it gave words to his thoughts as follows: 'If I was a way up in the sky, I could see the whole world—the angels take folks up—the angels are very strong.'"[10] Even the utterances of toddlers could evince a poetic tinge.

As children grew old enough to form words on paper, parents encouraged them to write down literary thoughts for others to read. An editor's wife praised her sons' efforts to fashion items for their annual holiday book exhibit. "Charlie as usual produced his Franklin Library which appeared in fine order, fifteen or twenty new books written principally by the children themselves," she declared, promising to her traveling elder son, "You will have a great deal to do to read up when you get back." Such literary rituals became centerpieces of parent-child relations. Children's literary output sometimes became more formalized, as when they created their own newspapers, wrote copy for them, and invited others to contribute. Looking back upon his own "Scrap Bag," one seventeen-year-old thanked his family for their support. "I am greatly obliged to all of you who contributed towards its interesting columns," he acknowledged after his mother mailed some copies she had saved from a decade past. Other young folks founded literary clubs for compositions that were read aloud. "This evening, I formed a plan, for the Literary Box," a vacationing student noted. "Fan and Cornelia, wrote their compositions, but I have deferred mine till tomorrow."[11] Having ready audiences greatly encouraged fledgling litterateurs.

Children's production of original writings at home was reinforced through schooling once basic handwriting and grammar were mastered. So frequently were essays assigned that one student claimed at the end of his senior year to "have written 60 since I have been in the high school." Composition was required in common schools, private academies, seminaries, high schools, and normal schools, depending on when students began or resumed their education. First compositions in particular became a rite of passage commonly noted. "The girls read compositions for the first time in Sanford's school," a Vermont woman chronicled of her younger sisters' accomplishment. But for some older students, especially rural folk who neglected the classroom in youth, first writings came hard, as Persis Sibley Andrews reported on the homework progress of two such teens boarding with her: "Our School boy & girl sit here (one on either hand) with laboring brains & long anxious faces making a first effort at writing school Composition. . . . These are young persons about 18 years of age of good abilities—by nature—but long neglect to commence the useful practice of putting their tho'ts on paper renders them about as ineaqual to the task now as they wo'd have been at 11 or 12 years of age." The practice was not only academic but also stimulated idea formation and sociability, as she observed: composition "learns them to think & to converse." Like her charges, other students dreaded writing, fearing the inevitable judgment that came with it. A twenty-two-year-old farmer still in school described his befuddlement in intending to "write composition": "[H]ang me I can not pen a single idea. My thoughts have all gone to bed or gone out a visiting." It was the subject matter that often left students trembling. Charlotte Forten noted an assignment that horrified her grammar school classmates: "Wrote a composition—subject—antiquities. It was most amusing to see the dismal, desparing faces when our teacher gave us the subject. We were truly a disconsolate band of youthful, inexperienced antiquarians." Topics requiring ample imagination but little application of research or prior knowledge seemed especially challenging. "We had a fearful subject for Composition today—'Night,'" a student wrote home. "Mine's all done—but no sense. Brains giving out." If broad assignments could daunt, so could specific ones, like the mishmash of unrelated topical themes which perplexed one seminary student. "[W]hen we were going to write our compositions, [our teacher] said she would give us something new," the girl explained in a letter to her parents; "so she gave us a great many words very different from each other, such as church, carrots, silk, earthquake, beads. &c. these she told us to put into our themes, and that we might make them as amusing as we pleased." Such assignments could boggle youthful minds, but even the simplest theme successfully completed gave pause when students had to read the resulting composition aloud. Charles Cobb, already a prodigious scribbler at age seventeen, gingerly approached school composition even when the topic appealed to him: "I like to write as well as others like to read, but writing compositions to read in school, I much dread and abominate." When his piece "ridiculing the old schoolhouse" read aloud by an older student met with "'applause,'" however, he changed his tune. He concluded, "I believe I must some time attempt to write a story it being only fun to write."[12]

Making composition sociable eased the pain and pushed the pen. Some students formed clubs for presenting original work; one Boston "debating society," for example, coordinated writing and speaking around controversial topics like the righteousness of capital punishment, the abolition of slavery, and the politicization of the pulpit. More casual after-school self-help groups added a high dose of sociability to the work, especially if one member supplied the brain power for the rest. "That's a way they have of doing here—Bel furnishes the ideas of half the compositions written," a boarding school student explained to her mother, mimicking her lazy classmates' ardent pleas for help: "Now Isabel, you are a lovely girl, just tell me how to express this—'The father of the stars after he made the light'—

what comes next?"[13] These unmonitored meetings saw a vibrant exchange of ideas and were helpful in easing diffident authors' fears.

Students further honed their sociability and writing skills in conducting and contributing to school newspapers, most of which were only modest handwritten productions. "The Manuscript," a New Hampshire sheet, betrayed its format in its title. Others, like "The Student's Meditations" from Hallowell, Maine, resembled printed counterparts with ruled columns, headlines, and editorials. Handwritten papers were organized by a few motivated student contributors and read or "published" before a limited audience of students, teachers, and, perhaps, a few interested outsiders. "The 2d. number of this sheet was read last Wednesday," one editor announced, boasting, "I had a number of lady visitors that afternoon who came in to hear the paper read." Audiences fluctuated, however, as did editorial staffs and contributor bases—often one in the same. Staffs varied from the skeletal to the elaborate. "This afternoon Alice Vincent came here to write a little school paper with Mary called the Meteor," a thirteen-year-old printer's daughter recorded. Less than two weeks later, the columns were finished and ready to be "published." "After school I read the paper (called the 'Meteor')," one editress's sister proudly asserted. Delivering these papers before mixed crowds could unnerve young women sensitive to the era's proscriptions against them speaking in public. One who read aloud "The Star of Hope," found "it was rather a task to read before so large a number, but hope it [was] to my benefit."[14] The social reticence instilled in girls from birth could be eroded by such experiences.

School papers were only as good as the contributors who faced, perhaps for the first time in their lives, deadlines outside of adult supervision. If contributors were lax, the paper floundered, as was the case with Lexington Academy's "Normal Experiment." Its editor, after a long lapse between issues, noted despairingly that students "are backward about handing their communications in." One reason for this problem was that initial enthusiasm often waned. The first issue of "The Flower," issued from Smithfield, Rhode Island, for example, served up original poetry, political editorials, essays, and announcements, but by its second and last issue, it too had dwindled to paltry essays, mostly by the editors, on celebrated writers (fig. 3.1). Contributions, such as thank-you letters from community members, were not as likely to dry up, but they hardly enlivened columns. Some papers' popularity undoubtedly was due to their often irreverent pieces. A spoof, "An Eighteener['s] Reasons for Going to Church," probably meant for a high school paper, targeted both adolescents who stayed at home on Sabbath to read as well as those who went to church for the wrong reasons: "Felt remarkably inquisitive in the morning, and wanted to know what kind of bonnet the deacon's wife had, as I heard she had just bought a new one—wanted to see all the new styles—expected

THE FLOWER.

VOL. I.] [NO. I.

PUBLISHED SEMI-MONTHLY BY
THOMAS A. BUFFUM.
OFFICE NO. 2 UPSTAIRS
WILLIAM O. BARTLETT, EDITOR.

TERMS
One approved Communication,
OR 3 CTS. PER NO. FOR READING.

The following article is from the pen of our new correspondent. We shall be pleased to hear from the same source again.

There are few of the myriad sources of enjoyment which nature unfolds so many equal to those afforded by twilight. There is something in this hour so tender, so holy, so fraught with simple, yet sublime associations that it belongs to heaven, rather than to the earth.

The selfish interests and common-place distractions of the day are gone by; the heart of man yields up its obstinacy, and gives way to its softening influences.

In this calm, pleasant hour the heart sways the past; the dead, the absent, and the estranged, come thronging back on our memory with force that we cannot control, if we would. The blessings of twilight are every where felt and experienced. Upon the hills, in the valley, and by the brook-side it pours its richest treasures; but in the narrow crowded lanes of the city it is no less refreshing and acceptable—

After the bustle of the day is past and all feelings of ill-will are shut out of the heart, how delightful it is to hold sweet communion with the spirits of the air. We look back on past years, think of those of our friends who have left this sinful world, and gone to the country where there is neither sin nor corruption to disturb its peace and harmony—

What heart has not acknowledged the influence of this sweet and soothing twilight, the hour of love, the hour of adoration, the hour of rest when we think of those we love, only to regret we had not loved them more—when we remember our enemies only to forgive them.

H.

Iona. Asher &c. &c. received sometime since, we have though best not to insert

Debating Society

The Scholars are respectfully requested to meet at the office of Bartlett & B[illegible] this evening, to form a society of the above description.

W.O. BARTLETT
Late Sec.

Fig. 3.1 ✦ This manuscript newspaper, which was read aloud before groups of listeners, was sold at "3 cts. per no. for reading." *Flower* 1:1 (1836): 1. Courtesy of the American Antiquarian Society.

all the beaux would be out it was such a fine day—knew it would be a fine chance to show my new bonnet—too pleasant to stay at home—had no novel to read; and a new preacher, young, handsome, and unmarried." Although students usually wrote copy for school papers, outsiders sometimes added some lines, with no less trouble. One accepted a "polite invitation" to contribute to the "'Literary Journal' a periodical conducted by the pupils of our High School" as a chance to "brush up my literary-ments a little."[15] By reaching beyond students, these papers became neighborhood forums for sociabilities.

Writing for social ends did not end with school graduation. It flourished in the many adult literary societies both men and women organized. These societies ranged from the most informal clubs that met in a participant's home on a regular basis to town lyceums, library associations, church groups, or private institutes. Members contributed essays, compositions, and other pieces for their own edification and the benefit of the group. Recent seminary graduate Mary Pierce Poor presented a composition on "the rights of woman" to the Bangor "spinster's club . . . , an association of seven young ladies who meet at each others houses, for improvement." She also belonged to a mixed-gender association of friends and neighbors called "The Bouquet," which derived its name from an original verse in which "each one of the young ladies & each of the gentlemen are compared to some flower or tree"—gathered together, a bouquet. These clubs invited participants not only to compose but also to ponder ideas: "After the compositions were read we had quite a metaphysical discussion upon innate ideas and first truths—A Mr Warren remarked that he thought the mind when first created nothing but a mere *capacity* for receiving ideas, which it afterwards compares with each other and draws inferences from their relations to each other—'Then,' said Mr Harlow, 'I suppose according to your theory the mind may be compared to a great sponge which draws in ideas like water.'" Informal clubs such as The Boquet sprang up everywhere and included almost everyone. A cabinetmaker's apprentice matter-of-factly told his sister, "I have joined a Debating Society which meet once a week to debate read compositions &c." A diffident farmer's daughter disclosed to her sister of a rural club event, "O dear you don't know how like a fool I have felt for a week past. . . . [N]ext Wednesday *poor me* has got to get up [and] read it [a composition] before all the ministers and doctors and half the other folks in town." Poorer rural lyceums that met at public halls or school houses usually could not afford to pay acclaimed lecturers, so members themselves debated, discussed, declaimed, read compositions, or delivered lectures. A fourteen-year-old country parson's son, for example, attended weekly meetings of the Granite State Debating Society, at which women read aloud the club's newspaper. There he frequently declaimed and eventually presented a lecture on slavery. Indeed, some societies formed around an abolitionist theme. The Juvenile Garrison Independent Society was a self-help group for young African American men devoted to the cause, among whom was William Lloyd Garrison's future *Liberator* comrade, William C. Nell. There, the sixteen-year-old son of a former ship steward reportedly showed "exceptional ability as a speaker and writer." Up and down the social scale, New England was abuzz with literary societies promoting composition.[16]

Literary associations advanced writing for public edification, but everyday scribblers often found enough incentive within more intimate and private networks of personal relations. The strongest push came from composing pieces expressly for other people on various occasions. Sometimes holidays such as Valentine's Day and May Day elicited a profusion of writing, itself considered a gift. At Christmas and on New Year's Day, writers penned notes to accompany presents. At other times, birth, marriage, death, or relocation occasioned a piece of verse or prose. This literature appeared in forms other than pen and paper; yarns, paints, flowers, and fabrics were combined in various ways to spell out love, cheer, adieu, or mourning. Whatever their form, these "literary gifts," addressed to friends and family filled a space uninhabited by other forms of social writing. Literary gifts unlocked a place in the heart devoted to recollections of loved ones, a place inscribed with the words: "I remember you; please remember me."[17]

Perhaps no other holiday elicited literary gifts more than St. Valentine's Day (fig. 3.2). Though mass-produced cards, especially ones with printed messages in verse, had long been available, they were not yet popular. Indeed, one normal school student derided the holiday's commercial face: "Today is St. Valentine's Day. How the eyes of young men and maidens sparkle as they think of the 'pretty nothings' which will doubtless be sent to them today, nicely written on tastefully ornamented and sweet scented note-paper. This custom once so beautiful is like others of a similar nature becoming very much of a nuisance, by means of those hideous representations of monsters for surely they cannot be intended to represent human beings which we [see] suspended in shop-windows and which are sent either to mortify or insult." Her repulsion at malformed cupids on cards was no doubt widely shared, for they could undermine the sender's sincere expression of sentiment. Personalized valentines persisted despite manufactured alternatives because they performed significant social work. Not merely romantic tokens for lovers, they might be distributed at benevolent fair post offices or sent to family members, cherished friends, or classmates as a measure of special regard. A Boston Irishman's daughter who relocated to Georgia, for instance, reaffirmed affection toward her brother back home via original stanzas decorated with painted flowers on a blank card resembling a piece of lace. Valentines to nonfamily members were often anonymous, even if recipients' guessing made secrecy never entirely assured. "I got my Valentines this morning, one a very pretty piece of poetry," a young woman exulted, adding, "Author unknown but strongly suspected." Writing on a friend's note paper and envelopes or using their seal might further veil authorship, yet not staunch curiosity. Sleuthing to identify authors could get out of hand, as shopkeeper's daughter Calista Billings found. "I had 2 Valentines one from William [. H]e thinks I sent him one Monday night," she explained, recapitulating his logic: "Rebecca was sick & I asked . . . for some brandy & William heard me. He was in another room & all through the evening he was talking of Brandy & in his Valentine there was something of brandy." It dawned on her that this was more than coincidence, as "he said when he first began reading it he did not suspect me but when he came to the end [of the poem] he knew it was me. (I did not send it)."[18] His close textual analysis was only misleading.

With anonymity seldom secured, love-struck amateur poets gingerly approached the holiday. Like one young lawyer confessing, "St. Valentines day; have an idea of sending one to ——— give it up," others surely stopped themselves short. The ability to charm with words was often judged harshly, especially if the writer seemed lackadaisical. One young woman complained, "Received two letters ('Valentines') through the Post Office—should not require a very great effort

Fig. 3.2 ✦ The excitement generated at the post office and at home on 14 February is captured in this illustration from a popular literary magazine. "St. Valentine's Day," *Ballou's Pictorial Drawing-Room Companion* 10 (16 Feb. 1856): 97. Courtesy of the American Antiquarian Society.

of the intellectual powers to write such as mine were—they *are passable* to be sure." Overly effusive writers could also meet with rebuff. "Received a miserable love sick letter from some fool purporting to be a Valentine, poor dolt, he needs looking after," a Vermonter snarled. The most fainthearted, nevertheless, penned verse only to keep it to themselves. "St Valentine's day has come again, / Making sad havoc of Cupid's pen, / For as he sits scribbling hour after hour, / Leaving far behind our noted steam power," an academy student poking fun at his clumsy muse scrawled, obviously struggling. The lad confessed that his ideas lacked sophistication. "I wrote them just to see what I could rhyme," he apologized, "& you see the effects. Henry [my brother] told me to keep on my boots so the ideas could not get through my thick soles . . . but I did not think that there would be much difference whether they were kept on or were taken off." Though verses might never be sent, they still occasioned the sardonic scrutiny of critics at hand.[19]

Despite complaints about lackluster valentines, most recipients were happy to get cards for the sociability they represented. Recipients usually said something nice and made sure to record the name of the sender, if known. Calista Billings not only kept track of who sent cards but also tallied up the numbers as they came in throughout the month. "Edward brought me another valentine very pretty I have 4 now this year," she chronicled. Even married, older people removed from the network of exchanges sensed the excitement. "Valentines circulate briskly to day," a Portland lawyer remarked. Expressions of the heart became a form of social capital, so not getting cards sent the opposite message: social marginalization. A nineteen-year-old rural teacher who felt alienated from her students was "disappointed" in finding no valentines at "the Post Office this morning," only "the weekly papers." Charlotte Forten, frequent victim of classmates' racial bigotry, also lamented the day: "Valentine's Day; but no one has remembered me."[20] The sting of these cards' absence suggests their importance as vehicles of socioliterary bonding.

Other occasions also called for literary gifts of verse. Throughout the month of May, leaves of poetry accompanied "May baskets" hung on the doors of friends and family. These gifts could become communal projects, as friends joined together to pick flowers and write. "[A]fter school we concluded to hang some May baskets," Calista Billings explained. "So, A tied 4 bouqets[.] [S]he is going to hang one to William & so is sister & I am to return Franks so we spent the rest of the afternoon in writing poetry." Sociable distribution of baskets could invite unwelcome frolicking: "The first time we went out some boys chased us and we ran back to Mrs. Goodwin's," a Sabbath school student wrote of classmates while delivering baskets. "The next time . . . we succeeded nicely. They did not catch us."[21] These baskets, like valentines, were often reciprocated, and so they ensured a flow of sociability during a time of year lacking gift-giving holidays.

More intimate than valentines and May baskets were birthday verses. Usually sent within letters, these contained specific references to the receiver, such as life events, date of birth, or number of years lived. A young woman from a Rutland farm family received one of four pages in verse that recalled a night at the local lyceum: "One night to debate we all went together, / In the beautiful, bright, frosty, cold winter weather. / The walk home at night perhaps you will remember / How warm you were though it was in cold December / And the gloves which you needed your hands to protect / Had been left in the 'Cademy all by mistake. / The history of base-ball you heard at that time / But I will not enlarge upon that in my rhyme." By jogging the memory of past shared experiences, such writers, if even miles away, made their presence felt. Not all birthday verse was composed for distant family members. John Park wrote some for his daughter still living at home but away in Boston. By repeating her birth date at the end of stanzas, he tailored them to the occasion: "Let others call the world a dream, / And all its transports visionary, / One blessing I substantial deem, / *That* of the seventh of February." The time, thought, and care that obviously went into constructing birthday verse expressed senders' love.[22]

As much as original verse, the notes that accompanied gifts, notably ones exchanged at Christmas and New Year's Day, could be as valued as the presents themselves. This was true even among wealthier recipients used to lavish gifts. "I received a handsome pocket-book from Mrs Lieber," a scion of a bank president wrote of a yuletide gift from his boardinghouse mistress, "and a note, which I much prize, and shall always preserve." Similarly, a poor widow cherished a note from her children's schoolteacher to them so much that she copied it into her diary. It stood out among many other objects received around New Year's Day: "Rec'd this evening a pr of shoes for Henry from his Uncle Rufus & a beautiful little Book from Ella to the children & a note from Miss Little to them. . . . I will copy Miss Little's note to them as some future day perhaps they will like to see it."[23] Such were the value of scribbled sentiments that the note alone was deemed worthy of special archiving.

While holiday notes spread good cheer and kind words to acquaintances, the gift of love in verse form might be given at any time of the year. One golden wedding anniversary of a Maine farm couple saw "poems written for and well adapted to the occasion" by their children, mostly mill workers, who delivered them at the celebration. Love also inspired literary expression by spouses, such as one whose wife recorded that he wrote "two pieces of poetry to *me,*" for no apparent reason, a year and a half after their wedding. Courtship poetry demanded greater tact lest it arouse skepticism. Harriett Low received an unexpected love poem, an acrostic "To Miss Low" from an anonymous but easily identified admirer. It read, in part: "Something there is that as an unseen power / Subdues the wonted current of our thought / Leaving the heart all passive—But one hour / Of *thy* sweet converse, and the Soul is fraught / With feelings of a cast, oh! *too* deeply wrought." In diary marginalia, she dismissed this fulsome cant as a "foolish affair." Some people even wrote poems warning recipients of falling too quickly in love. One counseled her apparently head-over-heels-in-love sister with a poem titled "To Haste."[24] Thus love, like all strong emotions, was approached cautiously with verse in hand.

Although joyous everyday literature abounded, sad missives did, too. Farewell messages promised a lasting memento of people one might never again see. Examples can be found in the many friendship albums often started by young women about to graduate from school or enter marriage. A graduating student dedicated hers thus: "Album, / The world is before thee / And like a child of one and twenty years / From parent care set free, thour't thrown / Upon the troubled elements of time. / Thou are now to seek thy fortune— / To gather treasures from afar and store / Them up for other days." As her verse explains, albums, although owned by one person, a "parent," were circulated or "set free" to "gather treasures." Among them were farewells from classmates as well as sentiments written by friends, relatives, and neighbors passing through her life before she moved west with her husband, a mechanic, eleven years later. This text composed of inscriptions by many hands was a store of remembrances. As one of her scribblers wrote, "Sacred sure this book must be, / to the charms of memory." These compositions often said good-bye by fixing in their recipient's memory a shared past. One album versifier bade a fond farewell to her friend by bringing up some common but unforgettable experiences: "When you may far from Newbury be / And these few lines may chance to see / Then think of friends and people here / And Scenes before you will appear." Albums allowed their "parents" to reenact lost social relations.[25]

Farewells appeared on other media, even on cloth. In one instance, an unnamed mill operative gave "a touching farewell address, written on the end of the last piece of cloth woven by her for" her departing employer. Fabric was an ideal medium for transmitting words of farewell, especially for those working with it every day. Ever burdened with sewing, communities of women literarily enlisted their needles to say good-bye to newlyweds or migrants. "Did you ever hear of an album bedquilt?" one seamstress asked a friend: "The ladies . . . have been making one. . . . Each lady makes a square of calico with a white line centre, on which is written with indelible ink a verse of poetry, a quotation from prose, or a motto with their own name. Should you not think it would be a pretty present, particularly for a bride, a lasting remembrance of all her friends?" Like albums in book form, literary quilts demanded coordinated effort to assemble various contributions, but entire quilts were not passed around for inscription. First, each uniformly sized square had to be cut and inscribed in ink by various people, and only then were the squares sewn together. Quilts inspired inscriptions ranging from mere signatures and dates to evidently original verse, like that written by one contributor: "Accept my friend this little pledge / Your love and friendship to engage / If ere we should be called to part / Let this be settled in your heart / That when this little peace you see / You ever will remember me."[26] As these inscribed squares testify, quilters transcended the limits of writing paper to fashion collaborative literary artifacts.

Literary remembrances became a constant feature of some traveling occupations, such as seafaring. One captain's embarkation summoned a poem that not only wishes him luck in travel—"Success all your voyages / Forever may attend / Until your crossing the ocean / Shall come to an end"—but also looks forward to his retirement: "Then the last of your days / Be enjoyed the Best. / At home with your consort / From the Ocean to rest / With your offspring around you / Your table forever spread / And all your descendants / Be abundantly fed." Before setting off on a whaling voyage, a seaman inscribed some lines in John Pierpont's *Airs of Palestine,* given as a farewell to a young girl: "And when a leizure moment you do spend / In reading 'Pierpont's' works, my pretty friend, / Wherein I am, on land or o'er the sea— / I hope Miss Ellen, you'll remember me." These lines that he later deemed "silly" became for him, also, food for remembrance—a unique token of a friendly relationship.[27]

Death, of course, being the ultimate separation between persons, inspired even greater poetic outpouring. Chapter 2 showed sympathizers clinging most tightly to published texts when enclosing verse in letters, for fear of meddling with grief. If an author wished to offer original sentiments, however, then she or he might make a delicate attempt to remain anonymous. One writer did this by leaving his poem on a doorstep. This versifier, known only as "Amicus," postscripted his poem with "These few, quick-wrought, imperfect lines, the family . . . will accept, from the unknown hand." When mourning verse was signed, it was usually by close friends and family. In "Lines Written to Susan Trowbridge on the Death Of Her Sister," Elizabeth Jocelyn projected the sense that she understood well how the recipient, her dear friend, might feel at the loss of a beloved sibling. Repetition of the deceased's name, "Harriett," and a sense of peering into intimate domestic spaces, marked this poem with a distinctive, personal sense of affection: "And when upon your fireside hearth, / You mournful sit alone, / The vacant seat beside you there, / Will say that 'Harriett's gone.['] / She's gone, yet every passing hour / Brings some remembrance dear, / Which seems with silent voice to say, / That 'Harriette is not here.'" Long-term relationships, especially if alluded to in the poem, might encourage writers to sign, as did one bereaved poet recalling past ties to a beloved friend's sister: "From childhood's hours we've lov'd thee well / And, must we, Charlotte say farewell— / Must we resign thee to the skies, / And no murmuring thought arise."[28] The tenderness of this poem derives from its allusions to a relationship that blossomed in youth and remained vibrant through correspondence—that same avenue bearing news of the woman's mortal illness.

Sometimes verse was written by those knowing death was impending. In these cases, the poems seemed especially cherished by the survivors, who copied them in diaries or read them aloud at funeral services. These literary gifts, from the dying to the living, served as a final testament to the ties that bind. A minister's wife, for example, copied the last poem written by a parishioner. The wife explained that the lines "were sung at her funeral at her request in the tune of Sweet Home." In the song, the deceased warned survivors against excessive grief, even as they heard the melodious strains: "My dear friends, do not weep that on Earth I'm no more, / But rather rejoice that my trials are o'er, / And when my dear friends, you approach that bright shore, / My spirit will wait thee, to watch you safe o'er."[29] "Fare-thee-well literature" touched audiences in ways that most published forms could not, insofar as it spoke directly to its readers, those people who knew the author. It was a final and ultimate gift of words, a one-of-a-kind tribute to the collective memory of a departed soul.

Conclusion

From the first rhymed utterances of children learning to read to last words rendered in poetic form, everyday writings were not conceived within a literary vacuum. Common authors' verse, essays, compositions, news columns, lectures, and eulogies all addressed traditional forms, revealing a knowledge of published authors and at least an attempt to imitate them. Often readers were moved to write after perusing a book or poem. If they were not directly induced to write by their reading, ordinary writers nonetheless tapped into the same sources of inspiration that their favorite authors, particularly genteel and romantic poets, drew upon: natural wonders, complex, deep emotional states, or sacred meditation. Everyday writers found in daily events the same enchantment that eighteenth-century writers such as William Cowper sought in mundane observations. Some common writers even tried to emulate the intuitive grasp that Transcendentalists cultivated. Like those who quoted and transposed lines of poetry and prose, these ordinary authors also played with literary forms; but part of the fun in dallying with well-known pieces, such as "Woodman Spare that Tree," was cleverly substituting new words. These words sometimes were tailored to fit the meter of well-known melodies or to mock the tone of flamboyant oratory. The humor, of course, largely depended upon readers' familiarity with the original.

Although everyday writers shared with published authors similar wellsprings of inspiration, they seldom achieved the same polished product. Their verse was usually spun out in simple lyrics of a few stanzas, with "abab" or "aabb" rhyme schemes and the singsong of iambic tetrameter or trimeter. Their essays seldom surpassed academic standards applied in the seminaries, high schools, or common schools. Their manuscript newspapers often died within a year for lack of interesting and varied contributions. But even though these everyday poets and prose stylists rarely, if ever, wielded the pen with a power that matched their idols, they pushed to the limits the human capacity to appreciate and, ultimately, create literature.

These everyday writers should not be measured against literary giants, for they were not trying to fill the shoes of a Byron, Walter Scott, or Daniel Webster. Rather, they accomplished within their own vicinities what the great authors could not. They wrote within the constraints and incentives of their social settings; they drew upon personal experiences but also submitted to community guidance. If at first they wrote under supervision in homes or at schools, where original ideas and words were nurtured and honed into more lucid thoughts on paper, they soon gained independence enough to enter a broader literary world. Both town lyceums and literary clubs provided forums for writing. Amateur newspapers conducted in schools, public meeting halls, or private homes, helped scribblers "publish" their work but also drove home the production realities of literature—meeting deadlines, submitting to editorial judgments, sustaining output, and, most of all, satisfying a reading "public." Whether in newspapers or in more private spaces, ordinary authors satisfied the literary needs of society. Nowhere can this social impact be better seen than in custom-made literary gifts created for birthdays, Valentine's Day, May Day, farewells, and mourning. These writings—on lacy cards, pieces of fabric, or scented paper—often spoke directly to their readers. They were composed with certain persons and events in mind and called upon a pool of memory that included shared thoughts, activities, and sentiments.

A few of these everyday scribblers saw pieces printed, if only a letter or two in a local newspaper, while others realized more sustained efforts. Domestic versifiers, such as Elizabeth Jocelyn, published in local periodicals; Charlotte Forten's poetry found a larger forum still in national abolitionist vehicles, such as the *National Anti-Slavery Standard* and the *Liberator.* Yet as these amateurs began to see pieces appear in print, they continued writing, sometimes for their own edification and sometimes for other people, without the end of professionalism in sight. Their creative impulse, although more broadly received, was not always broadly conceived. It was sustained by their community but not necessarily by wider, remote, and impersonal audiences. Although these published writers never achieved either the public standing or recompense of a professional author, they filled a quiet niche in a publishing industry craving original copy by talent nurtured on home soil. Yet with so many opportunities available in local forums to get into print, why did

Frances Merritt Quick abandon her "poor unfinished poem" about a comet—a poem that might have entered the pages of some minor periodical had she persisted? Quick, yet unmarried, taught school, and perhaps time devoted to those relatively impractical matters, such as writing, caught up with her. As Mary Pierce Poor wisely observed of her own "regular 'cacoecthes scribendi' . . . , the 'not practical' is the death knell of all such aspirations."[30] What was practical was using literature to maintain a world of social relations. In this, these writers achieved far more than even the most renowned authors.

Part II

Dissemination

Antebellum New Englanders not only produced reading material but also extensively disseminated it. Indeed, diarists and correspondents more frequently mention receiving it from kin or neighbors via loans, gifts, or oral presentations than from commercial outlets like booksellers, general stores, or traveling agents. A single publication's readers thus could far outnumber its purchasers or subscribers—net sales or circulation figures say little about actual readership. And not all print material was disseminated equally, so simply multiplying these figures by some standard factor only misleads more. Some relatively rare titles passed through many hands, while abundant ones sat virtually unread and ignored.[1]

Why did people disseminate literature more than buy it? It was not always much cheaper to do so. The postal system had greatly expanded by the antebellum period, doubling the number of its offices between 1845 and 1860, but using it could be expensive. Sending some newspapers cost almost as much as purchasing them, while mailing letters cost even more because correspondence traveled at higher postal rates. Not until 1851 did postage become affordable, when it dropped to three cents for prepaid letters sent within three thousand miles. It was even more expensive to send books, usually in bundles delivered by private express companies. Above all, it was vastly more trouble to send material than to buy it from a local vendor.

Although transportation was improving, especially with railroad development from the 1830s on, little of this was integrated. Ever-changing schedules and connections, varying rules, and service start-ups and shutdowns confounded senders. Express companies who kept track of options charged considerably, and even they were not always reliable. By any account, it would have been simpler, and usually cheaper, especially if time is added, to rely on one's own literary purchases.[2]

The immediate costs of getting literature somewhere distant did not faze local disseminators, of course, but they faced troubles recording who got what from whom and who was owed a return favor. Although libraries that circulated books were scattered about the region, they were mostly small, specialized, short-lived ventures funded by members or blatantly entrepreneurial. Most folks either preferred to or were obliged to borrow gratis from each other. In so doing, however, they also ran the risk of bidding permanent farewell to an item they thought they loaned only temporarily. In the case of printed items given as gifts, donors treaded carefully lest they create a sense of financial obligation on the receiver's part. But the resulting obligation to read something not of one's choosing could be as trying. Reading aloud, the simplest form of dissemination, required physical exertion, and listeners had to demonstrate attentiveness, even to dull readers. Why not just curl up with a book and read silently?[3]

We see in Part II that people accepted the expense and effort of disseminating literature because they used it for social ends. It coursed through everyday socializing: social calling, letter writing, newspaper exchange, and sending "care" packages—the theme of chapter 4. Chapter 5 shows people more formally giving print material as presents on special occasions, as donations for worthy causes, or as tokens of personal persuasion. In all, human relations outweighed monetary value, for diarists and letter writers usually esteemed even the cheapest gift for the social relations it expressed. Loaned and borrowed literature also coursed through social webs, as chapter 6 describes. Literature itself became infused with traces of social exchange and, ultimately, meaning. Perhaps the most socially intimate form of dissemination is covered in chapter 7: someone reading aloud or otherwise performing a literary piece as listeners and observers shared the experience. Oral reading did not die out with region-wide near-universal literacy at century's turn but vigorously continued.[4] *Throughout Part II, it is often difficult to tell what mattered more: getting literature from person to person or using the conveyances to do so as an excuse for making and keeping contacts with friends, kin, and neighbors. Thus, while Part I showed how literary these people were, Part II explores the social drives inspiring them to be that way.*

Chapter 4

Everyday Dissemination: Literature Sent via Letters, Newspapers, and Bundles

A Martha's Vineyard sea captain away from his wife and their toddler for over two years decided one November to ship them some tokens from Honolulu. He selected locally produced goods—including "one Fan[,] one silk apron, 4 handkerchiefs, one Piece of Grass Cloth which you can make yourself a dress"—and carefully packed them into a bundle, along with a copy of a local newspaper, the *Friend,* which "the Seaman's Chaplain" had given him the previous day.[1] While the grass fabric was certainly a novelty for his wife, so, too, was the Hawaiian temperance paper that she otherwise would not have seen. Both represented a transfer of affection as much as of exotic goods.

The periodical's origin was the only unusual aspect of this shipment, for New Englanders routinely disseminated literature to maintain social ties. They packed up periodicals, books, and other pieces of literature, just as the captain did, and shipped them off to friends and family overseas. Sometimes they sent cargo on trains headed out west or down south. Even more often, they mailed letters, their very own "texts of life" filled with literary quotes, excerpts, transcribed poetry, and newsclippings. In lieu of correspondence, they frequently sent newspapers containing contraband enclosures violating postal regulations. Literary disseminators sometimes scooted around the postal system altogether by having pages deliver items in person. Dissemination of all sorts took planning, care, and timing, but it was worth it to keep communication lines open and literature on the move. In this way, communication and literature became inextricable.

This chapter looks at out-of-market literary dissemination by focusing first on letters, then mailable print matter, and, finally, packages. Avenues of dissemination, such as the postal service, express services, shipping, and paging, are considered throughout. Vendors, including booksellers and peddlers, play a relatively minor role here, for people most often received literature from friends and family members, not directly from commercial outlets. As will be shown, dissemination was no easy matter, and that people so willingly shouldered the burden suggests how much literature's role in maintaining social ties meant to them. Collectively, their efforts reached grand proportions: a massive movement of texts and literary references, propelled by sheer willpower through dense webs of social relations stretching over the region, across the nation, and, indeed, at times around the world, as the captain's Hawaiian package testifies. When his wife received it, two hearts in Martha's Vineyard and Honolulu were, for a moment, intimately connected.

Dissemination in Letters

Letters more than anything linked people separated by space and time with handwritten messages containing literary quotations, excerpts, and clippings. Assembling these often took as much if not more thought, care, and time as writing down the latest news. But the trouble was worth it. Correspondents bonded through shared literary interests. Literature provided better glue for holding relationships together than mere reportage, for it conveyed not only an essential part of one's daily activity—reading—but also the thoughts, feelings, attitudes, and deeper values surrounding it. Literary experience simply "traveled better" and said more about a person than humdrum details. People were thus encouraged to delve ever more deeply into literature, to identify with it, and to disseminate it as freely as possible.[2]

Beyond creatively deploying quotes to underscore a letter's point or enhance its meaning, people also transcribed literature simply because they wanted to share it with their correspondents, who might not otherwise have had access to the material. These handwritten copies substituted for the printed originals that, for any number of reasons, could or would not be sent. For example, excerpting saved transcribers from having to part with a book even temporarily. A minister's daughter visiting Boston excerpted for her adoptive father back home some stanzas from Tennyson's hot-off-the-press *In Memoriam,* which she "procured" while there. She included the classic lines "'Tis better to have loved & lost / Than never to have loved at all" and might have copied more had she not run out of room on her sheet crowded with other news. Copying from much-desired but rare texts provided an essential service to one's correspondents, but there were limits upon extractors' time and energy. "But I must stop at once as . . . I might as well copy the whole book," a woman scolded herself after she devoted a page to an extract from Joseph-Marie Degérando's *Du perfectionnement moral.* She had to balance delivering a rare foreign-language text with sociable chitchat. Not all transcriptions in letters were literary; they could even encompass other private letters, public speeches, or legal documents. Copies of these sent in letters with but few words from the correspondent, however, might require at least a short apology. After black abolitionist Charles Lenox Remond spent three pages transcribing the "Proceedings had at a Town meeting" that passed resolutions against interracial marriage, he begged his addressee's forgiveness, as "my time & engagements will not permit me to remark upon them I must leave them in all their disgracefulness!"[3] Extractors precariously juggled dual roles as impartial scribe and familiar correspondent.

Rather than spend time and use precious space to transcribe literature, correspondents often sent enclosures, discrete items such as newsclippings. These had the obvious advantage over transcriptions in that they could be easily separated from the letter with which they were packaged and could take on an independent life. When a college student sent "interesting pieces from my old . . . papers" to his sister at a Shaker commune, he knew her friends, deprived by the sect's dictates against secular reading, would devour them. "[I]t is astonishing with what eagerness their young people, especially girls, seize upon old newspapers or anything readable," he observed, "& pass them from hand to hand till they have gone the round of the whole community." Enclosures could breach walls where books could not go, but they also could provide recipients with glimpses of their senders' everyday lives. A Yorkshire immigrant inserted "statistics of the Manufacturers of Lowell for the year 1847" to tell his parents he was doing well tending looms in a carpet mill. "They have increased very much during the last year, and are still doing so," he assured them.[4] Enclosures thus could bear as much social significance as the letters they accompanied.

Letters with literary extracts and enclosures arrived through two main avenues: the local post office or couriers. The former, the most common, usually required recipients to "tend out" to the post office, even in snow or rain, to send or pick up mail for themselves and other people. Post offices thus became regular stops on daily errands. One Kennebunk mill worker routinely walked down to the waterside to mail his letters and pick up a few other items. "Pleasant—Forenoon Go to the Port—put a letter in the post office. . . . Buy some Paint," he recorded after a typical excursion. Proximity to a post office only encouraged letter writing. "I guess you will begin to think I write you often enough but I am living at the *Post Office* now and can send as many letters as I please if I only *pay* for them," a rural Maine domestic servant wrote to her father. She explained, referring to her sister, that "the folks that Maroa & I are keeping house for, keep the P.O. in their kitchen." Although she bemoaned postage costs, most correspondents probably would agree with one mill worker who complained of people giving the "excuse that the postage was to[o] high." He queried, "Who would prize a few cents above the deep anxiety of endeard Parents, for the welfare of their children?" One way to avoid that excuse was to stuff stamps into envelopes. "As to the postage stamp," one young man responded to a friend's not-so-subtle hint for a reply, "you are a regular old *Scallywag.*" Correspondents short of cash could always pass on costs to recipients, for prepayment was compulsory only from 1855 on. Letters by private courier, of course, bypassed charges of commercial carriers or the postal system, and so correspondents eagerly availed themselves of any traveler going in the right direction and hastily scribbled to meet the exigency. "A man has just called at Mr Nichols who will pass through Gilmanton on his way to Tamsworth & would take a letter home or paper," a New Hampshire woman wrote, adding that she "couldn't resist the inclination (or as Hannah would say 'cant control my nerves') to write a few words."[5] Couriers were cheap but happenstance, while the postal service offered regularity at a price.

Another advantage of using the post office was the culture of sociability it engendered. Nearly everyone had to fetch mail in person or by proxy unless they paid for delivery service. Jaunts to and fro could enhance a day filled with social activities, especially if a bounty of letters awaited. Friends or family might provide company on sometimes dreary walks. "Met Frances . . . and went to the post-office with her," a New Haven woman wrote of an evening stroll with her sister in the center of town. "Arrived home about dusk, but were not afraid *at all,* though *York Street* is quite gloomy in a dark night." For one student, an excursion to a Boston post office became part of her everyday recreation with classmates during "exercise hour." Sociabilities occurred not only en route but also inside post offices. In one instance, a group of students in Concord, New Hampshire, "met in a corner of the post office and, over a pot of boiling 'lasses candy, discussed the merits of the respective colleges they represented."[6] Clearly, these were more than places for transacting postal business.

Not all postal encounters went so smoothly. Persis Sibley Andrews, in her husband's absence, "had to 'tend out' as usual upon the P.O. & Official business w'h I like well enough if it were not for baby." Besides having to lug the child, she complained of "the mud & rain" and "Mails arriving late" on cold winter days. Paying postage due was another minor irritation. Although senders often left it to recipients to pick up the charges, some prepaid out of consideration. Charles Cobb once felt neglectful that he did not do so: "These 3 letters I sent down by Hiram to be mailed & forgetting to give him 9c, they didn't go post-paid." Enclosures could weigh down a letter, making it more expensive than anticipated, so careful correspondents learned to estimate. "I . . . may slip-in a scrap containing some specimens, if I can do it without making this letter overweight," a father enclosing pamphlet clippings told his daughter.[7]

People gladly suffered the inconveniences, in most cases, because they valued the information that letters contained. By transcribing quotations and extracts or sending newsclippings and other enclosures, correspondents carved out a special role for letters as conveyances of literature. In letters, literary information and personal news often merged when people recommended titles, inquired about unusual books or periodicals, asked for old books, or commissioned new purchases. Through their correspondence, these folks did as much, if not more, than the book trade did to encourage literary pursuits. For compared with sending and receiving letters, purchasing books and periodicals was rarer—certainly not something one did everyday. Precisely because letters were so commonplace, they gave reading matter a familiar yet vital place within the social dramas of daily life.

Exchanging Periodicals

If letters were the most common and intimate vehicles for distributing literature, periodicals mailed by friends and loved ones at a distance ("transient papers") followed closely behind. Some weeklies, like so-called story papers, virtually eschewed news for entertaining belles lettres, while most other papers, even specialized religious, agricultural, or partisan ones, featured much literature beyond evangelical, business, and political intelligence. Packed into huge pages with tiny print were verses, short stories, speeches, songs, jokes, book excerpts, lectures, reviews, recipes, celebrity vignettes, and miscellaneous "fillers." "Read the paper which Marcellus sent me & found some very pretty stories," a schoolmistress recorded. Because these non-news items frequently turn up pasted in scrapbooks or transcribed commonplace books, diaries, or letters, it is clear that people indeed read them and thought them worthy of remembrance. As explained in chapter 11, these items often acquired deeper meaning as tokens of the sender and tributes to the social bond. Rereading them thus reenacted the relationship.[8]

Beyond furnishing shared reading material, transient papers mirrored letters in their social uses. Indeed, papers sometimes substituted for letters, insofar as their mere arrival could signal tacitly understood messages of well-being and personal remembrance. Moreover, like letters they could contain news of senders, recipients, and their social circles. As an inexpensive communication mode, they might be preferred over letters since they traveled with ease through the postal system, usually at much lower rates.[9] Yet because papers did not as easily bear the sender's personal impress as letters, creative ways were found to transform these printed materials into one-of-a kind statements, sometimes by adding federally prohibited marginalia or other marks. Thus, when disseminated by ordinary people, publishers' products originally addressed to an anonymous reading public took on private meaning for senders and recipients—a social handshake at a distance.

Diarists duly noted newspaper arrivals as if they were valued pieces of correspondence. Receiving papers could mark important anniversaries shared with the sender. "[T]wenty nin[e] years to day since my mother died. Mary had a paper from Otis," a New Hampshire woman chronicled. Sending a paper could also be shorthand for "I'm thinking of you" absent time for letter writing, as Persis Sibley Andrews found after arriving in a town to teach school: "Have rec'd a letter, & a vol. of the Common School Library from J. L. S., & a paper from S. G. from Gardiner—so I am not forgotten by my friends tho' I am from home." Such mailings were not usually one-time events but signaled the start of reciprocal exchange. "I have now a good opportunity to find who cares about hearing from me as I take it for granted that if one sends me a paper they wish to have it returned," a pupil starting school remarked. Thus fraught, exchanges could be negotiated beforehand. Charles Lenox Remond, the busy black abolitionist lecturer, wrote to a friend concerning a couple whose acquaintance they shared, noting that "if the press upon my time deprives me the privilege of writing either of them you will oblige me by saying to them I shall always be glad of a paper from them."[10] Such small postal gestures offered ample social investment.

Several people recorded newspapers sent and received as if accounting credits and debits of the heart. A schoolteacher heartbroken on leaving home to begin a new job tracked exchanges involving at least seventeen persons and thirty-two papers from May to August 1841 alone. For her, transient papers became a lifeline in sea of loneliness. After only a few days at her new address she started receiving them, the beginnings of a two-way flood that on a single day could involve several paper exchanges. The day after she reported that she received "two papers, one from [sister] Ellen & the other from S. B. R," for example, she returned the favor and mailed "three papers, one for S. B. R., one for Julia & one for Ellen." Her exchanges at times had circulation patterns like those of chain letters. "Received a paper from Ellen," she once jotted down, "the one that Edwin sent her." Exchangers expected similar quality of papers returned, but politeness dictated that at least something, even if lesser, be sent back, as she revealed: "Mailed a paper for Samuel a very poor one in return for the good one he sent me, but the best I could get."[11] These friendly interchanges clearly thrived upon disseminating good reading matter.

Quality or not, newspapers could signal that "all is well." Sending them saved busy travelers time in writing while in transit, so they were mailed en route or at journey's end. "I did receive the newspaper you sent me upon your arrival at Bangor and knew by that means that you must have arrived there in safety," Mary Pierce Poor assured her traveling fiancé. No news was usually good news, so, ironically, sending a newspaper instead of a letter meant there was nothing negative to report. "We received Thursdays paper this morning, and as we got no letter we presume you are all well," a Bostonian sojourning at Saratoga Springs told her children. A recipient could coolly rationalize the disappointment of receiving only a paper, as did one Connecticut farmer: "Last night rec[d]. a paper from Sister E. [in Wilkes-Barre.] I suppose she is well because if she had not been she would have written a letter."[12] Newspapers heralded social assurances, if, at times, little more.

But they might also bear grim tidings. Survivors often announced deaths by sending newspapers with relevant obituary notices instead of writing painful letters or enclosing clippings. Upon the death of his wife, a poor country minister let papers bear the news to distant family and friends: "Sent papers with the notice of Mrs. Arnold's death to the Post office to Mary S. Matthews . . . and to others—11 in number." Needless to say, recipients were astonished if not first primed for the shock via a letter. As one reader explained, the "papers . . . sometimes pierce the heart with intelligence of the sudden death of friends whose loss we dreamt not of." The blow could be especially severe for those, like Persis Sibley Andrews, who received newspapers simply for greetings' sake. "I have just rec'd a paper from brother Reuben bringing the sad news of the death of his only daughter Hannah Elizabeth aged 18 months," she once reported, observing, "How unfortunate he has been. My heart aches for him. Lost a wife & three children."[13] Opening a sent paper was akin to spinning a roulette wheel of life and death.

Since newspaper exchanges so much signaled news of loved ones, correctly identifying the sender was essential, but postal regulations made this difficult. Because any handwriting on newspapers subjected them to extra charge, they usually traveled incognito. "[W]hen you send a paper you must not put the initials of your name on it," a Lowell mill worker warned her sister. "It is against the law and we have to pay postage on it." In light of these strictures, senders' identity was necessarily obscured. One confounded farm hand gave up conjecturing altogether and registered enigmatically, "Received a paper from somebody." But because mailed papers had to be addressed, handwriting on their shipping wrappers gave some clue. Another way to discern senders was through the mail's place of origin. For example, from this evidence one young woman figured it was a beau who sent her a newspaper: "Received a paper from Hudson [New York]—I suspect who sent it." Some senders manipulated the very address on the wrapper to send a message. One shopkeeper visiting his sister settled upon a name for his newborn son back home through paper exchange: "[S]ent a paper to my boy last night with the name I & sister selected for him upon the envelp 'Geo Washington.'"[14] By cleverly addressing the paper to his son instead of his wife, he got across his message about naming the child "George" without scribbling extraneous words on the paper and thus subjecting it to extra postage.

Many senders wrote on their papers hoping that postmasters would overlook marks, for by law wrappers had to be open on one end to reveal contents to postal inquisitors. Among these covert additions even simple marks could be packed with meaning. A subtle sign on a paper to a dry-goods clerk helped him identify both the sender and her invitation to an educational event: "Rec^{d} paper at P.O suppose to be from Susan W. Beard showing by a mark when N° 26 Primary School would be examined." One clergyman asked his correspondent to send a coded message concerning the date of her visit "on the wrapper in figures, (as 8.24 for Aug, 24th . . .) to save the trouble of writing." Such coding could backfire; the mill worker who warned her sister against extraneous markings was mystified by one reprobate's initials: "I received a paper last week from Haverhill with the initials of H. A. P. on the wrapper, just as I have wrote it here, and now pray tell me who it is, I cannot think of anyone."[15]

Bolder folk violated newspaper margins with lengthy missives or extensive markings. "[A] few words from my dear father on the margin of one," Harriett Low remarked of papers from home, "was better than all the rest." Persis Sibley Andrews even discovered a marriage proposal—"Will 'no never,' under any circumstances whatever always remain an obstacle insurmountable forever?"—written inside a newspaper sent to her by "'the *handsome* Lawyer' of Augusta" whom she would marry in 1842. Marginalia could carry bad news, too. One Lowell mill operative opened a newspaper only to find a mix of good and upsetting intelligence about two English relatives: "I received a day or two since a Leeds Mercury from Rowland with the announcement of Benson's marriage on it, and a few remarks in pencil on the top of it, he says Arthur has been badly [ill], but is better." Some markings were not textual, for newsheets' large size made them ideal for dressmaker patterns. "Will you be so kind as to ask Lucy to send Feroline the pattern of Fred's bosoms & dickeys?" Mary Pierce Poor requested of her husband. "She can send it marked in a newspaper."[16] If the U.S. government offered such a cheap conveyance, why not use it, even if it was not for the ends intended—even if it meant stretching the law a tad?

Scofflaws faced an obstacle, though: postmasters on the lookout for marginalia and hidden enclosures. Hence, heavy enclosures sometimes did not survive the passage from sender to receiver. "I am sorry to hear that you did not get the almanack which I sent you in a news paper on the 24th May," a Connecticut farm boy apologized to his father mining in California. Small, flat, and lightweight insertions were less likely to be detected. One woman "received a paper . . . containing two samples of silk" from her sister's future husband, while a schoolteacher found enclosed "a sample of the Oxford Cap which have become prevalent with students of Harvard University of late." Literary enclosures, too, could be snuck in. A collegian discovered one of his early amorous verses—"a certain piece of poetry to a certain 'Harriett'"—inside a *National Trades' Union* sent from a friend, which "called to mind . . . certain old affairs at" his preparatory academy.[17]

If violations were detected, the extra postage due vexed newspaper recipients because cost differentials between the usual one- to three-cent postage and inflated extra charges stood out in high relief. Throughout 1839, some residents of tiny Bridport, Vermont, learned just how dear extra postage could be from a postmaster who scrupulously inspected papers. *A New York Herald* for example, cost, if clean of markings, one cent to retrieve from the local post office. The same paper, sent with "writing inside" cost the recipient a whopping thirty-seven and a half cents. A *Telegraph* "extra," or special sheet, without writing also cost only a cent; with writing inside, the charges mounted to twenty cents. One man had to shell out fifty cents for his "Detroit paper" with contraband writing inside, the highest price paid for that infraction. Lightweight enclosures did not apparently inflate rates too much, for an Illinois paper with "writing and Flowers inside" cost its receiver twenty cents to claim it. After August 1839, papers entering the post office with writing inside waned; either recipients warned neighbors and correspondents about the post master or he was replaced by a more forgiving successor.[18]

Far more troublesome than penalty charges were papers lost or filched in transit. These were more likely to disappear than letters, especially when sent from afar. After a year during which a Maine Forty-niner had "not yet received one single Newspaper or Pamphlet from Dexter or any other place since I left that place," he implored his wife, "I now charge you not to pay those naughty *Post Masters* one cent more for Newspaper postage." He aimed a parting shot at corrupt postal workers: "let somebody get their reading somewhere else." Because papers so often lost their way, acknowledging receipt became essential. "Please send us aurora of the 12$^{th.}$ of Jan," a Vermont carpenter in Wisconsin wrote back home, "the one E T sent us has probably miscarried." Words such as "miscarried" that vaguely pointed an accusing finger entered the vocabulary of victims unable to nail culprits losing or lifting papers. "I was much grieved to think that the papers were not to be found there," a dismayed black abolitionist wrote to a colleague. "[T]here seems to be some mistake some where."[19] The postal pathway for paper exchangers was strewn with potential or real mistakes.

This was particularly true for New Englanders having to send papers to loved ones abroad where communications were unreliable and circuitous. Even so, people struggled to get out papers, as they continually scanned dailies for notices of ships' departures and destinations to track potential delivery routes. "I keep a constant look out in the New York and Boston papers for a ship to Genoa or Leghorn, but I never see notice of one," an editor's wife told her traveling brother. "I should like to send you newspapers." It took about two months to find a more certain avenue: "I have discovered in the New York papers that vessels sometimes go from there to Genoa, and I have also learned the name of the Merchant who generally advertises them, so I am going to make up a pacquet of Newspapers."

Much easier was getting shipments to England via regular service that in the 1840s made the crossing in about fourteen days. Two abolitionist friends, Bristol's John Bishop Estlin and Boston's Samuel May Jr., for example, availed themselves of this avenue to exchange a steady stream of periodicals. Yet getting newspapers to or from ports overland might pose a problem in some areas. In Mariposa, a Yankee Forty-niner depended upon an "express rider" traveling regularly to Stockton or San Francisco.[20] That people strove so mightily against the uncertainties of transoceanic communication suggests their deep commitment to staying in touch with loved ones through literature.

Receiving papers might be no simple matter, either. Most seamen had to wait patiently to dock before hearing word from home, so to them even favorable trade winds might portend papers to come. "We have just got into the trades, and are going along finely," a lonely ship's boy on his first voyage entered in his journal. "We hope soon to reach San Francisco, and there to receive a good bunch of letters, and papers from home." His thoughts turned wistfully homeward: "I should like to look in upon Mother tonight, and see what she was doing, and how she is." Yankees in the South contended with a different obstacle: censorship of antislavery papers so severe that some supporters, fearing postmasters' confiscation or exposure of the addressee's convictions, hesitated sending them. "[T]he Evangelist is too warm a friend of the Slave to enter your atmosphere with safety," declared one Maine woman wanting to mail a transient paper to her brother in New Orleans. Even in some free states, radical papers like the Garrisonians' *Liberator* were eyed with suspicion and hence, if discovered, could endanger traveling recipients. "I think we are in a nest of slaveholders & slavery lovers," an abolitionist visiting Philadelphia informed her husband in Boston; "so do not send any more Liberators."[21] Papers were subject not only to the hazards of distance but also the prejudices of postmasters and carriers on the way.

Facing all these obstacles, why did people persist in this elaborate system of exchange? Because of widespread intra- and interregional migration, papers, like the letters they often replaced, helped maintain former face-to-face relationships over distances. For migrants, papers were artifacts of the home left behind that gave them a sense of participating in life there. As much as transient papers were enmeshed in the fabric of everyday social life, so were the practices of sending and receiving them. The very dailiness of the flurry of papers in the mail afforded constant social opportunities, more so than did relatively infrequent letters. Social obligations to mail papers could be heaped on to anyone destined to pass near a post office. "After school carried a newspaper for Mr Dixwell to the Post Office," a Boston student recorded of a trek with a classmate. Picking up newspapers for other people was also a social act with definite obligations, as Charles Cobb explained: "When one gets another['s] paper for him from the Post Office, it seems he is expected to immediately go & carry it to him." Having held on to it a few days, he had invited the recipient's suspicion that he read it before delivering it. The very access the system allowed postmasters checking for contraband could be easily taken advantage of, since the recipient would never know if the paper had been read along the way, something much more difficult to do with sealed letters. Because they were expected to deliver immediately, tenders dropping in suddenly risked embarrassing recipients. "[T]his morn I got up and slipped on my old sacque and went down to breakfast," a Lynn schoolmistress divulged of her state of half dress; "pretty soon Geo Crossman called with the 'Reporter' and said he guessed I was just up."[22] People retrieving papers felt licensed to visit unwary addressees at any time. In most cases, however, recipients welcomed direct but informal delivery of papers, for it enhanced social ties with both the messenger and sender.

Exchanging Bundles

Letters, periodicals, and pamphlets might carry volumes of meaning, and so, too, could books, but they were even harder to send. They often traveled in cumbersome packages called "bundles" that frequently included nonliterary items. For much of the period, books could not pass easily through the mail, for only after 1851 did the post office deem them "mailable," and then the postage was expensive. In any case, for convenience, most senders wanted to package books with other goods, and these large bundles the post office refused. So senders usually relied upon private express companies, less formally organized services provided by stage drivers, couriers, rail companies, and steamboats, or personal pages to deliver bundles domestically. For people with relatives in Europe, clippers and steam vessels assured shipment regularly to Great Britain and less frequently to the Continent. Whatever the conveyance used, parcels cost more to send than letters or newspapers and required greater skill in packing. But most folks who could afford to send them felt the time and trouble were worthwhile if it meant keeping connected.[23]

Anything and everything went into these bundles. They often contained books commissioned to be purchased. The close transatlantic relationship of Samuel May and his friend Estlin was forged not only over the papers they exchanged but also through the books they commissioned for one another. "I wish I could get the other volumes of this 'Miscellany of Useful & Entertaining Tracts,' bound in the style of the one you sent me," May once inquired of Estlin. "If you could," he continued, "I expect to know the whole cost to you and would gladly send you in return any American books you wished for." Commissioned items were usually reimbursed even by close relations. One Maine widow paid her brother beforehand for purchasing a few cheap books for her in Boston; he carefully accounted for the expenses, down to the last penny. "I have bought you books. 2 at 15c. each & one at 20c—so I have 10c left which is subject to your order," he calculated. "I shall send them the 1st opportunity." Apart from commissions, gift packages from city dwellers mixed rare goods and everyday items, such as expensive dried fruits and mundane newspapers. One Bostonian sent his aunt back home in a small rural town "a few articles," including "9 oranges 1 1/2 lbs raisons, 1 1/2 lb figs, 1 lb dates, Newspapers, L[egal] Documents and any thing else I can get into it for I intend to fill it full." An Irish American salesman expressed to a woman, "[b]y way of keeping up good old acquaintances and friendship," a basket with "a small quantity of Boston fruit for your special benifit, also a copy of that somewhat amusing book 'nothing to wear.'" In such cornucopias, recipients found feasts for minds as well as palates. The association of food with reading material beyond the obvious, that each might be obtained more easily in cities, suggests that both were meant to be sociably shared with others. Occasionally, boxes were meant for individual consumption, as when Persis Sibley Andrews, hearing that her little nephew "fell from a load of boards where he had climbed unobserved," sent him "some picture books" for to read during his convalescence. Other packages played a role in courtship rituals. A beau stationed in Canton shipped Harriett Low in Macao "a bundle of books, notes &c. . . . *[s]ome poetry too,"* a too-extravagant token of love that left her "in doubt whether the youth had taken leave of his senses or not."[24] That whatever book-length printed matter was inside these bundles far exceeded in cost both inexpensive newspapers and the raw materials of letters made it comparatively luxurious and worthy of note.

Lacking postal service for packages or the money to ship them express, senders did their own carrying or asked acquaintances and family members to do the work for them. Everyday social calls often occasioned book delivery. "Phebe Young came down & brought us some reading matter," a Vermonter noted in a typical diary entry of this sort. "Martha A. Rogers called to bring my book," a forlorn shoe binder remarked of a visiting friend. "She was very kind to think of me, and I love her because she is good." It was, after all, not just books as presents that were meaningful, but the very social presence delivery entailed. Short of direct presentations, travelers passing near package destinations left bundles at local addresses. An accountant wishing to send a book to his fiancée corralled a visiting brother who would pass by her on the way home: "Purchased the 'Young Lady's Friend' yesterday, & intend to send it to Martha by brother Albert when he pays me his visit which he has promised to do next Saturday." Planned visits provided chances to retrieve books left behind. "Please dear Papa when you come do not forget 'Tom Brown at Rugby' I saw it last on my bed," a daughter requested while traveling.[25] Paging books could mean summoning familial obligations.

Personal delivery in some cases would not do, so senders turned to commercial shippers. Some bundles were, according to one dispatcher, "too bulky & cumbersome to send" by personal page or they could not be delivered in timely fashion by the sender in person or by household members or neighbors traveling in the recipient's vicinity. "I return a number of the Review des deux Mondes, which I took with me to read on the way & found rather amusing," a diplomat informed his nephew. "Supposing that you might like to read it, and not exactly knowing when I may be at Boston again, I thought it best to transmit it by Express." Senders rarely identified the specific express company, however. One Bostonian listed having bought "Virgil for C." at "[$]1.30" and mailing it by "Bucks Express," while Worcester's John Park "returned his [Boston friend's] 'Life of Mozart . . .'—by the Express-man, Mr. Lewis." But when Park recorded that "the Providence stage driver" conveyed packages to and from his daughter there, or when a Portland lawyer called upon "Watson & Means" to send "a package of books" to New York "by steam boat," one can only surmise how much express companies were involved. Most senders left the matter unclear in their diaries and letters, perhaps because the options were so limited in most areas that they warranted little explanation. Since express companies provided little better assurance of items going astray than other delivery services, senders often obsessed over precise instructions. A Marbleheader in Boston needing some books from home specified how his sister should address it: "send it by express—these are the directions— . . . 'To J. Wooldrige, No. 15 and 17 Fulton St. Boston; to be left till called for'—now be sure to put this all on."[26]

As this young man realized, senders had to designate pickup stations, for, like mail, delivery was not usually door to door. Freight packages could be conveniently retrieved at transportation nodes if people lived nearby, as did a Roxbury schoolboy who "went up to the Toll Gate station after a bundle." More often, stations were places of businesses, particularly bookstores. "Will you send Charlotte's Ollendorf[f]'s French Exercises which is on one of the shelves in the back room?" one woman visiting a Boston suburb requested of her sister. "[I]f you can find no private opportunity to send it, will you be kind enough to send it by Express, and direct it to J. Munroe's & Co.[?]"—a major local bookseller. When Samuel May asked Estlin to send him "'Miscellany of Useful & Entertaining Tracts'" from England, he noted that they should be directed "to care of *Crosby & Nichols* in Boston," another bookstore. This was not something peculiar to Boston booksellers, for in smaller cities parcels were also received at business establishments. There might be confusion over which stations expressmen used as depots, as one schoolteacher revealed when he asked his sister to retrieve a parcel of "Swedenborgian books" in Lowell: "they are either at Merill & Heywoods, or at Mr. Hales' at Hales Mills. Will you . . . go to the bookstore and enquire for them, and if they are not there, go to Hale's Mills and get them?" Bookstore proprietors no doubt were delighted at the stream of recipients led into their store to pick up shipped items. Besides bookstores, periodical offices were good stations, especially since the papers they published could announce arrivals. Once, when a book from England for Frederick Douglass was delivered to Boston's *Liberator* office, Samuel May informed the sender, "It is not yet forwarded to him, but by this week's Liberator he will get notice of its being at our office." May went on: "I could have sent it by Parcel Express, without much expense, but as the line hence to Rochester is not under the management of one and the same company, I feared that so small a packet might get lost."[27] It was safer to wait for someone to fetch it than to send it.

As May noted, shipping costs for a single book or small package could be relatively inexpensive, at least for local transactions. A Boston woman paid only sixty-three cents for an 1859 bundle, while a Springfield candlemaker spent fifty cents on one in 1856. Shipments to out-of-the-way places cost more. In rural New Hampshire, a schoolteacher instructed his sister to hold off forwarding material because of shipping costs: "The bundle you have just sent cost nearly a dollar for transportation," he explained in 1845. "I want the books, but you better wait a while." Rates on books sent via postal service after 1851 were more predictable, insofar as they were based on distance and weight, as can be seen from an 1853 calculation of a Bible's shipping costs based on the formula "one cent for the 3 1st ounces, & 1 ct an ounce for more." "Abby's bible," the sender concluded, "w'd cost 18 cts, as it weighs 20 oz."[28] Cost-consciousness may have deterred some senders, but most accepted postage and other fees as tickets of admission to the system of informal social dissemination.

Whatever the means of conveyance or the cost of delivery, sending bundles involved more planning and care than either letters or newspapers. Packing was deemed a necessary social skill to acquire; recipients in turn appreciated careful handling of precious books. For women, particularly those from the middle class, it was a form of etiquette mastered at an early age, because as adults they were often charged with the family's packing duties. An eighteen-year-old was relieved when a meticulous family friend approved of her tidy bundle: "I was very glad that he liked our packing of the books." It was a skill attractive to suitors. "When I can fold, seal & direct a letter, pack the 'Annual Register,' & direct a dinner table to suit him, I shall think I know how to please a somewhat particular gentleman," she mused. One young woman, proud of her abilities to pack "a neat little pasteboard box" to send overseas for the holidays, gave to her brother a detailed description of its "varied contents" that included a "clove bag" filled with the fragrant spice, Indian moccasins, handcrafted needle books (cases for needles of various sizes), and a "number of the Almanacs, several tracts and a Seaman's Hymn Book." Pride gave way to tedium as older housekeepers packed as part of domestic routines, described by one woman as "hounding the errand-boy, scrubbing lettuce, skirmishing with twine & paper, & bundles for the Express, & notes to shopkeepers, & Book-Club books." Fussy recipients sometimes instructed young women in the art of packing. "[S]ee that my gold pen is in—and that those three books with green covers full of poetry or stuff (just as you think) are in it—," one student commanded of his sister, "do not let any of my letters or papers or little scraps drop out and wrap it up in several thicknesses of paper." This small bundle little troubled the sender; indeed, some packers preferred to limit contents. A Boston matron refused to send to her Staten Island boarding school daughter a commissioned historical tome. "I do not like now to increase my package," she explained. Fit as much as weight might concern senders. "To pack the box snugly & well, it was necessary to put into one parcel only those books or pamphlets which were of uniform size," Samuel May explained on one occasion of a shipment to England. A "box [that] was packed in a terrible hurry" could worry a conscientious packer like him.[29]

Even the best packed books were subject to weather hazards and shippers' reluctance to indemnify. Rain alone might forestall shipping, as one Bostonian explained to a sister in Maine awaiting a package containing Swedenborgian tracts: "I have not sent the Views for it rains so I am fearful of them being injured." Snow, ice, or water damage could be even worse. Samuel May described the state of one package traveling express for fifty cents between Philadelphia and Boston. The "bundle had been badly wetted, & the larger part of the books more or less damaged," he moaned, noting the "stains on the covers." His efforts at getting recompense were futile: "I have twice called on Harnden's Express, to pay me for the damage; as yet, they do nothing." Still, he continued to try. "I hoped to get at least 17 cts., & perhaps 20 cts., each,—i.e. $10," he griped. Finally, he decided to cut his losses: "I cannot now get more than half of that." In the end, he collected only "*three dollars.*"[30] Expressmen, like the weather, were intractable, unmoved by either ardent pleading or solicitous cajoling.

All these problems were tolerated in the name of circulating literature within social networks of friends and family members. Erratic ship schedules, high delivery rates, remote pickup stations, and the exigencies of bundle packing were equally annoying. With surprising grace and patience, however, people abided by the rules of the dissemination game. Winning, of course, meant losing a few game pieces; a couple of rain-damaged books, a lost package here and there, or an exorbitant fee were all small prices to pay for the chance to send literary goods and receive them from distant loved ones. Like any other game, it became easier with practice. Indeed, it became a way of life.

Conclusion

Sending reading materials, no matter how subject they were to the vicissitudes of fate, was so much a part of life that it seemed odd to refrain from doing it. "I should have sent the Oration before but I did not think of it," a bewildered down-easter apologized to his sister for not mailing her an item she had requested, even though he had visited its author. "And what was stranger than all. I dined with Mr. Chandler at his house . . . and did not think to ask him for a copy. . . . I wonder I did not think of it then."[31] The habitual observance was signaled by its rare breach. The forgetful times, however, were far outnumbered by the times people remembered and acted. The hole left in their lives by social neglect would have been too deep to fathom.

Whether it was a mailing a letter stuffed with clippings, wrapping a cheap penny daily, paging a magazine, or lugging a heavy bundle of books to a depot, New Englanders categorized literary dissemination with other routine but essential, everyday activities that required constancy, some skill, and not a little conscientiousness. It was done as a matter of course along with other chores, but especially with acts of social intercourse: letter writing, trips to the post office, and calling on neighbors. Indeed, sending literature was so tied to most forms of communication that it was almost an unwitting act, done primarily in the name of maintaining intimate ties. But these folks were both social and literary, so a bond created over a sent newspaper or book was as strong a link as could ever be forged.

Chapter 5

On Account of the Donor: Presenting and Receiving Literary Gifts

Twelve years after William Craft and his wife fled slavery in Georgia, he remembered the two gifts presented to them by Unitarian minister Theodore Parker upon officializing their marriage: "a weapon to protect our liberties, & a Bible to guide our souls." One was highly unusual for a wedding—a sword—but, then again, so too were the circumstances: a nuptial between fugitives in the shadow of an 1850 law that threatened to force their return south as property of their former master. The Bible was a more typical present signifying Parker's esteem for the couple. "I have that bible before me now," Craft explained. "I shall ever prize it most highly, both on account of the donor & the circumstances under which it was given as well as for its contents."[1] In this sense, the Bible demonstrated, perhaps more than the sword, Parker's regard, for it was a lasting tribute that, when read, would always keep him in the hearts of his two friends. By contrast, the sword symbolized the tragic price of ending human bondage that Parker and the Crafts were willing to pay.

If the sword would sever unwilling bonds, the Bible, like all literary gifts, symbolized voluntary ties of love and appreciation. Books, especially, but also pamphlets and even periodicals were presented upon marriage, during courtship, on birthdays or anniversaries, at Christmas and on New Year's Day, or during moments of mourning and parting. Sometimes gifts were bestowed simply for friendship's sake. These gifts, like the Crafts' sword and Bible, embodied not only the sender's good wishes but also the relationship between giver and recipient. When people disseminated literature as gifts, then, they not only circulated the printed word but also represented themselves, as if they were "written" into the book's very pages. In turn, recipients cherished the literary object "on account of the donor" every time they read or merely beheld it. In this sense, the text in the gift mattered less than the social relations it conveyed.

Not only intimates received literary gifts, however, for they also might be presented for the general welfare of society, to unfamiliar but needy folk, or as charitable donations to institutions. Some givers proffered persuasion through freely disseminating political propaganda or religious tracts, but in so doing, even here, they often socialized, albeit briefly, with the strangers they engaged. In their diaries and letters, benefactors described these ephemeral encounters as forging a tangible social connection where there was once only an abstract one. While this free distribution carried no obligations to give anything back, many recipients felt moved, perhaps impelled to return the favor, whether through service, donations, or even gifts of food, thus further strengthening ties to the giver. Through such transactions, literary dissemination intended for abstract transpersonal ends became intimately social.

This chapter looks at literary gift giving in three of its permutations: informal and occasional gift giving, benevolent donating, and ideological propagating, distinct practices that range from the seemingly trivial to the significant, from the secular to the religious, from the apparently frivolous to the somber. No matter how disparate, all these forms of gratis dissemination held something in common: they carried no definite obligation but merely invited recipients into deeper social relations with givers. Recipients thus valued literary gifts for much more than what they cost; social value imbued these transactions with a depth of meaning not usually associated with gifts today. Because of this difference, below we first consider the general value of literary gift giving before we discuss, in turn, presents delivered in person and from afar. Throughout, we refer to the occasions and personal significance of giving and the modes of presentation. Personal exchanges, charitable donations, and persuasive initiatives are interwoven, for diarists and correspondents discuss them in ways too strikingly similar to merit separate treatment. Whether gifts were given face-to-face or from afar, to celebrate holidays or to propagate ideas, the practice was, overall, an important avenue of heartfelt social communication.

The Value of Literary Gift Giving

When New Englanders used the word "gift" or "present" with regard to literature, they usually referred to published books, specially selected and given away to other people as gestures of love or friendship. Yet the terms could apply even to newspaper snippets sent everyday through the mails, old periodicals brought over on a social call, or bundles of cheap novels packed off to sea, all worth only pennies. Certainly, too, the original writings discussed in chapter 3, such as valentines and birthday poems filled with personally meaningful allusions, occasionally earned the label. Of course, "gift" could also mean a talent or aptitude, such as possessing the "gift of poetry" or having "spiritual gifts." These intangible gifts—talents, inspiration, faith—were highly valued, freely acquired, and priceless. Most literary gifts, like the Crafts' Bible, held qualities in common with spiritual gifts in that they were also gratis items of inestimable personal value, if not always monetary worth. "God's blessings," an ailing Sunday schoolteacher wrote to some former students, "often rest on one whose gift is small. . . . You remember the verse,"

> 'Tis not the gift, but 'tis the spirit
> With which 'tis given,
> That on the gift confers a merit,
> As seen by Heaven.

This "merit" of gifts, based on the spirit of relations, thus must be distinguished from material values reducible to a bottom line. People seldom tallied up gifts received against those given. The very idea, given the immeasurable social and personal value that they assigned to their literary presents, would seem vulgar. In fact, literary gift givers seldom used the word "exchange," which instead, for them, usually referred to "exchanging" books at libraries, "exchanging" pulpits with ministers, bartering goods, or making cash transactions.[2] Whether or not they used the word, exchange in gift giving, however, was not uncommon, but it operated on a subtle level, more akin to reciprocity in social relations than the haggling of a marketplace.

Even exceptions to the usual silence concerning exchange highlight this. For example, an eighty-year-old spinster kept a rare, detailed account of "Articles given away" and "Articles received" for the year 1857. She probably wanted to remember, not tally, the flow of gifts, including books, into and out of her hands. Her record suggests that not all gifts were reciprocated; when they were, the monetary value was not in most cases equal. In exchange for the many needle books she gave out on New Year's Day 1857, she received back from recipients some other small items at various times during the year, including a "lofe of Cake," a "bottle of currant wine," a pamphlet, *Daily Food for Christians,* and in one case, a 360-page hard-cover book, *Twenty-Two Years a Slave and Forty Years a Freeman.* Furthermore, she reveals that a "reciprocal" gift could come at any time of the year, thus playing down that recipients "owed" a gift on a particular occasion.[3] So when given the chance to balance credits against debits, even an impecunious woman like her did not do so.

Some people remarked yet more explicitly on exchange, but they treated it perfunctorily. Exchange among children—through adult intercession, of course—

seemed more obvious and natural than that between adults. "Purchased a book for little Nelly as Harry's gift," a widow wrote on New Year's Day, anticipating an exchange between her son and baby daughter. "Harry had a book from 'Nelly,'" she simply recorded the next day. Although this exchange was probably equal, as it often was among children, that between older and younger, or adult and dependent, was not. Most gifts passed from older to younger hands; but when the tables were turned, the value of the gift was often not on par, yet there was no recognition of the disparity. For example, when one novice school teacher exchanged a handmade gift for a pricey set of books from her mother, she matter-of-factly recorded, "Mother presented me with Mrs. Ellis works for my Christmas present. Returned the same in the form of a cap." Most recipients were female, but occasionally wives exchanged with their husbands. A Cape Codder on the Wisconsin frontier who depended upon her husband's income, and he upon her domestic skills, recorded that she made a fair exchange: "my Christmas present of a hymnbook from my husband. And in return I crocheted him a pair of slippers for a New Years present." This was more in the spirit of mutual assistance (a domestic throwback to traditional "changing works") than a demand for gift accounting, as is further shown in exchanges involving more than two persons. Frequently, an adult friend sponsored a child's gift to the parents, with money and help in selecting it. In these cases, the exchange between parent and child was really one between two adults, but parents nonetheless hoped at least to match their child's gift. "Mrs Farrar sent C. ten dollars, so that she had an opportunity of making presents to her family and others who had been kind to her," one woman reported to her sister of her fourteen-year-old daughter's windfall. The girl transformed the monetary gift into one cherished by her mother, who depended on correspondence to keep her in touch with her far-flung family: "I am writing on the Christmas present she gave me, a nice mahogany writing desk, price 3 dollars and a half." The unusual cost accounting was no doubt due to the role the original gift of ten dollars played in the story, but she also observed an uncommon parity between the gift she gave her daughter on this occasion: "My present to her cost the same, 'Uncle Tom's Cabin,' illustrated," the mother recounted, highlighting its relative expense. Noting the serendipity that led to the parity, she absolved herself of any obligation to give her daughter fine presents: "We neither of us knew anything about our presents until the day arrived." It would have been shameful if she had calculated costs beforehand so she had to explain the chance circumstance to her sister. Some recipients directly confessed to obligation, usually, though, not as part of a gift-for-gift exchange but from a larger sense of being socially beholden to the giver. "Will you do me the favor dear sister to accept the copy of Southey's works I send as a slight expression of my rememberance of your kindness & of my sense of obligations?" a woman inquired of a sister-in-law.[4] This gift, like so many others, was proffered out of remembrance and obligation, "on account of the donor" as much as for that of the recipient. The essential value was in the spirit of giving.

Face-to-Face Gift Giving

For this reason—that the spirit of giving was more important than the gift itself—diaries and letters most often capture gift exchanges in which both giver and receiver are present. The in-person delivery of literature discussed in the last chapter provides only some instances of everyday gift giving; in some cases the overall patterned flow of presents might be instrumental in constructing relationships. A rural brick mason, for example, kept account of the gifts he received from a young neighboring farm woman during rounds of calls. Among "2 lumps of butter and some soap grease" was "a present of a little book called 'Daily Food.'" "I esteem it very highly," he reflected. As he watched his fondness deepen with every present he received, the gifts themselves became inseparable from his affection for the giver. "I love her—but this is a secret," he confessed after still more gifts.[5] Though he would eventually marry someone else before moving west to become a lumberman, small gestures as these secured social ties with literary lacings.

If everyday social calls occasioned literary gifts, even more so did holiday socializing, especially around Christmas and New Year's. That latter holiday saw more gift exchange than Christmas since many New Englanders still maintained a traditional suspicion of yuletide merriment; if they celebrated the holiday at all, they accepted it as a holy day not to be corrupted by material concerns. Increasingly, during the late 1850s, however, strictures relaxed and Christmas gifts became more common, though recipients continued to value the sociabilities as much, if not more, than the presents. "Received a beautiful Book as a New Years Present," a schoolmaster's widow recorded, only to exclaim thanks for her thoughtful acquaintances instead of the gift: "O may I be grateful to my Heavenly Father for so many kind & precious friends." The presence of usually absent household members could also seem like a blessing that gifts only enhanced. "Santa Claus came with various presents for children," wrote one housewife whose husband had during the previous year spent most days away from home attending to editorial work. Although she cherished his gift of "Aurora Leigh by Mrs Browning"—"I am delighted with it. It is a *real* poem"—she underscored the more important event: her husband "was at home *all* day which was the greatest feast to us."[6] A real loved one was even better than "a real poem."

Some face-to-face holiday gift exchanges combined social calling with acts of charity. On a round of holiday calling, one minister and his wife "gave a quantity of biscuit & sundries including [her] beloved 'Testament & Psalms' to a poor, aged, sick colored woman in Mr. Martin's woods." Thinking the ill woman would need the Bible more than she would, the benefactor gave away not only a text that would provide nourishment for an ailing spirit but also a chapter in her own life history—a book that was "beloved." Face-to-face exchange based upon charity was therefore one of mutual satisfaction: the giver gratified that he or she was positively affecting someone's life, the needy recipient appreciative for the largess. One Maine widow, who did the holiday rounds dispensing gifts among less fortunate neighbors, brought her tikes in tow to learn benevolence. "I think it very useful to take my children on such excursions," she observed. That yuletide she was moved by a touching scenario involving her son that resulted from her lessons: "Henry carried to a little deformed boy we go to see, a little book which he bought for 6 cents, five of which, he found in the shed among the chips & grandpapa told him he could have it to buy a Christmass gift with & of his own free will he proposed buying a book for a poor child."[7] Rather than buying a book for himself, her son, an avid reader, imagined the many people he often called upon who might enjoy having it instead and settled upon the most needy child. For his mother, the choice testified to her son's social and moral development.

Benevolent literary gift giving and holiday socializing also coincided at institutionally sponsored holiday parties reaching out to people of all ages. One woman attended annual soirees given by her Gardiner, Maine, ladies' society, where all, even the uninvited children, were remembered with books. "Christmass evening Mrs Hoskins gave a very pleasant party & the ladies as usual, exchanged presents," she once recorded, noting a gift of "a little book called 'Inquisitive Jack'" for her children. Churches sometimes hosted more elaborate affairs, as was the case with one held in a Thomaston, Maine, church vestry at which, as one attendee put it, *"Every one got something,"* even though gifts exchanged hands in a flurry; "friends—put presents on the tree for friends—teachers for scholars &c." Even the minister "received a dressing gown—and a book." She went on to describe the printed gifts presented to her twelve-year-old brother and herself: "Vinnie's Sabbath School teacher McInston put on a very pretty clasped bible for Vinnie, I received . . . an A.B.C. book and a larger *picture book*—for children." Gift distribution to children had to avoid the slightest hint of partiality, so to stave this off, at some parties every child got the same book. "On New Year's day, Mr. Bowditch, had a tree in his house with presents on it for every scholar in the primary school," a witness reported of a gathering among immigrant laborers' children. "He had a book printed on purpose for them," she continued. "One of Miss Edgeworths tales, and a little beautiful horn full of confectionary." She concluded: "How those poor little Irish children will love Mr. Bowditch." Using an evergreen as a prop for gifts was not unusual, for in communal settings, the tree did the "giving," diverting responsibility away from any one person.[8]

On other occasions, wherever presents went, sociability followed. Although birthdays usually passed by as just another day—"My birth day," a seaman remarked, adding that he "spent it in ripping up sails, and have that now for a business"—they sometimes were celebrated with presents from everyday social callers, who could drop in with unexpected bounty. "My birthday," an eleven-year-old clerk's daughter began her diary entry. "In the evening Freddy & Ann [Bartlett] came up with a wreath[,] a boquet[,] some poetry & a plant." For teenagers, it all could amount to little more than simple fun; for adults, a birthday gift might feature complex layers of social meaning acquired over generations. For example, John Park commemorated son-in-law Benjamin Franklin Thomas's thirty-sixth birthday with a vintage literary gift at a family gathering. "I gave Mr Thomas Boileau's Works, in two volumes, which I purchased in Philadelphia, in 1802, of Dufief, with whom, Mr [Benjamin Franklin] Bache, and heir of Doctor Franklin had deposited a part of the Doctor's Library for sale," the elderly Park explained of the book's genealogy and its relevance for the recipient, a grandson of Revolutionary-era printer Isaiah Thomas. "The gift appeared to be highly gratifying to Mr Thomas, as the work was once the property of him for whom he was named." In this case, the gift's value was enhanced not only by the social setting in which it was presented but also by its own long history in which public and private significance intertwined.[9]

Besides birthdays, farewells and homecomings were surrounded by literary gifts. A worthy memento, like a religious text or beautifully bound poetry, could memorialize migrants who might never return. Surprisingly, even long after the development of photography around 1840, New Englanders often chose a book instead of a daguerreotype as a farewell present. Four days before moving with her husband from Massachusetts to Connecticut, a millwright's wife "[s]pent the afternoon in making calls" and, at one home, "[p]resented a Bible to Martha Gouch," a comb maker's spouse. More often, migrants received a book from friends who wished the traveler well. "The last day in beautiful N[ew] England," Charlotte Forten exclaimed with sorrow before heading South to her family home in Philadelphia, where she dreaded facing that city's intense racial segregation. "Helen gave me a Longfellow in blue and gold [binding], and Sarah P.[itman] gave me Bayard Taylor's 'Poems of the Orient.'" On her train journey south, she salved her pain by reading "Longfellow's sweet and musical rhymes." As with farewells, homecomings prompted literary gifts, too, but usually the traveler brought these, sometimes rare items not available locally. Back from Europe, a Bangor lumber merchant's wife, for example, presented "all [Jean Paul] Richter's works in 4 large volumes" to a German-speaking neighbor. Usually, receivers felt little obligation to reciprocate gifts from travelers; after all, they were procured under special circumstances and the occasion was not one necessarily enhanced by exchange, but by the spirit of reunion.[10] These treats from travelers helped solidify bonds cut asunder by time spent away from home, for they represented continuing ties in the face of disruption and the proof that the receiver remained in mind during separation. Furthermore, literary gifts during reunions focused conversation that was necessarily strained by the spaces of intervening time.

Even more interpersonal negotiation was, of course, required by courtship, and, not unexpectedly, it too saw much literary gift giving during social calls. The case of two of New Haven's Jocelyn sisters, Frances and Elizabeth, shows how extensive romantic parades of presents could be, but also the different gift strategies, pious and secular, pursued by their respective divinity-student suitors, David Peck and James Bradford Cleaveland. As the relationship between Frances and her beau intensified, so too did his gift giving, which included Thomas Dick's *Philosophy of a Future State,* "a beautiful volume of *'Pilgrims Progress,'"* and, on her twenty-fifth birthday, "a present of a beautiful Hymn Book." While Peck demonstrated his piety to Frances through his selections, Cleaveland, four years his junior, displayed to Elizabeth his facility with secular material such as Thomas Babbington Macaulay's *History of England,* "some French papers," and several sheets of printed sheet music, especially Jenny Lind songs. Yet of all his gifts, it was a "Greek Testament with a note" from the student that seemed to elicit the most affection from Elizabeth, who told her diary, "I prize it very much on the giver's account, aside from the use it will be to me."[11] A mountain of printed words given as gifts thus provided both foundations for romantic relations and opportunities for judging givers' worthiness as potential husbands. That both men's initiatives succeeded suggests the differences had to do with hitting just the right note with the two sisters' contrasting personalities.

Such prior "testing of the waters" was not unusual, for women needed to be sure of their lasting affections during an era when divorce was virtually unthinkable. The engaged schoolmistress we encountered in chapter 3, still yet pursued by her "Cousin Bill," was given a telling literary gift by him, Ik Marvel's *Reveries of a Bachelor,* in which a single man muses upon the women he would have married. Clearly, he wanted her to reconsider her betrothal by imagining an alternative course down the aisle with him, especially since she felt disappointed at her wedding being postponed. "I listened with as much interest as I could command," she divulged after he proceeded to read aloud his gift, "but I could'nt help wishing it was *another's* voice which was falling on my ear—soon may I listen to its music." Before long, his ceaseless social calling became an annoyance to her. Desiring to read the novel without the giver's tempting presence, on another occasion she recorded, "Came home intending to spend a quiet evening in reading 'Reveries'—but Cousin Bill interrupted again—He is a great talker—quite entertaining—and I enjoy his society—though I think he rather intrudes by the frequency of his calls." Still, the persistent man ignored her discomfort and visited the next day and two days thereafter, including, as she expressed it with exasperation, "the last night of my *girl life!*"—the eve before her wedding day.[12] His last-ditch effort having failed, she went to the altar with her fiancé. The story of whom one did and did not marry thus could often be told through a recounting of literary experiences during courtship visits.

Besides courtship and marriage, death was another life-cycle event marked by literary gifts. Mourners were brought books to comfort them and provide reading matter to soothe heavy hearts. Only days after Elizabeth Jocelyn's five-year-old brother passed away, the "Doctor brought over a hymn book . . . , in which were the verses, that the children sing at Sunday School, when one of their number is dead." In the wake of her four-year-old son's death, one grief-stricken mother was given a mourning book by her pastor during a call to alleviate her suffering. After a hiatus from her favorite leisure activity, reading, during the boy's illness, she finally picked up what the clergyman left her: "Have been reading a book that the bishop brought me a few days since, 'A Gift for mourners.'" He returned to visit the mother a few months later to find her still inconsolable and unable to read much; she could only record, "I feel that there is no source of comfort in the world." Sometimes it was the terminally ill themselves who offered literary gifts before their deaths as solace for soon-to-be mourners. Mary Pierce Poor witnessed such a scene filled with tears, biblical quotations, and tender words about books at the deathbed of a neighbor. "She seemed to think of everybody & everything, selected a little book & some birch bark slippers she had had ever since she was a little girl to be given to Caro," Poor recorded of a bequest to her niece. She noted another gift to her brother in law: "She gave Mr Hedge 'Longfellow's voices of the night' which was the last present she had received."[13] The valuable parting gifts, from one of her first childhood books, to the very last gift she accepted in her adulthood, told a long history of gift exchange charged with personal associations. The gifts she presented gained new life as mementos in the hands of the living. Just as lovers wended their way to the marriage altar with books in hand, so, too, did the bereaved trudge with literary mementoes on their lonely way to their own deaths and hopeful reunions.

Not all transactions of the sort were so gravely intimate. The power inherent in social calls to transform literary gifts into repositories of personal and social meaning was appropriated by disseminators whose ideology, whether religious, benevolent, or political, motivated them to give away free literature to the public. By visiting even total strangers in their homes, these advocates imbued gratis reading matter with a familiar air that suggested gift giving rather than propagation of ideas. No wonder distributors of free Bibles and other religious works often referred to a stop along the way within a tract district as a "call." One New Haven tract distributor blended concepts of religious duty with the terminology of sociable calling. "[T]o my task," she roused herself one morning; "and then with my bundle of tracts start to make that visit." Although she knocked on strangers' doors, she also tapped on those of acquaintances. During one round of calls, she "looked up" a Sunday school pupil to whom she "gave away my tracts." A rural Congregationalist circuit rider reported that he called "on Solomon Kellys family—found an old backslid[e]r—talked & prayed with her," "gave a tract viz the New birth[.] May it help her to decide wethether [*sic*] she has been born again." Some callers left cards; evangelically minded ones left propaganda.[14]

Visits that erased lines between sociability, gift giving, and ideological dissemination could be deployed for partisan political ends, of course. That the hoopla surrounding the 1840 Log Cabin campaign, for example, coincided with the sixth U.S. census, afforded ample opportunities to press partisan material into people's hands during canvassers' stops at neighborhood homes. "Estabrook has been round taking the census," a staunch Whig woman fumed when one Democrat made the rounds in Worcester, "and carried with him to every house where he dares to leave it, [Pennsylvania Democratic senator James] Buchanan's two last speeches." One Whig partisan expected her daughter during that election to "distribute among y' friends" campaign engravings of presidential candidate William Henry Harrison. Risking infractions of social etiquette, politicos even proffered their paraphernalia at newspaper offices or reading rooms. A country teacher, for example, got more than he bargained for during a trip to read some papers at the *Brattleboro Republican,* where "the foreman filled my pockets with old & new speeches."[15] Visiting during the heat of political campaigns might tinge customary sociable literary exchanges with partisanship.

Although many face-to-face gift exchanges took place in domestic or business environments, disseminators of gratis literature found eager recipients during excursions away from home, too. Tract distributors, for example, could easily dispose of their pamphlets to passengers in need of reading material as occupation after conversation ran dry during long, monotonous journeys. "Our boat company is remarkably quiet," observed a passenger among bored fellow travelers on the way to Niagara Falls. One colporteur "distributing some tracts all over the boat" enlivened the tedium in that he "furnished every idle loon with good reading." Traveling distributors themselves noted the effects of their efforts, as in the case of one on a stagecoach reporting she was "favored with an excellent opportunity for tract & paper distribution" via "[t]wo pretty young ladies" into whose hand she placed an evangelical paper. She was gratified that after a tavern break "when they were again seated in the stage, [they] commenced reading, very diligently, to themselves." Their reading then prompted pleasant conversation with a "gentleman, on the back seat, who had hitherto remained silent." She paraphrased a passage from Thomas Parnell's 1722 poem "The Hermit" (a popular tract society item for children) to describe the sociabilities among strangers that followed: "'word followed word, from question answer rose.'" Catching people on the move, whether traveling in stages or on boats, or walking about on their everyday routes, seemed to work as well for some distributors as the convention of social calls. Even recreational outings afforded chances for the ideologically committed. Always ready to convert people to the antislavery cause, one ardent abolitionist brought propaganda with him on a Mount Moosilauke excursion with friends, who were also advocates: "We were equipped with a knapsack, containing an enormous chunk of Graham bread, a tin-cartridge-looking box for flowers, a basket, some bundles of cheap Abolition publications, which we distributed along both to children & grown people as occasion offered."[16] Like literary Johnny Appleseeds, these folks sociably broadcast the printed word on their cross-country treks.

For those staying put, one way to further literary dissemination was to enlist the face-to-face sociabilities characterizing benevolent activities in order to procure money for associational book purchases. Skilled in organizing social events and making handicrafts, women particularly devised creative schemes for selling their wares to raise money for this purpose. Exhibitions might be held, say, to fund a supply of Sunday school books for a Universalist society or other denominational end, while many other events sprang from sewing society members pooling their talents for equally good causes. Sometimes, though, the cause was simply collective self-improvement. One Cape Codder explained to her friend, a machinist's wife, that "the young ladies here have be[e]n A triang [*sic*] to git A town library this winter by having what wee call The Young Ladies Library Association every week. [W]e hav made a lot of fancy articles and last month had A fair rased mony enoph to git two hundred and fifty [books?] for the first start[. W]ee are in hopes that by that the next winter to git there twice as menny and so increse until wee git A large library which is somthing wee vary much need." Clearly, if this farm daughter's orthography and folk usage are any indication, that need for local literary uplift may have been great indeed.[17] At these public events, donors, who purchased the handmade items at fairs, socialized with one another and their solicitors, forging one more link in the interpersonal chain of socioliterary experience.

Literary Gift Giving from Afar

The immediate reactions that receivers registered at public meetings, in private homes, or at holiday parties upon seeing their literary presents, obviously were lost to givers sending their literary gifts in bundles by express or ship to faraway friends and relatives. And although most gifts described in letters and diaries were handed out by someone, givers were not always on the scene; they often relied upon others to buy or page their gifts. Donors, too, particularly those who gave money for books, seldom got a chance to experience the effects of their gifts upon beneficiaries. These distant givers of all sorts could only vicariously experience what people who gave in person did. Since the locus of giving became the note attached to a present or a thank-you letter, writers commonly attempted to replicate the words and gestures of face-to-face gift giving. It comes as no surprise then, that recipients often valued these notes more than the gifts themselves.

Little wonder, too, that presentation notes challenged givers' literary skills to render feelings into words. Sometimes the result was humorous wordplay alluding to the gift's literary content. When the aforementioned Irish American salesman sent his bundle of dried fruits and the book-length poem *Nothing to Wear* to a lady friend, his note redeployed the title's words—something he might have said if present—to wish the recipient continuing material and spiritual prosperity: "I cannot send them off without adding. . . . I most sincerely hope that you at least will find no trouble in the matter of having 'nothing to wear,' while sojourning through this brief life, and when you shall have entered upon that life which is eternal, you there shall have to wear a crown that shall never fade." In other instances, cover notes imagined how their gifts would be used. After a Granite Stater presented her Vermont sister-in-law with Robert Southey's works, she ventured, "I hope it may serve to amuse some of your lonely hours, as I know books are your chosen companions and indeed with those at hand you are never lonely." Another way of personalizing a literary gift was to recount the selection process in light of recipients' wishes or needs. The note in one bundle sent by a Chelsea, Massachusetts, woman to a family member in Maine explained why she bought one certain book, an edition of Fénelon, for her aunt: "I remember, she expressed, a wish to own [it]." The cover note was the handshake that personalized the literary gift, which otherwise might seem cold and impersonal. Other senders hoped some aspect of their own life would be captured and imparted through presentation notes. While in the nation's capital on business, an editor sent a gift to his friend back home, which said something about the cultural life and social airs of political spouses and daughters: "There is an immense quantity of pretty girls and pretty women at present in Washington. I will send you the Huntress, which contains sketches of some of them." Had the unusual periodical, Anne Royall's scandal-mongering *Huntress,* been delivered without explanation, the gift's full import might have been lost. Previously used literary gifts carried a history of social meaning, so presentation notes might point out that genealogy. "I send you a little book which M[rs] [Lydia H.] Sigourney handed me last Fall for you," a minister informed his daughter; "if it does not interest you now, it will I think when you are older, do *preserve* it *with care,* for the sake of the Author, a much valued friend of mine." Literary gifts presented by the elderly or ill prior to impending death bore the indelible stamp of the owner's life, and so notes accompanying these mementoes reminded recipients that the item, no matter how trivial, was not to be treated lightly. John Park guaranteed gifts entrusted to him by a seventy-year-old prior to her death would retain her spirit. "She had prepared little memorials for many—a suitableness in every thing," he relayed to his daughter in a note announcing the bequest; "you will see by the Pen-wiper, which she had allotted for you and which I am sure you will value a thousand times its worth."[18] Even small tokens like personal writing implements, insofar as they signaled moments of communication, could be denoted as socioliterary mementoes of the departed.

Literary gifts, even those freshly purchased, quickly acquired a social history of their own, for they did not always arrive in a pristine state; they differed in this respect from transient papers, which were not supposed to be read en route. Gift notes recounted how books, even volumes hot off the press, were sometimes first read or admired before wending their way to recipients. "Mother sends you Miss Parks' Joanna of Naples," a Bostonian told her sister, "which we have been reading to [sister] Ellen, & like very much." A student who was asked by a gift giver to send a book to her sister, explained a similar situation. "Yesterday afternoon I went to see Miss Burdett," who "wished Alice to accept this book," she wrote, adding, "She would have brought it down, when she came at Thanksgiving, but a friend was reading it." When a retired politician sent a copy of a pamphlet, his edition of astronomer Maria Mitchell's correspondence concerning an award she received for discovering a comet in 1847, as a New Year's gift for his niece Lucretia by way of her mother, not only she but also her son read it first. "I read yesterday with the deepest interest the volume you sent to Lucretia. . . . I kept it for one day for my own satisfaction," the mother admitted. "The volume carried me back so fully to the years gone bye . . . that I seemed to live it all over again." Her enthusiasm spread to her son, who "sat up half the night to read it after he got home from his work." After both readers quickly indulged their curiosity, she directed it on its way the next day.[19] The mother and son could not keep their hands off the pamphlet perhaps because they knew the author, yet there was no sense that the gift had been devalued by this prior reading; in fact, it had gained in worth as it passed through the hands of loved ones.

Thank-you letters, as opposed to delivery notes, attempted to describe the pleasure of receiving to distant givers as if they were present upon opening gifts. Letters of gratitude usually spared no affection and spotlighted the relationship between givers and recipients. Often recipients stressed that their appreciation for the gift was one and the same with their deep valuation of the giver, thereby placing the human relationship, carried on at a distance, at center stage. William Lloyd Garrison Jr. demonstrated this when he ended his lengthy thank-you letter for a plain Bible sent in 1859 by his renowned but chronically impoverished abolitionist father on New Year's Day with a tender reassurance: "Rather would your children inherit the noble legacy of your example than the wealth of an Astor or the fame of a Napoleon." Garrison was not unusual. "*Pecuniary* value is not the true standard by which a token of good will should be estimated," a Swedenborgian congregant wrote to a minister's wife after she sent him a copy of her late husband's sermons for a New Year's Day gift. "It is the motive or affection which prompts it, & the manner of expressing it that gives it its true value. . . . [T]he Volumes now received will be encreased in value to me because they have been made the expression of the acknowledgment of a respected sister in the Church." A Maine woman's thank-you note to two of her brothers suggested that the power of affection, not only conveyances like steamships and coaches, transported gifts to her. "Have I ever thanked you for all the kind presents since your absence which your love has bestowed?" she asked and specified them: "The beautiful work-boxe from Spain—the Shakespeare from New Orleans, and all the joint tokens of love from dear Nat and yourself most precious and valued by your beloved sister." Notes highlighting relationships could also recount methods of delivery. "I received your kind letter and present by Mr Hedge, who was good enough to bring them up the evening of his arrival," a minister's daughter informed her brother. "I began to read the book immediately." Saying "by" whose hand a gift arrived was a standard acknowledgment of receipt, but some notes replayed the moment it came, as when Samuel May helped his friend Estlin visualize the final steps in his package's journey after it had crossed over the Atlantic: "Last eve$^{g.}$ as we sat at tea, a little parcel was left at the door, & brought to me at the table—which proved to be the 13th volume of Chambers' Miscellany—your daughter's kind and very welcome gift to my little girl."[20] The "at the table" conveyed his anxiousness to view the package's contents, while it gave the sender a sharper mental picture of the gift's opening.

Thank-you notes also commonly portrayed the pleasure of receiving, especially when they came from an eyewitness other than the recipient. Letters written by adults for children were particularly careful to let the giver know what delight the gift brought to the youngster. "[T]hanks for my letters—& my pear—& Willy's paper—the children's thanks also—they were delighted with the bag & books," a Brookline matron told her sister. These words of gratitude written by adult amanuenses, also often carefully animated the loving relationships between youthful recipient and giver by approximating childish words. Mary Pierce Poor caught the charm of a child, in this case, her coy three-year-old daughter, who, though thankful for her gift, thought more of the givers than the book she obviously cherished: "Agnes talking about Grandpa said he was very kind & she loved him because he gave her a little book—she said she loved Grandma too though she didn't give her a book." Such third-person representations could reassure the giver not only that the gift was welcomed but also that the relationship it signified was appreciated. Thank-you notes like these could also position the literary gift as a prop upon the stage of the recipient's everyday life. "My husband bids me thank you for the Medical Almanack it will be very useful to him," a physician's wife informed her brother. "The boys are spelling—telling *riddles* &c & I wish you could look in upon our happy group." Sometimes the witness provided a picture of how a literary gift abetted the child's social growth beyond the family circle, as captured by a merchant's wife writing to her cousin: "My daughter is very much pleased with the tokens you sent to her[;] . . . she has learnt several hymns in her hymn book and has read and lent the 'Boquet' to the most of her schoolmates." Charitable donors, too, sometimes learned of the effects of their beneficence from letters portraying reception. A Sunday school teacher in Arcadia, Maine, described in a letter to her father the joy her pupils felt upon receiving some tracts: "The children here are quite eager for books, & I often wish uncle J. T. could see how much interested they are in the small publications of the Tract Society he so kindly gave me."[21] In this way, a note of gratitude from interested observers could bring givers into an intimate scene of the object's use, making them feel a part of it.

Seldom mere vehicles of flattery, thank-you notes could express displeasure about the gift's text. It, after all, was only a secondary feature in the entire value-laden package of personal and social meaning; in these cases, the underlying significance remained unmarred. Sometimes indirection was the course of choice. One recipient offered qualified thanks for a densely written book sent as a gift, which, she claimed, "I read with a great deal of pleasure in spite of its involved passages & pages." But when the recipient held little back, it could push the giver, in reply, to balance apology with defensiveness. After getting a perhaps too-candid letter about his gift of Henry Wadsworth Longfellow's *Evangeline* to John Estlin, for example, Samuel May kept up the dialogue in the spirit of friendship: "I admit much that you say about it. The cumbrous Hexameter is ill-suited to our language. Many of the expressions are so commonplace as to give a ludicrous air to certain passages, especially when taken in connection with the elaborate measure. But, notwithstanding all, I was deeply affected by the Poem, or *story,* or whatever else it be."[22] The frankness usually only added to the value of the relationship, if not to the gift.

Of course, overly passionate dislike could hurt the giver. Privately expressed opinions of gifts, confided only to a diary, could cut and scathe at a literary present without risking anyone's feelings. Surprisingly, gift annuals, often elaborately bound, lavishly illustrated and in gilt-edged editions, filled with stories and poetry, struck some readers as but "slipslosh stuff." Certainly, Persis Sibley Andrews felt not only that the sentimental and trite reading matter in annuals was condescending to women but also that the idea of such a lavish gift, coming from suitors at

Christmas time, was presumptuous: "[H]ow astonishing that a man sho'd think of making so expensive a book as 'The Token for 1841'—containing such puerile, trashy matter, & no more that is valuable. 'The Rose of Sharon' is better, but this contains too large a proportion of *love—lover* & *beloved*—tho' the sentiments are mostly woven into religious tales." Andrews continued to fume at this. "I have had a New Year's present of Byron's poems in one vol.," she wrote on the next 1 January. "A thousand times more valuable than the trashy works I had last year." Harriett Low reacted in the same manner when in 1832 an impetuous suitor left her "2 annuals" as a love token along with a passionate note. "[S]o ceremonious it alarms me," she remarked of the gushy gesture. "Oh dear what animals men are," she observed in light of his gift. "They are certainly *incomprehensible.* I do think I have had some *odd specimens* to deal with."[23] In these cases, the spirit of giving was wrapped up in artificial sentiment and reflected back in the superficial gloss of giftbooks easily digested and quickly forgotten. Along with the insincere men who sent them, ostentatious gifts were disregarded.

But recipients remembered the social relations of literary giving long after the gift's bindings frazzled, the pages yellowed, and texts faded from memory. Like William and Ellen Craft, who, as we have seen, prized their Bible "on account of the donor & the circumstances under which it was given" for many years after their marriage, others, too, treasured their gifts as safeguards of memories. Certain events might reanimate the memories of givers and occasions for giving. For the Crafts, it was the death in 1860 of Theodore Parker, worn down by his decades of struggle to end slavery, which sparked their reminiscence. For one whaler, it was writing his retrospective diary. Stopping to think of his first whaling voyage in 1816, he recalled a gift, one of the few that survived years of a peripatetic life, from a distant relation, John Park. "My Boston friends treated me kindly," the seaman recollected in 1834, "particularly Dr. Park, who made me several presents. . . . My 'Bowditch's Navigator,' which I now have was one of them." For an eighteen-year-old New London shop clerk, the death of a friend who convinced him to lead a pious life refreshed the memory of a gift. "I hird of the Death of my True Friend Miss Elizabeth R. Coit who talked to me so faithfully," he fondly remarked; "at the time she gave me Abbots Young Christian." For a local historian, it was a reperusal of an old book that summoned up a childhood scene and lessons about making wise choices. The day after he finished helping his Michigan-bound parents pack up to leave their native New Hampshire, he recorded that he had "re-read Franklin's admirable autobiograph[y]," and noted, "I well recollect how I came into possession of this work. I was a small boy, when I asked my father to purchase for me a pair of skates. He told me, if I would relinquish the skates he would give me this life of Franklin, and on my compliance did so. I read the work many times and have received much advantage from it." Upon his family's final parting three days later, he sighed, "I may never again meet them." Though he was evidently right, the book at least remained with him; he read it again a month later—upon it he would eventually base his first lyceum lecture.[24]

Conclusion

As New Englanders traveled through the years, thoughts of once newly received presents were thus safely deposited in the libraries of memory, where the spirit of giving lived on with each recollection "of the donor." This spirit, as we have seen, wafted through occasional as well as charitable gift giving, the latter through tract dissemination and monetary donations for books. It moved both the social caller and bundle maker to imbue their gifts with affection and esteem for the receiver. Recipients in turn adopted the spirit and welcomed it into their hearts. They reciprocated with literary gifts of their own or priceless words of gratitude. No matter how unbalanced in monetary worth, the exchange between givers and receivers was almost always on par, for everyone gained as everyday ideas flowed freely through the spirit of giving. The greatest benefit, however, was the maintenance of the social bonds of literary experience among antebellum New Englanders who gave and received, who read and remembered.

Chapter 6

Through Many Hands: Lending and Borrowing Reading Material

On 15 March 1852, Charles Cobb went about his usual duties, which included a walk to his Uncle Henry's to help out around the farm. This particular winter day there was little to do after driving some steer from one neighbor's farm to Solomon Briggs's nearby property, so Cobb occupied his spare time at his uncle's by having his aunt grease his boots and by reading one of the books he found lying about the house. "I came from Brigg's over to Henry's & read in a 'Classical Dictionary' there that belongs to Loudon Smith," he recorded that evening in his diary after returning home. Intrigued by the encyclopedic volume that Smith had lent his brother-in-law Henry, Cobb returned the next day to borrow the dictionary. "I wanted badly to find out about Babylon, Nineveh, Palmyra, Persepolis[,] . . . Jerusalem, Thebes, Memphis &c.," he explained after getting it. He transcribed extracts in the form of a "Geographical Historical and Statistical Dictionary" a few days later. Eventually finishing the large volume, he drew his own conclusions about historical time lines that contradicted biblical accounts. "From reading that classical Dictionary, I have got the impression that we know of things that took place 12,000 years ago, and that 8,000 years ago the world was almost as civilized as it is now—but as the Bible says the world was created only 6,000 years ago, historians make every thing come down to it." He added, "This is the impression I got, but I ain't certain of anything."[1] His calculations thus led him to conclude that the biblical account of human history was seriously flawed. One act of borrowing, in this case a book that happened to be available at a regular stop along his path through an ordinary day, led to an intellectual discovery.

Although it seemed almost destined to happen, borrowing this particular book was but one link in a random chain of events: a volume in Loudon Smith's possession found its way to his sister, then to Charles Cobb. He also chanced to glance at it and wanted to read more. From his reading, he not only acquired information about ancient civilizations but also sharpened his critical thinking skills to produce an idea about the age of the earth.

Everyday ideas, culled from borrowed reading materials, frequently formed haphazardly among ordinary people as books, magazines, and newspapers unpredictably filtered through social networks. Lending, even more than purchasing and gift giving, supplied people with a range of materials they could not otherwise afford or that escaped local booksellers, shops, and peddlers. The spread of information in this manner defied the logic of the literary marketplace, which decreed that wherever publishers, booksellers, and printers ventured, readers were sure to follow. With seemingly only one small shop on Woodstock green from which he very rarely bought or rented a book, and no free or public libraries within easy reach except for a tiny Sunday school library, Cobb depended primarily upon non-institutional borrowing for his extracurricular reading. And so too did the people of his village, who passed among one another the few and valuable texts they had. But in larger towns and cities with sometimes more institutional libraries (municipally supported free public libraries were only slowly emerging),[2] book borrowers and lenders persisted in interpersonal exchange, risking all its intrinsic perils: losing materials, damaging costly items, or never reaching the book's conclusion just to return it in time. Obligations were inscribed heavily on each book borrowed and lent. Yet even as lending or borrowing a book surely led people into webs of social responsibilities, the entanglement was a welcome part of everyday life among folks hungry for both varied reading materials and the human trace impressed upon books passing through many hands.[3]

This chapter explores borrowing and lending practices via person-to-person exchanges, conducted primarily through social calling. Although borrowing and lending were closely interdependent, each had distinctive traits. We first briefly consider interpersonal exchange as part of an ongoing interflow in which participants acted as both lenders and borrowers within the characteristic give and take of social relations. Afterward, we shift the focus to the borrowers' unique viewpoint upon such transfers in homes and workplaces. Then we turn to lenders for their version: the reasons for letting a book circulate and its modes of dissemination. We conclude by assaying methods for returning or getting back books in good order. Throughout we highlight the myriad social acts and codes governing this informal system of dissemination and the tremendous level of trust people placed in one another to allow it operate successfully. Book borrowing facilitated social relationships to such a degree that one can never be sure if such exchanges were mere excuses for getting together. Yet as books passed through many hands, they acquired ever-deepening layers of social meaning, just as relationships themselves deepened through constant contact maintained by these and other literary practices.

Social Exchange through Reading Material

Most borrowers were also lenders, and vice versa. Readers usually acted out the two roles at some point in their lives and thus understood well the exigencies of either. Although Charles Cobb borrowed from his Uncle Henry's well-stocked bookshelf, including, beside the classical dictionary, music, lecture notes, and a volume of Byron's poetry, the farm boy also lent out from his small holdings. For example, he once jotted down: "Oramel was up too A.M. and borrowed 8 Posts containing 'Viola—a tale of the Far Southwest' . . . by Emerson Bennett." He added, "'Tis a grand story," as if proud to lend out such a worthy text. These two-way exchanges were often seen as so important that neither rain nor sleet nor snow could stop them. One miserable February day, a Vermonter risked walking through muddy streets both to borrow and lend: "It rained all the forenoon, I carried a book up to Daniel Young to read, borrowed some in return."[4] Simultaneous lending and borrowing ensured steady circulation.

Meeting to exchange books afforded opportunities for socializing and group-inspired intellectual development. The practice was often generated from within families as children witnessed it. A temporarily unemployed printer's apprentice looked back upon the constant relay of books and, with them, ideas, among his kinfolk, as instrumental to his own budding intellection. "The taste for Reading I always supposed myself to have imbibed from a desire to imitate my elder brother and cousins who lent books to each other, and talked much about their reading," he recalled of his school days. Because the dual identity of being both borrower and lender would be simultaneously internalized by those taking part in these informal systems, it leveled the terms of exchange—no one was always entirely beholden. Necessity was often the bedrock of these relations, especially during school years, when expenses for books mounted. As a seminary student in the mid-1830s, for example, Mary Pierce Poor exchanged reading material with at least two other frugal classmates. "We go upon the mutual accommodation system & lend each other books to save buying so many as we otherwise should," she explained.[5] Having many amenable friends could mean having ample books for people with limited budgets.

While a mutually beneficial relationship was struck up based upon economy in this case, other reciprocal borrowing and lending relationships reflected and reinforced bonds of growing intimacy. Demonstrations of mutual respect for one another's property particularly fueled feelings of trust during courtship when lovers typically tested the strength of the relationship. Emma Gannell, a young English immigrant in Concord, New Hampshire, saw her 1851 courtship progress through exchanging materials with ornamental coach painter John Burgum. At first, he regularly "call[e]d with some books and papers" as loans or gifts for her and seemed to delight her elderly aunt. Encouraged, Gannell in turn loaned him materials throughout that summer. On 4 August, she wrote, "M^{r}. Burgum calld with papers, I lent him a book. My Aunt was pleased that he called on me." A few days later, however, one of his offerings, perhaps an unorthodox religious text, aroused suspicion: "M^{r}. Burgum calld at seven with a book. . . . Aunt was not pleased at it." After a subsequent visit on the eighteenth, during which "Aunt rang the bell in his ears"—a rude way to announce to her niece of his arrival—the lovers agreed to rendezvous nearly every day on the banks of the Merrimack, sometimes at five in the morning, or during walks to and from church, away from her aunt's disapproving gaze. Promises to exchange books, scrapbooks, and newspapers sealed their secret agreement. "M$^{r.}$ B. came to the bank at seven with my book on the sabbeth," she reported on 3 September. In the cold mist of a late October shower at sunrise, she waited for her suitor to get back her clipping collection and to continue courting: "rainy saw M$^{r.}$ B. at five he returned me my scraps." As winter approached, the clandestine couple persisted. "Saw M^{r} B at 8 A.M.," she recorded a few days later. "I returned him my scraps." As October rain turned into icy November snows, the smitten woman remained ever true: "Snowy saw M$^{r.}$ B at 6. [A.M.] gave him the scrap book." Less than a year later the two married, while the aunt stayed at home.[6] Gannell's and Burgum's success story exemplified the intimate possibilities of literary exchange.

Into the Borrower's Hands

Beyond symbiotic relationships, like the one between Gannell and Burgum or between Mary Pierce Poor and her school chums, in which borrowers and lenders traded roles in a continuum of exchange, most readers borrowed books without immediately lending. Certainly, they did not add up loans against charges with any single person. Needs changed with time and the situation: students, for example, usually borrowed more than schoolteachers; urban, middling folk with large libraries were more often lenders than, say, poorer mill workers. Therefore, most relationships that coalesced over temporary literary exchanges can be understood from the different perspectives of either borrowers or lenders.

Borrowing was both practical and social. Practically, it was a surrogate for ownership. While literate New Englanders valued large home libraries, most were not able to afford them or find storage space for many books; many folks simply did not wish to purchase every book they longed to read. Frugality, even among the well off, often prevailed. "I want you to get from Westerton & read, not buy Miss Adelaide Procter's 'Legends & Lyrics,'" a Bostonian wrote, directing her sister to a London bookstore where, though she was sufficiently well off to afford the expensive two-volume book, she was advised either to rent or read it on premises. But a well-filled purse could not always access certain titles. Rare books, for example, commonly could not be gotten at any cost, but even latest editions could elude purchasers. Underdeveloped transportation networks and uneven distribution meant that locating and buying books often required substantial investments of time. Still, the urge to read books and periodicals which were out of reach nagged at prodigious readers, and the need to procure certain texts surfaced on occasion. Borrowing, if possible, was the obvious solution. But borrowing almost always tied one to a lender. For all of their pragmatism, borrowers relished the human connections that were part and parcel of book exchange, as suggested by one diarist referring to a neighbor's visit: "Miss W. loaned me a book. I like her *much.*" Lending and affection were effortlessly linked.[7]

For the poor or the frugal, borrowing rather than purchasing made sense. Shortly after her marriage, one impecunious minister's wife begged her much wealthier mother to lend her some titles that would otherwise drain precious income. These included "'The Christian Laym[an'] of which I spoke before 'The Listener' & if brother can spare them for a time 5 or 6 of the last reviews." She explained that her husband "feels the want of books, but hardly knows whether he can afford . . . them." She assured her mother that "he will be careful that we return them all." Another newlywed going into housekeeping remarked to his usual bookseller, "I have stopped buying books, & depended on borrowing, wh. I must contrive to do, until I have paid my debts, which will take a year longer, & perhaps some what more." Although newlyweds felt the burden of setting up a new home, financial considerations might even force borrowing by long-married spouses, as one Boston editor's wife found as stirrings of the panic of 1837 pressed upon her family. "Do you own Goethe's Faust and will you lend it to [my son]," she implored her brother. "His German class are to read it . . . and we have not got it." She knew how popular books seldom stayed on library shelves for long: "I may possibly get it from the Athenaeum but there is such a rage for German now prevailing that it is next to impossible to get such a thing from a public library." But the last resort, purchasing, was untenable. "The alternate of buying," she moaned, "is one to which I am loth to resort."[8] Why buy when one can borrow?

If inability to purchase books was the most logical reason for borrowing, it was not the most common. Rather, readers who did so were usually opportunists in quest of new and varied reading who took advantage of emerging circumstances and easily available materials. Although they might sometimes borrow distinct titles, they mostly wanted to add variety to their reading diet and so asked for materials that their family, friends, and neighbors had immediately on hand and were willing to lend. Sometimes providers granted borrowers free reign to ransack a library. When an apothecary was suddenly called away out of town, he offered a fellow boarder "the key of his parlor" and an open invitation to "his books & his easy-chairs." She jumped at the chance: "[W]e obligingly unlocked his door, & went into his room & helped ourselves from a book-case filled with most well-selected volumes, & criticised his pictures & admired his mantel ornaments & came away with books enough to last us a fortnight." Whether or not the man ever wanted the volumes to leave his parlor is uncertain, but she felt confident that he would not mind if she whisked a few titles into her own room. It behooved borrowers to strike up relations with people who owned many books. But when such generous friends packed up their libraries to move away, frequent borrowers could starve. "Do you have as many new books to read now as you did when Mrs Gray was near you?" Mary Pierce Poor wondered when her friend lost a steady-supplying acquaintance. Simply changing jobs could afford new opportunities for literary borrowing, especially if employers had large libraries. Starting work in a South Boston weaving room, a newly hired dollar-a-day young clerk remarked of its owner, "Mr Mann has a good library of useful books which I can obtain," and concluded, "I think . . . I shall not be in a great hurry to leave him." A nightwatchman in a Lowell mill had a similar reason for staying on, but had more free time to take advantage of his situation: "I am most of the time nights in the 'Counting Room,' with lights, fire, pens, paper, books a[n]d Newspapers furnished. So I enjoy myself at study nights almost as well as though at school."[9] Through such borrowing, the line between work and self-education could blur.

Most readers either did not know or did not live close enough to people with well-stocked private libraries and so took whatever was available and near at hand. One of simplest ways to borrow was to appropriate texts lying about at home. Parents constantly "borrowed" in this way from their children who received gifts from relatives. A housewife noted that she had "been reading a book that [daughter] Jose's uncle . . . gave her" as an eleventh birthday present. "[I]t is excellent," she concluded, judging its merit for youngsters. Any unattended book could be a tacit invitation to borrow. "I laid down this afternoon & read Adam Bede. You forgot to take it," a woman wrote to a recent visitor and confessed, "I'm sorry, though I find it quite a consolation to have it to read." Close friends sometimes assumed that borrowing without asking would be granted, especially if a literary relationship had been long established. So it was not unthinkable to snatch books openly displayed. "What did you think of my carrying off your little book?" one young woman queried her friend. The two friends who had corresponded over years about their reading, while sprinkling their letters liberally with literary quotes, understood one another quite well. "I meant to have asked you to lend it to me that night I last saw you, but entirely forgot it, I felt sure you would say 'take it' and therefore used no ceremony," she explained, concluding, "I hope you have not wanted it." Some opportunistic "borrowing" within the home environment proved consequential for one's future reading habits. For one farm girl, seizing one of her brother's books without asking resulted in a lifelong interest in history. She recalled that "one bright morning . . . I flitted away to school with a strange-looking, unbound book hidden in my satchel," Jane Porter's *Scottish Chiefs*. "I had surreptitiously borrowed it from my brother's table, where he had left it by accident," she confessed decades later, explaining that it "was destined to create within me a new want, and to turn my thoughts to the reading and study of history. In this historical reading I had very little help or sympathy, either at home or at school," she remembered of a time when many women were discouraged from undertaking serious study. No wonder she slyly slipped the book away instead of asking for it.[10]

As simple as it was to usurp a vulnerable text, most borrowers called upon more formal conventions, namely, social calling. During calls, hosts sometimes read aloud to their guests, allowed them to peruse materials themselves, or showed off new purchases or stately libraries. Visitors often went home with an unexpected literary prize tucked underarm and promises to return it, perhaps in exchange for another. After Charlotte Forten visited a sick acquaintance, she exclaimed, "To my great joy she lent me [Charles] Reade's 'White Lies,' of which I *devoured* the two first vols. this eve." A book lent during social calls might be a memento of their sociabilities, but some literary acquisition during visits seemed more unintentional. One ninety-year-old's stroll on a mild February day, for example, produced an unexpected loan: "A Beautiful clear Warm and Pleasant day for the season; I took a Walk after Breakfast . . . to Friend Kings. His Wife lent me a Book the Guide." As in this case, diarists do not exactly say how they got around to borrowing but record only the act itself as it emerged from unrelated encounters. Frances Jocelyn Peck's call upon a neighbor's newborn baby somehow yielded reading matter: "Called at Mrs Norton's. Saw her little son, four weeks old. Borrowed two books." Still, spontaneous loans were not always entirely serendipitous, for callers often knew who had books to lend. A Beverly woman showed this when she visited her friend, a fellow shoemaker working at home who recalled the event in her journal that night after a hard day: the visitor, referring to the diarist's brother, "said she wanted ~~some~~ a book to Read, so she [k]new where to come for J[oshua] has so many books." Although borrowers could visit to browse, many called for specific titles. A fifteen-year-old student, a seaman's daughter, "went up to" a classmate's "to see if she had a copy of Parker's Geographical Questions," while Charlotte Forten "[w]ent to Mrs. Mannings for some of Whittier's books" to lend to her bedridden teacher. Borrowers apparently kept mental checklists of a community's private holdings to draw upon in serving both themselves and others.[11]

At times it becomes difficult to sort out social calls from those geared toward borrowing. "I had a very pleasant call from" a couple, a woman told her diary, noting that the husband "borrowed my tune 'the pilgrim Fathers,' & 2 no's Spirit of the Pilgrims. I valued this call the more because I owed [them] one there." She should have returned their earlier call, but did they ignore customary reciprocal visiting just to get the loan, or did she press the loan upon them for her not calling? Conversely, seeking out lenders seemed an excuse to socialize. For instance, Charles Cobb's mother Lucia, an enthusiastic caller and a fiction aficionada, frequently fled from her endless kitchen duties to fetch new reading material from people within her social network. "Mother got another lot of novels from Ches Raymonds to read yesterday," he noted. On another occasion, she "went down to the flat . . . —brought home a romance by Walter Scott named 'the Pirate' from Jo Darling's to read." "Friday evening Mother brought home a novel from Lish's named The Witch of the Wave o[r] the Corsairs Captive which I read through Sat. A.M.," he wrote a year later. Each title retrieved represented not only a boon to him but also an unseen moment of neighborhood sociability for his mother.[12]

Outside of social calls to homes, workplaces saw much borrowing. This took place even in factories, as one operative's experience at the Pepperell Mills, on the Saco River, indicates. He described one day's activity: "In Mill—Borrow Miltons 'Paradise Lost.' of Mis—[.] [C]ome out at half past five. Read the first book of Paradise Lost." A dry-goods clerk intent upon becoming a Mason borrowed a relevant book from his employer at work: "Hosford lent me a Book on Masonry—Tressle Book." For agricultural workers borrowing books from farmers, the line between working and socializing was often very fine. A Maine ploughman borrowed "some numbers of the Boston Cultivator" from a gentry farmer who gave the young man credit on land and occasional odd jobs in the field. Another laborer, who "workd" on a Glastonbury, Connecticut, farm and presumably once helped his father "split logs 2 hours" for the elderly owner, borrowed her *Liberty Almanac* (an antislavery publication) the next day. The informal circulation of print thus lubricated the machinery of labor. This was also true on ships, the workplace for ship's boys and captains alike, who borrowed reading matter to help pass idle hours. Seamen rarely referred to appropriating books in ship's libraries, captains' or mates' holdings or newspapers that were relayed by passing ships as "borrowing," but occasionally the term signified what was commonplace. Having risen from second mate to captain, John R. Congdon was one exception to the rule. "I read most of the time," he journalized on one voyage. "Yet I have but few Books. [From] Mr. Arnolds I Borrow—, one I have been reading the sketches of a whaling cruise." Arnold, the supercargo, in turn borrowed from Congdon:

"M[r] Arnold has just come in and got my Bible and is now reading aloud on deck; From Pauls 1st Corinthians: 2 chapter." Passengers also borrowed from seamen as Congdon's daughter did while traveling with her father and mother through the Isles de Chincha. A list of "Books borrowed from Capt. Irvine" she recorded included "Scotts Poetical Works," "Coopers novels—The Bravo [and] The Spy," "Count of Monte Cristo," "Never too late to mend," "Lady Evelyn," "Ways of the Hour," "Love me leave me not," and "Charles O—Irish Dragoon." With one borrower on another voyage complaining, "Very little amusement can be found for me on board this ship except reading," it is clear that whether at sea or on the larger voyage of life, literary borrowing could enrich even the emptiest hours.[13]

From the Lenders' Hands

Obviously, borrowers craved extra reading matter, but why did lenders oblige them? Charles Cobb provided some clue. "Mr. Grow stopped in here on his way to Church and left me a book on the 'observance of the Sabbath' to read," the impious farm lad once complained. "I guess he thinks I don't observe them much." Such lending could be dogged. "In the vain hope of saving our souls," Cobb explained, Grow regularly lent a slew of Sunday school books probably charged out from the church library. At every turn, he confronted the old man who would not rest until satisfied that he had converted the infidel. "I ventured to go up to the old house and get a pail of apples," an exasperated Cobb scratched in his journal. "Grow had me take home another Sabbath-school book to read."[14] Determined lenders were not to be dodged.

As Cobb knew well, all voluntary lenders anticipated the literary needs of other people and went about fulfilling those needs by temporarily supplying reading materials. In this case, as in many, the lender wished to influence with a text that the borrower probably would not read on his or her own, much less purchase. These texts, usually containing religious or political messages, were attempts to change the nature of the relationship between lender and borrower toward one which embodied the tenets of the loaned text. For unlike gift givers, these lenders expected the book to be returned accompanied by conversation about its contents. Aggressive social calls like these made one Universalist shop clerk short tempered with a similarly conservative religious zealot. "A particular friend of yours Mr ———," he wrote to his fiancée working in the textile mills, "was in the store to see me the other day, he lent me some newspapers . . . (you probably know what kind) so that I might get right on my religious views."[15] Loans easily spelled coercion rather than amicability to hapless targets of well-meaning but assertive lenders.

Other lenders, even the most ideologically motivated, were more subtle and hence more effective than Grow or the annoying "Mr ———." One Yale Divinity student, for example, watched a black abolitionist quietly try to persuade passengers on a Connecticut River steamboat to borrow his copy of the *Liberator.* The man, he noted, "said but little to any one . . . [;] he constantly carried about in his hand a paper which he seemed very much inclined to lend to any one who was desirous of reading it." John Park followed a similarly unobtrusive path by lending out a newspaper article on the Fugitive Slave Act of 1850 threatening all runaways with forcible return to former masters. The most astute lenders who wished to disseminate ideas, however, often first gauged readers' receptivity before pressing books into their hands. For one farm laborer aspiring to the ministry, books given him by his clergyman, after a screening interview, offered necessary encouragement. "In the evening I went to see Mr. Allen—the minister of our Congregational Church—in his study," he wrote one Christmas Day, and "had a long and good conversation with him respecting myself." Having ascertained the young man's wishes, his pastor presented him with "the 'Thirty-Second Annual Report of the American Education Society' whose object is to render assistance to indigent young men preparing for the ministry" and gave him continuing incentive for further social contact: "He also promised to lend me another book."[16] Books could be a wedge into the heart of a would-be cleric.

Not all lenders who aimed to persuade did so over religion or politics. One schoolmaster fashioned himself a minor prophet of Transcendentalism—a persuasion that appealed to very few people—by sending a book by his acquaintance Ralph Waldo Emerson to family and friends back home. "By the way, when all the folks get through with Emerson's Essays, & c., I wish you would *carry* them to Julia Wells," he wrote regarding a friend to his brother in rural Connecticut. Not content merely to spread the word, he wanted to know how it was received: "Write me soon,—telling me your experiences & c.—the effect of Emerson's works on Uncle Sam'l's mind, about which I feel quite inquisitive." Social networks of lending were tapped into by reform tract distributors, too. Receiving a temperance pamphlet, one traced its circuitous route on which no person held sole responsibility for lending:

> Grandpa sent it [the tract] up on the plain to Deacon Israel Clark. . . . Mr Levi Wright, son of old Deac. W.[right] carried the book, & on the resolution to read it himself before handing it to Deacon Clark. Old Deacon W.[right] found it on his son's table & took it to read. . . . He rested not till he had read it tho' *5 times* & then carried it to *Deacon Clark* his next neighbour, (where it was originally sent,). . . . Deacon C.[lark] having read it, & being much interested therein, it was next despatched to neighbour Sheldon's where it was instrumental in leading *him* to a resolution of total abstinence, & afterwards came back

> to Grandpa. It has now gone over to South St. to be perused, I hope profitably, by another church member who thinks it no harm to drink a little poison daily. Success attends its progress.[17]

Such contagions of lending effectively disseminated literature into many readers' hands.

Beyond advocacy, some lenders preferred instead to bond with borrowers on common literary terrain. Sharing enjoyable literary works with another person who would be almost certain to like them was reason enough; in turn, these loans created pleasant bonds of trust between borrower and lender as well as mutual respect for certain items of reading matter. "Called to see Mrs Lassell and carried her, 'Light and Shadows of Scottish Life,'" a housewife declared. "It is a great favorite with me and I hope she will like it." Predictions of what a borrower might like could always fail, however, as when one ingenue complained that a family friend "besought me to read 'Verdant Green', & lent me his copy, which I am wading thro'." The jocular tome about Oxford freshman life "isn't the funniest thing under the sun," she disclosed to a friend before comparing it to a humorous pronunciation-mangling character from Dickens's *Pickwick Papers.* "Sam Weller beats it, rayther—but *boys* think there is nothing like it for wit & humor." Reading such unwanted books became more a social obligation than a pleasure. Despite the occasional misfire, lending texts already previewed by a reliable reader to family and friends with similar reading habits saved them the trouble of buying or seeking out promising titles in shops or libraries, an often tiring and sometimes fruitless task. At times, the selections were so limited that any book voluntarily lent was counted as a blessing. "We had been speaking of books & their scarcity up our way," a ship's carpenter's daughter explained to her diary, "& Trumbull in the afternoon brought us several books to read." Sometimes loans were made upon temporary contingencies. "I send you with this the 2d vol. of Malte Brune—which W. Merrill has lent me for you until I can get a copy from Philadelphia," a lawyer wrote his daughter, eager to read the concluding volume by a then-popular Danish geographer but frustrated by the unpredictable literary marketplace. Sometimes when readers made it clear that they were in search of a lender for a particular title, hints were often not picked up, even when coming from well-known professional authors. "I have been in a raging fever to see 'The Hour and the Man,'" author Lydia Maria Child declared to a friend about Harriett Martineau's fictionalized version of Toussaint L'Overture's life. "I thought *every*body must know I was in a fever; and I thought *some*body would have lent me the book, for a few weeks, when they had done with it," she griped. "Again and again we have inquired for it. . . . We might have as well have gone to the Dead Sea to catch whales."[18] Book fevers, no matter how severe, were not always easily quenched by lenders.

Attentive to the needs of other people for new reading materials and the difficulties and expense involved in procuring them, most lenders expeditiously gave useful or appealing titles to people facing extenuating circumstances. One mill worker realized that a good time to loan a friend a good book was just prior to traveling, when fears of long, boring coach or steamboat rides overtook even the most seasoned trekker. "Talk with Miss [Sadie] Lowell—she returns . . . Tennyson and [Gerald] Mas[se]y which I lent her before she went to Bangor," he wrote. He maintained the lending relationship with this mill worker and boardinghouse mate to whom he often read Thomas Moore and other romantic poets aloud at night by furnishing her that day with a new book of poetry: "I lend her Leigh Hunt." Lenders with extensive or specialized libraries also sent books to students in hopes of defraying expenses. A Hartford businessman, for instance, lent "Julius['] greek Dictionary or Lexicon to Frank Parsons for his son John who is now at Yale College."[19] Needs were often fulfilled by lenders with just the right books.

Lending might supply curatives for the ill or balm for the emotionally wounded. Hearing that a young printer's apprentice had accidentally "jammed three fingers" in a press that subsequently indelibly "printed some letters on one of them," a fellow worker's wife paid him a visit. The seriously injured boy's sister recorded that the ensuing encounter produced an invitation for a literary loan: "He was much better, and she said that she had some books at home, called 'The Constable's Miscellany' which she said she would lend him if he wanted them." The combined effect of lenders' friendly visits and prospective hours of therapeutic reading worked wonders. When Charlotte Forten once took time off from school to recover from an illness, her teacher thought the perfect antidote was a few good books to fill her long, empty hours. "Miss S.[hepard], with her usual kindness, brought me some books,—three volumes of 'Queens of England,'" she acknowledged. "Commenced reading 'Katherine Parr.'" Unlike literary gifts meant for long-term use, therapeutically loaned books urged recipients to read them immediately to imbibe the soothing properties as needed. After one seamstress, grieving over a child's death, finished reading *The Token for Mourners,* she loaned it to a household member. "Feel since reading that[,] little Susan's death was for our benefit," she observed, and explained, "It shows the shortsightedness of man to me, for I had formed a plan according to my own mind, and it has fallen." Affected deeply, she "[c]arried the book upstairs to Nancy, thinking that she might find comfort in reading it."[20] The mere act of lending was an empathetic gesture perhaps more eloquent than the comforting words in *Token for Mourners.*

Retrieving Loaned Materials

Lending to a person within the same household, as this mourner did, kept the book "at home" and therefore in safekeeping. However, most people allowed their reading materials to take up temporary residence with borrowers. How then did lenders ensure the safe and timely return of their property? Indeed, how did they remember if they lent a book at all? As one confused farmer once wondered about a missing item: "'tis either loaned or mislaid." For some lenders, the best way to keep track of materials was to make some kind of record, no matter how brief, of each loan. Most people who kept such records simply recorded the fact of lending among their diary entries. The entry would track the date of the loan, the title, and the person who borrowed. One widow, for example, jotted down under her 23 September 1852 entry, "Aunt Cady here, lent her Euthanasy," while a rural stagecoach driver aided his memory of a loan to his neighbor Spofford with a quick note under 6 December 1828: "lent Emerson Spofford kate." Since these jottings would be hard to recover from dense diary pages, more systematic methods were called for. Mary Pierce Poor, like a few other, more careful lenders, also kept a separate list devoted only to lending. On a blank page near the back of her 1850 pocket memoranda book, her list "Books lent" showed appropriate strikeouts for returned items, including Walter Scott's novels, chatty published letters from a physician in Paris, a bizarre Faustian poem, a Swedenborgian tome, and a Dickens classic.

~~Mrs Hewson?~~
~~1 vol of Scotts'~~ works.

Mrs Haley—New wine
in old bottles. [sic]

~~Mrs Cox—Festus—~~

Mrs Barnard.
True Christian Religion—

~~Mrs Chichester—~~
~~David Copperfield~~

Presiding over a private collection more extensive than most public libraries, John Park used a similar accounting method but marked an *X* next to returned titles. To encourage book returns, owners often pasted name labels, sometimes finely engraved ones, on inside covers. Branding books in this way helped keep them from going astray when lent, but all the labeling in the world could not ensure that loans would come back quickly—or at all, for that matter. "Of all kindness it must be confessed that lending books is the one which meets with the least return!" a scrap in a diary read. A rural itinerant entertainer simply entered, "The wicked *borrow* & return not."[21]

Despite the truth of such maxims, most lenders had faith in borrowers' good intentions to return all items. Because of this trust, general rules governing book borrowing were understood but not often voiced. One of these, that materials were handled with care, went without saying. Another was that primary borrowers could usually allow a secondary borrower to read the book. Added to this was the understanding that only limited numbers of items were taken away at any one time with a silent agreement that upon their return, other loans would follow. A final rule was that items should come back within a year unless they were rare books or when time constraints were stipulated; this rule was usually honored without much negotiation. One tolerant lender, however, waited "two or three years" before demanding a book back. These rules were apparently learned in childhood when borrowing began as a way of instilling a love for reading and a regard for the property of other people. Persis Sibley Andrews was proud of her six-year-old's conscientious habits: "She feels an amusing responsibility when she has borrow'd books—to keep them nice & return them soon."[22] The dutiful and often silent observance of these canons only underscored the social nature of literary exchange.

In the case of newspapers, however, which usually were assumed to be nonreturnable, lenders had to state specific borrowing conditions, otherwise they might forfeit the loan. When Holy Cross's James Healy "lent a paper to F[athe]r. Early with Rufus Choate's speech . . . on 'thoughts suggested by McCauleys History[,']" he concluded, "I never expect to see it again." As precaution, before mailing newspapers, lenders stipulated when or why they should come back. A Newburyport shop clerk did this when he asked his Andover mill worker fiancée to send back some. "I send you a few religious newspapers thinking your mother, and perhaps you would like to read on the Sabbath," he ventured, adding, "I should like to have you return them as all but two of them belong to my Father." A banker's wife announced a similar request. "I recd a London paper containing sketches & descriptions of the Pomp & ceremonies attending the baptism of the . . . royal infant Albert Edward," she wrote to a friend, while insisting, in a rather roundabout way, that she wanted it back: "[I]n the course of the week I will send it to you before I circulate it in the family as you are prompt in your news reading."[23] Periodicals' cheapness and timeliness meant they likely would not return without owners' insistence.

Unwritten rules and special injunctions aside, borrowers were sometimes sluggish, forgetful, or neglectful. In these cases, the lender asked directly for the item back. One embarrassed lender eager to get the popular novel *Three Experiments of*

Living back from her uncle to return it home revealed her strategy: "I have named it many times." When such an indirect method of "naming" the title of the book in passing did not work, some lenders took to bold written requests. A Holy Cross instructor sternly posted a "notice . . . for the person that took his Byron." At other times, letters did the trick. Charles Cobb was relieved that correspondence brought back some sheet music: "Last Saturday Father got me another letter from [Uncle] Norman—in answer to mine last August—he sent back the Queen of Diamonds as requested." Putting the word out was sometimes the only hope of retrieval. Lenders who lived near their borrowers often asked, as discretely as possible, for books back in person. Elizabeth Jocelyn took the opportunity during an amble with windblown friends. "Hariette lost her bonnet on the corner—but I soon regaining it, we went on, as I wished to ask her for a book I had lent her," Jocelyn recounted. As borrowed and owned books mingled in the home, they sometimes became difficult to distinguish—that is, until someone called in their loans. "I went up to Henry's," Charles Cobb wrote, where he encountered a neighbor who "carried off Uncle Tom's Cabin's which were his books it seems." The coveted two-volume work subsequently was lent to Cobb's mother.[24] Owning a best seller conferred status within tiny Woodstock via selective lending.

Lenders usually did not have to hunt loans down, for most borrowers returned them, either through calls or via courier. Several diarists referred to this practice as bringing or sending a book "home," suggesting it was a virtual family member that occasionally went a-visiting. Cobb once recorded that he "went up to Henry's at night to carry home Lord Byron." A country minister said he went to "Deac. Vilases—[and] carr[i]ed home an book that I had borrowed." An elderly Free-Soil woman "sent home Pamela's Fremont" after finishing it, while her daughter reported she had "been to carry home Mr Judd's book," *Margaret,* a local interest item attacking Calvinism. Sending a book home, like borrowing it, could mean a brief stop or extended hours of enjoyable time. "This evening Susie, Mary and I went over to Jerusha's to carry a book called 'The rebels,' (which I have read to-day), and staid a long while," a printer's daughter wrote, describing a summer's night she returned Lydia Maria Child's novel set in pre–Revolutionary War Boston. Returning a book in person often resulted in borrowing another, a chain of events linking borrowers and lenders together in a series of sociable calls. In this way a Boston domestic servant enriched a relationship with her minister, Edward Norris Kirk: "Pleasent[.] [C]arried some gloves to be cleaned[;] called on Mr Kirk[,]" she wrote and added that she brought "back book I borrowed[;] he lent me some others." When one farm laborer returned the "2nd [volume] of U.T. Cabin" he borrowed, he pried from the lender Ik Marvel's *Dream Life,* and when he returned that he came back with an issue of "Godey's Book for self," the latter a ladies' magazine whose contents complemented the gossipy chitchat he exchanged with his lender. Even though bringing a book home spawned sociabilities, borrowers might regret returning it. Some borrowers grew unduly attached to visiting volumes, as one confessed after finishing the *Young Lady's Gift:* "It is an admirable book, I do not wish to return it again." Others rued that they could "not quite finish" their borrowed items before due dates. Borrowers at distances from lenders sometimes held onto books longer by promising to return them in person rather than by express. "Speaking of books," a schoolteacher coyly wrote nearly a year after a book-borrowing visit to a friend two counties away, "reminds me that I have a great pile of books belonging to you which I mean to call and return, this summer or fall. 'Walden' is one of them." She explained: "I like to pick up one of 'Hennery's' thoughts now and then, very much."[25] While promises and procrastination could merge for distant borrowers, the warmness of a returning social call was preferable to the relative coldness of a shipment.

Despite good intentions, even the most conscientious people committed infractions of customary rules. Borrowers were horrified if they damaged a book and went to extraordinary measures to make amends. Having "been very much interested in reading Columbus" by Washington Irving, which a sister-in-law lent her, one borrower "felt quite mortified in having them get so much soiled, and in the future will promise more care, as there is nothing more provoking than to have books that you lend abused." But there were indeed things more provoking: losing books and, sometimes, secondary lending, which permitted them to disappear into vast social webs. A young businessman found himself in an embarrassing predicament when a lender called in a rare Richard Brinsely Sheridan edition after several years: it had been, in the meantime, lent to someone else. He requested that a sister "ask Miss Sarah Woodbridge if she can find Sheridans Plays which I lent to her sister Julia some two or three years ago & if she can if she will give it to you." He revealed he had tried in vain to replace it: "I have been to every book store in New York & am informed that the edition is out of print." Such was the penalty for losing a borrowed book, but shame of ever facing the lender again could also haunt. Charlotte Forten declared that she "should not have been able to meet" one lender "could I not have replaced" a lost book borrowed of her. Forten went to extremes to buy a new one, even venturing out "in the midst of . . . [a] storm to several book-stores trying to replace" it. She herself was "unsuccessful," but a Boston friend found a copy. In the end, all went well, for the lender "spoke very kindly about the lost volume" upon receiving its surrogate, much to Forten's relief. "Feel exceedingly obliged to her," she wrote after the ordeal was over.[26] Such were vexations of losing books and, possibly, friends.

Both borrowers and lenders clearly had their share of anguish as books circulated through many hands. Yet the joys by far outweighed the sorrows. Reading materials remained good capital for investing in social relationships. Borrowing and lending added an important element to visiting rounds—even to the extent that books, magazines, and newspapers became themselves visitors destined at some point to call and "chat" awhile and then go home.

Conclusion

Extra-institutional borrowing and lending was much more than simply a practical and far-reaching system for disseminating books among folk unwilling or unable to subscribe to libraries—most of the population. Books loaned out were tokens of the lender's self to be remembered by borrowers in acts of reading. The self represented in loans could be a proselytizing crusader or, just as likely, a generous spirit wanting to fill social needs for reading materials. Lenders would also have, eventually, when the item was returned, the satisfaction of knowing someone else who read the same book. To make the system work, informal lenders and their borrowers, like librarians and their patrons, abided by certain rules, albeit unwritten ones. Rules were seldom tested, however, for the social pressure enforcing them was great: when a borrower broke one, he or she violated not only a personal relationship with a lender but also the trust of the larger circle of local book owners, privy to the many dense social webs of exchange. For a good reputation as a borrower was an invitation into a virtually limitless store of reading material owned within the community and ready for dissemination.

Yet there was another, less risky, and arguably more socially satisfying way to disseminate books, as we will see in chapter 7, and that is through oral reading and reciting. By doing either, a text was effectively "loaned" without sending it away from "home." While sociabilities certainly attended lending, through calls that could last for hours in bringing home or receiving books, or conversations over the mutually read ones, reading aloud necessarily ensured a relatively lengthy and direct interpersonal engagement over a text. The actual act of lending could last but a minute in an otherwise long social call, but the act of reading to listeners was likely more prolonged, sometimes into hours. Furthermore, the oral reader's or disseminator's ethos was immediately imported into the text as he or she breathed life into mute words on a page. Conversely, the audience's response was palpably received by the reader who verbally "loaned" texts. The literature that could and did pass through many hands, could as well—and more resoundingly—ring in many ears.

Chapter 7

Literary Performances: Dissemination through Reading Aloud, Recitation, and Enactment

Shortly after the New Year's Day 1851 rang in, Abigail Pierce wrote her sister a letter brimming with holiday spirit: tales of social calling, chatting, literary gift giving, and reading. She recounted visiting a neighbor, an Irish omnibus driver's wife named Abigail Dillon, who read aloud verses from the *Pastor's Offering:* "'*Stranger,* I read it in thine eye, / And in thine accents meek & mild, / And in thy faith & charity, / That God hath chosen thee his child.'" Pierce told her sister that "it reminded [Dillon] of you. She will never forget your kindness."[1] The sister had obviously left such a lasting impression that a piece of poetry could evoke her image, so strikingly the neighbor wanted to share it with Pierce, who perhaps would never have read the piece herself. By reading aloud, Dillon not only disseminated literature but also expressed her fond feelings—better, perhaps, than her own words could convey.

Oral performances like hers were simply part of the everyday social relations of literary dissemination. Alongside gift givers and lenders, oral readers, too, imparted the written word. They did so, however, not to recipients who would have to wait to read the gift or loan at their leisure, but to a captive audience of listeners. In their role as disseminators, oral readers thus actively shaped receivers' responses. Only by Dillon pointing out the affinity between the *Pastor's Offering* poem and the sister it evoked, for example, would Pierce have grasped its meaning. Conversely, listeners' reactions in the moment—in this case, Pierce's attentiveness and recognition of the similarity—could affect the reader's performance as it unfolded. An oral performance was collaboratively and uniquely produced in the reading moment by all participants who influenced it with their own interpretations and interests. As such, literature was finely and, as we will see, intricately interwoven into the social context of its performance.[2]

This chapter explores the social dimensions of not only oral reading but also other literary performances, including recitation and theatricals. First, we examine the ubiquity of reading out loud before delving into reasons why people did so and the various occasions upon which the activity took place. We next attend to the critical expectations surrounding the practice. Not all literary performances occurred with book in hand, however, so we then consider recitation from memory—dissemination based upon recalling sometimes imperfectly committed but frequently well-rehearsed and emotionally charged words that, perhaps more directly than texts read aloud, linked speakers and listeners. Finally, we look at parlor theatricals, a type of dissemination in which performers visually represented characters created by published authors or dramatists. These seemingly disparate forms held one thing in common: the disseminator literally embodied the text by either speaking its words or acting out its parts. In this way, literary performers, as human media, disseminated authors' ideas into the everyday social world.

Reading Aloud in Everyday Life

The word "reading," when it appeared in diaries and letters, as likely meant a verbal performance before groups as a silent act for oneself alone. For this reason, it is difficult to determine exactly just how often people read aloud, but diarists and correspondents sporadically testify to the extent of the practice when they generally characterize their daily routines. Every now and then a diarist provides a single, easily overlooked key to unlock the larger day-to-day pattern. Only after three years of dense diary entries in which John Park mentions "reading" hundreds of titles at his retirement boardinghouse did he reveal, referring to his wife, that he "read[s] aloud to her a portion of every day" (fig. 7.1). Hints about reading aloud appear in newlywed Mary Pierce Poor's letters to her parents, too, but one piece of correspondence characterized it as a household routine occurring at appointed times of the day. "Between nine and ten Henry comes home, [and] reads aloud or talks," she described her nightly regime with her husband. While Persis Sibley Andrews similarly depicted her reading relationship with her husband—"He is constantly at his Office during the [day] but his eve'gs are spent in reading aloud at home"—her diary reveals that not only did the pattern persist until his death after ten years of married life, but it was resumed when the late husband's law partner took up residence as a boarder in the widow's home. "Eve[gs.] Mr. Black spends with us invariably—reading aloud to me—or I to him," the widow

Fig. 7.1 ✦ John Park, who routinely read to his wife, was never more at home than with his books, a small portion of which are shown with him here. Portrait of John Park (Ms.qAM.1352 vol. 5). Courtesy of the Boston Public Library/Rare Books and Manuscripts Department.

wrote. "It is solace to know that he is coming—as the curtains of eve[g.] begin to gather about us. He has lodged here ever since My poor dear Charles came home so sick." The bond strengthened by oral reading was great, indeed, for a few years later, she married Alvah Black, who continued to read to her and the children. Writers like Park, Poor, and Andrews provide qualitative evidence of reading aloud together, but a few meticulous record keepers permit a firmer quantitative sense of the day-to-day proportion of oral to silent reading. One of these was Daniel Child, who, in his decades-long diary, specifically noted whenever he "read aloud" a certain title in contrast to when he registered that he had simply "read" one. In this manner, he recorded 1,078 acts of reading, of which 51.76 percent he orally delivered at home or while visiting. The percentage would probably be higher if he recorded most of his daily newspaper reading, something seldom captured by other diarists, as we will see, because they dismissed it as desultory.[3]

If precise diarists like Child can represent the whole, listeners would be spotted inside domestic settings at least as often as solitary readers. Printed words thus were probably spoken or heard as much as they were silently scanned. Indeed, it may reasonably be assumed that if diarists and correspondents record "reading" occurring in the presence of other people, a very common occurrence, it probably was oral. When added to oral readings in churches, schools, and public halls, spoken dissemination far exceeded silent reading. This prevalence suggests that even silent and solitary reading could be experienced performatively and socially, as readers so habituated to oral renderings could almost hear the words on the page. One wonders, too, what social images flashed through silent readers' minds when they anticipated a possible future oral reading among family or friends. Did they imagine how it would be received? Certainly, family members often reminisced about being seated among loving listeners. "Did I talk to you, before I left, of 'Up Country Letters?'" one woman asked her aunts after returning home from their farm: "If you want to read something racy and full too of tender and beautiful and good things do get it. [H]ow I should enjoy reading some of it aloud to you."[4] Such oral readers missed communicating with distant relatives over a book as much as they yearned for one-to-one conversation with them.

Beyond families, any set of persons living within daily reach of one another could habitually read aloud together. For example, one mill worker befriended a boardinghouse companion, a female operative with a taste for poetry, to read to during evenings. He read aloud to her on different occasions Thomas Moore's "Fire-Worshippers," Tennyson's "May Queen" and "Locksley Hall," and Henry Wadsworth Longfellow's *Golden Legend.* Much regular group reading also occurred in boarding schools and seminaries. During extracurricular hours at places like Miss Porter's or Mrs. Sedgwick's schools, some teachers daily read varied works, from history to fiction, to their pupils, who might return the favor by using their sharper eyes to read tiny newspaper columns aloud to their teachers after class. One student informed her brother that her boarding school mistress "frequently gets me to read the Times to her." At seminaries like Holy Cross, students read aloud during meal time in the refectory. James Healy noted his private and public reading, as on one occasion when he reported, referring to a book by Washington Irving, "I amused myself with the 'tales' of a traveller until near supper-time and then (as I am reader for this week) I continued Martin Luther." The young men covered such works as Byron's *Childe Harold,* Antonio Francesco Mariani's *Life of Saint Ignatius,* and James McSherry's *History of Maryland.*[5] From boardinghouse to academy to dining hall, readers routinely disseminated literature to listening ears.

Some people joined clubs at which members took turns reading aloud at regularly scheduled gatherings. Many were held at members' homes, where reading was laced with conversation, snacks, political gossip, and music and thus offered sociability along with self-improvement. "There was more music than reading," an attendee once reported. One Jocelyn sister held winter "reading parties" at her New Haven home, where she read aloud "Lima & the Limanians" from *Harper's Magazine, Macbeth,* and Lajos Kossuth's speeches. So popular was a Bangor club at which Walter Scott's *Tales of a Grandfather* and other works were read that its female members "refuse[d] invitations to parties on Wednesday that they may attend it." These clubs often emerged spontaneously from groups of friends or family members. An eighteen-year-old shop clerk "formed a Reading Society" with his friends one evening after he "closed the Store." During the weekly meetings over three months they read aloud Eliza Farnham Lee's recently published *Three Experiments of Living* and "Object of Life," a poem from John Todd's *Student Manual,* among other works. Who might or might not be invited into these clubs was a socially delicate matter. A member of one said that two sisters not yet voted in "resent it to such a degree they wont speak to Win [the president] or Bill [a member]." When a group excluded, it was time to form one's own "in-group." Charlotte Forten, often shunned by her white classmates, began her own reading club with fellow African Americans; Agnes Strickland's *Queens of England* was the choice for their first meeting. Other African Americans formed societies to counter white exclusion, such as those in Boston's "Minors' Exhibition Society," where texts were read aloud, memorized, and recited, in the latter case by members who may not have been able to read.[6]

One of the most common body of texts called upon by reading clubs were those by Shakespeare. Reading the Bard lent itself well to the purpose because members could vocalize different roles. "We read last week 'Merchant of [V]enice' my part being *Jessica*[,]" a physician's daughter wrote about her Charlestown "Reading Club" to a friend in Maine, and beamed, "It was read very well so the audience said, we number some 30, now and still they come." As she indicated, these performances often attracted outsiders as spectators. "Mrs. L . . . is a member of a Shakespeare Club, which was to read that evening and she wished me to attend," bonnet-factory hand Martha Osborne Barrett who heard one society read *Richard III* explained, adding that she "enjoyed it quite well, several good readers. . . . Mrs. L. took the part of Queen Margaret."[7] Like many circles, this one probably did not endure and was superseded by others within the ever-changing local literary landscape.

Opportunities to engage less formal oral reading sessions were as many and as varied as the groups that formed. And informal groups coalesced everywhere that people, willing and able to read aloud, found those desiring to listen. Of course, the two usually exchanged roles, like borrowers and lenders, or gift givers and receivers, and so one understood the other's experience. After all, a reader heard the same words read aloud as listeners and responded to the text along with the audience. Also, readers comprehended well the limits of listeners' attention spans, and listeners, the physical stress of reading aloud. As we will see, in many other ways, the two roles complemented each other to such a degree that reading and listening need to be considered together.

Reasons for Oral Reading and Listening

The most common reason for group oral reading sessions was to pass time while performing tedious tasks like sewing. "I have lived in one unvaried round of sewing, sewing," Persis Sibley Andrews complained shortly before getting married. Her cry resounded widely, for virtually every female old enough to have learned knitting or sewing and healthy enough to have acceptable vision, made their own or other people's clothing. The age of mass-produced garments awaited the future. Many women could read to themselves while sewing, but if the option of having someone read aloud presented itself, they most gratefully welcomed it. Charlotte Forten disclosed, "In the evening did some more sewing, of which I must confess I am beginning to be heartily tired; I think it would be different if I had some one to read to me while I sew." The quiet tedium of sewing alone sparked desires for sociable reading. Mutual enjoyment of reading and sociability brightened the dreariest day. With rain tapping upon her windows, Mary Pierce Poor recalled "some of those dull forenoons when father used to read aloud to us & mother would sit with her basket full of stockings to darn & [sister] Elizabeth would be 'too busy' to sit down and listen." Overwhelmed with her own sewing, Poor befriended a neighbor with time on her hands to read aloud: "[W]hen I find anything interesting that I should like to hear I take my work and sit with her while she reads it to me." Since Poor brought over titles the neighbor might not otherwise see, both women benefited by the situation in which work and leisure came seamlessly together. Seamstresses so much valued this service that it naturally became part of courtship rituals. David Peck, who, as we have seen in chapter 5 brought his betrothed Frances Jocelyn literary gifts, also read to her. On at least two of the many occasions he read out loud, she reported that she sewed, but it is likely she did on others, too, without mentioning it. In this exchange, she demonstrated that she was attentive to her future husband, home loving, steady, skillful, industrious, and not partial to frivolous sociabilities; he showed his steady devotion with frequent calls during which he was willing not only to read aloud but also accommodate his future spouse's literary tastes. When she wrote after their marriage, "Finished my bag this evening while my husband read from 'Uncle Tom,'" she revealed that the habit continued.[8]

David Peck's service to his wife suggests the important role men played in the reading and sewing connection. They often participated in the period's many sewing-and-reading societies that produced garments for charitable causes. One young man was invited to join a club which, as he explained it, "consists of a few young ladies who meet once a week to Sew for poor Sabbath School children, & about an equal number of young gentlemen . . . who generally drop in and spend an hour in reading & social chat." This clerk decided "I think I shall accept the invitation, as it will give me an opportunity to get acquainted with some worthy young people." While he probably welcomed the chance to read, boys and men sometimes came solely for the merry atmosphere conducive not only to socializing but also to flirting. The romantic connotation delighted some swains, like one teenager who reveled in the beauties he encountered at Boston sewing circles, while it terrified others, like the painfully bashful Charles Cobb. After comparing "'sewing circles' [to]—kissing parties &c.," he confessed, "Darn it, I would jump from a tenth story window if I was at one, and couldn't leave any other way."[9] Such parties nonetheless reflected common domestic scenes that could set even him at ease—readers with time on their hands and sharp eyes to lend to seamstresses.

Projects undertaken during oral performances tended to be relatively simple, but there is little evidence that participants sought out "easy listening" readings to accommodate sewing. Different needleworkers were treated to, among other challenging works, Thomas Carlyle's *Life of Friedrich Schiller,* Andrew Combe's *Physiology of Digestion,* Thomas De Quincey's *Klosterheim,* and Charlotte Brontë's *Villette*—even, in one sitting, "Pope & Byron & Cowper." To listen sociably to these performances, seamstresses could not be visibly distracted by complex handwork. No wonder that a boarding school student reported that during reading hour "we plain sew—No fancy work is allowed at that sacred time." Simplicity was usually self-enforced. "[E]ve$^{gs.}$ we do plain sewing while they read or read while they listen" was how Persis Sibley Andrews divided women's from men's roles in her family.[10]

The reading-sewing link would not be severed even by the arrival of domestic sewing machines, for these had limitations. While they could "accomplish a yard of beautiful even stitching in two or three minutes," they could not cut fabric, pin, press, fit, rip or unravel mistakes, crochet, knit, quilt, embroider, or create other fancy work. Nevertheless, a few families purchased and used sewing machines before 1861, but apparently, no one listened to oral readings while hand cranking and feeding fabric into the noisy "wild beast." The whispers of cloth, needle, and hand did not compete with a reader's voice the way a machine could. Therefore, sewing machines desocialized reading in small but insidious ways. Women could not easily take machines with them to "sew and listen" at a neighbor's home. Sewing and reading circles could hardly be composed of women at machines.[11] Machines, of course, eventually made those who sewed by hand obsolete, and with them passed an era of persistent domestic oral reading.

Other household chores beyond sewing, such as cooking and childcare, could occasion listening to readers. Some mistresses read to their cooks. One matron encouraged her daughters to read to and listen with servants during their laboring hours. "Mary reading aloud in the kitchen, Polly [the live-in domestic], Elizabeth, and Abigail [another servant] for auditors," she recounted; "an hour or two is passed in this way, almost every day, how much preferable for a young girl like

A.[bigail] C. to be a listener to what will improve, than to be visiting about to the detriment of heart as well as head." Listening kept her away from the local kitchen gossip mills. The care of newborns also demanded labor that afforded time for listening to reading aloud, with the boon that oral reading rhythms could provide a lullaby. Shortly after her daughter's birth, a Bostonian recorded that she "settled down" in her room "with Miss Holt & baby for the next five weeks—mother reading aloud, I in bed." Three months later, a similar arrangement worked when a friend stayed over: "Maggie read Mrs Inchbald's 'Simple Story' aloud—baby sat on the bed—I sewed." As babies grew to toddlers, they could be incorporated into the family reading pattern even before they learned to read. An oral reading of a Bible or other religious work could enrich child and adult alike, making it a reciprocal activity. One mother believed that the Bible had an additional advantage: a soothing effect upon her six-year-old. When she "sat down to read in the room where the children were playing together & commenced reading aloud the 9 chap. of Mathew," her usually boisterous child "at once left his play & came & sat in my lap & kept remarkably quiet till I had finished reading the chapter. We were both affected by the sphere of the word. I held him awhile after I had done for he appeared in such a quiet subdued state it was pleasant to hold him."[12] Thus children experienced oral reading in social settings virtually from birth. Little wonder that when they grew up they sought after social reading experiences and reported loneliness while reading alone.

People with impaired vision particularly benefited from oral readers, since texts written in Braille were rare and expensive. By listening to books and periodicals read aloud, the blind entered the reading public on par with those who were sighted, especially since so many with good vision experienced the printed word orally anyway. A lawyer's fiancée, for example, over a four-year period regularly read to her blind neighborhood friend, even on one occasion noting that she "accomplished nothing but to read to Miss Gammell." The blind, in turn, proved to be extraordinarily acute listeners and sensitive respondents, as described by a New Haven schoolteacher who "called on old Mrs L[awson] a remarkably pious and devoted colored woman who lives all alone, and is nearly quite blind." For this reader, the experience was not merely a service, but a delightful and spiritually profitable undertaking: "I love to go in and read to her, for I feel that I derive benefit myself from her calm, christian conversation." Short of blindness, the chronic visual dysfunction endemic to some eyesight-dependent occupations could summon reading aloud. Cynthia Sprague, who operated a tailoring and dressmaking shop with her mother, wrote in the journal she kept for her seafaring fiancé John R. Congdon, "have not enjoyed myself at all to day my eyes are so weak. I cannot read as I wish and I have no one to read to me. John I wish you were here I think you would read for me." The elderly, too, garnered help from oral readers, but they sometimes rued the dependency. "My eyesight is too poor to read," seventy-six-year-old Hannah Hicock Smith moaned. "[T]ho's L[aurella] reads to me sometimes," she remarked about one of her daughters, "I do not like to ask her, she has so much to do for me."[13] A prodigious silent reader, she pined for the autonomy she formerly enjoyed but, like most of the elderly with failing eyes, welcomed the assistance.

As might be expected, oral readers also ministered to the depressed, sick, and dying, and their families. "M[rs] B is quite down or low spirited," Second Mate Congdon noticed of his captain's melancholy wife; "it is so rough she cant be about the deck and she is rather lonesome[.] Cap[t] B reads to her and does all he can to amuse her but still I guess the time passes heavy." For people attending to the physically infirm, reading aloud was a way to feel effective in desperate situations. "I was really unable to do any thing," the mother of a sick child sighed, "but read to, and in various ways try to amuse the dear little boy, who was certainly a very patient sufferer." Although literary medicine was impotent in the face of death, people read to comfort both themselves and the terminally ill. "[T]hough I knew he could never recover," one woman recalled of her brother, "yet I was happy in being able to pay him so many little attentions . . . [;] I could read to him, and every thing that I read, or saw, or recollected, was treasured up to entertain some of his lonely hours, and even when it wearied him to hear me read, yet he felt interested in my occupations." Loved ones who read to the dying maintained socio-literary relationships to the end. Afterward, some readers enshrined the deceased through literature. "The last thing I ever read to our dear Sarah," a mother wrote beneath a clipping inserted in her diary of "Two in Heaven," a Fanny Fern poem. "It was the day before she fell asleep." In this case, reading aloud became her final memory of her twenty-year-old daughter, who died of consumption. Knowing how literature could ease painful life transitions, oral readers soothed the bereaved. One woman nursed a neighbor's despondency after her husband and daughter died, leaving the home empty. She "said she would prefer to spend the remnant of her days, alone in that house . . . but this would not be best," this minister's daughter explained. "I read to her Mrs Hemans' 'Deserted House,' & she felt it deeply."[14] Reading aloud then, gave purpose to many people's lives even as listening provided the best elixir for others in need.

Whether emotionally or physically ailing, blind, or preoccupied by handwork, listeners found willing readers who parceled out, with each spoken fragment of literature, measures of diversion, respite from work, comfort, and compassion. Readers became in these cases, surrogates for failing eyes and preoccupied hands, props for weak constitutions, and flagging spirits. They also allowed their audience to "read" by listening when it would have otherwise been impossible. However, they sometimes played roles that, while not crucial, were nonetheless purposeful within the everyday social world. They led devotional services in the home, commemorated special occasions, gave informal instruction, and entertained hosts or callers during social visits. Reading aloud was thus one of the most versatile and practical of all dissemination methods. And the ability of readers to take on a variety of roles, lent them, as performers, authority in diverse situations, even acting within religious offices.

Leaders in prayer or other home-based devotionals were often oral readers. These laymen performed religious roles by uttering the words of theologians, ministers, or the Bible itself in group settings. At his boardinghouse, one Baptist clerk participated in a Sunday morning round of reading and prayer with a father and five children. "[E]ach one," he noted, "took a Testament, & then beginning at one end of the ring began to read a chapter each one by turns reading two verses until the chapter was finished." The father then "read a hymn," which was followed by prayer. At breakfast, he "repeated a verse from the Bible" and then elicited one "by each of his family." Two readings of Scripture by the children and a sermon by the father followed, before all trudged off to church. Such collective readings that allowed family members to trade roles of listener and reader usually augmented churchgoing, but sometimes, especially during bad weather, it could replace it. One Congregationalist read to her husband on one of these atypical Sabbaths. "Unpleasant this morning. I have not been out to church to-day," she reported in midwinter. "This morning read aloud in the scriptures to my husband." Alongside the Bible, other religious works became part of these "observances," as when the mother of one stay-at-home family during a spring "N.[orth] E.[aster] Storm" recorded that she "read in the mor^{g} to the family a sermon of Mr Buckminsters on 'habit' in the aft several chapters in 'Acts.'" Other conditions, besides inclement weather, allowed lay readers to step, temporarily, into ministerial shoes. On the northern frontier, where certain religious congregations could not sustain a regular clergyman, home meetings became the only alternative, as Persis Sibley Andrews found in Dixfield, Maine. Under conditions of clerical scarcity, some liberal protestants like her, used to hearing ministers deliver tightly structured written sermons, simply refused to attend services by more conservative preachers speaking extemporaneously. "I went to Church this morn'g. Quimby, the Methodist, was there. He took a text, but he didn't preach—t'was nothing but rant-rant-rant," she registered, resolving to avoid his evening services. "I have staid at home this P.M. & read Unitarian Sermons to Husband, & I think the time much better spent."[15]

It was not unusual for women to appropriate the role of religious reader in this way, and indeed, some liberal denominations might allow women to make the transition from participant in private devotions to preacher at public meetings. This happened to Eunice Cobb, the wife of a Universalist minister. In a natural evolution from her behind-the-scenes religious activity and her lecturing to women on physiology and temperance, she entered the pulpit at age fifty-three. Her diary entry from the next day captures her exhilaration at breaking new ground: "[F]or the first time, have I stood up before a christian audience, to speak in the capacity of a christian Preacher. . . . [N]ever before, did I enter the sacred desk, and attempt to speak from a 'text,' and interest a congregation, on the holy Sabbath! But now, I have done it!" Although her husband "made some remarks, stating . . . that I was no *'woman's right's man,'* but would speak to the mothers, and daughters, showing *not* woman's rights, but her *duties,* and her *sphere,"* she availed herself of the opportunity: "I then gave my lecture, and spoke with perfect ease, and confidence, my voice growing stronger, and stronger, to the last."[16] Despite her husband's disclaimers, she effectively publicized a woman's right to disseminate both scriptural text and her meditations upon it.

Lay religious reading took place during formal services seemingly anywhere absent ordained clergymen. Early in the century, the paucity of priests even in larger New England towns sometimes deprived Catholics of Sunday Mass, and so they, too, created their own services without rites. During an 1826 trip to Portland, Boston's Bishop Fenwick visited "the room hired by the Catholics & in which they are in the habit of assembling on Sundays, to recite their prayers & to read spiritual books." The makeshift church, he thought, "bespoke . . . the poverty of the Catholics in this place." Like these congregants propagating their faith under dire conditions, captains or other crew members often assumed ministerial reading roles on board their ships when no man of the cloth was at hand. A supercargo on a homeward-bound brig spent one Sunday "reading aloud on deck . . . all the chapters in Pauls first teaching in 1st Corinthians" to those who "sat to hear him." Capt. John R. Congdon's daughter reported that her father "read the church services" on a clipper ship headed for Havre. "I read & sang my favorite hymns, those I have sung many times in the choir," the seventeen-year-old added to show her role in the meeting.[17] These provisional religious services, whether on the high seas or on the borders of settlement, no doubt satisfied both the "preacher" and ardent listeners who together formed a temporary "congregation" of readers.

Although oral disseminators performed essential tasks, including leading prayer, comforting and healing, reading to the blind, and muffling the constant drone of domestic work, they often simply read to their listeners for no other reason than to amuse them. Reading aloud, therefore, appeared wherever leisurely social activity took place. Books accompanied picnics and even strolls where they could be read in scenic spots. "This morning took a very pleasant walk with Miss Shepard . . . through Harmony Grove," Charlotte Forten wrote. "Miss Shepard read several exquisite poems written by the sister of Mrs. Hemans." Scenic vacations, too, inspired other readers to disperse literary morsels. While on a spring trip to her aunt's, a young woman was treated to a poetry reading amid a dramatic setting: "After tea we stood at the window viewing the sky at sunset where Mr. C. read us a beautiful verse from Wordsworth." At home, romantically inclined readers set themselves against the backdrops of their own yards to highlight their spoken words. Lucy Colby perched near her window sill to entertain her friend Martha Barrett, a schoolteacher and soon-to-be factory worker, with poetic words illuminated by an early summer sunset. "Have been up to Lucy's," Barrett wrote, "sat a while by her chamber window and we converse of the good and the beautiful. She read to me a sweet little poem . . . [:] Pictures of Memory (By Alice Carey)." Barrett was led to muse: "This beautiful Sabbath day has passed away beautiful not outwardly but inwardly. How pleasantly tranquil its hours have been. May I have many such."[18]

Reading aloud often played an important role in social calling. As with Lucy Colby, sometimes it was the host who entertained the guests. One schoolteacher, for example, "finished Julia[n?] aloud to a listening fireside of friends" at her Lexington home one Saturday evening. If a gift giver came to call, reading the present out loud was one sign of appreciation, even from receivers who had some reservations. The day after the aforementioned pesky suitor, "Cousin Bill," gave his victim Ik Marvel's *Reveries of a Bachelor*, she read it to him: "[He] called and spent an hour or two with us this afternoon—I read a 'Reverie' to him and the rest of the company." Like gift givers, readers understood that the spirit behind the presentation meant far more than any fancy wrapping. Charles Cobb allowed guests to read material, however humble, aloud whenever the spirit moved them, as when one caller "read a song which he had in his pocket—out under the shed." Guests sometimes made special calls just to read material they found interesting, as when a schoolboy made a quick trip "to friend Jona's to read him a story on kissing taken from Knickerbocker Magazine." He recorded later that day that they "had a merry time over the story by an 'amateur,' & a good one too, if his tale is to be relied upon." Visitors sometimes carried personal journals to read aloud, a practice that enabled them to reveal only selected portions. Oral readings could keep cherished memories alive. If guests arrived without book in hand, they could simply pick up any in sight if struck by the urge or, in some cases, the need to read. One visitor to a family circle who wished to deflect attention away from unpleasant talk of his health, grabbed the nearest book within reach as a sidetrack. In order to "stop the discussion . . . he took up a volume of Miss Barrett's poems which lay on the table," a witness reported to her sister; "he turned to one which he liked particularly, & *read it loud* from beginning to end." Seizing a host's book in this way was not unusual, but reading it without some kind of prologue was. "[T]hink how different it was from the manner of the generality of morning callers, to read a poem so, without the slightest preface or preamble," she remarked. "It was so simple & easy,—& so like him."[19] A bit of literary impropriety was yet sociable.

Methods of Reading Out Loud

As this observer understood well, reading aloud to company was not a simple matter. Certain conventions interceded between conversing and beginning to read, including a pithy introduction. Once reading started, however, the audience could audibly react to the performance. Most readers enjoyed the breaks, as did schoolteacher Persis Sibley Andrews when a sea captain who helped her with classwork came to call: "I pay him by reading 'Two Yr's before the Mast' to him—every sentence of w'h seems to call up an association from his sea life, & every few pages I stop to hear some corresponding passage from his own experience. O, *this* is pleasant." Interjections, even playful ones, signaled listening and so helped dissemination along. On a visit to a cousin's, a schoolgirl ganged up with his wife to force him to read aloud, against his will, Josiah G. Holland's novel about female amateur authorship, *Miss Gilbert's Career,* when he customarily gave them more serious fare: "Dick sacrificed himself and read Miss Gilbert aloud to us." They rewarded him with vocal reactions: "We interrupted him occasionally by saying—fool!—think of that! how mean!—&c &c."[20] Such were the sociable delights of interruption.

Yet listeners could be highly critical, cognizant of the timing, tone, pronunciation, and style used to disseminate their favorite author's words. Sometimes the keen evaluation was positive. "I love to hear her read," a normal school student conceded of one classmate who stood before the class to deliver a poem "as she has so ^much command of her voice, and reads with great distinctness, also with variety of intonation." Such kudos went not only to peers, but to younger folk, too. "Little E[lizabeth] read 'Hiawatha' to us. She reads beautifully, with an evident appreciation really wonderful in so young a child," Charlotte Forten remarked. These appreciative sentiments were doubtless either voiced or they became evident to the oral reader, while negative judgments were usually confided only to diaries or letters. Students, being listeners much of the day, became especially acute judges; they even took gibes at their teachers who tried to entertain pupils with extracurricular reading. "She galops along—its as much as I can do to follow her," one pupil snapped, while another grumbled about a teacher plowing through Walter Scott's *Marmion,* declaring that "she reads it too much like a common thing." Faltering over words or incorrect pronunciation made some listeners squirm. Correcting a poor reader, however, was unthinkable. "He reads aloud the daily news, as opportunity offers, or anything else of interest, but makes some strange pronuncial blunders," one young woman jeered at her boardinghouse keeper. "On seeing me take down something in my note book, he asked if I kept a *dairy.* I could hardly refrain from" responding sarcastically, "but I very soberly and truthfully answered *no Sir.*" Because they often wore both hats, that of the listener and that of the reader, criticism could easily turn upon the self under the strain of comparison. When a divinity student and a minister's daughter "read aloud alternately" to her grandfather, she chided herself by noting that "his voice is pitched upon the right key & mine, unfortunately, is not."[21]

Within this critical environment, self-consciousness could become so great that would-be readers became frozen by the terror of performing aloud before a group of people. Thus some folks simply declined when asked. "[W]e tried to make Lizzie read a story but she would not & so I read," a frustrated Calista Billings wrote of an afternoon spent with several of her teenaged friends. Some people with less than adequate literacy skills flatly refused. A Maine farmhand with little education balked at the idea of reading aloud before his employer's guests. Because he dug in his heels, he received a whipping and subsequently ran away from his boss's boardinghouse. "Now William is a poor scholar," the boy's mill worker brother opined, rationalizing his behavior, "and it appears not at all strange that he should dislike to read before company—neither does it appear strange to me if Mr Downing gave him a flogging and kept him without his dinner."[22] His punishment for not serving the wishes of guests and employers meant less to him than his dignity. Such were the embarrassments of poor oral readers.

Because reading out loud was so often expected, even demanded, in everyday situations, many people set out to rectify early deficiencies. Although reading was taught in schools and academies through oral practice, parents outside of school urged children to become aware of their performance at an early age. Mary Pierce Poor enrolled her nine-year-old daughter in a private class after hearing some elocutionists perform at a reading party. "Agnes is taking lessons of Mrs Lesdernier, who says she will make a splendid reader," she reported to her sister. Although Poor gave her child a head start, it was never too late to master oral dissemination. One nineteen-year-old soon-to-be mechanic enrolled with an elocution tutor. "[T]he evening we had a lecture on Elocution by Mr. Russel[l], a gentleman who proposes to give us a course of 5 lessons 2 hours each at 1.00 for the course, have not decided whether I shall go or not," he wondered. Feeling it worth the money, the next evening he "attended the 1st. lesson in ellocution from 8 to 10[;] he practiced us on the diferent tones of voice and part of us read." Although low-cost elocution classes were available, most people learned to read aloud well through informal drilling, listening to expert speakers, and following elocution manuals. Immigrants like one successful Irish businessman understood that elocution oiled upward mobility and accordingly beseeched his son to practice the art while alone. "Be very fond of reading aloud as often as you conveniently can do so," he enjoined. "Read as though there were half a dozen listening to you and you were very anxious that each one should hear you very distinctly." He added specifics, such as "learn to vary your voice ascending to the meaning and expression of the subject. Manner and suitable expression of the face and feelings have a great effect in oratory." If all else failed, there were guides such as those by William Russell, Jonathan Barber, or John Walker.[23]

Along with manuals, self-monitored rehearsals, and emulation of role models, oral readers sought out amateur counsel of well-meaning listeners. At some reading clubs, such as the one Mary Pierce Poor attended, members welcomed helpful comments. "We criticise each others reading & pronunciation," she noted, "so that if we do not improve at these meetings it is our own fault." Informal advice came from within the household as well, where women, supposedly more endowed with eloquence, advised children, brothers, and even spouses. "I have often noted that when a fine woman[']s mind derives sustinance from books the delicacy of its structure refines what it feeds on which seems to be softened by transmision," a lawyer wrote to a sister. "If I had such a little wife as you," he continued, "I should read to you that you might correct any intonation that was bad." Mistresses sometimes helped their domestics to read out loud with aplomb. Persis Andrews tutored some of her domestics: "John is a fine promising boy—a very fine scholar, & strictly moral. He reads so well that he relieves husband often when reading to me o'even'g[s], & we aid him by making the numerous little corrections that a boy always needs, in way of pronunciation &c."[24] Rhetorical polish could be a product of such informal channels of socialization.

For all oral readers' practice, skill, and inclination, they might still face impediments, especially irritated throats caused by illness. That they persisted against them suggests the great social value placed upon reading aloud. Burdened with a bad cold, John Park admitted that he was "too hoarse to read aloud long at a time." Lengthy reading sessions also strained the larynx. Although one daughter "often read to [her] father six hours at a time" without missing a beat, many people grew weary. "Read aloud to the children till I was hoarse," a businessman complained one evening. "Laura has just come up in a state of exhaustion, after reading to Mrs. S.," a student sympathized with a classmate who assumed the task of reading to her teacher. Charlotte Forten, who "[r]ead aloud the 'Maniac,' a scene from 'Julius Caesar,' and some of Whittier's spirited A.[nti] S.[lavery] poems, till I was breathless," may have either been physically or emotionally exhausted.[25] Of course, these performers who strained their eyes, lungs, nerves, and passions might necessarily turn, at least for a time, into listeners.

Reciting as Dissemination

Listeners, whether exhausted readers giving their vocal chords a respite or seamstresses too busy with a project to pick up a book, were occasionally privy to hearing other people recite from memory. Chapter 2 showed that both skilled readers and children learning to read commonly created mental editions by memorizing printed pieces. Although some of these found their way into extract books, letters, or diaries, some were disseminated orally as well, often for the same reasons as reading aloud. So when a businessman counseled his son to become an eloquent reader, he also advised him to master an allied art: recitation. "[C]ommit to memory several choice pieces or extracts from elegant Authors and Orators," he recommended; "be able also to repeat them verbatim in true Classick Style for your own edification or that of others. This in fact for a scholar or gentleman is indispensible." But what was indispensable for a man of social standing was also requisite practice among literate folk from various stations, especially where religious works were concerned. On a visit to the Canterbury Shaker community whose members apparently read their "well-thumbed copy" of Scripture many times through, one college student observed that they were "able to repeat whole chapters, almost the whole Bible." He noticed that "both old & young, can quote scripture, to my shame be it said, much better than I can, or even most people in the world." Religious words memorized through constant devotional reading found verbal outlet on diverse occasions or at various life-cycle passages. The sick or dying found peace in repeating biblical passages, sometimes their last words to loved ones. People sprinkled everyday, casual, conversations with religious quotes, too, but like most mental texts, even the most sacred were subject to corruption of time, memory, and, of course, new, sometimes sardonic interpretation. Charles Cobb was amused that his neighbor carried a strange edition of the Bible in her head. After one visit, he recalled that "Mrs. Holmes has found a passage in the 'Holy Bible' where it says something like this.—And in the last days Hell shall come and get the very elect if possible but darn'd if they can get her." There were, however, always memorizers who knew their texts so well, they could repeat them unconsciously. "Joe Callanen said the Litanies in his sleep last night," James Healy mused of a classmate.[26] Like the sound of oral reading, reciting could be heard in the most unlikely places, even in dream states.

Occasions for recitation could be unpredictable. People might run into someone with a virtual library stored in memory, ready for verbal lending at a moment's notice. While visiting some poor children in Belfast, Maine, Persis Sibley Andrews, then a teacher on a charity mission, seemed surprised to find an impoverished but literary woman with a flair for recall: "At one garret I call'd, the woman told me that she was born in the Highlands of Scotland. . . . She has read some, particularly Scott's novels, & remembers every word of them." Listeners might hear unanticipated recitation emanating from streets below. Elizabeth Jocelyn caught an African American stranger, obviously versed in classroom dialogues, practicing some lines while out walking. "A negro was as he approached the house, talking, with all the eloquence he could command," she reported. "His subject, was the schoolroom, and he commensed first, with the questions, and then the answers, which we generally hear, between the teacher, and younger scholars." While some folks rehearsed lines into thin air, others practiced ad-libbing by weaving quotes into conversations during social encounters. Reciters traveling in public conveyances might spike the humdrum with revered quotations. On a stagecoach, a librarian met a friend with a "memory . . . most prodigious" who "repeated from Milton, Shakespeare and Byron" as they "discussed various matters, pertaining to literature and the law." Of course, some people plotted their delivery or asked their guests to prepare recitations for more formal presentations, which was just as fun as impromptu quoting but probably less stressful. "Mrs. P.[utnam] wishes each of us to learn something to recite when we meet again," Charlotte Forten jotted down after an evening of political discussion with friends. On subsequent visits, she heard "[N. P.] Willis' 'Sacred Poems'" and other unnamed poetical pieces.[27]

Everyday recitation, for all its drama and impressiveness when used in conversation, played other roles. Recitation, like oral reading, helped housewives pass the time. "Today we have been ironing, and have enjoyed ourselves extremely," Mary Pierce Poor wrote, "repeating poetry and flourishing hot irons; we finished before dinner, and considered ourselves very smart." Brothers sometimes importuned sisters to listen to them rehearse qualifying recitations for college and professional schools. "I began on the 4th inst. the Conversations on Chemistry by Joyce to recite to [sister] Elizabeth which will be pleasant to us both & we mean to continue it," one medical school hopeful explained. By practicing with his sister, both reciter and listener learned the lines well; she, like so many women of the time, imbibed a college-level education second hand. Expectations were such that extracurricular entertainment in the schools was also well rehearsed. The seminarian who could pray in his sleep was also successful at amusing his classmates as they dined. "Jos Callanen spoke something original in the refectory to-day together," James Healy recorded, "with little [Joseph] Boudar of Virginia, who had a selection from [O]vid." To Healy's dismay, the "latter young gent hardly knew his piece by heart."[28] Sloppy recitation and reckless performance spoke louder than the undisciplined clatter of words; it bespoke disregard for listeners.

Something memorized and recited was, after all, something shared. Although words repeated exactly demonstrated self-discipline as well as respect for an audience's sensibilities, the earnestness of delivery often had greater impact than practiced elocution. "M[ary] A. B[igelow] repeated me the other day a sentence wh. she met with in the newspaper & liked extremely," one young woman wrote before transcribing what she heard: "The greatest pleasure in life is love / [The greatest] treasure [in life] is contentment / [The greatest] possession [in life] is health / The best medicine *a true friend.*" Moved by the lines, she reflected upon them: "Poor Mary has a great deal of feeling & is herself *a true friend.*" Recitation, even of simple words, had a complex effect because it was a unique performance. Unlike reading aloud, the speaker, sans book, disseminated an author's words not only vocally but also visually, through gesturing of the eyes or body. Reciters could at times mysteriously embody authors or characters as if channeling their words and sentiments. "Late in the evening, Maria repeated sweetly two ballads—one, in which occurs the lines 'And what will you leave to your brother John?—A gallows high to hang him on!'—& another, . . . 'Binorie O Binorie'," a lawyer recalled after a social evening. "She looked lovely as the heroines of her poetry."[29] The combined visual and oral effects of recitation transported the little company out of the parlor and into the romantic highlands of Scotland.

Theatricals as Textual Dissemination

Like sensitive reciters, actors in amateur theatricals disseminated literature to audiences by creating literary illusions. As impersonators who literally donned costumes and read lines from plays or staged a "living picture," they breathed life into characters lying dormant in books. At times these performers freed themselves entirely from the spoken word and silently conveyed their literary message. Whatever the proportion of oral to visual, staged events were a particularly challenging, but also amusing, way to disseminate literature which left one matron raving "*mad* about the theatricals." Performed in homes, churches, schools, and even on ships, these disseminated literature with varying degrees of faithfulness, from verbatim renditions of published plays to projections of vaguely literary allusions in omnibus entertainments. Performances of the sort included costumed drama; tableaux, or "living pictures," composed of outfitted models who posed and froze their actions as if in a snapshot; charades, which were pantomimes of words or concepts but also of fictional characters and literary scenes; and "dialogues," set pieces, usually formal conversations, meant to highlight contrasting positions or qualities. Even costume parties, such as the "famous party—'the last of the Mohican's'" Charles Cobb once held, or the various masquerade balls filled with characters from the novels of Charles Dickens which plagued him during his American tour, drew upon literary themes and allowed people to assume fictional roles.[30]

Because theatricals were meant to lighten social gatherings, they often featured suspense-filled dramas or humorous pieces. Farces were popular; the "Four Sisters" and the "Laughing Hyena," for example, were enacted by one Lynn amateur theatrical club. Tableaux tended to portray more serious literature, but even these could produce mirth, as happened to John Park's boardinghouse neighbors when they once staged a piece after attending a lecture: "Barnes as a ghost or phantom, and Mrs Putnam as a witch, stirring a cauldron of some flaming stuff, which gave their countenances a most deadly hue." Despite the macabre theme, he claimed, "we were all laughing until I believe . . . every side ached." Actors, even in serious parts, were not immune from chuckles. One actor "was chained & he shook like a leaf & breathed *so* hard," thespian Calista Billings recorded of Byron's "Parisina," a tragic poem about ill-fated lovers, "I thought I should die from laughing but I managed to keep my head down & sober." In an equally serious tableau from Schiller's *Song of the Bell,* one actress in a wedding scene "laughed & spoilt the picture." But mishaps only added to the frivolity. During a night filled with ominous appearances by Shakespeare's Ophelia, a threatening Turk, Lady Russell "writing to her husband upon the even[ing] of his execution," and a soon-to-be scalped "Miss McCrea," a partygoer reported she "had a delightful evening notwithstand[ing] that people would run against a certain troublesome string and pull down nearly the whole scene & the candles would burn out." Perhaps the often dubious transformation of well-known faces, everyday settings, and ordinary objects into extraordinary literary scenes produced irresistible comic effects.[31] To work well, a tableau had to spark recognition in audience members with prior knowledge of the literary allusion, or else it might fall flat.

Thus, jovial as it was, turning ordinary objects into convincing illusions demanded no small creativity. One amateur "producer" saw theatricals as a "canvass to put my glowing fingers on." From start to finish, they demanded not only planning but also skills such as sewing and set design, not to mention at least a bow toward acting. In still lifes particularly, costumes, gesture, attitude, and props had to tell the story. If scenes portrayed were well known, as they usually were, then discrepancies in minute details might be noticed. A seaman's daughter obsessed over portraying a literary image that was known in Boston, where her friend lived, but had not yet reached her Lynn hometown, so she fervently solicited him, explaining that she and her companions "want to have Dante & *Beatrice,* the picture is in all the engraving stores & can probably be seen at Parkers window in Cornhill, will you just give me an idea of it, position, dress &c. by *description* or *pencil* so that I may receive it Friday morning which I shall if put in the [post] office early *Thursday."* Regardless of the familiarity or obscurity of their subjects, performers lavished more attention on appropriate costuming and props than any other aspect of theatrical performance. After many decades had passed, one matron still recalled the outfits garnered for her childhood theatricals in Boston. "At Grandmother Elliot's we used to have all sorts of frolics," she recalled in 1882. "We played theatre there. . . . I remember once we played Miss Hannah More's 'Search after Happiness.' Eliza Otis and I were shepherdesses, in white dresses trimmed with flowers, and crooks in our hands." Some women imaginatively altered clothing or hand sewed outfits from scratch, as when a mother spent part of a day "Preparing Euginas dress for the Tableaux." The challenges players faced can be glimpsed in the variety offered during one single evening's entertainment staged by Calista Billings and Massapoag Hotel residents in Canton outside Boston, who performed scenes from *The Vicar of Wakefield, The Balcony, The Village Amanuensis, Don Juan,* and *The Corsair.* She described the latter: "Alonzo sitting on a couch in Turkish costume Adelaide crouching beneath his dark frown."[32] Out of a hodgepodge of wardrobing and mishmash of furnishing emerged a delightful mélange of literary cameos.

Some depictions apparently owed to facial contortions or posturing rather than costuming. "Rob. puffed out his cheeks capitally as Mr. Vincent Crumles," a participant mused. "Mary & Rob. represented beautifully the murder of Miss McCrea, & R. looked fierce enough to frighten any one." Some tableaux performers "cheated" and added silent motion to animate a sparsely adorned still-life image. A youngster described an "amusing" captivity narrative involving a teacher and several of her deaf students at Hartford's American Asylum. "Miss Dillingham pretended that one of the boys was her husband and they had a little baby, and as they were talking together an Indian came and stole the baby and a few moments after he had got out of sight," she narrated, "the Father got up to see it, and he found it was not there, and he made signs to his wife that the baby was gone, and then they put their handkerchiefs up to their faces and pretended to cry." Because tableaux did not require sound, they allowed the deaf to participate on an equal footing with people who could hear. In dialogues, even minimal props, like the few pieces of cloth and toy doll the asylum players employed, were absent, as performers had to project through intonation and gesture often abstract personifications, such as that of "The Virtues and Graces."[33] All in all, a large dose of imagination was the main ingredient for bringing literature to life.

Creativity aside, actors and audiences approached theatricals critically. A sojourning amateur poet longing to hear gossip begged her sister, "Who acted well & what did they act?" One merchant's scion even kept a critical "Diary about the Theatricals." "Mrs. B. was capital," one entry reads, "but the debutante, Lizzie, being new deserves a word, her whole performance was one of great merit, correct without being stiff, and very easy on the stage without being familiar with the audience." Female amateur thespians faced special prejudice. "Mrs. Howe acted well," another theatrical participant wrote, adding, "I think any woman to appear on any stage must want delicacy, away from her husband too!" Similarly, a voyaging schoolmaster shuddered when the "ladies were not altogether harmonious in their deportment" as they acted roles from Hamlet and Othello at sea. Regardless of gender, some critics judged performances bluntly. "The acting was abominable," was one bachelor's sweeping verdict.[34]

Despite unforgiving critics, theatricals encouraged New Englanders of all ages to participate in a social world inscribed by literature. "[O]ften do I look back at the time when with them I have innocently & pleasantly beguiled many an evening which would otherwise have been tedious," a whaler, alias the actor "Slipshop," recalled of his boyhood neighborhood drama group called the Gander Club. For Charlotte Forten, acting with Salem's Putnam family provided confidence and relief from harsh realities of race and class. "The hero and heroine of the play were a duke and duchess," she wrote of the play *The Honeymoon,* in which she performed. "I had the honor of being a sister of the latter." She added with a sardonic edge, "Of course I did not fail to appreciate my newly-acquired dignity."[35] For Forten, then, disseminating literature through acting was but one short step away from role playing—trying on clothing worn only by the privileged. Theatricals could affirm relations and inspire social possibilities; they also could, at least for a moment, permit fictional and fabled characters, like spirits from the Great Beyond, to communicate directly with the living. By filling their leisure hours with literary reenactment, performers created social spaces inhabited not only by family, friends, and neighbors but also by characters from novels, romantic heroes, and long dead kings and queens. The two sets of players, real and virtual, together disseminated literary ideas on the stage of everyday life.

Conclusion

Oral readers and reciters, like theatrical performers, also evoked these elusive literary persons who inhabited the printed page—through articulation, gestures, and the emotional sensibilities brought to performances. They took on authors' voices and infused them with their own inflection, meaning, and understanding. Reciters who memorized authors' words could at any time summon them and communicate through them. These performances in sound and sense could never simply replace dissemination of manuscripts, printed books, pamphlets, and periodicals through the mails, interpersonal borrowing and lending, or gift giving—written words in material form spoke directly to possessors in intimate book-to-reader bonds that replicated close social ones. But the intervention of oral readers, reciters, actors, and other textual performers added an entirely new dimension: bonding over a text in its moments of unfolding. Like Abigail Pierce and her friend Mrs. Dillon, who united over a spoken poem filled with personal meaning, many other antebellum New Englanders forged deeper ties in those fleeting minutes of reading aloud, reciting, or acting. These special social moments, as brief as a line from a poem or as long as an epic journey, added to a lifetime store of memories.

Part III

Reception

Antebellum New Englanders received the written word into their everyday lives in many ways. Reception started in infancy, through learning to recognize and write the alphabet, create words, listen with attention, understand concepts, and react to texts. This kind of domestically based reading instruction dated back to pre–Revolutionary War years but persisted even with the rise of the common school. Early instruction provided foundations for adult reception, as people first visited and then revisited literary works, stored them in memory, and retrieved them as occasion demanded. Once reading and listening were mastered, people could stockpile ideas culled from an ever greater variety of written materials encountered throughout the years. As one normal school student saw it, "'Every book which a child reads with intelligence, is like a cast of the weaver's shuttle, adding another thread to the indestructible web of existence.'" In other words, as people read more and more literature, they accumulated new ideas that became part of their intellectual fabric. However, with each idea contained in a book, story, poem, or prayer that readers admitted into their lives, they themselves produced new ideas through their response—a kind of mental conversation with authors that might get written down in a diary or shared with correspondents through a letter. For example, the introduction to this book showed Charles Cobb recording his reaction, a lengthy discourse on the mind-body split, to an 1853 Harper's *story about galvanically induced life forms. The ideas about life and death, mind and matter laid out in the story "add[ed] another thread" to his existence and prompted him to think more deeply about his own spiritual attitudes and how his own beliefs resonated with the larger society around him.*[1] *Thus did ideas play through production, dissemination, and reception.*

Part III treats philosophical ruminations similar to Cobb's but among varied responses, including emotional, aesthetic, devotional, and even somatic ones. Although ideas contained in texts might stimulate thinking, often the artifact—the book itself, or its bindings, paper, ink, and even its wear and tear—could provoke fresh and complex thoughts.[2] *In pursuit of this story, Part III moves from general reception practices (chapters 8 and 9) to a discussion of reception itself (chapters 10 to 12). Chapter 8 examines how children gained literary proficiency in the home and practiced it as adults encountering and developing different modes of reading, such as study and desultory pursuits. It also explores how illiteracy was experienced in a highly literate society. Chapter 9 contrasts readers' ideal reception scenarios with their common literary habits practiced amid less than perfect conditions for absorbing books and periodicals. It shows how people adapted their work and leisure schedules to accommodate reading. In leisure time, one literary activity in particular caught New Englanders' attention: public lectures. Such lectures increasingly proliferated after the 1820s, when local lyceums were founded across the region. Auditors at these developed a vocabulary of reception and a set of social values specially suited to this popular form of oral dissemination, the subject of chapter 10. In chapter 11, we turn to viewers' responses to imprints as valued physical artifacts laden with visually appealing characteristics but also layers of social meaning. Finally we examine readers' responses, both emotional and intellectual, but always socially informed, to the artifact's text.*[3] *In all, social sensibilities blended so much with literary-mindedness that reception is revealed here as nothing less than the social production of meaning through literature.*

Chapter 8

Receiving the Word: Literary Socialization and Modes of Reading

After moving in late December 1845 from Dixfield to Paris Hill, Maine, with her husband and two-year-old Lotte, Persis Sibley Andrews met with disappointment. The house was too small and neighbors had made her kitchen, pantry, and clothes closet their own. She grew depressed, and so did her daughter. To revive Lotte's spirits and her own, she hit upon the seeming worst solution: she uprooted herself once again by traveling back in time and space to her childhood environs of Freedom, Maine. Surprisingly, it worked. There, playing with grandparents and an eight-year-old cousin, the baby forgot, for a while, the pangs of loneliness. Andrews observed the improvement while watching her daughter and nephew have "a fine time over a box of picture books . . . w'h amused & delighted the early years of my brother & myself." The scene evoked curiosity in the children and memories in Andrews: "I have seldom been so entirely carried back to early days as since I have been writing this—interrupted every moment as I have been by 'see Mother—O see how pretty'—'Aunt Persis—whose was this—who made this one[?] Aunt Persis look this is best of all.'" It all summoned her earliest encounters with the printed word: "I well remember the days when I looked upon this same box of treasures with their enthusiasm, & I remember the very language as well as the stories of these little books—better[,] much better than my later readings." These old toy books had a powerful effect, indeed. Lotte found a new literary wonderland to walk through, while Andrews traversed a long-familiar one. In doing so, the mother rediscovered the first reception of written words into her mind, heart, and memory; it remained as immediate an experience for her as witnessing Lotte's literary inculcation. Contrasting these initial experiences with her later ephemeral reading led her to posit a generational shift in the social value of books since she was girl. "My brother & I *kept every thing*—were taught by our parents to destroy nothing," she recalled. "[B]ut this second generation will never learn this lesson to much purpose," she opined, concerned that social strictures ensuring book preservation would erode. "They seem to have the organ of destructiveness—the children—in these latter days—more fully developed than used to be the fashion." She could not see the power of her example over precept, for Lotte, like so many of her generation, learned to treasure her books just as her mother had and became "a good girl to learn," an eager reader (fig. 8.1).[1]

This chapter considers people such as Andrews and their varied modes of receiving the printed word. It first follows them from their earliest literary engagements into later childhood to see the growing value they placed upon print material. The chapter then briefly weighs the social costs to those beyond the pale of

Fig. 8.1 ✦ This miniature of Persis Sibley Andrews and her six month old, Lotte, was painted about two years before she ransacked her mother's childhood books in Freedom, Maine. Miniature portrait of Persis Sibley Andrews and her daughter, c.1844 (no. 271). Courtesy of the Collections of Maine Historical Society.

English literacy: what happens when the word could not be received and the expected nexus of social expression and literary practice did not exist? The chapter's concluding section pursues the nature of socioliterary experience through different modes of adult reading. Throughout, we see social considerations mediating even basic cognitive interactions between readers and the printed page.

Learning to Receive

"[T]hirty days has September, / April June & November / All the rest have thirty one, &c. is a couplet which is very frequently repeated, as the last of a month approached," a Boston schoolboy etched in his diary. "Its age I do not know, but as long ago as I can remember (which to be sure is not very great) I had those lines repeated to me." The Latin school student, far advanced in physical as well as mental growth from those early years, continued his recollection: "And afterwards when able to read I re[me]mber with what delight I used to . . . say them over & over again, holding an old dilapidated almanac, or a Webster spelling ~~book~~ . . . minus covers, in my hand." He recalled getting carried away with it: "Pleased with the jingle of the rhyme, & raising such a clatter, as was suddenly stopped by the . . . gentle touch of my Mother's hand, in the region of my ear." Like Persis Andrews's fondest memories of things past, his own earliest remembrances formed a tableau of himself as a child and his first books. The student, like Andrews, captured a specific social relation, in this case with his mother, who restrained his self-absorbed chatter. Intervening years doubtlessly eroded his memory, yet the literary sensibility of his cameo from the past remained lucid. He probably learned to read at home from his mother, who read aloud from primers and spellers and gradually taught her son to listen well, memorize, recite, and, finally, recognize words on his own. For him, the written word first quietly entered his life by way of the nursery door, before he received it in classrooms. By that point, his reading had become deeply imbued with social associations drawn from his home learning.[2]

Whether they attended poor district schools or expensive academies, finished their education in elementary classrooms or pushed on through college, most children learned basic reading at home under household members' eyes, particularly mothers'. However, neighbors, relatives, and correspondents also encouraged literacy by recognizing, praising, and taking part in a child's advancement. That outsiders involved themselves was in turn welcomed by mothers as a strong incentive toward their children becoming both literate and social. The array of instructors seldom followed any formalized outline for instilling literacy, but all saw to the child's general development as a prelude to it. With preliminaries in place by the time the child was between three and a half and five, learning to read occurred among activities that included memorizing texts as well as visually recognizing and reproducing alphabetic letters, storytelling pictures, and simple words. So tightly interwoven into everyday sociabilities was literacy training that many adults forgot the precise moment when they first learned to read.

That literary socialization long preceded literacy acquisition explains some of the forgetting. Before most children read their first words they received much attention and affection for healthy physical development, uttering words, and performing endearing actions—first signs of literary things to come. In short, early facility in social communication predicted a later seemingly natural path from preliterate relations to ones infused with literary sensibility; literacy was but a step along the way, not an end in and of itself. Indeed, literacy acquisition was naturalized as an expectation of maturity not unlike the unfolding development of psychomotor skills. Even learning how to walk—a harbinger of mental as well physical dexterity, for example—prompted some mothers to anticipate their children's futures as readers. "She does not walk alone but pulls herself up by things," a former mill girl noted of her yearling; "if she was a little older I should recommend to her reading [Thomas] Carlyle's translation of Goethe's lines commencing 'Keep not standing, fixed and rooted / Briskly venture, briskly roam.'" As if walking and reading were in a single line of development, she reflected, "I hope she will be fond of reading."[3]

Domestic teachers often recorded these milestones of maturation with care, as mementoes for themselves, family members, or for their children in years to come. "I thought it would be pleasant for my children to know after they are grown up something of their *sayings* & *doings,* when they were small," a widowed mother wrote. By denoting what was being registered as "sayings and doings," she was already transferring fledgling experience into literary form, for writers of both biographies and autobiographies (some comic fictions) frequently used the phrase in their titles. Such memorializations, of course, were also records of progress in language acquisition as a prelude to reading. That phrases of greetings and salutations such as "Howd'ye do" and "Good bye" were among the first word clusters learned (at a stage of development when names of parents and pets were still uttered as single words like "mama" or "dog") suggests the degree to which children were early made aware of social niceties. Frances Jocelyn observed her baby nephew's awakening to the social and literary world around him: he "speaks quite plainly such as Horse, Book, If you please, Aunt Trisy, &c."[4] Given the premium placed upon literary and social progress, little wonder that "book" was one of his first words, alongside the socially delicate "If you please."

More than being mere words, these verbal spurts might signify interest in books, for they often accompanied first encounters with print matter. Babies commonly received toy books or picture books as gifts—a first step toward sociabilities of literary dissemination. One seven month old yet unable to recognize words, for example, "received his little book called 'The Sabbath,'" while a one-year-old received "for a birthday's present 'memoirs of a London Doll,'" a 152-page illustrated children's book. These books, of course, were not read by children but visually scrutinized by them as socially meaningful objects. In turn, a child's visual preoccupation with book illustrations delighted domestic caretakers. "Mary 14 months old to day can say a number of words, has eight teeth [and] is much interest[ed] in looking at pictures," a proud mother declared. Mary Pierce Poor bragged to her parents that her ten-month-old "Agnes was highly diverted by looking at the pictures in 'Fox's book of martyrs,'" potentially disturbing but nonetheless visually complex. When adults read or "showed" books to children, they advanced listening and comprehension, preconditions for literacy. Evidence of these, too, was carefully noted by guardians as they watched for "interest" in texts, a response that demonstrated mental awareness, nascent comprehension, and social engagement with readers. A mother noted that her two and a half-year-old was "much pleased" by a "Scripture Print" of "Samuel & Eli" sent by a distant uncle. She believed "it a great help in teaching the scriptures to him," which he "seems much interested in hearing me read."[5] For the mother, interest signaled fledgling literary motivation. For the child, a complex network of socioliterary relations was present: the uncle sending the print in light of the knowledge that the boy had progressed enough in his catechism to grasp the biblical story pictured, and the mother attempting to forge associations in the child's mind between the print and Scripture she read aloud.

Thus the "interest" in reading shown by children denoted an emergent sense of belonging to a community bound by texts. This was most evident when illiterate children mimicked adults reading correspondence aloud. "She reads loud with great volubility and always wants the letters we receive to look over," a fourteen-month-old's mother observed. The girl obviously did not "read loud" but blurted out words at the sight of a letter as if longing to partake in the sociability of reading correspondence to listeners. Young children's interest in reading could further be seen in short-term memory exercises. Ability to recite stories read aloud indicated the development of comprehension which attended bonding to caretakers through texts. Some patient oral readers encouraged their little listeners to commit a text as a reading session unfolded. One mother described her toddler listening to his older brother read: "One day Wallace took his little book about 'My Father' and read it slowly, so that Frederic repeated it after him." Thus through memorization, preliterate listeners imbibed stylistic conventions of published prose, filtered through siblings' or parents' voices. One two-year-old, for example, joined in the family ritual of listening to his older brother's homework recitation of a heroic ballad of the Greek Revolution by Fitz-Greene Halleck and surprised the family by memorizing a few lines and chiming in. The boys' father told his sister, "This morning I was hearing Willie rehearse Marco Boz[z]aris—and where he had said[:]

> Strike till the last armed foe expires
> Strike for your altars and your fires
> Strike for the green graves of your sires.

"Eddy bawled out with the voice of a young Stentor 'God and your native land.'" Regarding the younger boy correctly supplying the last line, the father explained that "as we had never heard any thing of the kind from him you may easily conceive that we were not a little astonished and amused." Having memorized sounds from his brother's rehearsal, Eddy no doubt little understood what he said, but within the social context of the moment he realized it was appropriate.[6]

Memorization provided the foundation for literacy instruction. The prevalence of adults reading aloud assured that children had learned literature by heart before they could read it themselves. The presence of children in the oral reader's lap or at his or her side, as attested to by many contemporary engravings of domestic scenes, encouraged them to associate words spoken with those on the page (fig. 8.2). Remembering visual and aural linkages often led the child to begin spontaneously recognizing alphabetical characters, numbers, and simple words. Persis Sibley Andrews reflected upon her Lotte's third birthday, "What she knows she has learnt mostly from observation." With the child's interest thus piqued, she wanted to verify the budding connections between sound and printed word; "she begins to bring her book[s] & inquire about them," Andrews recorded, concluding, "I think I shall soon take a little more pains to learn her." The child's bookish interest had to be manifest to the mother before the first deliberate if halting instruction in the alphabet began, possibly by way of a primer. Less than a month later, the mother was surprised that Lotte "has learned her letters very easily—I hardly tho't of her learning them yet—merely intended to ^show them to her a few times, but she was pleased with the new thing & kept to it until she is mistress of the alphabet—except the 'b's & 'p's she 'don[']t like to read.'" The next step was to move from associating memorized images of alphabetical characters with their corresponding sounds, to connecting printed words with their pronunciation. Eight months later, Lotte could read aloud simple passages without much help. "Our little daughter is learning to read of her own accord," Andrews mused, yet she indicated that she still monitored the performance: "I hear her in whatever book or paper she brings to me—wishing to read." What Lotte was probably doing, with book in hand, was essentially reciting from memory passages her mother had once read aloud, for her mother immediately added, "Her memory is very retentive." The child perhaps pointed to each word she enunciated, asking for verification.[7]

Fig. 8.2 ✦ Although it is an idealization of motherhood, this engraving illustrates the socially interactive process of teaching children how to read in the domestic setting. "The Young Mother," *Ladies' Companion* 12 (Apr. 1840): 253. Courtesy of the American Antiquarian Society.

While Andrews let Lotte set the pace for her literacy acquisition, other domestic instructors adopted more regular regimes. Such "reading lessons" signified a systematic, routinized approach marked by daily, scheduled exercises and a serious attitude distinguishing reading time from play. Little wonder that several home teachers recorded the day formal lessons began, usually when the child was between three and a half to five years old. "I am beginning to teach Eva to read," Mary Pierce Poor announced when the girl was just five, while a schoolmaster's wife declared of her three-and-a-half-year old, "This last week I began teaching her to read—and find it a very pleasant employment." Half a year later, the mother noted how far the child had come: she identifies "a great many words," "reads short sentances," and "writes a few letters." Apparently, reading and writing some alphabetical characters coincided, for the child could "write Abby very well," her own name, by age four. Still, since getting children to read took precedence over early writing acquisition, spelling instruction was initially lax. When one rural wife "began teaching" her four-year-old "to read as a daily exercise," her daughter "was previously familiar with the alphabet." But knowing it did not automatically lead to spelling lessons or teaching through phonetics. Once the girl learned the alphabet, the mother "adopted the plan of teaching her words, instead of going through a long course of spelling ~~syllables~~ lessons." The result: "In a very few weeks she was reading little stories with great interest," and a month later "she commenced reading a verse in the bible at morning prayers."[8]

Such advancement pleased the mother, but like many other folks, it worried her, too. "I began teaching her to read as a daily exercise, more for the sake of forming habits of attention & order, than with any wish to push her forward," she explained. "Perhaps the time directly devoted to her reading did not exceed five minutes a day." The girl's very rapid progress, however, troubled this mother all the more, fearing mental fatigue or unsociable obsession would follow: "She became so much interested that I was apprehensive she would injure herself by her application & felt it necessary to overrule her plans of reading so many stories by taking away her books." Excessive drilling was discouraged for older children, too, lest they develop into hermetic pedants rather than socially engaged intellectuals. "Be as happy as you can & dont read too much," Mary Pierce Poor warned her precocious ten-year-old. Acceleration made for a shallow scholar; one cooper's daughter observed of a young cousin who sped through his classroom exercises that he "seems to learn words but not ideas." Mental work's physical side effects were also cause for concern. "[I] think it well that he should not be kept at studdy too closely," one man advised his sister upon hearing that her eleven-year-old nephew developed chronic headaches. "But do not let him acquire idle habits," the man quickly added.[9] Reading showed industry if not carried to an extreme.

Forming gainful habits often coincided with learning to read. Sewing was by far the most common of these and was taught at about the same age as reading. For example, one three-year-old could thread a needle and "began sewing patchwork" about six months before she received lessons in reading. Such instruction was not confined to girls. "Little boy trying to learn to sew," a widow recorded when her five-year-old son first wielded needle and thread. Needlework was taught as an essential domestic skill but also to stimulate mental development. Sewing, like reading, focused children's attention in sociable settings. The mother who classed reading and sewing with "habits of attention & order" confessed that "much more [time] was spent in instructing her [daughter] in the use of the needle" than in reading. Clearly, some domestic instructors privileged needles over books, but when alphabetic samplers were stitched, learning letters literally interwove with sewing lessons. Yet not only thread and yarn were woven but also social relations: children applied sewing skills for social ends by handcrafting useful gifts and, of course, by easing the household's needlework burden.[10]

Children's communications with their peers brimmed with references to their achievements in sewing and reading. "I am anxious to know what Susy[']s accomplishments are," one mother asked her sister about her five-year-old niece; "pray how far has she got in reading, how much can she spell & what sorts of sewing do. Can she read a little story by herself?" Apparently, this woman's own five-year-old wanted to know, as she explained, "I have promised S. I would ask you." Such queries in letters which brought children into social networks of other young people learning to read quickened progress and made practicing more enjoyable. Even in statements of parental pride one can discern children looking over the writer's shoulders. "Perse sews ten stitches *every* day, reads, spells & has some other simple exercises daily," Persis Sibley Andrews wrote in her diary. Like the numbers they learned to cipher or the alphabet letters they inscribed, children measured progress in daily numbers of stitches. "[S]usie says 'tell Nathan I *don't* sew only five stiches a day' she sews quite a long piece—," a newspaperman's daughter was sure to note in a letter to her brother written with the five-year-old scholar at her side; "also 'Tell him I have got two new lessons in French & Arithmetic,'" she added proudly at Susie's request.[11] The competitive tone of such statements suggests yet one more social motivation for children to learn to read.

Because of home instruction, most children starting primary school, usually at about age five or six, already had basic skills in receiving written words. Yet school entry did not end outside encouragements. After all, home and community provided ongoing literary socialization to inspire further progress in reading, whether in school or elsewhere. Lotte Andrews "read at home once every day" after beginning school until she was able to "read little stories in her little books &

understand them, with very little aid." In her mother's opinion, the district school helped little in this progress: "I did not think of her learning much at school," she wrote. The home efforts remained crucial. Another pupil turned his schoolroom reading skills to religious ends in his domestic circle; "every Sunday evening" this five-year-old "would get the Bible, and try to read, two or three chapters before he went to bed." Students not only exercised domestically a skill acquired or honed in classrooms but also demonstrated a change in consciousness toward literary matters which visibly influenced behavior. After school started for one lad, for example, he continued to listen to his mother read aloud and responded to what he heard by applying the lessons in social intercourse with his sister and his friends. "[I]n his conversation [with his sister] I could see the effect some of the little stories I had read to him have had upon his mind," his mother perceived. Such shared experiences provided powerful motivations for developing reading skills. Conversely, children attending school could suffer from any lack of literary socialization by care givers. One six-year-old, for instance, complained to his teacher that he "had no Father or Mother to read his lessons to him or he could get them better." Succor could only come from above; "'if I am a good boy my Father in Heaven will take care of me,'" he added as encouragement to learn despite the odds.[12] Those outside the scope of family-generated literacy were indeed at a distinct disadvantage.

Illiteracy in a Literary Society

For a few students, of course, the ability to read never progressed beyond rudiments, due to a lack of education in the home, an inability or resistance to teach oneself, or spotty attendance at school. New England had the highest basic literacy rates of all regions in the country for both men and women; according to 1850 U.S. census returns, the ratio of illiterate to literate white adults ranged from Connecticut's 1 in 568 to Rhode Island's 1 in 67. Still, some adults remained at the most elementary levels of reception. Not only were the illiterate or marginally literate handicapped in reading the written word, but they often stood at a social disadvantage within a region that valued silent reading, oral performance, and literate elocution to such an extent that it became tied to human relationships from the neighborly bond to the marriage partnership. "I am sure we should feel no interest in a hero now, let him be ever so gallant," the bookish Harriett Low declared during a discussion about true love with a friend, "if he knew neither how to read or write." Such was power of literacy that even suggestions to the opposite were hurled as insults in public discourse. "'Lyman Kinsley! can he read[?],'" Free-Soil politician Charles Sumner insinuated during a speech in which he slung mud at a local politician from the opposition Whig party. Conversely, so powerful was reading's appeal that Jingua (i.e., Çinque), leader of the Amistad slaveship mutineers, entreated one abolitionist for his freedom on the basis of literacy. He promised her that if he were liberated from prison, he would bring back to Africa his newly acquired ability to read and write. "[N]ow since I be here in jail," Jingua explained in a letter to her from his New Haven cell, "I hab learn a good deal to write and read and makes de pen and count all my fingers—and when I learn to count all de mens fingers poor Jingua ever see—then I try tell you how many black men like me cant read and write." He requested help "so all our people learn to read in de good book and write Koran-Koran till de get it all by heart."[13] His people would learn to read from their foundational religious text, the Koran, a parallel to using the Bible as a reading primer.

With the Bible so often used for this purpose, some people equated illiteracy with irreligious behavior or superstition and, therefore, social marginality. One Protestant missionary from Andover, Massachusetts, stationed in Canada, for one, confused a mere six-year-old girl's inability to yet read with paganism and used her as an example to other children. "She cannot read any, she cannot say any verses in the Testament or hymns," the woman warned her former Sabbath school pupils in a letter directed to them. "She could not say the Lords prayer: I asked her who made her. she could not tell me[;] I asked her who made the trees, & the rock? she said she did not know." Conversely, strict orthodoxy, when combined with illiteracy, could also mark a person as peripheral. After the funeral of a sixty-year-old Calvinist who could not read or write, Charles Cobb alleged that he and his wife "were horribly superstitious, believe in ghosts and so forth . . . and abominate and despise all the horrible critters called infidels." Cobb further stated, "They have a terrible dread of playing cards." "Not one of these things," he explained, "superstition, a DREAD of the Truth, of the Bible, and an abomination of unbelievers, contributes in the least towards making a Christian, but on the contrary are everyone on the entirely opposite side."[14]

Although Cobb probably exaggerated the man's mental myopia, the orthodox often limited their literary horizons to the Bible and religious texts, relative to liberal Protestants. The latter were less likely to keep strictly spiritual or weekly Sabbath diaries but were more prone to writing letters with purely secular content; furthermore, they recorded reading (and probably owned) a greater number and wider variety of texts. Indeed, some attributed their lapse from orthodoxy to reading widely. "The truth was," John Park admitted, "I had been educated in the dogmas of Calvinism, as essential points of Christian belief. Reading and reflection had induced me to abandon them as shocking to reason, and incompatible with our notions of the attributes of Deity." "Heaven be praised for so much progress!" a Unitarian convert rejoiced. "In childhood, I played with the 'History of the

Devil,' yet I came out, *intuitively,* on the *liberal side.*"[15] For her, childhood immersion in Daniel Defoe and other Calvinist writers gave way to her diverse adult reading filled with both secular writings and liberal social reform material.

No matter what their religious beliefs, illiteracy was a liability. It severely hindered workers, for example in both their ability to earn living wages and their social relationships with employers. We met in the previous chapter the farmhand, "a poor scholar," who accepted a thrashing from his boss rather than read aloud before company. There were ways around not being able to read and write, as an illiterate Lowell mill worker, ridiculed by fellow operatives, found. "Being green in many respects boarders call him 'right from hum' but fact is he was an orphan and had none, and did not learn to read & write much," farm boy–turned–mill worker Charles Cobb sympathized. Cobb reported acting as his amanuensis: "I've written from his dict[at]ion to his brother at Nashua N.H. & lady-love at Wells River." Marginally literate domestics distressed mistresses such as Persis Andrews, who preferred ones who could read to her and who, by being more worldly, were better help. "I have a little girl—15 years old now—she will be honest if nothing more," she observed. "She has hardly ever been out of the woods—cannot read & knows as little of things in general as an infant." Of course, for some workers, illiteracy added to class and race prejudice to make alienation unbearable: "'I do begrudge your education,'" an African American steamboat porter confessed as he cleared a sojourning college student's lunch table. "'I would steal your learning if I could.'" "Poor fellow," the traveler observed, "there is little opportunity for one of his color, however disposed."[16]

Like that traveler, many folks discerned deeper intelligence beneath marginal literacy or illiteracy. Eloquent speaking and perceptive listening were, after all, as much well respected among adults as among children. This latitude especially extended to minorities. Perhaps no speaker exemplified the illiterate's potential for dignity and verbal fluency better than former slave Sojourner Truth. Although several people recorded having heard her, Martha Osborne Barrett, herself a working-class woman frustrated by limited opportunities, saw Truth as someone to emulate. "In the evening we all went to hear Sojourner Truth lecture at Union Hall," she wrote. "Sojourner can neither read or write having been brought up in the most abject slavery in the state of New York. Was emancipated by the act of the State abolishing slavery in 1828. She is possessed naturally of a powerful intellect, and for her acute reasoning and sound sense often put the educated to shame." Illiterate Native Americans also impressed auditors at lectures, prayer meetings, and church services. "I am going to the Indian meeting," a dressmaker wrote in her journal, afterward reporting, "They talked extremely well and it was really wonderful to hear them speak of the bible and bring forward their illustrations[,] Ignorant and unlearned as they were." Illiteracy hampered neither their eloquence nor piety:

"One of them could not read a word[;] he was the best speaker and one to have heard him would have supposed him well versed in the language of scripture."[17]

Examples of illiterates' intelligence doubtlessly motivated some volunteers to teach them to read. The very word "benevolence," after all, encompassed this motive. One schoolgirl defined it in an 1842 composition as "a disposition to [do] good to others" and, more specifically, as giving away both material goods and knowledge. "Sometimes we could give to the poor, and at others, we could instruct them," she explained. And she proposed a curriculum typical of domestic instructors who used books, needles, and thread: "We might find the poor and learn them to read and write and sew, and it would be a great help to them." Some benevolent workers concentrated on literacy without sewing, especially the army of Sunday school teachers who saw reading as a prerequisite for devotional exercises. Children and adults alike profited by these lessons, and certain ethnic groups, particularly African Americans, often first received the word through them—if obstacles did not block class attendance. One Yale Divinity student attempted to convince a reluctant illiterate African American man to take advantage of sabbath school instruction. "The man was unable to read himself," the student noted during a charity visit; "we tried to persuade him to attend the sabbath school, but he said he had been once, but could learn nothing." Although he "promised that he would try to do better," commonly segregated classrooms offered little encouragement. Because institutional settings might be otherwise off-putting, some volunteers set up makeshift classrooms in their homes. "[Y]esterday I had a number of poor boys in the lower parlor whom I hope to teach something," a Boston associate's son wrote in his diary one Saturday. "[T]hey live about hatters' square, are catholics & cannot all read, & are pretty dirty," he claimed. "They promised to come again Sunday morning—& I have purchased a bundle of little books for them." One benevolent volunteer discovered how to interest local working-class children in the printed word enough to develop their reading. "I have found a new way of entertaining the children when they breakfast here now, it is reading stories out loud to them," she reported to her aunt. Just about anywhere—kitchen, parlor, or even ship deck—could transform itself into a makeshift classroom. One seafaring wife saw Sunday as a fit day for combining religious and reading instruction when she "commenced giving lessons to the [ship's] boy in reading."[18] Thirst for reading, no matter where it occurred, usually attracted a willing teacher.

Strictures on slave literacy, however, frustrated benevolent instructors traveling in the South. While in Charleston, the captain's wife just mentioned confronted laws not only forbidding slaves from learning how to read but also punishing their teachers. "This morning while [the house slave] Caty was cleaning my room," she noted, "she took up a box that lay on the table, and tried to read the label." The slave must have sensed the woman's sympathy to risk such a bold gesture. The Bostonian "asked her if she could read," and Caty replied, "O no . . . I wish I could." The next day, on a walk with a slaveholder's daughter, the Yankee "asked her if her father's slaves were taught to read; she said they were not; but that they were instructed from the catechism, and were permitted to go to church every Sabbath: she and her sister taught the young children to repeat hymns." In this case, the words received were circumscribed by the master and his family. Awareness of those limitations led some travelers, like one Connecticut schoolgirl, to ponder slaves' mental world. Passing through Alexandria, Virginia, she heard a conversation: "Uncle inquired of the servant 'if there could no[t] be procured any cooler water?' 'No!' he said 'for the water was brought half a mile, and they had no ice in this Summer.' When asked where the ice was procured, he replied, 'It all comes from Greenland.'" She concluded that "all he may ever have heard of religion, or religious subjects, might be the Missionary Hymn commencing 'From Greenland's icy mountains,' where his idea probably originated." She did not see him as foolish, but, rather, as highly imaginative within slaveholders' limits upon writings available to slaves—forms of bondage in their own right yet eradicable through literacy. Small wonder that news of the Amistad rebels "learning to read . . . [with] indefatigable perseverance" spread through newspapers and personal accounts testifying to triumph over both illiteracy and enslavement. "[O]ur company on board the Boat consisted in part of the Amistads," the same observant student noted while on a steamboat ride to New York City in 1841. "I heard one of the little girls read from the Bible which they did very well considering their opportunities to learn since their arrival in this Country."[19] Slavery and illiteracy were viewed as related thralldoms.

Modes of Reading

With literacy so highly valued socially, no wonder people paid close scrutiny to the ways they read. While literacy acquisition seemed easy and natural for children, for adults reading became fraught with social significance and, at times, self-chastisement. Reading for self-improvement especially meant hours of hard work, struggle, and determination to excel. Because of this, the word most likely used to describe such learning was "studying" rather than "reading." Thus several diarists and letter writers paired the two activities as if to highlight the distinction. "Have stud[ied] some, read some[,] smoked 'one' and made myself generally useful," a Vermont deeds clerk entered in his diary one night after work. "In the evening I read and studied," a New Haven student noted. "Studied little read considerable," a college student wrote one evening in his Yale dormitory, while a rural businessman stated, "Studied and read the Bible" one Sabbath. A schoolteacher even portioned out her time along the lexical divide: "4–5 Study[;] 5–6 Read."[20] Although at times the two words were interchanged, and one activity could and did easily evolve into the other, the message was always clear: reading a book was quite different from studying it.

But what distinguished study from reading? Subject matter often had little to do with it, for the dichotomy reflected two different modes of engaging the written word, no matter what form it took. New Englanders could "study" just about anything. Mary Pierce Poor, for example, studied her sister's letter; it "was indeed *worth reading,* and even *studying,* her style has a great deal of finish—elegance united with a beautiful simplicity." One housewife spent "[m]ost of the Morning in the kitchen rocking chair, studying the cookery book," while one spinster "studie[d] the newspapers & her Bible." Infants could be found "studying" Mother Goose, and adults "studied" Shakespearean plays. Obviously, the academic status of the person reading or studying mattered little, for even though students were more likely to draw a line between study and reading, especially where mathematics, geography, languages, and the sciences were concerned, autodidacts and people long out of school also drew the distinction. "I succeed admirably in studying & reading—about as well as you & in going to school!" a pieceworker wrote to her sister. Self-motivated "studiers" (the neologism includes people who studied but were not institutionally affiliated students) like her often devised a home-based "course of reading," a phrase that always referred to disciplined "study" of a subject, not a light reading spree. Although autodidacts might occasionally slacken in their "courses," students were as likely to lapse. "I don't believe I shall go to school much this winter after all, but when I do go I shall study," Charles Cobb predicted. "I don't believe any scholar will learn a cent's worth this winter, by the way they study."[21]

If subject matter and academic status had little to do with contemporary definitions of studying and reading, then what did? The contrast implied differing levels of attention and mental focus applied while reading and whether or not a text was fully deciphered, engaged, and remembered regardless of how interesting (or tedious) it might be. Study usually required full mental attention that banished extraneous thoughts; it was therefore a good remedy for depression. "I need the discipline of routine and close study," one woman distracted by her physician father's recent death told her farmwife friend. Although "study" automatically implied strict attention, there were varying degrees of it. One could "pretend . . . to study" or study "'some,'" which was tantamount to not studying at all. More appropriately one would "read hard," another phrase for study, or "study most diligently." Other phrases included "studied hard," and even "studied very hard"—"too hard" in fact "to be kept up much longer," for study sapped the energy. "O I am exhausted," one collegian wrote, "in this interminable sea of human thoughts and—books."[22]

Although voluntary study often required effort, relentless academic study was the most tiresome of all.

Demanding such energy, study was easily frustrated. A beautiful day might win out over books for attention. "It is hard to study when the air is so pure and refreshing," Charlotte Forten confessed one May day. Watching a setting sun that "darted its last rays into the room . . . till it sank" wrested Frances Jocelyn away from her school books. Vaguer distractions could make one feel incompetent. "When I attempt to apply my mind to any particular study," a divinity student complained, "my thoughts are flying off to something else every moment." "It is exceedingly difficult for me to concentrate my whole mind upon the lesson," a bank teller admitted while teaching himself Latin after work. "It wanders continually, thinking of a thousand & one different things; but I am determined to break that bad habit." Furthermore, because studying meant building ever greater stores of knowledge on a particular subject, lapses in memory, as well as concentration, were rebuked. "I can do nothing with my studies," a law student chastised himself while plowing through a tome on English jurisprudence. "Even now I have read some hundred pages of Hammond, respecting which I know nothing definitely. . . . I am *ashamed.* . . . Grossness, & stupidity seem to have gained a complete mastery of my mind." The very panic that fuzzy-headed study induced only made things worse. Persistence was an essential ingredient. "The same employment day after day might be supposed to create a dislike for books and study after a while, but I still find it a pleasure to peruse my studies," a country schoolteacher averred. Like teachers, lawyers constantly found themselves, day after day, awash in a sea of books to study. No wonder that so many took up poetry or belles lettres for relief. As a law student explained, "[I] [m]ust do something to open my heart which is completely clogged with Law & History & French, so I read some Milton."[23] In this way, study and reading could work together.

Because study chewed up more time per page than reading, it was not as efficient a way to engage a book. "It requires more time than I allow myself to read it—it requires study," a retired physician's wife said of Thomas Carlyle's *Sartor Resartus,* a densely woven philosophical satire that eluded even its most erudite readers. So, too, works with specialized or technical vocabulary demanded time to study them. "Reading Mrs Somerville—a book, however, not to be read, but studied," John Park realized after beginning the scientific text one summer. "The authoress appears to be thoroughly familiar with her subject—wonderfully so," he continued, "but her style is so very abstruse it is necessary that her readers should already be astronomers, in order readily to understand her."[24]

Regardless of dense prose, enigmatic phrases, and ambiguous meanings, most readers believed that authors strove to be unambiguously understood; studying texts would assuredly unlock authors' meaning. Without faith in this socioliterary pact between author and reader, people would not have valued studying as much. In printed media, they believed they could replicate the mutual understanding that characterized their face-to-face relations; the more that misinterpretations and ambiguities could be reduced, the closer the relationship could become and the better the communication. And if ever they lost faith in an author's comprehensibility, they would have abandoned study, in much the same way they would try to extricate themselves from a relationship with a dissembling, untrustworthy person. The author-reader pact, of course, was based upon an ideal form of communication that could never be fully realized.

Yet struggling to "understand" a difficult text often meant neglecting everyday communications; that study could completely arrest the mind made the activity prone to being antisocial. "I have been shut up in my room the larger portion of the time giving my whole attention and study to Latin and Greek," a college prep student noted, while a normal school pupil moaned, "It is so lonesome to set alone 2 hours and study, and think most of the others have company." The loneliness could be abated by enlisting other people to help or by studying in groups. Daniel Child often read while his children studied in the same room with him, stopping at times to help out, while one mother allowed her boys to study in her chamber while she sewed. For some people, a social atmosphere helped them concentrate, especially when study departed from silent engagement with a book and demanded oral reading or recitation. One bank clerk felt that if he had someone to share a self-determined "course of Reading on Physiology" with him, he would not only banish loneliness, but his time would be spent profitably. "I try to improve my spare hours in a beneficial manner," he told his mother, "but I lack a companion to study with." Other people simply could not get past the "hard parts" without help. The downside of studying in social groups was straying from their purpose. James Healy reported that "during studies we laughed a good deal at an old toenail of mine which came off last night," and studying with a friend, one student "spent the remainder of the afternoon, & a part of the evening . . . learning Caesar, filling the pauses & spaces between the letters, the words, the lines, the sentences, the paragraphs, the pages, with conversation on various topics as they were suggested." A neophyte instructor also succumbed to the playful conversation that interjected itself into study, when a mischievous friend called after class hours: "Campbell & myself in dining room together writing & studying—when our friend of the Cloak entered with permission & joined the studies a somewhat comic scene—three of us about the round table—glancing from our books to each other & back again with affected interest in our occupation." The pace of study could be undermined through routinized interruption, as when Calista Billings would make a "joke" after "every two line[s]" of school lessons she delivered to her cousin.[25] Since sociability could not but help triumph over studiousness, most studying was done in silence, if not alone.

Study, then, could make all other activities peripheral. Studiers remained locked inside their own cognitive universe for long periods of time, until knowledge was released in the classroom or tested in conversation. What was gained by studying was lost upon human relations, unless they were recruited to help study. Yet intervention, while often helpful, just as easily complicated matters, making it that much more difficult to concentrate. No doubt, thoughts of other people coincided with studying: fathers who helped cram, for example, or sisters who had studied the same Latin text inevitably came into focus. But these were digressions away from the subject matter rather than enhancements to learning.

Reading, by contrast, invited sociability. As an activity, it was largely communal given that most reading was probably done aloud, bringing dissemination and reception together in a single moment. The person reading aloud received the words just as readily as listeners, yet reception differed between the two. The very performance of a text clearly meant that oral readers could not respond as fully to it as listeners. Instead, they had to concentrate on reaching the proper tone and pitch of voice, maintaining stamina, and, in general, keeping their listeners interested. Above all, an ability to pronounce words correctly and deliver them audibly was what counted. Therefore, emotional responses were necessarily repressed if they inhibited reading. Catharine Maria Sedgwick's *Home* so overwhelmed one housewife that she found it was "very hard to read the conclusion aloud, I was obliged to pause frequently before I finished it." One story was "so deeply interesting" by the end that tears nearly halted John Park's reading to his wife and neighbor. "I cannot read it without faltering," he averred. Boredom was yet another obstacle for oral readers. "Have you ever seen the Weekly Eve^{g} Post?" a boarding school student asked her mother; "let me say its soporific tendencies would be undoubtedly excellent. —but Mad. gives approving little grunts, every once in awhile which wake me up, & I read on, & on, in a machine-like way." If tedium was detrimental, laughter was ruinous. "I laughed so much at Stevenson's description of the wife of a Spanish Commandant who was 4 ^{ft} 6 inches in height & so many around the waist," James Healy recorded of his turn reading aloud in Holy Cross's refectory, "that I could hardly keep on reading and was obliged to omit the rest of the description."[26] How much the jollity may have infected the listeners remains a mystery.

As much as oral readers had to check their responses, listeners had to give themselves over as fully as possible. After all, listeners had to signal oral readers that the text was indeed being received. Grateful readers might perceive that listeners' effort exceeded even their own. "I think I should be completely wearied with confining my attention to half as much as he does," a minister's daughter wondered at her grandfather's capacity for listening to her read. Such receptivity repaid readers' efforts, as part of a sociable exchange, so they consequently welcomed reactions such as weeping, sighing, or laughing at germane parts of the text. Even swooning over romantic passages was permissible, if the reader was a gallant young man and the auditors were schoolgirls; one was embarrassed that her roommates "presented a most ridiculously sentimental aspect to the reader" upon listening to Samuel Taylor Coleridge's overwrought poem "The Improvisatore," which a beau delivered aloud to them. More sober listeners wished for spaces of "time to dwell upon striking sentiments or new trains of thought" elicited by the reading and showed interest through moments of silent pondering, if the reader allowed it. With listeners' roles so clearly defined, impolite deviations stuck out. Rude reactions such as inappropriate laughing or fidgeting destroyed the social trust between reader and listener. "Johnny Glover is reader this week," James Healy noted when a classmate delivered "an acct of the ceremonies of the Pope's Chapel during Holy Week" in the refectory. "Chubbs got 20 lines [of translation] for laughing at his manner of reading at diner-time." The seminarian added that his classmate "Devlin said that he missed his breakfast by excess of laughter. [W]hat a wonder."[27] The isolation into which Chubbs was sentenced as he wrote his lines was fit punishment, at least in this strict academic setting, for someone who violated listener etiquette. Anything that interfered with concentration diminished mutual interest and thus sociability.

If oral performances and listening necessarily brought groups of people together over a shared text, could silent reading acts do the same? New Englanders frequently mentioned in their diaries and letters that they "read together" with someone, but this usually meant doing so out loud. As we will see in the next chapter, two or more people sitting together in a room at home reading different things to themselves was unusual unless one of them was studying, but reading silently in the same room with people who were writing, sewing, or playing piano, was common. One stone mason's wife, for example, described a typical domestic tableau combining reading and writing: "[H]ere we sit[,] A[nn] Maria and me at the table knitting mittens[,] she reading Shakespeare while I am writing[.]" Readers seeking solitude stayed in their bedrooms or retired to the home library, attic, barn, or yard. But these sequestered readers—often people living alone, left home alone, in mourning, or sojourning—were by far rarer than readers surrounded by social activity. Isolated reading usually meant isolated people. Nonetheless, solitary readers attuned themselves to any social resonances they could discern. "I was glad to find you were reading it [Scott's Napoleon] at the same time," one European traveler wrote to her Boston sister-in-law; "& that although so widely separated we participate at the same moment of time the same amusement." Some readers even scheduled an agenda with their correspondents. Thoughts about other people became part of responding to literature, so even silent solitary reading could have social connotations. Indeed, discourse in letters about commonly read books united people together in social acts at a distance. Correspondents' and diarists' discourse about reading revealed a vocabulary of modes and methods for silently receiving the written word. One of the most often used terms was "reading with attention." "Read one of Channing's sermons and the little book sent per [the ship] *Roman* . . . with double attention now I know you all like it," Harriett Low told her sister back home. The very "attentiveness" Low and others paid to texts shows how much they wanted to communicate about them, but others simply hoped concentration would allow them to grasp a text fully. "I have taken up [Richard] 'Baxter's Call' meaning to read it with serious attention in the hope, that I might profit by it," a widow wrote to her cousin of the dry evangelical text by the seventeenth-century divine; "but I cannot feel that it interests me as I wish, & as it ought." Religious texts like these were seen as potentially uplifting to their readers, who would not presume to treat them lightly. Accordingly, attentiveness was associated with private devotions, another mode of reading that, oddly enough, was mostly referred to simply as "reading" and much less often "studying," despite the mental focus and engagement it required. Its ritualized aspects set it apart, yet devotees were just as quick to point out any lack of attention.[28] Inattentive devotional reading could verge on impiety, and it would certainly disrupt the clear transmission of the word from text to devotee, so the practice was avoided.

The faith that people had that they could understand through study applied to reading, as well. Proper education, well-developed literacy skills, and full attention were all that was required. Time to read and reread, if necessary, "digest," and ponder also helped comprehension, especially for foreign-language texts, philosophy, or dense prose. It comes as no surprise, then, that readers were easily frustrated by Transcendentalist authors who believed in intuitive reception of concepts and words. "I know what they *say,*" John Park complained after acquainting himself with some writings by the German theologian Friedrich Schleiermacher, who influenced the American Transcendentalists. "Their words are intelligible words, but when arranged by them into positions, I am confounded; my mind can find nothing to grasp." Park, an avid reader who found few texts too difficult to comprehend, threw up his hands on Theodore Parker and Ralph Waldo Emerson: "[S]pare me Transcendentalism," he cried; "give me something that can be distinctly comprehended, and I am willing to study hard." Yet "study" was precisely what the Transcendentalists attempted to bypass though direct intuition. As one sympathetic reader of Emerson's *Nature* explained it, there is "a mysterious analogy between thoughts & words, between all spirit & matter." Most ordinary folk disagreed; for them, the relation between ideas and words was concrete. Words, if used adroitly by authors, had a stable meaning for all careful readers. An attentive reader could grasp even the most difficult work if the author had acted sociably enough as to be understandable.[29]

Much of the time, however, readers were not fully attentive to texts. Nor did all texts merit full concentration. Readers often gave a "perusal," "ran through," "glanced" at, "coast[ed]" through, and gave a "cursory examination" to many literary items. These words were usually called upon by otherwise attentive readers to describe hasty textual encounters; they were not the preferred ways of reading, and readers often confessed their shallow skimming to their diaries. But glossing over texts sometimes served a purpose. A disabled and unemployed tax assessor, for example, first took some time "running through" a text "to see whether it was worth a careful reading or not," and John Park decided only to "wade through" *Memoirs of Count Grammont,* "a disgusting detail of licentiousness," instead of dwelling upon the unsavory accounts of Charles II's court.[30] Because perusal implied glancing at most pages between the covers of a book, a reader could feel satisfied at having acquainted oneself, albeit superficially, with an entire piece of writing. Most readers prided themselves on finishing books, even if only shallowly.

While it was not the best kind of reading, perusal carried a more virtuous connotation than desultory reading: jumping around between works within a single sitting, reading only parts of a book without intending to finish it, or flitting through diverse items such newspapers, short stories, and texts of a "light" nature. It is true that some people preferred to read two or more books at once, "changing every other day" to promote mental agility, but readers who adopted this understood that both books would be read cover to cover, even if it took months. But when fatigue, illness, or lack of time frustrated the best of intentions, readers fell into a "desultory" mode. This assured immediate gratification with the added benefit that such reading demanded moderate amounts of mental focus for only short amounts of time. "To be sure I read a little occasionally," Martha Osborne Barrett conceded after a long day in a millinery factory; but it was "merely a desultory, rambling kind of reading, a light story, or the news of the day, nothing that will improve my mind." Barrett once wrote in her diary that "Dr. Johnson is said to have had very desultory habits of study, and was never in the habit of reading [a] book through," but she nonetheless aspired toward full attention. Desultory readers like her actually completed texts, an entire newspaper issue or short story, but described their efforts as ill sustained. Evidently, time spent reading had little to do with defining desultory, for hours devoted to one long book were worth more than the same amount of time apportioned out to many shorter texts. One usually studious collegian, weakened by a long bout of illness, disparaged his desultory reading even though he was completing many full texts. "I was reading a good deal though my reading was too light & desultory[,]" he divulged. "Went through every newspaper that came to the reading room." Sticking with a long book connoted steady habits and mental fortitude, and, therefore, desultory reading was the bane of studiers, one of them who vowed to "settle down on one or the other of" the many books before him, "as this reading everything dont answer the purpose." Jumping from one text to another also suggested nervous tension, an anathema to the peace of mind necessary for concentrated focus. Some people went so far as to think that desultory reading, or the "habit of reading so many exciting stories so hastily," could cause nervousness through "difficulty . . . in fixing . . . [the] mind on any one subject for any length of time."[31] Despite the supposed ill effects, readers constantly glanced at excerpts or ephemera, as they turned from this text to that one and aborted dull texts half way through. Even firm resolutions could not change the way these folks most commonly received the word.

What was the remedy for the problem? The simple answer was to limit reading to a few worthy books, but that was easier said than done. In an "age of many Books," there were simply too many choices. "There is such a round of books to read that it takes me half the time to think what I shall take up," a lawyer's widow wrote to her sister. "I don't want to begin any thing that is not worth reading & am therefore in a fair way to read nothing at all."[32] Rather than "read nothing at all," the weary, the overworked, the chronically ill, and the nervous—just about all New Englanders at some point in their lives—took to so-called light imprints: news columns, short fiction, and other easily and quickly digested material good for one night's barely attentive, often hasty reading.

Despite the grumbling, the literary spirit was kept alive when the instability of everyday life called for unstable reading. It was welcomed into the private spaces where solitary reading took place in brief, leisurely moments—into the kitchen chair by the stove, under the bed covers, inside the hammock in the pine grove, and out onto the window sill—wherever reading materials were taken. And then they were digested, responded to, and shared in letters and diaries to create a literary legacy of social connection. In this way, even fleeting initial engagements could have a rich afterlife.

Conclusion

Ideas in written form penetrated the everyday world, no matter how briefly and how supposedly imperfectly they were received. But New Englanders berated themselves for reading "imperfectly," for not living up to their part of the bargain: to apply themselves fully to comprehend an author's words. The perfect reception that seemed so attainable in childhood, when time and effort expended in learning how to read promised the complete grasp of written words at some future date, somehow always remained out of reach. Multifarious life experiences and socially produced meanings complicated what seemed like a simple relationship between the written word and the reader. Even reading instruction varied so as to create diverse reception. In adulthood, everyday distractions, including claims of kin and neighbor, competed for attention during study. The likelihood for social intercession into acts of individual intellection was ever present, complicating text-to-reader transmission. No wonder Persis Sibley Andrews could "remember the very language" of her "little books—better[,] much better than . . . later readings," which were informed by years of socially mediated reception.[33] Falling short of youthful dreams, however, these folks read on, without fully comprehending how much the social "perfected" their understanding.

Chapter 9

Personal Ideals and Social Realities: Finding Time to Read

One morning a bored Elizabeth Jocelyn attempted to transform routine rug cleaning with a literary allusion. "There was a very pretty appearance in the heavens just after breakfast," the twenty-two-year-old noted with the keen eye of an engraver's daughter. "In the region of the mountains" north of New Haven, "a very small portion of the 'blue sky' was so completely encircled by white clouds, that it had the semblance of a blue lake embusomed in a circle of snow white hills." Summoning an image from a favorite poem, she mused, "You could even imagine, incongruous as it may seem, [Walter] Scott's heroine, the 'Lady of the Lake,' guiding her fragile bark over its calm surface." After her momentary flight of fancy, she wryly observed, "Quite a digression. It is said that 'there is but a step from the sublime to the ridiculous,' and I realized the truth of the remark, as I descended from my castle in the air and took a view of the kitchen carpet, which lay in an uninviting mass at my feet." She concluded, "True, it is that 'cleaning house time' is not a fit one to 'soar aloft on eagle's pinions.'"[1] Although she savored the ironic collision in her daydream of two seemingly irreconcilable facets of life, popular literature and household labor, they were not nearly so incongruent as she thought. She frequently read or listened to others read while she sewed, cooked, and cared for children; as she went about yet other household duties, such as rug cleaning, memories of her reading remained. Her diary entry thus exemplified the tiresome workdays filling most New Englanders' lives as well as literature's place within the everyday hustle and bustle.

Whether working at home, as Jocelyn did, or in offices, factories, or classrooms, New Englanders engaged literature during much of their day, though they seemed so unaware of it that they believed they gave too little attention to such matters. This chapter is devoted to observing readers in their "natural habitats" snatching bits of time here and there for books. Though quite different from the ideal conditions they craved, daily routines nonetheless could be conducive to literary engagement. We first describe readers' persistent longing for ideal conditions promoting concentration: peace and quiet, long stretches of time, adequate lighting, good health, near-perfect eyesight, and a well-selected stock of reading material. As we will see, these personal ideals were compromised by social realities that yet still allowed for much reading to occur. So the remainder of the chapter finds these people combining other activities with reading, first at work or school, then during leisure at home or on the road. In fact, so many and varied were the ways to labor or relax with a book that few nonliterary activities went thoroughly unallied with literary ones. Accordingly, few sites were incompatible with reading. Usually reading spaces and places—whether kitchens, nurseries, train depots, attics, passenger cars, gardens, or ship's cabins—were socially defined, insofar as reading took place in groups or during an activity that was itself social in nature. For example, ship's cabins were communal places, and kitchens saw food preparation for the household, yet reading occurred in both. Alone or in groups, readers whisking books into work and leisure spaces were socially immersed and rarely isolated. For readers on the run, social involvements could compensate for never quite reaching their optimal literary experience.[2]

Ideal Conditions for Reading

But what was that best-of-all-worlds reading experience? It should not have been desultory but regular and devoted to worthy, not overly light literature. Some people made resolutions to this effect on New Year's Day or important anniversaries. "Rose in good season this morning, four o'clock, consequently have had three good hours for reading," one accountant congratulated himself for keeping a New Year's resolution to "expand the mind." "If I would always rise at the time I did this morning (& I see not why I cannot) how much useful knowledge I might acquire in one year," he reasoned as he proceeded to calculate his bounty: "1000 hours at least yearly, wh is nearly 42 d[ay]s."[3] Ill-fated resolutions like his usually concerned study, devotional reading (especially of the Bible "in course" or all the way through),[4] or other solitary literary engagement. Seldom were resolutions made regarding a group activity, such as oral reading or attending lectures, for they involved assuming responsibility for other people's commitments. Perhaps because resolutions were private, however, they usually were broken, for reasons including shortfalls in the optimal conditions supporting reading: excellent vision, ample lighting, good health, and, of course, abundant time.

Good vision was of paramount importance, for without it, readers necessarily became listeners. Readers longed for perfect eyesight yet dreaded eyeglasses. They avoided them for various reasons, among them, vanity—one college student called them "those *vile spectacles*"—and because they were a nuisance. Furthermore, glasses did little if anything to strengthen vision, a common misconception. "My new glasses have not cured my eyes, I read so much," seventy-nine-year-old Hannah Hicock Smith defiantly asserted. Some people even thought "glasses might rather injure than other wise," and that damage extended to one's purse. Smith's daughter, whose income came from working on the Glastonbury farm, bought her obstinate mother the very pair that disappointed her for "half a dollar," a dear sum for a spinster who probably made much less than a dollar a day, while one fifty-four-year-old farmer paid more than twice as much. The investment proved to be a good one for Smith, an avid newspaper reader, the type most likely to complain of eyestrain from small print. Glasses were not only bothersome and expensive, but they symbolized aging. The elderly deemed it a gift to retain good vision. John Park marked his seventy-second birthday by assessing his eyes: "My sight is so good, I can read a newspaper without spectacles." A ninety-year-old likewise was thankful. "[C]an see to read without Glasses," he wrote, adding that he was "Greatly blessed in the decline of Life." Weakening eyesight heralded potential dependence, too. "I had several times offered to read to him, but he declined," a minister's daughter noted of her octogenarian grandfather's insistence upon "looking [the Harvard catalogue] over very attentively," which brought on a dizzy spell.[5] Reading to himself meant self-determination.

Clearly, people cherished being able to read unaided, even preferring natural light over artificial illumination. Some people made daylight reading a matter of principle. One unemployed clerk followed the advice of spiritualist Andrew Jackson Davis that "all thoughts born at night are nocturnal and skattered." The clerk therefore resolved to "retire at about 9 o'clock at night, and to do no hard reading in the evening." Most readers favored daytime reading simply because sunlight gave the brightest light—so much that even train passengers sat "on the shady side" to read and voyagers did the same under the "shadow of one of the great sails"—and it was the most convenient and cheapest source, albeit not always available.[6]

When it was not, readers could rely upon candles, rushlights, fireplaces, and lamps. They favored lamps for providing more direct and brighter light but feared oil spillage and recoiled from the smoke. Though cheaper than gaslight, oil-based illumination was still expensive; focused study lamps might cost 62 cents, and radiating solar lamps, "with fram & shade," as much as "$3.38." Oil lamps, moreover, seemed unsociable; they could hardly compete with a "cheerful little party round the fire" for bonhomie or romance but were best for lonely studiers and solitary readers well serviced by the limited aura. Lamps exuded a more dubious mystique, too. "Studying by lamp-light I find is attended with many evils," a student pronounced after an hour of homework. Chief among them was extending reading time into late night, resulting in excessive study or obsessive desultory reading. One reader quoted Hannah More, who metaphorically summoned a lamp to excoriate undisciplined readers: "'Too much reading . . . & too little meditation may produce the effect of a lamp inverted, w'h is extinguished by the very excesses of the aliment, whose property is to feed it.'" Lamplight excesses led to self-lambasting, for reading up late could benumb the mind. "[W]ith exceeding foolishness again read Belinda, a thing that does me no possible good," one woman moaned. "And now it is between the solemn hours of 11 & 12—The old novel has taken reflection out of my head."[7] Burning the midnight oil for novel reading was but folly.

Lamps also were blamed for eye problems. "I am suffering very much with my eyes at present," a schoolgirl told her sister. "They pain me very badly, & seem very much as if the measles were coming on," she continued. "I attribute it to reading by lamp light." There may have been some truth to this, for lamps were often so dim—seldom better than modern sixty-watt bulbs—that readers supplemented them with firelight to aid night vision. Indeed, a bright and shining moon gave off as much illumination, and one woman even mistook it for lamplight upon her choir book during an evening service, which inspired a quote that began "The moon hung out her silver lamp on high." Moonlight resembled lamplight in another regard: it was often too soft for weak eyes or lengthy bouts of reading. For those whose eyesight was already failing, reading by lamplight became impossible. "My eyes are so weak," a seamstress confided to her fiancé at sea, "I must deny myself the pleasure of reading by a lamp and this will be a very great cross as evening is the only time I can spare to read." One spinster refusing to wear glasses was "obliged to give up reading by lamp light, also sewing," according to her mother. Yet "lamplight is better for books than needle w[or]k," another woman concluded. She was probably obliged to put down her project and give full attention to oral readers after a certain amount of time spent in sewing and listening by lamplight.[8]

Reading was affected by health, too. One Vermonter identified the most common malady: "Read but little, had the head ache." Headache could doubly disable literary seamstresses—"neither read nor sew nor fit work," one wrote during a bout—and it could frustrate study. "I am exceedingly afflicted with the headache; I can study but very little at a time," a Yale student disclosed. Any kind of pain could undermine even light concentration. The nagging interruptions of a cold—taking medication, applying remedies, and hacking away—could also chip away at reading. "Cough-cough-cough all day, and pour down quantities of lemonade.—can read but little," John Park griped. More serious illness weakened the body and mental focus, making it impossible to sit upright with a book. "I am so tired of pain," a twenty-one-year-old barely scribbled in her diary. "I have had the tic-dolereux tonight, could not read, laid down upon the sofa and got a nap." Mortal illnesses like consumption brought reading to a halt. "I never, in my life, was so inefficient as for some weeks this summer," a dying young woman explained. "I *have been* unable to do any thing, *to read,* or even to look at anything—without fatigue." In these grave cases, picking up a volume might signal improvement and occasion rejoicing. After her daughter was severely burned in a fire, one farm woman took some hope when her little girl "began to want her book of which she has been very fond this summer." With it in hand, the child "seemed much more like herself than she had done," and she improved shortly after her literary encounter.[9] In extreme cases such as these, books and reading became powerful tokens of health, well-being, and, indeed, life itself. Complaints about glasses, lamplight, and colds seemed trivial by comparison. So, despite the annoyances, readers grasped at whatever imperfect time with books they had, as if their lives depended on it.

Work and School Activities Allied to Reading

In busy lives, time for reading was of the essence, but it was hard to come by, for paid and unpaid work drained concentration and time. Most laborers faced twelve-hour days or longer without access to oral readers or long breaks for reading. After quitting her job as a schoolteacher for work in a Danvers machine shop, Martha Osborne Barrett rued her diminished leisure hours. "I have been very ambitious, and dreamed of a life of pleasant leisure, devoted to literature and its kindred pursuits—but how differently am I now situated," she regretted, fatalistically conceding in the words of Alexander Pope, "Well, 'whatever is, is right' says the poet and we must all sooner or later make the same conclusion." Added to time lost was mind-numbing tedium. "I cannot bear to jog on in this dull Portsmouth life and find no time to do any thing but distribute, set, Press: distribute, set, press and no time to study," a New Hampshire printer confessed. "I must try to do something more than I now do with my mental powers." Professionals and other middling folk worked fewer hours, but they too were often sequestered away from their literary acquisitions, home libraries, and group reading sessions. Yet even women laboring at home were kept as busy as their male counterparts and unable to dip into books. Their work, although not divided into on and off hours, was nevertheless a constant drone, with unpredictably dispersed rest time. At any moment household workers could be called away from reading by what one woman called "many interruptions and various trials" that scuttled her plans to tackle Euclid, Kames, and the Bridgewater Treatise.[10]

Absent ideal conditions abetting both mental concentration and uninterrupted time with books, people combined reading with other activities. These were usually social, even when done alone, because the ends were usually for other people and the activity done with them in mind. Readers were not isolated literary selves rising above everyday constraints, like Jocelyn's Lady of the Lake nestled in the clouds, nor did they in recording their activities elevate literary over mundane matters. Rather, they describe combinations of reading and work as a tight alliance.

Such alliances were both conceptual and actual. Conceptual pairings juxtaposed reading with a proximate, not simultaneous activity, usually within a specific segment of the day. Women, for example, often paired sewing with reading. "Every day exactly the same—reading and sewing in the morning, reading & sewing in the afternoon," a newlywed described her monotonous diurnal regime involving solitary reading.[11] Because women like her often did both tasks within a certain time, one usually followed upon or was relieved by the other. In a similar vein, people conceptually linked "reading and writing," two similar literary acts performed beneath lamplight before bed which could not possibly happen at once. However, many women could with practice simultaneously sew and read, just as men, say, could smoke and read—such alliances were actual ones, as was the sewing while listening discussed in chapter 7. Record keepers seldom drew a line between conceptual and actual alliances, but because they recount dexterously juggling books with other paraphernalia, they hint at the difference. One thing is clear: academic study easily allied with no other activity except, occasionally, smoking. Study demanded all the focused concentration one could marshal, whereas reading allowed less than full attention and absolute comprehension and thus could interpenetrate other experiences and sociabilities.

This can be seen in the ability to sew and read at the same time. With pages open to view propped in front, seamstresses wove needles through cloth or, more commonly, knit without watching their hands while they read. Harriett Low discovered her ability to do so one day in the absence of a neighbor who usually read aloud. "Spent this morning in reading and sewing, both at once. Caroline went to Mrs. M's and I was sitting alone. I wanted to sew and read together," she explained, "and I managed very well." Not all people came upon this on their own; usually someone taught them how to do it. Mary Pierce Poor, for one, picked up the trick from her aunts and, in turn, taught her daughter how to perform "knitting and reading" at the same time. Other women went beyond merely mentioning having the skill to describing its practice. A seamstress working for pay at home "succeed[ed] admirably in studying & reading" during a busy winter. "Last week, I set up a volume of Malt-a bruns Geog[raphy]—^the size of father's bible on the opposite side of a thicket of cloth of various kinds & shapes," she explained, "hoping that by next w'k . . . I could commence, to get through, over or around it." Once the skill was mastered, it could become an enduring feature of family life. One woman recorded, "Pass[ed] the evg reading an interesting little book called the Swiss Family Robinsons written for children & in knitting . . . at the same time." Years later, the routine of "[r]eading . . . with knitting & sitting close to the fire" still persisted among her growing family, who doubtless forged a memory of their relative with book and needle ever in hand.[12]

One variant was memorizing while sewing. A fourteen-year-old committed "a great deal of Wordsworth's poetry" this way. She explained to her cousin, "I find when I am sitting in my room, and sewing I can learn it perfectly well, and it is a very agreable employment." Looking up from the page to fix lines in one's memory afforded momentary glances at the handiwork, and thus the task was easier to master than sustained reading while sewing. Consequently, some intrepid needleworkers, like Charlotte Forten, became adept at learning literature by heart. "This week while sewing," she once recorded, "have learned among others of Longfellow's poems, 'The Golden Mile Stone' and 'Santa Filomena.'" The diary entry was typical of others recounting works she memorized while doing what she called "destestable [*sic*] sewing!" The danger was that the poetry might be seductively distracting. She tried to memorize John Greenleaf Whittier's "Moll Pitcher" while sewing "but found it not very easy to do; my eyes and thoughts would wander to the beautiful poem, and the work was forgotten. At last I gave up both in despair."[13] Tensions between sewing and reading could lead to doing neither.

Children's caretakers could not as easily abandon their charges and thus had to avail themselves of lighter reading materials parceled out in snippets of time—and to tolerate interruptions (fig. 9.1). Nonetheless, one husband seemed bewildered by his wife's ability to read while minding children. "I have not had time to read the Caxtons," he declared of Bulwer-Lytton's popular novel. "Margaret has read them much as Mother used to read now darning stockings and now trotting the baby," he observed. "I am astonished often to know the amount of reading she accomplishes." Though infants demanded more immediate attention than older children, they napped longer in the nursery. Being on call there, while not always called, caretakers found some time to read. One woman reported that she "took care of babe & read & sewed in the nursery." Some childcare was minimal enough to allow for simultaneous reading, as one older sister described: "In the afternoon, I rocked the baby while I read, the 'Companion for Youth.'" Even men off from work babysat and read. "At home till five P.M.," one father wrote. "Spent the time taking care of baby, reading and ornament[ing] in a blank book." Of course, the quality of time spent reading depended entirely on children's behavior. If placid, it permitted intensive reading. "I read 'Martin' nearly all day," one mother claimed, regarding Eugene Sue's sensationalistic novel, and immediately added that her "Babe as good as he can be." If bad tempered, infants could ruin a reading session. "P.M. Reading Carlyle & resting," a relieved housewife wrote after passing on the baby to her nurse. "The baby fretting the whole time." A low adult-child ratio caused by a deficit of help could also disrupt. "No reading as we had so many young ones to take care of," a mother complained when her "Nurse went to meeting" at church. Conversely, a baby's bawling could precipitate nighttime reading by keeping its victim awake. During one interminable episode, a ship's passenger scribbled, "I employed myself in reading Cooper's Pathfinder."[14] No doubt, too, many drowsy caretakers read in wee hours amid crying babes.

Reading similarly passed time for people caring for the sick. Hannah Hicock Smith recorded of an ailing daughter, "I have been in her room reading Josephus," the ancient Jewish historian. Reading helped nighttime attendants stay awake, too. One woman surprised by her lack of "drowsiness" during one long watch, told her diary, "The cause of this phenomenon I hasten to explain,—I have owned the

Fig. 9.1 ✦ Child care, listening, and reading out loud naturally configured in New England households. "Salem Town," *The Progressive Pictorial Primer . . .* (Boston: Oliver and Ellsworth, c. 1857), 63, detail. Courtesy of the Digital Research Library, University Library System, University of Pittsburgh.

'Course of Time' since September, but have found no leisure to read it. Last night I commenced & finished 3 books." Other watchmen of the night were not so wide eyed after a few hours of reading, but they were nonetheless ready for nursing at a moment's notice. "I sat up all last night with Brother Beers," a college student who pulled an all-nighter during his classmate's illness wrote of an evening spent with Robert Burton's *Anatomy of Melancholy.* "Whether I slept much during my vigil in the sick man's room I cannot judge," he went on to explain. "I was awake a good part of the night . . . on the sofa, reading Bob Burton his laborious and pedantic volumes, but good withal, turning over the pages and culling here and there a flower." Reading this treatise on despondency evoked a sad reverie about a fellow student: "Anon I would drop the book in listlessness and *think.* The place, the room of Beers, and formerly of Brother John Heath called to mind the beloved form of the latter, and I could even fancy that he was sitting there in my company, just as we have often sat together in times gone by."[15] In the solicitude of a sickroom, this upperclassman could not help but recall social relations once animating it.

Reading while sewing or caretaking was acceptable, even laudable, but doing so silently while eating in the presence of others was not. So inviolable was this proscription that an American traveler thought it odd that London hotel boarders read, wrote, conversed, and ate—all in the café. At home, however, a silent reader at the table acted unconscionably. A pompous physician was irked that his wife read at breakfast: "O What a miserable taste, to prefer looking at blotted paper, to looking at one of the Lords of Creation, with his head full of literature & overflowing." Reading while eating signified lack of companionship. One sea captain, for instance, played upon a favorite passenger's sympathy by threatening to "take a book to dinner" if she refused to sup with him. As we have seen, however, etiquette allowed reading aloud in school refectories and elsewhere during mealtimes because it was social, not selfish.[16]

When done while cooking, solitary reading denoted lackadaisical work habits, so it was rarely reported. Listening was much more likely an occupation for cooks than reading. Domestic servants, while preparing food or washing dishes, could listen to their employer read, but they were discouraged from turning kitchens into libraries on their own initiative. Mistresses, however, read while fixing family meals themselves. With her own cook away at Sunday services, for example, one reported that she "sat in the kitchen & kept one eye on the roast beef & the other on Dewey's Discourses." Harriett Low concocted a similar recipe for reading and cooking. "Well I made my Candy, which was pretty good and at the same time read *Lara,* or the second canto," she recorded of a session making molasses confections, "stirring my *'lasses'* with one hand and holding *Lord Byron* in the other."[17] Her own homesickness was seemingly sweetened by the concoction of candy making and poetry reading.

Many allied activities so far considered—cooking, caring for the ill, childcare, and sewing—took place in the home. But most men who worked in fields, factories, offices, on ships, and some women who were teachers, operatives, servants, and seamstresses, spent much time away from domestic settings. Even craftsmen with workrooms within or near the home worked in a space apart. These workers were less likely to ally reading with their paid employment; for most, reading became an off-hours activity because reading on the job was usually not condoned. By contrast, lawyers, teachers, clergymen, and other professionals were occupationally required to read in their workplaces, usually to the neglect of recreational reading.[18] Often enough, though, on-job-related reading was woven into work time.

Employees with little autonomy, such as mill operatives, were least likely to read during work hours. Still, a few claimed to be able to during lulls in routines, including one nightwatchman who tended a large factory complex near Lowell while he squeezed in study between bursts of activity: "[F]rom 8.30 to 12 oclock at night I alternately ring the bell—9, 10, 11 and 12 and 'drive pins' at 8½, 9½, 10½, and 11½—every half hour. This takes perhaps each 3 or 4 minutes on the average," he explained. "The rest of this time 8½ to 12, I have to study, &c." After 2:30 A.M. he entered what he called the "leisure part of the time" in which he was "most of the time . . . in the 'Counting Room,' with lights, fire, pens, paper, books a[n]d Newspapers furnished." Nightwatchmen, of course, had less supervision than factory operatives, like one from Maine whose repetitive "Worked and read" diary entries usually meant time at the Laconia or Biddeford textile mills during the day and reading at home at night in Saco, Maine—the two activities that engaged most of his time. Occasionally, however, he registered "Read in mills" and referred to specific titles, as in one entry: "Have read today in the Mill from Whittier's Poems." He also read there "Whittier's 'Bridal of Pennacook,'" diverse articles "from the Atlantic," and "'The Lady of Lyons' a drama by Sir E. Bulwer Lytton." It is not clear whether he read outside during breaks at work or in the workplace itself while waiting for tasks to be assigned during slow periods. Counting rooms and other houses on the plant had newspapers and periodicals, so it was not unusual that one stagecoach driver "went to mill in the morning [and] amused myself by reading." Besides print matter, literary engravings adorned some mills, such as the "illustrations of Milton" on the walls of one at Newton, Massachusetts. Although books were usually forbidden at factory work stations, some people snuck in newsclippings of poetry to memorize while tending machines. In fact, a former mill girl later testified that "no objection was made to bits of printed paper" and reported on one young woman who "took to pieces her half worn-out copy of Locke on the Understanding, and carried the leaves about with her at work, until she had fixed the contents of the whole connectedly in her mind." The woman was not unusual, for it was "a common thing for a girl to have a page or two of the Bible beside her thus, committing its verses to memory while her hands went on with their mechanical occupation."[19] Of course, memorized texts undetectable by overseers might always follow workers into factories.

Away from such supervision, agricultural and rural workers often had many more chances to read. A recently immigrated Jewish peddler was shocked that the New England "farmer, himself, unlike the German farmer who works every minute, is able to sit down for a few hours every day, reading his paper and smoking his cigar." Seasonal patterns of intense labor followed by longer periods of inactivity allowed for this reading. Sugar makers' loose springtime schedule, for example, surprised Charles Cobb. Awaiting to accompany his literary-minded Uncle Henry "to the sugar place," Cobb reported that the farmer "would sit and read after breakfast and not finish his chores till 11 o'clock." Still, the uncle desisted: "Then he would talk with me about philosophical things (!!) which I didn't know but a darn'd little about and cared less till two o'clock—(dinner time)." That meal was followed by more talking and reading—only then at 4 p.m. did the sugar journey finally begin. Once while his Uncle "Henry [was] tapping & boiling," Cobb reported that he "read the 'Pirate' which I had in my pocket some." Hoeing also left him an hour after breakfast in which he "read and rested" and early evenings for reading and napping. But even on the job he learned a few tricks. He found that by taking books with him to the orchards, woods, and fields, he could read at intervals. "Father and I (with Don Quixote in my pocket) went over & dug some apple-trees," he wrote. "I read Don Q. near where Lysander Raymond and Chauncey were sowing oats." On another occasion, Cobb "slept in the bee-house, read & c (watching bees) till 5 o'clock." Uncle Henry had a supply of good things on hand, including a borrowed *Uncle Tom's Cabin,* which Cobb read during cherry-picking season.[20] He was always ready with a book.

Other farm workers read tracts and Bibles in the field, barns, or stables. One farmer moonlighting as a coach driver once "stayed at the Stable and read tracts"; at another time he "tended stage horses and read my Bible" (fig. 9.2). Seemingly sacrilegious, the practice may not have been so uncommon, nor offensive. A Congregationalist divinity student back home in rural Connecticut expressed satisfaction at seeing a farm boy "8 or 10 years old driving a team who had something in his hand reading. I asked him what he was reading—he replied 'a tract.'" Another observer remarked of the Shaker farm commune he visited in Canterbury, New Hampshire: "So far from ignorant of the Bible, you can go to no room, not even the men's workshops, where you won't find a . . . copy."[21] Of course, excessive reading while farming, especially of novels, signaled indolence and met with reproval.

Like farmwork, work on rivers and high seas left time for reading. One whaler assured his father that besides reading a chapter a day in the bible "which you gave me before I left home," he could "occasionally take a peep at other books," including "several . . . in the Latin, French & English languages . . . [during] the time, that is not devoted to ship's duty." Longer spaces opened up for seamen approaching port, as a passenger noted nearing San Francisco: "[All] hands are busy doing something big[:] writing, reading, washing . . . making money Belts and Purses, Pants Tooth Picks &c." Shipboard libraries could provide material, but often

Fig. 9.2 ✦ Hack drivers, like many other workers, found time to sneak a glance at the news between bouts of labor. "Hack-Driver," *Harper's New Monthly Magazine* 21 (Nov. 1860): 761. Courtesy of Cornell University Library, Making of America Digital Collection.

seamen brought books or borrowed them on board. One cook and sometime-violinist took with him on a fishing vessel a Testament, "music books," and an "Indian War book." Seamen might have listened to music such as that he provided, but they listened to readers, too. A California-bound "ship's boy" would on occasional Sundays spend "most of the day reading to the sailors"; frequently he "spent the day" during weekdays reading to shipmates. He himself had time to read when he "did not have much to do all day," and on one occasion he reported, "I have been reading Naval History & Homer's Iliad." Besides these, he read Dickens's *Pickwick Papers,* Captain Frederick Marryat's works (including his *Mr. Midshipman Easy*), *Harper's,* and Robert Bonner's story weekly, the *New York Ledger.*[22]

The higher the status of the seaman, the greater time with books. One supercargo, for example, took "about 125 vols." with him on a voyage from Boston to Singapore. "I pass but a comparatively small portion of my time on deck and a good part of the time on the sofa, reading," he noted. Similarly, as seamen like John Congdon advanced up the ladder from ship's boy to captain, they found more and more time to read. While he was a second mate, he usually only had time for his Bible or Sunday devotions. "I awoke about 5 A.M.," he wrote one Sunday in 1841 while en route to Calcutta, "seated myself on deck in a chair had nothing to do as we washed the decks down last night, got my Bible and began to read." If he was lucky, the moonlight was bright enough to "read [Scripture] on deck" during night watch. Reading by the curious phenomenon of fish light was also possible. "[F]rom 8 to 12," he reported one evening, "it was . . . quite light enough to read a book." "The light, under our bow," he explained, was "caused by large schools of fish deep down in the water being in motion" and reflecting the moonlight on the resulting foam. After being promoted that year to first mate, he read more frequently and more diversely on weekdays and wrote to his wife of his new-found time, meted out in pages of print: "[S]at down in my room and read Some," he scrawled in March 1846; "so [you] will See my C[ynthia] I am having an easy time now." Three years later, Captain Congdon concluded, "My C. I dont have enough to do hardly for exercise. I read most of the time." And in 1850, he penned with irony, "I have hard work to employ myself[;] days I set and read until my back side gets tired and sore from setting then I get up go on deck walk and look around until I am tired then come on again." Reading kept him isolated in his cabin, away from the commotion on deck that was also the heart of a sailor's social life, filled with storytelling, yarn spinning, and singing. Scrimshaw artists even etched favorite literary heroines, such as the "Female Pirate" Fanny Campbell and poet Robert Burns, on whale teeth in the company of fellow seamen.[23]

Just as increased opportunity for reading accompanied Congdon's move from the bustling quarterdeck to quiet captain's cabin, landlubbing professionals, managers, and clerks sometimes read in the isolation of their offices when time was free. Upon being promoted to overseer of a Lowell carpet loom, one Yorkshire immigrant boasted of his newfound autonomy to his parents, "On Tuesday afternoon while at work, I took up the Boston daily paper." What was a new habit for him had been routine for one twenty-three-year-old engineer who always read papers before hunkering down to work. "As usual I went into the office," he told his diary, "read the news of the day, and attended the business of my vocation." Law offices, replete with reading materials, beckoned lawyers to escape from Blackstone's *Commentaries* into the dailies. One Brattleboro student reading law with an attorney went "to the office & read & finished first volume of Evidence & read the papers." Newspapers, of course, were available because they kept lawyers abreast of political twists and turns, economic upticks and down, and the flows of cases through the courts, but these papers also contained plenty of other information and entertainment. Office readers could bring their own items with them. "I have nearly finished . . . 'Extracts from Fenelon,'" an accountant claimed. "[I] shall take the book to the counting room, for I can find time to read much in the course of the day by improving every spare moment." A Worcester politician also used spare moments on the job—in this case it was half-listening to long-winded political speeches in the United States House of Representatives, of which he was a member—to read a slew of family letters. "I recd a most excellent letter from [you] one from your Grandpa, one from Otis & one from Mr. Baldwin, all in a bunch," he surreptitiously scribbled home to his son Georgy, "and read them all while a big man from Kentucky was making a speech about affairs that I knew all about before."[24] He saw his time more usefully spent in reuniting with family through correspondence rather than listening to political opponents.

This method of reading "by stealth" was also practiced by students who engaged extracurricular literature in the classroom, as one did after purloining her brother's copy of *The Scottish Chiefs* and "concealing it under my text book during school hours." She explained, "My quiet attitude led my teacher and others to suppose I was absorbed in study." More often, stealth reading circulated via groups. Readers took to "passing a paper round the study-room" when supervisors' backs were turned or flipping pages "of a small song and picture book" under a desk for those who "sot near." Sometimes materials mysteriously "found their way into our recitation room," where readers, not owners, took responsibility if caught. Only careless readers left evidence behind of their secretive doings. The "prefects in searching the desks found some immoral & immodest papers in Jimmy Bergen's desk," Catholic seminarian James Healy recorded; "& the [C]rimes of London were in Barnet[']s possession which nearly resulted in the expulsion of said gentlemen."[25] That the two were the sole readers of this scandalous material, including a British knock-off of Eugene Sue's *Mysteries of Paris,* is unlikely, but they took sole responsibility.

Just as reading materials, both trashy and genteel, were smuggled into classrooms, clerks, with less dire consequences, brought novels into their shops, where time often hung heavily. Slow business, for example, allowed a Gloucester dry-goods clerk to finish several books during work hours. "Not much trade," he wrote of a typical day on which he picked up a bestseller on New York street life. "I borrowed 'Hot Corn' of my cousin and commenced reading it. Read about 204 pages. Shut up about 8 o'clock." He read on days when rain kept the customers away or when "business was dull." On such days, he reported, "Didn't have much to do read some." In this fashion, stealing a bit of time here and there, he made slow but steady progress in Richard Henry Dana's *Two Years Before the Mast* and "finished the 'Royal Greens,'" a cheap paperback adventure tale of the Revolutionary War. Similar monotony motivated one Boston shipping house clerk to read on the job. On several weekdays, he recorded some variations of "was not busy at all[.] Sat about reading & organizing papers &c." to describe his mornings and afternoons. At times he "sat about reading the papers & directing circulars," or when he had "nothing to do," he "[s]at about reading & copying the numbers of teazle casks." The ennui of shopkeeping that allowed for both reading and the performance of boring tasks was just the thing for a Vermonter working in his uncle's store in Jacksonville, Illinois, sometimes late into the night. The work gave him time to "read or write to [his fiancée] or sit and think or anything else"—the things he preferred to "Nite society." Charlotte Forten also read at a business establishment, the Putnams' Salem hair salon where she worked. "This afternoon, kept store for Mrs. P.[utnam] and became deeply interested in 'Dombey and Son,'" she remarked of Dickens's novel. She spent other days at the shop, "alternately reading and weaving." One slow day she lent a listening ear rather than a helping hand—hearing Joseph Putnam read pieces like "the first no. of Charles Reade's new story, 'Jack of all Trades'" or "an account of the great mechanic, Stevenson [i.e., George Stephenson], who, little by little, 'inch by inch,' won his way upward."[26] These social literary groupings within otherwise empty stores helped fill an otherwise uneventful day.

Uneventful days were rare for domestics who worked long hours but whose sometimes diverse tasks included reading aloud. "My girl proves a good one," Persis Sibley Andrews pronounced after hiring a young woman to help her during her pregnancy. "She reads aloud to me half an hour each day—under my instruction—so we combine pleasure & profit. She is reading Pilgrim's Progress now, & I am reading Milton aloud." Mary Pierce Poor had a similar arrangement with her domestic. "I do not know what I should do without her," she wrote, "she reads to me a great deal & helps me in various ways." Poor had earlier in life witnessed an inversion of the situation, with members of her family reading to her nanny, Polly. "I suppose brother sometimes reads to her when she is comfortably seated in her arm chair before the fire," Poor remarked as a schoolgirl away from her Brookline home. The same reversal of roles, employers reading to servants, also lent one wealthy Boston Brahmin family's home production of the *Spoil'd Child* a deeper class dimension. Not only were "[t]he parts . . . rehearsed for the edification of the domestics," but some members of the elite family lineage were costumed in livery.[27] In the imaginary world of theatricals, the distance between worker and employer could be temporarily narrowed.

By engaging books as part of scheduled work time, as some servants did, or while at the workplace during respites, as clerks could, employees transcended the boundaries between labor and leisure, if only momentarily. But texts read in supervised settings or during stolen moments seldom offered the same degree of satisfaction as those read in repose. There were only so many leisure hours in the day, however, and too few moments were left for reading after social calls, parties, nights out at the theater, and church. So during time off from the shop, factory, nursery, kitchen, or office, New Englanders found ways to ally reading with other leisure activities.

Reading and Leisure

Leisure time alliances did not require the adroit coordination of tasks or time that working and reading did. Men who smoked and read after hours, for example, naturally linked relaxing activities. "[W]hen all my work is over," one physician explained to his wife while he was away on professional duties, "I have nothing to do but read, & think & smoke!" One deeds clerk who liked to "read & smoke, and run around the streets" after work, rationalized the habit, with tongue in cheek: "Set down to read. Had to smoke to keep off the vermin." Once "reading and using the 'filthy weed'" took hold, it was hard to kick. One shop clerk who recorded that he smoked and read no less than 140 times over two years tried in vain to quit. Sociability made the habit stick; with his friend he regularly "smoked & read french till a late hour." A less addictive but equally seductive alliance with reading was napping. Although the two obviously could not be done at once, reading efficiently transported weary students, tired workers, and retirees alike into a state of rest. After all, reading made falling asleep easier. That same nicotine-addicted shop clerk, for one, often succeeded in slumbering and reading, but the ritual did not always work. One warm July evening he "came home: laid in the hammock and read and tried to go asleep but could not." The alliance, though it unfrazzled nerves, was naturally seen as nonproductive, and, accordingly, one Boston student castigated himself for his "highly intellectual occupation of napping, [and] filling up interstices by reading Extracts from the life of the poet Byron." Nappers fell asleep over almost anything, including fiction, but seldom religious texts. Of course, some readers tried to keep sentient but drowsed off nonetheless. "After shaving & washing this evening I sat down to read, but instead of reading was soon asleep," an accountant complained after a long day. "I am a sleepy dog, cannot sit more than fifteen minutes without nodding," he went on, and quipped, "To be sleepy is said to be a sign of good health, if such is the fact I am sure that I am remarkably healthy."[28] Humor over lapses might do as much to nourish literary experience as dogged persistence.

Reading just before drifting off was a private, solitary extreme; at the other end of the spectrum was literary engagement during social calls. As noted in chapter 7, it was common to read aloud during these occasions, but hosts could also use them to show off books, which guests would not so much read as admire or peruse. Some folks even made special visits to do so, as did one friend of a grain dealer who "called to look over my library. He staid till dusk." No library was too small for attracting guests. "Ad [Holmes] wanted to see my picture books," an embarrassed Charles Cobb recorded after a friend came to call, "but I told him I hadn't any at which he was surprised and grieved." Hosts with large holdings were compelled by etiquette to invite guests into the library. Charlotte Forten was overwhelmed when Theodore Parker treated her to his enormous private repository. "It contains *ten thousand* volumes, in almost every language," she exclaimed. "It was delightful to see so many books. I wanted to spend weeks there." The mode of "seeing" these books, rather than sitting down to examine them, served conversation. John Park frequently used his extensive library to this very end. On one occasion he displayed his maps to a group of touring Native American performers with whom he "had quite a sociable visit"; through an interpreter "they readily pointed out their country" on a U.S. map. Park, in turn, enjoyed other people's collections. "We took tea and passed the evening at Col. Richardson's," he wrote, "much engaged in examining and admiring his splendid collection of Books."[29] Peeping into one another's library bonded friendships as much as borrowing and lending books or the gift giving that often graced social calls.

Before callers even arrived, however, hosts readied themselves by reading. Callers dropped by unannounced within a range of hours set by convention; therefore, preparedness was essential and reading and sewing were good occupations in that they could be put down at a moment's notice. Sometimes people waited for callers by a warm stove or in comfortable bedrooms from where they could be easily summoned. However, many people positioned themselves in more formal but not always practical places, such as parlors or sitting rooms. Calista Billings, a sociable teenager eager for visitors, consistently "read & sewed" downstairs in her uncle's parlor waiting for evening callers, the lack of which disappointed her deeply. "[I]n the eve sewed & read no one came," she recorded, dismayed, one night shortly after her alcoholic father had scandalously died in an apoplectic fit.

One Salemite carried to Macao the same custom of waiting for friends or "some strangers . . . [to be] announced" while "sitting by with a book and [needle]work" in the sitting room. Not being prepared with something industrious in hand led to embarrassments such as an eighteen-year-old Bostonian in Europe experienced when a suitor dropped in unexpectedly. "This evening . . . we ladies had some cold chicken and meringues brought in to satisfy our hunger," she confessed. "I was partaking of the cold chick . . . , when Antonio opened the door and said in a loud whisper . . . MR. SANFORD!! My chicken flew . . . the meringues rushed behind the curtain and we all seized books and began very diligently to read, from which I gained much information as I had Galignani [a newspaper] upside down."[30] It was hard lesson in receiving calls with literary style.

Using reading to fill time efficiently while anticipating calls was equaled in frequency only by travelers waiting for connections, spending long hours in transit, or crossing the ocean. This was so common that at least one regular commuter thought "he hurt his sight by reading in the cars." And a long voyage, such as that from New York to San Francisco, allowed one passenger with "no cares or extraneous matters to engage the mind[,] fetter its thinking, and nullify its intellectual digestion," time with "at least 12000 pages of romances, poetry, poems, sketches and history." As one Forty-niner from Maine explained, "Very little amusement can be found for me on board this ship except reading." The most coveted amusement was to "talk . . . all the way" of the journey, but many garrulous people could not find willing listeners and so took up a book. One traveler, for example, said he "found no company to converse with . . . & returned again to Macaulay," the British historian. Another who "saw no familiar face . . . , opened my book, and wandered back to dear old Scotland and the 'days of Bruce.'" Sometimes passengers "spoke not a word to any one but looked out of the window & repeated poetry" to themselves instead. Anticipating loneliness, travelers usually brought along diverse items to read: newspapers, dictionaries, speeches, tracts, the Bible, devotional calendars, personal letters, biographies, Charles Rollin's *Ancient History,* novels like Hawthorne's *House of the Seven Gables* or Barbara Hofland's *Decision,* or poetry such as James Thomson's epic *The Seasons* or any of Longfellow's works—anything in fact that was owned, specially purchased among "Articles wanted" for a trip, borrowed, or given as a gift to fill idle hours. While short-term train and stage riders could easily manage a book or two of their own, ship passengers often resorted to reading in cabins equipped with libraries, a communal respite that ideally was "well ventilated and light enough to read in with the doors closed." Books easily tumbled from shelves, however. The "ship rolled so, that every-thing in the cabin was rolling around," a captain's daughter observed, moaning that "first the books went." Passengers on ships borrowed books from the captain, from fellow travelers, and at port stops where they also could purchase reading materials.

Sometimes a passing "[b]rig threw a line on board and a bundle of papers." For train travelers, a connection stop or missing a train could allow for plenty of time to go "to a bookstore, [and] select . . . a book" or to the depot for periodicals such as *Gleason's Pictorial.* Above all, reading materials were available from omnipresent hawkers. During a stop at Springfield, a busy transfer hub, a Granite State farmer noted that "books are frequently passed through the cars by smart looking lads . . . reiterating as they hasten along, '*Apples, apples—Daily-News—Daily-News*' &c." He "bought 'Appletons' Railway and steam Navigation Guide'" from one vendor; a week later, en route to Saratoga Springs and knowing "not one face," he "bought a book, called "our Summer retreats" for "25 cents." The routine train fare—"Cake, Apple, Reading, nap, *ad libitum*"—which paled before human interchange, kept passengers occupied if not satisfied.[31]

Once a book was in hand, travelers read "with ease & pleasure" on trains, but water transport presented problems for those without their "sea legs." While one sea captain's wife "ate very hearty as usual, . . . [and] read a little" during her voyage, a landlubbing schoolmaster "ate not—I shaved not—I conversed not—I read not—" during "[t]hree or four days & nights of high winds [that] blended into one *nauseous mass* of existence." For some "Sea sick" people, like one Connecticut farmer on his way to Australia, books were the only relief: "lettle appetite," he penned, "most of the time Spent in reading during the day." Conversely, with a calm sea, ennui set in, producing "a sort of listless feeling which always overpowers you," making it "not a good place" for "studying on board Ship." Consequently, "all day dozing & reading" became a common diary entry at sea.[32]

Travelers keenly observed their fellow passengers' reading habits—an amusing way to interact without interloping. "How very literary and industrious some people will be sometimes when they are observed," a schoolteacher remarked while on a train from New Haven to Boston. "There sits a lady busily knitting," she remarked. "I dare say she spends hours in idleness and gossip when at home, and there is a young pedagogue learning Geography from a map he has just hung up over his seat." While railroading through Connecticut, a Boston matron played literary guessing games. "I could not make out whether he was an old bachelor trying to find out what would be expected of him . . . or a husband seeing how he should mend his ways," she wondered while watching a man "who had bought . . . and could not wait to read . . . 'The Young Husband,'" a Christian marital advice manual. Sometimes observers were able to wrest information about readers who piqued their curiosity. A "very attentive" young man who read to "a young lady . . . in a very low voice" inspired one traveling teenager to muse, "I was making sundry conjectures, who she could be, & imagined they were engaged." After she got "a peep at the book . . . & found it was Coleridge's Table Talk," she "then indeed . . . felt interested in him," learned his name, his profession, and that the two were married.[33] Books thus could become the glue, sometimes the only kind of adhesive, for social interactions in otherwise anonymous situations of empty time spent in transit.

Conclusion

Whether on ships, trains, in factories, churches, or in the home, literary experience was influenced by the places and conditions in which it transpired and the activities to which it allied itself. Occupations like sewing, childcare, tending to the ill, working, and resting, blended into reading which, in turn, came to connote more than an isolated encounter between words and readers through its association with pursuits of everyday life. Paraphernalia related to reading therefore included not only books, eyeglasses, and adequate lighting but also needles and threads, flour and molasses, cigars and "teazle casks," sailcloth and ropes. Likewise, readers' comportment in these situations was hardly that of sitting erect in plush chairs surrounded by Victorian "culture and comfort": a warm fire, quiet and adoring children, a handful of servants, and leisure time to spare. As we have seen, most folks read in real spaces, not ideal places.[34] Although they enjoyed leisurely, solitary moments with books, the ideal—a plethora of good reading material, quiet babies, and undivided time—was seldom achieved. For the ideal required alertness, calm, quiet, and isolation, all of which the typically active day could not accommodate; at night, sleepiness waged a battle with consciousness. Quiet, solitary time with books sometimes induced sleep that defeated the goal of reading. Weariness after a day's work crossed purposes with the drive for self-improvement.

Yet most people preferred recruiting an unconventional moment, an unusual setting, or an allied occupation to accompany their reading, for such activities reflected engagement with other people, having a family, or secure employment. When unemployment struck one mill worker ever fond of the "companionship of books," he could only equate his newly found weekday reading time with "loaf[ing]." "Would be glad to go to work if I had any thing to do," a jobless plat maker rued, resolving, "What leisure I have I shall devote myself to study with great diligence." For women also, too much time alone with books often signaled loneliness, a life of isolation. A minister's wife reflected upon her marriage: "I once thought a solitary life the true one, and contrary to my theory was moved by influences from without to give [up] the independance of an attic covered with books for the responsibilities and perplexities of a parish and a family. Yet I have never regretted the change." For most folks, society and, with it, the inevitability of sociable reading was far more desirable than solitude, whether it be listening, reading out loud, or silently perusing literature with another person in mind. Even one hermitlike engineer, whose library was his "sacred sanctum," spent his time there not only reading but also thinking of his dear friend, noting that "although he is several hundred of miles from me; still he is very near to me in spirit." Like him, the nightwatchman who claimed to be "as contented as though at home, or as though I had a dozen companions" while reading at work, confessed that he was unusual. "Persons like you and me," he wrote to another loner, "who are so much in a 'brown study'"—a state of mental abstraction—"are not troubled much with lonesomeness."[35]

There were, of course, times when books were not badges of lonesomeness but antidotes for social saturation. For active debutantes, time with books was time off from display and performance. "I have been reading a good deal," one explained during a lull from the whirlwind of courtship activity. "It is a great solace to me, that of loving solitude & a book." For some highly sociable people, enforced solitary reading could merely fuel social sensibilities. "Impossible as it is to live—/ really live / without society," one woman reminded a friend confined by the flu; "we must have the materials for society—which can only be gathered in retirement—conversing with the 'mighty dead' and studying one's self." For one Forty-niner, the sole companionship of books was a luxury in San Francisco. "Mid the jargon of tongues and bustle of business here select reading would be almost useless, unless a man is rich and can retire into his own room and be alone when he pleases," he averred.[36]

For the self-elected, temporary recluse, books indeed functioned as ideal companions. For these isolated readers, the adage "Book as friend" was more than an empty platitude. But it could just as easily mean "Book as only friend." "There are times," Harriett Low wrote her sister, "when books, work and amusements fail, when nothing is required but the society of one dear *friend.*" Persis Sibley Andrews felt the same way after her siblings left home, thus affording time for her to spare: "Tis pleasant to feel so much freedom—leisure—time to read, but I miss society,—O how much." Even Martha Osborne Barrett, the factory worker who felt economically limited in her literary ambitions, complained, ironically, about too much time with books and too little sociability. "Read awhile, then closed my book. . . . I was lonely, felt a strong yearning for society," she conceded, blaming only herself: "[I] suppose it is my own fault, because I make such a recluse of myself, stay so much at home." While the book-as-friend metaphor alluded to flesh-and-blood companionship, it could never represent true human bonding—with all its joys but also its trials, responsibilities, burdens, and restraints upon the individually determined literary life. Books as friends were compliant, undemanding, unintrusive, and good for making resolutions, but they were also lifeless and cold unless animated by social intervention. No one better expressed the irony of this adage than Charlotte Forten, when she wrote, "And hence are books to us a treasure and a blessing unspeakable. And they are doubly this when one is shut out from society as I am, and has not opportunities of studying those living, breathing, *human* books, which are, I doubt not, after all, the most profoundly interesting and useful study." As she so eloquently reminds us, it was indeed "a very social time" in antebellum New England, but not for everyone.[37] The very books and periodicals that could play such a central role in forging and maintaining bonds between people could become the lonely succor left to desocialized unfortunates who, to their chagrin, were more likely to have at hand the ideal conditions for isolated reading so valued by people more immersed in the realities of everyday socioliterary experience.

Chapter 10

Within the Collective: Receiving Public Lectures and Readings

After spending the summer with her sister in Bangor, Maine, eighteen-year-old Mary Pierce returned home to Brookline, Massachusetts, with fond memories of reading club meetings, lyceum lectures, and new acquaintances—in particular, the young lawyer Henry Varnum Poor. Having fallen in love with him, Pierce continued their courtship through correspondence, sometimes writing twice a week. Wishing to maintain her literary relationship with Poor, who had treated her to the lyceum, Pierce wrote to him about her reading and lecture-going back home. All the while, however, she cleverly tested their compatibility as marriage partners. Under the guise of literary discussion, she teased out his opinions on everything from professional goals to gender roles; one lyceum lecture she heard particularly prompted exchange on a highly charged issue. "A propos to weddings," she coyly told him in a letter that segued from a merry description of a friend's nuptials into more dangerous territory—women's rights, "we had a lyceum lecture last week from Prof[essor Simon] Greenleaf of Cambridge on 'The legal rights of women,' and quite an interesting lecture it was too." She explained,

> The Prof. was amazingly complimentary to our sex save in one fatal instance which very nearly lost for him the good graces of his lady auditors, i[.]e[.,] he said that if ladies were allowed to take part in public meetings and share the debates in the halls of Congress, those same hallowed halls would become scenes of riot and confusion filled with a ceaseless clamor and strife of tongues. Perhaps the good Prof. is in the

> right, at any rate I agree with him in thinking it is not best for females to hold public offices, do not you?

Pierce here straddled the political fence by both acquiescing to Greenleaf's conservative opinions and pointing to the disapproval they caused among the women present. In this way, she tested her lover's sympathies with (or indifference to) women's rights. The ball was now in Poor's court.[1]

Oral performances such as Simon Greenleaf's often caused a stir within lecture halls as auditors hissed and hooted, clapped and cheered, or otherwise responded. But performances resounded beyond the walls as audience members discussed and corresponded about their experiences, the ideas they heard, and the new ideas they formulated. Performances had a larger impact still as they penetrated human interactions as platforms for discussing larger issues and exchanging ideas. For Mary Pierce and Henry Poor, a lecture provided common conversational ground about contemporary debates on women's legal and political rights. For other attendees, the same lecture might have sparked different ideas, discussions, and resolutions among those hearing it firsthand or vicariously through conversations or letters.[2]

This chapter considers audiences' experiences of public lectures and readings that took place not only in lyceums but also in lecture halls, churches, theaters—just about anywhere. Although we focus on lectures from manuscripts and readings of published works because they were so often obviously literary, it is well to remember that original writing with claims to being literature could be encountered in political speeches, debates, sermons and other "preached" texts, scripted panoramas, and staged plays, to name a few. Much of what we say below may pertain to any of these other oral performances, yet each form has its own peculiarities and so merits separate treatment that space cannot afford. These diverse presentations shared a literary sensibility that derived from not only their authors' attempts to construct a text for oral delivery but also performers' invocation of rhetorical forms, literary allusions, and oratorical strategies.[3]

Audience members' experience of lectures and readings was often constructed through social relations, both inside and outside the venue. Indeed, performances themselves blended into other sociabilities in diary entries. "Willie and I have been to eight dances this winter," a typical one went, "we have seats and go to [church] meeting; go to lectures; have callers; made some calls and have had quite a nice time this winter." A nineteen-year-old similarly streamed together performances and private gatherings in her account of one Christmas week: "the . . . party, visit to Eliza's, Mr. Holmes lecture, Mr. Eddy's preaching & taking tea at E's— . . . the Lyceum of Monday last by Dr. Cox on History," to which she added hosting her own tea. She asked, "[A]re they not all chronicled on my mind's tablet?" Like the other activities, lecture-going was social and sociable. Because of this, group considerations shaped how individuals received literary events: why they attended them, how they reacted to performances, and how they formed from them ideas on the "mind's tablet." The social drama surrounding performances encompassed exchanging tickets, extending invitations, planning for attendance with other people, and getting to and from the event with them. Accompanying sociabilities, like sleigh rides or visiting, also had their impact on attendees' overall reception. Amid performances, auditors became active participant/observers, alternately standing apart—as they evaluated audience composition, behavior, and mass reaction—and merging with fellow listeners by, say, taking part in experiments or applauding, laughing, or even rioting. The audience member's responses were hardly individualized, for they were developed with other people in subsequent discussions or letters to distant family members or friends. Thus attendees acquired a communally influenced understanding.[4]

This chapter explores audience experience in light of its social operations. We reconstruct the path of socioliterary experience from planning attendance to its aftermath. After describing how audiences assembled for an event, we turn to auditors' take on performances and then examine the criteria by which audience members collectively and individually assessed what they heard and saw. Finally, we contextualize attendees' response, through their post-event discussion and writing, among families, friends, and communities.

Social Logistics

People rarely determined on their own to attend public performances. Nor did they go alone and amble back home unaccompanied, only to crawl silently into bed after a nightcap. Rather, deciding who or what to hear, securing tickets, inviting guests, getting to and back, and arranging for food and accompanying entertainments all involved groups of people. Attendance was seldom spontaneous; rather, it demanded mutual negotiation and planned coordination—the sum of "social logistics."[5]

Events first came into view through favorable gossip about performances and performers. "At the instigation of Philbrick I went to hear him," a law librarian explained after listening to the "cold-water warrior" John B. Gough, of "whom I had never heard, but of whom I had heard much." Such persuasion and guidance entered into letters by gratified attendees. "If you *can* hear G.[eorge W.] Curtis, go," a Boston antislavery advocate entreated her daughter. "I never heard so *entertaining* a lecture as he gave us on Monday night." Notoriety, eccentricity, or even infidelity ignited curiosity, as in the case of Transcendentalist lectures. "Mother does not let me go to Mr. Emerson's lecture[s] this winter," an eighteen-year-old daughter of high Unitarians complained in 1838, "but I hear all about them, & they are very interesting." Excitement over such literary events was not confined to cities, where lectures proliferated, for it took hold even in backwaters. "All the talk about the town is Animal Magnetism," Persis Sibley Andrews in tiny Belfast, Maine, told her diary. "Everybody went to the Lecture *'knowing'* that they sho'd be deceived, & determined to find out the deception, but all came away puzzled." Alongside gossip, newspaper notices and lecture transcriptions also drummed up interest, and accordingly, some people used them to lure distant loved ones to come out to see a performance and pay a visit. "You see by the papers what great things the Waterbarians are doing," one young button-factory operative from Waterbury, Connecticut, exclaimed to her brother; "dont you want to come to those *Lectures?"* Invitations like this are more common in diaries and letters than recommendations, probably because they better served social ends. After all, New Englanders loathed to go to lectures unaccompanied. As one avid patron succinctly expressed it the night of one lecture she eschewed, "Mr. Abbott spoke on amusements but I was lonesome to go alone."[6] Little wonder group attendance was vastly more frequent than individual forays.

Most social invitations were informally made, just prior to the event, in person among local friends or family members. Some amounted to little more than agreements between people to go to a performance together. "Tomorrow eve Theodore Parker lectures at the [Salem] Lyceum," a ship's chandler's wife, who held a season ticket, observed. "Mrs. Thompson came in after the service, and engaged me to go with her to hear him." Although lecture-going often arose from such brief social encounters, it frequently occurred as part of dating and courtship. One teenager at a Boston party seized an opportune moment for romantic solicitation: "while conversing with Miss Lizzie White . . . [,] invited her to go to the next Mercantile Lecture." Though these dates on the fly often led nowhere romantically, formal courtship required making calls to family homes, where beaus sometimes enticed sweethearts with promises of a literary evening out. "About 12 oclock Mr Fresell called and invited me to attend a lecture on Phrenology by Mr [George] Combe," one twenty one-year-old reported; "accordingly I went—was very much pleased with the lecturer." So complementary was lecture-going and courtship that a manufacturer's daughter fancied that her uncle's penchant for being a literary escort cast him in the unlikely role of suitor. "Prof. Silliman is delivering lectures on Chemistry . . . [and] I go with Uncle Lee & Lizzie," the sixteen-year-old wrote. "Uncle Lee has become quite a beau, he goes to all the Lectures & concerts with 'the Ladies.'"[7] Lecture halls thus were either forums for expressing one's affiliation with groups or arenas for negotiating romantic relations. Confusing the two naturally could lead to humorous (or potentially scandalous) results.

Those who invited guests at the spur of the moment had obviously already acquired tickets or passes. "Simeon has a ticket for two and this eve invited me to go," one seamstress explained to her fiancé after hearing a lecture on "Transcendentalism" at the East Greenwich, Rhode Island, lyceum. Single admissions were usually available, however, but people often procured passes for each family member to ensure they could all go together. For example, John Park took "one for Mrs Park 75—one for [daughter] Louisa 75—one for myself 1.25" for the 1837–38 Worcester lyceum season. Because multiple passes usually bore no names, different people could fill the slots. "Cousin W. H. S. purchased a family ticket for the course" of lectures at the Northampton Town Hall, one granddaughter of a dry-goods retailer explained, "& takes Sarah & Frances & the 2 lads in the store." Complimentary tickets were frequently issued in sets, too. Sex education lecturer Cloye W. Gleason gave away some to a rural businessman and his wife for a course of his lectures, while a clerk's wife, who won a set of passes in a lottery, distributed them among her family, according to her husband: "Wife having drawn three tickets of admission to the lectures of the Lowell Institute, on Botany, by Prof. Nut[t]all, she, with sister Fisher and Sophia attended the first lecture of the course this afternoon."[8] As she demonstrated, such bestowments could be used for socializing.

Even if the giver did not attend with the recipient, the gift still represented social exchange. Boardinghouse dwellers might get tickets from housemates, as in the case of one mill worker who recorded he went to a "Lecture this eve by Whipple of Boston subject Joan of Arc," and explained, referring to his boardinghouse keeper, "Mr C—gave me a card of admission." A ticket gained, however, was only as valuable as a performance given, for cancellations were rife. One impoverished Maine farm laborer "was greatly disapointed" when the "lecture from the Franklin Association at Salmon Falls," for which he was offered a free ticket, was called off because the state had decided to hold its Thanksgiving on that day. That tickets were often expensive only deepened the disappointment for him and other financially strapped beneficiaries. For this reason, perhaps, employers often gave them to their employees to encourage their intellectual development. For instance, one dry-goods shopkeeper presented his clerk "a ticket to go to the Lyceum" as a friendly perk. A politician's wife supplied her African American gardener with money for tickets to demonstrate her liberality. "There is a Lyceum for the Ladies & gentlemen of color," she informed her husband, reasoning, "I gave Sam nine pence to buy a ticket for I thought it should not be laid at your door that you shut your people out from these benefits bestowed by liberal and enlightened philanthropists." Given that blacks could be barred from attending performances, the support offered by ticket givers far outvalued the price of admission.[9] Like other literary gifts, tickets reflected the best of social connections and, conversely, the worst of social maladies.

These gifts often came in the form of season passes or other tickets that would otherwise go unused. Season passes were said to be "lent," as if they were a book, even though the borrower inherited the monetary value of a single admission. Incapacitated by a "wounded heel," John Park complained, "I cannot therefore attend the Lyceum Lecture, by Mr Hall. . . . I lent my ticket to Mr Burt." A Lynn farmwife down with the "sick headache" reported that she "lent . . . ticket to Irene," a neighbor. Such tickets could thus shore up social relations through a "free" gift requiring little payback other than providing a service to the giver: to get the full money's worth from the ticket. There were plenty of willing recipients on the lookout. Unexpected guests, for example, obliged hosts to go out on hunting expeditions for unused tickets. "Have you any tickets to the Lecture to-night?" a journalist's wife pleaded with her brother. "We have enough for our own family," she affirmed, "but the girls have two young ladies staying with them, who they would like to take."[10] These complex scenes of negotiation between tickets holders and recipients created social dramas of their own, long before performers uttered their first words.

Social ties enlivened and even motivated lecture attendance. Accordingly, attendees, often "Quite a party of" them, gathered at certain destinations that saw a mélange of dating couples, other invitees and their hosts, last-minute joiners, regular goers, social callers, and even passersby. They could assemble just about anywhere, as one businessman on "riding home to supper" found when he accidentally encountered some lecture-going friends and "joined them supperless." Most groups, however, gathered in homes during social calls immediately prior to evening lectures. Callers sometimes arrived in groups to negotiate transportation or coordinate arrival. "Maria and Lydia Page and their cousin Mary Sawyer of Hamilton came over from Danversport and attended the lecture," Martha Osborne Barrett, who lived near the Peabody Institute, explained. Attendees gathering before performances often took meals together. John Park's daughter, for one, regularly took tea at her father's before going to the Worcester lyceum. But dinner parties also set the mood for more fun, and when the guest of honor was the speaker, all were in for a special treat. "At Dinner with us, R. W. Emerson, D^r. Francis, Mrs. F., Car'y Sturgis, Augusta King," a Boston abolitionist lawyer rostered his guest list. "We talked of Goethe. Mr F. compared his liberality with Coleridge's intolerance towards unitarians." As intellectual as the conversation was, the evening's finale remained the highlight: "In the Even.^g. R.W. Emerson's Lecture on Heroism." Smoking and sewing also accompanied performance going, much as they did reading. "We smoked & then I went down to hear Gough at the Hall (Faneuil)," one young man said of an evening spent with a friend. Like smoking, sewing wove through performance days as well. Just as seamstresses waited for callers while sewing and reading, so too did they anticipate drop-in guests on lecture evenings with needle, thread, and book in hand. "Read 'Picciola' and sewed," Charlotte Forten scribbled. "Mr. G.[ilbert] came in very unexpectedly, and accompanied us to the Lyceum." Women seldom if ever brought their sewing but instead ventured out unfettered by domestic labor.[11]

Further sociability beckoned as people packed into train cars, huddled in coaches, or walked together. Simply to ride evening trains opened opportunities for encounters with lecture-goers; they were so common that one passenger lamented the missed chance to sit with a literary-minded friend in transit. "I regret that I did not see you in the cars on the evening of Mr Thackeray's lecture," he apologized. Walking to or from a performance could be every bit as enjoyable as riding providing the weather complied. With fair weather, performance-goers preferred walking over other means for its ease and reliability. Of course, spring and summer excursions to lectures had special charms. "Lecture again this eve[g.]—subject Metals," Persis Sibley Andrews recounted. "A large class . . . & a social, pleasant interview & a most delightful walk—this very personification of 'balmy June weather.'" For one newspaperman's wife, an April stroll with her husband even redeemed "a lecture from Prof. Frost, a pedantic school boy performance," as she called it; "but we had a nice walk down . . . ," she concluded. Conversely, "very bad walking"—extreme weather conditions, such as heavy rain, deep snow, and frigid cold—commonly caused auditors, especially women hindered by voluminous dresses, to stay home. "Edwin has gone to the Lyceum & Lecture," a Connecticut farm woman noted of her husband with envy one January day; "if the roads & weather were good I should love to go. I should enjoy it—*but I can not.*" Bad walking's impact on attendance could be noticeable. "Considering the state of the streets," John Park recorded on one March night, "the Lecture was well attended, though many ladies were afraid to venture out." Male speakers, however, could walk through ten inches of snow to avoid unpredictable transport.[12]

The social logistics of getting to a public performance meant that performance was enveloped in social meaning before it even started. Social interchanges—through recommendations and invitations, procuring and exchanging tickets, calling and cajoling, by meeting on trains or going by sled or on foot—all would condition the performance atmosphere. The audience's reception of the event thus stretched far beyond stage and lecture platform to pre-performance activity. Individual reception continued to be collectively inspired at the event itself. Audience members watched one another as much as the speaker and responded with the crowd. As we will see, this collective audience response was being formulated from the moment auditors entered the door. And it had a yet richer social afterlife when everyday ideas, culled from within the lecture hall, were disseminated through diaries and letters.

Inside Venues

Once inside lecture venues, audience members were greeted by various sensory experiences: gas lighting "like groups of stars," decorations, spaciousness, "echoes, [in] dark, dirty & dilapidated" halls, the sounds of debates that amused an audience waiting for a tardy speaker to arrive, and "Music before & after the lecture." That most performances were held in familiar multipurpose venues, however, little moved veteran auditors to comment upon physical surroundings, yet newcomers might do so. "Wednesday night Wm. and I went to the Lyceum at the City Hall," a Manchester mill worker informed her sister. "[A]s I entered the room I heard some beautiful music, upon looking around there was stationed a band of music that plays there every night at the Lyceum," she continued. "I thought of you, how you would like it." The lecture venue was experienced through the eyes and ears of a distant loved one. Alongside such remembered though absent friend or kin, fellow audience members made the first and most lasting impression upon auditors. Attendees searched for familiar faces. One Boston schoolboy, ever on the lookout for rival beaus and pretty girls, "saw many acquaintances, among them saw George Dana with a lady," at one Mercantile Association lecture. "Miss Richardson, Miss C. White & Miss R. Walker & many others, all putting on their best looks." Because they were scrutinized, attendees, even poor ones, paid special attention to appearances. "J. M. Spear lectured at the spiritual meeting," Charles Cobb recorded. "Mother had to borrow some clothes of Aunt Barney to wear there!" Reconnoitering offered more than grist for gossip; it made auditors feel secure in largely anonymous public settings. One young woman, for instance, was delighted that "[n]early all my acquaintances were present" at a Beverly lyceum lecture.[13]

Audiences were the very heart of performances, and a good showing was one thing attendees noticed most. They often referred to abundance, or paucity, when estimating crowds. "Full house" was only one of many terms suggesting plenty, profusion, and surfeit. "Every nook and alley and the galleries were filled," John Park noted when Caleb Cushing spoke on "the English Empire in Hindoostan" at Worcester Town Hall, while one teenager at a Boston lecture observed that the hall "was covered to jam." One Universalist preacher's wife noticed the crowd's social complexion as well as its size when she reported seeing "a large and respectable" audience at a "reading of Mrs. Stow[e]s 'Uncle Tom's Cabin' dramatized by Mrs. Webb, a colored lady." Of course, crowds were not always large. Of all reasons attendees gave to account for low turnout, the most common was inclement weather. "Wm Wells Brown read his drama here, last Thursday evening," a shoe clerk reported to his brother. "It rained quite hard, but he had a pretty good audience." Like him, one Portland lawyer weighed inclemency against good speaking when he attended a "lecture at Lyceum by Mr. Thoreau" buffeted by an "Equinoctial storm." Although the performer, who previewed his *Walden,* was deemed "queer, transcendental & witty," this observer conceded that he drew "quite a good audience notwithstanding the storm." The excuse of bad weather, however, commonly let unpopular speakers save face. "Mr Caswell's lecture on the Results of Machinery, was attended by only about 25 persons last evening in consequence of the snow storm," a Providence industrialist testified, but he alluded to "the want of skill of the lecturer," too.[14]

Despite the bad weather that could keep them at home, women managed to attend lectures in great numbers, so their presence did not go unnoticed. Because of lectures' role in dating rituals, it is not surprising that bachelors surveyed the assemblage for prospective spouses. At a temperance lecture, for example, one remarked, "Saw about three hundred ladies—what a good opportunity to select one for life." Whatever attendees' motives, public lecture crowds in which the sexes freely intermingled were becoming so common that some women chafed against the occasional gender-segregated seating they encountered in the form of "ladies' galleries" at other events. "Sarah and I went to [the Yale] Commencement this afternoon," Frances Jocelyn penned, but observed, "No lady was allowed to sit down stairs, and the gallerys were very crowded." Disappointed, she concluded, "We could get no seat and we soon left the church." Four years earlier, however, her sister Elizabeth watched a few disgruntled women wander outside their commencement ghetto to hear a dissertation upon national poetry. "Some of the ladies, in the afternoon, took one row of seats in the gentlemen's gallery," she blithely remarked. "Harriette and I were invited to go up there, but preferred to sit in our morning seat." But sometimes seat hopping was checked by literally barring admittance. "[T]here was a fearful crowd of ladies who attempted to get in after the galleries were filled & the doors closed," one daughter of a jobless clergyman complained to her friend a few days after Edward Everett delivered his eulogy on John Quincy Adams. "I know several ladies who were in the crowd but only two who got into the Hall," she continued. "They had tickets & were admitted early." Segregated seating notwithstanding, getting there well beforehand was sometimes the only way to secure "good seats"—or "any seat" at all, for most tickets were not issued with seat numbers.[15]

Arrival times often determined where people sat regardless of status. "The worst of it is that folks go tremendously early," one newspaperman's daughter complained of ticket holders for historian Jared Sparks's lecture course. "Last time we went at half past 6, the lecture begins at 7, and we could only get a seat 4 from the top of the Hall." Due to seating overflows, auditors might have to stand, often "in one position . . . [which] was very fatiguing," or they were directed to makeshift "benches behind the other seats" or to the far corners of a hall, where speakers became inaudible. "The great convention for Women's Rights assembled today in Brinley hall," John Park announced on 15 October 1851. "I went over this afternoon, but the hall was crowded to the utmost, so that I could get no farther than the door, and heard a woman's voice, but not a word she said." Stragglers also paid the penalty of not being able to select their company. "We did not get there till late so we had to sit back," a schoolteacher moaned after a lyceum lecture in Lynn; "and we could not hear on acc[oun]t of some young men who sat in the seats behind us; who talked all the eve." For performance-goers intent upon hearing something, one closed door might lead to another open one. "Evening husband and sister Catharine walked to the State House, where, in the Representatives hall there was an adjourned meeting of the Mass. Anti-Slavery Society," Daniel Child reported; "on arriving there[,] however, the hall was so crowded that we could not enter." But all was not lost: "So we thence . . . attended a lecture on mesmerism by Rev. J. B. Dod[s]. Two subjects, both young men, were magnetized." The entourage was fortunate enough to find available seats for such an exciting performance before a crowd "estimated at 2000."[16]

Responding to Performances

Whether literally mesmerized or only figuratively entranced, audiences responded to the performance on three levels of engagement: as a totality, as congeries of small groups, and as individuals within the collective. Audiences as a whole might react with unambiguous displays of concerted approval or protest. Small groups might offer competing social dramas to the main performance through near-at-hand chitchat and across-the-room intergroup gestures. Individually audience members might have their own unique reflections upon performers as both textual producers and verbal disseminators. Listeners might variably point to well-written or -organized texts, clear and concise delivery of new ideas, effective oratory and refined elocution, deft use of visual props, successful execution of experiments, and even a performer's appearance if it enhanced presentations. While some auditors drifted into half-conscious reveries, others felt a close, almost intimate bond with the speaker. So, far from being a uniform experience for all participants, public lectures could elicit a host of multivalent responses.

Collective audience response was gauged by various measures. The most general arose from observers who described a palpable spirit permeating the hall independent of other oral or visual indicators. Charlotte Forten claimed that such unarticulated audience response was indeed perceptible. "[I]t seemed to me as if I could *feel* the half suppressed sensation which it occasioned," she told her diary after hearing Theodore Parker speak. Other auditors drew conclusions from their affinity with the crowd—one's response *had* to be the audience's, too. "No one, with a soul, could have heard him this afternoon, without saying in his heart, *Kansas must be free!!!*" was one woman's response to an address on containing slavery delivered by that state's governor. What they may have discerned were degrees of "attentiveness," a commonly used word to describe audience interest. One Danvers lecturer holding forth "on the matter and manner of reading," was "listened to with attention," according to one listener. What type of lecture kept the crowd attentive? It was not always subject matter as much as lucidity. "It was very clear and interesting," was the way a college president's daughter described naturalist Louis Agassiz's lecture on glaciers at which the "audience were of the first class & very attentive." Concrete examples and simple syntax aided concentration. Of course, expressive delivery helped audiences focus for long periods, usually more than an hour. No one could do so better than temperance crusader John B. Gough. "He was very eloquent at times and commanded the attention of the audience for an hour and a half," a New Haven artist attested after hearing him speak. So, too, did "elegant gestures" enhance the "'*magic oratory*'" of this popular temperance speaker who, according to an enthralled Frances Jocelyn, "held the audience for nearly two hours in *breathless admiration* if I may use the expression." Conversely, poor performances were associated with audience inattention. "But few persons were present & those few looking tired & sleepy," an attendee reported of a lecture by "Mr Mills the Physiognomist."[17] Collective snoozing denoted extreme inattention, the most passive form of audience resistance.

Visual and aural clues indicating general audience response were not lost upon observers. Some were subtle, as "the hundreds of earnest faces" Charlotte Forten gazed on during one lecture by Wendell Phillips or "the gentlemen" who nervously "bit their lips" when a female commencement speaker charged, "Eve only tasted the apple[—]'was it not Adam who devoured the rest?'" More commonly noted were obvious reactions, such as appropriate laughter. A port collector, for instance, admired John Gough's ability to "convuls[e] the audience with laughter." Applause, of course, offered customary approval for all but the most solemn lectures, such as public memorials. At secular events, applause came in varying strengths, from the "thunders of applause" one woman heard at a temperance lecture to the "suppressed applause"—clamorous enough in its quiet disapproval—a locomotive-firm treasurer noted at the close of Ralph Waldo Emerson's address "on cause and effect." Besides intensity and timing of clapping, duration sent a distinct message, such as the "repeated and long continued applause" enjoyed by English actress Fanny Kemble at one of her readings. Not all applause, however, was genuine or indicative of appreciation. Audiences sometimes spontaneously conspired to give a mock ovation to tedious speakers. That this mass ridicule could be so closely orchestrated attests to the audience's self-consciousness as a totality improvising in concert. "[A]t every pause of the speaker, the audience stomped & clapped," a schoolboy noted after he attended a lecture he "could not find head or tail to." He explained, "This was done for variety not for their commendation of what they heard; and the best of the joke was the orator thought it was on account of his sayings."[18] The cleverly synchronized sham opaque to the hapless speaker suggests the degree to which an audience might exhibit a collective will of its own.

Stomping was only one type of raucous reaction that could signify enthusiastic participation or impassioned dissent. "One of the liveliest, best meetings that I ever attended," a dry-goods shop clerk remarked after coming home from a lyceum debate on some constitutional questions. "The audience becoming livid . . . and hissed so that Mr Hatch could not proceed." Sometimes collective mirth rather than contentiousness overwhelmed speakers. A chemistry lecturer in rural Maine once caused mayhem by administering laughing gas to illustrate his points. "Several have respired the exhilerating-gas—w'h afforded much sport," Persis Sibley Andrews wrote with delight and described the ensuing bedlam: "Leavitt the Tailor quoted from Shakespeare with an eloquence that astonished *all*—Some sung—some danced—others fought." Word apparently got around, and two days later the performance was reprised to a packed house over which the lecturer lost control. "[N]oise & confusion have been more conspicuous than anything else," she stated, before applying an apt quote from Milton: "The Lecturer tried to *drive* them to be still w'h rendered 'confusion worse confounded.'" Her conclusion was no doubt based upon behavior witnessed at other lectures gone awry: "He doesn't understand the New Englander—he isn't to be driv'n,—not he."[19] The audience, according to her, had not only a will but also a mind of its own.

More contentious riotous outbreaks were all too familiar to witnesses at abolitionist and other politically charged performances that provoked violent reactions from opponents. Auditors at these events were ever on the lookout for any signs of tension. "[A]ttended at faneuil hall a meeting called to give a publick reception to Geo. Thompson Esq. of England," a clerk scrivened, with his careful hand, of a noted abolitionist; "but as there was a good deal of commotion—left before Mr. Thompson had spoken." Peaceful onlookers who stayed might stand by helplessly only later in their diaries to chastise perpetrators. "[H]ad a very interesting lecture," one country schoolmaster noted, "but many were enraged and endeavoured to disturb the peace and make a riot" at a Methodist Meeting House where a Boston black abolitionist spoke. "The man was shamefully treated, and many disgraced themselves by their injudicious conduct towards him." The spell that transformed socially acceptable dissent into violence was at times only broken by threat of force—to anxious auditors' dismay. When Wendell Phillips once addressed a "densely crowded" Boston Music Hall on "'Mobs and Education,'" he, ironically, sparked "a row . . . by a considerable number of evil[ly] disposed individuals who had intruded themselves with that design." A businessman witnessed the outcome: "The presence of a Police force however checked any considerable development of the mob spirit."[20] The reaction of a minor contingent within the audience threatened to shift the "spirit" of response from that intended by the speaker to that manipulated by dissidents.

Of course, not all mobs were small, nor were all small groups within audiences aiming to disrupt performances. Indeed, audiences were largely composed of the small sociable coteries that had assembled prior to events and had taken seats together at the venue. During performances, these lecture-going parties played out their own, more intimate dramas, which occasionally defied speakers' public claim on their attention. Some intergroup interludes were silent, simulated through binoculars obviously surveying the crowd and beckoning other spies to rejoinder—but the game took courage. After spotting a pretty girl before one lecture and striking up a brief conversation with her, a schoolboy equipped with lorgnette considered peeping upon her from afar once the lecture began, but demurred. "I did not use the glass I had with me being in rather a conspicuous place," he confessed. "I was strongly tempted to take it out of my pocket many times, but was prevented . . . , knowing that if I used it she would also." Similar cat-and-mouse games doubtless fluttered through any crowded hall, especially among attendees seated adjacently. Such interactions necessarily chipped away at the group's attentiveness to speakers. "I was much amused to find myself seated between Mr W. & Harry Oxnard," a debutante mused at one Boston lecture. "I paid almost undivided attention to the latter whom I really like," she confided, "& he too seems to possess a *penchant* for me, how long it will last I know not." She philosophized and set her course: "Men are so fickle, there is no trusting them. I however am bent upon amusing myself as much as possible."[21] Speakers, whether they knew it or not, competed with such audience sideshows.

Whether or not she and her beaux disturbed other people sitting near them with audible chatter remains unclear, but it was not unusual to hear a sociable buzz among parties of lecture-goers. Attendees felt that chatting among themselves while performers spoke was entirely permissible. After all, as we have seen, similar conversations accompanied home-based group oral-reading sessions, the difference being that the reader joined in while the lecturer could not. "[W]e sat in the gallery," a young woman reported, "& between quizzing, frolic[k]ing & listening to a description of St. Peter's church by Mr. Butler the evening passed on." Bad seating could account for the buzz. "We could not hear what the (female) speakers said," a woman attending an antislavery society meeting averred, *"so talked ourselves."* Some people deliberately sat "near the door" to have "quite a lively time" without bothering other people, while other placements veiled bouts of giggles at poor speakers. Attending one "ridiculous" Bangor lyceum debate with her fiancé and a friend, Mary Pierce Poor welcomed "the high sides and post" which "concealed us in a great measure from view" so "we could laugh as much as we pleased unnoticed." Audience members did not always find babble among groups disturbing, perhaps because it was an integral part of socioliterary experience. "I was much amused by the conversation of a couple behind me, & the actions of one in front," the student who refrained from using his lorgnette admitted after hearing a lecture on the history of Boston. Despite witnessing this set of social dramas, the young man nevertheless found "it was the most useful lecture of the course so far."[22] Sociability could complement not compete with lecturers.

At times, members of even the noisiest groups of lecture-goers focused their attention on speakers and mentally formulated their own response, which they afterward recorded in their diaries or letters, alongside reports of audience and group reaction. These post-lecture accounts may not entirely reflect what the writer was thinking at the moment the performance was experienced, but they show how the event resonated with one's larger life story and the surrounding social world. Record keepers strove to capture the gist of their response to give their correspondents access to it and, through diaries, to allow their readers and themselves to reexperience it. Thus individual response inevitably rested upon a social foundation, especially since many lecture-goers knew they would write down their thoughts afterward. In other ways, extrinsic influences shaped the way auditors experienced performances: diverse literacy levels, differing knowledge bases, unique backgrounds, and specific, internalized communities of family, friends, and neighbors to which any personal interpretation paid respects. This community came into view as individuals listened, thought of other people, and invited them to respond in conversations and letters to what was heard. "I wished that my dear teacher had been there to hear the lecture," Charlotte Forten reflected during a talk on early New England clerical life; "she had a most enthusiastic love for the old Puritan fathers, and I knew she would appreciate it."[23] In this way, performance-goers ventured out with recollections of loved ones ever carried within.

Responses, however, were not idiosyncratic, for they shared a common vocabulary. It consisted of spare words or terse phrases critically summing up performances and rendered with often space-saving precision. Even writers who went on at length prefaced their reviews with the shorthand. Performances could be "very good," "pretty good," "liked very well," "first rate," "most splendid," "excellent," or "one of the best" ever heard. Variants of "interesting," however, were most often used, with "transcendentally interesting" being a high compliment. Like "reading" (as opposed to "studying"), listening to a performance was ideally effortless. As one iron-foundry clerk explained of an antislavery lecturer, "He was very interesting & held me very still for about two hours."[24] One could hardly "master" an orally delivered text like a written work that was studied, for words rushed by with little hope of recapturing them. Most auditors therefore had lower expectations of retention. Performances, after all, were respites from work and study which promised refreshment, moral or spiritual uplift, and useful information imparted in an entertaining fashion.

As easily digestible an interesting lecture might be, however, it was not to be confused with an insipid or abstruse one. At the opposite end of the spectrum from performances deemed interesting, then, were those that were *"foolish,"* "silly," "not interesting," "dull," "tedious," or "dry" enough to send auditors who "could not stand it" scurrying out of the hall or wishing they were at home with a good book. Victims of boring performers often candidly described their inattentiveness or flights of fancy. A less-than-interesting declamation pushed a teenager into erotic fantasy. "In Imagination," he scratched in secret code in his diary, "My bodily presence being at the Howard," where "Madame Turnes a splendid rider" displayed her "Glorius form so full the curious could see her bubbys quite well."[25] He joined with his imagined ogling crowd, to witness, at least to him, a much more interesting performer.

Responses often clustered around what maintained interest, for once established, engagement with performers followed. But what, exactly, engaged the audience member? Many of the same things that pulled in entire crowds, such as well-written scripts, expressive delivery, and, of course, new ideas. These three criteria were complementary and often inextricable, and they all were rooted in a good manuscript.

As producers of everyday literature themselves, auditors could spot well-crafted writing. Ideal texts for delivery were "neat" (meaning concise), "truly finished and sensible," and "evinced much thought." They were also "focused and scholarly" and "showed great research & considerable ingenuity in arranging . . . material." "It was quite a learned work and must have cost him great labour," a politician's wife remarked after a lecture "on the origin of the Nations of Europe, and the formation of the English language." Listeners valued a lucid, tightly woven, conventionally organized text with a strong, logical thesis, over "desultory" or "aimless productions." Many Transcendentalist lectures, in stressing intuition over reason, particularly challenged convention—so much so that one delivered by Emerson in Worcester was, to John Park at least, "chiefly a disconnected series of vague dogmas & paradoxical sentences, wrapped up in . . . imposing diction." One young woman, after hearing Emerson "on the subject of Worship," simply threw up her hands and admitted, "I have no idea of what I think of his lecture." A Portland lawyer forgave the writer's eccentricities, his "epigramatic style" in this case, in lieu of his "brilliant thoughts."[26] He distinguished between argument, construction, and research on the one hand and quality of ideas on the other. The two were usually accorded different critical standards.

However disagreeable, lecturers' ideas and presentation provoked speculation about their originality. "I guess he wrote his lecture after reading the 'Childs 1st book of History,'" a schoolteacher condescendingly surmised while listening to a former Massachusetts governor's lecture. Other hearers compared styles of writing to make critical judgments. "It was evidently written in a hurry and was not what it should have been," a college student commented upon a lecture. "I remember a little book I used to own, called the Child's Good manners Book," he continued, "which was brought to my mind by Mr Stone's address filled with ridiculous, starched, unnatural rules in relation to superiors, inferiors & equals—just such distinctions of caste arising from *wealth* &c." Even lecturers who could easily draw upon unique experiences, such as a veteran of the first U.S. diplomatic mission to China, were charged with having nothing new to say. His lecture on that nation was "much the same we have heard & read in the newspapers" was one attendee's verdict, while another griped, "the principal information he gave, and much more in detail, may be found in the two volumes of John Francis Davis's 'History of China and its Inhabitants.'" Firsthand information clearly did not necessarily translate into originality, yet this quality was not always necessary for enjoyment. "[W]e all went into town to hear Mr Emerson lecture on Genius & Talent," an architect's wife wrote of a night out with dinner party guests. "It was a very pleasant lecture, though with nothing especially original in it." Eloquent speakers might modify the demand for novel material. "Heard a blind man lecture," a farmer's daughter wrote to her sister of an encounter with the Methodist U.S. Senate chaplain; "most of the History I knew before, but it made it more interesting, I thought."[27] If the treadworn information did not instruct, hearing it from a blind speaker did.

Audiences longed for new ideas, not hackneyed thoughts. "New ideas in abundance" was the phrase a country schoolmaster used to characterize a stimulating lecture on "the Macbeths, Lord and Lady." Fresh insights culled from performers accumulated like coins in a mental storehouse of intellectual profit. "Gain many good ideas," Martha Osborne Barrett, then a schoolteacher, commented after hearing a phrenologist speak on "the training and development of the selfish and social organs in children," as if she had come home with treasures. "I learned a great many useful things about the laws of health which I knew not of before and which I would not forget," a mill woman exclaimed to her sister of one physiology lecturer. A farmwife likewise learned something new from a lecturer about history. "He paid a passing compliment to the Goths (calling them an abused people) as instruments for . . . establishing, or rather planting the seeds of liberty," she reported, pointing out the novelty: "It [was the] last thin[g] I ever thought of the Goths, but I suppose it was [becau]se I [gave them no] thought at all." Fresh ideas could multiply, as auditors thoughtfully responded to them. This was especially true for heated contemporary issues, like woman's "proper" sphere or slavery. A textile magnate's daughter, for one, posed a lecturer's ideas on women against her own. "According to Mr Dana's ideas a woman's sphere is but a limited one; or rather instead of playing an active part she is doomed to spend her days in indolence & ease," she scratched in her diary after hearing lawyer-litterateur Richard Henry Dana Sr. "In my humble opinion she shld exert due influence over those around her & give her opinion as should a responsible being," she countered, conceding, "However I may be wrong." By confronting contradictory ideas other listeners learned to make keen distinctions. "[T]he lecturer spoke eloquently of the haytians," and "I was beginning to think him an earnest friend of freedom," abolitionist Charlotte Forten wrote of antislavery speaker Benjamin C. Clark, "when he proved to be a colonizationist and then a very decided and unpleasant 'change came o'er the spirit of my dream.'"[28] Upon such shattered dreams, however, personal convictions often grew stronger and thrived.

Part of the speaker's art was to sway listeners' sympathies through not only well-written words but also inspiring delivery. Eloquent speakers were as much admired as skillful authors. While auditors could locate "an able writer" beneath "a fluent but not graceful speaker," they thought that words were given more power when delivered well. Coarseness obviously was not conducive to listening, but neither was coolly rendered, pedantic argumentation. "Though he aims at the orator he does not rise above the rhetorician," a minister's wife gibed at ponderous historian George Bancroft's lecture on the Weltgeist. Public speaking, at its best, mirrored everyday talk. "The true standard of public lecturing," John Park declared, was "a person in merely earnest conversation." Genuineness and intimacy lay at the core of other positive traits, such as sounding simple, being "[s]mooth-flowing-graceful," having "force & good emphasis" or "animation," and, especially, exhibiting "eloquence." The opposite was "too boistrous," "ranting & bawling," "dry," "*ostentatious* or *commanding,*" and "too pompous," along with speaking too loudly or softly, overusing slang, or erring in pronunciation or grammar. The occasional "droll mistake" among foreign-language speakers was easily forgiven, but for native speakers, lapses could prove fatal. "Last evening I attended an Antislavery lecture in the meeting house," Mary Pierce Poor explained of a Baptist minister; "was very much surprised & even shocked at many things he said, it was some of it quite low & almost vulgar. He seems not to be a man of education, using such expressions as aery one for either, *them men,* &c." Even highly educated lecturers could reveal vernacular roots. "I went out Friday eve[g] to Mr. Norton's Astronomical Lecture," Persis Sibley Andrews jotted; "—highly scientific—but he mixed in some other matters where he *exposed* his *'bringing up.'"*[29] Lecturers had to run a gauntlet of finely discriminating hypercritics.

But obvious transcendence of lower-class upbringing, race, or educational deprivation, could deeply inspire listeners, too. "I never heard a piece read with better pronunciation and emphasis," a Providence industrialist commented after a factory girl of Irish extraction read some poetry during his classroom visit to a "public Evening School"; her "style" he claimed, "would have done credit to any person of the most cultivated education. Indeed, I never heard a piece read with better pronunciation and emphasis, and judicious expression of tones of feeling." African American speakers could also receive strong commendations amid more tempered criticism. "[S]he does not distinctly sound the s," an audience member noted of Mary Webb, the black public reader, though he deemed her "quite graceful in her manners & with a good voice." Likewise, Persis Sibley Andrews declared that black physician David J. Peck lecturing on psychology epitomized good speaking: "Elegance itself," as she described him.[30]

Because of the era's strict proscriptions against women speaking in public, the very sight of them at the podium sparked an immediate negative reaction. Women speakers' messages therefore were often muffled by audience members' ideas about propriety. Some verbally assaulted the women. One man complained of "'crabbed old maids going around asserting their rights'" while abolitionist and women's rights activist Lucy Stone was lecturing, "but she let that pass with dignified silence." Auditors paid more attention, it seems, to the speaker's comportment, style of dress, and femininity, or lack thereof. Of Stone, one rural schoolteacher proclaimed, "It was a novel sight, to see a woman rise up before such an audience—with all the *undaunted courage,* which we are accustomed to think belongs exclusively to the sterner portion of mankind." "I believe that she is *out* of *woman's proper sphere,"* was her judgment, but she conceded, "I presume she is sincere in thinking her duty calls her into the field." She was hardly unusual in her ambivalent assessment; women could be admired for their passionate crusading and denounced for their brazen defiance of gender norms. A shopkeeper's granddaughter pondered the mission of one Indian rights activist in similar terms: "She was really eloquent, & although I should be unwilling that a lady should plead in public, I should like much to have her gain the private ear of some influential characters." Even women who spoke in public themselves, like the aforementioned Universalist preacher Eunice Cobb, were not free of contradictions on the issue. "Do tell me Sis Brown, what you are lecturing upon," she inquired of her friend in Cleveland, Ohio. "Will you not come on to Boston, and let us hear your voice in our midst? Here woman has a 'right' to utter her own sentiments, without fear of molestation." Yet Cobb, on another occasion that year, decried physician Harriot Kezia Hunt's visceral exposition at Boston's Female Physiological Institute. "Miss Hunt occupied the time," Cobb complained, "and so perfectly repulsive is she, to me, in *every* respect, I do not enjoy going there at all." Some women's chastising response to women speakers could sputter into inarticulateness. "I had the—not pleasure, [(]I hardly know what you might call it) of hearing Miss A[bby] Kelly of . . . Lynn, & another woman get up & make speeches!" a befuddled farmer's daughter jotted down, referring to a prominent abolitionist. Like many other auditors, she did not know what to make of it. A "modest & graceful" or feminine woman lecturer might allay suspicions of gender radicalism, however. An antislavery lecture "from a young Lady of New York" led a rural Vermonter to declare, "She was really quite eloquent and as she did not meddle with politics, I pronounced it quite supportable." But he gave as his final reckoning, "She was pretty and intelligent."[31]

Male lecturers, too, were critically eyed for their looks, but more for the way they matched the content of their presentations. A "captivating appearance" worked well for one male politician who, according to an observer, "produced a decided effect" visually. Charlotte Forten melded poet James Russell Lowell's "extremely unpretending" "personal appearance" with "the great beauty of his thoughts and language." Physical oddity, however, could turn otherwise attractive speakers hideous. "[He] seemed to labor hard in the delivery of his discourse—owing . . . to his physical constitution," one woman opined, "being very bulky and rather corpulent." A schoolgirl criticized orator Edward Everett because "His gestures . . . are infantine, [and] [h]e moves about too much." Many listeners, though, discerned speakers' intellects beneath the off-putting façade, as did Forten when she described Emerson as "a very peculiar-looking man" but added that he "is a fine lecturer." Likewise, a schoolteacher remarked, upon seeing lecturer Henry Giles, "There is a perfect contrast between his body and mind. He is a dwarf indeed—hunchbacked but has a mind worthy of the fairest tenemant of clay."[32] Cosmetics mattered little; good ideas usually shone through.

The importance of visual presentation was underscored by the use of props that could focus audience attention. John Park was highly amused by freedom fighter and author Christophoros Plato Castanis, who at his lecture "wore his Greek military costume, and the identical sword belonging to Lord Byron." Diarists especially relished recording lectures on anatomy featuring illustrative artifacts such as a "manikin," "Skeleton," "representations in wax, of the various organs of the body," or a "paper man." One mill woman marveled at a physiology lecturer who "had many splendid manakins which he took to pieces and explained." These often startled viewers both for detailing how "'fearfully and wonderfully made'" the human body was and for their workmanship. "It seemed to me it must have taken a *lifetime* to prepare and make that most perfect representation of the human form," a Maine woman attending a medical lecture excitedly relayed to a friend; "every part *correctly colored* also, every blue vein, every ligament and bone was fearfully natural—the principal point to which he directed attention, last night, was the use and power of the *muscles.*" She probed the model's make up, consisting of "*the pulp used* for making paper, dried and *hardened,* and *varnished,*" and ended by quoting the speaker: "[I]t is . . . 'a most perfect representation of your own bodies, with the exception of the *screws,* these *nature needs not for her handywork.*'" Hokey models, by contrast, could be devastatingly boring, as one newspaperman's wife found: "Buchanans lecture was full last night but dull, consisting of an expose of his particular views of Phrenology illustrated by skulls lighted up [in] the manner little boys use pumpkins."[33]

Experiments also made for more interesting performances. Demonstrations of gasses, electricity, machinery, galvanization, condensation, and mesmerism were commonly featured at scientific presentations. Insofar as they involved audience participation they made speakers' words palpable. During a lecture on "the solidification of carbonic acid gas," a doctor "distributed the gas among the audience in the form of pure hard snow." Some phrenologists administered "a public examination of heads after the lecture," as in the case of Martha Osborne Barrett, whose cranium was scrutinized by noted phrenologist L. N. Fowler—"'I have a dense brain'" was the verdict (fig. 10.1). Phrenology had gained some legitimacy, but the jury was still out on mesmerists. While a country schoolmaster deemed a lecture by one a "humbug," he thought the hypnotist's painless tooth extractions "quite successful." Seeing was also believing for one clerk: "A very considerable number of the audience was influenced, by the speaker's *lecture* alone," he claimed, "so as to be completely under mesmeric subjection, and several individuals were led, some by the hand and others by the will to the stage where very wonderful results were produced," including yet more dental procedures.[34] Pseudoscientific miracles stimulated audience escape fantasies, whether of control over others or simple surcease from suffering.

As much as human subjects became entangled in hypnotic demonstrations, well-drawn illustrations proffered excitement to audiences. "Illuminated Diagrams," "transparent views," or models of historical places, enhanced verbal descriptions with visual images. Some illustrations were even printed on tickets for referral during lectures; an invalid venturing out held one such stub sporting a "map of the Holy Land" in her hand at one exhibition, "so we can have it before our eyes all the while [the speaker] is describing it." Viewers approached these, like they did props and experiments, skeptically, and even relished detecting hoaxes, however transparent. Writing home during a visit to Bangor, Mary Pierce Poor bore witness to one such travesty. "One of *his* (the lecturers) illuminated diagrams representing a street in ancient Babylon, exactly represented a part of Washington street, Boston, the Old South Church rearing its venerable head in the distance,"

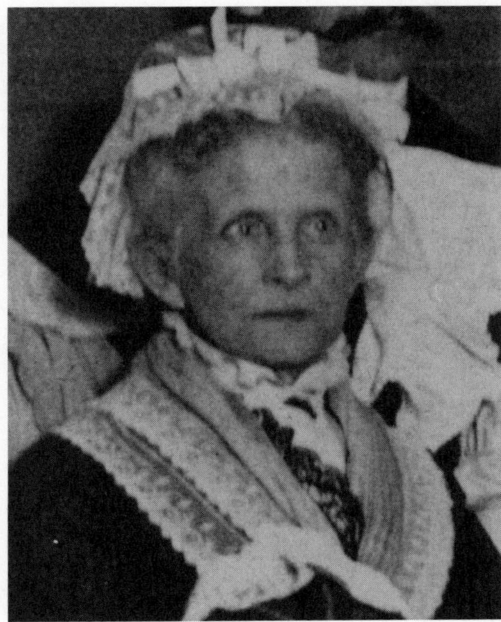

Fig. 10.1 ✦ Martha Osborne Barrett, pictured here in old age, once had her head examined by famed phrenologist L. N. Fowler at one of his lectures. Photograph of Martha Osborne Barrett, 1890. Courtesy of the Peabody Historical Society.

she recounted. And the anachronisms only mounted: "In the foreground were two ladies riding on horseback, mounted on *side saddles* with fashionable caps and habits—Beltshazzar's feast was a company of about a dozen men dressed in the Turkish costume, seated in *chairs* around a table covered with a white table cloth." She concluded that "it was nothing but a rid[ic]ulous farce which would not be tolerated in the vicinity of Boston."[35] By implication, it might be tolerated in rural backwaters, so hungry were folks there for mental stimulation and everyday ideas.

Capturing Ideas

Performers' physical traits, visual effects, and verbal delivery helped get ideas across, but once received, auditors above all wanted to hold onto them. As discussed in chapter 2, audience members struggled to write down what they had heard at the first opportunity, but this could only produce dim traces of the performance. Another solution was to seek out written versions of orally delivered texts. One black abolitionist, for example, thought that some ideas proposed in an 1842 lecture refuting the Millerite prediction that the end of the world was nigh would be useful "for discussion before the Adelphic Union Library Association," a Boston

African American literary society. He solicited from the lecturer "the favor of Your allowing me [to] look at those *facts* if you have them in manuscript." Some lecture-goers anticipated published versions of what they heard. Charlotte Forten went to "Mr. Stone's lecture on the 'Song'" and afterward wrote, "I hope these lectures will be published. I want to study them." Relatively few lectures went this route, despite the demand, because once in print the lecture could no longer be delivered orally. Speakers waited as long as possible to publish lectures in order to milk the circuit. After all, paid lecturers made more money this way than from publishing the same material.[36] From the audience's perspective, however, printed versions both gratified lecture-goers with a permanent record and reached a readership that missed hearing the original delivery.

Correspondence was the best way to nail down what one heard, for, as we discussed earlier, lecture-goers often listened knowing they would have to recap lectures for one's social networks. Writing about lectures allowed friends and family not attending to receive the same ideas as the audience did. One woman, for example, gave the gist of two of archeologist Francis L. Hawks's lectures on American antiquities in a long letter to a friend. "He cannot, he says, suppose God recreated animals for this Continent," she reported, "and there is no other manner of their arriving here, the passage across the Behring Strait being too cold." Those on the receiving end were usually glad to get this kind of report given the rarity of some appearances. "You give us very pleasant accounts of the lectures you attend," an attorney acknowledged of his daughter's letters, "and I doubt not they will be the means of very valuable additions to your stock of useful information—and will give you a good idea of the style of thought and expression of the most eminent literary men of the city." By exchanging anecdotes and fuller accounts of lectures, correspondents could widen their ken of fresh ideas. Folks in proximity to performances who did not attend almost felt obligated to apologize to interested correspondents who wanted feedback. "I was sorry I did not go that I might give you some account of it," a farmwife informed her husband the day after Buck Oowatie's 1832 Cherokee fund-raising tour reached her town; "but [I] hope those who were there will do it."[37] So predictable were letters about a good lecture that she could rely on others' reports.

Of course, many conversations took place while lectures were still fresh in mind. People returning often told stay-at-homes what they missed. "Rebecca has just come in from the Lyceum, and gives me glowing accounts of Mr Judd's lecture that [I] feel almost provoked that I did not go," Mary Pierce Poor, inhibited by a particularly frigid night in Bangor, lamented over not hearing the Transcendental novelist. "But Rebecca says she would not think of the cold after such a lecture." Realizing that glowing ideas could melt even the hardest snow, she exclaimed,

"Behold the triumph of mind over matter!" Once at home, attendees greeted nighttime social callers with the latest news from the lecture hall. "[F]ound Mr Champlain here," Sarah Jocelyn recorded after returning from a New Haven lecture with her date. "Tisdale came in—made a few remarks on the lecture." Being well immersed in the day's main literary experience, post-performance callers naturally emphasized related topics; after hearing one of "Proff Nuttal[l]'s lecture at the Odeon" in Boston on botany, a clerk and his nephew sought out more information by visiting a neighbor: "On our return from lecture, called at Mrs Langley's in Bennet St. to see a beautiful cactus, which she brought from Cambridge Port." While Child's eyes were treated to a rare botanical specimen, the visit gave him a chance to fill his host's ear with what he had just heard. Conversations could extend into the following days or weeks as auditors dropped by. "Mr Frenchs [daughter] Mary came over for an hour," a businessman explained a day after hearing abolitionist Wendell Phillip's lecture in Hartford. "Lent Mr French Toussaint L'Ouvertures life by Dr Beard—Very glad to find that . . . Lecture last evening had very materially diminished Mr Frenchs admiration of Napoleon Bonaparte." Both the borrowed book and the discussion related to the antislavery talk.[38] The chain of spoken words, from performer to listener, and from listener to discussion groups, was broken only by time, as ephemeral performances faded from memory. In the aftermath, interpersonal relations, thus furthered, remained firm.

Conclusion

As we have seen here and in chapter 2, auditors found ways to render ephemeral performances more permanent. Transcriptions of half-recalled words and once vibrant sentiments about performances filled pages of diaries and correspondence. In them, we hear not only barely audible utterances of eloquent and dull speakers alike but also the responses of ordinary people to those ideas and their delivery. We also discern the social ambience surrounding attendance logistics—invitations, tickets, transportation, and ancillary entertainments—all prompting interactions that, like shavings to a magnet, clustered around the main attraction. During performances, social dramas played out before the eyes of the speaker, who, perhaps unaware of the exchange of spyglass glances, or muffled giggles, went on as if all ears were attuned and all eyes were riveted to the podium or stage. Of course, many times, everyone was catching every word and pondering every new idea as a collective whole that could burst forth at opportune moments in audible response. At other times, the audience member defied group opinion or drifted away in imagination to another time and place where familiar faces beckoned or emotions soared.

Transcriptions and written responses provided only shadowy glimpses of true experience, and, accordingly, auditors yearned for more permanent records of fleeting literary events. While published versions allowed listeners to study what the ear could only briefly take in, they also materially expressed evanescent speech—no other evidence retold the tale in so manifest a form. Ticket stubs, sometimes tipped into diaries or other texts of life, seldom elicited reminiscence of a night out at the lyceum.

Unlike tickets, however, reading materials—books, tracts, Bibles, periodicals, newsclippings, and, especially, the full array of texts of life—offered never-ending literary experience. Each time they were studied, read, rendered orally, lightly perused, or shown to guests, the texts were revived and reexperienced and so were the social relations surrounding items: their original donor, first oral reading, and genealogy of borrowers, lenders, and inheritors. With a printed text's use and countless reuse, its social meaning deepened such that a single imprint could stand for generations of users. Although they were no less socially embedded, performances came and went, like a day in a life. Recollections refused to cling easily to such ephemeral spoken texts. But writings could live on forever and with them, memories—or so it seemed to those who once created, possessed, and inevitably relinquished to "Old Mortality" their cherished literary objects.[39]

Chapter 11

Social Imprints: Reception of Books and Periodicals as Objects

George W. Stacy, one-time printer of the short-lived *Groton Herald,* had long moved on to other ventures when local antiquarian Samuel A. Green sent him a missive asking if he was willing to sell any back issues he had. The paper having failed in 1830 after only one year, as did many, he was eager to part with reminders of his back file. "As it is a memento of *'hard times'* to the printer, and seems to bring to mind hard work without a bit of joy," Stacy assured him, "you shall have it for $100 which will pay the expense of binding." While sifting through the musty piles to prepare them for sale, he snuck a glance here and there, and, finally, became himself fully enthralled. Five days later the deal was off. "Excuse my weakness, as well as apparent indecision," he began a note to Green. He explained: "In looking over the 'Herald' which I was led to do, after the receipt of your line, I have found so many mementoes of the past, that I am rather unwilling to part with this volume." The reason was not craft pride, but something more intimate: "I find the record of my first union with a loved companion a native of Groton, who has gone to the spirit land." Instead of selling his precious possession, he offered "a loan of the papers," which Green, himself born in that town, could read at a nearby establishment upon promising to "preserve the file safe."[1] For Stacy, printed words about his departed spouse increased the newspaper's value well beyond its market worth. Fond memories transformed its associations with hard times to those of close relations. What had changed his mind, once so filled with disdain for the paper bearing his imprint, was the more compelling human trace upon its pages.

Publishers' imprints began to turn into social ones the moment they were used by people reading them, displayed on library shelves for visitors to see, lent and borrowed, given away as gifts, or simply cherished as mementos. Not just industrial products for quick consumption, imprints acquired traces of social life in palimpsest fashion, as layers of use accumulated. Vestiges of wear and tear branded the pages, as did marginalia, inscriptions, or defacements. Added leaves of human design, such as dried flowers or clippings, might be tipped into books. And there were less visible tiers of social meaning—traces of times items were lent, read aloud to guests, brought along on a picnic, or tossed into a bundle for shipping. These can be reconstituted through records left by people, such as George Stacy, whose imprints grew so dense with social meaning as to invite emotional and intellectual response to them.[2]

Because literary items were so amenable to human manipulation and social interpretation, people cherished them for their substance as well as their spirit. The care—in the form of maintenance, repair, and display—that these folks expended upon their books, periodicals, and even clippings was proof enough of their value. At times, however, the material object was prized for its inherent properties as much as its social significance. Its elements—paper, ink, bindings, typeface, paint, frontispieces, gilt edges, even jewels—might be savored by beholders. Some people so admired bookmaking that they emulated the craft. The flourishes, such as bindings, covers, drawings, paintings, and mastheads, which everyday writers added to texts of life, further mimicked publishers' products.

As both substance and symbol, commodity and concept, material and memento, few other cultural products were as highly esteemed for their varied meanings. Whether to contemplate books for their beauty or to consecrate them as storehouses of memories, their users seldom separated literary form from social authenticity. Thus they evened out any imbalance between symbolic value and material worth. Cheap ephemeral forms, such as newspapers and clippings, were often enhanced with bindings or placed in decorative scrapbooks. Shabby but beloved books were repaired, covered, and given new life on elegant bookcase shelves. Conversely, expensive and sumptuous editions gained social import when they were inscribed, given as gifts, shown to visitors, or loaned to neighbors. The "old and valuable book" similarly was treasured like an old friend that had traveled far and wide. True, literary users unevenly portioned out their affections upon certain items, yet they usually erred in favor of embracing an imprint's human history rather than its material façade. Seldom did literary aficionados entirely divide their attention, or their consciousness, between bibliographic descriptors and social meaning. The physical object became the embodiment of socioliterary experience.[3]

This chapter examines how people received literature as both material object and social artifact. While New Englanders were not blind to literary objects' monetary worth as possessions, they commonly accorded to them values based on visual elegance, age, rarity, and, especially, the ability to evoke memory. After all, a book or periodical could acquire meaning as one returned to it repeatedly over a lifetime and marked the difference and similarity between prior and present biographical associations. Moreover, as they passed over time through successive users' hands, literary articles acquired generational associations and thus became repositories of broader social memory. As such, memory became the most social of all sources of value. First, we explore the diverse values users placed upon literary items and then move on to practical responses to valued objects as expressed through activities, like caring for and maintaining literature as well as storing and sheltering it. As we will see, responses to literary objects emerged from beholding or envisioning them as part of the dense social networks they coursed through or as implicated in literary socialization. This kind of meaning making did not necessarily relate to words on the page, but rather, simply, to the artifact itself.

Meanings of Literary Value

In light of this meaning making involving artifact and memory, New Englanders generally conceived of the books and periodicals they owned as a form of social, not monetary, capital accumulation. While it is true that books were relatively expensive luxury items and that large home libraries were priceless investments, literature nonetheless fell into a special category of value that transcended cash equivalency. Hence, it is not surprising that children were taught to regard literary items apart from other commodities among which they might have to select. "Freddy chose books instead of Fire Crackers," a proud father recorded after a gift-bearing relative tested the boy's self-restraint. Buying a book was seen as making an enduring commitment, and its cost potentially was a lifelong investment. "How much books cost!" schoolgirl Mary Pierce Poor moaned to her parents after purchasing textbooks. "I have been obliged to give $1.37 for a book today, but it is one which will be of use to me through life."[4]

The social uses of literature help explain why families with limited incomes struggled so hard to own books and periodicals. Even Charles Cobb's dirt farm family owned, by his reckoning, literary possessions that included several music books and ledgers together worth about thirteen dollars, along with other cheap books among "thousands of little things that cost a ninepence apiece" and a bound run of Philadelphia's *Saturday Evening Post*—"This is the best and cheapest paper we know of, and we must have a paper," he once explained. Libraries of poorer and even middling folk were similar in that they had a few inexpensive titles dotted by perhaps one or two costly books, such as an heirloom treasure or a rich family

Bible. Exceptions were always evident, of course; one Beverly shoemaker evidently owned a large set of books from which his sister's literary friend borrowed; and we already saw in chapter 2 printer and fish-yard worker Enoch Hale's extensive library—so large he devised a catalogue to keep track of it. How did this material show up in households that could ill afford it? Clearly, many factors besides income were at work. Inheritances, gifts, and long-term loans could suddenly expand a paltry collection. Conversely, sudden losses through theft or fire also skewed correlations between a library's size, its quality, and the owner's income. Of course, downward mobility or the inevitable "retrenchment" accompanying financial hard times might stanch a library's growth. People reflected upon such fluctuations when they recorded their own excursions up and down the economic ladder, as did one impoverished rural Granite Stater. Having been left behind to fend for himself when his family moved to Michigan, he could barely buy food and school books during college, when he got by on a librarian's meager salary. Much later, having a law degree in hand and a well-established practice, he measured his success by the size of his library. Calling the previous year "quite useful & profitable" in bringing him "nearly four thousand dollars from legal & professional services, and seven or eight hundred from other sources," he noted, "My library has increased by more than one hundred valuable books, some of which I have read carefuly, and all of them looked over."[5] He valued his library not only for its size but also for its intellectual worth and use value.

The aim was, after all, to read, even study, one's books. Therefore, rich and poor alike wanted only books "of consequence enough to be put in your library" and so purchased them selectively. One voyaging Bostonian accordingly "directed" a Jewish immigrant toward two essential books he should purchase first: Joseph Addison's *Spectator* and Hugh Blair's *Lectures on Rhetoric.* Such books served as building blocks. "[E]very book assists and does its respective part in the formation of a library," a novice engineer opined; "and I trust that ere I am many years older I shall . . . have a respectable looking if not a select library, and trust that many of their contents may be transferred to my vacant mind." One newlywed clerk, too, thought patience and discrimination were key. "Most of our library is composed of Books of a Moral character of which kind we have a great number," he wrote. "We now need to make a good selection [of] some good histories & Scientific works." He continued, "However the world was not built in a day, neither can nor expect to obtain with our present means, a complete library in a day."[6] The denial was only temporary.

Literary deprivation afflicted most people during certain life stages and it often signaled being cut off from society. As a first mate with insubstantial earnings, a lonely John R. Congdon despaired of getting even a newspaper to remind him of the types of reading material commonly available back home. While anchored at Mobile one Christmas Day, he recorded: "I . . . sent by [one of our men] 10 cts to buy me NY or Boston news paper that I might have something to take up my mind this PM, when he came back he said he could not get one less that 25 cts, and I am sure I could not afford that." After receiving a care package from home, one poor minister's wife, who "in dread of debts" refrained from "taking one or two papers or reviews," wrote to her wealthier mother about the social value found in the bundle: "Thanks dear Mother for those papers. I read with interest about Uncle Joseph—& I only wish you had sent a dozen more for papers & books are *treasures* to us both." Even once-prosperous academy teacher John Park was forced to give up some subscriptions when the Panic of 1837 unsettled his finances. "Having taken Newspapers for nearly forty years, I find the discontinuance of all mine at the close of the year rather a privation, & hope it will not be always necessary," he wrote. Fortunately, his son resubscribed "for the Courier and Messenger, to July 1st as a birthday present," and he was able to keep in touch with the world as presented in two dailies from Boston, his former longtime home.[7] Whenever he read them, he would see his son's imprint and value them on "account of the donor."

Bargain hunting was one way to stave off literary privation for folks with limited means. Bargains were always relished in an era when books were often referred to as luxuries, so purchasers could easily recognize, as one diarist put it, "what Yankees call a good *speck.*" His was "the Biographical Dictionary, bound in calf, worth 4 dollars," which was thrown in an old barrel with other miscellaneous articles all bought "for *four pence.*" It was easy to find used books like these among sundry other items, sold at private auctions, "Library Auction[s]," or at flea markets. At a book auction house in Lewiston, Maine, one mill worker usually found a good speck. His best buys were "'The school boy' by Charles Dickens cost five cents," originally at twelve and a half cents, and, at half off list price, "The history of the hen fever at .50," a recently published humorous account of the introduction of boutique chickens into America. He bought his books one at a time, but when purchased in lots, a single item could be very cheap indeed. At "Leonards sale of Books" near Boston, a gaslight engineer bought "50 of which I purchased in one lot for 6¢ per volume." But the buyer had to beware in such cases, because there was no telling what was included. A Hartford evangelical located within the mass he purchased at auction a "book whose tendency I could not approve." Because he lived in an extended household of twelve members whose ages ranged from six to seventy, he feared such material might fall into the wrong hands, so he "destroyed it, that it might never waste precious time or be the occasion of evil." Evidently, buyers of these grab bags had no chance to inspect them. "Some of them," he admitted, referring to the selections, "I did not know enough of to place them in my library without examination."[8] Old, used, outmoded, and "immoral" books, no matter how cheap, were not a good buy if they diminished a home collection's social capital.

Because readers invested so much personal and social value in literary artifacts, they believed that their form should ideally suit their deeper significance. For example, crude books—usually cheap, small-sized editions—were affordable but poor encasements for meaningful texts of life. "What an awful looking book this is," a mariner's daughter scribbled while writing the day's events in her Marsh's Pocket Diary. As much as size, an attractive binding elevated a valued book's appearance. Samuel May Jr. was certain that the "elegantly bound" French translation of Frederick Douglass's autobiography "will rejoice his eyes." Beyond the binding, a book "printed in an elegant style" could also be admired for its comeliness. One Irish immigrant ordered up from the old country a special Catholic Bible fit to be an heirloom, "elegant in paper binding, and type . . . [and] plates." It was a format worthy of recording a family's record of births and deaths. A book's elegant dressing, according to some folks, enhanced the reading experience, and for that purpose alone, quality bibliographic features were sometimes taken into consideration when purchasing books for other people. One seminarian, who anticipated a bookish life "read[ing] together sitting side by side" with his future wife, explained his book selection method: "you know my peculiar extravagance—I take care always to get such editions that I can never become dissatisfied on the appearance of any other; for I know that to you as well as to myself there must be an increased satisfaction in reading an elegantly printed book." Charlotte Forten, a prodigious reader, wholeheartedly agreed. Upon receiving "an English copy of Longfellow's poems" from her teacher, she exclaimed, "The engravings, the printing and the binding are executed with the greatest elegance, and enhance, if it can be enhanced, the fascination of the poetry."[9]

More was obviously at work than charming veneers in increasing the pleasure of reading. Elegant books, epitomized by "the attractive form of English editions—large print and clear paper," as described by one sojourner in the Far East, were also easier on the eyes. Small or blurry print on coarse paper made for a cheaper edition that strained vision. Large-print editions were indeed available to folks with failing eyes; one ninety-year-old read the life of Christ in "Large Letter press"; issued in numbers, it ran to about "Eight hundred Pages . . . of Quarto size." The larger the print, the more space it took up on the page, resulting in more and larger pages that, taken together, amounted to more expense. One need only compare the 1844 English edition of Charles Dickens's *Christmas Carol,* replete with hand-colored plates, engravings, and 166 sixteen-centimeter pages of text, with the cheap, unadorned Harpers' edition, which squeezed the same amount of text into 31 pages—less than a fifth the length of its English counterpart. One woman who acquired "Dickens Christmas Carol, in the Harpers cheap literature edition," informed her son; "you who have not seen the nice English edition may like it, but it is enough to make any body sick who *has* seen the other as some folks have—however the story is pretty, print it up as you will." To make matters worse, the cheap editions had small margins which taxed the eyes. But large, clear print framed by wide margins demanded more paper still. However, these could mask a skimpy article passing as a book and so devalued a text. A college student decried Rebecca Theresa Reed's *Six Months in a Convent,* with its "Narrative which might be contained on one page of a respectable newspaper," spread out, with an introduction comprising about one-third, over 192 pages. "By the half of coarse type & large margins, it makes a very respectable book," he concluded.[10] Most of the time, publishers did not need to beef up texts, for many were long, too long, in fact, for a single volume. Readers who valued their eyesight, needless to say, usually favored the same text in several volumes if they could afford them over one compressed edition.

Books that strained the eyes were problem enough, but most newspapers were even worse. Editors crammed as many lines of tiny typeface as possible usually into the standard four-page format, perhaps believing that more copy would best competitors, but the compression led only to eyestrain. "[I]t tires me a little & hurts my eyes, that horrid print of the Times," a boarding school student fussed about her nightly reading duties for her teacher. For seventy-nine-year-old Hannah Hicock Smith, who, as we have seen, sometimes refused to wear her badly needed glasses, some newspapers were undecipherable. "Emily brought Trib.," she inscribed; "not much intelligence in it & so fine print that I cannot read what there is—but it is as good a paper as any I can get if it was readable." Fine print was not always to blame, however. A Quaker journeyman compositor complained that one issue of the *Worcester Daily Spy* "was so poorly printed that I was unable to read some of it"—worn type was often blurry. Whenever periodicals bought new type, sometimes as often as twice a year, they proudly announced the "new dress," yet for readers, new type was more than ornamental. The "new leading" of the *Catholic Observer* noticed by James Healy, or the "new type & press" of the *Oxford Democrat* welcomed by Persis Sibley Andrews, meant an unhampered read as well as a fine finish.[11] Affordable periodicals, as cheap as a penny each, in whatever "dress" they came, were welcomed additions to the library of those unable to buy many books.

One of the physical features garnering much commentary was the book's or periodical's illustrations, for these remained relatively rare, especially before the emergence of fully illustrated monthlies in the 1850s. Perhaps because of their scarcity, responses to these images reflected a limited and simple vocabulary centering on variants of "beautiful," "pretty," "elegant," or "fine." Value resided in rendering ideas beautiful, only secondarily in the reproduction's quality. Thus even reference works could provide visual entertainment, as a businessman recorded: "Got out Websters Dictionary to look at the illustrations." Insofar as some pictures told stories they, too, enchanted readers. One housewife noted, "Have just got the 'Ladies Companion' for May" and immediately added, "It has a beautiful engraving, 'The Young Chief's First Ride.'" Charles Cobb was equally enthralled with the "striking pictures in" a magazine which he picked up while visiting a neighbor. Like him, one elderly woman mentioned only a "beautiful mezzotint portrait" of Scottish geologist Hugh Miller in "the Eclectic Magazine" instead of the articles within. Readers like these seldom pondered interactions between word and image.[12]

It was not that illustrations left the beholder dumbstruck, for they otherwise could spark lively discussions. When a group of hearty seamen got hold of a copy of the *Ladies' Companion,* for example, they extensively debated upon the latest fashions and assayed the effect of constraining undergarments on the female form (fig. 11.1). John Congdon described the incident to amuse his wife, an accomplished seamstress who knew all about corsets and bustles:

> I am in my room writing for my C[ynthia], Mr Hobrook is reading in the Ladies companion[;] there are some beautiful engravings there. One of a young mother with a little girl in her arms reading A B C[.] [T]hey of course made comments on that, which I shall not mention—another of the Fall fashions, they commented on that, on their shapes &c says Mr C take off them traps they will appear quite different. Capt B says what do you call that which sits them out so behind[?] One says bishop another tunic[;] . . . Mr Congdon what do you call it[?] I said I believe some called it bishop other[s] tunic, bishops properly speaking were worn in the sleeves. [H]e said, yes, it is so, if I understand right.[13]

Cynthia Congdon, who would have confirmed her husband's understanding of "bishop sleeves," also made her imprint upon the recorded scene when she later read about it in her husband's journal. And so, social imprints accumulated: the several discussants, the presence of Cynthia in John's mind to inspire him to think the event would interest her, his bemused immortalization of it in his diary, and the final exchange of life writings upon John's return when he and Cynthia could reexperience together this moment and probably chuckle over these old salts' debating high fashion plates on the high seas.

"Every thing *Old Fashioned* has been the new fashion of late years, & this fashion has continued longer than usual," a retired physician's wife concluded in 1840. "People are yet hunting up *old fashioned* articles, some, merely to be in fashion & some to shew ancient splendour which has passed from them." Old books, too,

Fig. 11.1 ✦ The tightly corseted look popular in the 1840s became the topic of conversation for some seamen who mocked this engraving's finely rendered but exaggerated depiction of narrow waistlines. "Fall Fashions for 1840," *Ladies' Companion* 13 (Sept. 1840), opposite 211. Courtesy of the American Antiquarian Society.

were sought simply because of their long life span. Having survived time's ravages, they matured like fine wine, taking on distinctive character in an era of increasing mass production. More new editions than ever were being published on steam-powered presses in runs exceeding the muscle pull of pressmen of yore. Yet many imprints were discarded immediately after being read, as made clear by their omnipresence in train cars at journey's end. New production methods cheapened the look of many books: less durable papers with more pulp content, uniform machine-cut pages, standard edition bindings with cloth rather than leather covers, and, often, typographical compression through less generous leading between lines, smaller margins, tighter and less artful kerning, and lower point sizes. The physical differences between new and old books were thus obvious. Little wonder that "old & valuable" sometimes described ancient volumes as if the two words were synonymous. "The book is very rare & I value it very much," a captain's daughter declared when her uncle gave her an eighteenth-century edition of "'Clark[e]'s Scripture promises.'" These books' rarity charmed observers, who often gave the year of publication (anything older than fifty years was noteworthy in a market seasonally flooded with new titles). One schoolboy, for example, who read his parents' "'Selections from Nature' by St Pierre," stated that "it is very old: being printed in 1799." Books, like people, had genealogies. Tracing them often meant describing age or appearance. While visiting a cousin, a New Hampshire farmer "looked . . .

over" a "Bible that was our Grand Father's, George Abbott, which was printed in London in 1712." He discovered that although "somewhat shattered," it was in remarkably good shape with "but few, if any, whole leaves gone." One did not have to have ancestries inscribed in old books to admire them. At Amsterdam's "Bible Hotel," that was "over three hundred years old," John Congdon saw "one of the first Bibles" printed there and contemplated its producer's dire end: "The poor printer lost his life." Books might summon authors as much as printers. "I should like to see in some magic mirror the man who wrote it, and the apartment in which it was done," John Park's daughter ruminated upon seeing "a superb old quarto missal, highly illuminated" which "bears [the] date 1466." "Perhaps it required many hands; and I think there is internal evidence of more than one artist," she mused. "In some of the miniatures, the expression of the countenances is wonderful; and in the little embellishments of flowers, birds, &c nothing can be more delicate than the work and finish," she marveled. "[T]he coloring and gilding seem to be fresh as ever." She concluded, "If people could not do so many things in the olden time, what they did was done for a 'permanancy,' not a 'temporary.'"[14] Old books expressed their producers' mentality—craftsmen creating for the centuries.

Fine finish, elegant binding, beautiful engravings, or even clear type did not give texts their deepest value, however. While material properties figured in everyday socioliterary practices, symbolic value assigned by users acting within their social universe lent print artifacts more enduring significance. That value most often registered as personal meaning: what made items special beyond their age, rarity, price, and appearance to owners, beholders, or borrowers. Meaning was sometimes idiosyncratic—so singularly fashioned from unique life experiences intersecting with imprints that it escaped even intimates' full comprehension. "I met with this volume among some old books, the other day," a woman explained to her brother; "and though its intrinsic value does not appear to be great it has your name in it, and thinking you may have some association with it I send it to you." Usually, however, even singular associations found meaning only socially, through discussion or correspondence. Within these communications, people negotiated collective response to reading materials as mementoes. Such materials housed memories of gift givers, as described in chapter 5, but also of past homes, childhood, and the deceased; indeed, any kind of remembrance could make its social imprint. Print artifacts also invoked, and at times consummated, ongoing social relations, yet even here charging printed objects with meaning usually took time. The longer they were owned, used, or thought about, the more value they assumed, as one normal school composition underscored: "'Our attachment to every object increases in general with the length of our acquaintance with it.[']"[15] Such meaning might require decades to layer in and ripen, but it could be reaped instantaneously by the very sight or thought of a personally charged printed object.

Memory-rich literary artifacts proved useful in bringing continuity to disrupted lives. Yankees well deserved the peripatetic reputation they had acquired, for they often changed residences to live at a school dormitory or boardinghouse, to travel abroad, to go away to sea, or to seek their fortunes in new towns, states, or countries. First-time brides understood most acutely the pain of permanently departing from childhood homes and kin. Reading materials, which seemed stable amid change because they were portable and ideal vessels of social meaning, reminded wanderers of people, places, and activities from home. Local newspapers, as we have seen in chapter 4, were sent to the uprooted to give them information of doings at home, but sometimes the physical artifact itself sparked past connections. The mere "sight of a Salem paper was really refreshing" to a traveler from that home town. Mary Pierce Poor, away at school, likewise responded to papers from home by conjuring images of domestic activity. "How I wish I could look over Sister Abby's shoulder when she is reading one of neighbor Pierce's newspapers & read a little of the Boston news!" she exclaimed. "I very seldom see a B.[oston] newspaper, & when I do it seems quite like an old friend."[16] The value was in the remembrance.

Because books were so precious as reminders of home and family, sojourners often took with them texts and accompanying insertions. When Cynthia Congdon joined her seafaring husband on an 1852 voyage to California, she left behind her school-aged daughter but brought some books into which her little Mary had tipped some mementoes unbeknownst to her mother. "I took my trunk out and looked at my clothes, to see if they were mouldy," the mother penned about three months after embarking. "I opened a little Hymn book, while looking over my clothes, and the first that met my eye, was Mary's paper baby, that she cut and put there." She paused—"the tears came in my eyes in a moment." As if by incantation, the paper doll immediately summoned the daughter: "It brought the little creature right before me, and home and all its scenes, came into my mind with renewed freshness." So vivid was the apparition that she directly addressed the girl: "Dear little one how glad would I be to see you, and know of your Welfare. God bless you all, and take care of you, and bring us home in safety and Peace." The Congdons did return safely and brought both Mary and her books along on their 1854 voyage.[17]

If books, newspapers, and insertions could invoke thoughts of home, conversely, memories of past residences brought back images of books. When travelers returned to childhood scenes, old books awaited them to refresh memories. "I am at home," a Westering stonemason wrote to a friend during a visit to his former Maine home. "The very desk at which I write, the chair in which I am seated, the pictures that greet my eyes as I raise them for a new thought and the familiar look of the books as they range along the shelves of the time-honored Old

Bookcase," he declared, overwhelmed with nostalgia, "all conspire to bring me back from the care and turmoil of a life of reality into the dreamland of an early home with the aircastles of boyhood's days." After her father died, Mary Pierce Poor avoided visiting her family home precisely because his room for reading and writing would provoke grief. "I feel as if it would be very sad for me to go to Brookline again," she confided to her sister-in-law. "The dear old study seemed so full of Father's presence that I seemed to feel him nearer to me when I was there than I did anywhere else." In most instances, books had been displaced along with the former inhabitant, yet traces of their arrangement within a room could almost magically reappear. "One circumstance struck me as somewhat mystical and was certainly unexpected," John Park revealed to his diary after a stroll in which he happened upon the Boston apartment he long ago left. The "association of former times was so strong," he wrote, "that it obliterated the consciousness of eight years absence, & particularly as I passed my former residence in Mount Vernon, it seemed as certain, that if I entered the house, and should go into the parlours or chambers, I should ^find the furniture, desks and books as they had ^been before my eyes for twenty years."[18] Books on remembered shelves and desks swept through the dustiest mental cobwebs.

Sounds were recaptured, too. Through literature, time travelers tried to remember loved ones' very voices, as in the case of one whaleman's childhood friend soliciting an old essay written by his former schoolmate. "I regret not only your loss, but even the pleasure I have received in society with you in reading those scientifick themes but especially that one which you delivered in the exhibition of the Philo Dramatic society," he wrote of an informal extracurricular club. "I suppose it would be in vain for me to ask a copy of that performance, but I really wish I had one." Echoes of laughter rather than recitation filled Samuel May Jr.'s recollection of a brother-in-law enjoying a comic work, *Obadiah Oldbuck:* "he was mightily amused with it, and used to read it over & over, & sit & shake his sides" in hilarity.[19] Such sensory clarity after years of dormancy testified to social imprints' inexhaustible vibrancy.

Small wonder that books once owned or favored by the deceased were particularly valued. Enoch Hale's first thoughts after his five-year-old sister "[*d*]*ied,* at half past 2 o'clock, this morning" turned to her reading materials as if they would resurrect her. "We bring the book, in which she read her little tales,—she does not claim it—we bring her playthings—but her hand lies motionless. What shall arouse her?" One bereaved woman also located vestiges of a late friend in books. "I shall never look at the volume which interested her, without recalling that which has given to it a tenfold value," she predicted in a sympathy letter. "I love dearly to . . . see every thing to remind me of him," one widow revealed shortly after her husband died, when she discovered his literary footprints everywhere in the house, from storage boxes to the attic. On one occasion she went "up garret with Agnes to clean up a little, found some of dear Henry's school books among my box of books & papers, two were when he was learning book-keeping, 14 years old." Even merest shreds of mundane educational exercises possessed near talismanic power. The lack of literary mementoes, conversely, could long rend the heart. Four years after her father died without specifying the fate of his books in his will, Mary Pierce Poor still felt bereft, for Reverend Pierce's eldest son, an Illinois migrant, had carted off the lion's share of them. "I feel badly about his carrying so many of dearest Father's books out West," she confessed to her sister and unburdened her misery: "How I should have valued them!! I have not one single book that was my father's, with his name written in it in his own hand, but a hymn book & that I value above price." She referred to the late John Park's beloved daughter who had just received his bequest: "When I heard of Mrs Hall's carrying home her portion of her father's books I was too envious." Poor then broke down: "Oh Lucy! my heart is always crying 'My father oh my father shall I *ever* see you again?"[20] A book of his might make his spirit if not his body once again visible.

More anguish surrounded discarded items that, after generations had passed, would have become all the more valuable. An African American–Native American farmer wished he had held on to his maternal grandfather's favorite mid-century periodical, apparently kept by the family after the patriarch's death in Lyme, Connecticut, in 1875. "My Grand father once took a little green-covered magazine called the American Missionary—and I regret very much now, that I never kept—even one of them," the grandson wrote in his memoirs. "There were also many other old relics, that were destroyed, but I am very glad the old Quassia cup, or bitters cup, as we always called it, is still in my possession, as it still makes its own Medicine, with out drugs, as it did more than 100 years ago."[21] The cup might heal the living, but it could not illuminate, as the lost and lamented magazine could have, the mental life of the dead.

Even more than printed possessions, of course, manuscript texts of life, including diaries and letters, could do this. After a son of hers died in Florida, one woman hoped that his belongings, being sent home to Boston, would contain at least one piece in his hand. "His things have been packed up and are on the way here by water," she informed an in-law. "I almost dread to see them, but I hope we may find among his papers something written after his last letter which was several days before his death." Like letters, diaries and poetry held special appeal because they contained the departed's direct mental imprint. Aware of this, some writers explicitly addressed their progeny. So, too, could commonplace books, like the one left by one Connecticut farmer wherein he inscribed, "I leave you here a little book / For you to look upon / That you may see your Fathers face / When he is dead & gone." So closely associated with him was his record of literary experiences—he mentions reading "Novels by Cooper" and the "Works of Washington Irving"—they could stand for his very visage. To underscore for posterity the sincerity of what he wrote, he added, "The following sketches are the result of deep thought and long experience." His descendants could vicariously share his "long experience."[22]

When a literary item came to signal social bonds or to represent the deceased, its text was often less important than its role in life's social dramas. Literary items were valued precisely because they so ably conducted both individual and interpersonal associations. Elegant imprints were not only tokens of human relations but also instrumental in weaving and reweaving them.

Safeguarding Value

Because people so highly esteemed reading matter in so many ways, they carefully preserved and stored it. Methods for covering and repairing pieces of literature circulated within communities like time-tested recipes. Owners who could afford professional conservation enlisted bookbinders using quality material and tools; those who could not, took up needle and thread themselves. Cabinetmakers could be called upon to construct elaborate bookcases to shelter literary items, but most folks hammered together their own shelves and racks for the purpose. The haves and the have-nots shared, however, similar dilemmas of organizing volumes on shelves. Lacking modern library classification schemes, owners had to devise unique arrangements to avoid a hopeless confusion of titles. Just as books fell into disarray, they also fell into danger, especially from the ravages of fire. Overall, the life of a printed artifact—be it book, pamphlet, magazine, newspaper, or even ephemera—and, therefore, its social imprint, was prolonged as long as possible through conscientious safeguarding.[23]

Unsurprisingly, amateur bookbinding was common. "This morning my little Henry Clay came into the office with his new Spelling book, and asked to have it covered," a country doctor wrote of his son. "I put on a strong paper cover, and fastened it with a needle and thread," he explained of his surgery upon unbound pages. The outcome: the lad "was pleased with it, and said, 'we do every thing nice, dont we father?'" As pleased himself, the man gave thanks that his boy had learned to value reading materials enough to want to care for them. "It is said, in heaven, every measure will be full," the father reflected. "It may be so on Earth sometimes with individuals, for my little son appears perfectly happy with his new covered *book.*"[24] The simple operation that had magically transformed printed pages into a "book" hardly required a surgeon's steady hands; folks with far less skill frequently turned their periodicals, newspapers, and manuscripts into books as well.

The idea was not only to fashion a book out of once jacketless printed pages but also to shield valued pages from wrinkling, tearing, dampness, and other signs of wear. "Cover all your books"—such solemn enjoinders as issued by one mother to her daughter echoed throughout New England. Books were sometimes sold at retail or given as presents without hard covers; owners supplied their own encasements or reinforced flimsy paperbacks. Daniel Child, for one, sent "Goodrich's 'Cabinet Library,' presented to the children by their grandfather," sans hard covers, to a Boston bindery, from which it came back as "twenty pretty volumes." Old books could go for rebinding with new or sturdier covers. Binders might be variably entrusted with "sacred rolls" and other religious texts, along with bunches of newspapers, magazines, sheet music, illustrations, school catalogues, pamphlets, or tracts. Over a seven-month period, one mill worker carried his issues of *Ballou's Pictorial* and *Waverley* magazine to local bookbinders, while one poor neophyte schoolteacher had her "[Godey's] Lady's Books bound." When she retrieved one volume, she dubbed the result "a delicate boquet." Inexpensive paperbacks were in this way ennobled by the casing that turned them into beautiful editions—at least in beholders' eyes. Any number or combination of ephemera, sometimes cut to achieve uniform size or left untrimmed, were bound together by professionals to make unique "texts from texts."[25] By having the discrete items bound together into books, one could devise a library from miscellany.

Sending inexpensive periodicals and other materials out to binders may have been costly and could even exceed the outlay for the material being bound, so people with limited incomes had to devise their own ways of protecting their prized literary possessions. Quality book binding took the precise skills of a leatherworker or paper cutter as well as access to high-grade materials such as boards, leathers, threads, cords, tapes, and equipment for gilding, embossing, and stamping—all out of reach to most amateurs. Do-it-yourselfers did their best, however. They learned what they could from one another about covering techniques, assembled materials at hand, and often enlisted help from family and friend in homes, classrooms, churches, and even professional offices, where supplies might be more readily available. Although instructors, such as one at Framingham Academy, sometimes "gave . . . teaching exercise[s] on 'Book binding,'" few people could do more than stitch together sundry reading materials and fasten on a simple cover. Newspapers, made of thin paper, were easily handled. Hannah Hicock Smith "sorted & sew'd news-papers till tired, no pain," but when Charles Cobb attempted to sew denser items—"four printed music books together to save them from coming to pieces"—he finally asked his father to finish the job with his leather-crafting tools. Cobb merely "evened them down &c myself" to level the edges. "This being well done," the boy beamed, "they present the appearance of a large and first rate music book." Neither Cobb nor Smith stitched covers to their compendiums, but she certainly knew how, for she had on other occasions created cloth encasements for her journals and penny magazines. Apparently the starching process took as much time as binding. "5 o'clock [P.M.], have been starching a book cover," she recorded after spending one Fourth of July at home working; "it has taken up my time." While she sometimes used "new cloth" for her covers, another farmer handcraftsman swore by "Bonnet paper." He explained that it "makes a good covering for books to which if News papers for a Year or more be stitch'd it will contain many pleasing as well as interesting Matters & is as Good as a Magazine." Other amateurs used scraps of wallpaper, very strong paper, or readily available brown wrapping paper.[26] Paintings or pasted-on engravings could ornament a bland cover, however, while decorative name labels announced book owners.

The finest bindings and sturdiest covers, even if they could always be had, could not protect texts from rough or incessant handling. Not surprisingly, people spent almost as much time "fixing old books," or repairing them, as they did fortifying them. Preventive medicine, however, was more potent than any antidote, and so book lovers practiced, or at least preached, caution in handling books. "Father wishes you to take particular care of that Stearn Book & not *lose* the *loose* leaves," a newspaperman's daughter warned her brother in a letter tucked within a bundle of books. Children who received their first books through gift giving and borrowing imbibed principles of caretaking that they later tested against the practices of other children. "'Lotte goes to school half the day—comes home full of news & wonders," Persis Sibley Andrews remarked of her daughter; "she . . . expresses astonishment that children at school . . . 'dirty & tear their books . . . & all such very naughty things.'" So ingrained was the careful handling that the sight of adults mistreating books sometimes provoked a scolding. "This morning I was reading the Bride of Lammermoor from a fine English edition, which [Chancellor James Kent] thought I did not use with sufficient care," a law student clearly embarrassed by his laxity confessed to his diary. "So he chided me pretty severely, shewing his affection for his books," he continued; "he said to me, this book is quite frail, that[']s not the way I use my books."[27] Failing to treat books properly was a grave social impropriety.

Clearly, people left their imprints upon books through the care they lavished upon them. Indeed, it expressed their response to the object, particularly of the value they placed upon it—why else spend so much time, money, and energy on it? Binding loose leaves, newspapers, or pamphlets denoted they were worthy of extended life. Repairing damaged books meant they were deemed good enough to be used again. Carefully handling books recommended them to future users. Owners also registered their response through alterations in the look of their books; they often determined the type and color of paper or leather used in professional binding, and, of course, had full sway over homemade efforts. Because these maintenance procedures were often carried out in groups, personal imprints became social. They did so even for solitary interventions when the item was perceived and responded to by other people who read, borrowed, inherited, and, of course, further altered it. Between sojourns to borrowers' homes, reading circles, or sewing baskets, imprints needed resting places to protect them until the next user came along.

In responding to literature as valued artifact, owners spent much time and energy sheltering their books at home. Some people stored little used books away in chests, trunks, or boxes, in hopes that molds or insects would not get the best of them; wealthier folk hid some away in libraries or rented offices. But few people had so many books that they inundated their home; and even fewer wanted to segregate their books in lockboxes away from everyday life scenes. Instead, they preferred refuge space for unused items that left them visible and easy to retrieve. If the shelter could also organize volumes, which were ever prone to dishevelment, then it became ideal. Shelves approached that ideal insofar as they were the most decorative yet functional way to protect books. At once they sheltered books, maintained accessibility to them, and established their orderliness. Shelves took many forms, such as freestanding bookcases or boards "nailed very fast to the walls." Bookcases with glass doors kept out dust, while closets and secretaries with drawers for hiding away literature and writing materials were also good havens. Wooden or metal racks brought books within arm's reach across tables and desktops. These diverse sanctuaries could hold varying numbers of items depending on shelves' size and number; small table racks, for example, held only a few, while a large bookshelf set along a wall could hold dozens.[28]

Unlike the books they housed, furnishings garnered little note for their social value beyond, perhaps, usefulness, monetary worth, or workmanship. Few if any people expressed grief upon selling or giving them away or developed emotional associations with them; rather, they came and went with other outworn goods. "They wish to sell . . . a beautiful case for books and many other articles, all, but a few things which they reserve on account of some associations," one Rhode Islander relayed to a house-hunting friend. She was excited about the bookcase because such items were not always easy to come by in an age before much mass-produced wooden furniture. Nor were they cheap. A wealthy lawyer "tried to get a Book case but could not find one" for his college-bound son and "ordered . . . a book case [for] $25" instead—more than most workers' monthly wages. A schoolteacher's widow bought her "Bookcase &c" for ".28," considerably less but it was probably much smaller, of cheaper wood, and in very bad condition. Because these pieces of furniture were usually expensive household additions, diarists and letter writers mentioned purchases alongside other notable life events. A Boston domestic servant inscribed in her diary a purchase made possible by her recently deceased mother's legacy: "I took Mothers money out of the Bank 31 dol for Mary I bought Book shelves 1.25." After buying a few new books, one clerk gave them a handsome home: "I have just procured a Book Case, & have now quite a respectable Library." Bookshelves lent "respectability" to libraries by demonstrating that owners valued books enough to give them safe haven. To save costs some industrious folks made or repaired their own shelves, racks, or other containers. Octogenarian Hannah Hicock Smith could repair fences and bookshelves with ease, although she got "somewhat out of breath . . . fixing my shelves & placing my books on them," but she completed her work in about three days. She averred, "It was a job that tired me, but I have no pain," a remarkable feat since shelving books could exhaust even young folk. Book shelters may have looked simple to make or repair to novices, but experience proved differently. After making "a design for a reading frame," getting "some drills," and "cut[ting] out my side of book rack," one high school student admitted, "I am some what perplexed to know how to erect my book-rack" and spent another evening fixing his mistakes.[29] Vaunted Yankee ingenuity aside, the requisite skills for shelf making were not widely distributed socially.

Maintaining shelves was almost as much work as procuring them. First of all, books had to be arranged in some kind of logical order. With scant models from professional librarians, domestic caretakers had to invent their own taxonomies and sometimes even compiled their own catalogues. One schoolmaster, for example, kept in his diary a catalogue-like "List of Books in Library." His fifty or so books were slotted into categories that generally reflected various accomplishments in his life: as a student, a teacher, a lawyer, as a lover of poetry, and as an amateur musician. We have seen in chapter 2 how fish-yard worker Enoch Hale kept a diverse set of texts from texts; these were but a few in his large library. He organized it alphabetically according to subject and especially format, such as hardcover books and ephemera. Beyond setting upon a classification system for easy retrieval on the shelf, home librarians had to keep their books and shelves tidy. As often as twice a year, they sorted through newspapers, pulled books off their shelves, dusted them and rearranged them. The "ever dreaded anniversary has come!" announced a dismayed John Park on 1 November when annual library cleaning officially began. He sketched out the drill: "Take books and pictures down—up comes carpet—wash—scrub—I take refuge in a neighboring room." What was annoying for displaced inhabitants was exhausting for housekeepers. "I was working hard all the morning. Cannot remember when I have perspired so much with *working,* and what do you think I did[?]" Harriett Low posed to her diary, and replied that she "put all the books in order into the book case." She had little help and many knee bends: "The servants know nothing about books. And it is such a job, having to stoop to the floor to pick them all up." Such exertion also fell upon John Park as he "finish[ed] arranging *all* my books in their places" and likened it to a workout: "I have *done working,* as to bodily exercise." No one seems to have enjoyed the task that not only taxed body and mind but also consumed precious leisure time. For one busy overseer in the Manchester Mills, time had to be stolen from other activities. "Attended church half the day[;] arranged books & papers" was the way he described his doings one Sunday, while a hatmaker also reported his Sabbath activities as having "arrang[d] papers & Books all day."[30] Such efforts were necessary because a well-ordered library made a social statement for callers: the owner was a player in the game of socioliterary experience.

This was particularly true for people who could afford to devote a room in their home to their library, a far from common occurrence. These home library chambers—equipped with fireplaces, paintings or engravings, curtains and, of course, tables, chairs, and shelves—were scenes of social interactions as well as sites for housing books. As callers came to borrow, peruse, read, admire, or discuss literary possessions, libraries, like the books they sheltered, became stamped with distinctive social imprints. But libraries were also places to usher in guests, to "[s]pen[d] the evening" with a spouse, to converse "[a]fter dinner" and "f[a]ll asleep" with one's father, or to entertain a friend. Some of one engineer's fondest times with a friend were set in his library. "After breakfast, Nyck and myself retired to the library and there enjoyed ourselves in a manner only known to dear friends, having one heart and perfect sympathy of feeling," he gushed before his chum moved away. Lively places as well as quiet sanctuaries for study, libraries became repositories of past events as well as books. "I love to sit here in this cozy little library, it has very many pleasant associations connected with it," a sixteen-year-old told her diary. One Christmas Eve a businessman recalled family members who once enlivened the room: "Whilst quietly seated in the library during Christmas evening, we all felt the loss of the usual animated scenes of frolic with the children who are now absent in Europe." Libraries were often multipurpose, sharing functions as studies, drawing rooms, sewing rooms, and "memory palaces."[31]

Whether or not a home had a library chamber, books and their showcases inevitably spilled out into other rooms, which thus became library-like havens surrounded by the hum of everyday life. One woman's library could be found in her "boudoir, my sanctum sanctorum—my *snuggerie,*" as she described it to a friend. "At one corner stands a table, and upon the table . . . y'r letter that is to be, several books, an exquisite bronze inkstand . . . and the tiny camera obscura. Over me hang some bookshelves full of their natural dwellers." A "nic by the side of the fire place" in the parlor held a boardinghouse keeper's "side board & book case," along with "the sofa chair, table & glass," the only place in her rooms for storing books. One schoolgirl sometimes "looked over the chest of books in the attic," which contained "Miss Opie on Lying and the Family Encyclopaedia," while a deeds clerk picked over "the old rubish in the Attic in search of something interesting to read." Charles Cobb kept reading materials in the "entry . . . where we have a table against the door, with melodeon and books on it." He explained that "the room is used for a clothes closet, and having a large cupboard on the inner side it answers also for a buttery." In rural Maine, one woman placed a "small, mahogany, hanging book case" in "the back, of [the] dining room" along with the "two dinner tables, a work table, Piano-Forte . . ." and situated "a large Secretary well filled with 'standard works'" in a "passage between" the front parlor and the dining room. Despite the large bookcase in her drawing room that challenged her to arrange its contents, Harriett Low kept a slew of books on "a table 3 by 2" in the bedroom. "[It] is so crowded with literature or *litter* just which you may please to call it," she shamelessly punned. "It consists of lots of books, such as Spanish & English dictionarys, reviews, histories, drawings, etc." Here the books enjoyed the company of "an orange, a comb, keys, ink stand, 2 Cologne Bottles, a pair of gloves," a still life in which literature found its natural place. Like her, other owners let reading materials, precious as they were, fall into disarray for want of storage. Not everyone could afford shelves or find room; unbound newspapers and periodicals, resistant to standing up straight on shelves, posed special problems. One woman let her "newspaper hang" near the clock, while another kept the "English papers . . . behind the green curtain in the study close by the door" with "the old ones at the bottom and the later ones on the top" to prevent shuffling for latest editions. Some housekeepers "Cleared the libraries of newspapers & pamphlets" when tidying time rolled around; in and of itself it was "quite a tedious job." One avid newspaper reader advised her husband looking for a larger house: "You will want a space for your own use, and suitable accommodations for all the trumpery and newspapers that are accumulating in every corner of the house." Unpruned newspaper accretions filling every nook and cranny threatened to overwhelm subscribers, as did a profusion of books for owners with constricting space. Overflow sometimes went to storage space outside living quarters. After Park left his spacious home for a boardinghouse, he rented office space at "7.50" per quarter, for about 2,000 of his books—a room "I shall hereafter call my 'Library.'"[32] It seemed to offer a secure spot for his valued items, so he lovingly arranged his huge collection on the shelves.

As safe as it seemed, the office caught fire and with it his library. He fervently recounted the incident unfolding near his boardinghouse. "At our front door, I heard Col Richardson Exclaiming 'Dr Park's Library is on fire!'" Park rushed to the scene, but the fire had progressed: "I soon unlocked my door, but a smoke as dense as possible, prevented my entering." As he wondered what to do, the import sunk in, as he explained, "I knew that if the fire was allowed to go on unchecked for a few minutes more, my property would be entirely destroyed." That was enough to screw up his courage, so, "holding my breath, I made a plunge across my room—found and opened a window—there got breath—and turning round, saw the flames, like the mouth of an oven, under and behind one of my bookcases—the contents of which, mostly folios and quartos, were in full blaze." The few buckets of water his neighbors splashed did little to stop the conflagration that "was spreading along the wall and behind other bookcases." Fire engines were tardy, so with a strength provided only by those who understood well the value of books, most of the collection was heroically saved, as several of his friends "now seized such of my bookcases as were nearest the fire; and heavy as they were, with an effort which astonished me, they took five cases, books and all into Mr Thomas's Office, a few doors distant in the same entry." Rather than chance loss of life, he refrained from further help: "Seven cases remained, but as they had glazed doors, and would probably not be reached by the fire, we let them remain, though they contained most of my most valuable books." The engines finally showed up, "and in a few minutes, the water came down in a drenching shower, through all the ceiling of my room, so that I and the friends who were assisting me, were as wet as though we had fallen into a river." It was a mixed blessing, for it "damaged a great number of my books essentially, perhaps two hundred—some completely soaked." The next day, "visitors began to come" to the site to witness the destruction. Only two days after the fire could Park safely enter the room. "The appearance is deplorable," he gasped, "partly burnt, and *all* black with smoke." But he went about resurrecting it and his waterlogged books as best he could, spending about two weeks drying out the volumes "by our stove." In the end, most of Park's collection, the product of decades of building, remained intact. "When I see what I have lost, it makes me, for the moment, feel unpleasantly," he reflected, "but when I look at the treasure, unhurt, I think my escape most fortunate."[33]

Fires were one of the greatest hazards to personal libraries, for few buildings were entirely fireproof. While an unattended stove set the blaze that singed Park's books, one fire that "originated from the servant girl's going with a candle to a barrel of shavings" had a more devastating effect. "The Rev M[r] Spring . . . had his dwelling house burned to the ground entirely destroyed with almost all its contents," a farmwife reported; "scarcely was any thing saved[—he lost] his library all his sermons and almost all the clothing of the family." Fire could deeply affect other professionals, especially lawyers, for restoring their libraries was difficult and costly, and legal documents and bank notes were irreplaceable. Persis Sibley Andrews shared her husband's horror when a fire broke out at his Paris Hill, Maine, law office "where *all* his books & papers" were. When he and Persis arrived at the scene, a crowd had already gathered to save the valuable goods by pitching them out the windows. "[O]ut [came] the great chest with all the contents—the book-case & many of the books—throwing many of the papers from the desk &

shelves from the window many of wh[ic]h picked up—but some caught & were burnt as they came down," she nervously wrote, as if she were reliving the horror. One can almost feel her pen pause before she summed up the damage: "The chest is charr'd & the papers within much singed. Many books even acc't books were thrown out w[hic]h had one cover burnt off. & Most of them terribly scorched—burnt at the back so as to need rebinding—& some ruined & other some burnt to ashes."[34] Yet enough was saved, thanks to his neighbors' sociable valor, that he could continue his practice.

Conclusion

It must have seemed strange that objects surviving decades could disappear in an instant. What did that mean then for the layers of social meaning invested in them? Memory retained some of that significance, but the vessel for the meaning—the books, periodicals, and pamphlets incinerated—had vanished forever. Most personal libraries, however, were spared such dire fates. And everyday efforts to preserve and shelter reading materials kept them mostly safe from less fatal hazards of molds, dust, water, and, of course, mistreatment. The care lavished upon these artifacts was itself an investment in meaning.

Yet reading materials were composed of more than the elements that gave them form. They had texts as well—authors' words that could not be so easily obliterated as an irreplaceable and valued book. The same text could be reread and reexperienced repeatedly in new formats or under new conditions and responded to in vastly different ways, often by the same reader on different occasions. Like the literary objects these people invested with memory, texts were imbued with social meaning as well—when people read aloud or listened in a group, when they thought about other people while silently reading, when fictional characters reminded them of someone dear, or when they discussed a favorite book with someone else. Texts in this sense were more elastic than their containers, for the ideas they put forth were continually being reconceived and reconstructed through the initial response at the moment of reading or through reflection in years to come. One thus could not judge, or fully glean the social imprint of, a book by its cover, nor its binding, paper, type, or material format.

Chapter 12

The Sayings and Doings of Nobodies: Everyday Reception of the Printed Word

While still living in the rural backwater of Freedom, Maine, Persis Sibley Andrews received a call from a former neighbor who had moved to a bustling market town. "[S]he has made good improvement of her mental qualities ever since she went to Calais," Andrews observed. And being of like spirit, she naturally engaged her friend in literary talk, especially about Charles Dickens, who had just finished his 1842 whirlwind tour of Boston. "We have made a learned criticism upon all recent 'works'—Boz., & all," she explained in her diary that night, "& I fear he wo'dn't be as much flattered, co'd he know what we s[ai]'d as he was by the toasts of the great dinner given him by Bostonians." She reflected upon the incongruity of ordinary talk about extraordinary celebrity. "What matters it what *we* s'd—in that lowly cottage—here in one corner of the world—what *we*—the 'nobodies' s'd?" she inquired, and expounded: "Sayings & doings are spread abroad & valued not in consequence of intrinsic worth, but in proportion to the *elevation* of the author." To her, however, homespun literary criticism by two "nobodies" was as valuable as gossipy reports of Dickens's "sayings and doings." "It was a treat in the way of a conversation so different from anything I have been in the habit of enjoying in Freedom," she remarked, "that it seems richer than the richest wo'd any where else."[1] While the two women's literary chat was perhaps more learned than what could be heard that night in the tiny town's other sitting rooms, it was hardly singular.

These so-called nobodies, the region's ordinary people, usually had much to say to one another about what they read. Ideas formulated through reading were advanced and even conceived in social settings, where they took root and blossomed. Firmly planted in these nobodies' daily existence, they might have vanished had not a few of them been written down; even then, only tantalizing traces of everyday ideas often remain. Andrews, for example, never recorded exactly what she and her friend said about Dickens, only what they did not say: "We did not say that he has not merit." And she only hinted that the two compared some of his works with those of others. "Comparison & contrast have much to do with our opinions—our enjoyments," she observed.[2] Other nobodies in their role as everyday writers were more explicit about their "sayings and doings" at barnyard salons, sitting-room debates, and kitchen lyceums.

This literary encounter between Andrews and her friend stands as one among many that challenge the common modern reductive view of response as an immediate transmission of meaning more or less intact from a particular text to the reader's mind, where depending on the individual, it is then either accepted or subverted. Such narrow focus cannot encompass reader response to textual corpuses, such as, in the case of Andrews and her conversant, Dickens's oeuvre. Their discussion of it must be seen as its own type of shared and negotiated response between two readers reacting to their experiences of several books, not just one. And those initial readings of Boz were probably, as we have seen, not individual but mediated through a group listening to a text being read aloud. Moreover, with half or more of all reading taking place orally, even silent reading could not silence the remembered din of voices reciting and reacting. In other words, individual readers responded in a group-mediated way.

As but one stream in the flow of collective experience, literary and otherwise, response can be seen as having a past, present, and future—the three-part scaffolding of this chapter. Response began even before reading a text, for example, as its reputation or that of its author preceded it. For Andrews, her prior knowledge of Dickens's works influenced the manner in which she received reports of his Boston visit. In other instances, advance notice from friends and family created a social envelope in which texts would be received. Such associations echoed through response in its "present manifestation," the moment of reading. Also shaping present response, if reading was performed orally, were immediate group interactions and influences. But whether reading took place aloud or silently, memories of one's social world and previous literary experiences intervened in reception of the text. To be sure, evidence of such in-the-moment response, other than perhaps marginalia or other annotation, is rare; it usually must be reconstructed through retrospective written records. Still, diarists and letter writers insisted they captured their immediate reactions in writing. Response was not confined to the moment eyes were on the page, however. Long after reading ended, response continued, as, say, allusions to what was once read came to mind and were applied to one's ongoing experience. Response could continue intermittently over years after only a single reading. By situating textual response within a continuum of past, present, and future, we hope to complicate its study, restoring its proper social multidimensionality and interpersonal context.

Response Prior to Reading

While New Englanders preferred to read a text for themselves before judging it, they often formed prior opinions about it. To be sure, information came through advertisements, prospectuses, reviews, and published extracts, but informed correspondents added gossip and recommendations. Prior fulfilling engagements with certain authors or genres, too, naturally predisposed readers toward similar works. Overall, prejudgments emphasized textual aspects over the material qualities discussed in the last chapter; readers rarely preevaluated a text based upon its encasement alone. Elegant looks seldom biased textual reception. Recommendations from friends and family, however, did, in that they predisposed a reader to enjoy a text.

Endorsements came in all forms, not all of them explicit. They inhered in unsolicited literary gifts, loans, clippings, and extracts—items presenters "picked out." On account of donors, receivers usually did read these and so implicitly followed the tacit advice. Readers also fielded verbal and written recommendations, many of which queried unpresupposingly, "Have you read . . . ?" A Manchester law student began his solicitation with "You *'yena disse'* you—Have you read Longfellow's 'Hiawatha'[?]" Then came the hard sell: "I advise you to if you have not, if nothing more you will get an excellent collection of endearing little epithets out of it to apply to your friends—*vide* the strange word above," which meant, according to the book's glossary, "an idler and gambler; an Indian dandy." Such entreaties were made to socialize over common textual ground. Enthused by Elizabeth Sara Sheppard's *Charles Auchester,* one woman advised a sister to "Buy it and read it and then we will talk about it." Some invitations suggested that recipients read something so they could envision recommenders' present circumstances. On a Swiss tour, a brother bid his sister in Maine to scan Samuel Taylor Coleridge's "Hymn Before Sun-Rise, in the Vale of Chamouni" and "imagine one enjoying all that and more in reality." He believed she would, through poetry, vicariously experience his own European wanderings. Sometimes the mere mention of an enjoyable literary experience was its own recommendation, sparking enthusiasm in fellow readers. "I spoke of a book I have been reading," factory worker Martha Osborne Barrett wrote of her visit to a friend, "and she expressed a desire to read it also."[3]

Beyond endorsements, prior literary experiences could favorably (or unfavorably) dispose readers to certain authors. "I was so much pleased with 'Olive,'" John Park asserted, "that I begin 'The Ogilvies' today by the same author," Dinah Craik. Previous good encounters influenced book purchases, of course. The mill worker who picked up Charles Dickens's story *The School Boy* at an auction did so on the assumption that "it[']s worth it if it is any[thing] like Nicholas Nic[k]leby." Other readers paged straightaway to a favorite writer's story among the throng of others in magazines. "Here comes Thomas with the 'New Mirror,'" rejoiced one housewife, who "greatly admire[d] [the] writings" of its famous editor. "We will turn to the last page and see what [Nathaniel Parker] Willis has to say first." If predispositions toward authors could be reconfirmed through subsequent reading of their work, those against were far from fixed. "I have been reading Hiawatha and . . . even Mother who dislikes Longfellow[']s writings so much, likes this," a captain's daughter remarked while sailing across the Pacific Ocean with her parents.[4] Shipboard book scarcity caused the mother's prejudice to fall away.

Like regard for an author, interest in a topic, genre, or concept could set readers' expectations. "I know that I shall like it, as I do everything that relates to England," Charlotte Forten maintained after starting Thomas Babbington Macaulay's *History of England.* A newspaperman's wife was equally certain in that she would enjoy Thomas Keightley's study *The Fairy Mythology,* "a kind of a book I am always fond of." Only a few moments with Johann Wolfgang von Goethe's *Leiden des jungen Werthers* convinced one woman that it "will suit me exactly," for "it is dreamy and full of fancy, which is what I like." Differences between authors and readers hardly dampened inquisitiveness, however. "I took it up prejudiced against it," a sixty-year-old widow averred after completing the *Memoirs of Margaret Fuller,* "but notwithstanding many things which I could not wholly approve, I read it with absorbing interest."[5] As she discovered, prejudices and previews might poorly predict final judgment after attentive and thorough reading.

Although experience taught readers to follow their predilections, they resisted being confined by prejudice. Many sure-fire portents proved false, long-trusted personal "literary sages" occasionally gave poor advice, and public opinion often faltered, so some readers adopted a devil-may-care attitude toward others' opinions. For example, after reading Walter Scott's *Letters on Demonology and Witchcraft,* a young woman remarked, "I had heard it was a dull [book] but was very agreeably disappointed." The book's bad press had left her undaunted. Most folks would agree that the only way truly to evaluate a text was to read it oneself—and thoroughly, at that. When asked if it was a good book he was reading, a Glastonbury farm boy, tract in hand while plowing, "said he could not tell because he had not read it through." All were determined to make up their own minds with full evidence before them but were otherwise reticent to give opinions.

Unfairness was to be rooted out, so opinionated blowhards raising ruckuses received sharp rebuke, even in private, domestic settings. After railing unmercifully against Thomas Carlyle's *Sartor Resartus* without looking at it, a retired physician received a lashing by his wife. "But you say that you have not read the book, so your criticism is not quite fair," she declared. Having studied it herself, she charged the offender with dismissiveness: "It is a Book of some reputation & by an Author of reputation, & I think if you could interest yourself in the work that you would find much to admire."[6] According to her, interest, even if forced, was the entrée to full attention and, eventually, informed reception. But her husband had slammed the door tightly shut. Most people would have agreed with her because she appealed to reputation and, hence, society's reception of the work. Sociable readers avoided singularity.

Reading and Responding in the Moment

When engaging a text, readers experienced an unpredictable stream of emotional, social, and intellectual currents impelled by what they read. Certain words, passages, and, especially, the cathartic end paragraphs of texts, could evoke tears, laughter, or melancholy, but also thoughts about textual features or authors' arguments and philosophy. Much reading, however, was simply rowing toward those points of heightened response, sometimes merely on faith they would soon appear. If the trip were interesting, it would keep one going; if not, it would be a hard row. Below, we consider first conditions hindering or abetting that interest, and then, in turn, emotionally charged, socially activated, and critically analytical responses to both the texts and their authors.

Readers wanted a book to interest them enough that they could easily read it from cover to cover. Because they prided themselves on being careful, thoughtful, and thorough—in other words, not desultory—they aimed to finish whatever they started. It was easier said than done, for while some texts pulled readers in like magnets, others were so unattractive that readers abandoned them; this itself must be read as a type of negative response. The road to completion was indeed strewn with obstacles, for there were a host of distractions: an "aching head," "noise and excitement," "persons . . . talking," a "clap of thunder," the "intru[sion]" of "anxious troubled thoughts," "recollections of the past," other extraneous ideas that "dart into [the] mind," and, of course, sleepiness. But when conditions were right, the book itself often was to blame. Length, an obvious deterrent, prevented some people finishing. Failing to read the Bible through in course stands as a classic example, but plenty of secular texts were as long and as difficult to complete. Embarrassed that she could not plow through one tome, a Rhode Islander coyly asked her sister, "Did you ever read Spenser's Fairy Queen through[?]" She confessed, "I had no idea it was so long a poem" and took comfort in her neighbor's tongue-in-cheek survey that "there are [not] 3 people in Providence who have read it through." If length did not detour interest, then prolixity might. Tired, "dull," dry, or formulaic narratives might cut short the journey, but so could even heart-rending stories. "It is really quite affecting-touching," a journalist's daughter observed of Charles Dickens's *Master Humphrey's Clock.* "I am afraid when mother reads it she will say 'she shan't read any more' as she did of Oliver Twist." Considering that lack of interest was not really the problem, she predicted her mother would finish this time, as "she will have to in spite of herself." Readers at times felt ashamed of stopping, as one did when she declared that "we're very sorry indeed" that she could not make it through a "slow, not to say muddled" tome by German theologian August Neander. By contrast, when texts proved to be "too *stupid"* such that a reader "cannot get through with them," or were "so nearly worthless as to be destroyed," then reading came to a cheerful suspension—with no regrets at all.[7]

Confronted with a meritorious yet excruciating text, however, some readers opted for the desultory solution rather than admit full defeat. One scanner "skip[ped] about a little & read here & there as I could," while another "passed over the most abstruse passages." Some texts, though, were suited to readers who liked to dip in and out. "[I]f you don't like it, shut the book & you lose nothing," one woman opined of John Horne Tooke's *Epea pteroenta,* a book with which she occasionally "diverted [her]self to see how the *Learned in languages* get excited in their play with *Words,* with their Nouns, articles, Prepositions, & Conjunctions." Newspaper and periodical grazers likewise lost nothing from partial immersion, but readers of discrete texts—an entire speech or story published in a newspaper—at least tried to maintain enough interest to get through every word without having to say, "'Will this never end!'"[8]

Yet as often as readers aborted texts, they cried, "It ends much too soon" or "[A]las! We are at the last chapter." It was usually "interest" that led them to long for a never-ending text. True, persistent folk did trudge through "tiresome," "commonplace," "tedious," or "excessively long" texts, but interest sustained effortless, swift, and, indeed, compelling rides. "I did not go out[;] read the Lamplighter & completed it[;] was much interested," a Vermont woman explained. Within diarists' and correspondents' compact argot, to "like" or "enjoy" a text, or to find reading it "pleasur[able]," "entertaining," "delightful" and "amus[ing]," was often tantamount to finding it interesting. So, too, were judgments like "excellent," "very fine," or *"good."* Still, interest had wider meaning, for unlike pleasant texts, interesting ones could be "very sad" or "melancholy"; similarly, a book could, paradoxically, be "intensely interesting tho' often very absurd & sometimes quite bad."[9] Interest was its own sensation.

Readers more likely revealed how than why something interested them. Although interest could be mild, when it was extreme, people often reported feeling consumed or overtaken. They used words or phrases like "absorbed" or "absorbing interest," "deeply immersed," "deeply plunged," "bewitched," "engross'd," "enchained," and "bound up." A daughter depicted *"Mother, head & ears* in 'Uncle Tom.'" Full absorption could put everyday activities on hold, as when one congenitally disabled plat maker became so fascinated with the "very interesting" novel *The Experience of Life* one morning that he found "I can hardly put it down to eat my breakfast"—probably out of sympathy for the book's heroine, "a deformed young lady." For interested readers, time vanished. While reading a volume of Shakespeare, Persis Sibley Andrews claimed, "I am so fascinated with it that I forget all time, & never lay it down unless compelled by some duty." Compulsive interest was a kind of enslavement under which readers chafed. "Last night I came into my room, looked under the bed and into the closet, and then sticking the scissors over the door latch as usual, sat down to finish a story I had borrowed of Miss B. the other evening," a New Haven schoolteacher remorsefully began her own captivity tale regarding a romantic novel by Fredrika Bremer. "My old mania of reading seemed to return again with violence," she continued, "and long I read, and leaf after leaf I turned of the 'Neighbors,' till I was almost spellbound." Upon finishing the story the next morning, she resolved, "I'll never read again till I learn to control myself."[10]

Because intense interest was often solitary, it could, like study, be deemed antisocial, as readers became oblivious to people around them. It is not surprising, then, that some of the most extensive analytical responses occurred after such sessions as an attempt to reintegrate one's experience into the social realm by sheepishly rationalizing what would otherwise seem bizarre behavior. A part-time writing master and farm laborer in rural Maine reported his enthrallment with an antislavery novel:

> This morning I happened to be in at my Uncle Rose's . . . where I took up a volume of Uncle Tom's Cabin. Soon I was all absorb[ed] in its interesting pages and was bound down captive by this by this ingenious production. Much have I heard and read about this same book, but, but never have I before had the pleasure of feasting, mentally, upon its enticing pages. The picture is so exceedingly lifelike that the characters which figure largely in this work seem almost visible before my eyes. I seem to be gazing in astonishment upon the scene as it passes before in all its variety of phases. Eagerly I devoured the first volume regardless of the presence of those to whom at any other time I should have been happy to have tendered my whole attention. I

> disregarded all the rules of Ettiquit. I read untill the flickering lamp and my bedimmed eyes warned me that it was time to desist and lay aside all books for that time at least.

With the second volume, he was still "so completely bound up" that he "[r]ead until nearly midnight."[11] To complete an interesting book was to walk the fine line between resignation and resistance. Competing social tugs were rendered ineffective.

Readers of serialized stories could not, of course, hope to finish at a sitting. Such texts dripped out in installments did not necessarily save readers from groggy mornings—the penalty for going "to bed [at] 11 after reading a continued story" in the *New York Ledger,* as one sleepy-eyed store clerk remarked the next day in his diary. Life went on between installments, yet readers anxiously marked their progress. Given all the waiting, groups were more likely to coalesce around serials (and share in their distribution) than other works. Charlotte Forten, for instance, read chapters of John Townsend Trowbridge's novel *Martin Merrivale,* published in parts, with her teacher, who loaned it to her. Suspense so much mounted for them that for two weeks in a row she noted the unfolding novel "increases in interest." A much-awaited issue, however, could disappoint even intensely interested readers. "We are not so well pleased, that is Agnes & I, with the last number of the Professor's story," Mary Pierce Poor complained to her sister after a daughter-and-mother reading session of the Oliver Wendell Holmes's *Atlantic Monthly* tale "The Professor," which dubbed the New England elite "Brahmin." "Is Elsie Venner a rattlesnake in the form of a girl? Else why does she bite, & why do her eyes have a cold glitter? I dislike all snakes."[12] Through Holmes's use of metaphor, she had discerned the novel's key premise: a snakebit woman begets a snakelike daughter.

Whether characters, plot, or tone interested readers, absorption allowed them to escape temporarily from responsibilities and cares of everyday life into an imaginary world. Readers of epic literature might lose themselves in a time and space inhabited only by mythical heroes. Upon taking up Alexander Pope's translation of the *Iliad,* Charlotte Forten wrote, "Find it delightful to leave this matter-of-fact, every-day world and soar into *his* world of grand old heroes and gods and goddesses." Travel books were particularly adept at transporting readers. Imaginary travelers might even accompany travelogue writers. "It is so lifelike, so natural, and takes one right amid the scenes which she saw and makes one feel almost acquainted with the people whom she met," Martha Osborne Barrett, working as a factory hand, observed of Harriett Beecher Stowe's *Sunny Memories of Foreign Lands.* "With her this day I have wandered over Scotland's heather, amid her mirrored castles, Melrose Abbey and Classic Ha[w]thornden. I've visited, roamed by the Avon, where gentle Shakespeare dwelt, entered the palaces of princes and conversed with England's best nobility." Her reading fed a long-held aspiration, virtually hopeless for the laboring woman: "It has been a cherished dream, even from my childhood to go to Europe. Alas! I fear it will be but an unrealized dream." At least, literary visitations like these made the harsh realities of her underpaid factory job fade into the background. Such therapeutic distraction was not confined to laborers, for students availed themselves of it, too, to relieve tedium. "There are some days when I feel as if every energy were drained and I cannot write," a normal school student despaired amid her studies. "Dipping into Milton's sublime thoughts brought a recreation, for it was a change and a true pleasure." Literary escape could narcotize as much as stimulate, as in the case of one recent widow for whom Julia Kavanagh's *Madeleine: A Tale of Auvergne* "was like four hours mental Chloroform to her." For Charlotte Forten, even a geography once led to an emotional crash after an initial high. With hopes of mentally entering a free country that such a text offered her came the inevitable letdown: the realization that she remained where African Americans were either enslaved or treated with severe prejudice. "I cannot even *think* of those beautiful, distant lands without a longing so earnest to behold them as makes the thought almost a painful one," she explained of her perusal through a geography of France: "I wish that I could cast away some of these day-dreams—forget these vain hopes of the Future, which I fear too often prevent me from engaging earnestly enough in the actual labor of the Present. There is so much to be done, and I can do so little—this feeling often oppresses and saddens me, and almost unconsciously I seek relief in the indulgence of those delightful dreams of days to come when great good shall be accomplished, and the glorious principles of Justice, Liberty and Truth everywhere triumphant."[13] Literary fantasy's ostensible deliverance from social injustice was but a deceptive emotional detour.

Although interest was the most basic and most commonly written response, it was only the stage upon which more nuanced reactions played. Often it was emotion that fueled interest, as readers reacted with tears, laughter, knee knocking and teeth chattering, or even disgust. Subtler emotional reactions, too elusive even to record, were of course evoked, but these can only be glimpsed through more circumstantial evidence. Obvious and dramatic emotions appear more often and are better delineated in diaries and letters that subtle ones. One of the clearest, yet most powerful and all too common, was shock, especially that received as a blow from tragic news stories, while another was excitement, produced by distressing news in print but also by literary texts, especially novels. In contrast to the evocative prose employed to describe these heightened responses, a social ethic of restraint governed most other less clearly drawn emotions, as we will see.

Fiction and other belles lettres could spark exhilarating excitement, though readers avoided succumbing to mere thrilling literary invention. A rousing but didactic text nevertheless could appease conscientious readers. "I read 'never too late to mend,' in vacation," a teacher told a friend about a penal-reform novel, hot of the press. "Isn't it exciting, harrowing, the prison scenes?" Stimulating yet pious novels such as those in William Ware's biblical trilogy spiritually uplifted rather than profaned readers. "Have been reading 'Zenobia' today," a schoolmistress acknowledged in her diary; "was really excited at some of the thrilling details of the betrayal and fall of Palmyra." Some readers felt sullied by literary excitement, especially when it raised the heart rate and, consequently, the temperature. "It excited me to such a degree," Charlotte Forten wrote after perusing English novelist Charles Reade's *White Lies,* "that I was obliged to take a walk to 'cool my fever.'" The flames ignited by one novel went instead to a farm daughter's head, as she disclosed she "read this day History of a flirt & it has nearly set my brain on fire." One woman was certain that reading the "too exciting" novel *Amabel* "is not healthy for me." Ideally, authors redeemed readers' lapses into excitability with some sobering, uplifting, or calming textual antidote. According to Mary Pierce Poor and a few of her contemporaries, Dickens had that ability to lead the reader through various moods. She described her emotional state in reading through *David Copperfield:* "[Y]ou do not experience the sentiments of horror or regret that you feel when the heroine of a tragic play or novel meets with a sudden or violent death. Then you are excited, wrought up, but Dickens moves & melts that he may reach the heart & implant a love of all that is pure & holy."[14] Unmitigated tragedy for little purpose other than sheer sensation seemed inexcusable.

In contrast to emotional responses elicited by authors, those in reaction to news of actual events, especially shock, all fed upon interest in reading about real people, an interest that grew from often disturbing revelations. In addition to newspapers being mailed to addressees as a way of announcing friends' or relatives' deaths, they told too of shipwrecks, crimes, fires, epidemics, and natural disasters. Readers accordingly searched through their pages with a mixture of trepidation and anticipation. Any paper, of course, whether read at post offices, periodical depots, or neighbors' homes, might contain personally significant news to set off emotions. It appeared so regularly that a factory girl could write of a carriage maker's wife, "I read the death of Mrs Caroline Halenbeck . . . aged 23 disease consumption . . . [;] thus it is each week brings the tidings of the death of . . . some acquaintance or friend."[15] Readers simply resigned themselves to constant shockingly bad news.

Printed news about people, of course, ranged from exceptionally good to neutral to devastating and thus, at the far ends, would seem to elicit commensurate extreme sensations. However, this was true only for negative and impersonal positive tidings. Both positive and ordinary social intelligence printed in newspapers seldom provoked much more than a statement of fact. Good news printed in papers left readers cold because they preferred to hear news first through correspondence. As one avid newspaper reader explained of intimate letters, "A newspaper may tell you of a caucus or a fire, but who except a friend can tell you of the family concerns of those you love[?]" Print simply did not get to the heart of the matter. Superlatives and exclamation points usually applied to impersonal news relating to technological advances (like the telegraph), geographical discoveries, or election returns. One of many examples includes Charles Cobb's exuberant ejaculation upon hearing that Franklin Pierce won the nation's presidency: "Glory to God!" Negative news, by contrast, evoked strong statements of emotion; it could be described as "distressing," "appalling," "horrible," "terrifying," "afflicting," or "astonish[ing]." Several folks described bad news as a kind of lightning bolt—being "much struck," as one put it. So detrimental was one emotional blow that a reader wrote, "[M]y heart died within me." Perhaps people utilized a more finely tuned vocabulary for shock because they had greater need to express it in writing.[16]

Readers who spent much time with newspapers constantly worried—about travelers, distant relatives, or friends at sea. In most cases, people immediately turned to columns of direct relevance, such as passenger lists or notices of ships' progress at sea. "I looked for Ship news the first thing," one seaman's lover explained of her habit. The distressed shoe binder scanned the papers, even ones used as wrapping paper, for news on ships' clearances and arrivals. The most obscure intelligence could bear upon a loved one's fate; indeed, some people drew nearly irrational correlations. Worcester's Eliza Davis went through an emotional wringer wondering about her son during a voyage. "Where can George be that we get no intelligence?" she fretted absent correspondence; "reading over the names of passengers I see that of J. H. Davis, and for a moment hoped it might be a mistake & it should have been G.," she confessed to her husband after glancing at the ship arrival columns that routinely appeared in the papers. "Then again I read the list of deaths the names of—Davis. I could not fill it with George—God forbid." What made things worse for people riveted to newspapers was tenuous reportage, contradictory statements, and, sometimes, utter inaccuracy.[17] For many anxious newspaper scanners the worst imaginable fate never panned out, but, on occasion, riding emotional waves of news stories with hopes for the best instead left readers, like the aforementioned shoe binder who soon learned of her lover's death, shipwrecked.

One such reader was a Catholic South Bostonian caught up in the 1834 tsunami of news after a mob torched a Charlestown, Massachusetts, convent. While on an August hunting trip in the White Mountains with some friends, he by chance picked up a newspaper at an inn near Lake Winniepesaukee. "[F]ound there first Boston News since we left Concord & were as much astonished to find the news of the burning of the Charlestown Convent as at any thing during our whole time," he scratched in his travel journal; "became somewhat anxious to get home to ascertain the origin of this savage outrage on law & humanity." After calling a "meeting of Boston boys," who resolved "that we will stand on our heads & eat fire in commiseration of our Catholic brethren," the vacationer rushed home, only to find his father injured: "passed round to the Convent & through Charlestown—& arrived at home in Boston at 2 PM. where we found father bleeding & in peril of his valuable life requiring the skill & attention of 3 physicians." The man concluded, "[T]hus ends a passage in the ever changing allotment of life . . . we had risen elated the hills of Hope & arrow sunk into the vale of tears."[18] Life, it seemed, was as transient as the news.

And, indeed, life's pageant often unfolded in newspapers. Hearing upsetting news from editors rather than acquaintances was all too common in an era when newspapers could travel faster than letters. Persis Sibley Andrews was dealt perhaps the harshest blow of this sort. In early 1852, upon her husband's denial of worsening health, she shrugged off rumors that he was dying of consumption while away serving as a U.S. congressman from Maine. But on 31 March, she learned the truth during a shopping trip: "Bangor & Portland papers announce, as fact, that he is dying dangerously ill at Wash[n.]" The information cut like a sword. "These notices in the papers were shown me," she wrote several days after the shock died down, "& tho' I had great reason to believe I was better informed—they were too startling not to have an effect on me—took away my strength so that I co'd not sit up in the carr-coming home." Charles Andrews soon returned to Maine gravely ill. "O Heavens!" Persis inscribed in her diary after yet another shock, Charles's demise on 30 April 1852, had barely subsided. "Am I a Widow? The very name freezes me."[19] Newspapers bore tidings of loved ones' well-being or ill fortune and were highly valued for their personal meaning. They were no less than texts of life—and death.

These cases, though not unusual, were few and far between for any one person. After all, most tragic intelligence was not personally relevant. One schoolteacher realized this when her own heart was broken by shocking news. While other newspaper readers went about their everyday lives as if nothing had changed on 26 January 1860, she was transformed. "My heart is full of sad news that came to me this week, that I can hardly think or write of anything else," she revealed to her former Sunday school students. "A little cousin in Texas is burned to death." She explained, "Such announcements are common," and then she drew out the moral significance:

> We may read them in almost every paper; but they make very little impression upon us, because the sufferers are not our brothers or sisters, or in any way related to us. They did not even live in the next house; nor were we accustomed to see them day by day in the school or in the street. Their very names seem unfamiliar, as we carelessly

> glance at them, and go our way, little thinking of the mourning ones left behind, or of the dead who are gone. But some times our turn comes to weep and shudder, and we feel that we can join hands with all afflicted humanity.[20]

Tragic newspaper accounts, like the one that overwhelmed her with grief, were so commonplace that she feared readers might become immune to them, as some surely had.

Yet enough newspaper readers remarked upon calamitous events and the anonymous lives affected by disasters to give this teacher reason to have faith in her contemporaries' compassion for unknown victims. Like her, Charles Cobb, upon reading accounts of a local fire, made the emotional step from sympathy to empathy for the unknown name on the page: "I am . . . strongly impressed with the idea that every fire which occurs is a loss to every citizen of the country, and hate to read accounts of 'em." As much as they hated to see the shocking accounts, newspaper readers could not avoid them nor the feelings they stirred. "This Eve. B. came up and I read an account of the Steamer San Francisco, which was lost in the last storm on her way to California," a Lynn schoolteacher inscribed in her diary; "it was shocking to read what must it have been to those on board!" She probably knew none of the passengers, yet an emotional jolt surged through her. Disinterested social shock at human catastrophe often registered in the numbers that diarists felt compelled to record. "[T]he steam Boat Lexington destroyed by fire on Long Island Sound & about 150 Lives Lost," a Taunton farmer scribbled in his journal. "An awful calamity at Lawrence Mass. A large factory fell in & killed 200 persons," a shipping clerk noted. Exclamation points succinctly and emphatically conveyed shock. "The papers within a few days have announced the destruction of four vessels, by burning, blowing up, or stranding," John Park chronicled, "resulting in the loss of above a thousand lives!!" He reflected that same day, "Disasters have of late abounded to a melancholy extent." Daily dire accounts piled up into insurmountable heaps that only sustained and deepened momentary shock. Newspapers inspired perceptions of ever accumulating misfortune. "[P]apers are full of disasters," a farmer brooded after an 1841 night's reading; "the burning of the Erie, the explosion of the Louisiana with the loss of 15 or 20 lives, an explosion in [S]yracuse NY with the loss of 25 or 30 lives, murder of Miss Rogers in NY, the awful murders in Illinois committed under Lynch law &c." To this Congregationalist, divine judgment seemed imminent. "Wo to our country if a few years bring no change," he prophesied.[21] Extensive newspaper reading led to incessant handwringing.

As news of war or other calamities unfolded, a collective "excitement"—akin to agitation rather than pleasure—became the catchword. "Political excitement" was aroused by various events, but especially by the declaration of war on Mexico in May 1846, the arrest of Anthony Burns under the Fugitive Slave Act in June 1854, the sudden deaths of presidents in April 1841 and July 1850, and the Civil War's outbreak in April 1861. To newspaper readers, the tumult seemingly never ceased. "Have you observed what a constant state of excitement people have been kept in for the last two years?" the daughter of an unemployed man asked a correspondent in 1849. "There was the famine in Ireland, our war with mexico, the revolution in France, & disturbances throughout the rest of Europe. Then came our Presidential Elections with which our papers have teemed."[22] That she and others grouped campaigns with disasters is telling, for partisan battles were indeed vicious, disturbing, and, at times, bloody.

Probably the era's most exciting, violent, and widespread news story concerned the 23 November 1849 murder of Boston physician George Parkman by his colleague, Professor John White Webster, and the latter's ensuing trial. According to one Lynn bank cashier, the "report of the trial is daily read perhaps by half a million of people." Like a serial novel, the gruesome scene-of-the-crime details, day-to-day judicial proceedings, and "minute account" of the murderer's execution, were dripped out by the press from early December 1849 until 30 August 1850. Although interesting, the unfolding tale was nonetheless nightmarish. "[O]h it is horrid, too horrible to record or even to think of," a Beverly magistrate's daughter ached with incredulousness on 1 December 1849; "it seems to me the most awful thing I ever heard." While collective shock would increase and spread with each installment, excitement took hold even with the first announcements of Parkman's suspicious disappearance. John Park was convinced as early as 4 December 1849 that the "city and vicinity have never been in such a state of excitement since the commencement of the American Revolution." By February 1850, it had become "the event of the winter, an horrible one too & for weeks the all absorbing topic." When Webster was pronounced guilty on 30 March 1850, the "announcement came like a thunderclap upon the city," according to a Boston schoolgirl. Although locals at first were most likely to be affected by the excitement, the "dreadful intelligence" soon spread to other New England cities, where agitation followed and quickly moved outward further still to their hinterlands and beyond. As early as 9 December, Persis Sibley Andrews observed from isolated Paris Hill, Maine, that all "New England is in a state of unparalell[e]d excitement about the murder of Doct. Parkman of Boston." Even tiny Woodstock, Vermont, was caught up in the furor by mid-April 1850, just after Webster received the death sentence. Charles Cobb explained that as he "was carrying up Henry's Christian Messenger," he met an acquaintance who asked to see it, saying, as he confused sentence with execution and victim with perpetrator, that "he wanted to look at the deaths to see if Doctor Parkman was hung, but couldn't find them."[23]

When the denouement, the execution, did take place in August, it became the event's most widely noted aspect. One reason for this was that capital punishment had strong opponents, such as Boston abolitionist businessman Daniel Child, who, much to his relief, "was set aside, from serving on this trial, for having anti-capital-punishment opinions." The shock of Webster's hanging induced in one woman an ethical dilemma. "What an awful tragedy—the execution of a fellow creature," she recorded on 5 September; "yet I am not convinced that capital punishment is not necessary to answer the ends of justice—and to act as a wholesome restraint upon the violaters of peace in the community." Other folk, such as Frances Jocelyn, grieved for the murderer. "Poor Professor Webster was executed on Friday," she tersely reported, referring her diary to the "Further particulars in the mornings paper." A Boston associate's daughter worried about the family's fate. "Before this time he is probably executed," she reflected. "His poor wife and daughters!"[24] Readers, although thoroughly saturated by this news event, fashioned new ideas from a singularly horrific crime transmogrified into an all-too-familiar story.

The collective shock inspired by national crime reportage had its counterpart in communal emotional responses elicited by small group oral readings. Of course, group response pales before the magnitude of collective shock, but nonetheless, together readers and listeners generated a collectively felt reaction that was probably intense due to the multiplication factor of several people at once being affected. For example, as John Park struggled to steady his voice while finishing the moving *Stranger,* he discovered upon looking up that he was not alone: "When I finished, my auditors, Mrs Richardson and Mrs Park, I found were both sniffling as well as myself." Similarly, Mary Pierce Poor witnessed the deep sorrow felt by two young servants over an instruction manual. "My Mahala . . . has very tender feelings," she observed of her country domestic; "the other day she had Abbott's 'child at home' & Mrs Dodd's girl came to see her, & they read loud together." Poor looked on as "they cried so over the story of the girl who was sent to the house of correction . . . that they could not go on."[25] They cried because of the sad story, but also because one another did so; emotions swelled interpersonally.

Readers separated by distance formed virtual communal response groups similar to actual ones. Letter writers anticipated, envisioned, and sometimes imagined themselves seated with their correspondents, watching and sympathizing with their reactions to touching texts. In this way, intimacy was expressed through a tacit understanding that response would be shared, or at least understood. "I suppose you have read another tale by [James] Thomson," an Irish immigrant's daughter teased her love-struck sister as if she had caught her in the act of reading proto-romantic literature yet again; "oh methinks I see you now reading that exquisite pathetic piece the tears rolling down your cheeks your large bosom heaving with sup[p]ressed emotion." Correspondents sometimes bonded over commonly shed tears, even involving a third party, that were assumed to flow while reading a moving story. "Have you read & cried over 'Uncle Tom's Cabin?'" Mary Pierce Poor asked her sister Lucy. "I have been writing home to advise Elizabeth not to attempt it," a half-serious Poor declared. "I am afraid it would kill her. I never read anything so affecting in my life." While emotional responses to literature could, in extreme if rare cases, prove fatal, sometimes, when letter writers could not be certain what their addressee's response to a particular text might be, they couched their overtures in disclaimers to discuss it in tentative terms. In querying whether a correspondent back home had read Fredrika Bremer's *Brothers and Sisters,* one unemployed man's daughter cautiously explained that emotional response was at times entirely relative to both readers and authors. "I think the degree in which one likes Miss Bremer must depend very much upon the character of the reader & on their state at the time of reading her," she reasoned, aware that the book had gotten some negative reviews. "Her writings are among those which we judge of more from the affections than the intellect, it seems to me."[26] Although emotional reactions seemed to be written into the text, as if it contained an invisible script prompting readers to respond in definite, often uncontrollable ways, readers, she believed, had some power to affect these directives.

If readers or listeners sometimes mediated the writer's emotional cues, they even more readily invested a text with inscribed meaning of their own, as they mentally tailored it to elicit more intimately charged emotions. Readers detected personally meaningful messages between lines, as if authors planted a secret code to jar innermost thoughts and memories. This was illusionary, of course, for they drew upon their own storehouse of memories to reinvent what they read. With a little imagination, printed texts easily reflected back images from everyday social life. Rereading a book could recall conditions and people associated with its initial encounter; first-time reading likewise summoned up social ties, especially familiar faces within readers' worlds.[27]

Of all conceivable ways to recall one's past, rereading a book was a sure-fire bet. Some people simply wanted to refresh a once-profitable literary experience, but as Persis Sibley Andrews explained, a person also reread a text "for the associations it brings up on auld lang sine." John Park, for example, who read Cowper's poem *The Task* in his "thirteenth and fourteenth years," revisited it in old age to discover that "[m]any passages in the 4th and 5*th* book, especially . . . sound like old friends, and give me a favorable impression as to my early taste." Other people found that rereading made them cognizant of how much their reception had either modified or continued unchanged. Most discovered that while the text remained the same, they themselves were not. "I read the 'Sorrows of Werter,'" a newspaperman's wife reported after a disappointing reunion with Goethe. "I brought it home from [brother] John's remembering how I once wept over it . . . and [now] found it very sentimental and silly, and not to my taste." Communal settings might reaffirm the sense of transformation. One spinster experienced a new appreciation of Hannah More's *Cœlebs in Search of a Wife* when she read it in a social setting—with a reading club: "I think there is much instruction to be derived from it, but I well remember how dry I thought it was, when I was a child, & I had not seen it since."[28]

Readers could just as easily revitalize the past on first readings. To fan the flames of former relationships, some readers situated themselves in texts. One elderly Hartford woman read *Recollections of a Lifetime* by Connecticut native Samuel G. Goodrich and experienced "much pleasure, recalling many pleasant occurrances of my own life." Associations did not have to be evoked by content specific to time and place. Some readers entered their pasts through an emotional connection to what they read. Reading William Wordsworth's poem "Characteristics of a Child Three Years Old," though it likens the toddler to the beauties of the English countryside, caused one collegian to review his socially deprived childhood on a New Hampshire farm. He was taken with the following lines: "'Solitude to her / Is blithe society, who fills the air, / With gladness and involuntary songs'." He explained that these "were lines which strongly reminded me of my own early childhood, when, brought up in the woods of Northwood, without a brother or a companion,—I nevertheless found company in every thing—in the birds, in the old cat, the cow, the inanimate objects, and my little cubby-houses were built with as joyous hands and as laughing glee as tho' my labors had been shared by another."[29] His response to Wordsworth had everything, and nothing, to do with what the poet wrote. Universal in its appeal, the poem captured childhood bliss; particular in its application, it invited him to reminisce about his own life.

Present as well as past relationships came to mind while reading. Fictional or historical characters could spring to life, as readers compared them to people they knew, plucking them from pages and plopping them down amid their social circles. Among friends, lovers, teachers, or family members, these characters interacted as pseudo-entities. One of many examples occurred when Harriett Low "[c]ommenced Rob Roy" and immediately "[c]ompare[d] my friend Caro to Die Vernon. " She penned, "Think in *spirit* and *independence* she is very like her. Many traits of her character are very similar." In some cases, the resemblance was more than accidental, for people often modeled themselves upon exemplary characters. While reading the biography of Rugby School's Thomas Arnold, Frances Merritt Quick discovered that her own teacher had patterned his pedagogy upon the clergyman's. "I have discovered Mr. Stearns' model in Dr. Arnold," the normal school graduate ascertained: "The Senior class were to Mr. Stearns what the Sixth Form was to Dr. Arnold—they were co-workers with him for the good of the school." In most cases, however, direct emulation could not account for such melding.

Indeed, why characters seemed so like real persons is sometimes inexplicable, but it might be clearly understood between two readers. "Did not Walter in the second volume remind you of sister E.?" Mary Pierce Poor inquired about her sister's resemblance to a male character in Wilhelm Martin Leberecht De Wette's *Theodore,* without giving clues to her reasoning. Sometimes name coincidences led to comparisons. Tikes were particularly struck by encountering appellations in print similar to those of people they knew. Adults played the same name games that invited thoughts about loved ones. "In reading in the 'Times' I found the following poem 'to Lizzie' and as I know a 'Lizzie' very similar to the one there described," a cooper's daughter confided to her diary without spelling out the similarities. "I determined to copy it." The poem was easily applied to any cheerful, industrious young woman, but serendipity led her to make it her own particular memento.[30]

Thus, whether reading was done alone or in groups, it was essentially a social act in that literature provided a canvas on which to project personal relations. To fasten on images of loved ones, readers even inserted themselves or other people into narratives by replacing characters. In this way, they creatively turned impersonal narratives into life stories. While reading *Recollections of a Southern Matron* while at sea, John Congdon "found John and [his wife] Cynthia pictured in it." He continued tailoring one tale to his own vision: "I there saw domestic comfort, happiness, love, represented in man and wife." He promised her, "I will show it [to] you if nothing happens when I get home[.] I [k]now it will please you, for it does me very much, [to] situate us as man and wife were there" in the book. Sometimes readers set real loved ones above lovable fictional characters. "I think I have the ideality to understand such things very well," a country schoolmaster declared after starting *Undine,* the German fairy romance about a water sylph. "But I would give more for the genuine spirituality of my own dear, dear Martha than all the Undines which imaginative Germany ever produced." Real was better than the ideal. Readers who linked characters to intimates had to be careful, though, for it might be taken as an insult. "Margaret says that Uncle Jack reminds her of me," a storekeeper reported with mock injury to his sister of his wife's comparing him to a character in Bulwer-Lytton's novel *The Caxtons,* "who has lost several small fortunes trying to make one large one." His wife, seeing what he was writing, nipped misunderstanding in the bud: "Margaret desires me to correct what I said about Uncle Jack in the Caxtons—she thinks it may give you a wrong impression." He then divulged, "I am happy my dear sister to say that I am doing much better than I thought I should."[31] Such "literary dueling" could call upon characters as weapons to sort out old marital tensions.

Desire to see distant or deceased loved ones often led to the personalization of literary content. It prompted voyagers and travelers to fly mentally back home over vast expanses on wings of literature. During an attack of "home sik[ness]" at sea, a Rhode Island captain's daughter read a history of Newport and thought "[as] it is so near home, it recalls many pleasant thoughts of kind friends who reside there, & our own dear home." During one voyage to San Francisco, a down-easter immersed in Grace Aguilar's *Home Influence* was "reminded . . . often of home sweet home." But the oddest text could be sentimentalized. In Marseilles, a traveling teacher read "Mr. [Martin] Vanburens Message" to Congress and suddenly it "seemed like being at home." Some evocations were even more idiosyncratic. While listening to *Lady of the Lake,* Charlotte Forten realized, "I never read it without thinking of home and Uncle W." Readers themselves could sometimes not understand why certain texts dredged up associations. "I have been reading Mr. [Sampson] Reed's 'Growth of the Mind' this afternoon, & that always makes me think of you," a young woman informed a friend. "I do not know why, but, believe that it is because I have heard you speak of it with a great deal of affection, & say that you loved to read it."[32] According to her, a person's literary preferences could forge lasting links between text and life.

Her reasoning was sound, for people often were so aware of loved ones' taste that they read with them figuratively looking over their shoulders. "I have thought an hundred times while reading it how much Mother would be pleased with it," a customhouse worker disclosed to his sister while reading the life of Walter Scott. Reading something once treasured by loved ones razed walls of separation. An editor's wife estranged from her husband wrote to a dear friend who had left a volume of poetry on a recent visit:

> . . . in the evening feeling very lonesome, and also being visited by some mournful reminiscences of our old home, and being "lang syne," I went involuntarily to the volume of Wordsworth, hoping to find something like companionship in passages marked with your pencil, and impatiently turning it over to find some traces of *yourself.* I accidentally met with *that one* as delicate, and affectionate, in its revealings, as the heart that dictated it. I cannot express my thanks, for words seem to me inadequate to express the sense I feel of your . . . *affection.* . . . I shall most certainly read, and *love* it, for the sake of the donor and as certainly fancy that there is something of communion between us when reading your favorite passages. . . .

Such markings could specifically address a recipient, as when one man mailing some sermons to his sister, explained, "You will by my marks [see] what are the thoughts which arrest and occupy your Brother[']s mind." Pencilings took on a different significance for later readers when the person who made them died, for they remained the only lines of communication with the living. For example, the widow we discussed in the last chapter, who prized her late husband's books as mementoes, also cherished their marked texts. "[T]ook out Byron and Webster's Dic't," she inscribed in her diary; "read some of dear Henry's favorite passages." Fortunately, he indicated those very lines. She also found in his Bible "passages marked in it which I shall often read." The living might do the same to communicate their reading experience.[33] In *X* marks, a volume of social meaning resided.

Readers thus summoned social relations even while isolated and having only a book as a companion. This social meaning was as evident to them as any other message conveyed by authors. After all, response was collaborative insofar as people on readers' minds influenced reception. In this way, reading encompassed much more than a one-to-one relationship between writers and readers; texts were platforms for maintaining everyday social ties upon which writers indeed might play only supporting roles.

Still, most readers believed an author intended to impart specific ideas and that they could comprehend them, indeed, collect and savor them like strawberries in June. But just as texts were open to reinterpretation to suit social ends, so, too, were they tractable enough to inspire new ideas. Readers applied ideas, experiences, and social relations to texts to make them their own. They critiqued features such as characters, narratives, and style. They brought prior knowledge to bear upon authors' factual representations, research, and argument; they determined, too, whether texts were useful. While engaging a text, however, readers looked beyond its form to ruminate on its ideas, usually an exercise in meditating upon everyday life. Texts, too, could be springboards for reflecting upon personal dilemmas or larger ethical, religious, political, and social issues.[34]

First and foremost, however, readers wanted to cull authors' ideas, not create their own, and they criticized them only after thoroughly understanding them. Like lecture-goers, readers wanted "many new ideas." This meant more than facts. "All learning and no thought" was a charge leveled by one reader at some magazine essays, and similar complaints weave through other diaries and letters. To show both learning and thought was a big bill to fill, but hungry readers found most literary food laid before them to be satisfactory. Because they desired as much new knowledge as possible, they tried to cram authors' ideas into memory. As one young woman jested after completing William Stirling Maxwell's *Annals of the Artists of Spain,* "[I] have attained a number of ideas which will probably remain in *my* noddle several weeks during which time I shall enjoy a sense of knowing something." Selectively storing ideas became its own form of response through sifting for worthwhile ones to remember. If memory was faulty, commonplace books could come to the rescue and give opportunity for digesting ideas. Yet despite readers' valorization of precise understanding and recall, they were hardly literalists; otherwise, they would have taken proper precautions to make more exact transcriptions. One clerk who "improved" upon some lines he recorded from Emerson's "Gifts" clearly eschewed slavish iteration in favor of original ideas. For example, after his mistranscription he mused upon gift giving. "A bouquet of flowers is better than jewelry," he maintained, "because the selection and arrangement of the flowers is your own and the receiver can see somewhat of your own skill and talent in it, and thus really gets at your mind and heart." Readers like him opportuned themselves of indeterminate spaces between lines of texts to insert new ideas. Frances Merritt Quick, for example, found Robert Pollock's poem *The Course of Time* conducive to creative thinking. "It occurred to me while reading, how much more we draw from an author than even he himself intended," she noted. "It seemed verily so in this instance. Every word suggested a topic of thought." She contended, "I believe here lies the power of an author." For the same reasons, a rhetoric teacher appreciated Emerson's work: "I do enjoy reading what he has to say, always,—because he gives you so much room to think in." One Congregationalist divinity student even "got a new idea from Matt. 11:30," a text long familiar to him, while performing his routine devotions.[35] Countless improvisations like this made the region a seething cauldron of new ideas.

Ideas that may have begun cooking in a single reader's mind came to a boil through communicating them. Readers recorded their impressions for others to read or set their ideas out for discussion and debate in open forums—during oral reading sessions or social calls, or at church groups and reading club meetings. In social settings, they recalled past reading experiences, derived literary allusions, and applied ideas. Such dissemination made individual literary experience ever interpersonal.

Most folks believed that ideas were rooted in experience, so they seldom abstracted them from material existence, emotional response included. As Martha Osborne Barrett, then in a boot-and-bonnet factory, explained, "I am no critic, I only know what touches a responsive chord in my own heart, and that which touches the most deeply I call *good.*" Yet the mind-body quandary perplexed most readers as it did Charles Cobb, who could not, as we have seen, reconcile that man was "1st what he eats, lives on, & has in his body . . . and 2dly what he knows, i.e., his mind."[36] Despite the impasse, much of what was received and ruminated upon was grounded in everyday social life. Mind and matter were one and the same in the sayings and doings of nobodies, and this sensitized them to textual features as vessels of ideas.

From authors readers above all asked for verisimilitude—the closest, most believable replication of reality—and deemed texts with realistic settings, plot, and characters as worthy. Credible characters most often captured interest. As a newspaperman's wife saw, "Truths brought out in characters meet the sympathies of more people perhaps than in any other way." An author's best chance at getting ideas across was to personify them, yet not at reality's expense. *Uncle Tom's Cabin* enraptured the aforementioned writing master and day laborer, for example, because it was lifelike, not fanciful, "almost visible before my eyes," as he asserted. Anything that undermined credibility, like impossible perfection, could kill interest. "[T]he principal characters are so much nearer perfection than any real persons are," complained a farmer's daughter "disappointed" with Susan Warner's *Wide, Wide World.* "Arthur Blague is so excruciatingly pious!" a miffed schoolgirl wrote of the hero of *Miss Gilbert's Career.* Like most of her contemporaries, she preferred characters with flaws, in other words, those who had traits in common with real people. Reading about characters one might daily meet was thus hardly escapist but social. Since they acted as surrogates for known types, discussion of characters thus easily blurred into commentary on social life. "We do get out of all patience with good Lady Nickelby," Mary Pierce Poor's fiancé admitted of Dickens's *Nicholas Nickelby,* "as we do with an hundred good ladies in real life that we meet." A Lynn grade school teacher saw "real life" villains in a T. S. Arthur story, "'The Minister and the Merchant,'" in her Sunday school book, noting that "too true I fear, many men are like the merchant." Similarly, a country schoolmaster averred that Parson Abraham Adams in Henry Fielding's *Joseph Andrews* "is a finely drawn character; and I have seen his counter part in a layman."[37] Readers expected fictional characters to react as they would under similar social circumstances.

Credible characters both shared common traits with real people and were, paradoxically, "entirely original." Since they were not formulaic, they seemed unique among real and fictional creations. "Most of the . . . characters are, in their way, inimitable," Charlotte Forten claimed after reading Dickens's *Old Curiosity Shop.* "There could not be a lovelier, a nobler conception than Little Nell." Upon hearing *A Midsummer Night's Dream* read at her literary club, Frances Merritt Quick realized, "Every character of Shakespeare's is indeed a unit, unlike each and every other." Authors were scolded for mass producing their own stable of characters. "Have been reading Say and Seal by Mrs. Elizabeth Wetherel & as I read I wondered why she would have her heroines all so much alike," a farmer's daughter reported with a critical eye; "was not interesting [*sic*] in it after all." "I know what I should like," she offered; "to know of *homely girls,* how they get along &c &c. I am thinking of a story I read some time ago of a poor Factory Girl."[38] Fictive depictions that reflected both common human flaws and diversity ironically appealed most. That very blend of typification and particularity is what made them so much like real people.

Good biographies and histories did no less, and readers knew that authors painted even nonfictional "characters" in literary colors. "The character of Columbus is represented far more noble and excellent, than I had before thought it," a spinster wrote concerning William Robertson's account of New World conquest. "The exciting scenes of the history, the valor, courageous and ambitious

Fig. 12.1 ✦ While a student at Holy Cross College, James A. Healy wrote down his response in his diary to several books, including William Hickling Prescott's *Ferdinand and Isabella* (1837) and Agnes Strickland's *Queens of England* (1840–48), and to the Boston newspapers he read for recreation. James A. Healy, carte de visite, Worcester, Mass. Courtesy of College of the Holy Cross Archives.

characters of Cortes and Pisarro were calculated to attract the attention." In other words, Robertson did the calculating. James Healy (fig. 12.1) saw each of Agnes Strickland's players in her *Queens of England* as a pure manifestation of some quality the author wished to portray: "Henry VIII of England . . . only wanted bristles to make him a hog," "(Katharine) as then spelt, of Aragon was a noble high-minded & pious lady," and "Ann Boly[ne] a vain and fickle ~~lady~~ woman, spiteful and unforgiving in her revenge," Healy observed. To this Catholic seminarian, authorial biases necessarily shaded the images, and in Catharine Parr, Strickland created a "paragon of Protestant perfection." In so doing, she "probably overlooked" that queen's "hysterics about being accused."[39] As they pondered character delineation, readers also thought critically about assumed audiences and marked their distance from them.

Readers might so much identify with characters, whether fictional or real, that they wanted to be like them or have a relationship with them. "O may I emulate him" was the conclusion a reader drew from "the Life of Rev David Stoner," one of several spiritual biographies he read, including fellow Methodists William Bramwell's and John Wesley's, that stayed close enough to their subjects' own writings to be like "a transcript of their minds." Heroes and heroines might be conflated, as one young woman explained after reading Grace Kennedy's *Dunallan;* "there is nothing strained or unnatural or even unattainable in the piety of the hero. . . . You feel yourself identified with both himself & his young wife." As if this doubling were not confusing enough, she triangulated herself with the couple, noting that "one yearns for communion with such choice spirits." Such longings for "communion" might resemble intimate ties. "*Cora* was one of *my* models for a *wife,* and, of *course,* I should feel somewhat attached to her," Eunice Cobb declared just after finishing *Cora and the Doctor.* "Hero is a most splendid creation—I am horribly in love with her and some half dozen others—real and imaginary," a law librarian claimed of the heroine in the *Adventures of an Attorney.*[40] Literature ably provided imaginary objects of affection to take their place among real ones.

Like realistic characters, credible plots and reliable narratives were sought after. Although readers wanted a "fascinating narrative" to carry them through, they valued tenable ones. John Park used this standard when he compared two novels by G. P. R. James: *The King's Highway*'s "incidents . . . [were] not forced against probability," but *Gowrie*'s "incidents . . . are romance" merely. The "very unnatural . . . plot" of that author's novel *The Robber* so disgusted one reader that she dubbed it "the *James* defect." Factual accounts were subjected to the same scrutiny. Samuel May Jr. appreciated Jonathan Walker's "thoroughly *'unvarnished'* narrative" of his Florida trial and imprisonment for helping slaves escape. "The weak and silly plot" in Rebecca Reed's *Six Months in a Convent* ". . . I never believed," a college student testified of the supposed exposé. Substance or novelty might serve in lieu of mimesis, but even these were often lacking. "A most unsatisfactory plot" or "miserable story" in *Corinne* displeased two readers, the "slight story" of *Mary Barton* dissatisfied another, and an all-too-predictable ending of an unnamed story of southern life left one more cold. "I cannot say I liked the plot," he explained. "Thought the terminus was just what I expected it would be after I learned the Characters of the Actors." Stories that "unravelled too quickly on the last page" could also annoy, as might "too horrible" or "far too sad . . ." surprise endings. Conclusions should leave satisfied smiles, wistful thoughts, or awakened consciences.[41]

Many texts featured no character other than their authors' own persona as manifested in their style. A good one made reading flow easily by being "simple," "plain," and "clear" enough to suggest conversation. Frances Merritt Quick saw this in Henry Rogers's *Greyson Letters:* "I like his talk; there is no tinsel wordiness in it." For similar reasons, a rural deeds clerk "like[d] the stile" of Irving's life of Washington "very much, [as] he is not so prosey." Simplicity was valued even among highly educated folk. A collegian admired essayist Benjamin Rush's "plain, practical style," from which he "gathered much information." Plainness meant getting to the point for one country schoolmaster, who thought Robert Peel's speeches were "concise and have nothing which does not tend directly to advance the matter or idea in hand." In being direct and accessible, however, wit helped, for it more finely delineated authors' personas. Byron's cleverness in his "Vision of Judgement" was appreciated by Charles Cobb, who vouched, "Every line or two brings some Bible idea up so that it appears most infinitely ridiculous." It tickled his fancy, too: "[I]t is the most laughable thing I ever read. And [it] don't make a person laughs . . . with a fool's reason either." Byron and other witty writers were simply good friends and allies to have around, yet wit giving way to vulgarity alarmed readers. Coarse language, "slang," or other "offenses against good taste" were routinely condemned. "Beautifully written, but somewhat obs[c]ene manners portrayed!" was a lawyer's reaction to an unnamed play by Henry Fielding. Sometimes colloquial phrases—for example, the "Yankeeisms" in Orville Dewey's *Discourses*—"would shock" the more refined, according to one reader.[42]

Good style was not enough, as overall tone had to be right, too, though it was more elusive and variable. After all, tone was an effect produced by style interacting with other textual elements and readers' own predilections. An ever waggish (and frequently penniless) mill worker sensed a "devilish" tone to a story entitled "Money." The pious Frances Merritt Quick, who would eventually marry a minister, thought that the "spirit and tone" of Pollock's *Course of Time* "seems to me a truly poetical beauty." She averred that the "richest poetry draws its essence, its vitality from spiritual conceptions." Even more than poetry and fiction, tracts and speeches exuded strong tone. On the Civil War's brink, a partisan businessman was moved to "record my cordial approbation of . . . [the] tone & character" of New York Republican senator William Seward's speech on the state of the country. A rabid anti-Jacksonian farm woman was "delighted with . . . [the] manly independent tone" of a U.S. senator from Maine's 1830 speech against the president's spoils-of-office activities during a Senate recess. It would be wrong to conclude, however, that readers appreciated tone only when a text suited them. Hannah Hicock Smith, who deemed congressmen "upholding war & slavery" nothing but "rascals," in 1848 allowed that South Carolina senator John C. "Calhoun's speech [on the Mexican War] has more sense & soundness than all congress . . . ," but added that "there are many defects in it."[43] Tone could not bridge vast ideological differences.

Characters, narration, plot, style, tone, and other textual features were but the wrapping in which the information and ideas readers so desired came. They therefore thought about the fullness or scantiness of what a text had to say and whether or not it had "new matter" or "many new facts" instead of old tired ones. While fact-filled books could certainly be dull, readers prized those that were both "interesting & informing" or, as Charlotte Forten deemed Plutarch's *Lives,* "[r]ich in interest and information." New facts could be received as exciting discoveries. "I never thought of any such thing before I studied the book," a normal school student exclaimed upon learning the "[b]est time to take exercise" from a physiology text. Cynthia Congdon, who found "much useful information" in Edward Littell's *Living Age,* learned that her hometown's name, East Greenwich, originated in the "Saxon word, Greena Wir or, green Creek." Charles Cobb was "Much astonished" to find out from a piece on fence making that wood "conveys moisture up it while alive, & so it does afterwards if it stands butt down, but if top down it can't." He wryly concluded, "I don't know everything yet." Folks with prior reading on a topic employed contrast-and-compare techniques. After spending one morning with the "Memoirs of Madame Junot," during which time she was "very much amused and entertained," Harriett Low conceded, "I cannot put confidence in many of her opinions and statements because they are at variance with everything I have ever read before." A primer so displeased a retired doctor that he cried, "Here is the Devil in a New Spelling book." It is "full of errors & absurdities," he griped, pointing out inconsistencies with previous authorities.[44]

Most newspaper readers weighed the credible against the "equally incredible" to find that news was often "exaggerated," "shabby," or manufactured from "statements [that] are entirely untrue." Errors were sometimes deliberate. "Last eve'g I counted the different slanderous articles in one small sized newspaper ('Republican Journal[']) & they were 29," Persis Andrews avouched. "These attacks on private reputation, such as now fill some prints, . . . are really sickening," one reader fulminated. Maligned readers had reason to rant, but most targets of sloppy journalism were merely annoyed. "They have put me into the account of the Fancy Dress Ball, in the Herald, as being only ten years old," a sixteen-year-old socialite grumbled; "and in another paper they say, I wore a magnificent pearl head-dress. They must have confounded me with mother." John Park thought it absurd that the

Boston Post had erroneously reported that his healthy son "died . . . of cholera, after a few hours illness!" Readers spotted omissions as well as mistakes. "The papers never say any thing about the thousand of poor fellows that can[']t earn their board," a Forty-niner noticed while reading propaganda about California.[45] Clearly, newspaper information was not always informative or useful.

If newspapers' usefulness could be dubious, what then of fiction? Surprisingly, it could be considered useful if it taught a lesson. Religious or moral instruction could come from spiritually "informative" novels such as Elizabeth Missing Sewell's *Experience of Life,* which one woman found to be "very interesting & very useful," or Hannah Farnham Sawyer Lee's *Three Experiments of Living,* which for a clerk "embodies . . . much valuable instruction." To be instructive or useful, didactic fiction had to be mimetic, or else it would be open to the charge one postmaster made against *The Lamplighter*—that it was of "no utility" because of its supposedly strained characters. A clear moral also made fiction useful. A physician's son viewed *Ellen; or, Forgive and Forget* as "very instructive" because it "prov[ed] that innocence will triump[h], and the wicked be found out." Decades after Susanna Haswell Rowson's 1791 tale *Charlotte Temple* was published, a farmer declared, "It may safely be asserted that a more useful Novel was never written to be put into the hands of young females in order to guard them against imprudent confidence in the plausible professions of artful seducers." One small-town port collector learned from Shakespeare's *Othello* that "it behooves every married man to beware of jealousy."[46] Lessons there were aplenty in fiction.

Texts could act instrumentally for moral ends insofar as they gave readers an image of themselves and a compass for their placement within society. Martha Osborne Barrett pondered her search for wisdom under economic difficulties while reading *Farmingdale,* a tale of an orphan who "struggles upward." The hardworking machine worker expanded upon the story's theme to fit her case: "I feel I can yet accomplish much. Sometimes I feel almost desponding[;] the thought of wanting so much intellectually and physically almost unnerves me." She then situated herself among other people with similar handicaps and wondered "how many have had to do more than I have to, and have succeeded[?]" Like Barrett, an unemployed plat maker ruminated upon his own sagacity and future hopes while reading an old issue of the *Dial.* "It is a very good volume to read now although it has attained some considerable age," he opined. "But that is the case usually with works of real merit; they are like wine—they improve by age." One can almost see his pen falter for a moment before he turned the lesson upon himself: "So may I I [*sic*] grow wiser and better as life wears away." Spiritual fullness rather than intellectual wealth was coveted by a Congregationalist minister, who, while reading India missionary letters, "felt that I ought to be more devoted to God than I am." Harriett Low's disdain for artifice was aroused by tales set in medieval times: "I always wish when reading books that bring to mind the days of Chivalry and romance that I had lived *then.*" Chafing under rules of feminine propriety in British-dominated Macao, she looked longingly backward to what she thought was a freer time. "Then it was no harm for a lady to show forth her best feelings and be herself. Oh but times have changed," she mused. And she cast a cold eye upon contemporary mores: "All must be heartless, *made up* creatures, without feelings of any kind."[47] As if magic mirrors, texts reflected back one's innermost thoughts and desires.

But texts were not entirely malleable. They firmly stated and often clearly demonstrated ideas that, when held up against readers' own notions, could either controvert or support them. As Martha Osborne Barrett explained, "How often in our readings do we meet with thoughts that seem so like our own . . . and can scarcely persuade ourselves that they were not the product of our own brains." But concordance between reader and text was not always possible. For this reason, readers often found themselves agreeing or disagreeing and explicating at length points of convergence or divergence. "One article [from the *New York Ledger*] on the measure of manhood represents my own views precisely," a chronically unemployed man maintained, before going on at length to explain how. Another reader declared without qualification of writer Hannah More, "I exactly agree with her opinions." Religious texts usually evoked more than simple affirmatives or negatives. They confirmed or deepened beliefs, on the one hand, or tried toleration, on the other. Harriett Low, for example, worked her way through several Trinitarian works in her quest of doctrinal certitude but fell back upon those of her own persuasion: "I find all my sentiments which I have formed from my own reason and as I understand the Scriptures agree when I compare them with the Unitarian writers." She earlier confessed, before she had made up her mind about orthodoxy, "I cannot bring myself yet to believe in the Trinity" but conceded that "Arguments strong on both sides quite puzzle me." While Low read to reconfirm her beliefs, Cynthia Congdon simply read whatever works were on hand, only to find herself confronted with unfamiliar doctrine. "I have been reading a Catholic book, named sick calls," the Methodist remarked. "I like the most of it very much, but there are some things with which of course I cannot say I am satisfied, but I would not by any means condemn the Catholic because he does not believe as I do." Political tracts especially invited intellectual accordance or repudiation. "He is a very good writer, and shows his principles to be of the right sort in my humble opinion," a printer thought while reading a newspaper article on the 1848 presidential candidates. "I agree with him in almost every part of his piece."[48] Even in agreement, partisan readers were discriminating.

Yet ideas came in all colors, not just black and white, so astute readers assessed authors' skill in arguing their theses. Hinton Rowan Helper's book *The Impending*

Crisis put forth, by Charlotte Forten's abolitionist reckoning, "[o]ne of the best arguments against slavery I've ever heard." Not all writers addressed sympathetic audiences, of course. To budding Catholic theologian James Healy, a "sermon in the N.O. Delta tring to prove the non-existence of hell" was "a miserable bungle of assertions founded upon mere ignorance or upon a desire to mislead." An orthodox minister found one writer for the *Unitarian* to be "more expert at assertions than in reasoning." Sometimes when cherished viewpoints were not at stake, readers like Frances Jocelyn hailed an author's ability to sway skeptics with facts. "It proved without a shadow of doubt to my mind that Louis 17th son of 'Marie Antoinette,' is resideing in this country," she claimed of a magazine essay, "'Have we a Bourbon among us[?]'" Evaluations of argumentation could be more equivocal. A printer's apprentice saw in one electricity advocate a linguistic gamester rather than a clever challenger to the theory of gravity. "I believe the author attributes the phenomena Newton ascribes to *attraction of bodies,* to *Electricity,* in two different states—positive and negative," the craftsman began, before rejoinding: "If he is correct (as I have belief he is) I don['']t see that he *overthrows* anything of Newton's theory but some of its *phrases.*—the whole thing is but just the same, in the end." This reader may have made a halfway concession, but others fully considered authors' cases only ultimately to decide against them, as did elderly John Park, when heard "a rhapsody rather than an argument" in William Mountford's *Euthanasy* offering to salve his worries about death: "The alleged proofs are, for the most part, mere assumptions." If lack of argumentation could undermine a palatable message, reasoning and evidence were closely scrutinized by some disinterested readers. This was especially likely when authors seemed to "go . . . too far," as Mary Pierce Poor believed Unitarian George Frederick Simmons did in his tract *Who Was Jesus Christ?* "[He] explains some [Bible] passages, altering them," Poor told a friend, "when I think they would not injure his argument were they left as they are." Even fiction played in the contest of ideas. "It seems to take an opposite view of things from what Harriett Beacher Stow [*sic*] does," a schoolteacher was quick to notice while reading Caroline Lee Hentz's *Planter's Northern Bride.*[49] Contrasting the two refined her understanding of the antislavery issue.

Through comparison, readers integrated the text before them into their past reading. Readers most likely assayed two or more works by an author. "'Evangeline' is a perfect Gem," a mill worker wrote of his affection for Longfellow to a companion: "Hiawatha I like much—it is great and original—But the Golden Legend[,] Eureka! it is the best of all I have read." Another common point of comparison can be seen in James Healy's evaluation of one author's style against another's. "I read one or two of [William Pitt, earl of] Chatham's speeches and admire his logic extremely," the seminarian told his journal. "Also [Edmund] Burke's to the Electors of Bristol but his style has not the fire & ardour of Chatham although his sentences are longer and more harmonious." One did not have to read extensively to pronounce a text the best among its peers. One young farmer read an account of a polar expedition and confidently concluded, "Though not able to compare them with other works of arctic adventure and discovery, I do not believe that it is surpassed in interest & value by any thing of the kind."[50]

Rather than simply comparing, agreeing with, or disputing texts, readers used them to forge ideas of broad social significance. Such rumination might extend authors' arguments or comment upon printed statements of fact, but it involved even solitary readers in public discourse. In their thinking, readers frequently brought to bear current news stories. "Let the zealots in religion—break up the churches—destroy communities—nay *burn down Convents,"* a farm woman, with an eye to the aforementioned 1834 anti-Catholic incident, wrote, chastising her daughter for accepting prejudiced accounts. Amid oblique references to specific events exemplifying religious bigotry, the mother held out one hope: "Let the politicians in politics—embroil neighborhoods, violate the laws and overturn constitutions—but let the family compact remain unbroken." Religious zeal's destructive power was recognized, too, by a ship chandler's wife when she confronted dire newspaper predictions of war with the Utah Mormons. "There is nothing that will rouse to desperation more easily than religious controversy," she claimed. "A man will fight for his religion when nothing else will rouse him to strike a blow." A Bible passage allowed Charlotte Forten to formulate a plea for abolition. "The third verse of the last chapter of Hebrews—'Remember them that are in bonds as bound with them' suggested many thoughts to my mind: *Remember the poor slave as bound with him."* The text revealed to her that the movement had yet far to go. "How few even of those who are opposed to slavery realize this!" she wondered. "If they felt thus so ardent, so untiring, would be their efforts that they would soon accomplish the overthrow of this iniquitous system." Women's rights and gender issues also traipsed through everyday cogitations. While reading the life of a minister's wife, Mary Pierce Poor opined, "It is well to see what a woman can do, without genius, & in a purely feminine sphere." She then pronounced on women's roles: "There are some noble women in the world yet, & women too who make no fuss about their goodness or their rights. The *doers* are better than the *talkers . . . ,* though both are well in their place." Some women celebrated the "talkers," though. Reading Elizabeth Barrett Browning's *Aurora Leigh* inspired a woman rhetorician to mark the public emergence of women's intellect as evidenced by the poem, its main character, and the author: "I think woman is *some body* in these days, if all the talk and writing lessons do any thing." She pointed to Fredrika Bremer's novel *Hertha* as "in the same *progressive* strain."[51] Ideas from texts were grist for both social inertia and change.

Given the heterogeneous universe of print that catered to this intellectual curiosity, texts, if widely and earnestly engaged, offered instruction in social toleration and, at times, almost cultural relativism. We already know how Charles Cobb viewed the mind-body split after reading "The Tree of Knowledge": that people can believe whatever they want, whether "the Bible, Koran, book of Mormon Swedenborg & the spirits, or Thomas Paine." That relativism also framed one Episcopalian's ideas as she pondered reading's relationship to faith during an engagement with Emerson's first book of essays. "I have felt the emotions he describes on the chap. on Friendship," she avowed, almost despite herself. "I should think it very odd to change the principles of ones religious Faith because you find pleasure in the perusal of one of a different persuasion," she maintained. But she cut room for the infidel: "These seem . . . scriptural let them emanate from whatever source." Certainly, for pious believers like her, a mere brush with Emerson or other heterodox thinkers seldom undermined faith. But some readers wrestled more strenuously with repugnant ideas; they corralled and confronted them, then subjected them to further analysis. One Baptist weaving-room clerk, for example, formulated questions about the liberal doctrine of universal atonement as espoused in a sermon he read. "He argues," he wrote of the author, "that if a man does not do the thing strictly honest, . . . the upbraiding of his own conscience will surely follow." The young man declared, "How far this is correct I will not say, but that it is strictly so I very much doubt." He refused to let it rest there, as queries followed one upon another: "Do we not see men acting dishonestly day after day? Does not the same person commit fraud upon fraud? . . . Is it not apparent to impartial observation that some become so callous, so hardened in crime, they do not feel the sting of conscience when they do wrong?" When all was said and done, he reaffirmed his belief in judgment after death, but he nonetheless traveled through unfamiliar territory to reassert his claim. In so doing, he granted viewpoints unlike his own the respect of not dismissing them out of hand but engaging them on a field of reason and experience. Not every person walked this pathway, for religious, racial, ethnic, economic, gender-based, and other forms of intolerance chronically flared up, as they did in every other part of the country. Yet for many, reading, precisely because of its social inflection, often led the way out of bigotry and fanaticism and, for some, toward abolition, women's rights, and other liberal reforms. Most enlightened readers would have agreed with one woman who, questing for spiritual knowledge, earnestly but skeptically read some Swedenborgian texts loaned to her. "The search after Truth is long & laborious," she observed, "& we must be content to gain it by little & little, & often thro' painful experiences. . . . [A]nd we need to struggle and die every day, or we cannot gather increase of life."[52] The very idea that truth itself was elusive sharply struck this spiritual pilgrim during her reading. And as she well knew, new ideas gathered from the tree of knowledge were lethal to obdurate hearts and minds.

As these readers engaged texts, they continually picked ideas like pieces of fruit, tasting and feeding upon them, even if it meant a kind of death to old notions. The fruits of knowledge, however, just as often multiplied as readers planted their own ideas between lines of text. Much passed through readers' minds as they winnowed what interested them from what did not. But once interest was established, and texts were engaged emotionally and intellectually, there came a time for reaping new ideas and incorporating them into one's outlook. Yet the harvesting, it seemed, never ended, as new ideas continually surfaced.

Outside of the Text

With reaping over, readers digested their store of new ideas. Ideally, they had acquired something valuable, lasting, and useful. Intensive study, of course, almost always yielded memorized excerpts, some mastery over subjects, or at least new funds of ideas from which to draw. General readers wanted the same, but to a lesser degree, and both they and those who studied wish to hold on to as much as possible. "I wish that I may remember what I have read or at least some particular things," was the way a shopkeeper put it.[53] Replaying memories thus was the most common after-the-fact response to texts.

Often, against readers' wills, textual traces stuck like glue, with continual intellectual, emotional, and even physical impact. A Methodist minister, for one, could not shake off Henry Glassford Bell's *Life of Mary Queen of Scots.* "[I]t occupies my thoughts considerably," he realized even when the book was put to rest. "My head is so susceptible of delicate feeling that even small things . . . bind me by almost invincible chains." Because readers so valued retention, they welcomed lingering impressions of informative texts, such as John Lloyd Stephens's travels in the East. "I shall not soon forget his interesting description of the ancient temples, tombs and pyramids," Charlotte Forten was pleased to state.[54] She had engraved the book's literary renditions of antiquities upon her mind.

Although information filled the mind for days to come, literature also supplied lasting corporeal, emotional, and spiritual benefits. A Boston matron swore that Dickens's *Christmas Carol* "has quite soothed my headache this morning." A merchant's daughter used texts to mend a broken heart; when her fiancé broke a date, she "read a sermon 'Retribution,' & felt worse" and then read "'Mary Barton' and felt better"—the dismal tale of English factory laborers perhaps a reminder of her relative good fortune. After reading Longfellow's *Hyperion* on the anniversary of her close friend's death, a distraught Martha Osborne Barrett, while in an ill-fated stint as a schoolteacher, conceded in the language of its poetic prose that "to night its calmness has been imparted unto me." Religious texts, too, acted therapeutically as they "cheered up . . . spirits considerably" and dispelled "mean & groveling tho'ts." One Jewish pedlar, who in "a mood of depression" reluctantly resorted to reading "some beautiful prayers in the English Bible," claimed that it "relieved my heart," although he "pledged that [he] would not spend another sacred holiday in this manner." Such healing worked only on those receptive to its puissance. "I expects something plagues [the captain], and he has no other way to ease his mind but to growl with us around him," first mate John Congdon fumed. "I see he reads his bible sometimes but I don't see as it does any good he is no better for it."[55] Taken in small doses, texts, perhaps, were impotent.

Yet at times, even small measures of vile textual potions darkened readers' spirits, sometimes for days to come. Violent texts, like parts of Walter Scott's *Fair Maid of Perth,* so much "left a horrid impression" upon one reader that she admitted days later that "the memory of it still rides like the night mare upon my mind." Other troubled readers reported nocturnal tossing and turning. "I *could not sleep* all night," John Park grumbled, blaming a heterodox *Christian Examiner* article. Selections from the *Spiritual Telegraph* gave Charles Cobb sleepless anxiety one night. "I had read about 'Luminous manifestations of spirits' and about 10 P.M. I was astonished to see a light on the wall over my bed, moving round, and I began to sweat in full expectation of seeing a specter," he confessed. "It is impossible for one who don't sleep alone to get an idea of the effect of any such thing on one who does." The antidote was to modify one's reading. "I have such horid dreams & they are so connected with my reading that I fear I shall have to give up Shak[es]p[ea]re until I get better," Persis Sibley Andrews promised herself after reading *Richard III;* "never did his diabolical depravity so horrify me—his consummate duplicity is exactly portrayed." Literary nightmares could cast dreamers in imaginary social dramas. The night he read the part of *Noctes Ambrosianæ* that gives "Hogg's account of his sleeping between two ghosts," an abolitionist attorney dreamed that "on returning from a party with L. [his wife] the carriage set us down at my office"; he found the "whole building seemed blazing with light: and on looking in at the window below, I discovered that it was Ghost-Ball—All were dancing in their white shrouds. The horror awoke me, instantly."[56] Such were the perils of unconscious response.

Not all literary dreams terrified, of course, although they usually unsettled, as Harriett Low's make plain (fig. 12.2). She once "dreamed of Napoleon . . . , and all those *'critturs'*" after reading *Memoirs of Count Lavalette.* "[M]y dreams were *anatomical,"* she chronicled the night she thumbed through some books on physiology. Upon reading a life of Anne Boleyn, she had ludicrous, if not horrifying night visions of her head being figuratively on the chopping block: "I dreamed that I was to be crowned Queen of England of all things in this world! Never should I *deign* to think of it in my waking hours: hardly tolerate it in my sleeping moments." Her most taxing dream, however, transported her from steamy Macao back home momentarily to Salem through a textual vehicle, James Fenimore Cooper's novel *The Spy,* and the character whom that author made famous, Leatherstocking himself, Natty Bumppo. "Felt rather melancholy when I awoke this morning, for in my dreams I was in America," she began, and explained, "I

Fig. 12.2 ✦ In this portrait painted while she was living in Macao, Harriett Low holds a book, perhaps one of the many she read and wrote about in her diary kept for her sister. Portrait of Harriett Low by George Chinnery (M18709). Photograph courtesy of the Peabody Essex Museum.

was in Salem and was to stay there till Monday Night when Natty Bumpo's play was to be performed called The Spy." Her homesickness registered: "The next day I was to take the stage for New York with Father who was then in Salem—but alas I awoke and found myself in China still."[57] In her literary dreams at least, Low was reunited with her family through a favorite fictional character-cum-playwright. The allusion to *The Spy,* set in the Revolutionary War era about a peddler suspected of being a British spy, doubtless reflected Low's alienation from her largely British social set in Macao.

Texts read long ago, such as *The Spy,* which Low probably encountered before living in Macao, were employed for creating allusions to everyday circumstances. Through them the social world became suffused with literary sensibility and literature took on social meaning. If living people were ever in mind while reading, what one read was ever in mind while living. Quotes extracted from memory or excerpt books could allude to everyday life. A concise one, for example, might efficiently sum up personality traits or flaws that otherwise required a flood of words. "Oh dear! 'I'se so wicked'!" Mary Pierce Poor indicted herself for gossiping in a paraphrase of *Uncle Tom's Cabin*'s African American "imp," Topsy. A schoolteacher used allusion to reveal his feelings about an estranged uncle. "I cannot give over hoping good from Uncle Sam[l.] on the principle laid down by Carlyle that 'the Dunce is the *only fatal* person,'" he wrote, meaning that because his uncle was not stupid, there was hope for him. Allusions captured delight upon receiving letters. "Like Desdemona listening to Othello's story," a European sojourner replied to a correspondent, "I did with 'greedy eyes devour up your discourse.'" Well-selected quotes also applied to political turmoil. Caught up in proslavery forces' routine nighttime ambushes of antislavery settlers in bleeding Kansas, a Yankee migrant "recalled the perfect imagery of the phrase" from Whittier's "'Pass of the Sierra'": "'Beyond their camp fire's *wall of dark*.'"[58] All was darkness beyond her antislavery aura of safety. Sometimes short excerpts said more by suggestion than wordy tomes.

Many literary allusions were more general or conceptual. Rather than being drawn from specific lines, they assumed understanding of a text's themes or characters. Readers could "awak[en] from the Rip Van Winkle sleep," for example, "feel" as a military academy instructor did, "like the Ancient Mariner" during a "drought [that] is terrible," or feign to be as "exhausted as Christian in Pilgrim's progress." A returning student and an "old classmate" would "be the last of the Mohicans" in a class full of newcomers; Calista Billings in a fearful moment looked "very much like Bachelor Butterfly when his lady love made an attack upon him" (a reference to one of the nation's earliest comic books); John Park had an "interview . . . as good as a volume from Sir Walter Scott"; a merchant's son returned tired and seasick "from [a] Robinson Crusoe expedition." These diverse, simple references to titles, characters, or themes, which by their very easy currency suggest how much literature and life mixed, sometimes carried complex and often scathing messages. Charlotte Forten noted this when she deemed her aunt "wicked enough to call" a bare-headed young woman "bent on enjoying the cool of the day" by the name "'Jane Eyre.'" Charles Cobb referred to a classic to indict some slovenly farm animals. "Our pig pen is a perfect Paradise Lost," he complained; "the water is up to the pig's belly anywhere in it." Literary allusions succinctly sketched the social vacuum of loneliness. John Park's daughter had only to mention the name "Ulysses" to describe the feeling in coming home after a trip to "find none but the dog rejoicing to see you." Biblical allusions helped westward migrants make sense of their journey. After crossing the Great Basin, filled with "several hundred teams" on the Oregon Trail, one New Hampshire pioneer was "reminded . . . of the Pilgrims progress of Bunyon"; upon seeing whirlwinds in Mormon territory, the same traveler "was reminded of the wandering of the children of Israel as they were led by a pillar of a cloud by day" (Exodus 13:21–22). Literary allusions eased guilty consciences, too. "His empty cushion upbraids me as Banquo's chair did Macbeth," John Park wrote after putting his rheumatic canine Fido out of his misery.[59] Allusions were like pigments on a palette fit for painting life in literary colors.

As readers colored their world, fiction supplied as much allusive paint as nonfiction. Using it usually meant setting social reality against fictionalized illusion. A schoolboy, for instance, distinguished real-life from textual goddesses. "There may not be that heavenly beauty (we read about) in her countenance," he wrote of an object of his desire, "yet there is an expression . . . which can not be described, but which must be seen to be felt." Clever allusions were fed to hopeless romantics as strong doses of reality. An Irish immigrant's daughter did this when she warned her infatuated sister that her predilection for novels clouded her good sense. "[D]oes the soul of the lover dear Sarah live in the body of another as some author beautifully describes it[?]" she asked rhetorically; "all this sounds pretty when read but you know nothing gives pleasure unless we know it to have its foundation on truth."[60] These critical references to a fictional land in which women are unearthly beauties and where love beats true in all men's hearts pulled distracted readers back to social reality.

Readers' textual engagements spurred them to act, follow up, and learn more. In this manner, Longfellow's *Hyperion,* with its Teutonic references, ignited a fire in Charlotte Forten to learn German. Harriett Low wanted to study history after reading the fictionalized *Philip Augustus.* It is, she wrote, "rather a good thing to read Historical novels as it induces you to search out the real history of the parties concerned." One twelve-year-old Massachusetts boy, conversant in "all Dickens' works," wanted to "find the places" mentioned in the novels "on the map [of London]." Most fundamentally, people inspired by their reading were roused to undertake more by the same author. Indeed, mastering authors' oeuvres could be a long-term response to a single reading. Some readers resolved to act not for themselves but upon others. A storekeeper's granddaughter found that the *Memoir of Catharine Brown,* an early Cherokee convert to Christianity, "awakened in my heart an ardent &, I trust, invincible desire to dwell with & instruct that injured race" of American Indians. *Visits of Mercy* inspired Frederick Gleason to "distribute" money "in a way to . . . releive much suffering" among prisoners. More mundane affairs, like health, were altered by persuasive writing. After reading John Balbirnie's *Philosophy of the Water-Cure,* a machinist's son sent a letter to a New York bookseller from which he got the book, on behalf of his brother, afflicted with typhus fever. "Do you not think cold water to be applicable to his case[?]" he asked. Charles Cobb reported that a friend with whom he "took lesson NO. 2 i[n] swimming yesterday" at the reservoir resolved to "swim about every day" to keep fit after reading the *Water Cure Journal's* nostrum to do so. A clerk "determined to confine myself to one cigar a day and that after the evening meal" upon reading an article on "Smoking" in Thomas Webster's *Encyclopædia of Domestic Economy.*[61] He and his contemporaries indeed wanted to activate their post-reading reception on the stage of life—to make it part of their social experience.

People furthered socioliterary experience by honing their post-reading response through discussion. Among small groups, readers refined thoughts, sharpened comprehension, and effected ideas in the everyday world. Several folks believed such conversation furthered social and intellectual development. After reading Francis Wayland's *Elements of Political Economy,* one clerk remarked, "It w[ou]ld be more pleasant if I could have some one to help me[;] society, if of the right kind, is beneficial & by conversing upon what I read it would fix the subject more strongly in my mind." Whether it was one attentive pair of ears or a group of gregarious, hometown literati, society alone could give literary experience its most enduring meaning. Readers, therefore, craved opportunities to engage in literary discussions. Home was the most likely place to find conversants, especially if group reading was the norm. Persis Sibley Andrews, a member of an active family circle reading group, observed that "where we all hear the same we are more apt to converse about the subject, & thus its most prominent features are fixed in the mind, & new ideas elicited upon it." More intensive literary interchange took place when two readers built their relationship upon such discussion. As we have seen, Charles Cobb could expect some literary chat at his uncle Henry's house, while Martha Osborne Barrett could call upon her well-read friend Lucy Colby to "have a literary talk with her." Mary Pierce Poor also forged a literary relationship—with one of Margaret Fuller's students, Mary Ann Jackson. "Our conversations are generally suggested by books we have read," she informed her fiancé Henry Poor. "When last she was here we talked about a number of the dial we had both been reading." Her own courtship with Poor was conducted through literary discussions. After they married, she came to rely upon him for equilibrium. "Some of my acquaintances are going mad upon the subject of the Sovereignty of the Individual," she claimed after a whirlwind of talk concerning Elizabeth Cleghorn Gaskell's novel *Ruth,* about a fallen woman making good. "Henry's conversation acts as a sort of balance wheel to keep me from undue extravagances."[62] Readers thus juggled intersecting and sometimes conflicting communities of discourse about books.

Alongside literary discussion in long-term relationships, conversations might also occur at the drop of a hat. As Harriett Low explained, "One must . . . read the novels of the day for small talk." She maintained that "they certainly serve for conversation every where." Unlike performance-goers who discussed presentations on walks home or over a snack after a lecture, readers opportuned themselves of visits or social meetings whenever they occurred, during which they summoned recollections of recent reading experiences. Fashionable dinner parties often resounded with literary banter of "authors, translators of the recent German works—M^{rs} [Sarah] Austin, M^{rs} [Anna] Jameson, Miss [Harriett] Martineau[.]" Passengers on stagecoaches, railroad cars, steamboats, and ships, and every other conceivable conveyance whiled away the hours or only "a few minutes" together talking about "Milton, Shakespeare, Longfellow & Tennyson" or other authors. Bookstore drop-ins might expect to overhear a literary discussion in full swing or put forth a new topic. Anything, from political jawboning to the "talking over . . . the introduction" to Nathaniel Hawthorne's *Scarlet Letter,* could be heard in reading rooms, college dorms, or newsrooms. Literary talk filled just about any public space. Social callers could expect no less, so they came always armed with literary ideas. When a ship's carpenter daughter was unexpectedly "introduced" to a new family acquaintance, the two "had quite a conversation concerning various books and authors." The seaman John Congdon's lonely fiancée was happy to have callers, such as one, who, on one evening, "conversed on various subjects[,]" including "the rise and fall of the Roman Empire the History of Greece, the Colonizing our Mother country from Rome[,] [Flavius] Josephus[,] and other Histories interesting to us." Literary chats were often the highlight on days during which "nothing worthy of notice took place."[63]

Discussions about reading, however, could set off class tensions. Underlings were not always at liberty to join in literary conversation. A Catholic Irish domestic in a protestant Boston family was fired after offering her unsolicited opinion of a news story about the unjustly accused Father Gillespie on trial for assault. "She overheard a remark mother made to me," her employer's son claimed after reading an article on the case, and "like lightening us[ed] more rich expression than the times press can issue in a hour. Her tongue went in plain English like thunder." The family's father "asked her what she meant by thus talking, she being a servant, & ad[d]ressing, even when she was not addressed." The boy did not record her indecipherable reply, but that the woman was eventually sent packing suggests it was not a very apologetic one. Often, though, conversations between servant and mistress were more open and allowed for disagreement. "I asked my girl how she liked *Rosanna—,"* a physician's wife wrote after lending out the short novelette to her servant, "she replied 'I don't think much of it. If I read, I like to read books that will teach me something. I did'nt get any thing from that.'" The mistress took her domestic's word at face value and derived a lesson in democracy from it. "I have observed that it won[']t do to give your girls a small sized book, if they are grown up girls," she wrote. "It implies, or they so interpret it, inferiority. I shall profit by her remark, & let her chuse from among a number of all sizes.—A kitchen library won[']t do in a Republican Country!!!!"[64] Workers claimed the right to share with employers a common literature.

Literary conversations on board ships invited commentary from those in all walks of life, passenger and seaman alike. Before he became ship master, John Congdon, for one, fell into spontaneous discussions with travelers, fellow crew, the captain, and his wife, especially after newspapers arrived on board from home. Literary chats continued after he ascended to the captain's cabin. "[T]his AM we was all on deck . . . discussing various subjects," he wrote while on his way back from the Indian Ocean via Cape Good Hope. "Among the rest, a work written . . . by a celebrated man named Andrew Jackson Davis." Talk about this spiritualist book left an impression on Congdon, who soon took part in a contest of ideas in this ocean-bound lyceum. "The work belongs to M[r.] Weeden one of our Passangers who is a great advocate of it," he wrote, launching into his blow-by-blow account. "We had a great argument this AM[:] he commented on the Book[,] I was down on it, and had most all against me." Down for the count, the seaman acknowledged his handicap: "M[r] Weeden is a man 37 years of age has read much and can recollect well what he reads; therefore I am no match for him on most arguments."[65] Textual discussions ended with some winners and losers, no doubt, yet all gained in exchanging ideas.

Debates were less common than groups of readers mutually puzzling through what they read. Veterans might elucidate fine points of political squabbles. During these sessions in which texts were explicated, social bonds were forged and strengthened. "Elliot takes such pains to be pleasant to Charlie that it does my heart good," an architect's wife noted of her husband's fraternal interest in her nephew. "He gave him a long talk about [Charles] Darwin's book Saturday & Charlie seemed really interested to know his opinion." She weighed the intellectual as well as social benefits to her nephew: "This pleases me because I think Charlie's interests so far have been apt to be in trivial subjects & I like him now to have his ears open to larger ones." Inevitably, however, overly zealous readers pontificated upon texts to the dismay of those targeted for conversion. Mary Pierce Poor was one such victim of her sister's enthusiasm for Sarah Josepha Hale's *Lecturess,* a cautionary tale "illustrating the unhappy effects of wives not yielding implicit obedience to the wills of their lords and masters," according to the obviously disapproving Poor. "Elizabeth has been quite stirred up by it and has pounced upon my innocent head a torrent of advice and council so that I fear she too may turn a lecturess," Poor divulged to a friend as she hoisted the sibling on her own petard. Fearing that her jibe at Elizabeth would become public information, Poor issued the directive: "These [pages] I wish to be destroyed and not read by any one." The recipient, of course, disobeyed her friend's wishes, kept the letter, and later added her own impish bit of marginalia: "You see dear how cautious I was!"[66]

And so countless voices raised in response to texts survive through letters that to their producers sometimes seemed brazen, but more often they were so trivial as to be meaningless to posterity. Yet letters, like face-to-face discussions, invited epistolary response. As we have seen, written discourse about reading usually began with one correspondent's query concerning a favorite author or recently read book. Such queries also facilitated formation of response after reading. That posited by a mill worker to his friend in a bobbin factory was typical: "By the way have you ever read Longfellow?" The sequence that followed was typical, too: "[I]f so write me how you like him[.] As for me I can speak freely—I think him the greatest Poet that I have ever read." The mill worker then disclosed, "Have been looking over Longfellow complete this A.M. Have read and re-read it this winter." He then dangled a bevy of poets, hoping to lure his correspondent into literary exchange: "[I] have also read Tennyson who is tip top[,] Gerald M[a]ssey[,] Charles Swain[,] and Leigh Hunt besides [Thomas] Moore[,] [Robert] Burns[,] [Nathaniel Parker] Willis and last but not least James Russell Lowell[.] His Bigelow [*sic*] Papers are the best of their order." After this fusillade, he could only disclaim, "Please excuse the above if not interesting." Whether his friend responded is not certain, but correspondents often sought out reaction in an effort to forge a consensus or confirm opinions. "But, oh, Louisa, the church service! . . . it was so cold—so cheerless!" John C. Park described his reaction to a service he was reading, as he elicited his sister's response. "[I]f you have it in the house, read it, and tell me—was it my own highly wrought feelings, or is it the inherent defect of the service, that it operated upon me, as such a chilling sedative." Most people who did read the text in question wrote back, usually with some kind of meeting of mind, to brace the social bond. "I have read the Log Cabin and I agree with you about the hero," a teenager told her cousin and then used the heroine as a focal point for discussing marriage; "and I do not think I should relish much, such a bridal as Ellen's, I should have preferred to have such arrangements deferred, a while. Don't you agree?" The discourse of affirmation became more complex when third parties were involved.

"What you say of H. Ware's Memoir met my feelings exactly," abolitionist Samuel May Jr. parlayed back his thoughts on the less-than-sympathetic portions to John Estlin. "I had said the same to my wife," he continued, as if including his correspondent in an ongoing domestic discussion. "She begged me not find any fault with so beautiful a book. . . . But I would not have you think she is not a good Abolitionist!"[67] The scythe of readers' associations with the books they read could cut both ways concerning noxious texts.

As platforms for discussion, texts allowed correspondents to bring up personal concerns as much as political issues. During their courtship in 1840, Mary Pierce and Henry Poor tested each other's fidelity, in one case by discussing "Plato's treatises upon 'Love.'" "If you will believe his reas[on]ing," he wrote her, "that just in proportion as we really love, in the proper sense of that term, the good and the beautiful in the whole sex becomes the object of one affection, and no *one personification* or *embodyment* of the charms and graces appropriate to the sex, more than another equally beautiful, engages our love!" In other words, a person loves all comely women or handsome men when he or she loves one. An alarmed Pierce, convinced that "our own hearts are better guides than any system of philosophy," retorted back defiantly. "I do not like Plato's idea of loving all alike who are equally good and beautiful," she quipped. "I do not believe Plato had any heart or he would not have gone to work so deliberately and coolly to speculate upon the sensations of that organ."[68] Pierce's friendly but firm response ended Poor's philosophical speculation on love; their widely disparate responses signaled possible deeper incompatibilities.

These literary discussions taking place long after texts were laid aside were as much a part of reception as response at the moment of reading. Through these interchanges, readers came to understand both the texts and one another better. Communicating literary experience gave response a social dimension that was immediate and tangible rather than vicarious. And it usually involved the array of response as it developed through the three phases discussed above: prejudging texts and authors, forming ideas while reading occurred, and, finally, making ideas part of one's social life after initial reading.

Conclusion

Thus, together, people produced meaning. Only through social relations could ideas take root, grow, and fully blossom in everyday life; otherwise, ideas might have just vanished like seeds in the desert winds of the solitary mind. These readers, as self-conscious, social beings, could not, of course, have thought otherwise. Other people were present when readers heard about things to read, they were in mind when reading took place, and, afterward, they were there to discuss and activate response. In this trajectory of response, ideas gleaned from literature remained always grounded in social reality. Yet just as textual response developed along a social continuum from preconception to post-reception, so too did one's reception meld into social production. Producing ideas in social settings, writing texts of life, fashioning literary items, even establishing new habits—a veritable universe of creative activities—often had their genesis in textual reception. Reception was hardly passive, even though it demanded accommodation to authors' ideas—self-diminishment in the name of intellectual growth, not only one's own but also of one's social relations. In light of the questing reader who concluded that "we need to struggle and die every day, or we cannot gather increase of life," it becomes clear that Charles Cobb's "tree of knowledge," so seemingly poisonous to body and mind, was merely an agent of transformation.[69] Its magic elixir turned personal encounters with the written word into socioliterary experience.

Epilogue

Cannonballs and Books: The Civil War and the Fate of Socioliterary Experience

Altogether it was the saddest scene I have ever witnessed. Most of them are young men from the best families, & they are going to actual war. The parting seemed heart-rending. I never saw so many men *shedding tears. Some of the fathers & male friends abandoned themselves to grief, & wept like children. Most of the Mothers & female friends took leave at their homes. O War! War!! Might not this war have been spared? Where are the peace-makers? Everybody is for war.*

—Persis Sibley Andrews Black,
at South Paris Hill, Maine,
Train Depot, 28 April 1861

After one eight-year-old Bostonian requested a "cannon-ball or a Secession dollar" in an 1862 letter to his father, a U.S. Army surgeon in Virginia, the boy's brother received a book, the more traditional antebellum-era present for children. Although the dutiful son replied with a thank-you note—"I am very much obliged to you for getting me that book"—he prefaced his gratitude with an eager plea for any Confederate stamps his father might find. His fascination for the paraphernalia of combat persisted despite his father's recent written exhortation: "I wish my little boys all of them could be here that they might learn what a horrible business war is, & that they might never want to have their country engaged in it."[1] The boys were too young to have understood fully the dire consequences of the Civil War and their father's sense of repugnance toward it, but they nonetheless knew that it had affected most facets of everyday life, including literary gift exchange. Like many of their contemporaries in 1862, they coveted war relics over reading materials, cannonballs over books. In the face of a war that took their father far away from them and limited their communications to an irregular correspondence stretching over four hundred miles to the battle front, books seemed to the boys irrelevant compared to emblems of the distant struggle.

However far removed spatially from New England the war was, it became almost omnipresent culturally, so much so that it changed the very nature of literary experience. To civilians, wartime social disruption often registered, sometimes most keenly, through literary encounters of various sorts, from reading and studying to gift giving and book borrowing.[2] With the outbreak of hostilities, representations of war in print, through correspondence, or by word of mouth infiltrated civilians' mundane experience in an essential way: literary encounters that had been largely locally oriented and socially motivated before the war were now redirected outward toward national affairs and propelled by more abstract political concerns. Literary sociability faded before patriotic duty.[3]

Although the social and the literary were ultimately destined to part ways regardless of the war, due to the worldwide emergence and valorization of solitary and atomized reading practices later in the century, the war foreshadowed the separation.[4] During the war, the literate New Englander began to divide his or her literary self into distinct modes of consciousness: one in solitary pursuit of self-edification through literature during leisure time, another devoted to formalized, institutional study, and yet another assuming the role of the literary patriot who identified with an often anonymous, indeed, abstract society of Unionists caught up in the furor of war. Of course, each New Englander may have experienced all modes in varying degrees and emphasized any of them, depending upon the available amount of leisure time, the quality of educational background, and the vicissitudes of political affiliation. Still, no matter how New Englanders focused or diffused their literary attentions, they could not elude the constraints that the war had imposed upon the social production of literary meaning. Below, we follow twenty-seven informants from the region into the war years in order to assay these changes.[5]

First, however, we need to address a critical question: Was the social nature of literary experience in decline anyway, without the war? The clear answer is no; if anything, the patterns we have described were not weakening but strengthening as the war approached. This can be seen in several areas. Nearly all New Englanders, even religious conservatives who had always left fewer and less-extensive literary testimonies than liberals, spent more time writing about their encounters with literature, especially secular material. And they were reading ever more widely and diversely, too. Traditionally, the middle and upper classes, with more leisure and money to spend on books, also wrote more about their varied literary encounters than the working classes, who, due to the rapid growth of lending institutions and the increasing availability of cheaper editions, nonetheless left more articulate records toward the end of the era than they did earlier. As part of the multiplying variety of reading on the market, a periodical boom in the decade before the war was expressed in almost every informant's diaries and letters through more references to this type of literature and more thoughtful responses to it, yet with little corresponding increase in discussion of the news that may have appeared in these vehicles. In short, the vast majority of New Englanders were more literary in their social relations in 1861 than they were in 1830, and they more frequently used literature instrumentally in them.[6] Thus, when war broke out, socioliterary experience was so much evolving in accord with religious, social, and economic change in the region that it seemed destined to continue for decades more. But as we will see, the war would prove to be a watershed in New Englanders' relationship to literature.

Production

The war strikingly affected production. Diarists and correspondents increasingly refrained from literary adornment of their writings about everyday events. War, and its close companion death, were simply the most important facts of life, and most thoughts about literature serviced those ends. Indeed, for many civilians writing to their diaries or composing letters, all matters besides war became trivial space fillers. "I am amused at the ridiculous manner in which I mix up home incidents with news of great public interest," one diarist chided herself after years of integrating public and private matters in her writings. Few people seemed cognizant of these drifts away from traditional substance. One exception was a sixteen-year-old schoolgirl who noted how the war coincided in her diary with the cessation of literary reflections: "Then, I used to tell what we had for dinner, my quarrels with the girls, . . . & in the midst of it all, would generally have a Bible verse."[7] Evidently, New Englanders, confident of a quick end to the war, dismissed stylistic changes as but temporary adaptations.

As the war years wore on, exigent deviations from prewar practices of literary production became inevitably habitual and permanent. Once-prolific diarists began to truncate their entries severely to mere lists of titles of books read, if any at all, wrote sporadically with large gaps, or simply abandoned journalizing altogether. Letter writing, by contrast, became more copious, especially, if not surprisingly, between soldiers' friends and families. Interest in commonplace and extract book production was being displaced by nonliterary compiling, such as keeping photo albums, which began to arrive in even outlying areas. "Photograph books are the fashion now," Persis Sibley Andrews Black could confirm in 1862 from her tiny rural village. These books did not always replicate literary albums as records of the written sentiments of loved ones. One boy wanted his book to be "filled up with *'notorious'* characters," that is, infamous Southern leaders. But some social uses remained, albeit put to new purposes. An army chaplain's wife kept a personal picture album for her husband and sent it to him on the front, where he inserted photos of men from camp. The literary fell away from other collecting practices in which it once held sway. As postage stamps increasingly became the international mode for mail transactions, making books of stamps from all over the world amused children once limited to scrapbooks of newsclippings. During the war, one avid collector amassed 233 numismatic items by June 1862; she traded with correspondents or asked family members in the South for Confederate stamps.[8] These fashionable books threatened to subvert dwindling literary production all the more.

For those who kept on writing, literary production was inflected with war. "'[V]erily, verily I say unto you they shall have their reward,'" one woman quoted Matthew 6:1–3 to her diary upon reading in February 1864 that "the servants of the rebel Jeff Davis have run away & that his house has been set on fire." An accountant uninterested in national politics and guarded about his partisan affiliation in the 1850s uncharacteristically inscribed a patriotic poem about the war at the back of his diary: "Our countrys' [*sic*] woes demand a sadder verse, / No time have we her sorrows to rehearse." Diaries that before the war featured original eulogies to the deceased now frequently memorialized kinsmen, even anonymous ones, who died in battle. One widow's diary read like an obituary column of Providence men she may have hardly known. For dissenters, the encroachment of war into the experience of writing was as painful. At one female academy, an abolitionist disunionist student squirmed at patriotic writing assignments, such as one in May 1861 on "the Benefits of War." "My ideas upon that point are exceedingly limited," she sneered, "but they will stretch, in big writing."[9]

Not surprisingly, New England noncombatants who, while away from home near battle fronts, cherished hearing about everyday family life and fancying nothing had changed, asked their correspondents to write about their literary reading among other details of home life, not their concerns about the war. "What have you been doing these many days? What have you been reading?" one U.S. Treasury official in South Carolina asked his daughters in Salem. "I now wonder if there is such a thing as time to read or ever was or ever will be for me?" Writing from Virginia on nearly the same day to his wife in rural Connecticut, a serviceman echoed the query: "Are you devoting much time to reading? You better make a selection of some choice books for a winter evening pastime." Despite changes in her everyday life, she and other women painted, as faithfully as they could, comforting vignettes of literary life continuing in the old way. "If you could just step into the parsonage you would find Mary, and myself sitting by the table in the kitchen," she wrote shortly after her spouse left home. "Mary has her sewing. I have the Atlas in my lap that you always used." One daughter reassured her father of his much-missed place in the family literary circle, as she wrote, "I glance almost instinctively at the large rocking-chair, as if I must see you there with books and newspapers." The efforts of these correspondents to produce letters striking an ever-cheerful tone led them to walk a tightrope between therapeutic remembrance to prop morale and sincere disclosure to maintain intimate relations.[10]

Dissemination

With the increase in letter writing came an increase in dissemination activity through delivery systems. Not only did home-front writers mail more correspondence and newspapers than before, they also stuffed their envelopes with clippings and other literary scraps of a patriotic nature and directed bundles bearing imprints through the ever-mounting number of express companies. Varied reading matter was often in short supply for Union armies; combatants relied upon what was available through tract societies, scavenging, borrowing, and a few limited army libraries. Newspapers were especially craved, but local and treasured papers were not readily available. When Charlotte Forten, now a teacher of freed blacks in the Sea Islands, received an old issue of the *Liberator* from a friend back home, she was gratified: "It is familiar and delightful to look upon as the face of an old friend." Papers from home towns carried with them local news about townsfolk as well as the personal "imprint" of the sender. Because senders knew how eagerly their missives and bundles were anticipated not only by the receiver but also secondary readers, often wounded men in hospitals, they feared misdirection and, accordingly, some civilians kept track of all shipments. Personalized communications in these and many other cases became selfless patriotic acts. Patriotism also engulfed many forms of charitable donations, from informal ones to those collected by organizations such as the Sanitary Commission. Generally, enthusiasts welcomed the chance to give away reading materials. Charlotte Forten, for example, solicited picture books for her South Carolina pupils from a friend back home, who readily complied. Even Persis Sibley Andrews Black seemed eager to join in with her village "awakened to the call" to donate "books, pamphlets, newspapers" and other items to a local district committee.[11]

While charity grew in importance, occasional literary gift giving declined. One reason was that New Englanders showed their support by economizing on luxury goods, and books were relative extravagances. Another reason was that photo albums supplanted other books as gifts at holiday season, a time when both blank books and fancy "gift annuals" had in decades past sufficed. Oddly enough, none of the informants considered here recorded giving away a book to a departing soldier as a memento, an act that would seem to evolve naturally from the antebellum era's practice of presenting literary gifts symbolizing the meaningful relationship between donor and receiver to sojourners before departure. Perhaps the pain of parting was too great to record any such transactions that took place. Given the deep social meaning that traditionally adhered to literary gifts, it comes as a surprise that books sent home to New England once owned by Confederates were prized at all, even as trophies or for their monetary value, something that would have repulsed Yankees before the war.[12] That such relics were acceptable is but another sign of the severance between social and literary experience and the appropriation of the two by patriotism.

Like gift giving, the activity of lending privately owned books slowed down, although social callers often carried newspapers, clippings, letters, and photographs with them to show to the host. One woman even fashioned herself into a walking lending library when she sported a published piece of war-related correspondence on her clothing. "I have gone about a good deal with the letter pinned on the front of my dress," she wrote to her sister, "& when I meet those who deserved it have allowed them to read it."[13] One could in this way become a billboard for the Cause.

Reading out loud continued during the war, but not as evidently as before. Ever fond of oral reading, Persis Black admitted in late 1862 that she had "not even the privilege of reading a single volume for the past year." A similar pattern was followed by a mill worker who formerly read aloud to boardinghouse mates but seldom, if ever, did so after he returned from the battlefront in 1863. In several other accounts, reading aloud was highlighted as a way of entertaining children or soothing the ill rather than as an adult recreation. Group reading probably waned due to the intrusion of "war talk" about the news or other intelligence from the battlefield into home-based sociabilities. "Do you remember how Captain Ames read to us from the New York papers, and what long war talks we would have?" one young Salemite asked her correspondent. Certainly, there is abundant evidence that oral renderings of news, along with telegraphs and letters from the front, occupied hours of adult reading and listening. Letters were even "loaned" to others to read. Insofar as personal correspondence often relayed information of value to other people, passing it on was only being responsible. "[A]fter the battle I hope that you will send a telegraph about all our friends, if possible," a wife begged her husband. "This waiting with a drawn sword over our heads is perhaps as trying to the friends here as it is to the soldiers themselves." Given the antebellum practice of letting others see or listen to letters, it followed that some candid writers rightly assumed (and often feared) a public airing of even intimate letters. "I am all the time thinking every word I write that others are going to hear it read," a man on the front confessed to his wife. "Yet I suppose you cannot avoid it."[14] With family and friends hanging on every word, letters had a more profound impact upon the reading public than ever before.

Perhaps because reading aloud and listening had suddenly become so pressing, doing so while engaged in other activities, especially sewing and knitting, was less likely to happen during the war years than before. Reader-listeners wanted to fix upon important letters, dispatches, and news without distraction. Yet the devoted concentration necessary for rapid home production of clothing and socks for soldiers in the first months of the war discouraged women from reading or listening while performing important handiwork. One student tried to do both—even if it meant studying and knitting—a rare alliance of activities in decades earlier. A classmate marveled that the knitter "is now rabid on the sock subject, & keeps losing her place in her lessons to pick up her stitches." As women's benevolent efforts became more institutionally coordinated, the vestiges of sewing and reading for patriotic ends all but vanished.[15]

Reception

The encroachment of war-related literature upon everyday consciousness cannot be overestimated. It registered as an obsession with newspapers that began as war approached, reached a high point in the first months of fighting in 1861, and nearly replaced all other forms of reading, let alone writing, throughout the conflict. "Nearly two months have passed away since I have opened this Journal to record the passing events," one industrialist wrote in July 1861. "Much of the leisure time I have is taken up in reading the daily news of the Rebellion." Women, too, honed their political acumen more than ever by focusing on the news. The once promiscuous reader Persis Black admitted in June 1862, "The extent of my reading is the daily newspaper." The first book she recorded picking up after 1861, at least two years later, seemed like a challenge: "I am reading 'Les Miserables' & it is a large work for me who never reads anything, but the daily paper." For some diarists, such as Charles Cobb, who so much fancied fiction, his accounts of perusing papers were the only evidence of any reading during the war.[16] Among the antebellum informants we traced who had been prodigious readers, only Charlotte Forten and a Union army veteran back at work in the mills rarely mentioned a piece of war news. That mill worker wrote as he did prior to his enlistment, in terse entries of titles read but little else about his everyday life, showing a consciousness already divided between his literary life and everyday political events around him.

For the majority who did capture their newspaper engagements, most kept a simple, sketchy, time line of war events that clustered around a few key periods, such as the firing on Fort Sumter, the Battle of Gettysburg, or the New York Draft Riots. These and other less prominent events were recorded both as a way of giving ephemeral newsprint more permanent form and to act as a reference guide for coordinating and evaluating often contradictory intelligence. Of course, record keepers were more likely to record what was relevant to their embattled loved ones.

Persis Black worried for her townsmen in the 1862 Peninsular campaign: "Yorktown evacuated & other battles won—but we have not particulars as to our Maine soldiers." But news readers mostly kept track of the war's unfolding events to participate in the ongoing related discussions that had come to eclipse all other social communications. Readers, of course, responded to events as individuals with ideas of their own or in highly personal, often emotional ways, but such responses were formulated with a keen awareness of the "many rumors" and "exaggerations & contradictions" circulating by word of mouth, telegraph reports, or the newspapers, as well as of government attempts at censorship. In response, local coteries pooled information from varied sources, such as letters, telegrams, and gossip during social calls. Newspaper readers, often deeply affected, responded with emotion and analytical commentary on what they read. After examining Abraham Lincoln's second inaugural address, one abolitionist despaired, "I am much disappointed at finding it unmistakably conservative." Many readers expressed their hopes for an end to the fighting. "The war continues, but it has assumed a different look to me within the last few days," Charles Cobb wrote in February 1862 between engagements as a traveling fiddler, "a look of caving on the part of the South, especially in Tennessee, but perhaps it is no such thing." In assessing public excitement, readers often blurred the line between their own opinions and the nation's mood, an unusual response in the antebellum era. One Bostonian used the collective "we" and the personal "I" almost interchangeably in her response to distressing news reports released during the summer of 1862. "We are expecting every hour to hear of a great battle," she wrote to her brother-in-law; "if we fail again . . . , I believe it will only be the signal for fresh efforts." Then she slipped into the first person plural: "More & more we realise that we are struggling for our national existence & that we *must* succeed at whatever cost."[17] Although she had been an astute political commentator since the early 1850s, she had never before so clearly identified herself with the nation.

Ironically, as civilians on the home front could seem quite willing to abandon patterns of antebellum socioliterary experience for patriotism's sake, servicemen facing battle struggled to keep those patterns very much in view by urging folks back home to discuss them as if they yet continued. Warriors wanted correspondence that would attempt to mirror peaceful hours once spent in reading together. Through exchanging literary enclosures or transcriptions of poetry in the mail, some combatants hoped to read the same thing as their distant loved ones. Others coordinated the exact time of reading. "You say you have commenced reading the bible in course," one man on the battlefront wrote his wife. "Can we not arrange it so that we can both read the same portion each day? I would suggest that we read three chapters per day commencing with the old testament." The two kept up their sessions, despite problems with synchronization, for at least a few months. Simulated reading circles that attempted to replicate old ways had counterparts in epistolary parenting and instruction carried on from afar. Through letters, children on the home front indirectly benefited from their embattled fathers' guidance, and mothers were reassured by spousal input. One parent enjoined his sons to "do your lessons & dont give your mother too much trouble in helping you," while another, tenaciously clinging to his role as teacher, apologized that his "dear little son is growing up without the care and oversight of his father." He implored, "Let father see how you have improved in knowledge and goodness, write to him and tell him what you have read, and what you think of your reading." The son would field his father's quizlike questions and submit hand-drawn maps and a personal journal for judgment, his progress marked by his mother's and sister's reports.[18]

Under the war's drastic dislocations, the subtle querying and inducements to study that marked antebellum letters gave way to strident goading and shrill competitiveness. One father working in the South went so far as to push his youngster academically by making invidious distinctions with a talented freedperson of around the same age under his charge. The steady habits, disciplined comportment, and lonely hours spent mastering lessons that characterized study were difficult enough for children distracted by the war. Even a twenty-year-old academy student explained that getting "the news from the telegraph office" was agitating: "I can tell you it didn't make it any easier to study!"[19] As the domestic authority figures in their life put studious reading on hold for newspaper scanning or the occasional retreat into leisurely perusal of books, students could perhaps sense their singular—indeed, isolated—experiences as readers in the domestic social setting. For study, leisurely reading, and war-related reading had taken on distinctive meanings, and the latter reading now had come to predominate over the other forms.

Conclusion

The alliance between everyday social intercourse and literature that antebellum New Englanders had crafted was threatened during the Civil War when they channeled both social and literary experiences into the Union cause. Because the war touched so many local and public forms of sociability, folks who remained both social and literary usually assumed the role of "literary patriot," one whose everyday production, dissemination, and reception of reading material related in some way to the larger conflict. Under the banner of literary patriotism, productive activity, such as diary keeping and letter writing, bore traces of the war in terms of both content and purpose, while dissemination of literature, especially to friends and kin dislocated by the hostilities, took on a sense of urgency. As literary reception became virtually synonymous with engaging war news and responding to it in writing, "war talks," or epistolary discourse, reading non-war-related materials was seen, relatively, as having trifling significance, as a leisurely, self-edifying pursuit invested with little social value. Even study, disconnected as it was from the concerns of war, seemed ever more removed from daily life.

Because the war consumed socioliterary experience and transformed it to serve patriotic ends, it lost an element of its once-disinterested purpose—the maintenance of social ties for their own sake. Literature instead had become instrumental to warfare, like cannonballs or rifles. Otherwise, it was dysfunctional to the cause, distracting to its devoted pursuit, and, ultimately, relegated to secondary importance, sequestered into a space of its own, where in time it came to serve individual rather than social ends. "Where are the peacemakers?" Persis Black wondered as her neighbors marched off to war in April 1861.[20] She could just as well have been searching for her literary companions, who likewise seemed to vanish with peacetime, perhaps forever. New Englanders like Black, who attempted to reconstruct their literary lives socially after the war, found it was impossible to repair that delicate chain that had once so intimately linked human relations and literary meaning. Ideas would never be quite so everyday again.

Notes

Abbreviations

Collections are cited by the following abbreviations followed by a dash and the abbreviation of the repository in which they are found. The many cited items not in specific collections appear in the notes with only the repository abbreviation.

AAB — Archives of the Archdiocese of Boston, Brighton, Mass.
- PBJF — Papers of Benedict Joseph Fenwick

AAS — American Antiquarian Society, Worcester, Mass.
- BBP — Boston Booksellers Papers, 1640–1860
- CFP — Cheever Family Papers
- JDP — John Davis Papers
- JMCC — James Munroe and Company Correspondence
- JPBP — Jotham Powers Bigelow Papers
- PFP — Park Family Papers
- SFP — Salisbury Family Papers
- TDFP — Taintor Davis Family Papers
- WFP — Wall Family Papers

AHS — Andover Historical Society, Andover, Mass.
- MALCL — Mary Ann Loring Currier Letters
- MARL — Mehitable Abbott Russell Letters
- MJAP — Mary James Abbott Papers

AJHS — American Jewish Historical Society, Waltham, Mass.
- ASWR — A. S. W. Rosenbach Collection of Early American Judaica

ATHM — American Textile History Museum, Lowell, Mass.
- MAP — Metcalf-Adams Papers
- MGLC — Mill Girls' Letters Collection
- ML — Miscellaneous Letters

BC — Archives, Boston College, Chestnut Hill, Mass.
- MAP — Moses Adams Papers

BHS — Beverly Historical Society and Museum, Beverly, Mass.
- EC — Endicott Collection

BPL — Boston Public Library Rare Books Department, Boston, Mass.; all materials quoted courtesy of the Trustees of the Boston Public Library

- CHC College of the Holy Cross, Archives and Special Collections, Worcester, Mass.
- CHS Connecticut Historical Society Museum, Hartford, Conn.
  - JFP Jocelyn Family Papers
  - MP McClellan Papers
  - PFP Primus Family Papers
  - SC Sykes Collection
- CSL State Archives, Connecticut State Library, Hartford
  - WWP William Wheeler Papers
- HU Harvard University
  - GEL Gutman Education Library, Special Collections
  - HL Houghton Library, Cartland Family Papers; all material quoted by permission of the Houghton Library
- LC Library of Congress
  - CCP Caleb Cushing Papers
- LHS Lynn Historical Society, Lynn, Mass.
- LxHS Lexington Historical Society, Lexington, Mass.
- MBEL Mary Baker Eddy Library for the Betterment of Humanity, Boston, Mass.
- MbHS Marblehead Museum and Historical Society, Marblehead, Mass.
  - RP Rogers Papers
- MeHS Maine Historical Society, Portland
  - BFP Brown Family Papers
  - CKNFP Cargill-Knight-Norcross Families Papers
  - JEHP Joshua Edwin Harris Papers
- MHS Massachusetts Historical Society, Boston, Mass.
  - AALP Amos A. Lawrence Papers
  - ALP Amos Lawrence Papers
  - AL2P Amos Lawrence II Papers
  - CFP3 Cary Family Papers III
  - CP Clapp Papers
  - DFCP Daniel Franklin Child Papers
  - DFP Dabney Family Papers
  - EEP Edward Everett Papers
  - ENP Everett-Noble Papers
  - FCLP Francis Cabot Lowell Papers
  - FCMP Frank C. Morse Papers
  - LFP Lamb Family Papers
  - LLWP L. L. Waterhouse Papers
  - SAGP Samuel A. Green Papers
- NEHGS New England Historic Genealogical Society, Boston, Mass.
  - HWCC Henry Wyles Cushman Collection
  - JHP John Hoyt Papers

NHCHS	New Haven Colony Historical Society, Whitney Library, New Haven, Conn.	
NHHS	New Hampshire Historical Society, Tuck Library, Concord, N.H.	
OCHS	Old Colony Historical Society, Taunton, Mass.	
PEM	Phillips Library, Peabody Essex Museum, Salem, Mass.	
	BFL	Elizabeth Ellis (Prescott) Betton Family Letters
	CLRL	Charles Lenox Remond Letters
	GFAPD	George Forster Allen Papers and Diaries
	PFP	Putnam Family Papers
	RFP	Rogers Family Papers
	TPP	Thomas Perley Papers
PPL	Portland Public Library, Portland, Maine	
PrPL	Providence Public Library, Providence, R.I.	
	BL	Beetle Letters, Paul C. Nicholson Whaling Collection
RIHS	Rhode Island Historical Society, Providence	
	CAGP	Christopher A. Greene Papers
	CFP	Congdon Family Papers
	DFP	Diman Family Papers
	HBDP	Henry B. Dexter Papers
	HLFP	Herreshoff-Lewis Family Papers
	MMC	Miscellaneous Manuscripts Collection
	ZAP	Zachariah Allen Papers
SCHS	South Carolina Historical Society, Charleston	
	MFP	Middleton Family Papers
SL	Schlesinger Library, Radcliffe Institute (Harvard University)	
	AFP	Almy Family Papers
	BHFP	Bradley-Hyde Family Papers
	BriFP	Briggs Family Papers
	BroFP	Browne Family Papers
	CAFP	Chamberlain Adams Family Papers
	CFP	Cabot Family Papers
	DFP	Dana Family Papers
	ECAFP	Elizabeth Cary Agassiz Family Papers
	EGLFP	Ellis Gray Loring Family Papers
	EGLP	Ellis Gray Loring Papers
	FMQP	Frances Merritt Quick Papers
	GFP	Gardiner Family Papers
	HC	Hooker Collection
	MGFP	May-Goddard Family Papers
	NSFP	Nichols-Shurtleff Family Papers
	PaFP	Parsons Family Papers
	PoFP	Poor Family Papers
	RSP	Robinson-Shattuck Papers

	SABRP	Sarah Alden Bradford Ripley Papers
	SEBP	Sarah Ellen Browne Papers
	SFA	Swanton Family Addenda
	SFP	Swanton Family Papers
	SFUP	Swanton Family Unprocessed Papers
SSC	The Sophia Smith Collection, Smith College, Northampton, Mass.	
	BFP	Bodman Family Papers
	GP	Garrison Papers
	HP	Hale Papers
	MJRNLP	Martha Joanna Reade Nash Lamb Papers
	MP	Munroe Papers
	PFP	Peabody Family Papers, Munroe Collection
	STPP	Sturgis/Tappan/Prout Papers
UV	University of Virginia	
	CWBL	Clifton Waller Barrett Library, Special Collections (Lucy Larcom Collection #7005-B)
VHS	Vermont Historical Society, Barre, Vt.	
	CFP	Clement Family Papers
	JBLFP	Joseph B. Leonard Family Papers
	MEBTP	Marion E. Blake and Tuttle Papers
	NTP	Nancy Taft Papers
	SFP	Sabin Family Papers
	STMP	Sarah Thankful Mars Papers
	WCP	William Chamberlain Papers
YUb	Beinecke Rare Book and Manuscript Library, Yale University	
	GWP	George Waldo Papers, Yale Collection of American Literature
	WSP	William Sherwood Papers, Yale Collection of Western Americana
YUs	Sterling Memorial Library, Manuscripts and Archives, Yale University	
	ADP	Albert Dodd Papers
	DMC	Diaries Miscellaneous Collection
	JLWP	James Lockwood Wright Papers

Introduction

1. Charles M. Cobb, 12 Sept. 1853, Journal, from a transcript in VHS, which houses the original. His mother borrowed another *Harper's* on 28 November 1853. "Tree of Knowledge." Webster had died less than a year earlier, on 24 October 1852.
2. On Cobb's stationery purchases, see 30 July 1851, 9 Feb., 16 May 1852, Journal, VHS. A retrospective entry for 1 December 1852 reports him buying an almanac on 27 January 1849 and a book on 19 October 1847. Dana, *History of Woodstock,* 549; De Bow, *Statistical View,* 342. Charles M. Cobb, 11 Feb. 1852, 17, 22 Apr. 1850, 15 Apr. 1851, Journal, VHS.
3. William Kelly Bartlett, 14 June 1837, Journal, NHHS; H. E. Beck to Harriet Jane Hanson Robinson, 7 Sept. 1846, RSP-SL; Christopher Keith, 16 Feb. 1858, Diary, MMC-RIHS; William Hoyt, 14 Feb. 1851, Journal, BPL; Philip Sage, 26 Feb. 1849, Journal, CHS; James Barnard Blake, 1 Mar. 1851, Diary, AAS; Harriett Low, *Lights and Shadows,* 30 Nov. 1832, 2:469; Sarah E. Trask, 31 Mar. 1849, Journal, BHS; Frances Merritt Quick, 16 Apr. 1855, Diary, FMQP-SL; Mary Pierce Poor to John Pierce and Lucy (Tappan) Pierce, 26 May in 25 May 1837, PoFP-SL; Benjamin Waterhouse Sr., quoted in Louisa Lee Waterhouse, undated entry after 15 May 1840, Journal, LLWP-MHS; Susan S. Johnson, 3 Dec. 1841, Journal, LxHS; Katherine Bigelow Lawrence Jr., 17 Sept. 1852, Journal, LFP-MHS; Mellen Chamberlain, 19 June 1843, Diary BPL; Ellis Gray Loring to Anna Loring, 26 Oct. 1851, EGLFP-SL. A textual focus on printed sources has shaped traditional antebellum intellectual histories, ranging from Miller's *Life of the Mind* and Welter's *Mind of America* to Perry's *Boats Against the Current.* These works analyze ideas produced in print by elite "quality" writers, on the assumption they saw matters more clearly and could better express themselves. *Popular* intellectual history departs from the history of ideas (e.g., Lovejoy's *Great Chain of Being;* cf. Ginzburg, *Cheese and the Worms* and note the similarity to Cobb's speculations); Gramsci, *Selections from the Prison Notebooks,* 323–43.
4. In a total regional population of 2,728,300, according to the 1850 U.S. census, only 8,097 native-born adults (.296 percent) could not read and write. Figures compiled from Inter-university Consortium, *Historical, Demographic, Economic, and Social Data.* Sweden and Scotland were among the few nations with comparatively high literacy rates; Lockridge, *Literacy in Colonial New England,* 99–100; Graff, *Legacies of Literacy,* 169, 223–27, 239.
5. This is by far the most extensive historical survey of testimony in diaries and letters of popular reading (and of other engagements with literature and imprints) ever attempted. Prior early American studies calling upon much smaller bodies of such material include Jackson, "Reader Retailored"; Kelley, "Reading Women"; Motz, "Private Alibi"; Nichols, "'Blunted Hearts'"; Sicherman, "Sense and Sensibility" and "Reading and Ambition"; and Zboray and Zboray, "'Have You Read . . . ?'" "Reading and Everyday Life," and "Cannonballs and Books." Reading seen in diaries figures prominently in Brown, *Knowledge Is Power,* 170–75, 207–11, 232–33, 238–39, 220–21; Shalhope, *Tale of New England,* esp. 42–46, Appendix 1; and Stevenson, *Victorian Homefront,* xvi. Other sources scholars have used to study reading in history include commonplace book entries (Berland, Gilliam, and Lockridge, *Commonplace Book of William Byrd II,* 4–6, 25, and passim), marginalia (Jackson, *Marginalia;* Jackson,

"Reader Retailored"), images of readers (Leonard, *News for All,* chaps. 1, 4; Docherty, "Women as Readers"), book inscriptions (Hayes, *Colonial Woman's Bookshelf,* 7–11), readers' autobiographies (Rose, *Intellectual Life*), library charges (Todd, "Antebellum Libraries"; Zboray, *Fictive People,* chap. 11; Pawley, *Reading on the Middle Border,* Chap. 3), and probate inventories (Gilmore, *Reading Becomes a Necessity of Life*).

6. Harriet Prescott to Elizabeth Ellis (Prescott) Betton, 8 June 1835, BFL-PEM; John Park, 11–12 Jan. 1845, Diary, BPL; Martha Osborne Barrett, 11 Nov. 1853, Diary, PEM; John R. Congdon, 24 Apr. 1846, 25 May 1841, Journal, CFP-RIHS; Forten, *Journals of Charlotte Forten Grimké,* 20 Jan. 1858, 279; Harriett Low, *Lights and Shadows,* 18 May 1831, 1:288; Mellen Chamberlain, 30 Jan. 1847, Diary, BPL; Joshua Edwin Harris, 18, 20 Feb., 10 May 1858, Journal, JEHP-MeHS; Elizabeth Dwight Cabot to Ellen Twisleton, 16 Apr. 1855, CFP-SL; Mary Pierce Poor to John Pierce and Lucy (Tappan) Pierce, 11 Mar. 1842, PoFP-SL.
7. Persis Sibley Andrews, 25 Apr. 1841, Diary, MeHS. The interdisciplinary genealogies of "the everyday" are many and varied, with one line descending from Lefebvre *(Critique)* through Bourdieu (*Outline*) and leading, on the one hand, to, say, de Certeau *(Practice of Everyday Life)* and Maffesoli *(Ordinary Knowledge)*, and, on the other, to the *Alltagsgeschichte* school (Eley, "Labor History"; Lüdtke, *History of Everyday Life*); cf. Douglas, *Understanding Everyday Life;* Goffman, *Presentation of Self.* While the historical literature on antebellum everyday life is rich (e.g., Larkin, *Reshaping of Everyday Life*), most of it is not informed by these more theoretical perspectives. A previous attempt at an intellectual history of everyday antebellum life, Saum's *Popular Mood,* uses "a couple thousand" personal testaments from a less diverse group of informants and does not explore the material acquisition and interpersonal interpretation of literary ideas (xxi).
8. On literary consumption and its social uses, see Zboray and Zboray, "Books, Reading." In the past two decades, some scholars have looked into early American reading and thus have provided a groundwork for studying popular intellectual life: Brown, *Knowledge Is Power;* Davidson, *Revolution and the Word;* Gilmore, *Reading Becomes a Necessity of Life;* Kelley, "Reading Women"; and our own "Political News," "'Have You Read . . . ?'" "Reading and Everyday Life," and "Transcendentalism in Print." Though treating a later period, Sicherman's "Reading and Ambition" and "Sense and Sensibility" contain insights applying equally to antebellum readers. The sources just cited deal with "real readers" who left records of their specific literary encounters; for consideration of these and other sources, see Zboray and Zboray, *Handbook,* 57–75. On modern "real readers," see Bleich, *Readings and Feelings;* Holland, *5 Readers Reading;* and Radway, *Reading the Romance.* Long, *Book Clubs,* sees even solitary reading as yet still essentially a social experience. On antebellum Americans' socially oriented versus individualistically centered character, see Saum, *Popular Mood.*
9. Gertrude M. Chandler quoted in Mellen Chamberlain, 5 Sept. 1845, Diary, BPL. The nature of socioliterary experience and its attendant practices remained mostly stable over the period. For cultural historians used to studying the *longue durée,* this is not unusual, but it needs explaining in light of the region's socioeconomic transformation, since, as we discuss later in the book, the threat to social relationships

posed by development seemingly fueled socioliterary experience. Most changes, however, were well afoot before the 1830s, when our book picks up (Gilmore, *Reading Becomes a Necessity of Life,* 1–113; Cott, *Bonds of Womanhood,* chap. 1; Kelly, *In the New England Fashion,* 4 n. 4; Dublin, *Transforming Women's Work,* chaps. 1 and 2), so initial cultural reactions may have already set in. While we are thus mostly concerned with persisting patterns, we duly note in appropriate spots any trends affecting the overall picture.

10. The ensuing discussion is similar to that in Zboray and Zboray, "Transcendentalism in Print," 311–18, but with slightly different numbers due to the inclusion of more documents.
11. Hansen and Macdonald, "Surveying the Dead Informant."
12. On amateur writers drawn from this set of informants, see our *Literary Dollars,* chaps. 1 and 2. Our selection criteria permit inclusion of some then-renowned people, such as Massachusetts governor John Davis. A tiny number of prominent literary figures contributed information about ordinary folks' patterns.
13. Lincoln and Guba, *Naturalistic Inquiry,* 202, 219, 233–35.
14. The number of subjects must be approximated because writers occasionally make vague references to groups, such as households, whose members cannot be counted, or to persons by first names only.
15. Since these letters and diaries are self-representations, it is possible that there were some literary activities deliberately not recorded, perhaps out of self-censorship or a desire to highlight only "useful" reading (Hunter, "Inscribing the Self"). But we do have many cases of people admitting that they wasted time in reading a book of "a bad moral tendency" or reading otherwise scandalous literature, so self-censorship is by no means absolute (John Park, 17 Oct. 1845, Diary, BPL). We paid particular attention to these revealing documents and tried to subject the less-than-forthcoming ones to intense critical scrutiny based upon their franker counterparts. Some practices, such as, in many cases, daily newspaper reading, were so commonplace as to be virtually invisible and hence not worthy of comment, yet "slips" in the record can be revealing, as when someone offhandedly mentions that a snowstorm prevented the arrival of a newspaper and hence "usual" reading has been interrupted.
16. There were 475 men versus 437 women, or 52.08 versus 47.92 percent, with the rest of the informants being institutions or groups; the slight imbalance is due to a few single business letters by various men which touch on literary matters. The 1850 census places women proportionally ahead, 50.22 percent to 49.77; figures compiled from the 1850 U.S. census (Inter-university Consortium, *Historical, Demographic, Economic, and Social Data;* De Bow, *Statistical View*).
17. We resisted the temptation to quantify the proportions of each occupation, which would be only meaningful by grouping the many categories into some scheme of upper, middle, and lower classes. While perhaps useful for comparative point-in-time studies, like those based on manuscript census data, such schemes become dubious when dealing with a profusion of points, not to mention the confusion of contemporary class trajectories.
18. Of 785,282 employed men over fifteen years of age in New England, the census reported the following percentages: "Commerce, trade, manufacture, mechanic arts, and mining"

(37.78), "Agriculture" (34.24), "Labor, not agricultural" (18.95), "Army" (0.02), "Sea and river navigation" (5.47), "Law, medicine, and divinity" (1.59), "Other pursuits requiring education" (1.67), "Government civil service" (0.35), "Domestic servants" (0.34), and "Other occupations" (0.54). Based on De Bow, *Statistical View,* 128, table CXXX.

19. Based on the information in the diaries and letters we consulted, along with the 1850 manuscript population schedules (via Ancestry.com), we were able to find occupations for 404 of the 475 men (as in the census, students were not counted). The percentages are as follows: Commerce (26.23), Agriculture (20.79), Labor (14.60), and "Sea and river navigation" (7.92) . With army personnel and male domestic servants below .5 percent of the total employed male population in the region, it is not surprising that they do not show up at all among our informants.
20. The percentages are 14.35, 8.66, and 6.68, respectively.
21. This is particularly true for the second category, "Other pursuits requiring education," which includes our male schoolteachers, for they were pivotal in socioliterary experience. Had we not included them, we would not have had a fully rounded picture of institutional literary socialization; moreover, a proportional representation of male teachers would have been so much overwhelmed by female teachers (most of whom should be considered working class; see Hansen, *Very Social Time,* 32) that it would obscure the underlying reality that the feminization of schoolteaching was not yet complete. Like teachers, clergymen and politicians provide insight into their communities' literary practices; besides, including clergymen of various denominations and politicos of every stripe allowed us to see if our generalizations depended upon some denomination or partisan variable. Above all, the professional groups included key informants who unlocked many mysteries of the larger population's literary experiences that we might not have otherwise uncovered.
22. There were 23,021 African Americans, 0.84 percent of the regional population in 1850, compared with their 2.37 percent showing among our informant base.
23. We were able to find probable birth dates for 597 informants, whose average birth year was 1812. The youngest children, of course, are more likely to be subjects than informants, so we have only 2 informants born in the 1850s. Twenty-four were born in the 1840s, while the vast majority were born before 1840: 81 in the 1830s, 130 in the 1820s, 103 in the 1810s, 125 in the 1800s, and 132 in the eighteenth century.
24. This is but the tip of a huge iceberg of material containing evidence of socioliterary experience which yet remains to be read—especially at the multitude of small-town historical societies scattered throughout the region.
25. Prior researchers using a few of our sources include Cott, *Bonds of Womanhood;* Hansen, *Very Social Time;* Kelly, *In the New England Fashion;* McGovern, *Yankee Family;* Rothman, *Hands and Hearts;* and Ulrich, *Age of Homespun.* We let the writers designate what constitutes a separate item, as when they page-numbered letters or as when a diarist stitched together unnumbered leaves. Six diaries were in printed form and 110 were archival transcripts. Since we used these, a few items have appeared in print or have been transcribed. A small number of this book's quotes appeared in our previous articles.
26. We used 2,816 letters, 798 diaries, and 185 other documents. Among the thirty-five archives at which we consulted these items, ten account for well over four-fifths of

the total: the Schlesinger Library (1,205), the Sophia Smith Collection (607), the American Antiquarian Society (350), the Boston Public Library (204), the Vermont Historical Society (190), the Massachusetts Historical Society (169), the New Hampshire Historical Society (156), the Connecticut Historical Society (113), the Rhode Island Historical Society (113), the Maine Historical Society (112), and the New England Historic Genealogical Society (86).

27. Pieces of textual material that fell under these categories were blocked and moved into separate word-processing text files, which we created in a subdirectory structure mirroring the nine-hundred-category hierarchy. We encoded each piece with informant and text-page location data. Each piece, sometimes as little as a sentence clause, had to be closely analyzed within its context before being sorted. A dBase IV database tracked each item's full archival citation information, while the text itself was imported into yet another database on the principle of one line equals one record. The resulting 271,342 records were also coded with informant and transcription page numbers, along with a date field. For every line of text, we could immediately know who wrote it when, and we could summon the archival description instantly. Without such information control, this book would have been virtually impossible.
28. For example, over three years at a Taunton, Massachusetts, social library, 280 patrons (counted as subjects, not informants) checked out books on 14,560 occasions (1,428 titles, for an average of just over 10 charges per title). The most frequently checked out item, *Harper's,* accounted for a mere 2.31 percent of all charges, while the leading book, a volume by Maria Edgeworth, represented but .63 percent of the whole. The most checked American-authored book was Washington Irving's life of George Washington, with only .55 percent. Individual lists are eclectic and widely differ from one another. Focusing only on popular items thus offers little insight into the typical patron's mind. Benjamin R. Dean, Taunton Social Library, Record of Books Circulated May 7, 1856–March 3, 1859, OCHS.
29. Our sample run included material from the Schlesinger Library and Massachusetts Historical Society, along with the Taunton library charges and the Bridport, Vermont, postmaster subscription list, VHS. By one estimate, American presses produced 733 book titles in 1853 alone (Zboray, *Fictive People,* 3). Items published in Boston dominated the region, even though it was only the third largest publishing center (Massachusetts produced a quarter of New York state's output by value; Zboray and Zboray, "Boston Book Trades," 213, fig. 1).
30. Via a wide and ever-changing array of university library databases at our home institutions, we tried to identify every title mentioned in this book and every quotation from printed sources our informants deploy.
31. Buell, *New England Literary Culture,* 3. On the literary publishing ferment, see Zboray, *Fictive People;* Zboray and Zboray, *Literary Dollars;* Charvat, *Literary Publishing;* Brooks, *Flowering of New England.*
32. We do consult six primary sources written later that are retrospective of the antebellum years.
33. Zboray and Zboray, "Cannonballs and Books."
34. On scarcity to abundance, see Brown, *Knowledge Is Power,* 270–86. The number of Boston book-trade firms, for example, expanded by a factor of forty-two from 1789

to 1850; Zboray and Zboray, "Boston Book Trades," 220, passim, and, on stationery and paper, tables 9 to 18, 232–39; see also McCarthy, "'Page, a Day,'" 122–24. On papermaking, see McGaw, *Most Wonderful Machine.* On out-migrants' letters, see Holbrook, *Yankee Exodus.*

35. Thirty-six items come from the period before 1820, 203 from the 1820s (88 of them from the last two years of the decade), 792 from the 1830s, 1,255 from the 1840s, 1,507 in the remaining years until the Civil War, and 6 after the war. Pre-1820 material usually deals with people who figure later in time, as does some from the 1830s.
36. A few informants from outside are not New Englanders, but they corresponded with people in the region and thus give insight into the patterns of those to whom they wrote. Our informants resided in Massachusetts (461), Connecticut (95), Maine (95), New Hampshire (59), Vermont (42), Rhode Island (27), the mid-Atlantic states (38), southern Atlantic states (19), old Southwest (5), Midwest (17), California (5), Hawaii (1), and at sea (9), with the remainder in other countries. Eighty-one percent (3,077) of our documents originated in New England, 194 in the mid-Atlantic states, 165 in the South, 58 in the Midwest and far West, 259 in other countries, and 46 at sea.
37. Blouin, *Boston Region,* 24–25. People in the Boston region contributed 1,811 items, with 1,266 from elsewhere in New England. On the information flow biases that predict more letters circulating from city centers, see Pred, *Urban Growth and City Systems.* Zboray, *Fictive People,* 72. When letters are subtracted, the percentage of diaries and other documents relative to the whole from the Boston region are proportional to its population measured against that of all New England (less than one-third in 1850). The 1,492 letters written in the Boston region hardly reflect only conditions there; indeed, many were written by transients from the upcountry.
38. We tried to account for intrastate differences by casting our net broadly. Items come from all but six of the region's sixty-four counties, the exceptions being Piscataquis (Maine), Coos and Stafford (N.H.), Bennington, Grand Isle, and LaMoille (Vt.), and Washington (R.I.). Most of the Boston region's 219 towns are included, too.

Part I

1. Studies of manuscript production in the age of print are only beginning to be undertaken. Beyond the works devoted to diaries and correspondence that appear in chapter 1, most of the scholarship focuses upon early modern Europe (e.g., Ezell, *Poems and Prose;* Hobbs, *Early Seventeenth-Century Verse*) or colonial and early American authorship (e.g., Blecki and Wulf, *Milcah Martha Moore's Book;* Miller, *Assuming the Positions;* Mulford, *Only for the Eye;* Shields, *Civil Tongues;* Stabile, *Memory's Daughters*). Although limited to early modern British authors, Ezell's *Social Authorship* provides a framework for studying writers who eschewed print. We extend Ezell's premise into antebellum America in our *Literary Dollars.* The writers we examine here may rightly be called social authors. Our ground-level consider-

ation of them has no real counterparts, but sources on other aspects of literary output in the period range from Brooks's *Flowering of New England* to Buell's *New England Literary Culture.* More popular literary forms are treated in Cohen, *Pillars of Salt;* our own "Romance of Fisherwomen" and "Mysteries of New England"; and Reynolds, *Beneath the American Renaissance.* On African American literary expression, see Cottrol's compilation, *From African to Yankee.* For a case study of famous writers being influenced by their families, see Cole's *Mary Moody Emerson.*

2. Shields, "History," 240; Kagle, *Early Nineteenth-Century American Diary Literature,* 3–5; Decker, *Epistolary Practices,* 88, 100–101.
3. Tebbel's *History of Book Publishing,* 386–457, entries in Dzwonkoski's *American Literary Publishing Houses,* and monographs on specific firms (e.g., Tryon, *Parnassus Corner*), give the best insight into the region's antebellum print production. For the industry's local structure and expansion, see our "Boston Book Trades," and on newspaper publishing there, see Fowle, "Boston Daily Newspapers." On that city's domination of regional printing, see Blouin, *Boston Region.* A few directories of the book trades in other cities exist (e.g., Phelps, "Printing, Publishing"). On the national trade, see Tebbel, *History of Book Publishing;* Zboray, *Fictive People;* Charvat, *Literary Publishing;* and Stern's *Imprints on History, Books and Book People,* and *Publishers.* On the international context, see Barnes, *Authors, Publishers, and Politicians.*
4. Ezell, *Social Authorship.* On professionalism, see Buell, *New England Literary Culture;* Charvat, *Profession; Dauber, Idea of Authorship;* Railton, *Authorship and Audience;* Loving, *Lost in the Customhouse;* Newbury, *Figuring Authorship;* Rice, *Transformation;* and, on amateurs, our *Literary Dollars.* Author-centered studies include Cayton, *Emerson's Emergence;* Fink, *Prophet;* and Williams, *Hungry Heart.* On women writers, see Kelley, *Private Woman,* and Coultrap-McQuin, *Doing Literary Business.* On economic changes giving rise to professionalism and publishing's expansion, see Temin, "Industrialization"; Clark, *Roots of Rural Capitalism;* Pred, *Urban Growth and the Circulation of Information;* and Pred, *Urban Growth and City Systems.*

Chapter 1

1. Charles M. Cobb, Copy of Memoranda, 11 Oct. 1848 in 29 Apr. 1850, Journal, VHS. The entry for 1 July 1849 is copied under 12 Jan. 1854; he began his major journal on 23 Feb. 1851; Charles M. Cobb, 15 May 1853, Journal, VHS.
2. Ezell, *Social Authorship.* While more nineteenth-century diaries than earlier ones approach literariness, not all, of course, do (see Motz's "Folk Expression" and Ulrich's *Midwife's Tale*). This focus has generally centered on prominent people. See Kagle, American Diary Literature, 20–25; Kagle, *Early Nineteenth-Century American Diary Literature,* 4–5. Miner, "Literary Diaries." On common women, see Culley, *Day at a Time,* xi, 17–21.
3. Bunkers, "Diaries"; Bunkers, *Diaries of Girls,* 18–19; Culley, *Day at a Time,* 3, 11–12; Druett, "Those Female Journals," 115–16; Hunter, "Inscribing the Self"; McCarthy, "'Page, a Day,'" 259; Kagle, *American Diary Literature,* 24–26; Kagle, *Early Nineteenth-Century American Diary Literature,* 5–6. Cf. Bloom, "I Write for Myself."

4. On the difficulty of defining what a diary is, see Kagle, *American Diary Literature,* 15–17; Matthews, *American Diaries,* x; Arksey, Pries, and Reed, introduction to *American Diaries,* xii.
5. Most antebellum diary literature studies focus upon women and explore their diaries' therapeutic or subversive value within woman's sphere constraints: Bunkers and Huff, *Inscribing the Daily,* 1–20; Culley, *Day at a Time;* Motz, "Private Alibi"; and Wink, *She Left Nothing.* Schlissel, *Women's Diaries,* compares women's and men's expression, as does Druett, "Those Female Journals," 121–24. McCarthy, "Pocketful of Days," reveals gender distinctions and similarities in forms and usage. For an overview, see Hampsten, *Read This Only to Yourself,* vii–28. Among studies inclusive of men are McCarthy, "'Page, a Day'" (she claims that women's diaries were generally no more private than men's supposedly public ones [256]); Kagle, *American Diary Literature;* Kagle, *Early Nineteenth-Century American Diary Literature;* Kagle, *Late Nineteenth-Century American Diary Literature;* August, *Clerk's Tale;* and Shalhope, *Tale of New England.*
6. Frances Merritt Quick, 2 Apr. 1857, Diary, FMQP-SL; A. K. H. B., "Concerning Hurry."
7. J. Reynolds Hixon, c. Mar. 1836, Diary, OCHS; Frances Merritt Quick, c. 21 Aug. 1858, Diary, FMQP-SL; Catherine S. Patton, 1 July 1845, Journal, CHS; Osman Cleander Baker, 29 Apr. 1831, Diary, NHHS; [Elizabeth W. Clement?], Journal, 1849, CFP-VHS; James Healy, 8 Dec. 1848, 14 Aug. 1849, Diary, CHC. Kagle (*American Diary Literature, Early Nineteenth-Century American Diary Literature,* and *Late Nineteenth-Century American Diary Literature*) has identified various types of diaries: exploration, frontier, life, multigenerational, courtship, situational, spiritual, Transcendentalist, travel, and war. Though most of our diaries fit these categories, we are more concerned with the diarist's reasons for beginning or maintaining one.
8. John Langdon, at the beginning of Diary, 10 Dec. 1844, NEHGS; Christopher Keith, 14 Nov. 1854, Diary, MMC-RIHS; the exact quote is "Each young and ardent person writes a diary, in which, when the hours of prayer and penitence arrive, he inscribes his soul" (Emerson, *Essays*). Nathaniel Morton, 8 Jan. 1842, Diary, OCHS; see, for example, Sarah Jocelyn, c. Mar. 1839, Diary, JFP-CHS; Daniel F. Child and Mary D. Child, 14 Nov. 1839, Diary, DFCP-MHS; for background, see Zboray and Zboray, "Reading and Everyday Life"; Kohn, "Jewish Peddler's Diary," 47–73.
9. Forten, *Journals of Charlotte Forten Grimké,* May 1854, 58; Low, *Lights and Shadows,* 20 July 1829, 24 May 1829, 1:39, 19; John Park, 7 Jan. 1838, Diary, BPL. Cyrus Parker Bradley, 2 Dec. 1835, 29 Mar. 1836, Journal, NHHS.
10. John Park, 26 Nov. 1838, Diary, BPL; Charles M. Cobb, 1 Mar. 1851, Journal, VHS; on models drawn from so-called diary fiction, see Emmeline Augusta Ober, 1 June 1850, Diary, BHS.
11. Lorenza Stevens Berbineau, 15 Jan. 1851, line-a-day Account Book, vol. 120, FCLP-MHS; Paul Atwood Gibson, 12 June 1840, 1 Jan. 1846, Pocket Memoranda, NHHS; James Healy, 15, 17 Jan. 1849, Diary, CHC; Charles M. Cobb, 16 May 1852, Journal, VHS; Lewis Brewster, 28 Oct. 1848, Diary, NHHS.
12. Frances M. Jocelyn, blank page before 1 Mar. 1850, Diary, JFP-CHS; Louisa Gilman Loring to Anna Loring, 2 Jan. 1855, EGLFP-SL.

13. Dorothy C. Walter, annotation to her transcription (194) of Seth Shaler Arnold, Journal, 13 Oct. 1839–19 Oct. 1843, VHS. For an example of a woman's handmade diary, see [Elizabeth W. Clement?], Journal, CFP-VHS. J. Reynolds Hixon, 13 Oct. 1836, Diary, OCHS; Charles M. Cobb, 8 Aug. 1852, Journal, VHS. On belated delivery of binding orders, see John Park, 25 Jan. 1851, Diary, BPL; Persis Sibley Andrews, 12 Jan. 1851, Diary, MeHS.
14. Hannah Hicock Smith, 11 Sept. 1845, Diary, CSL; Charles M. Cobb, 30 Dec. 1851, 1 Jan. 1852, Journal, VHS; Moses Adams III, Common Place Book, No. 2, c. 1835, p. 55, MAP-BC; William Kelly Bartlett, 18 Oct. 1838, Journal, NHHS; Clarissa Harrington, 25 Oct. 1840, "A Daily Journal," LxHS; Daniel F. Child and Mary D. Child, 30 Apr. 1860, Diary, DFCP-MHS; Hannah Hicock Smith, 14 Sept. 1845, Diary, CSL; Charles M. Cobb, 12 Dec. 1850, Journal, VHS. Between 1850 and 1869, the proportion of wood to rag gradually increased, making inferior paper; beginning in the early nineteenth century, machines made paper that could be used in writing, but it too was not as good as handmade paper (Gaskell, *New Introduction,* 222, 215). According to Carvalho, *Forty Centuries of Ink,* good writing ink flowed easily, permeated paper, and was durable (132); by the mid-nineteenth century, many companies manufactured cheap writing fluids that faded with time (210). On the introduction of steel pens, see Thornton, *Handwriting in America,* 46.
15. Hannah Hicock Smith, 19 Nov. 1849, Diary, CSL; William Lloyd Garrison Jr. to Wendell Phillips Garrison, 15 Nov. 1856, GP-SSC; Stephen Salisbury III, 2 Sept. 1853, Diary, SFP-AAS; Ellen Wright to Martha Coffin Wright, 30 Jan. 1861, GP-SSC; J. Reynolds Hixon, 10 Dec., 13 Oct. 1836, Diary, OCHS. Bowers, *Lengthening the Day;* Milan, "Refracting the Gaslier"; Schivelbusch, *Disenchanted Night,* 16, 40.
16. William Kelly Bartlett, 14 June 1837, Journal, NHHS; Martha Osborne Barrett, 7 Mar. 1849, Diary, PEM; Agnes F. Herreshoff, 29 Mar. 1848, Journal, HLFP-RIHS; Sarah E. Trask, 31 Mar. 1849, Journal, BHS.
17. Philip Sage, 26 Feb. 1849, Journal, CHS; J. Reynolds Hixon, 20 Aug. 1836, Diary, OCHS; William Kelly Bartlett, 12 Dec. 1837, Journal, NHHS.
18. Forten, *Journals of Charlotte Forten Grimké,* 14 July 1855, 136; Arozina Perkins, Sept. 1849, Diary, CHS; Agnes F. Herreshoff, 6 Mar. 1840, Diary, HLFP-RIHS.
19. J. Reynolds Hixon, 13 Oct. 1836, Diary, OCHS; Charles M. Cobb, 3 Oct. 1851, Journal, VHS; Lewis Brewster, 7 Dec. [1865?], Diary, NHHS; George H. Clark, 23 June 1847, Diary and Memorandum Book, HBDP-RIHS; John R. Congdon, 5 Nov. 1840, Journal, CFP-RIHS; John Foster, 2 Mar. 1856, Diary, NHHS; Persis Sibley Andrews, 3 Dec. 1841, Diary, MeHS; Cyrus Parker Bradley, 8 Jan. 1836, Journal, NHHS.
20. Low, *Lights and Shadows,* before 19 Mar. 1833, 25 Aug. 1832, 2:525, 431; Parsons Family, Gilmanton, N.H., "Home Journal," 1:3 (1 Nov. 1858), manuscript amateur newspaper, PaFP-SL; Caroline A. Stoddard, Journal, 1856, PEM; Charles Henry Charlton, Diary, CHS; I. W. Chapman, title page, Diary 1850–51, CHS; Mary Pierce Poor, Account Book, 1858, vol. 26, PoFP-SL; McCarthy, "Pocketfull of Days."
21. On verses, for example, Mary Coult Jones, 1 Jan. 1851–3 Feb. 1854, Diary, NHHS, and Mary Coult Jones, 12 Apr. 1855–31 Dec. 1859, Diary, CHS. Culley, *Day at a Time,* 14; Huff, "Reading as Re-Vision"; Druett, "Those Female Journals," 123.

22. Low, *Lights and Shadows,* 1 Aug. 1832, 2:421; Gibbins Adams, 18 Aug. 1841, Diary, PEM; John R. Congdon, c. 24 Mar. 1850, Journal, CFP-RIHS; Low, *Lights and Shadows,* 24 May, 16 June 1829, 1:19, 28.
23. J. Reynolds Hixon, 29 Mar. 1836, Diary, OCHS; Chauncey Thomas Botsford, 5 Nov. 1860, Journal, CHS; Lucy Charnley Bradner, inscription in Elizabeth Atwater Charnley, Journal, 1833–38, and Lucy Charnley Bradner, 9 July 1858, Journal, both in CHS; Amos A. Lawrence, 22 Sept. 1842, Diary, AALP-MHS.
24. Charles M. Cobb, 6, 7 May 1852, Journal, VHS; Sarah B. Mason Ruggles Eaton, 7 July 1833, Diary, RIHS.
25. Albert Gallatin Browne to Sarah Smith (Cox) Browne, 28 Nov. in 27 Nov. 1838, BroFP-SL; Joshua Edwin Harris, 29 Nov. 1856, Journal, JEHP-MeHS; Forten, *Journals of Charlotte Forten Grimké,* 17 July 1854, 87; Cornelia Jocelyn Foster, 23 Jan. 1861, Diary, JFP-CHS; Emmeline Augusta Ober, 10 Mar. 1850, Diary, BHS.
26. William Durkee Williamson and others, Album and Diary, 1826–48, BPL; Daniel F. Child and Mary D. Child, 27 Jan. 1861, Diary, DFCP-MHS; Sarah Anne (Chace) Greene, added entry, 28 Nov. 1853, in Christopher Albert Greene, Diary, CAGP-RIHS; Richard F. Fuller, added entries, 10 Jan. 1858–10 Jan. 1866, in Sarah K. (Batchelder) Fuller, Notebook, c. 1842, BPL.
27. Even the little work done on antebellum diaries dwarfs that on common people's personal letters, which tends toward women's practices. Decker, *Epistolary Practices,* covers the vast scope of early American history but focuses on Ralph Waldo Emerson, Emily Dickinson, and Henry Adams; on letters as literary forms, see 4–6, 20–21. On "the various rhetorical deployments of the letter" in American literary works, see Polly, "Private and Public Letters," 4. See Zboray, *Fictive People,* chap. 8, esp. on the letter's relationship to fiction, 115–21. On letter writing as women's work, feminine accomplishment, and self-expression, see, for example, Motz, *True Sisterhood,* chap. 3; Thornton, *Handwriting in America,* 56–57, 59–60; Cashin, *Our Common Affairs,* passim; and Eldred and Mortensen, *Imagining Rhetoric,* 7–8, 24, 37–40, 56–65, 73–75, 127, 129. Women's letter writing was both public and private, according to Gilroy and Verhoeven, introduction, 15–16, and the essays in parts 1 and 2, *Epistolary Histories.* On letters as vital communication vehicles across racial and regional boundaries, see Starobin, *Blacks in Bondage,* and Dicken Garcia, *To Western Woods.*
28. Mary Pierce Poor to John Pierce and Lucy (Tappan) Pierce, 30 Jan. 1842, PoFP-SL.
29. William Lloyd Garrison Jr. to Wendell Phillips Garrison, 3 Jan. 1858, GP-SSC; J[oshua] and Phoebe A. Ballard to Benjamin Russell and [Mehitable Russell], 31 July 1825, MARL-AHS.
30. Elizabeth Dwight Cabot to Elizabeth L. Eliot, 21 June 1846, CFP-SL; Catherine Prescott to Elizabeth Ellis (Prescott) Betton, 23 Sept. 1837, BFL-PEM; Alexander Hill Everett to Sarah P. E. Hale, 4 July 1828, HP-SSC.
31. Marginalia by Louisa Goddard in Anne Elizabeth Goddard to Mehetable May (Dawes) Goddard, 10 Feb. 1833, MGFP-SL; postscript in "Cousin Louise [Cheever]" to [Elizabeth B. Cheever], 9 Jan. 1837, CFP-AAS.
32. Edwin Leigh Furness, 9 Nov. 1848, Journal, MeHS; Joshua Marean, 20 June 1851, Diary, MeHS; Sarah Watson Dana, 24 Mar. 1859, Private Account Book, 1859,

DFP-SL; Sarah Smith (Cox) Browne, 18 Feb. 1853, Account of Family Expenses, 1853–57, and 11 Mar. 1851, Waste Book, BroFP-SL. Frances M. Jocelyn, undated recipe at conclusion of 1839–45 Diary, JFP-CHS; Sarah Watson Dana, 4 May 1853, Private Account Book, 1853–Jan. 1854, DFP-SL; Sarah Smith (Cox) Browne, 20 May 1853, Account of Family Expenses, BroFP-SL; Lorenza Stevens Berbineau, 5 July 1851, line-a-day Account Book, vol. 120, FCLP-MHS, Charles M. Cobb, 10 Feb. 1853, Journal, VHS; William Sherwood, 8 June 1840, 22 Apr. 1843, Account Book, 1840–44, WSP-YUb; Sarah Smith (Cox) Browne, 24 Oct. 1843, Family Account Book entries, 1834–45, BroFP-SL. Charles M. Cobb, 12 Dec. 1850, Journal, VHS. Sarah Watson Dana, 5 May 1853, Account Book, 3 May 1853–5 Jan. 1855, DFP-SL; George H. Clark, Sept. 1847, Diary and Memorandum Book, 1846–58, HBDP-RIHS; Annie B. Lawrence Rotch, Jan. 1849, Expenses, 1 Jan. 1849–8 Aug. 1850, LFP-MHS. U.S. Bureau of the Census, *Historical Statistics,* 807; John Davis to Eliza Bancroft Davis, 4 Dec. 1825, JDP-AAS.

33. Joshua Edwin Harris to Irving Curtis, 7 Dec. 1856, Letterbook, JEHP-MeHS; John R. Congdon, 4 Apr. 1848, Journal, CFP-RIHS; Mary Pierce Poor to John Pierce and Lucy (Tappan) Pierce, 30 Jan. 1842, PoFP-SL.
34. Mehetable May (Dawes) Goddard to "Children," 12 Feb. [postmark] 1833, MGFP-SL; Mary Pierce Poor to John Pierce, 28 Oct. 1841, PoFP-SL; Olive Gay Worcester, 17 Oct. 1846, Journal, SFA-SL.
35. Charles Lenox Remond to Loring Moody, [c. 1846], BPL; Wallace Clement to Sarah Fish Clement, 6 Nov. 1859, CFP-VHS; Charles Lenox Remond to Martha H. Usher, postscript to 22 May 1845, CLRL-PEM; Martha Russell Fifield to Benjamin Russell and Mehitable Russell, [1840], MARL-AHS. Frances Adams Chamberlain to Joshua Lawrence Chamberlain, 12 May 1857, CAFP-SL; Mary Pierce Poor to John Pierce and Lucy (Tappan) Pierce, 12 May 1836, PoFP-SL; Luella J. B. Case to Sarah E. Edgarton, 20 Jan. 1842, HC-SL; S. R. W[orcester?] to Mary A. Byram, Friday Evening [1830s?], SFA-SL; Mary Pierce Poor to John Pierce and Lucy (Tappan) Pierce, 6 Feb. 1849, PoFP-SL; S[arah]. B. Mason R[uggles Eaton] to Agnes F. Herreshoff, 11 Aug. 1834, HLFP-RIHS; Ellen Wright to Martha Coffin Wright, 8 Mar. 1861, GP-SSC. On handwriting as a mark of character, see Thornton, *Handwriting in America,* chap. 2.
36. H. E. Beck to Harriet Jane Hanson Robinson, 7 Sept. 1846, RSP-SL; Charles Lenox Remond to Mrs. Ellen Sands, 1 Apr. 1840, CLRL-PEM; Jane E. Shedd to Harriet E. Strong, 3 Dec. 1836, WCP-VHS; Mary Anne Loring to Mrs. J. A. [Louisa] Peabody, 25 July 1837, PFP-PEM.
37. William Lloyd Garrison Sr., quoted in William Lloyd Garrison Jr. to William Lloyd Garrison Sr., 3 Aug. 1860, GP-SSC; Cyrus Parker Bradley, 22 Nov.,16 Sept. 1835, Journal, NHHS; Mary Pierce Poor to John Pierce and Lucy (Tappan) Pierce, 11 Feb. 1842, PoFP-SL (she may be referring to John MacPherson, author of the play *Hodge Podge Improved*). A conversational tone in private letter writing was extolled in Hugh Blair's *Lectures on Belles Lettres and Rhetoric* (1783); see Polly, "Private and Public Letters," 10–11. Many contemporary manuals treated correspondence like any other belletristic writing; see Johnson, *Gender and Rhetorical Space,* 86. Weiss, *American Letter-writers.*

38. Persis Sibley Andrews, 2 Apr. 1842, Diary, DFP-MHS.
39. Eliza Bancroft Davis to John Davis, 8 July 1840, JDP-AAS. On Bristow, see Caroline W. H. Dall, *"Alongside,"* 38. Zboray and Zboray, "Gender Slurs," 429.
40. Charles M. Cobb, 15 May 1851, Journal, VHS; J. Reynolds Hixon, 24 May 1837, Diary, OCHS. On stolen letters and lack of privacy, see Peters, *Speaking into the Air,* 165–67.
41. Caroline Gardiner Curtis, 6 Jan. 1851, Diary, 1851, CFP3-MHS; John Park, 19 Jan. 1851, Diary, BPL.
42. Sarah Watson Dana, 12 Apr. 1834, Journal, 1833–35, DFP-SL.
43. Persis Sibley Andrews, 2 Apr. 1842, Diary, DFP-MHS.

Chapter 2

1. Enoch Hale, 13 June, 3 Aug., 20 Dec. 1849, Diary, PEM.
2. Charles M. Cobb, 5 May 1850, Journal, VHS; Olive Gay Worcester, 16 Feb. 1843, 25 Dec. 1846, Journals, SFA-SL; James Lawrence Whittier, 31 Aug. 1830, Diary, AAS; Elizabeth H. Jocelyn, 3 Oct. 1839, Diary, JFP-CHS; Elizabeth Atherton Clapp, 12 May 1852, Journal, CP-MHS. While ordinary folk's creativity in assembling textual materials has been largely overlooked, Capezzi's "From Reading to Writing" suggests an emerging interest in this area. Garvey, in her *Adman in the Parlor,* devotes a chapter to late-nineteenth-century trade-card scrapbooks; see also her "Scissorizing and Scrapbooks" (208, 224) for a take similar to the "texts-from-texts" idea: "gleaning" from "assorted preexisting artifacts to create a new work." On scrapbooks as women's self expression, see Buckler, "Silent Woman Speaks"; Buckler and Leeper, "Antebellum Woman's Scrapbook"; and Katriel and Farrell, "Scrapbooks as Cultural Texts." On abundance, see Brown, *Knowledge Is Power,* 270–86. Garvey, "Scissorizing and Scrapbooks," 209, claims scrapbook makers of a later time "adapted to this proliferation of print by cutting it up and saving it."
3. Frances M. Jocelyn, 15 Mar. 1854, Diary, JFP-CHS; Elizabeth Pierce to Mary Pierce Poor, in Elizabeth Pierce and Lucy (Tappan) Pierce to Mary Pierce Poor, 11 Feb. 1842, PoFP-SL. William Stevens Robinson, postscript to Lucy Robinson to Mrs. Martha Robinson, 1838, RSP-SL. On scrapboxes, see Elizabeth H. Jocelyn, 27 Apr. 1839, Diary, JFP-CHS; James Lawrence Whittier, 31 Aug. 1830, Diary, AAS. Emmeline Augusta Ober, 15 Dec. 1850, Diary, BHS. On amassing clippings, see Capezzi, "From Reading to Writing," 9.
4. An example of diaries turning into scrapbooks occurs in Sarah E. Trask, Journal, vol. 2, BHS. Recycling at century's end (Garvey, "Scissorizing and Scrapbooks," 215–17) was probably more common as books became cheaper. On recycling, see Olive Gay Worcester, Recipe Book and Scrapbook, 1827, 1828, 1838, and her Commonplace book, 1841, written and pasted over Harris, *Maine Register* (in SFP-SL). The common juxtaposition of recipes and political matter may represent a subversion of domesticity (Capezzi, "From Reading to Writing," 8). Charles M. Cobb, 5 May 1850, Journal, VHS. Aurilla Ann Moffitt, 8, 16 June 1847, Personal Journal, OCHS; Elizabeth H. Jocelyn, 28 Mar. 1839, Diary, JFP-CHS; Susan D. Tucker, 3, 4 Apr.

1851, Journal, VHS. On scrapbook making, see Buckler and Leeper, "Antebellum Woman's Scrapbook," and Buckler, "Silent Woman Speaks." Mark Twain advocated albums with adhesive columns that would eliminate making homemade pastes that were subject to drying up or spilling (Smith, "Consuming Passions," 69).

5. Harriet Jane Hanson Robinson, Scrapbook, 1850–78, RSP-SL; Elizabeth H. Jocelyn, 22 Mar. 1839, Journal, JFP-CHS; Sarah E. Trask, 22 May 1851, Journal, BHS; the piece by E. Curtis Hine appeared in *Flag of Our Union.* Garvey, *Adman in the Parlor,* 28–38; Smith, "Consuming Passions," 70–73.
6. Frances M. Jocelyn, 7 July 1840, 23 Oct. 1851, Diary, JFP-CHS; D. F. to William [H. Byram?], 24 Feb. 1851, SFA-SL.
7. On contributions, see Hannah R. Child, Commonplace Book, DFCP-MHS. Charlotte Rantoul to Elizabeth Abbot, 8 Sept. 1833, EC-BHS; William Wheeler, "Hints," Journal, 1833, vol. 5, 1833–35, WWP-CSL; Feroline (Pierce) Fox to Mary Pierce Poor, Nov. 1847, PoFP-SL. Scholars have just begun to treat commonplace books in other times or places (e.g., Stabile, *Memory's Daughters;* Blecki and Wulf, *Milcah Martha Moore's Book*). Miller, *Assuming the Positions,* includes nineteenth-century Virginians; see also Harris, *Courtship of Olivia Langdon,* chap. 1. Major figures predominate (e.g., Wilson, *Jefferson's Literary Commonplace Book*). Laborers kept them with content appealing to middle-class tastes; see Stainton, "Halifax Sailor's Taste." Unlike Moss, *Printed Commonplace-Books,* who argues that "the decline of the commonplace into the trivial and the banal . . . was irreversible by the nineteenth [century]" (2), we assume it still held personal meaning. Butler, "Commonplace Books," 503, maintains that it aided memory, ordered knowledge, stimulated imagination, and acted as a fact repository. On commonplacing as an active rather than passive intellectual exercise, see Knoles and Knoles, "'In Usum Pupillorum.'" Lockridge, *Sources of Patriarchal Rage,* 3–4 and passim, argues that they are important in identity creation. The quotations in this chapter are not always verbatim as the transcribers sometimes took liberties with the original or misquoted.
8. Enoch Hale, *Extracts in Poetry,* 20 Dec. 1849, Diary, PEM. Martha Osborne Barrett, 2 Jan. 1855, Diary, PEM; Sarah Everett Hale, Commonplace Book, vol. 1, c. 1837–50, HP-SSC; Annie B. Lawrence Rotch, Commonplace Book, 1834–?, LFP-MHS; William Paul, Commonplace Book, before 1845, MEBTP-VHS; Electa Kimberly, Copybooks, 1838, 1846–54, CHS; Sarah P. E. Hale, Commonplace Book, c. 1827–50. Joanna Rotch, Commonplace Book, LFP-MHS; Moses Adams III, Commonplace Books, Nos. 1 and 2, MAP-BC; Olive Gay Worcester, Copy Book, 1826, SFA-SL. Elizabeth Pierce, 30 Jan. 1830, Notebook [1825–28?], vol. 2, Extracts in Prose and Poetry, PoFP-SL. On these books' hodgepodge nature, see Miller, *Assuming the Positions,* 29–30, 35. According to Moss, *Printed Commonplace-Books,* 79–80, this characteristic seems to date to the seventeenth century. Antebellum New England commonplace books departed from earlier ones classifying excerpts topically (Lechner, *Renaissance Concepts,* 67–70, 233). On eighteenth-century coteries, see Stabile, *Memory's Daughters,* 9, 12–13, 63, 155, 233–34. On collaborative authors, see Miller, *Assuming the Positions,* 37–38, 175, 182. Crane, *Framing Authority,* argues that commonplacing in Renaissance England less promoted humanistic individualism than acted as a form of "cultural capital" for the socially mobile (6).

9. Martha Osborne Barrett, 22 Dec. 1854, 16 Dec. 1852, Diary, PEM. See, for example of segregated quotes, the two-page extract of "Rules for spending money by A. A. Livermore" and the half-page "Extracts from Channing" at the end of James Allison, Diary, NHHS. Little has been done on quoting, especially in history and by ordinary people. Garber, *Quotation Marks,* 14, traces the development of printed quotation marks in the seventeenth century; she maintains that writers and speakers quote primarily to gain authority but also to stimulate thinking or to make "an excuse for not thinking" (2). Fried, "Valves of Attention," posits an aesthetics of quotation and the act's relationship to death through its practice by major antebellum authors. See also Kellett, *Literary Quotation and Allusion.*
10. Arozina Perkins, 17 May 1849, Diary, CHS; Persis Sibley Andrews, 2 Jan. 1841, Diary, MeHS; Cyrus Parker Bradley, 3 June 1835, Journal, NHHS; Lewis Brewster, 1 Sept. 1848, Diary, NHHS; Mary Coult Jones, 30 June 1853, Diary, NHHS.
11. Forten, *Journals of Charlotte Forten Grimké,* 25 May 1854, 60; Kohn, "Jewish Peddler's Diary," [4 Dec. 1842], 65; Mary Hall, 13 Dec. 1831, Diary, NHHS. For religious references, see Lucy S. Baker, 9 Mar. 1848, Diary, BHS; Susan S. Johnson, 10 Oct. 1841, Journal, LxHS. On secular works, see Mary Elizabeth Fiske, 9 Jan. 1843, Diary, LxHS; Martha Osborne Barrett, 31 Aug., 2 Sept. 1854, Diary, PEM; Frances Adams Chamberlain to George E. Adams, 22 Sept. 1847, CAFP-SL; Forten, *Journals of Charlotte Forten Grimké,* 15, 17 Aug. 1856, 162–63; Frances Merritt Quick, 2 Jan. 1859, Diary, FMQP-SL.
12. "R.H.S," "Sympathy," in Mary Baker Eddy, Scrapbook, c. 1830–60, MBEL; see, for an example of this reticence by nonfamily members, Elizabeth Abbot to Hannah L. Rantoul, 20 Dec. 1839, and Lydia Baker to Hannah L. Rantoul, [7 Apr. 1853], EC-BHS; C[aroline] M[oore] Evans to Olive Gay Worcester, 1 June 1855, SFUP-SL.
13. Laura Smith to Jane E. Shedd, 15 Feb. 1841, WCP-VHS; S. B. Mellish to "Friend [Caleb] Wall," 15 June 1849, WFP-AAS.
14. Prudence Crandall Philleo to William L. Garrison Sr. 19 Mar. 1833, BPL; Sophia Ellsworth to Delia E. Taintor, 13 June 1859, TDFP-AAS.
15. H. E. Beck to Harriet Jane Hanson Robinson, 7 Sept. 1846, RSP-SL; Elizabeth W. Clement to Charles Clement, 1 July 1840, CFP-VHS; J[ohn] B. Herreshoff to Agnes F. Herreshoff, 6 Oct. 1832, HLFP-RIHS.
16. Lydia Baker to Hannah L. Rantoul, [7 Apr. 1853], EC-BHS; Garber, *Quotation Marks,* 20, calls repeated misquotation over time "quotation by free indirect discourse."
17. On the creativity of marks and on annotators as authors, see Jackson, *Marginalia,* 4–5, 203; chap. 8, 99–100. On reader response, see Jackson, "Reader Retailored"; Davidson's *Revolution and the Word* analytically incorporates marginalia (69–70, 75–79, 95, 182). On decoding marks, see Stoddard, *Marks in Books,* and Hellinga, "'Marks in Books' Project." Some scholars have examined canonical authors' marginalia (e.g., Cowen's *Melville's Marginalia*). On inscriptions, see Dickinson, "Creating a World," and Jackson, *Marginalia,* 67–69.
18. Elizabeth Atwater Charnley, 8 Feb. 1833, Journal, CHS; Watts, *Improvement of the Mind;* Mary Baker Eddy, Scrapbook, c. 1830–60, passim, MBEL; Cyrus Parker Bradley, 13 Nov. 1835, Journal, NHHS. Martha Osborne Barrett, 20 Sept. 1854, Diary, PEM. On marks for commonplacing, see Jackson, *Marginalia,* 184, and, on

marginalia's social nature, 82–88, 96, 100, 256–57. On giftbook marks and "social currency," see Dickinson, "Creating a World," 57, 60, 63–65.

19. Webster, *Elementary Spelling Book,* 39, 64 (in GEL-HU); Charles M. Cobb, 28 Feb. 1851, Journal, VHS; Cyrus Parker Bradley, 10 Sept. 1835, Journal, NHHS; Christopher Albert Greene, marginalia to Persy, *Elementary Treatise,* in CAGP-RIHS. Johnson, *Old-Time Schools,* 151–66.
20. Arozina Perkins, Sept. 1849, Diary, CHS; James Amsted Brown, 15 May 1859, Journal, VHS; Calista Billings, 23 Jan. 1849, Diary, SL. On marginalia and flirting, see Jackson, *Marginalia,* 72.
21. Frances Merritt Quick, 18 Mar. 1857, Diary, FMQP-SL; Patrick James Keegan to Dermot Warburton Keegan, 18 Mar. 1858, NSFP-SL; Charles M. Cobb, 1 Aug. 1852, Journal, VHS. The classical notion that the mind can create a library of its own continued into eighteenth-century America (Stabile, *Memory's Daughters,* 81). Nicolaisen, *Oral Tradition,* considers memorization of texts; McGillivray, *Memorization.* On the history of methods of memory improvement, see Yates, *Art of Memory.* For an example of a contemporary guide, see Miles's *American Phreno-Mnemotechny.*
22. Olive Gay Worcester, 17 Oct. 1845, Journal, SFA-SL; Persis Sibley Andrews, 13 Mar. 1845, Diary, MeHS; Harriet Prescott to Elizabeth Ellis (Prescott) Betton, 8 June 1835, BFL-PEM; Elizabeth W. Clement to Charles Clement, 1 July 1840, CFP-VHS; Annie De Wolf Middleton to Nathaniel Russell Middleton, 2 Sept. 1842, DMFP-SCHS. On children's memorization and recitation as part of everyday life, see Sorby, "Learning by Heart."
23. Elizabeth Pierce, 19 July 1828, Journal, PoFP-SL; William Kelly Bartlett, 13 Aug. 1838, Journal, NHHS; Low, *Lights and Shadows,* 2, 3 Jan. 1833, 2:486–87.
24. Ellen Wright to William Wright, [Nov.?] 1860, GP-SSC. Mary Belden to Sarah Watson Dana, 21 Dec. 1838, DFP-SL; Elizabeth Atwater Charnley, Journal, 1 Feb. 1833–8 May 1838, CHS; Frances Merritt Quick, 18 Mar. 1857, Diary, FMQP-SL; Augustus Dodge Rogers, 6 Apr. 1855, 13, 27 Mar. 1855, 9, 17 Apr. 1854, Diary, RFP-PEM; Forten, *Journals of Charlotte Forten Grimké,* 27 Nov., 30 Apr. 1858, 22 June 1854, 346, 306, 77; Wallace Clement to Sarah Fish Clement, 11 Apr. 1860, CFP-VHS; Moses Adams III, Common Place Book, No. 2, c. 1835, p. 27, MAP-BC. On recitations' prevalence in nineteenth-century higher academe, see Holifield, "On Teaching," 240–42, and in secondary schools, Windhover, "Literature in the Nineteenth Century," 29 (and on the view of "the mind as a muscle to be strengthened," 28); on poetry memorization as character building, see Rubin, "'They Flash,'" 276 (and on memorized words as something to call up as needed, 275).
25. Harriet Jane Hanson Robinson, 20 Aug. 1856, Diary, RSP-SL. On spiritualism and communication, see Barnes, *Long Distance Calling;* Peters, *Speaking into the Air.*
26. Charles M. Cobb, 18 Jan. 1852, Journal, VHS; William Cooper Nell to William Lloyd Garrison Sr., 15 Sept. 1851, BPL; Mary Pierce Poor to Lucy (Pierce) Hedge, 21 Jan. 1851, 1 Oct. 1854, PoFP-SL. Martha Osborne Barrett, 11, 13, 21 Nov. 1853, and, on the circle to which she belonged, 14 Oct., 26 Dec. 1852, Diary, PEM; Martha Osborne Barrett, Undated Poetic Communications, c. 1852–54, PEM. Weisberg, *Talking to the Dead,* 121; on automatic writing's 1850s upsurge, see Braude, *Radical Spirits,* 18; Jackson, *Spirit Rappers,* chap. 11.

27. Charles M. Cobb, 11 Feb. 1852, Journal, VHS; George Rodney Babbitt, 5 Sept. 1858, Journal, OCHS; Charles M. Cobb, 18 Jan. and 23 Feb. 1852, Journal, VHS; Mary Pierce Poor to Lucy (Pierce) Hedge, 9 Feb. 1851, PoFP-SL. On the Woodstock incident, see Zboray and Zboray, *Literary Dollars,* 10–12.
28. On changes in meaning when the spoken word takes on written form, see Ong, *Orality and Literacy;* see also Hindman's *Printing the Written Word.* For a case study, see Fielding, *Writing and Orality.*
29. Brasher, "James Freeman Clarke's Journal," 85. Frances M. Jocelyn, 27 June 1840, Diary, JFP-CHS (mention of lecture notes appear on 26 June, 6 July 1848, Diary); James Lawrence Whittier, 8 May 1831, Diary, AAS; Helen M. Warner, 22 Sept. [1851], Diary, NEHGS; on the practice among journalists, see Sarah P. E. Hale to Edward Everett, 30 Sept. 1842, HP-SSC; for examples of shorthand in diaries, see John Park, 4, 10 Apr. 1846, Diary, BPL; Ezra Warren Mudge, 16 Feb. 1850, Diary, LHS. For phonographic marginalia, see Stuart, *Grammar of the Hebrew Language* (ASWR-AJHS). Charlotte Henrietta Pettibone, 12 Dec. 1842, Diary, CHS. Popularized in the United States about 1844, the Pitmanic method was often learned via lectures and manuals (Landroth, "History and Development," 82, 69).
30. Annie B. Lawrence Rotch, 3 Nov. 1840, Diary, LFP-MHS; Sarah Watson Dana, 13 Dec. 1833, Journal, DFP-SL; Martha Osborne Barrett, 25 Dec. 1855, Diary, PEM; Forten, *Journals of Charlotte Forten Grimké,* 18 June 1854, 73–74; Persis Sibley Andrews, 22 Nov. 1846, Diary, MeHS.
31. See, for example, Unidentified Salem Woman with Husband in China, 6 Mar. 1853, Diary, BPL; Mary P. Howe, 18 June 1826, 9 July 1831, Diary, NEHGS; Paul H. Bixby, Diary, NHHS. Frederick Lathrop Gleason, 18 Sept. 1859, Journal, CHS; see also Daniel F. Child and Mary D. Child, 3 Oct. 1841, Diary, DFCP-MHS.
32. For one case of creative translation, see English, "'Genuine Transcripts.'" The nineteenth century saw greater regard for foreign language texts and, accordingly, theories of translation by Matthew Arnold, Wilhelm von Humboldt, and Arthur Schopenhauer moved away from literalness toward questioning precise equivalencies, preserving foreignness, and allowing multiple translations (Schulte and Biguenet, *Theories of Translation,* 3–6); see also Lefevere, "Translation." Whether everyday translators were literalists ("word for word") or more sensitive to the poetics of language is unclear. Lacking a history of American translating, readers must rely upon international overviews, such as Rener's *Interpretatio,* Kelly's *True Interpreter,* and Robinson's *Western Translation Theory,* and works on foreign cultures' national impact (e.g., Pochmann, *German Culture;* Leighton, *Two Worlds;* Blumenthal, *American and French Culture;* and Reinhold, *Classica Americana*); on New England, see Bauschinger, *Trumpet of Reform.* On foreign language instruction, see Watts, "Teaching of French," and Kelly, *Twenty-five Centuries.* On translation as production, see Lefevere, "Introduction," 10.
33. Hannah Hicock Smith, 28 Dec. 1847, Diary, CSL; Mary Pierce Poor to John Pierce and Lucy (Tappan) Pierce, 18 May in 17 May 1837, PoFP-SL; Sarah Ellen Browne to Sarah Smith (Cox) Browne, 1 Feb., 16 Mar., 1857, SEBP-SL; Lilly Dana, 8 Feb. 1860, Diary, DFP-SL; Forten, *Journals of Charlotte Forten Grimké,* 14 Apr., 5 Mar., 23 June 1856, 155, 151, 158; Ellen Wright to Martha Coffin Wright, 11 Jan. 1861,

GP-SSC. Latin and Greek instruction was rare in female schools before mid-century (Winterer, "Victorian Antigone," 73). French was offered at Norton Female Seminary, Mount Holyoke, Uxbridge Academy, and the Boston High School for Girls; it was on few Massachusetts public high school curricula before 1840 but was required after 1857 in towns with populations of over four thousand (Watts, "Teaching of French," 38, 40).

34. Cyrus Parker Bradley, 20 Apr. 1833, 22 Oct., 25 Sept. 1835, Journal, NHHS; for a summary of his Exeter academic work and on his acquisition of French at Dartmouth, see 18 Aug. 1832, 20 Apr. 1833, School Journal, NHHS; on translating Goethe, see his entry for 16 Dec. 1835, on de Staël, see 12 Nov. 1835, and on the classics, throughout; James Healy, 4 Mar., 15 Jan., 9 Feb., 21 Mar., 25 June 1849, Diary, CHC. Zboray, *Fictive People,* 93. French had been studied in college since the late seventeenth century (Watts, "Teaching of French," 61–88) and was "authorized" at Harvard in the eighteenth (Blumenthal, *American and French Culture,* 75). Carl Follen became Harvard's first German instructor in 1825 (Pochmann, *German Culture,* 114–15). According to Kelly, *Twenty-five Centuries,* 174, modern languages before the nineteenth century were mainly taught privately. Winterer, *Culture of Classicism.*

35. William Lloyd Garrison Jr. to Wendell Phillips Garrison, 7 Feb. 1856, GP-SSC; William Lloyd Garrison Jr. to William Lloyd Garrison Sr., 27 Sept. 1858, GP-SSC; Mary Pierce Poor to Laura Stone, 19 Sept. 1852, PoFP-SL; Annie B. Lawrence Rotch, 4 Nov. 1840, Diary LFP-MHS; Low, *Lights and Shadows,* 19 Aug. 1829, 2 Mar. 1831, 8, 9 Mar. 1830, 2 Feb., 6 Mar., 21 Aug. 1832, 16 Apr., 13 May 1833, 1:49, 198, 114, 288, 296, 2:430, 538–39, 551, and editor's introduction 1:3; Forten, *Journals of Charlotte Forten Grimké,* 20 May, 5 Jan., 18 Nov. 1857, 3 Dec. 1856, 219, 180, 267, 170.

36. Low, *Lights and Shadows,* 30, 31 May, 20 Aug. 1833, 2:558–59, 608; Mary Pierce Poor to John Pierce and Lucy (Tappan) Pierce, 20 July in 6 July 1838, PoFP-SL; John Park, 27 June 1842, Diary, BPL.

37. Frances Merritt Quick, 18 Mar. 1857, Diary, FMQP-SL.

38. Enoch Hale, 20 Dec. 1849, 30 July 1841, Diary, PEM; Charles M. Cobb, 27 Aug. 1852, Journal, VHS. He misquoted Ecclesiastes 9:10: "Whatever thy hand findeth to do . . ."

Chapter 3

1. Frances Merritt Quick, 30 Sept. 1858, Diary, FMQP-SL. Without historical studies of writing within literary genres for pleasure by common folk, researchers must turn to contemporary research on creativity, such as Talarico's *Spreading the Word,* Csikszentmihalyi's *Flow,* and Nebel's *Dark Side of Creativity* (the latter considers writer's block).

2. Of course, we cannot be absolutely sure that the everyday literature we cite in this chapter is indeed original. However, there were several indications of originality: (1) the material was signed; (2) writers elsewhere claimed authorship in their diaries or letters; (3) the piece contained internal evidence of nonstandard usage, stylistic

idiosyncrasies in line with the rest of the writer's letters or diaries, and, for verse, irregular meter; and (4) the prose or verse lacked quotation marks to denote it was written by another hand and passed our test of a global search of databases of published work (ProQuest's *Literature Online,* available via the University of Pittsburgh). We did not hold these writers to high criteria of originality, and indeed some of their work may so closely imitate (or parody) popular ballads, hymns, children's rhymes, or other verse, as well as commonplace passages of prose, that it may represent only minor deviations from standard literature. Especially in cases of oral tradition, we might expect a tension between formulaic expression and improvisation (see Lord, *Singer of Tales*).

3. Moses Adams III, Common Place Book, No. 2, c. June 1835, p. 101, MAP-BC; Charles M. Cobb, 7 July 1849, "The Vermont Collection," Extra, no. 6 under 4 Sept. 1852, Journal, VHS.
4. Martha Osborne Barrett, 27 Aug., 9 Sept. 1849, 24 Dec. 1852, Diary, PEM; on the friend, see Barrett's letters from the period and those of Lucy A. Colby in the Cartland Family Papers, HL-HU, and Hansen, *Very Social Time,* 60–61; John R. Congdon, Aug. 1846, Journal, CFP-RIHS; Low, *Lights and Shadows,* 13 Apr. 1831, 1:217–18; Cyrus Parker Bradley, 12 Jan. 1835, Journal, NHHS. Druett, "Those Female Journals," 116.
5. Mary Pierce Poor to John Pierce and Lucy (Tappan) Pierce, 26 May in 25 May 1837, PoFP-SL; Sarah Everett Hale to Nathan Hale Jr., 21 Sept. 1838, HP-SSC; unidentified Irish Catholic named Crowninshield, Hunting Journal, [c. Aug. 1834], NHHS. Frances Merritt Quick, 14 Oct. 1858, Diary, FMQP-SL; Leverett Norton, 11 Jan. 1858, Diary, SC-CHS.
6. Sarah E. Trask, 8 June 1851, Journal, BHS; James Healy, quoted in Foley, *Bishop Healy,* 23; Mary Coult Jones, 9 Feb. 1851, Diary, NHHS.
7. Nancy Taft, Poetry, c. 1840, NTP-VHS; Forten, *Journals of Charlotte Forten Grimké,* 19 Apr. 1857, 212; Caroline Barrett White, 29 Oct. 1849, Diary, AAS (for more on this episode, see Zboray and Zboray, "Romance of Fisherwomen"); Albert Dodd, 24 Mar. 1837, Diary, ADP-YUs; Katz, "1837," 1.
8. I. W. Chapman, "Spare the Albatross," 11 Feb. 1851, Diary, CHS; Calista Billings, 7 Oct. 1849, Diary, SL; Leverett Norton, 24 Jan. 1858, Diary, SC-CHS; Frances M. Jocelyn, 1 Feb. 1841, Diary, JFP-CHS; Rebecca Primus, "I've Lost a Day," poem, 15 Feb. 1854, PFP-CHS, reprinted in Griffin, *Beloved Sisters,* 16.
9. Leverett Norton, 14 Mar. 1859, Diary, SC-CHS; Giles Waldo to George Waldo, 6 Feb. 1843, GWP-YUb; W. E. Mars, undated fragment in Sarah Thankful Mars, Chip Basket [i.e., undated cookbook], STMP-VHS.
10. Mary Pierce Poor to John Pierce and Lucy (Tappan) Pierce, 2 Feb., 6 Apr. 1846, PoFP-SL; Daniel F. Child and Mary D. Child, 8 Mar. 1849, Diary, DFCP-MHS.
11. Sarah P. E. Hale to Edward Everett Hale, 25 Dec. 1844, HP-SSC; Henry Worcester to Olive Gay Worcester, 17 Oct. 1856, SFUP-SL; Elizabeth H. Jocelyn, 2, 11, 13, 24, 25 Apr. 1839, Diary, JFP-CHS.
12. Stephen Salisbury III, 22 Jan. 1852, Diary, SFP-AAS; Susan D. Tucker, 24 or 25 Jan. 1852, Journal, VHS; Persis Sibley Andrews, 9 Feb. 1845, 13 Jan. 1850, Diary, MeHS; William Kelly Bartlett, 2 Oct. 1838, Journal, NHHS; Forten, *Journals of Charlotte Forten Grimké,* 10 Nov. 1854, 109. Ellen Wright to Martha Coffin Wright, 2 Mar.

1861, GP-SSC; Mary Pierce Poor to John Pierce and Lucy (Tappan) Pierce, 27 May 1836 in 24 May 1836, PoFP-SL; Charles M. Cobb, 21 Jan., 8, 20 Feb. 1852, Journal, VHS. Histories of reading instruction usually only implicitly deal with classroom composition exercises, but see Schultz, *Young Composers;* Halloran, "From Rhetoric to Composition"; and Campbell, "'Real Vexation.'" Salvatori's *Pedagogy* situates composition in the larger nineteenth-century instructional context; see also Jackson, "Nineteenth-Century Elementary Composition." On older students' compositional activities, see Berlin, *Writing Instruction,* and Schultz, "Southern Women." On compositions' content, see Miller, *Assuming the Positions,* chap. 2; her Virginians wrote about "composition, language, and notably about the shift away from spoken to written forms of discourse" while exhibiting self consciousness in composition writing (83, 82, 87).

13. Charles F. Low, 6, 13 Feb., 13 Mar., 10 Apr. 1857, Diary, BPL; Ellen Wright to Martha Coffin Wright, 6 Mar. 1861, GP-SSC.
14. Cyrus Parker Bradley, 25 Mar. 1835, Journal, NHHS; "The Students Meditations," 8 Oct. 1851, CKNFP-MeHS; Carroll Norcross to Nathaniel and Nancy Norcross, 31 Jan. 1853, CKNFP-MeHs; Elizabeth Atherton Clapp, 22 May, 3 June 1852, Journal, CP-MHS; Martha Osborne Barrett, 22 Sept. 1848, Diary, PEM. Despite a paucity of studies on institutionally motivated creative writing, work on the amateur press stretches back to Spencer's *History of Amateur Journalism.*
15. Susan S. Johnson, 29 Mar., 3 Dec. 1841, Journal, LxHS. "The Flower": undated 1836 issues are in the amateur newspaper collection, AAS. The last issue number cited is 2. Persis Sibley Andrews, 6, Apr. 1845, Diary, MeHS. Another example of a normal school paper (and a comic piece) is in Rothermel, "Sphere of Noble Action," 50–51.
16. Mary Pierce Poor to John Pierce, 18 July 1838 in 6 July 1838, 9 May 1838 in 3 May 1838, 21 Nov., and 23 May 1838 in 14 May 1838, PoFP-SL; Russell Hall to Harriet W. Hall, 6 Feb. 1853, MAP-ATHM; Clarissa Angeline Bodman to Philena (Hawks) Bodman, 10 Oct. 1851, BFP-SSC; David P. Stowell, 13 Dec. 1853, 3 Mar. 1854, and on newspaper readings, 21 Dec. 1853, 20, 27 Jan. 1854, Records of Granite State Debating Society, NHHS. Horton and Horton, *Black Bostonians,* 62. The writing done for Lyceums and private clubs only flits through general works such as Bode's *American Lyceum,* but some recent dissertations, such as McCaughey-Silvia, "Lectures and Discussion Questions," consider it in depth (see also Radner, "Performing the Paper"). Kelley, "'More Glorious'" considers reading and writing circles that date back to the eighteenth century. Gere, *Intimate Practices,* deals with postbellum women's clubs, while Wright's "Extra-Institutional Sites" looks at informal venues for learning composition. On national African American societies that promoted writing, see McHenry, *Forgotten Readers,* 6, 12–13, 23–24, 48–49, 56, 58, 61–63, 76, 82–83.
17. Studies of self-produced literary gifts usually focus on Valentine's Day but seldom on other holidays. See, for example, Schmidt, "Practices of Exchange"; Staff, *Valentine and Its Origins;* and Leopold's *Allison Kyle Leopold's Victorian Keepsake* on the British case. Theoretical considerations of gift giving include Godelier, *Enigma of the Gift;* Hyde, *Gift;* and Schrift, *Logic of the Gift.*
18. Helen M. Warner, 14 Feb. 1851, Diary, NEHGS; on fairs, see 29 Jan. 1850. Sarah Ann Keegan, valentine, 14 Feb. 1856, NSFP-SL; Charlotte Brooks Everett, 15 Feb.

1846, Journal, vol. 16, EEP-MHS; Calista Billings, 17 Feb. 1849, Diary, SL; "New Fashion for Valentines"; Schmidt, "Fashioning of a Modern Holiday."

19. Augustus Dodge Rogers, 14 Feb. 1850, Diary, RFP-PEM; Sarah Jocelyn, 14 Feb. 1840, Diary, JFP-CHS; Susan D. Tucker, 13 July 1852, Journal, VHS (the shy sender evidently waited five months); William Hoyt, 14 Feb. 1851, Journal, BPL.
20. Calista Billings, 19 Feb. 1849, Diary, SL; William Willis, 14 Feb. 1848, Diary, MeHS via PPL; Mary Brown, 15 Feb. 1853, Journal, BFP-MeHS; Forten, *Journals of Charlotte Forten Grimké,* 14 Feb. 1856, 150.
21. Calista Billings, 24 May 1849, Diary, SL; Mary M. Dawley, 22 May 1857, Diary, RIHS.
22. "Aunt Mary" to "My dear little niece," 19 Sept. 1860, CFP-VHS; John Park, 7 Feb. 1837, Diary, BPL. On dates in birthday poems, see Stainton, "Halifax Sailor's Taste," 73. Sending birthday, mourning, and other verse was seemingly a more vibrant practice in the eighteenth century (Blecki and Wulf, *Milcah Martha Moore's Book,* xiii).
23. Stephen Salisbury III to Stephen Salisbury II, 25 Dec. 1856, SFP-AAS; Olive Gay Worcester, 9 Jan. 1848, Journal, SFA-SL. See also Elizabeth B. Cheever to Henry T. Cheever, 1 Feb. 1838, CFP-AAS.
24. "Golden Wedding," *Andover Advertiser,* 17 Nov. 1860, p. 2, MARL-AHS; Frances M. Jocelyn, 10 Apr. 1854, Diary, JFP-CHS; Low, *Lights and Shadows,* 22 Aug. 1832, 2:430–31; Susan S. Johnson, "To Haste," c. 1841, Journal, LxHS. On writing courtship poetry, see Stainton, "Halifax Sailor's Taste," 73–79.
25. Martha Joanna Reade Nash Lamb, 14 Feb. 1846, Autograph Book, 14 Feb. 1846, MJRNLP-SCC; the undated quote is signed "A. S. C." Lizzie Tilden, poem, 23 Dec. 1852, in Sarah Ann Keegan, Album, c. 1850, NSFP-SL. For albums, see Ockenga, *Women and Friendship.* Jabour, "Albums of Affection," 157, finds a greater propensity to write original rather than excerpted verse by the 1840s and maintains that blank albums were manufactured by 1850 (152); McNeil, "From Advice to Laments," 175, maintains that verse albums became popular after 1820.
26. Zachariah Allen, 1 Apr. 1854, Diary, ZAP-RIHS; Agnes Paine to Mary A. Byram, 9 Dec. 1845, SFP-SL; Harriet Downe to Mary J. Abbott, 24 May 1844, MJAP-AHS; M. E. A., 1847, quoted in Lipsett, *Remember Me,* 24.
27. Josiah Rogers to Capt. Elias H. Stacy, 28 Aug. 1836, RP-MbHS; Moses Adams III, "Lines written in a blank leaf of 'Pierponts, Airs of Palestine . . . ,[']" c. Nov. 1824, in Common Place Book, No. 2, pp. 101–2, MAP-BC; Jackson, *Marginalia,* 67–69; Dickinson, "Creating a World," 57, and on original poetry in giftbooks, 63.
28. "Amicus" [George Hood], poem to Robert Rantoul, EC-BHS; Elizabeth H. Jocelyn, mourning verse, dated 9 Mar. 1847, Diary, JFP-CHS; Martha Woodberry, "Thoughts, on hearing of dear Charlotte's illness," Jan. 1840, EC-BHS. For an introduction to the literature on death, see Douglas, "Heaven Our Home."
29. Frances M. Jocelyn, "Lines written by Miss Louisa Woodward . . . ," after entry for 19 May 1857, Diary, JFP-CHS.
30. Mary Pierce Poor to Lucy (Pierce) Hedge, 4 Mar. 1852, PoFP-SL. Junius Juvenalis is the source of the Latin phrase. On Jocelyn and Forten, see Zboray and Zboray, *Literary Dollars,* 12–13, 25, 46–57, 91, 173–74, 179.

Part II

1. Interdisciplinary work on how the dissemination of texts contributes to their meaning, or even alters or undermines it, ranges from Derrida's *Dissemination* to Stoneman's *Brontë Transformations.* Just about any study that discusses appropriation implicitly recognizes that the cultural production in question has traveled some distance from its initial inception and commercial release. "Dissemination," insofar as it is concerned with what happens to texts moving through space and time, competes with three other related terms: "circulation," "diffusion," and "distribution." The first is most associated with Greenblatt (e.g., "Towards a Poetics of Culture" and *Shakespearean Negotiations*), who, though indebted to Derrida, nevertheless metaphorically links the term to the way value circulates in a capitalist economy. The circulation metaphor implies a return to the point of origin, meaning how socioliterary experience influences the market and what authors and publishers produce for it. Circulation scholarship is thus often author-centered (e.g., Trotter, *Circulation*). Since our diarists and correspondents little cared how their literary dissemination influenced the market, the circulation metaphor obscures more than it illuminates. "Diffusion" has roots in a late-nineteenth-century school of anthropology and continued on as a minor concern of linguistics until its recent resurrection by "world historians" (McNeill, "Diffusion in History.") The wave metaphor summoned by diffusion is ideally suited to tracing the movement outward of significant news, like rings emanating from an object, the original source of the news, dropped in water (see Brown, *Knowledge Is Power,* chap. 10). However, the most common form of the movement of texts, as we discuss, was point to point, sometimes widely scattered over long distances. One difference between diffusion (and to some extent circulation) and dissemination, thus, is that of one text (i.e., information) going many places as opposed to many texts going to only a few. "Distribution" shares with circulation and diffusion the assumption of a single-point origination fanning outward, but rather than the text being mostly moved by receivers along the way, there is a greater emphasis upon deliberate propulsion from the point of origin, meaning, usually, the publisher. Hence, "distribution" carries the greatest connotation of marketing, whereas "circulation" implies metaphorical uses of the market, as well, but with less deliberation (indeed, determination) on the part of the publisher or middlemen like booksellers or jobbers specializing in distribution. General sources on nineteenth-century book distribution include Gilreath, "American Book Distribution"; Zboray, *Fictive People,* chaps. 2–5; Hackenberg, *Getting the Books Out;* and Fink and Williams, *Reciprocal Influences.* On amateur distribution, see Zboray and Zboray, *Literary Dollars,* chap. 4. On bookselling, see Boynton, *Annals of American Bookselling,* and Lehmann-Haupt, Wroth, and Silver, *Book in America.* Gilmore's *Reading Becomes a Necessity of Life* also shows how books got into people's hands. On peddling, see Jaffee, "Peddlers of Progress"; Wright, *Hawkers and Walkers;* and Benes and Benes, *Itinerancy.* The lesson in all of this is that one cannot link a specific type of reader with a type of book periodical on the basis of its physical properties or affordability. After all, we saw at the outset that Charles M. Cobb managed to read "The Tree of

Knowledge" in *Harper's,* often thought of as aimed at a genteel, middle-class magazine readership. Examples of other working-class folk reading this type of literature abound in this book, but for an example of a mill worker reading *Frank Leslie's Illustrated Newspaper* and the *Atlantic Monthly,* among others of the sort, see Joshua Edwin Harris, 20 Jan. 1860, 21 June 1858, 7, 21 Jan., 21 Feb., 5 Apr., 25 May 1860, Journal, JEHP-MeHS.

2. Kielbowicz, *News in the Mail,* 106, 86. Beyond person-to-person movement of texts largely outside of market-oriented distribution, diffusion, and circulation, some scholars study the history of "scholarly communications" (e.g., Johns, *Nature of the Book;* Dain and Cole, *Libraries and Scholarly Communication*). Of course, by their very nature such inquiries concentrate on intellectual elites', not common folks', dissemination, despite parallels between them. On the development of the region's transportation infrastructure, see Blouin, *Boston Region.*
3. Shera, *Foundations of the Public Library,* 55, 69, 71–75, 127.
4. If we set aside the concept of text and replace it with commodity or good, anthropologists can offer some theoretical insight into issues of exchange which point away from the functionalist assumptions of scholarship using the circulation metaphor. Hann, *Property Relations,* complicates the cross-cultural meaning of ownership, while Douglas and Isherwood's *World of Goods* argues that goods express social relations—the latter point, of course, supports our discussion of socioliterary experience (see also our "Books, Reading"; Godelier, *Enigma of the Gift;* Mauss, *Gift;* and Weiner, *Inalienable Possessions*). Baudrillard, *Symbolic Exchange and Death,* widens the exchange motif. On economic exchange in the region, see Geib, "'Changing Works.'" On earlier oral reading, see Fox, *Oral and Literate Culture,* esp. 36–39.

Chapter 4

1. Henry W. Beetle to Eliza Ann (Eaton) Beetle, 22 Nov. 1847 on back of 21 Nov. 1847, BL-PrPL.
2. The national extension of postal services encouraged everyday literary dissemination (John, *Spreading the News;* Foley, "Mission Unfulfilled"). On keeping up distant ties, see Fuhrer, *Letters,* and Dublin, *Farm to Factory.*
3. Frances Adams Chamberlain to George E. Adams, 22 Sept. 1847 [1850?], CAFP-SL; Sophia Peabody to Maria Chase, Mar. [1829], PFP-SSC; Charles Lenox Remond to Elizabeth Pease, Dec. 1839, BPL.
4. Cyrus Parker Bradley, 11 Jan. 1835, Journal, NHHS; John Wilson Jr. to Mr. and Mrs. John Wilson, 18 Feb. 1849 in 3 Feb. 1849, ATHM.
5. Although after 1825 mail could be delivered to private dwellings if receivers paid the postal carrier, most people opted to tend out (Cullinan, *United States Postal Service,* 39, and Bowyer, *They Carried the Mail,* 22). Joshua Edwin Harris, 12 May 1856, Journal, JEHP-MeHS; Mary Paul to Bela Paul, 8 Oct. 1856, MEBTP-VHS; Charles Hunton to Lewis Hunton, 26 Jan. 1846, ML-ATHM; Stephen G. Clarke to Chase P. Parsons, 17 Dec. 1855, PaFP-SL. Federally authorized postage stamps first appeared in 1847; Bowyer, *They Carried the Mail,* 25–26 (see also Rohrbach, *American Issue*). Mary Elizabeth (Parsons) Hidden to William M. Parsons, 1 Jan. 1845, PaFP-SL. After

1851, prepaid letters traveling within three thousand miles cost three cents; otherwise they cost five cents (*Laws and Regulations,* 104). On compulsory prepayment, see U.S. Post Office Department, *United States Domestic Postage Rates,* 56. On rates, see Cullinan, *United States Postal Service,* 38, 67.

6. Elizabeth H. Jocelyn, 17 Aug. 1839, Diary, JFP-CHS; Helen M. Warner, 17 Sept. 1851, Diary, NEHGS; Cyrus Parker Bradley, 23 Dec. 1835, Journal, NHHS. On post offices as social spaces, see John, *Spreading the News,* 115, 161–66.
7. Persis Sibley Andrews, 16 Jan. 1848, 5 Dec. 1847, Diary, MeHS; Charles M. Cobb, 1 Jan. 1854, Journal, VHS; Ellis Gray Loring to Anna Loring, 26 Oct. 1851, EGLFP-SL. *Laws and Regulations,* 104.
8. Kielbowicz, *News in the Mail,* 85–86, 89, 91, 105, and Leonard, *News for All,* 117–24; on agricultural journals, see McMurry, "Who Read the Agricultural Journals?" And on story papers, see Zboray, "Technology." Clarissa Harrington, 28 Aug. 1841, "A Daily Journal," LxHS. For nonnews items, see Mary Baker Eddy, Scrapbook, c. 1830–60, MBEL.
9. U.S. Post Office Department, *United States Domestic Postage Rates,* table V, 27–28.
10. Unidentified, 30 Sept. 1857, Diary, 1 Mar. 1857–2 Sept. 1858, NHHS; Persis Sibley Andrews, 7 June 1841, Diary, MeHS; Clarissa Angeline Bodman to Clarissa (Day) Bodman, 14 Aug. 1845, BFP-SSC; Charles Lenox Remond to "My Very Good Friend," 4 Sept. in 1 Sept. 1845, CLRL-PEM.
11. Clarissa Harrington, 25, 26 Aug., 30, 22 July, 30 Sept. 1841, "A Daily Journal," LxHS.
12. Leonard, *News for All,* 120–21. Mary Pierce Poor to Henry Varnum Poor, 15 Sept. 1839, PoFP-SL; Sarah P. E. Hale to Lucretia P. Hale and Nathan Hale Jr., 14 July 1843, HP-SSC; H. [L.] Wells, 31 Jan. 1844, Diary, CHS.
13. Seth Shaler Arnold, 13 Feb. 1841, Journal, VHS; Lucretia Anne (Peabody) Everett to Sarah P. E. Hale, 1 Apr. 1828, HP-SSC; Persis Sibley Andrews, 23 Sept. 1843, Diary, MeHS.
14. Ann Swett Appleton to beloved sister, 8 Jan. 1847, MGLC-ATHM; Paul Atwood Gibson, 1 Aug. 1846, Diary, NHHS; Sarah Jocelyn, 6 Apr. 1839, Diary, JFP-CHS; Horatio A. Chandler, 12 Nov. 1840, Invoice Book, NHHS. A handwritten initial on a paper did not mean extra postage after 1851 (Kielbowicz, *News in the Mail,* 105).
15. Fowler, *Unmailable,* 13–14; Kielbowicz, *News in the Mail,* 105. Paul Atwood Gibson, 27 July 1855, Diary, NHHS; E. W. Robinson to Deacon Joseph A. Metcalf, 20 July 1843, MAP-ATHM; Ann Swett Appleton to sister, Feb. [1847?], MGLC-ATHM. Writing in papers dates back to the colonial era; one sheet even provided blank areas for doing so (Leonard, *News for All,* 118–19).
16. Low, *Lights and Shadows,* 8 Mar. 1831, 1:203; Persis Sibley Andrews, 22 May 1841, Diary, MeHS; John Wilson Jr. to Mr. and Mrs. John Wilson, 18 Feb. 1849 in 3 Feb. 1849, ATHM; Mary Pierce Poor to Henry Varnum Poor, 27 July 1846, PoFP-SL.
17. William C. Sherwood to William Sherwood, 24 Sept. 1851, WSP-YUb; Sarah Jocelyn, 6 Feb. 1841, Diary, JFP-CHS; Mary Elizabeth Fiske, 17 May 1842, Diary, LxHS; Cyrus Parker Bradley, 11 Apr. 1836, Journal, NHHS.
18. Kielbowicz, *News in the Mail,* 86. Bridport, Vt., Post Office, Newspapers & Pamphlets Received, 1 Jan. 1839–30 Sept. 1841, VHS; cf. F. P. Fletcher, Postmaster, Bridport, Vt., "Post Office Book," 1 Oct. 1841–31 Dec. 1841, VHS.

19. John Hoyt to Elizabeth T. Hoyt, 22 Sept. 1850, JHP-NEHGS; B. B. Chadwick to Roswell and Mary Farnham, 4 Feb. 1861, HC-SL; Nathaniel Paul to William Lloyd Garrison Sr., 31 Aug. 1833, BPL.
20. Sarah P. E. Hale to Edward Everett, 30 Nov. 1840, 23 Jan. 1841, HP-SSC; Samuel May Jr. to John Bishop Estlin, 19 Dec. 1845, 26 Feb. 1846, 29 May 1847, and 7 Mar. 1848, BPL; William Sherwood to Esther H. Sherwood, postmark, 31 Mar. 1851, WSP-YUb; Paine, *Old Merchant Marine,* 149; Hyde, *Cunard and the North Atlantic,* 15.
21. David P. Stowell, 2 Dec. 1858, Journal, NHHS; Elizabeth B. Cheever to Henry T. Cheever, 27 Jan. 1837, CFP-AAS; Louisa Gilman Loring to Ellis Gray Loring, 17 May 1858, EGLFP-SL. On censorship of antislavery material, see Savage, *Controversy;* Curtis, "Curious History"; and Dickerson, *Course of Tolerance,* 81–113.
22. William Hoyt, 7 Feb. 1851, Journal, BPL; Charles M. Cobb, 18 Oct. under 3 Nov. 1853, Journal, VHS; Mary Mudge, 10 June 1854, High School Common-Place Book, SL.
23. *Laws and Regulations,* 106; Kielbowicz, *News in the Mail,* 132–34.
24. Samuel May Jr. to John Bishop Estlin, 19 Dec. 1845, BPL; Rufus Marble Gay to Olive Gay Worcester, 8 Jan. 1844, SFA-SL; John Perley to Sarah Perley, 2 Mar. 1838 in 1 Mar. 1838, TPP-PEM; William James Keegan to C. M. Clark, 26 Sept. 1857, NSFP-SL; Persis Sibley Andrews, 7, 11 Apr. 1846, Diary, MeHS; Low, *Lights and Shadows,* 29 Mar. 1832, 1:304.
25. Susan D. Tucker, 20 Nov. 1851, Journal, VHS; Sarah E. Trask, 7 Apr. 1849, Journal, BHS; J. Reynolds Hixon, 14 Jan. 1837, Diary, OCHS; Anna Loring to Ellis Gray Loring, 30 Apr. [1857 or 1858], EGLP-SL.
26. John Perley to Sarah Perley, 2 Mar. in 1 Mar. 1838, TPP-PEM; Alexander Hill Everett to Edward Everett Hale, 5 July 1844, HP-SSC; Sarah Watson Dana, entries for 18 May 1859, Private Account Book, 1859, DFP-SL; John Park, 24 Feb. 1846, 25 Jan. 1841, Diary, BPL; William Willis, 9 Nov. 1856, Diary, MeHS via PPL; William M. Briggs to Anne Briggs, 15 Oct. 1849, BriFP-SL.
27. Charles F. Low, 28 Mar. 1857, Diary, BPL; Lucy (Pierce) Hedge to Mary Pierce Poor, 30 Nov. 1847, PoFP-SL; Samuel May Jr. to John Bishop Estlin, 19 Dec. 1845, BPL; John Wesley Hanson to Harriet Jane Hanson Robinson, 1846, RSP-SL; Samuel May Jr. to John Bishop Estlin, 5 Sept. 1848, BPL.
28. Sarah Watson Dana, 18 May 1859, Private Account Book, 1859, DFP-SL; Jotham Powers Bigelow, 16 Aug. 1856, Pocket Diary, JPBP-AAS; John Wesley Hanson to Harriet Jane Hanson, 27 Nov. 1845, RSP-SL; Christopher Albert Greene, 29 Apr. 1853, Diary, CAGP-RIHS; Kielbowicz, *News in the Mail,* 134; U.S. Post Office Department, *United States Domestic Postage Rates,* Table V, 28.
29. Hannah Lowell Jackson Cabot to Sarah (Jackson) Russell, 6 June 1839, AFP-SL; Elizabeth B. Cheever to Henry T. Cheever, 22 Nov. 1837, CFP-AAS; Elizabeth Dwight Cabot to Ellen Twisleton, 16 Jan. 1854, CFP-SL; William M. Briggs to Anne Briggs, 15 Oct. 1849, BriFP-SL; Katherine Bigelow Lawrence Sr. to Annie B. Lawrence Rotch, 31 Jan. 1838, LFP-MHS; Samuel May Jr. to Richard D. Webb, 2 Mar. 1852; and Samuel May Jr. to John Bishop Estlin, 7 Mar. 1848, BPL.

30. Rufus Marble Gay to Dorcas P. Gay, 12 Sept. 1838, SFP-SL; Samuel May Jr. to Richard D. Webb, 1 Aug. 1853, BPL; Samuel May Jr. to Hannah Webb, 18 Sept. 1853, BPL.
31. Rufus Marble Gay to Dorcas P. Gay, 5 Mar. 1852, SFP-SL.

Chapter 5

1. William Craft to Samuel May Jr., 29 May 1860, BPL. Parker, *Discourse,* 76–77.
2. On newspapers as gifts, see Leonard, *News for All,* 118–24. Luella J. B. Case to Sarah E. Edgarton, 12 Apr. 1840, HC-SL; Daniel F. Child and Mary D. Child, 29 June 1856, Diary, DFCP-MHS; Harriet Prescott to Elizabeth Ellis (Prescott) Betton, 23 Sept. 1848, BFL-PEM; Frances Merritt Quick, 1 Apr. 1855, Diary, FMQP-SL; F. S. Lindsay to Mrs. Charles F. Tillinghast, 30 Sept. 1842, HC-SL; Elizabeth Pierce to John Pierce and Lucy (Tappan) Pierce, 6 Jan. 1843, PoFP-SL; C. L. Curtis to former pupils, 10 Mar. 1859, Letterbook of Deborah C. Burt, NEHGS. On uses of "exchange," see Abraham Joseph Warner, 10 Mar. 1842, Diary, CHS; Mary Elizabeth Fiske, 3 Feb. 1843, Diary, LxHS; Persis Sibley Andrews, 22 Oct. 1844, Diary, MeHS; Cyrus Parker Bradley, 14 Sept. 1835, Journal, NHHS; Seth Shaler Arnold, 26 May 1849, 26 Oct. 1835, Journal, VHS; Joshua Edwin Harris, 12 June 1856, Journal, JEHP-MeHS; Alexander Hill Everett, 19 Oct. 1840, Diary, HP-SSC; Elizabeth Dwight Cabot to Ellen Twisleton, 13 May 1860, CFP-SL. Serious consideration of antebellum gift giving, literary or otherwise, has been hampered by a lingering tendency to reify putatively modern patterns of "consumption for its own sake" onto a time period when older patterns remained strong. Zboray and Zboray, "Books, Reading," and Sicherman, "Reading and Middle-Class Identity," argue against this point, while Horowitz, *Morality of Spending,* highlights consumption modes' historicity (and the neglected importance of the antebellum years). Moreover, antebellum consumption stands in the gigantic shadow of Veblen, whose *Theory of the Leisure Class* and other works provided analytical categories of upper-class consumption motives which have trickled down, in the hands of scholars, to even the earlier lower middle class. Challenges to the traditional view of modern consumption include Csikszentmihalyi and Rochberg-Halton's *Meaning of Things;* see also Appadurai, *Social Life of Things,* 1–13, and Kopytoff, "Cultural Biography." Some scholarship on other times and places has been more analytical; see, for example, McKendrick, Brewer, and Plumb, *Birth of a Consumer Society;* Campbell, *Romantic Ethic;* and the essays by Breen, Vickery, and Campbell in Brewer and Porter, *Consumption.*
3. Electa Kimberly, "Memoranda," 1857, Diary, CHS.
4. Sarah L. Edes, 1, 2 Jan. 1852, Diary, AAS; Mary Elizabeth Fiske, 23 Dec. 1843, Diary, LxHS; Ellen Bassett ["C——"] to Maria Nash, 5 Feb. 1860, MJRNLP-SSC; Geib, "'Changing Works'"; Lucy (Pierce) Hedge to Mary Pierce Poor, 2 Jan. 1853, PoFP-SL; Sarah L. Chamberlain to Abigail Chamberlain, 2 Mar. 1847, WCP-VHS. While both men and women shared equally in literary gift giving, both were more likely to give to females. Among family members, daughters and brothers apparently received most of these gifts, followed by nieces, sons, sisters, and nephews. The least likely to

receive literature as a gift were grandfathers and husbands, who, perhaps being more financially secure than younger folk and women, did more dispensing than receiving.

5. Edwin Leigh Furness, 3, 29 May 1850, Journal, MeHS.
6. Sarah I. (McClellan) Webb, 1 Jan. 1848, Diary and notes, MP-CHS; Harriet Jane Hanson Robinson, 25 Dec. 1856, Diary, RSP-SL. Veblen's notion of the irrational (or quasi-rational) class maladaption to the logic of capitalism finds some expression in Schmidt's overview of American holiday practices, *Consumer Rites,* which ponders the relationship between Protestantism and the marketplace. Christmas, of all holidays, naturally has garnered much commentary: Waits, *Modern Christmas;* Restad, *Christmas in America;* and Golby and Purdue, *Making of Modern Christmas.* Nissenbaum, *Battle for Christmas,* treats the yuletide's middle-class kidnapping. Christmas gift giving overshadows that for other holidays (see our discussion of valentines in chapter 3), and there is little done on non-occasional presents (see, however, Ockenga, *Women and Friendship*).
7. T[homas] H[yde] to Sarah [Hyde], 19 Jan. 1854, BHFP-SL; Olive Gay Worcester, 27 Dec. 1845, Journal, SFA-SL. Veblen's critique of selfish privatization has obscured the connections between antebellum gift giving and public benevolent activity, despite recent scholarship on the emergence of a "humanitarian sensibility" that bridges the public and private. Haskell, "Capitalism," traces it to the internalization and moralization of capitalist logic—an advance, perhaps, from the Weberian overemphasis on the Protestant ethic's parentage of capitalism (and with it, that ethic's benevolent traditions) but neglecting traditional and radical sources of humanitarianism. A related issue is, of course, the public sphere interceding between the state and the private (Habermas, *Structural Transformation*), setting the stage for late-eighteenth- and early-nineteenth-century liberal bourgeois revolutions. Benevolence has thus become linked to middle class motivation or even social control (several essays in Davis's *Ante-Bellum Reform* reflect this), at the expense of probing its emotional and social roots. Bourgeois women's inclusion in the class analysis has tended to deepen its scope: see especially Ryan, *Cradle of the Middle Class;* and Boylan, "Benevolence."
8. Olive Gay Worcester, 27 Dec. 1845, Journal, SFA-SL; Sarah Ann Keegan to William James Keegan, 5 Jan. 1856, NSFP-SL; Abigail Pierce to Mary Pierce Poor, 3 Jan. 1851, PoFP-SL. Lacking contextualization in broader emotional expressions of social life, benevolence has been mostly studied from an institutional perspective, particularly from that of the various antebellum reform associations. On philanthropy, see Wright, *Transformation of Charity,* and Hall, *Organization of American Culture;* though these studies' leadership focus should be augmented with Jeffrey's rank-and-file study, *Great Silent Army.*
9. David P. Stowell, 22 Sept. 1858, Journal, NHHS; Martha Greene, 7 June 1849, Diary, NHHS; John Park, 12 Feb. 1849, Diary, BPL.
10. Rosina Rhoda Houghton Moore, 26 Mar. 1857, Diary, typed transcript, AAS; Forten, *Journals of Charlotte Forten Grimké,* 10, 11 Mar. 1858, 291–92; Lucy (Pierce) Hedge to Mary Pierce Poor, 22 Sept. 1839, PoFP-SL.
11. Frances M. Jocelyn, 2 Feb. 1849, 30 Oct. 1851, 10 Feb. 1849, 17 Nov. 1851, Diary, JFP-CHS; Elizabeth H. Jocelyn, 5 Nov. 1849, 10 Mar. 1852, 3 Apr. 1849, Diary, JFP-CHS. The suitor gave her Lind's song "The Child of the Regiment" on 14 Apr.

1849 and, three days later, the singer's "Song of Home." Fleeting references to gift giving appear in works on courtship: Zboray and Zboray, "Romance of Fisherwomen"; Lystra, *Searching the Heart;* Rothman, *Hands and Hearts;* and Harris, *Courtship of Olivia Langdon.*

12. Caroline Barrett White, 9, 13, 24 June 1851, Diary, AAS.
13. Elizabeth H. Jocelyn, [17 Feb. 1839] in c. 1 Mar. 1839, Diary, JFP-CHS; Aurilla Ann Moffitt, [29 July] after 26 July, 27 Sept. 1848, Personal Journal, OCHS; Mary Pierce Poor to John Pierce and Lucy (Tappan) Pierce, 11 Mar. 1842, PoFP-SL.
14. Arozina Perkins, 13, 12 Sept. 1849, Diary, CHS; Almon Benson, 8 Mar. 1841, Sketch Book, NHHS. Nearly all the work on the American Tract Society has been from the perspective of the New York headquarters to the neglect of the semiautonomous New England branch. The New York–centered view (itself complicated by the presence of many members with New England roots) is provided in several article-length works by Nord, including his "Evangelical Origins" and "Systematic Benevolence"; see also Thompson, "Printing and Publishing"; Schantz, "Religious Tracts"; and Thomas, "Reading the Silences." On Bible societies, see Gutjahr, *American Bible,* and Wosh, *Spreading the Word.* Scholarship on other evangelical groups' free publication activities is scanty, but see Pilkington, *Methodist Publishing House.* Boylan's *Sunday School* discusses the benevolent support of Sabbath school libraries. Scholarship on free literary dissemination by reform organizations is less extensive than that on dissemination by evangelicals, but see, for abolitionists, Wood, *Blind Memory;* Lapsansky, "Graphic Discord"; DeRosa, "Into the Mouths"; Roberts, "'Ten Thousand Tongues'"; and, for temperance advocates, Hampel, *Temperance.* Reynolds, in his *Faith in Fiction* and *Beneath the American Renaissance,* synthesizes these various evangelical and reform threads.
15. Eliza Bancroft Davis to John Davis, 10 June 1840, JDP-AAS; Katherine Bigelow Lawrence Sr. to Annie B. Lawrence Rotch, [late summer or early fall 1840], LFP-MHS; Mellen Chamberlain, 16 Oct. 1846, Diary, BPL.
16. Cyrus Parker Bradley, 24 June 1835, Journal, NHHS; Elizabeth Pierce to Lucy (Tappan) Pierce and John Pierce, 6 Jan. 1843, PoFP-SL; the actual quote is "Words followed Words, from Question Answer flow'd."; Cyrus Parker Bradley, 3 June 1836, Journal, NHHS.
17. Eunice Hale Waite Cobb, 17 Jan. 1839, Diary, NEHGS; Sarah E. Reynolds to Mary E. Buffington, 23 Feb. 1852, HC-SL. On a sewing circle event, see S. A. Whitman to Olive Gay Worcester, 3 Mar. 1856, SFUP-SL.
18. William James Keegan to C. M. Clark, 26 Sept. 1857, NSFP-SL; Sarah L. Chamberlain to Abigail Chamberlain, 2 Mar. 1847, WCP-VHS; S[arah] M. Davis to Olive Gay Worcester, 28 Sept. 1852, SFUP-SL; William Stevens Robinson to Henry H. Fuller, 27 Jan. 1842, RSP-SL; [George E.?] Adams to Frances Adams Chamberlain, n.d., CAFP-SL; John Park to Louisa Jane Park Hall, 22 Jan. 1846, in John Park, Diary, BPL.
19. Hannah Lowell Jackson Cabot to Sarah (Jackson) Russell, Jan. 1838, AFP-SL; Sarah Ellen Browne to Sarah Smith (Cox) Browne, 7 Dec. 1856, SEBP-SL; Sarah P. E. Hale to Edward Everett, 9 Jan. 1857, HP-SSC.
20. William Lloyd Garrison Jr. to William Lloyd Garrison Sr., 3 Jan. 1859, GP-SSC; N. B. Hoskins to Olive Gay Worcester, 1 Jan. 1850, SFA-SL; Elizabeth B. Cheever

to Henry T. Cheever, 27 Jan. 1837, CFP-AAS; Harriet W. Hall to "my dear brother," 8 Feb. 1855, PFP-AAS; Samuel May Jr. to John Bishop Estlin, 1 Dec. 1846, BPL.

21. Elizabeth Dwight Cabot to Ellen Twisleton, 1 Nov. 1858, CFP-SL; Mehetable May (Dawes) Goddard to Lucretia Dawes, 31 Mar. 1847, MGFP-SL; Mary Pierce Poor to John Pierce and Lucy (Tappan) Pierce, 2 Nov. 1845, PoFP-SL; Eliza Green to Amos Lawrence, 1840, ALP-MHS; "Cousin Sarah" to Elizabeth B. Cheever and Charlotte L. Sewall, 19 Feb. 1837, CFP-AAS; Elizabeth Pierce to John Pierce, 31 Dec. 1847 [i.e., 1846], PoFP-SL.
22. E. J. Hunter to Elizabeth Dwight Cabot, 28 Apr. 1857, CFP-SL; Samuel May Jr. to John Bishop Estlin, 16 July 1848, 7 Mar. 1848, BPL.
23. Cyrus Parker Bradley, 18 Dec. 1835, Journal, NHHS; Persis Sibley Andrews, 1 Jan. 1841, 1 Jan. 1842, Diary, DFP-MHS; Low, *Lights and Shadows,* 9 Apr. 1832, 1:311–12. On giftbooks, see Faxon, *Literary Annuals and Gift Books,* and Thompson, *American Literary Annuals.* For some observers, these expensive, often ornate, and sumptuous books might lend some credence to Veblen's notion of conspicuous consumption, but our informants did not universally see them that way. On gift books, see Lehuu, *Carnival on the Page,* chap. 4.
24. William Craft to Samuel May Jr., 29 May 1860, BPL; Moses Adams III, Common Place Book, No. 1, c. 1834, p. 130, MAP-BC; Frederick W. Treadway, retrospective entry under 9 Mar. 1837, Diary, CHS; Mellen Chamberlain, 20, 23 Aug., 24 Sept. 1843, 23 Jan. 1844, 5 June 1843, Diary, BPL.

Chapter 6

1. Charles M. Cobb, 15, 16, 18 Mar. in 23 Mar.; 25 Mar. 1852, Journal, VHS.
2. Traditional library histories need to be seen in the context of the widespread informal circulation discussed below (Zboray and Zboray, "Home Libraries"); see Ditzion, *Arsenals,* and Shera, *Foundations of the Public Library,* for institutional origins and forerunners. On one of the earliest tax-supported, free public libraries, see Whitehill, *Boston Public Library.* For other lending institutions, see, on circulating libraries, Kaser, *Book for a Sixpence;* on mercantile libraries, Augst, *Clerk's Tale,* chap. 4, and Ditzion, "Mechanics"; on social libraries, Gross, "Much Instruction," and Gross, "Reconstructing Early American Libraries"; on shipboard libraries, Zboray, *Fictive People,* chap. 10, and Skallerup, *Books Afloat and Ashore;* on school libraries, Culver, *Horace Mann;* on college libraries, Rush, *History of College Libraries;* and on adult education institutions' libraries, Kett, *Pursuit of Knowledge,* chaps. 2–4. Treatments of informal circulation include McHenry, *Forgotten Readers,* 7, 10; Kelley, "Reading Women," 55, 60; Kaplan, "'We Have Joys'"; Kaplan, "'He Summons,'" 550–53; and, for a later period, Martin, *Sound of Our Own Voices.* Charles M. Cobb, 30 July 1851, 18 Jan., 5 Jan. in 9 Feb., Sept. 30 under 11 Oct. 1852, 19 Oct. 1847 in 1 Dec. 1852, 7 Dec. in 8 Dec. 1852. On a purchase from a peddler, see 1 Oct. 1852, Journal, VHS. Dana, *History of Woodstock,* 510–11.
3. The borrowing and lending treated here is more a subset of economic anthropology, with echoes from the pre-capitalist world, than a pure expression of the circulation of capital or even a metaphorical refraction of it (Hann, *Property Relations*). Capitalist

issues of creditworthiness, compound interest, and so forth are far overshadowed here by more specifically social considerations, such as the formation and maintenance of kin and friendship ties, upon which it is difficult to put a commodity price (on local market consciousness, see Clark, "Economics and Culture," and Clark, "Household Economy"). This emphasis upon the continuity of traditional *mentalité* is not to say that such social relations lack economic consequences (Wilk, *Household Economy;* Gaughan and Ferman, "Toward an Understanding"). Rather, the operating principle is "use value," which, of course, has a good deal of elasticity depending on how useful the item is deemed by would-be borrowers; to complicate matters, the uses are not necessarily intrinsic to the printed item but can carry associations (e.g., valued because kinfolk or friend had previously used it), at times only confined to the particular act of borrowing. (For theoretical background, see Garnett, "Postmodernism.") Borrowing or lending can summon as much or more social value (e.g., a friendly chat) as the item itself; the exchange could be simply a peripheral excuse for an interpersonal encounter. On sociabilities over nonprint transactions, see Hansen's *Very Social Time,* and over exchanged papers, see Zboray, *Fictive People,* chap. 8.

4. Charles M. Cobb, 4 Feb. 1849, Pocket Memorandum, VHS; Charles M. Cobb, 6 June 1852, 3 Oct. in 19 Oct. 1852, Journal, VHS; Susan D. Tucker, 10 Feb. 1852, Journal, VHS.
5. Enoch Hale, Dec. 1841, Diary, PEM; Mary Pierce Poor to John Pierce and Lucy (Tappan) Pierce, 10 Dec. 1836, PoFP-SL.
6. Emma Gannell, 25 June, 2 July, 4, 11, 18 Aug., 3 Sept., 30 Oct., 8, 10 Nov. 1851, Pocket Memorandum, 1851, NHHS. Burgum, "John Burgum."
7. Elizabeth Dwight Cabot to Ellen Twisleton, 26 Nov. 1858, CFP-SL; Emmeline Augusta Ober, 2 June 1852, Diary, BHS.
8. Elizabeth Edwards to Rebekah S. Salisbury, 11 July 1840, SFP-AAS; Crawford Nightingale to James Munroe & Co., 18 Dec. 1847, JMCC-AAS; Sarah P. E. Hale to Edward Everett, 16 Feb. [1837?], HP-SSC.
9. Elizabeth Dwight Cabot to Ellen Twisleton, 22 Oct. 1854, CFP-SL; Mary Pierce Poor to Mary Hudson, 19 Feb. 1842, PoFP-SL; John Park, 27 Nov. 1838, Diary, BPL; J. Reynolds Hixon, retrospective, 2 Mar. 1836, Diary, OCHS; unidentified night watchman to G. W. Walton, 7 Apr. 1856, ATHM.
10. Aurilla Ann Moffitt, 5 Oct. 1851, Personal Journal, OCHS; Elizabeth Dwight Cabot to Ellen Twisleton, 3 June 1859, CFP-SL; Elizabeth Abbot to Charlotte Rantoul, 29 Oct. 1837, EC-BHS; Lamb, "Formative Influences," 54–56.
11. Forten, *Journals of Charlotte Forten Grimké,* 22 May 1857, 220, 30 Jan. 1858, 283; John Langdon, 26 Feb. 1845, Diary, NEHGS; Frances M. Jocelyn, 24 Jan. 1856, Diary, JFP-CHS; Sarah E. Trask, 18 Feb. 1849, Journal, BHS; Mary M. Dawley, 5 Dec. 1856, Diary, RIHS; Forten, *Journals of Charlotte Forten Grimké,* 11 Mar. 1857, 202.
12. Elizabeth Pierce, 20 Nov. 1830, Journal, PoFP-SL; Charles M. Cobb, 7 Mar. 1851, 6 Apr. 1852, 3 Jan. 1853, Journals, VHS.
13. Joshua Edwin Harris, 18 Feb. 1858, Journal, JEHP-MeHS; Paul Atwood Gibson, 10 Feb. 1858, Diary and Memorandum Book, NHHS; Edwin Leigh Furness, 23 Apr. 1850, Journal, MeHS; Hannah Hicock Smith, 5, 6 Dec. 1846, Diary, CSL; John R.

Congdon, 24 Mar., 23 Dec. 1849, Journal, CFP-RIHS; Mary R. Congdon, 26 Dec. 1861, Account Book and Diary, CFP-RIHS; John Hoyt, 9 May 1849, Diary, JHP-NEHGS. Skallerup, *Books Afloat and Ashore.*

14. Charles M. Cobb, 25 July in 27 July 1851, 15 Apr., 27 Oct. in 4 Nov. 1851, Journal, VHS.
15. Anthony D. Currier to Mary Ann Loring, 16 May 1835, MALCL-AHS.
16. James Lockwood Wright, 3 Sept. 1833, Journal, JLWP-YUs; John Park, 11 Apr. 1851, Diary, BPL; Edwin Leigh Furness, 25 Dec. 1848, Journal, MeHS.
17. Giles Waldo to George Waldo, 15 Jan. 1843, GWP-YUb; Zboray and Zboray, "Transcendentalism in Print"; Elizabeth Pierce, 6 Dec. 1830, Journal, PoFP-SL.
18. Aurilla Ann Moffitt, 11 Aug. 1851, Personal Journal, OCHS; John R. Congdon, 26 Jan. 1861, Journal, CFP-RIHS; Ellen Wright to "My dear Caddie" [Caroline], 8 Apr. 1861, GP-SSC; Catherine S. Patton, 22 Aug. 1845, Journal, CHS; John G. King to Augusta G. King, 11 Oct. 1833, EGLFP-SL; Lydia Maria Child to Ellis Gray Loring, 9 Feb. 1841, EGLFP-SL.
19. Joshua Edwin Harris, 15 Apr., 20 Jan. 1858, Journal, JEHP-MeHS; Julius Catlin, Oct. 1853, at back of 1854–57 Diary, CHS.
20. Elizabeth Atherton Clapp, 1, 3, 10 May 1852, Journal, CP-MHS; Forten, *Journals of Charlotte Forten Grimké,* 2 Dec. 1856, 169–70; Sarah G. Hathaway, 7 May 1843, Diary, OCHS.
21. Joseph Lucas to Caleb Cushing, 15 July 1840, CCP-LC; Sarah L. Edes, 23 Sept. 1852, Diary, 1852, AAS; Jonathan Danforth Meriam, 6 Dec. 1828, Diary, AAS; Mary Pierce Poor, list of books at back of Pocket Memorandum, 1850, vol. 19, PoFP-SL; John Park, "Books Lent," 13 July 1846–21 Jan. 1852, Diary, vol. 3, concluding pages, BPL; Zboray and Zboray, "Home Libraries," 63, 65, 75; for a discussion of book labels, see Samuel May Jr. to Richard D. Webb, 15 Apr. 1860, BPL; on the phenomenon, see Zboray and Zboray, *Handbook,* 60–61; and for an inscribed copy declaring ownership, see Stephens, *Incidents of Travel* (in ASWR-AJHS); Anne B. Barrett, Diary, c. 1830s, bound in section from the *Missionary Herald* 29, no. 11 (Nov. 1838) (in ATHM); L. E. Emerson, Diary 1853–55, MeHS. He paraphrases Psalms 37:21: "The wicked borroweth, and payeth not again" (KJV).
22. William Watson to Sarah Watson Dana, 23 Feb. 1838, DFP-SL; Persis Sibley Andrews, 12 Aug. 1849, Diary, MeHS.
23. James Healy, 20 Mar. 1849, Diary, CHC; Anthony D. Currier to Mary Ann Loring, 7 May 1835, MALCL-AHS; Sophia Tuckerman to Elizabeth Salisbury, [16 Mar. 1842], SFP-AAS.
24. Mary Cheever to Elizabeth B. Cheever, 27 Dec. 1837, CFP-AAS; James Healy, 2 Mar. 1849, Diary, CHC; Charles M. Cobb, 10 Sept. 1851, Journal, VHS; Elizabeth H. Jocelyn, 18 Sept. 1839, Diary, JFP-CHS; Charles M. Cobb, 2 Sept. 1852, 14 Apr. 1853, Journals, VHS.
25. Charles M. Cobb, 6 June 1852, Journal, VHS; Seth Shaler Arnold, 20 July 1849, Journal, VHS; Hannah Hicock Smith, 15 Jan. 1849, 21 May 1845, Diary, CSL; bringing a book "home" was a longstanding usage; see, for example, Low, *Lights and Shadows,* 22 Sept. 1831, 1:264; Elizabeth Atherton Clapp, 20 Aug. 1852, Journal, CP-MHS; Lorenza Stevens Berbineau, 5 Feb. 1851, line-a-day Account Book, 1851,

vol. 120, FCLP-MHS; Paul Atwood Gibson, 11 June, 18, 23, 28 Aug. 1852, Pocket Memorandum, NHHS. Aurilla Ann Moffitt, [15 Jan.] under 11 Jan. 1842, Personal Journal, OCHS; Cyrus Parker Bradley, 2 May 1835, Journal, NHHS; Lucy Larcom to Harriet Jane Hanson Robinson, 7 Apr. 1857, Diary, RSP-SL.

26. Ann Everett to Sarah P. E. Hale, 20 Feb. 1829, HP-SSC; William Watson to Sarah Watson Dana, 23 Feb. 1838, DFP-SL; Forten, *Journals of Charlotte Forten Grimké,* 31 Jan., 5 Mar. 1857, 187, 199.

Chapter 7

1. Abigail Pierce to Mary Pierce Poor, 3 Jan. 1851, PoFP-SL.
2. Although the predominance of oral over silent reading in antebellum literary studies is yet unexplored, there is rich theoretical scholarship on related issues of oral tradition and orality (e.g., Svenbro, *Phrasikleia;* Doane and Pasternack, *Vox Intexta;* Bahn and Bahn, *History of Oral Interpretation,* chap. 6; and Havelock, *Muse Learns to Write*). On secondary orality after Gutenberg, see Ong, *Orality and Literacy.* Much of this work emphasizes how orality structures printed texts, but less is done on the opposite flow of influence, which was also germane to our informants. For they had so internalized literary conventions due to their own identity construction and social formation through engaging print that the gap between "natural" speaking and literary expression closed; then again, the period's authors recognized the predominance of oral reading and, like medieval storytellers, incorporated verbal structures into their written prose (e.g., Fielding's *Writing and Orality,* Kenny's "Memory, Truth, and Orality," and related essays in Ruoff and Ward's *Redefining American Literary History,* 75–82, 115–54). Orality and literacy thus synergized; it would be difficult to trace which linguistic practice originated in one or the other. It is best to assume, then, that most of the printed texts our informants engaged had potential performativity.
3. On reading aloud at home, see Kelley's "Reading Women," Leonard's *News for All,* 19–32, and most of our recent articles, especially "Reading and Everyday Life," 285–323. John Park, 7 Jan. 1842, Diary, BPL; Mary Pierce Poor to John Pierce and Lucy (Tappan) Pierce, 30 Jan. 1842, PoFP-SL; Frances A. C. Small Douglass, 2–15 Mar. 1856, Diary, MeHS; Persis Sibley Andrews, 21 Jan. 1843, 25 Dec. 1844, 26 Jan. 1851 (their last oral reading), 18 July 1852, Diary, MeHS; Dibner, *Portrait of Paris Hill,* 101. Zboray and Zboray, "Reading and Everyday Life," 291, table 2.
4. Annie De Wolf Middleton to "My own dearest Aunts," 11 Jan. 1853, MFP-SCHS.
5. Joshua Edwin Harris, 20, 24, 31 Jan., 3 Feb. 1858, Journal, JEHP-MeHS. Lilly Dana, 8 Feb. 1860, Diary, DFP-SL; Ellen Wright to Martha Coffin Wright, 13 Nov. 1860, GP-SSC; Ellen Wright to William Wright, 26 Jan. 1861, GP-SSC; James Healy, 21 Jan. 1849, Diary, CHC.
6. Forten, *Journals of Charlotte Forten Grimké,* 12 Apr. 1857, 211; Elizabeth H. Jocelyn, 16 Jan. 1852, Diary, JFP-CHS; Frances M. Jocelyn, 16, 19, 20 Jan., 11, 25 Feb. 1852, Diary, JFP-CHS; Mary Pierce Poor to John Pierce and Lucy (Tappan) Pierce, 6 Aug. 1838, PoFP-SL; Frederick W. Treadway, 21 Nov. 1837, 23, 16 Jan. 1838, Diary, CHS; Lettie Lewis to Emma Brown, 26 Jan. 1861, BFP-MeHS; Forten, *Journals of Charlotte Forten Grimké,* 5 Apr. 1857, 208–9; McHenry, *Forgotten Readers,*

54, and on black literary clubs as "acts of resistance to the hostile racial climate," 17.

7. Lettie Lewis to Emma Brown, 26 Jan. 1861, BFP-MeHS; Martha Osborne Barrett, 19 Feb. 1860, Diary, PEM.
8. Not surprisingly, references to oral reading appear in histories of domestic sewing. Ring, *Let Virtue Be a Guide;* see also Kelley, "Reading Women." Informal and formal sewing get-togethers could include men as well as women; Hansen, *Very Social Time* (106–9); Lawes, *Women and Reform,* 62–63. Persis Sibley Andrews, 12 Mar. 1842, Diary, DFP-MHS; Forten, *Journals of Charlotte Forten Grimké,* 30 June 1854, 80; Mary Pierce Poor to John Pierce and Lucy (Tappan) Pierce, 18 Apr. 1842, PoFP-SL; Mary Pierce Poor to Lucy (Pierce) Hedge, 2 July 1841, PoFP-SL. Frances M. Jocelyn, 29 May, 25 Nov. 1851, 27 Sept. 1852, Diary, JFP-CHS (the two married on 8 Sept. 1852). Men might listen while crafting items; boys commonly applied the skill to bookbinding, garment making, and leatherworking (e.g., Sarah B. Mason Ruggles Eaton, 20 May 1840, Diary, RIHS).
9. For an example of literary dissemination and benevolent sewing work, see Young Ladies Sewing and Reading Society, Pittsfield, Mass., Records, 1840–70, SL, which includes entries such as "Amount of money sent to Mission Institute by the Young Ladies Reading & Sewing Circle April. 1840. Sent 25 dollars to which was added 5$ by Mr. Benjamin Mills[;] Value of it in Illinois $33.00" and "April 1841. Sent 38$ value in Illinois nearly 41$." Lawes, *Women and Reform,* 47, 56. Elizabeth Pierce, 16 June 1830, Journal, PoFP-SL; John Park, 4 Aug. 1841, Diary, BPL; Agnes Paine to Mary A. Byram, 24 Jan., 23 Feb., 13 Dec. 1847, SFP-SL. J. Reynolds Hixon, 26 Sept. 1837, Diary, OCHS; William Hoyt, 13 Feb. 1851, Journal, BPL; Charles M. Cobb, 26 Mar. 1852, Journal, VHS.
10. Sarah P. Worcester to Mary A. Byram, 8 Jan. 1843, SFA-SL; John R. Congdon, 4 Sept. 1840, Journal, CFP-RIHS; Forten, *Journals of Charlotte Forten Grimké,* 24 Feb. 1858, 288; Pauline Agassiz Shaw to Sarah Cary, 7 June 1854–57, ECAFP-SL; Elizabeth Dwight Cabot, 4 Apr. 1853, Diary, CFP-SL. Ellen Wright to Martha Coffin Wright, 13 Nov. 1860, 3 Feb. 1861, GP-SSC; Lilly Dana, 18 Jan., 18 Feb. 1860, Diary, DFP-SL; Persis Sibley Andrews, 30 Nov. 1841, Diary, MeHS.
11. Elizabeth Dwight Cabot to Ellen Twisleton, 27 Mar. 1860, CFP-SL; Caroline Gardiner Curtis, 29 Apr. 1859, Diary, CFP3-MHS. Lewton, *Servant in the House.*
12. Lucy (Tappan) Pierce to Lucy (Pierce) Hedge, 13 Feb. in 29 Jan. 1840, PoFP-SL; Caroline Gardiner Curtis, 31 Oct. 1854, 30 Jan. 1855, Diary, CFP3-MHS; Olive Gay Worcester, 10 Dec. 1845, Journal, SFA-SL. On other domestic chores that could occasion oral reading, see Hoffert, *Private Matters,* and Boydston, *Home and Work.*
13. Caroline Gardiner Curtis, 5 Nov. 1849, 9 Oct., 6 Dec. 1851, Diary, CFP3-MHS; Arozina Perkins, 5 July 1849, Diary, CHS; Cynthia Sprague Congdon, 2 May 1841, Journal, CFP-RIHS; Hannah Hicock Smith, 6 Feb. 1847, 8 Dec. 1848, Diary, CSL.
14. John R. Congdon, 10 Sept. 1840, Journal, CFP-RIHS; Sarah M. Davis to Dorcas P. Gay and Olive Gay Worcester, 24 Jan. 1853, SFUP-SL; Charlotte Rantoul to Elizabeth Abbot, 2 Jan. 1832, EC-BHS; Eunice Hale White Cobb, clipping of Fanny Fern, "Two in Heaven," from the *Olive Branch,* 1853–55, Diary, NEHGS; Elizabeth Pierce, 6 Jan. 1831, Journal, PoFP-SL.

15. J. Reynolds Hixon, 26 Mar. 1837, reported on in entry dated 28 Mar. 1837, Diary, OCHS; Cornelia Jocelyn Foster, 24 Feb. 1861, Diary, JFP-CHS; Mary Gardner Lowell, 18 May 1845, line-a-day Journal, 1845, vol. 106, FCLP-MHS; Persis Sibley Andrews, 23 Apr., 8 Jan.1843, Diary, MeHS.
16. Eunice Hale White Cobb, 14 Apr. 1856, Diary, NEHGS. On women as preachers, see Brekus, *Strangers and Pilgrims.*
17. Benedict Joseph Fenwick, 9 Aug. 1826, Memoranda of the Diocese of Boston, PBJF-AAB; Willis, *History of Portland,* 700; John R. Congdon, 23 Dec. 1849, Journal, CFP-RIHS; Mary R. Congdon, 20 May 1860, Journal, CFP-RIHS.
18. Forten, *Journals of Charlotte Forten Grimké,* 8 July 1854, 83; Harriet Mary Brown Owens was Felicia Hemans's sister; Elizabeth Atwater Charnley, 31 May 1834, Journal, CHS; Martha Osborne Barrett, 8 June 1851, Diary, PEM.
19. Mary Elizabeth Fiske, 17 Dec. 1842, Diary, LxHS; Caroline Barrett White, 10 June 1851, Diary, AAS; Charles M. Cobb, 16 Mar. 1853, Journal, VHS; William Hoyt, 25 Mar. 1851, Journal, BPL; Sarah B. Mason Ruggles Eaton, 18 Feb. 1834, Diary, RIHS; Ellen Twistleton to Elizabeth Dwight Cabot, 15 July 1846, CFP-SL.
20. Persis Sibley Andrews, 29 July 1841, Diary, MeHS; Ellen Wright to Martha Coffin Wright, 19 Nov. 1860, GP-SSC.
21. Susan S. Johnson, 27 Mar. 1841, Journal, LxHS; Forten, *Journals of Charlotte Forten Grimké,* 7 Jan. 1857, 180–81. Ellen Wright to Martha Coffin Wright, 13 Nov. 1860, GP-SSC; Lily Dana, 29 Feb. 1860, Diary, DFP-SL; Sarah Brown to Cyrus S. Brown and Family, Sat. Eve. c. 1861, BFP-MeHS; Elizabeth Pierce, 21 Jan. 1830, Journal, PoFP-SL. Garber, *Quotation Marks,* 10, asks, "How does one indicate that one is speaking in quotation?" and discusses speakers' vocal cues (14).
22. Calista Billings, 26 Nov. 1849, Diary, SL; Joshua Edwin Harris, 29 May 1856, Journal, JEHP-MeHS.
23. Mary Pierce Poor to Lucy (Pierce) Hedge, 16 Mar. in 4 Mar. 1852, PoFP-SL; George H. Clark, 1, 2 Aug. 1847, Diary and Memorandum Book, HBDP-RIHS; Patrick James Keegan to Dermot Warburton Keegan, 18 Mar., 3 Oct. 1858, NSFP-SL; Helen M. Warner, 14 Oct. 1854, Diary, NEHGS; Melvin Lord, "Marsh and Capen," in "Boston Booksellers, 1650–1860" (in BBP-AAS); Emma Gannell borrowed Walker's work on 12 Apr. 1851 from a local bookstore (Pocket Memorandum, NHHS). Johnson, *Gender and Rhetorical Space,* 26–31, and Johnson, "Popularization," 139–57.
24. Mary Pierce Poor to John Pierce and Lucy (Tappan) Pierce, 26 July in 25 July 1838, PoFP-SL; William Watson to Sarah Watson Dana, 4 Apr. 1841, DFP-SL; Persis Sibley Andrews, 25, 5 Nov. 1843, Diary, MeHS.
25. John Park, 28 Nov. 1842, Diary, BPL; Dall, *"Alongside,"* 94; Frederick Lathrop Gleason, 13 Jan. 1861, Journal, CHS; Ellen Wright to William Wright, 16 Feb. 1861, GP-SSC; Forten, *Journals of Charlotte Forten Grimké,* 2 May 1858, 307.
26. Patrick James Keegan to Dermot Warburton Keegan, 18 Mar. 1858, NSFP-SL; Vicesimus Knox, *Elegant Extracts* (1784). Cyrus Parker Bradley, 23 Jan. 1833, School Journal, NHHS. Seth Shaler Arnold, 22 May 1852, Journal, VHS; Olive Gay Worcester, 17 Oct. 1849, Journal, SFA-SL; Charles M. Cobb, 23 Feb. 1851, Journal, VHS; James Healy, 24 Apr. 1849, Diary, CHC.

27. Persis Sibley Andrews, 11 Sept. 1841, Diary, MeHS; Elizabeth H. Jocelyn, 18 May 1839, Diary, JFP-CHS; Mellen Chamberlain, 3 Nov. 1843, Diary, BPL; Forten, *Journals of Charlotte Forten Grimké,* 14, 17 Sept. 1854, 26 Aug. 1855, 100, 138.
28. Mary Pierce Poor to John Pierce and Lucy (Tappan) Pierce, 16 Feb. 1848, PoFP-SL; Nathaniel Cheever to George Barrell Cheever, 19 Nov. 1839, CFP-AAS; James Healy, 30 Mar. 1849, Diary, CHC.
29. Hannah Lowell Jackson Cabot, 18 Jan. 1840, Diary, AFP-SL; Ellis Gray Loring, 25 Mar. 1838, Diary, EGLP-SL. He may be quoting the traditional ballad "The Cruel Brother; or, The Bride's Testament": "'What will you leave to your brother John?' / 'The gallows-tree to hang him on.'"
30. Mary Crowninshield Mifflin, 29 Jan. 1860, Diary, BPL; Isaac Webb to Sarah I. (McClellan) Webb, 30 Nov. 1840, MP-CHS; Charles M. Cobb, 19 Jan. 1849 (near 21 June 1852), Journal, VHS. Zboray and Zboray, *Literary Dollars,* 117–24; Halttunen, *Confidence Men;* Smith, "Introducing Parlor Theatricals"; Lewis, "Tableaux Vivants"; Elbert, "Striking a Historical Pose."
31. William Lloyd Garrison Jr. to Helen Frances Garrison, 6 Mar. 1861, GP-SSC; John Park, 7 Mar. 1839, Diary, BPL; Calista Billings, 12 Sept. 1848, Diary, SL; Hannah Lowell Jackson Cabot to Sarah (Jackson) Russell, 13 Apr. 1838, AFP-SL; Hannah Lowell Jackson Cabot, 30 Aug. 1839, Diary, transcript, AFP-SL. Durivage, *Life Scenes,* 178–79.
32. Susan Sturgis to Caroline Sturgis Tappan, n.d. [1847], STPP-SSC; M. Elizabeth Nutting to Wendell Phillips Garrison, Dec[?]. 1855, GP-SSC; Eliza Perkins Cabot, reminiscences taken 3 June 1882, CFP-SL; Mary Crowninshield Mifflin, 5 Mar. 1856, Diary, BPL; Lily Dana, 28, 29 Feb. 1860, Diary, DFP-SL; Mary Gardner Lowell, 31 Aug. 1843, Diary, FCLP-MHS; Calista Billings, 7 Sept. 1848, Diary, SL.
33. Hannah Lowell Jackson Cabot, [4 Sept.] 1839, Diary, AFP-SL; Mary Lavinia Cowles, [1850], Diary, DMC-YUs; for a dialogue, see Mary M. Dawley, 21 Feb. 1857, Diary, RIHS; Mary R. Congdon, 20 Feb. 1857, Journal, CFP-RIHS.
34. Caroline Sturgis Tappan to Anne Sturgis Hooper, 23 Jan. [1858?], STPP-SSC; Thomas G. Cary Jr., Diary, 1847, ECAP-SL; Katherine Bigelow Lawrence Jr., 2 Apr. 1851, Journal, LFP-MHS; Isaac Webb, 30 Nov. 1840, Diary, MP-CHS; Stephen Salisbury III, 15 Jan. 1855, Diary, SFP-AAS.
35. Moses Adams III, Common Place Book, No. 1, c. 1834, p. 45, MAP-BC; Forten, *Journals of Charlotte Forten Grimké,* 5 Mar. 1856, 151. On tableaux as self-fashioning, see Elbert, "Striking a Historical Pose," 236.

Part III

1. Kaestle and Vinovskis, "From Apron Strings to ABCs"; Moran and Vinovskis, "Great Care of Godly Parents." Mary Elizabeth Fiske, "Apothegms," 21 July 1840, Diary, LxHS; Charles M. Cobb, 12 Sept. 1853, Journal, VHS.
2. While reception theory dates at least back to the early-nineteenth-century romantics, the 1960s witnessed a spurt of as-yet-unabated interest. The sixties' legitimation crisis concerning authority naturally led scholars to ponder the relationship between receivers

and what they received. Is there but one best reading of the text and does it conform to its author's intentions? The negative answer to both questions was apparent even amid Vatican II's ecumenism, which summoned theories of reception of Scripture (Alberigo, Jossua, and Komonchak, *Reception of Vatican II*). Secular reception theorists look to Jauss's 1967 University of Konstanz speech, translated as "Literary History" (Jauss, "Theory of Reception"). His quest for a *Rezeptionsgeschichte,* or "reception history," of texts' actual readers must be distinguished from *Rezeptionsæsthetik* (Iser, *Implied Reader*), which looks for readers implied in texts, not the actual people who read them. Other scholars seek "ideal readers," those most competent to engage a text (Salado, "Lecteurs empiriques"). Jauss would hold that the reader is the text, while for Iser the text itself gives insights into its reader. Iser is thus concerned with plausible processes by which readers construed meaning from the printed page, whereas Jauss evinces contextualization as a way of understanding reader and text. Despite their differences, both shift the focus of literary study (and, by extension, humanistic inquiry) from authors to readers, a move abetted by Barthes, "Death of the Author." Some scholars use the text and biographical material to discern who authors actually intended to read their books (Kay, "Intended Readers"). A quite separate line from that of Jauss and Iser emerged in the United States from scholars of rhetoric and pedagogy (e.g., Booth, *Rhetoric of Fiction;* Cavell, *Must We Mean What We Say?* Fish, *Surprised by Sin;* and Fish, *Is There a Text in This Class?*). On constructed readers, see Mailloux's *Reception Histories.* Not all reception analyses are text-based (e.g., Kemp, *Betrachter*), or, as among many Cultural Studies scholars, influenced by Jauss and Iser (e.g., Scannell, Schlesinger, and Sparks, *Culture and Power;* cf. Garnham, "Political Economy and Cultural Studies"). In light of these peculiar disciplinary genealogies, reception study has remained largely defined by specific market-oriented cultural productions (i.e., a certain book or genre). Yet cultural reception is much broader than this, as Part III makes clear. For receivers, boundaries between the various arts, performing or visual, and letters are permeable, at times seemingly nonexistent. Little boundary, too, separates the reception of informal conversations, gestures, and sociabilities from that of more formal cultural productions, a fact implicitly recognized in Benjamin's abortive *Arcades Project.* Plus there is the added complication that instances of reception depend upon perception and discernment ineluctably shaped by previous experiences drawn from the vast field of cultural possibilities. A broader, subject-centered anthropological approach like the one employed here avoids the myopia of reception histories confined by disciplinary boundaries and focused upon single types of cultural production. Reception might be viewed as a subset of long-term ongoing processes like enculturation, socialization, or cultural reproduction (Bourdieu and Passeron, *Reproduction*). Cultural reception thus becomes but a particular moment, in itself not a very important one, within the larger process, which nevertheless can be analyzed together with similar and different moments to exemplify or symbolize widespread and recurring patterns. A problem occurs with the terminology insofar as it highlights cultural acquisition, thus constricting its application, and, worse, it brings with it a notion of a coded "authorized" culture writ upon the blank slate of the subject's mind—one reason, perhaps, why the terminology has fallen quietly out of fashion while subjects as agents have powerfully reemerged in anthropology (e.g., Clifford and Marcus, *Writing Culture;* Denzin and Lincoln, *Handbook*). With the demise of reductionist cultural determinism (Bennett's "Classical Anthropology"), culture has become, if anything, but a tendency, of variable strength, that can shape probabilities of group behavior and thought through an accretive effect experienced by non-autonomous socialized selves in close communication with one another (Sokefeld, "Debating Self"). Culture, rather than acting upon subjects, is something constantly enacted (or performed) and given new life, while reception is but one type of enactment.

3. On illiteracy, see Soltow and Stevens, *Rise of Literacy,* chap. 5. Bode, *American Lyceum.* Note that our concern here is informal literacy acquisition, not the formal types encountered in schools and other institutional settings which have their own rich scholarship.

Chapter 8

1. Persis Sibley Andrews, 1, 4, 25 Jan. 1846, 28 Jan. 1849, Diary, MeHS.
2. William Hoyt, 30 Apr. 1851, Journal, BPL. The "thirty days" rhyme is from Mother Goose. Memories of learning to read set the personal context for this chapter and influence how adults saw children's literacy acquisition. Given this achievement's pivotal nature, few scholars study its memory. Celebrities receive the most scrutiny (Furman and Standard, *Bookworms;* Gilbar, *Open Door*), but there are also some modern surveys of common folk: Sohn, "Gettin' Above"; Paterson, "Embodied Narratives"; and Roe and Vukelich, "Literacy Histories."
3. Harriet Jane Hanson Robinson, 1 Jan. 1852, Diary, RSP-SL. The quote is from the concluding verse in Thomas Carlyle's translation of Johann Wolfgang von Goethe, *Wilhelm Meister's Apprenticeship* (1828). The importance of home-based preliteracy that Roe and Vukelich ("Literacy Histories") and others find for today applies as well to antebellum New Englanders. The significance and centrality of learning outside schoolrooms (*paideia*) was noted in 1960 by Bailyn's *Education* and later picked up by Cremin, *American Education* (see also Monaghan, "Family Literacy"). Since then, the history of nineteenth-century informal education remains unexplored, except for women as educators in the home (Cott, *Bonds of Womanhood;* Ryan, *Empire of the Mother*).
4. Olive Gay Worcester, 25 Nov. 1845, 17 Oct. 1842, Journal, SFP-SL; Daniel F. Child and Mary D. Child, 30 Sept. 1843, Diary, DFCP-MHS; Frances M. Jocelyn, 16 Apr. 1844, Diary, JFP-CHS. On "sayings and doings," see, for example, Haliburton, *Clockmaker,* and Hook, *Sayings and Doings.*
5. Olive Gay Worcester, 20 May 1840, Journal, SFA-SL; Harriet Jane Hanson Robinson, 1 Jan. 1852, Diary, RSP-SL; Olive Gay Worcester, 17 Dec. 1842, Journal, SFA-SL; Mary Pierce Poor to John Pierce and Lucy (Tappan) Pierce, 14 Sept. 1843, PoFP-SL; Olive Gay Worcester to Rufus Marble Gay, 18 Feb., 27 Mar. 1842, SFP-SL.
6. Sarah Anne (Chace) Greene, 15 Feb. 1846, Diary, CAGP-RIHS; Elizabeth W. Clement to Charles Clement, 1 July 1840, CFP-VHS. William De Wolf to Annie De Wolf Middleton and Nathaniel Russell Middleton, 13 Apr. 1850, MFP-SCHS.
7. Persis Sibley Andrews, 15 July, 9 Aug. 1846, 1 Apr. 1847, Diary, MeHS. Rancière, *Ignorant Schoolmaster,* 29–32.

8. Some diarists claimed their children were "reading" before actual lessons began; Sarah Anne (Chace) Greene in her diary (CAGP-RIHS), for one, reported on 21 February 1847 that her daughter "reads a deal," but records that the girl began formal reading lessons more than a year later, on 30 April 1848. Mary Pierce Poor, 1 Dec. 1858, Account Book, PoFP-SL; Sarah Anne (Chace) Greene, 30 Apr., 10 Dec. 1848, Diary, CAGP-RIHS; Abigail Bradley Hyde to "dear Sister," 10 May 1840, BHFP-SL. Current school practice replays many nineteenth-century home-learning methods (Putnam, "Beginning Reading Methods"). On the alphabet, see Crain, *Story of A.*
9. Abigail Bradley Hyde to "dear Sister," 10 May 1840, BHFP-SL; Mary Pierce Poor to Agnes Blake Poor, 10 July 1853, PoFP-SL; Helen M. Warner, 12 Sept. 1851, Diary, NEHGS; Rufus Marble Gay to Dorcas P. Gay, 6 Feb. 1851, SFA-SL.
10. Sarah Anne (Chace) Greene, 25 Oct. 1847, Diary, CAGP-RIHS; Sarah B. Mason Ruggles Eaton, 25 Mar. 1834, Diary, RIHS; on a boy learning sewing in school, see Elizabeth H. Jocelyn, memorial to Isaac Jocelyn, c. Mar. 1839, Diary, JFP-CHS; Abigail Bradley Hyde to "dear Sister," 10 May 1840, BHFP-SL. Learning how to both read and sew continued after first school enrollment, although needlework, popular in eighteenth-century girls' curricula, eventually faded. Some teachers warred on craftwork in academic life (e.g., Sister Mary Benedict to Benedict Joseph Fenwick, Sept. 1837, PBJF-AAB). The link between socialized handcrafts and literacy training would have its counterpart later in John Dewey's educational philosophy and practice (Lagemann, "From Discipline-Based"). On the link in girls' education, see Ring, *Let Virtue Be a Guide.*
11. Sarah Watson Dana to Elizabeth (Watson) Daggett, 12 Oct. 1847, DFP-SL; Persis Sibley Andrews, 23 Mar. 1851, Diary, MeHS; Sarah Everett Hale to Nathan Hale Jr., 12 Dec. 1838, HP-SSC.
12. Persis Sibley Andrews, 8 Aug. 1847, 6 Feb. 1848, Diary, MeHS; Elizabeth H. Jocelyn, c. Mar. 1839, Diary, JFP-CHS; Olive Gay Worcester, 4 Nov. 1845, Journal, SFA-SL; Susan S. Johnson, 5 June 1842, Journal, LxHS.
13. Zboray, *Fictive People,* 196–201; Low, *Lights and Shadows,* 14 Aug. 1832, 2:426–27; Calista Billings, 6 Nov. 1848, Diary, SL; "Jingua" to "Missus Wesson," 10 Feb. 1840, BPL. A range of other influences, mostly socioeconomic, acted upon the attainment and quality of literacy. The fullest and most systematic consideration of these influences can be found in Gilmore's "Elementary Literacy." Historical issues concerning illiteracy and its social costs are assayed in Graff, *Literacy Myth,* and Graff, *Labyrinths of Literacy.* Literacy and literary practice have been considered for several groups: on white servants, see scattered references in Dudden's *Serving Women* and Sutherland's *Americans and Their Servants;* for Irish immigrants, see Handlin, *Boston's Immigrants.* Hurdles facing native-born working-class men questing after literary attainment can be discerned in Burritt, *Learned Blacksmith.* The slowly growing literature on Native Americans includes Wyss, *Writing Indians,* and Monaghan, "'She Loved to Read'." For African American scholarship, see Gundaker's *Signs of Diaspora;* Painter's "Representing Truth," and Cornelius's *"When I Can Read."* Garnering much less attention than African American literary culture is that of the Chinese and Jews. On the former, see Tchen, *New York Before Chinatown;* on the latter, see Ashton, *Rebecca Gratz.*

14. Mary J. Abbott to "Dr Children in Sab. S.C.," 1838, MJAP-AHS; Charles M. Cobb, 16 May [1854?], Journal, VHS. Unlike the link between manual skills and literacy, that between religion and literacy has faded. Lockridge, *Literacy in Colonial New England,* credits the Bible (and other religious) reading with the region's high white adult male literacy rates; children's reading of holy writ had a persistent history (Bottigheimer, *Bible for Children*). However, the religious aspects of literacy acquisition can be and has been far overemphasized at the expense of secular motivations and purposes, especially socioeconomic ones (Gilmore, *Reading Becomes a Necessity of Life;* Brown, *Knowledge Is Power;* Zboray, *Fictive People*).
15. John Park, 19 May 1794, Diary, BPL; Sarah Smith (Cox) Browne to Albert Gallatin Browne, 29 June 1855, BroFP-SL. Calhoun, *Intelligence of a People,* argues that antebellum evangelical Protestantism adversely affected the rationality of its adherents and undermined their ability to engage tightly reasoned sermons or technical documents.
16. Soltow and Stevens, *Rise of Literacy,* 24–25; Joshua Edwin Harris, 29 May 1856, Journal, JEHP-MeHS; Charles M. Cobb, 2 Aug. 1854, Journal, VHS; Persis Sibley Andrews, 7, 28 Aug. 1844, Diary, MeHS; Cyrus Parker Bradley, 2 June 1835, Journal, NHHS.
17. Martha Osborne Barrett, 24 Sept. 1854, Diary, PEM; Cynthia Sprague Congdon, 21 Mar. 1841, Journal, CFP-RIHS.
18. Sarah K. (Batchelder) Fuller, Notebook, c. 1842, BPL; James Lockwood Wright, 3 Feb. 1833, Journal, JLWP-YUs; Boylan, *Sunday School,* chap. 2. Amos A. Lawrence, 26 Nov. 1842, Diary, AALP-MHS; Pauline Agassiz Shaw to Sarah Cary, 15 Nov. c. [1854–57], ECAP-SL; Emily Wise, 13 Mar. 1831, Diary, NEHGS.
19. Emily Wise, 1, 2 July 1838, Diary, NEHGS; Charlotte Henrietta Pettibone, 25 Apr. 1842, Diary, CHS; "The Amistad Captives"; Charlotte Henrietta Pettibone, 22 May 1841, Diary, CHS.
20. James Amsted Brown, 3 Mar. 1858, Journal, VHS; Elizabeth H. Jocelyn, 26 July 1839, Diary, JFP-CHS; James Lockwood Wright, 2 Nov. 1832, Journal, JLWP-YUs; Henry Wyles Cushman, 8 Mar. 1835, Diary, HWCC-NEHGS; Sarah Watson Dana, introduction, Journal, 1833–35, DFP-SL. Little historical scholarship recognizes different reading modes, but see Stierle, "Studium"; and Sicherman, "Reading and Ambition." Rabinowitz, *Spiritual Self in Everyday Life,* hints at the devotional mode. Stewart, "Cultural Work," considers emotional response. Group reading is an often-overlooked and crucial mode, perhaps a rubric covering several modes; see Fish on "interpretive communities" (*Is There a Text in This Class?* chap. 6).
21. Mary Pierce Poor to John Pierce and Lucy (Tappan) Pierce, 27 Aug. 1836, PoFP-SL; Caroline Gardiner Curtis, 25 May 1852, Diary, CFP3-MHS; Elizabeth Dwight Cabot to Ellen Twisleton, 8 May 1855, CFP-SL; Eliza Bancroft Davis to John Davis, 3 Apr. [1836?], JDP-AAS; Frances Merritt Quick, 20 July 1858, Diary, FMQP-SL; Sarah Abbott to Mary J. Abbott, 10 Jan. 1839, MJAP-AHS; Lucy (Tappan) Pierce to Mary Pierce Poor, 6 [Feb.] in [1 Feb.] 1842, PoFP-SL; Charles M. Cobb, 30 Dec. 1851, Journal, VHS. "Study" differed from what our informants called "reading," even though today both technically involve reading. Confusion arises from some scholars' view of a succession of dominant reading styles since the 1600s (described in Engelsing's *Analphabetentum und Lektüre* and *Bürger als Leser*): from intensive (few books, deep knowledge of them) to extensive (many books, relatively shallow grasp of

them); see Hall, *Cultures of Print,* 36–78. Among the many weaknesses, both logical and empirical, of this view is that study is by definition obviously intensive, and yet some of the period's most studied texts, such as Noah Webster's blue-backed spellers, were extensively distributed (Monaghan, *Common Heritage*). Stiverson and Stiverson, *Books Both Useful and Entertaining,* shows that in colonial Virginia works could be *both* useful and entertaining, one not more worthy of study than the other.

22. Caroline A. Briggs to Ruth Elizabeth Weed, 10 May 1852, BriFP-SL; Sarah Watson Dana, 31 Oct. 1833, Journal, DFP-SL; George H. Clark, 25 June 1847, Diary, HBDP-RIHS; Stephen Salisbury III, 27 Mar. 1860, Diary, SFP-AAS; Katherine Bigelow Lawrence Jr., 23 Oct. 1851, Journal, LFP-MHS; Almon Benson, 19 July 1836, Memoranda, NHHS; Stephen Salisbury III, 18 Mar. 1853, Diary, SFP-AAS; George Burk to William Chamberlain, 5 Feb. 1820, WCP-VHS.
23. Forten, *Journals of Charlotte Forten Grimké,* 1 May 1856, 155; Frances M. Jocelyn, 11 Mar. 1839, Diary, JFP-CHS; James Lockwood Wright, 25 Nov. 1831, Journal, JLWP-YUs; William Lloyd Garrison Jr. to Wendell Phillips Garrison, 20 Sept. 1857, GP-SSC; Mellen Chamberlain, 30 July 1846, Diary, BPL; Frank C. Morse, 29 May 1856, Diary, FCMP-MHS; Mellen Chamberlain, 30 Jan. 1847, Diary, BPL.
24. Louisa Lee Waterhouse, after 10 Aug. 1839, Journal, LLWP-MHS; John Park, 8 Aug. 1846, Diary, BPL.
25. Carroll Norcross, 5 Mar. 1852, Diary, CKNFP-MeHS; Clarissa Harrington, 20 Oct. 1840, "A Daily Journal," LxHS; Daniel F. Child and Mary D. Child, 25 Jan., 3 Dec. 1856, Diary, DFCP-MHS; Sarah B. Mason Ruggles Eaton, 18 Jan. 1855, Diary, RIHS; Stephen Salisbury III, 16 Jan. 1852, Diary, SFP-AAS; William Lloyd Garrison Jr. to Helen Benson Garrison, 24 July 1857, GP-SSC; James Healy, 16 Dec. 1848, Diary, CHC; William Hoyt, 26 Mar. 1851, Journal, BPL; Sarah Watson Dana, 11 Oct. 1833, Journal, DFP-SL; Calista Billings, 25 Apr. 1849, Diary, SL.
26. Aurilla Ann Moffitt, 6 Dec. 1839, Personal Journal, OCHS; John Park, 20 Dec. 1841, Diary, BPL; Ellen Wright to Martha Coffin Wright, 2 Mar. 1861, GP-SSC; James Healy, 28 Mar. 1849, Diary, CHC.
27. Elizabeth Pierce, 7 Nov. 1828, Journal, PoFP-SL; Sarah Watson Dana, 29 Aug. 1833, Journal, DFP-SL; Mary Pierce Poor to Henry Varnum Poor, 4 Feb. 1840, PoFP-SL; James Healy, 2 Apr. 1849, Diary, CHC.
28. Phebe Beede Clark, 7 Nov. 1856, Diary, LHS. Lucretia Anne (Peabody) Everett to Sarah P. E. Hale, 8 Jan. 1828, HP-SSC; Low, *Lights and Shadows,* 15 Apr. 1832, 1:313; Sarah B. Mason Ruggles Eaton to Agnes F. Herreshoff, 11 Aug. 1834, HLFP-RIHS. On inattentive devotionals, see Persis Sibley Andrews, 4 June 1843, Diary, MeHS; Harriet to Delia E. Taintor, 19 Mar. 1833, TDFP-AAS; Osman Cleander Baker, 13 May 1829, Diary, NHHS; Benedict Joseph Fenwick, 1 Aug. 1826, Memoranda of the Diocese of Boston, PBJF-AAB; Low, *Lights and Shadows,* 8 Apr. 1832, 1:310–11.
29. John Park, 14 Feb., 8 Mar. 1837, Diary, BPL; William Francis Channing paraphrased in Hannah Lowell Jackson Cabot, 4 Sept. 1839, Diary, AFP-SL; Zboray and Zboray, "Transcendentalism in Print," 310–81.
30. On perusal: Sarah E. Edgarton to Luella J. B. Case, 21 Oct. 1841, HC-SL; A. Marsh to Sarah Watson Dana, 22 July 1842, DFP-SL; Osman Cleander Baker, 12 Jan. 1831,

Diary, NHHS. On running through: Sarah P. E. Hale to Edward Everett Hale, 9 May 1843, HP-SSC. On glancing at: Martha Osborne Barrett, 18 Jan. 1849, Diary, PEM. On coasting: Elizabeth Pierce, 12 Jan. 1830, Journal, PoFP-SL. On cursory examination: Cyrus Parker Bradley, 1 Apr. 1835, School Journal, NHHS; see also John Park, 27 Dec. 1847, Diary, BPL. Christopher Keith, 13 June 1858, Diary, MMC-RIHS; John Park, 11 Jan. 1848, Diary, BPL.

31. Mary Cary to Thomas G. Cary, 23 Dec. 1838, ECAP-SL; Low, *Lights and Shadows,* 22 May 1833, 2:555; Martha Osborne Barrett, 29 Apr. 1860, 8 Jan. 1849, Diary, PEM; Cyrus Parker Bradley, 20 Oct. 1835, Journal, NHHS; Mellen Chamberlain, 4 Feb. 1847, Diary, BPL; Frederick Lathrop Gleason, 1 Jan. 1860, Journal, CHS.
32. Lavius Hyde to Sarah Hyde, 22 May 1852, BHFP-SL; Mary (Watson) Willson to Sarah Watson Dana, 25 Mar. 1855, DFP-SL.
33. Persis Sibley Andrews, 25 Jan. 1846, Diary, MeHS.

Chapter 9

1. Elizabeth H. Jocelyn, 21 June 1847, Diary, JFP-CHS. She probably played here on the Aesopian fable of the Tortoise and the Birds, with its moral "Never soar aloft on an enemy's pinions."
2. Despite the fact that it has become a minor scholarly industry to expose how much Victorian realities fell short of the period's ideals, there has been a surprising neglect of doing so for reading and other literary experiences. Too often, norms voiced by some people are taken for everyone's actualities, as in the case, for example, of so-called parlor values, which would situate reading primarily as a genteel activity pursued within middle-class leisure time (see Stevenson, *Victorian Homefront*). Conversely, chastisements in public discourse, especially against the pernicious fiction-reading woman (see, for example, Harris, *Pernicious Fiction,* and Lehuu, *Carnival on the Page,* chap. 6), are too often mistaken for actual practices; but see Nichols, "'Blunted Hearts.'" Indeed, our diaries and letters reveal few differences between the types of materials men or women read, which is not surprising since so much oral reading took place in mixed-gender groups.
3. J. Reynolds Hixon, 13, 2 Jan. 1837, Diary, OCHS. The "self-culture" Hixon exemplifies was seldom denoted as such by our informants (Zboray and Zboray, "Transcendentalism in Print," 324–25). The peculiar flavor of this popular mid-nineteenth-century movement owes to a grafting of German-inspired idealistic egoism (Bruford, *German Tradition of Self-Cultivation*) upon a base of Calvinist conduct-of-life literature stretching back to English settlement, but kept continually in view by numerous self-help works such as Watts, *Improvement of the Mind.* Just as German romantic culture was impacting the region during the late 1830s, a new spate of prescriptive works appeared, such as Channing, *Self-culture.* Perhaps as a legacy from Germanic writers, the works more addressed young men than young women, but women were quick to adapt self-culture to their own ends, as can be seen in Irons, "Channing's Influence on Peabody."
4. Printed Protestant discourse presented a simplistic hermeneutic (sola scriptura), with syncretic accretions harkening back to medieval folklife, like reading the Bible

in course with its monastic roots (Masini, *Lectio Divina*). Space limits prevented us from laying out the full variety of antebellum devotional reading practices.

5. John S. Gardiner to "Carl Rufus" (i.e., Charles Gardiner), 18 Nov. 1853, GFP-SL; Hannah Hicock Smith, 31 Dec. 1846, Diary, CSL. On the "trouble" glasses cause, see Lucy (Pierce) Hedge to Mary Pierce Poor, 6 Dec. 1843, PoFP-SL. Hannah Hicock Smith, 30 Dec. 1846, Diary, CSL; Nathan Kilbourn Abbott, 16 Jan. 1854, Diary, NHHS; John Park, 7 Jan. 1847, Diary, BPL; John Langdon, 6 July 1845, Diary, NEHGS; Hannah Hicock Smith, 14 Nov. 1846, Diary, CSL; Elizabeth Pierce, 28 Oct. 1830, Journal, PoFP-SL. On corrective eyewear, see Rosenthal, *Spectacles and Other Vision Aids.*
6. Christopher Keith, 25 Oct., 5 Nov. 1857, Diary, MMC-RIHS; Catherine S. Patton, 3 July 1845, Journal, CHS; Anna Loring to Louisa Gilman Loring and Ellis Gray Loring, 3 Nov. 1851, EGLP-SL. Zboray, *Fictive People,* 14; Crowley, "Artificial Illumination"; Milan, "Refracting the Gaslier."
7. Sarah Smith (Cox) Browne, 30 Aug. 1849, Waste Book, 1846–52, BroFP-SL; Forten, *Journals of Charlotte Forten Grimké,* 13 Sept. 1854, 100; Susan S. Johnson, 2 Dec. 1841, Journal, LxHS; Elizabeth Pierce, 26 Jan. 1830, Journal, PoFP-SL; Sarah Watson Dana, 4 June 1833, Journal, DFP-SL.
8. Emma Brown to Sarah Brown, 31 May 1857, BFP-MeHS; Elizabeth Pierce, 8 Jan. 1830, Journal, PoFP-SL; Cynthia Sprague Congdon, 29 Apr. 1841, Journal, CFP-RIHS; Lucy (Tappan) Pierce to Mary Pierce Poor, 6 Dec. 1843, PoFP-SL; Agnes F. Herreshoff, 12 [Nov.? 1832?], Diary fragments, HLFP-RIHS.
9. Susan D. Tucker, 13 June 1852, Journal, VHS; Elizabeth Dwight Cabot to Ellen Twisleton, 3 Mar. 1859 in 29 Feb. 1859, CFP-SL; James Lockwood Wright, 11 Nov. 1834, Journal, JLWP-YUs; John Park, 6 Mar. 1847, Diary, BPL; Lucy S. Baker, 4 Nov. 1849, Diary, BHS; Charlotte Rantoul to Elizabeth Abbot, 8 Sept. 1833, EC-BHS; Chloe Metcalf to Sarah B. Adams, 20 Sept. 1831, MAP-ATHM.
10. Martha Osborne Barrett, 3 Aug. 1855, Diary, PEM; Lewis Brewster, 3 Oct. 1848, Diary, NHHS; Mary Belden to Sarah Watson Dana, 24 Oct. 1838, DFP-SL.
11. Caroline Gardiner Curtis, 6–8 Sept. 1852, Diary, CFP3-MHS.
12. Low, *Lights and Shadows,* 5 Oct. 1832, 2:445; Mary Pierce Poor to John Pierce and Lucy (Tappan) Pierce, 3 Nov. 1842, PoFP-SL; Mary Pierce Poor to Lucy (Pierce) Hedge, 14 Feb. 1859, PoFP-SL; Sarah Abbott to Mary J. Abbott, 10 Jan. 1839, MJAP-AHS; Agnes F. Herreshoff, 1 Mar. 1833, Diary fragments, HLFP-RIHS; Agnes F. Herreshoff, 14 Jan. 1848, Diary, HLFP-RIHS. Zboray and Zboray, "Books, Reading," 599–601.
13. Elizabeth Dwight Cabot to Elizabeth L. Eliot, 25 Aug. 1844, CFP-SL; Forten, *Journals of Charlotte Forten Grimké,* 27, 7 Nov., 30 Apr. 1858, 22 June 1854, 346, 343, 306, 77–78.
14. William De Wolf to Annie De Wolf Middleton and Nathaniel Russell Middleton, 13 Apr. 1850, MFP-SCHS; Sarah B. Mason Ruggles Eaton, 14 Feb. 1848, Diary, RIHS; Elizabeth H. Jocelyn, 2 Mar. 1839, Diary, JFP-CHS; Frederick Lathrop Gleason, 22 June 1860, Journal, CHS; Sarah B. Mason Ruggles Eaton, 21 Aug. 1847, Diary, RIHS; Elizabeth Dwight Cabot, 5 Aug. 1859, Journal, CFP-SL; Sarah B. Mason Ruggles Eaton, 13 Aug. 1848, Diary, RIHS; Alexander Hill Everett, 2 Apr.

1840, Diary, ENP-MHS. For a glimpse into childcare tasks, see Scholten's *Childbearing in American Society* and Hoffert's *Private Matters.*

15. Hannah Hicock Smith, 21 Dec. 1849, Diary, CSL; Elizabeth Pierce, 4 Nov. 1828, Journal, PoFP-SL; Albert Dodd, 14 Feb. 1837, Diary, ADP-YUs. On changing practices of care for the elderly, see Achenbaum, *Old Age in the New Land;* Fischer, *Growing Old in America;* Scott, *Growing Old in the Early Republic;* and Scott, "''Tis Not the Spring of Life with Me.'" The place of literature in the sick room is hinted at in Rothman, *Living in the Shadow.*
16. Stephen Salisbury III to Georgiana DeVillers Lincoln, 16 Sept. 1856, SFP-AAS; Benjamin Waterhouse Sr., quoted in Louisa Lee Waterhouse, 15 May 1840, Journal, LLWP-MHS; Katherine Bigelow Lawrence, 29 Oct. 1852, Journal, LFP-MHS. On meal-time reading to calm children, see Pauline Agassiz Shaw to Sarah Cary, 15 Nov. c. 1854–57), ECAP-SL; Olive Gay Worcester to Rufus Marble Gay, 18 Feb. 1842, SFP-SL.
17. Caroline Gardiner Curtis, 6 June 1852, Diary, CFP3-MHS; Low, *Lights and Shadows,* 25 July 1833, 2:592. Literary culture amid kitchen duties and eating awaits treatment, but theoretical work on the reading-and-eating metaphor abounds. See Radway, "Reading Is Not Eating"; Mailloux, "Cultural Rhetorical Studies"; Mailloux, "Rhetorical Use and Abuse"; and Gilbert, "Ingestion, Contagion, Seduction."
18. On professionals' literary experiences, see Bledstein, *Culture of Professionalism;* Geison, *Professions;* and Haber, *Quest for Authority and Honor.* On lawyers, see Fidler, " 'Young Limbs of the Law' "; see also Grossberg, "Institutionalizing Masculinity."
19. Unidentified night watchman to G. W. Walton, 7 Apr. 1856, ATHM; Joshua Edwin Harris, 7 Feb. 1857, 9, 20, 24 Jan., 19 Mar., 23 Aug. 1860, Journal, JEHP-MeHS; Jonathan Danforth Meriam, 30 June 1828, Diary, AAS; Eliza Perkins Cabot, reminiscences of the early Republic, taken at Brookline, 3 June 1882, CFP-SL; on factory libraries, see Ditzion, *Arsenals,* 111–12; Larcom, "Among the Lowell Mill-Girls," 603; Murphy, *Ten Hours' Labor,* 48; see also Bushman, *"Good Poor Man's Wife,"* 38–39, and Dublin, *Transforming Women's Work.*
20. Kohn, "Jewish Peddler's Diary," c. Oct. 1842, 62; Charles M. Cobb, 12 Apr. 1851, 10 Apr. 1852, 29 Apr. under 5 May, 19 July under 24 July 1851, 30 July 1852, Journal, VHS. Schob, *Hired Hands and Plowboys,* captures some literary practices of midwestern migrants.
21. Jonathan Danforth Meriam, 31 Aug., 28 Dec. 1828, Diary, AAS; James Lockwood Wright, 21 Feb. 1834, Journal, JLWP-YUs; Cyrus Parker Bradley, 23 Jan. 1833, School Journal, NHHS. Shaker reading is covered in Madden, *Bodies of Life.*
22. Moses Adams III to Moses Adams II, 1 Sept. 1822, transcript in Moses Adams III, Common Place Book, No. 2, pp. 65–66, MAP-BC; Seth C. Whitehouse, 21 Mar. 1850, Journal, MeHS; William Y. Sprague, "List of Things," in back pocket of Diary, 16 Aug. 1858–[spring?] 1859, CSL; David P. Stowell, 24, 17 Oct., 20 Nov., 1 Dec., 22 Oct., 9 Sept., 8 Oct., 22, 27 Nov. 1858, Journal, 1858–62, NHHS. On literary culture among seamen, see Springer, *America and the Sea;* Sherman, *Voice of the Whaleman;* Bolster, *Black Jacks;* and Skallerup, *Books Afloat and Ashore.*
23. Albert Thorndike, 14, 2 Feb. 1860, Log, BHS; John R. Congdon, 4 July 1841, 23 June 1844, 24 Apr., 20 Mar. 1846, 24 Mar. 1849, 18 June 1850, Journal, CFP-

RIHS. The cross-dressing Fanny Campbell appears as both man and woman in a piece of scrimshaw in PrPL; the source image is the cover engraving to Ballou, *Fanny Campbell.* PEM has several examples of literary scrimshaw, including Campbell, Robert Burns, Jenny Lind, Daniel Boone, Benjamin Franklin as a reader, the English stage actress Kate Bateman, and the cover illustration from a cheap novel (Jones, *Belle of Boston*). Thanks go to Lyles Forbes, Curatorial Assistant, Maritime History, for pointing out most of these.

24. John Wilson Jr. to Mr. [and Mrs.] John Wilson, 23 July 1849, ATHM; James Barnard Blake, 13 Oct. 1851, Diary, AAS; Mellen Chamberlain, 5, 10 Nov. 1846, Diary, BPL; J. Reynolds Hixon, 5 Oct. 1836, Diary, OCHS; John Davis to George Davis, 15 Jan. 1826, JDP-AAS.
25. Lamb, "Formative Influences," 54; James Healy, 14 Feb. 1849, Diary, CHC; Charles M. Cobb, 23 Feb. 1852, Journal, VHS; Cyrus Parker Bradley, 23 Oct. 1835, Journal, NHHS; James Healy, 9 Jan. 1849, Diary, CHC. Allmendinger, *Paupers and Scholars.*
26. Francis Bennett, 11 May, 5 June, 29 May 1854, Diary, AAS; Charles F. Low, 16 Feb., 5 Mar., 9 Apr. 1860, Diary, BPL; Wallace Clement to Sarah Fish Clement, 11 Nov. 1856, CFP-VHS; Forten, *Journals of Charlotte Forten Grimké,* 20, 21 Aug., 28 Nov., 22 Aug. 1857, 251, 269, 252. For clerks, see Horlick, *Country Boys and Merchant Princes,* and Augst, *Clerk's Tale.*
27. Persis Sibley Andrews, 22 Apr. 1843, Diary, MeHS; Mary Pierce Poor to John Pierce and Lucy (Tappan) Pierce, 23 July 1842, 25 Jan. 1837, PoFP-SL; Mary Gardner Lowell, 31 Aug. 1843, Diary, FCLP-MHS.
28. Samuel Cabot Jr. to Hannah Lowell Jackson Cabot, 25 July 1852, AFP-SL; James Amsted Brown, 6 Apr. 1859, 17 Aug. 1858, Journal, VHS; Albert Thorndike, 2 Feb. 1860, Log, BHS; Charles F. Low, 18 July 1859, 9 Jan. 1860, 6 July 1857, Diary (the two years mentioned were 1859 and 1860), BPL; William Hoyt, 15 Feb. 1851, Journal, BPL; J. Reynolds Hixon, 10 Dec. 1836, Diary, OCHS. Apperson, *Social History of Smoking.*
29. Frederick Lathrop Gleason, 1 Jan. 1861, Journal, CHS; Charles M. Cobb, 16 Apr. 1850, Journal, VHS; Forten, *Journals of Charlotte Forten Grimké,* 31 Jan. 1857, 187; John Park, 24 Jan. 1839, 29 Jan. 1844, 10 June 1848, Diary, BPL.
30. Persis Sibley Andrews, 20 Feb. 1842, Diary, DFP-MHS; Sarah Everett Hale to Nathan Hale Jr., 11 July 1840, HP-SSC; Calista Billings, 2 Oct., 18 Sept., 29 July 1849, Diary, SL; Rebecca Chase Kinsman to Parents and sisters, 6 Mar. 1844, MP-SSC; Katherine Bigelow Lawrence Jr., 29 Nov. 1850, Journal, LFP-MHS.
31. Mary Mudge, 24 May 1854, High School Common-Place Book, SL; I. W. Chapman, 27 Feb. 1851, Diary, CHS; John Hoyt, 9 May 1849, Diary, JHP-NEHGS; Stephen Salisbury III, 18 Feb. 1854, Diary, SFP-AAS; Alexander Hill Everett, 31 July 1840, Diary, ENP-MHS; Martha Osborne Barrett to Mary Paige Gove Cartland, 26 Feb. 1854, HL-HU; Hannah Lowell Jackson Cabot, 21 Dec. 1839, Diary, AFP-SL; Helen M. Warner, 16 Dec. 1850, Diary, NEHGS; Mellen Chamberlain, 23 Oct. 1845, Diary, BPL; William T. Gilbert, 17 Sept. 1860, Diary, CHS; James Barnard Blake, 3 Dec. 1851, Diary, AAS; Arozina Perkins, c. Aug.–Sept. 1849, Diary, CHS; Frederick Lathrop Gleason, 31 Jan. 1859, Journal, CHS; Nathan Kilbourn Abbott, 11 Oct. 1859, Diary, NHHS; Henry Clarke Wright, 24, 23 Feb. 1852, Journal, BPL;

Nathaniel Cheever to Elizabeth B. Cheever, 26 Oct. 1837, CFP-AAS; Georgina Lowell, 7 Aug. 1856, Journal, FCLP-MHS; Elizabeth H. Jocelyn, 14 June 1839, Diary, JFP-CHS; Catherine S. Patton, 3 July 1845, Journal, CHS; Forten, *Journals of Charlotte Forten Grimké,* 11 Mar. 1858, 291–92; William Sherwood, 25 Mar. 1853, Memorandum Book, WSP-YUb; John Hoyt to Elizabeth T. Hoyt, 20 Mar. 1849, JHP-NEHGS; Caroline A. Stoddard, 29 June 1856, Journal, PEM; John Hoyt, 21 Apr. 1849, Diary, JHP-NEHGS; Mary Pierce Poor to John Pierce and Lucy (Tappan) Pierce, 27 Apr. 1838, PoFP-SL; John Hoyt, 13 May 1849, Diary, JHP-NEHGS; Arozina Perkins, 4 Aug. 1849, Diary, CHS; Martha Joanna Reade Nash Lamb, expenses entered after 15 Aug. 1854, Memorandum Book, MJRNLP-SSC; Nathan Kilbourn Abbott, 3, 10 Oct. 1859, Diary, NHHS; Sarah Brown to Cyrus S. Brown and Family, Saturday Evening, [c. 1861], BFP-MeHS. On reading on the rails, Zboray, *Fictive People,* chap. 5, and Hayes, "Railway Reading."

32. Catherine S. Patton, 3 July 1845, Journal, CHS; Mary H. Snell, 6 Feb. 1839, Journal, PEM; Isaac Webb to Sarah I. (McClellan) Webb, 10 Nov. 1840, MP-CHS; William Sherwood, 10 May 1853, Memorandum Book, 1855 [includes dates from 1852 and 1853], WSP-YUb; Low, *Lights and Shadows,* 25 Nov. 1833, 2:661; Mary Gardner Lowell, 18 July 1851, Diary, FCLP-MHS.
33. Arozina Perkins, c. Aug.–Sept. 1849, Diary, CHS; Sarah P. E. Hale to Nathan Hale Jr. and other children, 16 Aug. 1843, HP-SSC; Elizabeth Atwater Charnley, 3 Aug. 1835, Journal, CHS.
34. Grier, *Culture and Comfort;* Heininger, *At Home with a Book;* and Kruger, "Home Libraries."
35. Joshua Edwin Harris to George A. Callahan, 19 June 1859, 2 May 1858, Letterbook, JEHP-MeHS; Christopher Keith, 3 May 1858, Diary, MMC-RIHS; Sarah Alden Bradford Ripley to George F. Simmons, 19 July 1844 in 16 July 1844, SABRP-SL; James Barnard Blake, 4 Jan., 30 Mar. 1851, Diary, AAS; unidentified night watchman to G. W. Walton, 7 Apr. 1856, ATHM.
36. Annie B. Lawrence Rotch, 31 May 1845, Diary, LFP-MHS; Fanny [Webb?] to Sarah Watson Dana, 24 Apr. 1838, DFP-SL; John Hoyt to Elizabeth T. Hoyt, 27 Dec. 1849 in 25 Dec. 1849, JHP-NEHGS.
37. Low, *Lights and Shadows,* 9 Feb. 1833, 2:504; Persis Sibley Andrews, 21 Nov. 1841, Diary, MeHS; Martha Osborne Barrett, 30 June 1850, Diary, PEM; Forten, *Journals of Charlotte Forten Grimké,* 1 Jan. 1860, 361–62; on books as friends, see Booth, *Company We Keep,* chap. 6; Haney, "Aesthetics and Ethics"; and Buell, "Introduction." Hansen, *Very Social Time.*

Chapter 10

1. Mary Pierce Poor to Henry Varnum Poor, 10 Oct. 1839, PoFP-SL. Harvard Law School's Greenleaf was adverse to married women's property rights. Avery and Konefsy, "Daughters of Job." On coverture, see Kerber, *No Constitutional Right to Be Ladies,* chap. 1–3.
2. Bode, *American Lyceum;* Cayton, "Making of an American Prophet"; Deese and Woodall, "Calendar of Lectures"; Scott, "Itinerant Lecturers"; Scott, "Popular Lecture";

Ray, "Pupils, Spectators, Citizens." While lecture-going had a history prior to the 1830s, most of it was open only to "exclusive or specialized audiences" (Scott, "Popular Lecture," 792).

3. The social and performance-oriented nature of churchgoing is underscored in Hansen's *Very Social Time.* On the lack of cultural hierarchy permitting these venues to be considered together, see Levine, *Highbrow/Lowbrow.* Below we consider all forms of lectures: those organized by lyceum or reform societies as well as those offered by entrepreneurs or self promoters (Scott, "Itinerant Lecturers," 70–73; Zboray and Zboray, *Literary Dollars,* 164–66).
4. Harriet Jane Hanson Robinson, 18 Mar. 1855, Diary, RSP-SL; Emmeline Augusta Ober, 24 Dec. 1851, Diary, BHS. Symbolic interactionists' work on intersubjectivity deals with collective reception (Hewitt, *Dilemmas;* Deegan, *American Ritual Dramas*), but few humanities scholars working on historical topics have explicitly tackled the concept. Work on crowd psychology emerging after Rudé's *Crowd* (1959) emphasizes collective action, not reception. The phenomenology of collective reception eludes work on collective memory (Neal, *National Trauma and Collective Memory;* Kammen, *Mystic Chords of Memory*). Kenneth Burke's dramatism has spawned some analyses of shared understanding and collective action called "consubstantiality" (e.g., Kimberling, *Kenneth Burke's Dramatism*). A Burkean analysis would see audience members as both participants and observers. "Participant observer," of course, derives from anthropology (see Stewart, *Ethnographer's Method;* Porter, *Seeing and Being,* applies it to historical insiders).
5. For background on the social logistics of these participant observers as they prepared to attend performances, see Hale, *New England Boyhood,* 152–58. On the circuit, see Ono, "Concord Lyceum"; Rowell, "Lyceum Sketchbook"; Cameron, *Massachusetts Lyceum;* and Putnam, *Petersham Lyceum.*
6. Mellen Chamberlain, 30 Nov. 1847, Diary, BPL; Morrow, *Tiger! Tiger!;* Louisa Gilman Loring to Anna Loring, 6 Feb. 1856, EGLFP-SL; Hannah Lowell Jackson Cabot to Sarah (Jackson) Russell, 14 Dec. 1838, AFP-SL; Persis Sibley Andrews, 24 Sept. 1841, Diary, MeHS. On advertisements for lectures, see Scott, "Itinerant Lecturers," 72–74. Sarah in Waterbury, Conn., to brother, 19 Dec. 1852, MGLC-ATHM; Emmeline Augusta Ober, 17 Aug. 1852, Diary, BHS.
7. Sarah Smith (Cox) Browne to Sarah Ellen Browne, 25 Jan. 1857, SEBP-SL; on the Lyceum season ticket, see entry for 29 Nov. 1856 in her Account of Family Expenses, 1853–57, BroFP-SL. William Hoyt, 6 Feb., 12 Mar. 1851, Journal, BPL; Sarah Jocelyn, 21 Feb. 1840, Diary, JFP-CHS; Hannah Lowell Jackson Cabot to Sarah (Jackson) Russell, 13 Mar. 1836, AFP-SL.
8. Cynthia Sprague Congdon, 10–12 Jan. 1842, Journal, CFP-RIHS; John Park, 7 Dec. 1837, Diary, BPL; William Willis, 10 Dec. 1845, Diary, MeHS via PPL; Elizabeth Pierce, 16 Dec. 1830, Journal, PoFP-SL; Henry Wyles Cushman, "Monday," Oct. 1860, Diary, HWCC-NEHGS; see also Daniel F. Child and Mary D. Child, 12 Mar. 1855, Diary, DFCP-MHS. The flavor of Gleason's sex-education lectures can be garnered from a sheet he circulated a week before visiting Norwich, New York: "Dr. Gleason, of Philadelphia, the well-known lecturer on anatomy and physiology, will deliver a chaste, amusing, scientific and instructive lecture to gentlemen only on the

anatomy, physiology and philosophy of healthy reproduction, and the laws of hereditary descent . . . , Illustrated with the largest collection of models . . ."; in Miner Medical Library, Univ. of Rochester, Rochester, N.Y. See also Gleason, *Seven Lectures.* Daniel F. Child and Mary D. Child, 18 Mar. 1840, Diary, DFCP-MHS.

9. Joshua Edwin Harris, 7 Feb. 1856, Journal, JEHP-MeHS. Edwin Leigh Furness, 15 Nov. 1848, Journal, MeHS; Francis Bennett, 29 Nov. 1854, Diary, AAS; Eliza Bancroft Davis to John Davis, 11 Dec. 1836, JDP-AAS; Forten, *Journals of Charlotte Forten Grimké,* 5 Sept. 1854, 98.
10. John Park, 9 Feb. 1843, Diary, BPL; Phebe Beede Clark, 26 Nov. 1856, Diary, LHS; Sarah P. E. Hale to Edward Everett, 10 Nov. 1837, HP-SSC.
11. Annie B. Lawrence Rotch, 1 Nov. 1839, Diary, LFP-MHS; Frederick Lathrop Gleason, 7 Feb. 1860, Journal, CHS; Martha Osborne Barrett, 1 Jan. 1855, Diary, PEM; John Park, 31 Jan., 21 Feb. 1846, Diary, BPL. Ellis Gray Loring, 22 Mar. 1838, Diary, vol. 4, 22 Mar. 1838, EGLFP-SL; Mellen Chamberlain, 30 Nov. 1847, Diary, BPL; Forten, *Journals of Charlotte Forten Grimké,* 23 Oct. 1858, 341.
12. J. W. Bush to Henry Wyles Cushman, 30 Dec. 1855, HWCC-NEHGS; Persis Sibley Andrews, 21 June 1841, Diary, MeHS; Harriet Jane Hanson Robinson, 6 Apr. 1855, Diary, RSP-SL. On bad walking, see John Park, 19 Mar. 1840, Diary, BPL. Mary Coult Jones, 22 Jan. 1856, Diary, CHS; John Park, 21 Mar. 1839, Diary, BPL; Mellen Chamberlain, 28 Feb. 1844, Diary, BPL. On urban transportation options, see Warner, *Streetcar Suburbs;* Binford, *First Suburbs;* and Cudahy, *Cash, Tokens, and Transfers.* Some hints about the advertising on these conveyances can be found in Henkin's *City Reading.* Despite these developments, all New England cities remained essentially "walking cities" (Pred, *Making Histories*).
13. Forten, *Journals of Charlotte Forten Grimké,* 30 Jan. 1857, 186; Deborah Weston to Caroline Weston, 27 May 1847, BPL; Susan D. Tucker, 13 Feb. 1854, Journal, VHS; Frances M. Jocelyn, 2 Jan. 1851, Diary, JFP-CHS; Ann Swett Appleton to beloved sister, 8 Jan. 1847, MGLC-ATHM. William Hoyt, 5 Feb. 1851, Journal, BPL; Charles M. Cobb, 1 Apr. 1853, Journal, VHS; Emmeline Augusta Ober, 8 Jan. 1851, Diary, BHS.
14. William Willis, 3 Mar. 1852, Diary, MeHS, via PPL; John Park, 20 Nov. 1845, Diary, BPL; William Hoyt, 5 Mar. 1851, Journal, BPL; Eunice Hale Waite Cobb, 6 Dec. 1855, Diary, NEHGS; Stowe, *Christian Slave;* William Lloyd Garrison Jr., 15 Dec. 1856, GP-SSC; (the drama to which Garrison refers may be Brown's work *The Escape*). William Willis, 21 Mar. 1849, Diary, MeHS via PPL; Zachariah Allen, 6 Jan. 1856, Diary, ZAP-RIHS.
15. On women at lectures, see, Pease and Pease, *Ladies, Women, and Wenches,* 64; Higginson, *Part of a Man's Life,* 78; Scott, "Popular Lecture," 800. Philip Sage, 26 Mar. 1848, Journal, CHS; Frances M. Jocelyn, 17 Aug. 1843, Diary, JFP-CHS; Elizabeth H. Jocelyn, 21 Aug. 1839, Diary, JFP-CHS; Agnes Paine to Mary A. Byram, 17 Apr. 1848, SFP-SL; John Park, 19 Jan. 1850, Diary, BPL; Annie B. Lawrence Rotch, 23 Oct. 1839, Diary, LFP-MHS. On African Americans' segregated seating, or exclusion from entertainments, see Horton and Horton, 73–74.
16. Sarah Everett Hale to Nathan Hale Jr., 17 Nov. 1838, HP-SSC; Helen M. Warner, 28 Jan. 1851, School Journal, NEHGS; Sarah Everett Hale to Nathan Hale Jr.,

22 Nov. 1838, HP-SSC; John Park, 15 Oct. 1851, Diary, BPL; Mary Mudge, 19 Jan. 1854, High School Common-Place Book, SL; Daniel F. Child and Mary D. Child, 26 Jan. 1843, Diary, DFCP-MHS. Pattie, *Mesmer;* Gauld, *History of Hypnotism.*

17. Forten, *Journals of Charlotte Forten Grimké,* 31 Jan. 1855, 126; Eunice Hale Waite Cobb, 17 June 1856, Diary, NEHGS; Mellen Chamberlain, 28 Feb. 1844, Diary, BPL; Charlotte Brooks Everett, 17 Feb. 1846, Journal, EEP-MHS; Elizabeth Pierce, 19 Mar. 1829, Journal, PoFP-SL; George H. Durrie, 18 Feb. 1845, Diary, typescript transcript of original, NHCHS, vol. 32, via DMC-YUs; Frances M. Jocelyn, 5 Apr. 1848, Diary, JFP-CHS; Annie B. Lawrence Rotch, 7 Jan. 1840, Diary, LFP-MHS.
18. Forten, *Journals of Charlotte Forten Grimké,* 31 May 1855, 136; Helen M. Warner, 22 July 1851, School Journal, NEHGS; Philip Sage, 9 May 1848, Journal, CHS; Elizabeth Dwight Cabot to Ellen Twisleton, 31 Oct. 1852, CFP-SL; Deborah Weston to Anne W. Weston, 22 Aug. 1840, BPL; Daniel F. Child and Mary D. Child, 6 Jan. 1861, 26 Jan. 1849, Diary, DFCP-MHS; Clinton, *Fanny Kemble's Civil Wars;* Burroughs, "'Be Good!'"; William Hoyt, 12 Feb. 1851, Journal, BPL.
19. Francis Bennett, 6 Mar. 1854, Diary, AAS; Persis Sibley Andrews, 30 Oct., 1 Nov. 1841, Diary, MeHS; "Confusion worse confounded" is from book 2 of John Milton's *Paradise Lost* (1674).
20. Daniel F. Child and Mary D. Child, 15 Nov. 1850, Diary, DFCP-MHS; Frank C. Morse, 8 Apr. 1856, Diary, FCMP-MHS; Cynthia Pratt, 6 Aug. 1834, Diary, LHS; Daniel F. Child and Mary D. Child, 16 Dec. 1860, Diary, DFCP-MHS. The relationship between antebellum audiences and crowds (or mobs) is subtle (Grimsted, *Melodrama Unveiled;* Grimsted, *American Mobbing*). The police force to whom fell the hapless task of controlling the Boston crowd is treated in Lane, *Policing the City.*
21. William Hoyt, 12 Feb. 1851, Journal, BPL; Annie B. Lawrence Rotch, 29 Oct. 1839, Diary, LFP-MHS.
22. Emmeline Augusta Ober, 4 Feb. 1852, Diary, BHS; Sarah Abbott to Sisters, 3 June 1840, MJAP-AHS; Elizabeth H. Jocelyn, 10 Feb. 1848, Diary, JFP-CHS; Mary Pierce Poor to John Pierce and Lucy (Tappan) Pierce, 25 Nov. 1838, PoFP-SL; William Hoyt, 5 Feb. 1851, Journal, BPL.
23. Forten, *Journals of Charlotte Forten Grimké,* 21 Nov. 1854, 112; Stanley Fish, *Is There a Text in This Class?* 171–73.
24. On variations of "good," see Calista Billings, 23 Feb. 1849, Diary, SL; Amos Armsby, 22 Mar. 1853, Diary, AAS; Annie B. Lawrence Rotch, 24 Nov. 1838, Diary, LFP-MHS; Francis Bennett, 7 Aug. 1854, Diary, AAS; Mellen Chamberlain, 9 June 1843, Diary, BPL; Eunice Hale Waite Cobb, 19 Apr. 1854, Diary, NEHGS; Francis Bennett, 14 Feb. 1854, Diary, AAS. Persis Sibley Andrews, 28 June 1841, Diary, MeHS; J. Reynolds Hixon, 7 Oct. 1836, Diary, OCHS.
25. On negative response, see Henry Wyles Cushman, 25 Mar. 1852, Diary, HWCC-NEHGS; Charles F. Low, 27 Jan. 1859, Diary, BPL; Katherine Bigelow Lawrence Jr., 2 Apr. 1852, Journal, LFP-MHS; Hannah Lowell Jackson Cabot to Sarah (Jackson) Russell, 14 Dec. 1838, AFP-SL; Annie B. Lawrence Rotch, 7, 18 Dec. 1838, Diary, LFP-MHS; Stephen Salisbury III, 14 Nov. 1855, Diary, SFP-AAS; James Barnard Blake, 6 Jan. 1851, Diary, AAS. William Hoyt, 11 Feb. 1851, Journal, BPL; on equestrian drama, see Hrkach, "Music, Drama, and Horsemanship!"

26. John Park, 25 Feb. 1841, Diary, BPL; Ezra Warren Mudge, 16 Jan. 1850, Diary, LHS; James Barnard Blake, 3 Feb. 1851, Diary, AAS; Martha Osborne Barrett, 19 Feb. 1860, Diary, PEM; William Hoyt, 5 Feb. 1851, Journal, BPL; Eliza Bancroft Davis to John Davis, 23 Mar. 1832, JDP-AAS; William Willis, 10 Dec. 1845, Diary, MeHS via PPL; Persis Sibley Andrews, 24 May 1846, Diary, MeHS; John Park, 3 Dec. 1840, Diary, BPL; Mary E. Webster to Caroline A. Briggs, 6 Apr. 1842, BriFP-SL; William Willis, 28 Mar. 1849, Diary, MeHS via PPL.
27. Mary Mudge, 6 Dec. 1854, High School Common-Place Book, SL; Cyrus Parker Bradley, 1 May 1835, Journal, NHHS; Annie B. Lawrence Rotch, 20 Nov. 1845, Diary, LFP-MHS; John Park, 8 Jan. 1846, Diary, BPL; Elizabeth Dwight Cabot to Ellen Twisleton, 15 Apr. 1861, CFP-SL; Emma Brown to Susan Brown, Nov. 1856, BFP-MeHS via PPL.
28. Mellen Chamberlain, 19 June 1843, Diary, BPL; Martha Osborne Barrett, 1 Feb. 1852, Diary, PEM; Ann Swett Appleton to sister, [1849], MGLC-ATHM; Eliza Bancroft Davis to John Davis, 23 Mar. 1832, JDP-AAS; Annie B. Lawrence Rotch, 14 Nov. 1840, Diary, LFP-MHS. Henry Wyles Cushman, 25 Oct. 1827, Diary, HWCC-NEHGS; Forten, *Journals of Charlotte Forten Grimké,* 28 Mar. 1855, 132 (the quote is from Byron's poem "The Dream").
29. Enoch Hale, 20 Oct. 1840, Diary, PEM. Sarah Alden Bradford Ripley to George F. Simmons, 7 Jan. 1844, SABRP-SL; John Park, 2 Feb. 1837, Diary, BPL; Stephen Salisbury III, 5 Mar. 1856, Diary, SFP-AAS; Caroline Barrett White, 7 Feb. 1850, Diary, AAS; William Willis, 23 May 1855, Diary, MeHS via PPL; Annie B. Lawrence Rotch, 3 Jan. 1840, Diary, LFP-MHS; George H. Clark, 10 Mar. 1853, Diary and Memorandum Book, HBDP-RIHS. On the antithesis of the conversational style, see John Park, 2 Feb. 1837, Diary, BPL; Eunice Hale Waite Cobb, 24 Jan. 1856, Diary, NEHGS; Susan D. Tucker, 20 July 1846, Journal, VHS; Annie B. Lawrence Rotch, 7 Dec. 1838, Diary, LFP-MHS; Persis Sibley Andrews, 29 Oct., 31 May 1841, MeHS; John Park, 13 Feb. 1840, Diary, BPL; Annie B. Lawrence Rotch, 11 Dec. 1838, Diary, LFP-MHS; Mary Pierce Poor to John Pierce and Lucy (Tappan) Pierce, 25 Jan. 1837, PoFP-SL. Persis Sibley Andrews, 31 Oct. 1847, Diary, MeHS. Cmiel's *Democratic Eloquence* discusses incorporation of working-class speech patterns into public discourse.
30. Zachariah Allen, 13 Feb. 1857, Diary, ZAP-RIHS; William Willis, 23 May 1855, Diary, MeHS via PPL; Cyrus Parker Bradley, 26 Apr. 1835, Journal, NHHS; Persis Sibley Andrews, 4 May 1851, Diary, MeHS.
31. Lucy Larcom to Mrs. S. A. Spaulding, 14 Dec. 1852, CWBL-UV; Caroline Barrett White, 13 Jan. 1850, Diary, AAS; Elizabeth Pierce, 7 Jan. 1830, Journal, PoFP-SL; extract of a letter to Mrs. H. F. M. Brown, 1 Jan. 1856, in Eunice Hale Waite Cobb, Diary, NEHGS; Eunice Hale Waite Cobb, 24 Sept. 1856, Diary, NEHGS; Sarah Abbott to Sisters, 3 June 1840 MJAP-AHS; Susan D. Tucker, 14 Apr. 1853, Journal, VHS; [Henry?] S. Chamberlain to "my dear sister," 3 Oct. 1833, WCP-VHS. Campbell, *Man Cannot Speak for Her;* Mattingly, *Appropriate(ing) Dress.* On women speakers (and on Truth and other African Americans), see Cutter, *Domestic Devils,* chap. 4, and 14–15, 72–77. "Woman's sphere" scholarship stresses the limitations preventing women from entering the public arena (Ryan, *Civic Wars*). Female public

speakers facing prejudice (e.g., Lerner, *Grimké Sisters*) thus can suggest the forces silencing less outspoken women—the majority. In this view, women turned to the one avenue left open: benevolence (Hewitt, *Women's Activism and Social Change*). But some scholars focus on women as partisan activists apart from benevolence (see, for New Englanders, Formisano, "Role of Women," and our "Political News" and "Whig Women").

32. Enoch Hale, 14 July 1840, Diary, PEM; Forten, *Journals of Charlotte Forten Grimké,* 7 Mar. 1855, 129; Caroline Barrett White, 1 Aug. 1849, Diary, AAS; Ellen Wright to Martha Coffin Wright, 26 Feb. 1861, GP-SSC; Forten, *Journals of Charlotte Forten Grimké,* 14 Mar. 1855, 130; Caroline Barrett White, 14 Mar. 1850, Diary, AAS.
33. John Park, 10 Jan. 1844, Diary, BPL; Mellen Chamberlain, 14 Nov. 1844, Diary, BPL; Ann Swett Appleton to sister, [1849] MGLC-ATHM; Persis Sibley Andrews, 19 July 1845, Diary, MeHS; Helen M. Warner, 22 Jan. 1851, School Journal, NEHGS; Mellen Chamberlain, 15 Nov. 1844, Diary, BPL; Ann Swett Appleton to sister, [1849], MGLC-ATHM; Mary G. Hoskins to Mary A. Byram, 22 May 1840, SFP-SL; Bedford, *Reports,* describes the model; Sarah P. E. Hale to Edward Everett Hale, 15 Mar. 1843, HP-SSC. On Joseph R. Buchanan, see "Neurology," 79–93.
34. Daniel F. Child and Mary D. Child, 18 Dec. 1839, Diary, DFCP-MHS; Aurilla Ann Moffitt, 19 Aug. 1842, Personal Journal, OCHS; Martha Osborne Barrett, 1 Feb. 1852, Diary, PEM; Mellen Chamberlain, 21 Feb. 1844, Diary, BPL; Daniel F. Child and Mary D. Child, 12 Nov. 1847, Diary, DFCP-MHS. Daniels, *Nineteenth-Century American Science;* Daniels, *American Science in the Age of Jackson.*
35. James Lawrence Whittier, 20 Sept. 1830, 11 Feb. 1831, Diary, AAS; Susan D. Tucker, 12 Mar. 1850, Journal, VHS; Sophia Peabody to Maria Chase, 31 Jan. 1828, PFP-SSC (she may be referring to Assheton, *Historical Map of Palestine*); Mary Pierce Poor to John Pierce and Lucy (Tappan) Pierce, 9 May in 3 May 1838, PoFP-SL.
36. William Cooper Nell to Rev. Amos A. Phelps, 20 Sept. 1842, BPL; Forten, *Journals of Charlotte Forten Grimké,* 23 Apr. 1857, 213; Zboray and Zboray, *Literary Dollars,* 166.
37. Mary Belden to Sarah Watson Dana, 13 Apr. 1839, DFP-SL; John G. King to Augusta G. King, 1833, EGLP-SL; Eliza Bancroft Davis to John Davis, 8 Mar. 1832, JDP-AAS.
38. Mary Pierce Poor to John Pierce and Lucy (Tappan) Pierce, 6 Feb. 1849, PoFP-SL; Sarah Jocelyn, 21 Feb. 1840, Diary, JFP-CHS; Daniel F. Child and Mary D. Child, 8 Apr. 1840, Diary, DFCP-MHS; Frederick Lathrop Gleason, 23 Feb. 1859, Journal, CHS; Beard, *Life of Toussaint L'Ouverture;* John Park, 20 Sept. 1847, Diary, BPL.
39. See the discussion of this Walter Scott tale in chapter 1; Frances Merritt Quick, 2 Apr. 1857, Diary, FMQP-SL.

Chapter 11

1. George W. Stacy to Samuel A. Green, 5, 10 Oct. 1852, SAGP-MHS.
2. Bibliographers use "imprint" in three ways, emerging from the process of producing the printed artifact (Tanselle, *Guide* 1:xii–xiii): (1) the name of the firm or person printing the item (McMurtrie, *Printers' Marks;* Mumey, *Study of Rare Books*), (2) the entire physical work as a production artifact rather than a text (Tanselle, *Literature and*

Artifacts), and (3) the publisher (Gaskell, *New Introduction;* Bowers, *Principles of Bibliographical Description*). The very definition of imprint, then, generates three questions: Who produced the item? Who made the basic decisions? And who executed those decisions? (McKenzie, *Bibliography*). Because the book as artifact thus represents the sum of all these decisions, the study of imprints often proceeds causally backward, from the finished product to the processes that produced it. Below we attempt to enlarge the definition of imprint further by adding to it the perspective of people who used the imprint, hence the coinage, "social imprints." After all, these folks share in the production of the book's meaning, contribute to its dissemination, and, of course, are the ones who receive it into their lives. For a consideration of imprints as subset of a history of meaning to which consumers and readers contribute, see Zboray and Zboray, *Handbook,* 57–75. The imprint as a historical artifact hardly can have a social life independent of its ultimate or potential users (a serious oversight in McKenzie, *Bibliography*). Even if it remains an aborted product sitting on the shelf undistributed—as countless stories of business failure discussed in Tebbel's *History of Book Publishing* attest—at some time an author thought of producing for readers and a printer or publisher believed enough of a market or public existed to justify producing the artifact. Apart from these exceptions, most books and periodicals indeed do pass through people's hands and are used up (see Stoddard's *Marks in Books*). In fact, some popular formats like chapbooks were so much used that few survive relative to the number produced (Neuburg, "Chapbooks in America").

3. When readers/consumers are included in the frame of analysis, imprints, like other goods, exhibit a multivalency that undermines usually futile attempts to unlock *the* meaning of an object based on evidence discerned in the object itself—that is, based on "reading" through grammatically based analysis what an object "tells us" (on the latter approach, see Berger, *Reading Matter;* Barthes, "Written Clothing"; Tilley, *Material Culture and Text;* Tilley, *Reading Material Culture;* and Hodder, *Meanings of Things*). For attempts to grapple with objects' multivalency, see Zboray and Zboray, "Books, Reading"; Upton, "Ethnicity, Authenticity, and Invented Traditions"; and Csikszentmihalyi and Rochberg-Halton, *Meaning of Things.* The move toward understanding goods' multivalency relies upon the changing epistemological status accorded to both individuals and communities in being able to devise meanings against or merely different from producers' intentions. A distinction of perspective must be drawn, however, between, on the one hand, constructions taken from the viewpoint of the product, as is the case with texts in Stanley Fish's concept (in his *Is There a Text in This Class?*) of the interpretive community that converges upon and, indeed, is called into being upon a group reading a particular text, and, on the other hand, the way communities operate in the real world, in which specific items, textual or not, are but small phenomenon in a larger field of experience. On bridging interpretive and real communities, see Murphy's "Doing Audience Ethnography"; on the problem of multivocality, see Conquergood, "Rethinking Ethnography."
4. Frederick Lathrop Gleason, 5 July 1858, Journal, CHS; Mary Pierce Poor to John Pierce and Lucy (Tappan) Pierce, 23 June 1836 in 16 June 1836, PoFP-SL. Printing's industrialization affected books' monetary value. On used books, see Cannon's *American Book Collectors and Collecting.* On production cost factors, see Tryon and Charvat,

Cost Books. The cost of standard first-edition American-authored publications (not paperback pamphlets) could be prohibitive—at between $1.25 and $1.50 per volume it was usually more than a full day's labor for even white, skilled male workers, especially those with families to support (Zboray, *Fictive People,* chaps. 1 and 2). Women, children, and members of some ethnic and all racial minority groups made considerably less, so the relative costs within their budgets were that much higher. That all groups still managed to read as much as they did testifies to both the premium they put upon enriching their socioliterary experience and to the strength of dissemination activities outside of the market. Relative prices are given in McCusker, *How Much;* on women's wages, see Dublin's *Transforming Women's Work* and Goldin's *Understanding the Gender Gap;* and on issues surrounding men's, Laurie, *Artisans into Workers.* The most systematic study of New England home libraries relative to other possessions is Gilmore, *Reading Becomes a Necessity of Life;* see also the place of books in Stapp, *Afro-Americans in Antebellum Boston.*

5. Charles M. Cobb, 8 Apr. 1852, 21 Sept. 1851, 19 Apr., 12 Dec. 1850, Journal, VHS; Zboray and Zboray, "Home Libraries," 268; Sarah E. Trask, 18 Feb. 1849, Diary, BHS; Enoch Hale, 20 Dec. 1849, Diary, PEM; John Park, 18 Jan. 1839, Diary, BPL; Mellen Chamberlain, 1 Feb. 1860, Diary, BPL.
6. Rufus Marble Gay to Olive Gay Worcester, 10 Feb. 1833, SFP-SL; Wise, "World of My Books," 151; James Barnard Blake, 15 Feb. 1851, Diary, AAS; J. Reynolds Hixon, 20 Dec. 1838, Diary, OCHS.
7. John R. Congdon, 25 Dec. 1845, Journal, CFP-RIHS; Elizabeth Edwards to Rebekah S. Salisbury, 27 June 1840, SFP-AAS; John Park, 5, 9 Jan. 1838, Diary, BPL.
8. Cyrus Parker Bradley, 24 Sept. 1834, School Journal, NHHS (he refers to Allen, *American Biographical and Historical Dictionary*); John N. Van Deusen, 3 Jan. 1853, Diary, DMC-YUs; Joshua Edwin Harris, 11, 15 Feb., 6, 3 Mar. 1856, Journal, JEHP-MeHS; James Barnard Blake, 30 Oct. 1851, Diary, AAS; Frederick Lathrop Gleason, 2 July 1858, Journal, CHS.
9. Mary Caroline Sweetser, 1 May 1852, Diary, MeHS; Samuel May Jr. to John Bishop Estlin, 5 Sept. 1848, BPL; Douglass, *Vie de Frederic Douglass;* Alexander Hill Everett, 7 Dec. 1840, Diary, ENP-MHS; Patrick James Keegan to James Keeghan Sr., 14 July 1843, NSFP-SL; Joshua Lawrence Chamberlain to Frances Adams Chamberlain, 20 May 1853, CAFP-SL; Forten, *Journals of Charlotte Forten Grimké,* 8 Jan. 1855, 121. On binding, see French, *Bookbinding in Early America;* Spawn and Kinsella, *It's the Ticket;* Spawn, *Bookbinding in America;* Tomlinson and Masters, *Bookcloth;* Groves, "Judging Literary Books"; and Wolf, *From Gothic Windows to Peacocks.* On papermaking, see Hunter's *Papermaking by Hand;* Bidwell, "Size of the Sheet"; and McGaw's *Most Wonderful Machine.* On typography, see Silver, *Typefounding in America,* and Wells, "Book Typography." On pamphlets, see Schick, *Paperbound Book.*
10. Rebecca Chase Kinsman to Parents and Maria Chase, 6 Dec. 1843, MP-SSC; John Langdon, 11 Oct. 1845, Diary, NEHGS (one edition that fits the description is the 802-page quarto by Cochem, *Life and Sufferings of Christ*). Sarah P. E. Hale to Nathan Hale Sr. and Edward Everett Hale, 25 Jan. 1844, HP-SSC; Dickens, *Christmas Carol;* see Eckel, *First Editions,* 110–12. Cyrus Parker Bradley, 25 Mar. 1835, School Journal, NHHS; Reed, *Six Months in a Convent.*

11. Ellen Wright to William Wright, 16 Feb. 1861, GP-SSC; Hannah Hicock Smith, 11 Oct. 1846, Diary, CSL; Joseph Southwick Wall to "Parents," 4 Feb. 1839, WFP-AAS. For an example of the repetition of the announcement, see Gleason, "New Dress Throughout." James Healy, 20 Jan. 1849, Diary, CHC; Persis Sibley Andrews, 10 Feb. 1850, Diary, MeHS.
12. On beauty, see Katherine Bigelow Lawrence Jr., 18 Jan. 1850, Journal, LFP-MHS. Aurilla Ann Moffitt, 22 Mar. 1844, Personal Journal, OCHS. On "pretty" or elegant imprints, see Low, *Lights and Shadows,* 9 Apr. 1832, 1:312; John Park, 22 Jan. 1840, Diary, BPL; Cyrus Parker Bradley, 7 Aug. 1833, School Journal, NHHS. Frederick Lathrop Gleason, 7 Mar. 1860, Journal, CHS; Aurilla Ann Moffitt, 8 May 1841, Personal Journal, OCHS; Charles M. Cobb, 9 Mar. 1853, Journal, VHS; Electa Kimberly, 12 Mar. 1857, Diary, CHS. Illustrations often increased the monetary and, often, emotional value of books. For theoretical background, see Benjamin's "Work of Art." Resources on illustrations include Weitenkampf, *American Graphic Art;* Peters, *America on Stone;* Hamilton, *Early American Book Illustrators;* Tatham, *Lure of the Striped Pig;* Pierce and Slautterback, *Boston Lithography;* Pierce, Slautterback, and Barnhill, *Early American Lithography;* and Smith, Hastedt, and Dyal, *American Book.*
13. John R. Congdon, 25 May 1841, Journal, CFP-RIHS. On the first image discussed, see fig. 8.2.
14. Louisa Lee Waterhouse, 11 Apr. 1840, Journal, LLWP-MHS. Zboray, *Fictive People,* 13, 69, 72–75; Gaskell, *New Introduction,* 189–273. Charlotte Henrietta Pettibone, 9 July 1841, Diary, CHS; Charles F. Low, 8 Feb. 1857, Diary, BPL; Cyrus Parker Bradley, 19 Aug. 1834, School Journal, NHHS. Nathan Kilbourn Abbott, 19 Dec. 1855, Diary, NHHS; John R. Congdon to Mary R. Congdon, 12 Apr. 1856, CFP-RIHS; Louisa Jane Park Hall postscript to William Hall, in Harriet W. Hall to William Hall, 8 Feb. 1855, PFP-AAS. The antiquarian book trade was also flourishing (Stern, *Antiquarian Bookselling;* Stoddard, *"Put a Resolute"*). Such veneration of handcrafted book production took place as it was fading due to industrialization (Comparato, *Books for the Millions;* Comparato, *Chronicles of Genius and Folly;* cf. Silver, *American Printer;* Hamilton, *Country Printer*).
15. Sarah P. E. Hale to Edward Everett, 1 Dec. 1851, HP-SSC; Helen M. Warner, 10 Nov. 1851, Diary, NEHGS. Valuing of objects merely for themselves must be distinguished from antebellum New Englanders' mode of consumption in which they cumulatively charged objects with social and familial meanings, a persisting but weakened pattern (Csikszentmihalyi and Rochberg-Halton, *Meaning of Things*); it had continued strongly until the turn of the century (Grier, "Decline of the Memory Palace"). Compare this attitude with the twentieth-century producer-oriented notion of "planned obsolescence"—goods produced explicitly to decrease in value over time (Packard, *Waste Makers*). Some books' genealogies can be traced through "provenance research" (Pearson, *Provenance Research*).
16. Rebecca Chase Kinsman to Parents and sisters, 16 Dec. 1843, MP-SSC; Mary Pierce Poor to John Pierce and Lucy (Tappan) Pierce, 25 Jan. 1837, PoFP-SL; see also Elizabeth Edwards to Rebekah S. Salisbury, 27 June 1840, SFP-AAS.
17. Cynthia Sprague Congdon, 30 Dec. 1852, Journal, CFP-RIHS. Mary R. Congdon, Journal, 24 Nov. 1854–26 Dec. 1854, CFP-RIHS.

18. George M. Gage to George Forster Allen, 20 July 1857, GFAPD-PEM; Mary Pierce Poor to Laura Stone, 3 Feb. 1850, PoFP-SL; John Park, 31 May 1839, Diary, BPL. See also Buckingham, *Personal Memoirs* 1:26.
19. I. S. Wheeler to Moses Adams III, 3 July 1820, transcript in Moses Adams III, Common Place Book, No. 2, c. June 1835, p. 31, MAP-BC; Samuel May Jr. to Richard D. Webb, 24 July 1855, BPL.
20. Enoch Hale, 5 Aug. 1842, Diary, PEM; Elizabeth Abbot to Hannah L. Rantoul, 20 Dec. 1839, EC-BHS; Sarah L. Edes, 2 Feb., 9 Jan., 8 May 1852, Diary, AAS. Mary Pierce Poor to Lucy (Pierce) Hedge, 18 Apr. 1853, PoFP-SL.
21. Joseph Caples, Memoir, c. 1948, p. 27, CSL. On the therapeutic uses of quassia cedron, especially for treating malaria, see Purple, *Observations.*
22. Sarah P. E. Hale to Jane Hurdock Hale, 23 Nov. 1850, HP-SSC; William Wheeler, Mar. 1831, Journal, vol. 4, WWP-CSL.
23. With imprints bearing social and familial value little wonder that folks struggled mightily to preserve them. Discussion of amateur preservation practices flits through recent technical works on archival studies and rare books librarianship, such as Berner, *Archival Theory and Practice;* Ford, *Archival Principles and Practice;* and Ogden, *Preservation.*
24. Thaddeus Kingsley DeWolf, 10 Dec. 1855, Diary, NEHGS.
25. Sarah Smith (Cox) Browne to Sarah Ellen Browne, 25 Sept. 1856, SEBP-SL; Gaskell, *New Introduction,* 146–53, 231–49; Daniel F. Child and Mary D. Child, 4 Apr. 1851, Diary, DFCP-MHS. Frederick Lathrop Gleason, 14 Apr. 1859, Journal, CHS; Sarah Smith (Cox) Browne, 24 July 1849, Account Book, BroFP-SL. On rolls, newspapers, magazines, sheet music, and illustrations, see Carson Dana Benton, 5 Dec. 1843, Diary, CSL; Seth Shaler Arnold, 15 Aug. 1848, Journal, VHS; Frederick Lathrop Gleason, 21 Feb. 1859, Journal, CHS; Helen M. Warner, 18 June 1851, School Journal, NEHGS; Julius Catlin, 7 Feb. 1846, Diary, CHS; Sarah Smith (Cox) Browne, 25 Mar. 1843, Family Account Book entries, 1834–45, BroFP-SL. Joshua Edwin Harris, 9, 23 Dec. 1856, 9 Feb., 18 May, 30 June, 24 July, 18 Aug. 1857, Journal, JEHP-MeHS; Mary Elizabeth Fiske, 23 Feb. 1843, 7 Apr. 1842, Diary, LxHS; Cyrus Parker Bradley, 21 Oct. 1835, Journal, and 3 Mar. 1835, School Journal, NHHS.
26. On binding costs, see William Willis, 19 Sept., 4 Oct. 1845, Diary, MeHS via PPL; Sarah I. (McClellan) Webb, 8 Feb. 1861, Recipes, Clothing Patterns, and Accounts, late 1850s to early 1860s, MP-CHS. On materials in an office, see William Hoyt, 19 Feb. 1851, Journal, BPL. Frances Merritt Quick, 24 May 1854, School Journal, FMQP-SL; Hannah Hicock Smith, 23 Dec. 1846, Diary, CSL; Charles M. Cobb, 22, 18 June 1851, Journal, VHS. Hannah Hicock Smith, 4 July 1849, 17 Apr. 1849, Diary, CSL; William Wheeler, Journal, n.d., vol. 5, p. 76, WWP-CSL. On wallpaper and wrapping paper, see Eunice Callender, Diary, 1808–24, SL; Seth Shaler Arnold, Notebook, no. 1086, VHS. Gaskell, *New Introduction,* 147–53, 231–49.
27. Hannah Hicock Smith, 16 Jan. 1850, Diary, CSL; Sarah Everett Hale to Nathan Hale Jr., [c. 1838–39], HP-SSC (she may be referring to Stearns, *Life and Select Discourses*); Persis Sibley Andrews, 20 June 1847, Diary, MeHS; Mellen Chamberlain, 7 Aug. 1847, Diary, BPL.
28. Helen M. Warner, 9 Aug. 1851, School Journal, NEHGS; John Park, 26 Aug. 1843, Diary, BPL. Molds and mildews are considered in Florian and Manning, "Ecology";

for other types of maladies, see Schechter's *Basic Book Repair Methods.* Petroski, in *Book on the Bookshelf,* ruminates over the most common storage system; Kruger's "Home Libraries" provides historical background, as does Heininger's *At Home with a Book* and Brooks's *Brief Illustrated History.*

29. S. W. Goddard to Annie De Wolf Middleton, 9 June 1852, MFP-SCHS; Stephen Salisbury III, 10 Sept., 8 Oct. 1853, Diary, SFP-AAS; Sarah I. (McClellan) Webb, 12 Jan. 1860, Recipes, Clothing Patterns, and Accounts, MP-CHS; Lorenza Stevens Berbineau, 14 Nov. 1854, line-a-day Journal and Almanac, vol. 123, FCLP-MHS; J. Reynolds Hixon, 7 Jan. 1837, Diary, OCHS; Hannah Hicock Smith, 10, 11 Dec. 1847, Diary, CSL; Charles F. Low, 1, 4–7, 9 Mar. 1857, Diary, BPL.
30. Levi Abbott, undated entry, Journal 1841–1863, pp. 200–201 NHHS; Enoch Hale, 20 Dec. 1849, Diary, PEM; Zboray and Zboray, "Home Libraries," 70; John Park, 1 Nov. 1849, Diary, BPL; Low, *Lights and Shadows,* 22 Apr. 1831, 1:221; John Park, 31 Oct. 1843, Diary, BPL (he began on 27 Oct. 1843). Daniel Stearns, 18 Apr. 1841, Diary, NHHS; Edwin Olmsted, 7 Nov. 1830, Diary, CSL.
31. Cornelia Jocelyn Foster, 15 Jan. 1861, Diary, JFP-CHS; Stephen Salisbury III, 20, 23 June 1860, 8 June 1852, Diary, SFP-AAS; John Park, 24 Jan. 1839, 1 Nov. 1849, Diary, BPL; Sarah B. Mason Ruggles Eaton, 26 May 1848, Diary, RIHS; James Barnard Blake, 29 June, 6 July 1851, Diary, AAS; Sarah P. E. Hale to Nathan Hale Jr., [1840?], HP-SSC; Lucy Charnley Bradner, 13 May 1857, Journal, CHS; Zachariah Allen, 24 Dec. 1855, Diary, ZAP-RIHS. Grier, "Decline of the Memory Palace." Histories of vernacular domestic architecture suggest the place of libraries amid the changing dispositions of interior space, but because these works are often based upon pattern books or floor plans, they need to be approached cautiously in light of actual uses (Reiff, *Houses from Books;* Fields, Zingman-Leith, and Zingman-Leith, *Secret Life of Victorian Houses;* Sweeting, *Reading Houses and Building Books;* Nylander, *Our Own Snug Fireside;* Bushman, *Refinement of America;* and Clark, *American Family Home*).
32. Sophia Peabody to Maria Chase, [11 Oct. 1829?], PFP-SSC; Sarah L. Chamberlain to Miss Abigail Chamberlain, 28 Mar. 1836, WCP-VHS; Helen M. Warner, 9 Aug. 1851, School Journal, NEHGS; James Amsted Brown, 16 May 1858, Journal, VHS; Charles M. Cobb, 19 Apr. 1850, Journal, VHS; the entry for the date also includes a floor plan; Harriet Prescott to Elizabeth Ellis (Prescott) Betton, 1 Oct. 1834, BFL-PEM; Low, *Lights and Shadows,* 28 Feb., 5 Apr. 1830, 1:109, 131; Clarrisa Angeline Bodman to Philena (Hawks) Bodman, 8 Apr. 1852, BFP-SSC; Sarah P. E. Hale to Nathan Hale Jr., [1840?], HP-SSC; Susan D. Tucker, 2 Nov. 1854, Journal, VHS; Eliza Bancroft Davis to John Davis, 12 May 1838, JDP-AAS; John Park, 31 Mar. 1845, 9 Oct. 1843, Diary, BPL.
33. John Park, 11–13, 23, 30 Jan. 1845, Diary, BPL; on other instances of drying, see 16, 21, 23, and 24 Jan. 1845.
34. John Park, 13 Jan. 1845, Diary, BPL; Sophia Ellsworth to Delia E. Taintor, 2 June 1858, TDFP-AAS; Susan D. Tucker, 11 Feb., 2 Mar. 1846, Journal, VHS; Persis Sibley Andrews, 16 Dec. 1849, Diary, MeHS.

CHAPTER 12

1. Persis Sibley Andrews, 28 Mar. 1842, Diary, DFP-MHS.
2. Ibid. Literary scholars seeking what reading in history means for textual interpretation provide essential background here. New Critics' close textual readings gave way to poststructuralists' including the reader (Machor and Goldstein, *Reception Study,* ix–xvii; Mailloux, *Interpretive Conventions;* Tompkins, *Reader-Response Criticism;* Tompkins, "Reader in History"; Suleiman, "Varieties of Audience-Oriented Criticism"; Davidson, *Reading in America,* 1–26; Davidson, *Revolution and the Word,* 3–14). Since most aimed to enrich, develop, or liberate literary criticism, they employed methods of historical analysis insofar as it furthered those ends. Some pointed to historical methodology's limitations themselves or summoned writers, such as Michel Foucault and Jacques Derrida, who did so (Armstrong and Tennenhouse, *Imaginary Puritan*). Machor's introduction to his *Readers in History* targets the less-than-historical aspects of such figures as Wolfgang Iser, Hans Robert Jauss, Stanley Fish, and Stephen Greenblatt as being "transhistorical" or "disappointing in terms of advancing our understanding of the . . . textual engagement of audience as historical phenomena" (viii–x). Though these studies share an interest in readers, they construct them differently. Some examine the discourse of criticism by applying "informed reader" analysis (Machor, "Fiction and Informed Reading"). Among these informed readers are reviewers (Baym, *Novels, Readers, and Reviewers*). Greater articulation is often one reason given for studying reviewers over common readers, based on the assumption that such readers are less articulate or their response is harder to find—an assumption which for antebellum New Englanders is unfounded. A rationale for studying the response of these readers and a demonstration of a technique for doing so can be seen in our "'Have You Read . . . ?'" Using readers' life writings to understand their reading response makes considerations of specific texts, writers, or genres seem much too narrowly conceived. In particular, such studies point away from the quest for, say, "the fiction reader" as a construct often undertaken in pursuit of a greater textual "indeterminancy" putatively yielding a response more worthy of study; see Iser, *Prospecting* and his *Fictive and the Imaginary.* As can be seen in our many cases of creative reading of nonfictional texts, this is not the case here; readers respond in essentially similar ways to both fiction and nonfiction; indeed, some of the strongest emotional responses are not to fiction but to newspapers.
3. Zboray and Zboray, "Have You Read . . . ?" Stephen G. Clarke to Chase P. Parsons, 17 Dec. 1855, PaFP-SL (he meant "Yenadizze"); Longfellow, *Song of Hiawatha,* 316; Feroline (Pierce) Fox to Mary Pierce Poor, 24 Feb. 1856, PoFP-SL; George Barrell Cheever to Charlotte Barrell Cheever, 20 Oct. 1838, CFP-AAS; Martha Osborne Barrett, 23 Sept. 1860, Diary, PEM.
4. John Park, 15 Mar. 1851, Diary, BPL; Joshua Edwin Harris, 6 Mar. 1856, Journal, JEHP-MeHS; Aurilla Ann Moffitt, 4, 7 Dec. 1843, Personal Journal, OCHS; Caroline A. Stoddard, 13 July 1856, Journal, PEM.
5. Forten, *Journals of Charlotte Forten Grimké,* 20 June 1854, 75; Harriet Jane Hanson Robinson, 3 June 1855, Diary, RSP-SL; Katherine Bigelow Lawrence Jr., 1 Mar. 1852, Journal, LFP-MHS; S. W. Goddard to Annie De Wolf Middleton, 9 June 1852, DMFP-SCHS.

6. Elizabeth Abbot to Charlotte Rantoul, 22 May 1833, EC-BHS; James Lockwood Wright, 21 Feb. 1834, Journal, JLWP-YUs; Louisa Lee Waterhouse, 10 Aug. 1839, Journal, LLWP-MHS.
7. Low, *Lights and Shadows,* 26 July 1829, 1:42; Helen M. Warner, 18 Oct. [1851], Diary, NEHGS; Charles M. Cobb, 10 Oct. 1852, Journal, VHS; Henry A. Worcester to Joseph E. Worcester, 31 July 1831, SFP-SL; Forten, *Journals of Charlotte Forten Grimké,* 21 Mar. 1855, 131; Rachel W. Stearns, 23 Apr. 1837, Journal, SL; William Wheeler, "Text Book," Journal, vol. 2, chap. 9, p. 78, WWP-CSL; J. Reynolds Hixon, 10 Dec. 1836, Diary, OCHS. Lucy (Pierce) Hedge to Mary Pierce Poor, 26 Mar. 1852, PoFP-SL; John Park, 14 Oct. 1851, Diary, BPL; Louisa Jane Park Hall to William Hall, 3 Apr. 1853, PFP-AAS; Sarah Everett Hale to Nathan Hale Jr., 1 Aug. 1840, HP-SSC; Elizabeth Dwight Cabot to Ellen Twisleton, 15 Aug. 1859, CFP-SL; Low, *Lights and Shadows,* 21 Aug. 1832, 2:430; Frederick Lathrop Gleason, 29 June 1858, Journal, CHS.
8. Elizabeth Dwight Cabot to Ellen Twisleton, 23 May 1854, CFP-SL; Elizabeth Pierce, 12 Jan. 1830, Journal, PoFP-SL; Louisa Lee Waterhouse, c. May 1840, Journal, LLWP-MHS; Caroline Sturgis Tappan to Ralph Waldo Emerson, undated fragment, STPP-SSC.
9. Aurilla Ann Moffitt, 18 June 1843, 4 Apr. 1850, Personal Journal, OCHS; Anna Davis Hallowell to Ellen Wright, 24 Dec. 1860, GP-SSC; Alexander Hill Everett, 27 Nov. 1840, Diary, ENP-MHS; Cyrus Parker Bradley, 16 Apr. 1835, School Journal, NHHS; John Park, 23 Feb. 1844, Diary, BPL; Alexander Hill Everett, 20 Sept. 1840, Diary, ENP-MHS; Susan D. Tucker, 1 Oct. 1854, Journal, VHS. On enjoyable reading experiences, see Isaac Child, 28 Apr. 1822, Diary, BPL; Mellen Chamberlain, 5 Dec. 1843, Diary, BPL; Aurilla Ann Moffitt, 2 Mar. 1850, Personal Journal, OCHS; Horatio A. Chandler, 26 Dec. 1840, Journal, NHHS; J. Reynolds Hixon, 15 July 1836, Diary, OCHS; Martha Osborne Barrett, 12 Feb. 1849, Diary, PEM; Cyrus Parker Bradley, 5 Mar. 1835, School Journal, NHHS. Aurilla Ann Moffitt, 25 June 1843, Personal Journal, OCHS; John Park, 28 Jan. 1848, Diary, BPL; Elizabeth Dwight Cabot to Ellen Twisleton, 22 Mar. 1859, CFP-SL. On interest and other criteria, see Baym, *Novels, Readers, Reviewers.*
10. On absorption and absorbing interest, see Feroline (Pierce) Fox to Mary Pierce Poor, 29 Nov. 1850, PoFP-SL; Aurilla Ann Moffitt, 24 Mar. 1844, Personal Journal, OCHS. James Healy, 29 June 1849, Diary, CHC; Cyrus Parker Bradley, 24 Nov. 1835, Journal, NHHS; Low, *Lights and Shadows,* 24 June 1831, 1:237; Hannah Hicock Smith, 3 Sept. 1849, Diary, CSL; Christopher Keith, 14 Feb. 1858, Diary, MMC-RIHS; Elizabeth Cary Agassiz to Mrs. Thomas Cary, 11 Mar. [1851?], ECAP-SL; Carroll Norcross, 27 Aug. 1852, Diary, CKNFP-MeHS. Sarah L. Edes, 12 Apr. 1852, Diary, AAS; Low, *Lights and Shadows,* 14 Aug. 1833, 2:605; Christopher Keith, 14 Feb. 1858, Diary, MMC-RIHS; Persis Sibley Andrews, 25 Feb. 1841, Diary, MeHS; Arozina Perkins, 12, 13 Sept. 1849, Diary, CHS.
11. Carroll Norcross, 26, 27 Aug. 1852, Diary, CKNFP-MeHS.
12. Paul Atwood Gibson, 19 Apr., 10 May 1859, Diary and Memorandum Book, NHHS; Forten, *Journals of Charlotte Forten Grimké,* 20, 22, 27 June 1854, 75, 76, 79; on *Martin Merrivale,* see Zboray and Zboray, *Literary Dollars,* 70–84. Mary Pierce Poor to Lucy (Pierce) Hedge, 20 May 1860, PoFP-SL.

13. Forten, *Journals of Charlotte Forten Grimké,* 10 May 1858, 309; Martha Osborne Barrett, 1 Oct. 1854, Diary, PEM; Frances Merritt Quick, 1 Nov. 1856, Diary, FMQP-SL; Elizabeth Dwight Cabot to Ellen Twisleton, 16 Apr. 1855, CFP-SL; Forten, *Journals of Charlotte Forten Grimké,* 27 Jan. 1855,124.
14. Lucy Larcom to Harriet Jane Hanson Robinson, 7 Apr. 1857, RSP-SL; Caroline Barrett White, 14 Mar. 1850, Diary, AAS; Forten, *Journals of Charlotte Forten Grimké,* 31 Jan. 1858, 284; Emeline Browne, 8 July 1860, Diary, CHS; Feroline (Pierce) Fox to Mary Pierce Poor, 16 Aug. 1853, PoFP-SL; Mary Pierce Poor to Mary Hudson, 27 Feb. 1842, PoFP-SL.
15. Mary G. Holbrook, 8 Aug. 1851, Diary of Personal Entries, DMC-YUs. As the number of papers in circulation mushroomed between 1830 and 1860, more and more tragic life stories potentially swarmed newsreaders' households (Dicken Garcia, *Journalistic Standards,* 49). Such news as a subject worthy of response analysis has largely eluded literary scholars, who naturally seek response to more literary texts. Some of the problem relates to news being seen as merely a vehicle of factual information, not as a rich site of social ritual; see Carey, *Communication as Culture,* 18, 21. Nord, *Communities of Journalism,* posits that traces of news readers elude study because the activity is "unremarkable" (19). True, there are a few studies that look at news events that influence literary texts (e.g., Fishkin, *From Fact to Fiction*). But response to news is more commonly traced by historians (Brown, *Knowledge Is Power;* Brown, *Strength of a People;* Cohen, *Pillars of Salt;* Leonard, *News for All;* Zboray and Zboray, "Political News"; Nord, *Communities of Journalism,* chap. 11; Dicken Garcia, *Journalistic Standards,* chap. 5). On reception of news's material aspects, see Barnhurst and Nerone, *Form of News.*
16. Elizabeth Pierce, 22 Dec. 1829, Journal PoFP-SL; Eliza Bancroft Davis to Mrs. Frederick W. Paine, 10 Mar. 1836, JDP-AAS; Charles M. Cobb, 5 Nov. 1852, Journal, VHS. On negative news, see Elizabeth Pierce, 19 Mar. 1829, Journal PoFP-SL; Charlotte De Wolf to Nathaniel Russell Middleton, 25 Sept. 1854, in Middleton, *Life in Carolina,* 86; Augusta G. King to Mrs. John G. King, 13 June 1830, EGLP-SL; Harriet Prescott to Elizabeth Ellis (Prescott) Betton, 8 June 1835, BFL-PEM; Lucy M. Nourse to Dorcas P. Gay, 7 Oct. 1839, SFP-SL; John Wilson Jr. to Mr. [and Mrs.] John Wilson, 23 July 1849, ATHM; Mary Pierce Poor to Mary Hudson, 20 Aug. 1842, PoFP-SL; Harriet Prescott to Elizabeth Ellis (Prescott) Betton, 24 Mar. 1835, BFL-PEM.
17. Sarah E. Trask, 29 May, 28 June, 10 Feb., 20 June 1849, Diary, BHS; Lucy S. Baker, 15 Jan. 1849, Diary, BHS; Eliza Bancroft Davis to John Davis, c. 1850, JDP-AAS.
18. Unidentified Irish Catholic named Crowninshield, [c. Aug. 1834], Hunting Journal, NHHS (whether his father's wound was related to the convent burning is unclear, but the juxtaposition suggests it). On the Charlestown convent burning, see Cohen, "Miss Reed."
19. Persis Sibley Andrews, 4 Apr. and 2 May 1852, Diary, MeHS.
20. C. L. Curtis to former pupils, 26 Jan. 1860 in Deborah C. Burt, Letterbook, NEHGS.
21. Charles M. Cobb, 25 Sept. 1853, Journal, VHS; Mary Mudge, 18 Jan. 1854, High School Common-Place Book, SL; Lemuel Leonard, 19 Jan. 1839, Diary, OCHS; Charles F. Low, 11 Jan. 1860, Diary, BPL; John Park, 4 Dec. 1847, Diary, BPL; James Lockwood Wright, 27 Aug. 1841, Business Journal, JLWP-YUs. At least 171 passengers perished when *The City of Erie* caught fire on Lake Erie near Silver Creek,

New York, on 9 August 1841; Mary Cecilia Rogers was murdered in New York in July 1841; vigilante "regulars" in Illinois's Rock River Valley executed two local bandits in 1841. Nord, *Communities of Journalism,* calls these individual chain reactions to diverse news stories, "linking" (254).

22. On political excitement, see Sarah Watson Dana, 11 Apr. 1834, Journal, DFP-SL. Agnes Paine to Mary A. Byram, 1 Mar. 1849, SFA-SL.
23. Ezra Warren Mudge, 25 Mar. 1850, Diary, LHS; Daniel F. Child and Mary D. Child, 30 Aug. 1850, Diary, DFCP-MHS; Lucy S. Baker, 1 Dec. 1849, Diary, BHS; John Park, 4 Dec. 1849, Diary, BPL; Annie B. Lawrence Rotch, 25 Feb. 1850, Diary, LFP-MHS; Helen M. Warner, 31 Mar. 1850, Diary, NEHGS. Mary Crowninshield Mifflin, 1 Dec. 1849, Diary, BPL; Persis Sibley Andrews, 9 Dec. 1849, Diary, MeHS; Agnes Paine to Mary A. Byram, 28 Mar. 1850, SFA-SL; Charles M. Cobb, 21 Apr. 1850, Memorandum Book, VHS. On the Parkman-Webster case, see Schama, *Dead Certainties,* 73–294. On regional crime literature, see Cohen, *Pillars of Salt,* and our "Mysteries." For unusual consideration of the "recreational uses of emotion in mid-19th-century reading" inspired by some of this sensationalism (or reflecting it), see Stewart, "Reading American Sensationalism," vi.
24. Daniel F. Child and Mary D. Child, 19 Mar. 1850, Diary, DFCP-MHS; Caroline Barrett White, 5 Sept. 1850, Diary, AAS; Frances M. Jocelyn, 2 Sept. 1850, Diary, JFP-CHS; Katherine Bigelow Lawrence Jr., 30 Aug. 1850, Journal, LFP-MHS.
25. John Park, 20 Dec. 1841, Diary, BPL; Mary Pierce Poor to John Pierce and Lucy (Tappan) Pierce, 13 Jan. 1842, PoFP-SL.
26. Activating the social through reading has a much less extensive scholarship than that for sensational response. Motz, "Private Alibi," looks at the instrumental role of reading and writing in two women's lives, while Sicherman, in "Sense and Sensibility," explores one family's reading. Kelley's "Reading Women" treats intellectual pursuits and sorority, and we, in our "Books, Reading" and "Have You Read . . . ?" consider the way the printed word was used to maintain social ties. Mary Keegan to Sarah Ann Keegan, 11 Feb. 1850, NSFP-SL; Mary Pierce Poor to Lucy (Pierce) Hedge, 18 Apr. 1853, PoFP-SL; Agnes Paine to Mary A. Byram, 1 Aug. 1848, SFP-SL.
27. Nord, *Communities of Journalism,* calls responsive forays away from the actual text "cuing" (252).
28. Persis Sibley Andrews, 4 July 1841, Diary, MeHS; John Park, 29 Oct. 1851; on an early encounter, see 19 May 1794, Diary, BPL; Harriet Jane Hanson Robinson, 4 July under 25 Nov. 1856, Diary, RSP-SL; Elizabeth Pierce, 18 June 1828, Journal PoFP-SL.
29. Electa Kimberly, 1 Sept. 1857, Diary, CHS; Cyrus Parker Bradley, 12 Sept. 1835, Journal, NHHS.
30. Low, *Lights and Shadows,* 29 Dec. 1832, 2:484; Frances Merritt Quick, 8 Oct. 1858, Diary, FMQP-SL; Mary Pierce Poor to Feroline (Pierce) Fox, 17 Apr. 1842, PoFP-SL; Persis Sibley Andrews, 13 Mar. 1845, 7 Apr. 1850, Diary, MeHS; Helen M. Warner, 11 Nov. 1851, Diary, NEHGS.
31. John R. Congdon, 13 Mar. 1847, Journal, CFP-RIHS; Mellen Chamberlain, 23 May 1845, Diary, BPL; William De Wolf to Annie De Wolf Middleton and Nathaniel Russell Middleton, 3 May in 13 Apr., and 13 Apr. 1850, DMFP-SCHS.

32. Mary R. Congdon, 20 May 1860, Journal, CFP-RIHS; Seth C. Whitehouse, 16 Jan. 1850, Journal, MeHS; Isaac Webb, 25 Jan. 1841, Diary, MP-CHS; Forten, *Journals of Charlotte Forten Grimké,* 23 May 1855, 134; Agnes Paine to Mary A. Byram, 15 Aug. 1846, SFP-SL.
33. Rufus Marble Gay to Olive Gay Worcester, 19 Feb. 1838, SFP-SL; Luella J. B. Case to Sarah E. Edgarton, n.d., HC-SL; Edward Tuckerman to Rebekah S. Salisbury, 17 Oct. 1840, SFP-AAS; Sarah L. Edes, 9 Jan., 26 Nov. 1852, Diary, AAS.
34. Perhaps because critics interested in readers were concerned with freeing interpretation from the authority of texts (the notion that texts in all circumstances mean one thing or have one best reading), they have focused on essentially "subversive" readings, those which go dramatically against the apparent "message" of the original text. Thus, for example, modern romance novels, which have often been seen as reflecting (and instrumentally effecting) women's traditional subservient role in society, spawn a range of interpretations among these books' readers that can include the undermining or challenging of that traditional role, at least when the readers themselves are interviewed; Radway, *Reading the Romance.* Davidson, in her *Revolution and the Word,* performed a similar reversal of expectations, but in this case for subversive readings of some seemingly conservative novels; Sicherman's "Reading and Ambition" shows how one woman's reading encouraged her unorthodox career; and Kelley, in her "Reading Women," applies Stephen Greenblatt's concept of self-fashioning. The insufficiency of approaches confined to texts without regard to their actual readers has been firmly established. We complement this scholarship by unearthing reading strategies beyond subversive and, especially, self-actualizing ones, but ones which also do not conform to the dictates of the text. Alongside their considerations of socially activating response, Kelley, Sicherman, and we, of course, do deal with intellectual response, for it is virtually unavoidable in the nineteenth-century northern United States. It is a point also underscored in Brown's *Knowledge Is Power;* Scott's "'These Notions'"; and Scott's "'Cultivated Mind.'" The larger bibliographical background, however, brings us back to the introduction, where we considered the possibility of an intellectual history of common folk.
35. Cyrus Parker Bradley, 5 Mar. 1833, School Journal, NHHS; Alexander Hill Everett, 2 Jan. 1839, Diary, HP-SSC; Elizabeth Dwight Cabot to Ellen Twisleton, 30 Apr. 1854, CFP-SL; John Park, 2 Mar. 1837, Diary, BPL. Christopher Keith, 12 Nov. 1854, Diary, MMC-RIHS; Frances Merritt Quick, 9 Apr. 1856, Diary, FMQP-SL; Lucy Larcom to Harriet Jane Hanson Robinson, 2 Apr. 1858, RSP-SL; Almon Benson, 3 Mar. 1838, Memoranda, NHHS.
36. Martha Osborne Barrett, 1 Oct. 1854, Diary, PEM; Charles M. Cobb, 12 Sept. 1853, Journal, VHS.
37. Sarah P. E. Hale to Edward Everett, 15 Nov. 1858, HP-SSC; Carroll Norcross, 26 Aug. 1852, Diary, CKNFP-MeHS; Ellen Bassett to Maria Nash, 21 Mar. 1855, MJRNLP-SSC; Ellen Wright to Martha Coffin Wright, 1 Nov. 1860, GP-SSC. Henry Varnum Poor to Mary Pierce Poor, 10 Feb. 1840, PoFP-SL; Mary Mudge, 17 June 1854, High School Common-Place Book, SL; Arthur, "Minister and the Merchant"; Mellen Chamberlain, 6 Dec. 1843, Diary, BPL.

38. John Park, 18 Feb. 1848, Diary, BPL; Forten, *Journals of Charlotte Forten Grimké,* 14 Aug. 1857, 249; Frances Merritt Quick, 1 Dec. 1858, Diary, FMQP-SL; Emeline Browne, 18 May 1860, Diary, CHS.
39. Mary Belden to Sarah Watson Dana, 13 Apr. 1839, DFP-SL; James Healy, 30 Dec. 1848, Diary, CHC; see also 11 Dec. 1848. On biography, see Casper, *Constructing American Lives.*
40. Osmon Cleander Baker, 29 Dec. 1832, 17, 20 July 1829, 6 Dec. 1831, 9 Feb. 1832, Diary, NHHS; Annie B. Lawrence Rotch, 19 July 1846, Diary, LFP-MHS; Eunice Hale Waite Cobb, 5 Oct. 1855, Diary, NEHGS; Mellen Chamberlain, 16 Feb. 1847, Diary, BPL; Zboray and Zboray, *Literary Dollars,* 96–97.
41. Sarah Jocelyn, 21 Apr. 1840, Diary, JFP-CHS; John Park, 9 July 1840, 12 Aug. 1848, Diary, BPL; Sarah Everett Hale to Nathan Hale Jr., 10 Oct. 1838, HP-SSC; Samuel May Jr. to Dr. John Bishop Estlin, 19 Dec. 1845, BPL; Cyrus Parker Bradley, 17 Apr. 1835, Journal, NHHS; Katherine Bigelow Lawrence Jr., 22 Feb. 1851, Journal, LFP-MHS; Mellen Chamberlain, 17 Aug. 1847, Diary, BPL; Mary Gardner Lowell, 13 Aug. 1853, Personal Journal, vol. 88, FCLP-MHS; James Amsted Brown, 27 Mar. 1859, Journal, VHS; Frances M. Jocelyn, 12 Nov. 1842, Diary, JFP-CHS; Charlotte Forten, *Journals of Charlotte Forten Grimké,* 30 Jan 1859, 352; Aurilla Ann Moffitt, 22 Sept. 1844, Personal Journal, OCHS.
42. On conversational style, see Elizabeth Pierce, 8 Jan. 1830, Journal, PoFP-SL; Christopher Keith, 29 Oct. 1857, Diary, MMC-RIHS; Ellen Wright to Lucy McKim, 16 Feb. 1861, GP-SSC. Frances Merritt Quick, 20 Sept. 1858, Diary, FMQP-SL; James Amsted Brown, 23 Feb. 1858, Journal, VHS; Cyrus Parker Bradley, 10, 12 Nov. 1835, Journal, NHHS; Mellen Chamberlain, 18 Apr. 1844, Diary, BPL. Charles M. Cobb, 28 Sept. in 14 Oct. 1853, Journal, VHS; Samuel May Jr. to Richard D. Webb, 9 Mar. 1860, BPL. Augustus Dodge Rogers, 2 Dec. 1852, Diary, RFP-PEM; Hannah Lowell Jackson Cabot to Sarah (Jackson) Russell, 27 July 1836, AFP-SL.
43. Joshua Edwin Harris, 5 Apr. 1857, Journal, JEHP-MeHS; Frances Merritt Quick, 9 Apr. 1856, Diary, FMQP-SL; Frederick Lathrop Gleason, 14 Jan. 1861, Journal, CHS; Harriet Prescott to Elizabeth Ellis (Prescott) Betton, 23 July 1830, BFL-PEM; Hannah Hicock Smith, 4 Dec. 1846, 14 Jan. 1848, Diary, CSL.
44. Sarah P. E. Hale to Nathan Hale Sr. and Edward Everett Hale, 17 Jan. 1844, HP-SSC; Elizabeth Atwater Charnley, 19 Jan. 1833, Journal, CHS; Louisa Lee Waterhouse, 14 Feb. 1840, Journal, LLWP-MHS; Forten, *Journals of Charlotte Forten Grimké,* 11 Nov. 1855, 143; Clarissa Harrington, 16 Oct. 1840, "A Daily Journal," LxHS; Cynthia Sprague Congdon, 15 May 1853, Journal, CFP-RIHS; Charles M. Cobb, 27 May 1853, Journal, VHS; Low, *Lights and Shadows,* 17 Aug. 1833, 2:606; Benjamin Waterhouse Sr., quoted in Louisa Lee Waterhouse, 26 June 1839, Journal, LLWP-MHS.
45. J. Reynolds Hixon, 25 Nov. 1836, Diary, OCHS; Mary Pierce Poor to John Pierce and Lucy (Tappan) Pierce, 6 Apr. 1846, PoFP-SL; James Healy, 26 May 1849, Diary, CHC; Nathaniel Morton to Seth F. Nye, 9 Aug. 1848, in Nathaniel Morton, Diary, OCHS; Persis Sibley Andrews, 2 June 1844, Diary, MeHS; Alpheus S. Packard to Amos Lawrence, 9 July 1840, ALP2-MHS; Katherine Bigelow Lawrence Jr., 3 Sept. 1848, Journal, LFP-MHS; John Park, 7 June 1849, Diary, BPL; Charles Henry

Charlton, to Sarah E. Charlton14 Nov. 1850, inserted in Charles Henry Charlton, Diary, CHS.

46. Caroline Gardiner Curtis, 27 Jan. 1853, Diary, CFP3-MHS; J. Reynolds Hixon, 10 Jan. 1837, Diary, OCHS; George Foster Allen, 24 May 1854, Pocket Memorandum, GFAPD-PEM; William C[owper] Boyden, 14 May 1848, Diary and Poetry, BHS; William Wheeler, Journal, n.d., series 1, vol. 1, WWP-CSL; Philip Sage, 6 May 1849, Journal, CHS. Nichols, "'Blunted Hearts,'" shows women read novels without guilt in the eighteenth century.
47. Martha Osborne Barrett, 21 Jan. 1855, Diary, PEM; Christopher Keith, 16 Feb. 1858, Diary, MMC-RIHS; Almon Benson, 20 Dec. 1836, Memoranda, NHHS; Low, *Lights and Shadows,* 22 June 1832, 1:351–52.
48. Martha Osborne Barrett, 22 Oct. 1854, Diary, PEM; Christopher Keith, 16 Apr. 1858, Diary, MMC-RIHS; Elizabeth Atwater Charnley, between 25 Feb., 5 Mar. 1833, Journal, CHS; Low, *Lights and Shadows,* 14 Apr. 1833, 10 Apr. 1831, 2:537, 1:214–15; Cynthia Sprague Congdon, 26 Dec. 1852, Journal, CFP-RIHS; Lewis Brewster, 24 Oct. 1848, Diary, NHHS; see also William T. Gilbert, 14 July 1860, Diary, CHS.
49. Forten, *Journals of Charlotte Forten Grimké,* 20 Apr. 1858, 302; James Healy, 23 Feb. 1849, Diary, CHC; Almon Benson, 22 Mar. 1838, Memoranda, NHHS; Frances M. Jocelyn, 21 Feb. 1853, Diary, JFP-CHS; Enoch Hale, 18 Mar. 1843, Diary, PEM; John Park, 6 Feb. 1850, Diary, BPL; Mary Pierce Poor to Mary Hudson, 9 Jan. 1840, PoFP-SL; Mary Mudge, 16 May 1854, High School Common-Place Book, SL.
50. Joshua Edwin Harris to George A. Callahan, 4 Apr. 1858, Letterbook, JEHP-MeHS; James Healy, 24 Feb. 1849, Diary, CHC; William Hawks to Luther Bodman Jr., 26 June [1857?], BFP-SSC.
51. Harriet Prescott to Elizabeth Ellis (Prescott) Betton, 24 Mar. 1835, BFL-PEM; Sarah Smith (Cox) Browne to Sarah Ellen Browne, 30 Oct. 1857, SEBP-SL; Forten, *Journals of Charlotte Forten Grimké,* 2 July 1854, 81; Mary Pierce Poor to Laura Stone, 2 Apr. 1853, PoFP-SL; Lucy Larcom to Harriet Jane Hanson Robinson, 3 Feb. 1856 [1857?], RSP-SL.
52. Charles M. Cobb, 12 Sept. 1853, Journal, VHS; Agnes F. Herreshoff, 29 Dec. 1847, Diary, HLFP-RIHS; J. Reynolds Hixon, 10 Mar. 1836, Diary, OCHS; Emma B. Ca[mpbell?] to Olive Gay Worcester, n.d., SFUP-SL.
53. Frederick W. Treadway, 7 June 1838, Diary, CHS.
54. Osman Cleander Baker, 1 Mar. 1832, Diary, NHHS; Forten, *Journals of Charlotte Forten Grimké,* 24 Sept. 1854, 101.
55. Sarah P. E. Hale to Nathan Hale Sr. and Edward Everett Hale, 22 Jan. 1844, HP-SSC; Caroline Gardiner Curtis, 7 Sept. 1851, Diary, CFP3-MHS; Martha Osborne Barrett, 31 Aug. 1854, Diary, PEM; Osman Cleander Baker, 26 Apr. 1832, Diary, NHHS; John Townsend Trowbridge, 14 Aug. 1853, Diary, BPL. Kohn, "Jewish Peddler's Diary,"[4 June 1843], 72–73; John R. Congdon, 19 Apr. 1846, Journal, CFP-RIHS.
56. Sophia Peabody to Maria Chase, 18 Feb. 1829, PFP-SSC; John Park, 3 Jan. 1852, Diary, BPL; Charles M. Cobb, 3 Mar. 1853, Journal, VHS; Persis Sibley Andrews, 8 Apr. 1841, Diary, MeHS; Ellis Gray Loring, 20 Mar. 1838, Diary, EGLP-SL.

57. Low, *Lights and Shadows,* 15 July, 6 Nov. 1833, 15 June 1829, 18 May 1831, 2:586, 2:651, 1:28, 1:228.
58. Mary Pierce Poor to Lucy (Pierce) Hedge, 14 Mar. 1854, PoFP-SL; Giles Waldo to George Waldo, 18 July 1843, GWP-YUb; Isaac Webb to Mr. Shailer, 25 Dec. 1841, MP-CHS; Charlotte Hyde to Sarah Amanda Ives Hyde, 23 Sept. 1856, BHFP-SL.
59. Frances Merritt Quick, 9 June 1855, School Journal, FMQP-SL; Christopher Albert Greene, 1 July 1853, Diary, CAGP-RIHS; Sophie W. Ripley to Caroline Sturgis Tappan, 23 Oct. in 3 Oct. [1845], STPP-SSC; Cyrus Parker Bradley, 27 July 1835, Journal, NHHS; L. Adelaide [Kinsley?] to Salome W. Kinsley, 26 Jan. 1851, BPL; John Park, 6 Oct. 1839, Diary, BPL; Caroline Gardiner Curtis, 30 Aug. 1851, Diary, CFP3-MHS; Forten, *Journals of Charlotte Forten Grimké,* 17 June 1858, 318; Charles M. Cobb, 9 Nov. 1852, Journal, VHS; Louisa Jane Park to Agnes Park, 29 Apr. 1832, PFP-AAS; Amos Bachelder, 16 Sept., 20 Aug. 1849, Journal, transcript, NHHS; John Park, 1 Aug.1838, Diary, BPL.
60. William Hoyt, 13 Feb. 1851, Journal, BPL; Mary Keegan to Sarah Ann Keegan, 11 Feb. 1850, NSFP-SL.
61. Forten, *Journals of Charlotte Forten Grimké,* 12 Oct. 1856, 165; Low, *Lights and Shadows,* 21 June 1832, 1:351; Elizabeth Pierce to Lucy (Tappan) Pierce and John Pierce, 29 Mar. 1843, PoFP-SL. Elizabeth Pierce, undated entry, c. Apr. 1825, Notebook, PoFP-SL; Frederick Lathrop Gleason, 15 Dec. 1858, Journal, CHS; George H. Clark to S. R. Wells, 1 Dec. 1846, HBDP-RIHS; Charles M. Cobb, 1 July 1851, Journal, VHS; Christopher Keith, 2 Mar. 1858, Diary, MMC-RIHS.
62. J. Reynolds Hixon, 6 June 1837, Diary, OCHS; Persis Sibley Andrews, 25 Apr. 1841, Diary, MeHS. We discussed Cobb's Uncle Henry in chapter 9; Martha Osborne Barrett, 21 Aug. 1849, Diary, PEM; Mary Pierce Poor to Henry Varnum Poor, 17 Apr. 1841, and Mary Pierce Poor to Laura Stone, 12 July 1853, both PoFP-SL. On individual sovereignty, see Noyes, *John Humphrey Noyes,* 187.
63. Low, *Lights and Shadows,* 14 Aug. 1832, 5 Mar. 1833, 2:426, 2:519; Annie B. Lawrence Rotch, 26 Mar. 1841, Diary, LFP-MHS; Frederick Lathrop Gleason, 19 Oct. 1859, Journal, CHS; Mellen Chamberlain, 29 Feb. 1847, Diary, BPL. Augustus Dodge Rogers, 17 Mar. 1850, Diary, RFP-PEM; Catharine S. Patton, 18 July 1845, Journal, CHS; Elizabeth Pierce, 11 Mar. 1830, Journal, PoFP-SL; Cynthia Sprague Congdon, 31 May 1841, Journal, CFP-RIHS; Philip Sage, 1 Mar. 1849, Journal, CHS.
64. William Hoyt, 19 Feb. 1851, Journal, BPL; Louisa Lee Waterhouse, c. 11 Apr. 1840, Journal, LLWP-MHS.
65. John R. Congdon, 18 Feb., 30 May 1841, 2 Feb. 1845, 20 Dec. 1849, CFP-RIHS.
66. Elizabeth Dwight Cabot to Ellen Twisleton, 27 Mar. 1860, CFP-SL; Mary Pierce Poor to Mary Hudson, 1 Mar. [1840?], PoFP-SL; Mary Hudson, marginalia, in Mary Pierce Poor to Mary Hudson, 1 Mar. [1840?], PoFP-SL.
67. Joshua Edwin Harris to George A. Callahan, 4 Apr. 1858, JEHP-MeHS; John C. Park to Louisa Jane Park Hall, 27 Mar. 1839, in John Park, Diary, BPL; Elizabeth Dwight Cabot to Elizabeth L. Eliot, 25 Aug. 1844, CFP-SL; Samuel May Jr. to John Bishop Estlin, 30 Mar. 1846, BPL.
68. Henry Varnum Poor to Mary Pierce Poor, 13 Sept. 1840, PoFP-SL; Mary Pierce Poor to Henry Varnum Poor, 19 Sept. 1840, PoFP-SL.
69. Emma B. Ca[mpbell?] to Olive Gay Worcester, n.d., SFUP-SL.

Epilogue

1. James Cabot to Samuel Cabot Jr., 29 Apr. 1862; Arthur Cabot to Samuel Cabot Jr., 9 May 1862; Samuel Cabot Jr. to James Cabot, 3 Apr. [1862?], all in AFP-SL. The epigraph is drawn from Persis Sibley Andrews Black, 28 Apr. 1861, Diary, DFP-MHS. By this time, Black is married to her second husband, hence the change in name. The epilogue is based on Zboray and Zboray, "Cannonballs and Books."
2. On home-front disruptions, see Silber and Sievens, *Yankee Correspondence,* 1–24.
3. Most accounts of reading focus on military life: Wiley, *Life of Billy Yank,* 153–57; Kaser, *Books and Libraries;* and McPherson, "'Spend Much Time,'" 7–18. Cf. Stevenson, *Victorian Homefront,* chaps. 1 and 2.
4. Chartier, *Culture of Print;* Cavallo and Chartier, *History of Reading;* Radway, *Reading the Romance;* Long, "Textual Interpretation."
5. Most of these informants played a role in previous chapters; a few appear for the first time as family members or correspondents of our antebellum informant pool. We read about 430 Civil War letters and volumes of diaries.
6. Two technological innovations occurred just before the war that hinted at later developments through their impact on specific practices, but they left the overall cultural pattern in place. One of these, as we have seen, consisted of noisy home sewing machines that in the late 1850s weakened the longstanding link between needlework and oral reading. The other saw photographic albums replace literary albums and commonplace books (Butler, "Commonplace Books"). Before the war, both innovations were limited in their impact and their social distribution. Indeed, some New Englanders—specifically, the poorest rural laborers—remained virtually unaffected by these.
7. Sarah Smith (Cox) Browne, 3 May 1862, Diary, BroFP-SL; Lilly Dana, 11 July 1862, Diary, DFP-SL. See also, for example, Elizabeth Dwight Cabot to Ellen Twisleton and Mary Parkman, 7 Apr. 1862, CFP-SL; Elizabeth Dwight Cabot to Mary Parkman, 30 Mar. 1862, CFP-SL.
8. Persis Sibley Andrews Black, 17 Aug. 1862, Diary, DFP-MHS. Sarah Smith (Cox) Browne to Albert Gallatin Browne, 4 Jan. 1864, BroFP-SL; Frank C. Morse to Ellen J. Morse, 2 Apr., 25 Mar., 28 Mar. 1864, FCMP-MHS; Lilly Dana, 17, 20 June 1862, Diary, DFP-SL; Alfred J. Bacon and Catharine E. Bacon to Lilly Dana, 20 Oct. 1862, DFP-SL; Alfred J. Bacon to Lily Dana, 29 Sept. 1864, 10 July 1865, DFP-SL. See also Ellen Wright to Martha Coffin Wright, 24 June 1861, GP-SSC; Sarah Ellen Browne to Albert Gallatin Browne, 30 Jan. 1864, SEBP-SL; Arthur Cabot to Samuel Cabot Jr., 9 May 1862, AFP-SL; Edward Cox Browne to Albert Gallatin Browne, 23 Oct. 1863, BroFP-SL. Davis, "'Terrible Distinctness.'" Trachtenberg, *Reading American Photographs,* 82–89.
9. Sarah Smith (Cox) Browne, 5 Feb. 1864, Diary, BroFP-SL; Christopher Keith, 16 July 1862, at back of Diary, vol. 2, MMC-RIHS; Abby Clark Stimson, 21 July 1861, 9, 13 Oct. 1861, 13 Dec. 1862, 22 Feb. 1864, Diary, DFP-RIHS; Ellen Wright to Martha Coffin Wright, 27 May 1861, GP-SSC; see also Christopher Keith, 2 Sept. 1862, Diary, MMC-RIHS; Ellen Wright to Lucy McKim, 2 May 1861, GP-SSC. Some amateurs applied their talents to wartime production and sometimes received soldiers' letters; H. B. Howe to [Caroline A. Briggs Mason], 22 Mar. 1863, BriFP-SL; Mason, "Soldier's Dream of Home."

10. Albert Gallatin Browne to Sarah Ellen Browne and Alice Browne, [17?] Jan. 1864, BroFP-SL; Frank C. Morse to Ellen J. Morse, 6 Jan. 1864, FCMP-MHS; Ellen J. Morse to Frank C. Morse, 25 Oct. 1862, 7 Oct. 1862, FCMP-MHS. Alice Browne to Albert Gallatin Browne, Nov. 1863, BroFP-SL; see also Frank C. Morse to Ellen J. Morse, 7 Jan. 1864, and Ellen J. Morse to Frank C. Morse, 28 Sept. 1862, FCMP-MHS.
11. Silber and Sievens, *Yankee Correspondence,* 2. Hannah Lowell Jackson Cabot to Samuel Cabot Jr., 29 Apr. 1862, 12 Apr. 1863, AFP-SL; Elizabeth Dwight Cabot to Ellen Twisleton, 17 June [1861], CFP-SL; Elizabeth Dwight Cabot to Mary Parkman, 19 Oct. 1863, CFP-SL; Ellen Wright to [Frank Wright?], fragment [c. Sept. 1861], GP-SSC. Forten, *Journals of Charlotte Forten Grimké,* 27 Nov. 1862, 406–7. McPherson, "'Spend Much Time'"; Kaser, *Books and Libraries,* 78, 26–29. Daniel F. Child and, 2 Nov., 1, 28 Dec. 1862, 7, 19, 25 Jan. 1863, Diary, DFCP-MHS; Ellen J. Morse to Frank C. Morse, 7 Oct. 1862, FCMP-MHS; Frank C. Morse to Ellen J. Morse, 15 Nov. 1862, FCMP-MHS; Hannah Lowell Jackson Cabot to Samuel Cabot Jr., 2 May 1862, AFP-SL; Seth Shaler Arnold, 11 Aug. 1862, 27 Apr. 1863, 3 Mar., 9 Feb. 1864, Diary, VHS; Lilly Dana, 4 Aug. 1862, Diary, DFP-SL; Elizabeth Dwight Cabot to Mary Parkman, 20 Dec. 1863, CFP-SL; Alice Browne to Albert Gallatin Browne, Nov. 1863, and Sarah Smith (Cox) Browne to Albert Gallatin Browne, 1863, BroFP-SL; Caroline Gardiner Curtis, 19 Oct. 1864, Diary, CFP3-MHS. Attie, *Patriotic Toil,* esp. chap. 4; Forten, *Journals of Charlotte Forten Grimké,* 5 Nov. 1862, 4 Jan. 1863, 394, 435; Persis Sibley Andrews Black, 27 Oct. 1861, Diary, DFP-MHS.
12. Frank C. Morse to Ellen J. Morse, 26 Aug. 1862, 15 Oct. 1864, FCMP-MHS; Sarah Smith (Cox) Browne to Albert Gallatin Browne, 13 Oct. 1863, BroFP-SL. Sarah Smith (Cox) Browne to Albert Gallatin Browne, 3 Oct. 1864, Diary, BroFP-SL; Albert Gallatin Browne to Sarah Smith (Cox) Browne, 4 May 1865, and Albert Gallatin Browne to Edward Cox Browne, 14 Feb. 1865, BroFP-SL.
13. Ellen Wright to Beverly Chase, 29 May 1861, GP-SSC; Elizabeth Dwight Cabot to Ellen Twisleton, 11 Nov. 1861, CFP-SL.
14. Persis Sibley Andrews Black, 18 July 1852, 16 Nov. 1862, Diary, DFP-MHS. Joshua Edwin Harris, 20, 24, 31 Jan., 3 Feb. 1858, Journal, JEHP-MeHS; Caroline Gardiner Curtis, 12 July 1863, Diary, CFP3-MHS; Sarah Ellen Browne to Sarah B. Howard, 20 Nov. 1862, BroFP-SL. Daniel F. Child, 28 Dec. 1862, Diary, DFCP-MHS; Hannah Lowell Jackson Cabot to Samuel Cabot Jr., 21 Apr. 1862 in 20 Apr. 1862, AFP-SL. Frank C. Morse to Ellen J. Morse, 12 Oct. 1862, and Ellen J. Morse to Frank C. Morse, 20 Oct. 1862, FCMP-MHS; see also Sarah Smith (Cox) Browne to Albert Gallatin Browne, 12 Jan. 1863, 30 Dec. 1864, BroFP-SL.
15. Elizabeth Dwight Cabot to Ellen Twisleton and "Millsey," 3 June 1861, CFP-SL; Elizabeth Dwight Cabot to Ellen Twisleton, 14 Oct. 1861, CFP-SL; Ellen Wright to Martha Coffin Wright, 20 June, 20, 31 July, 21 Sept. 1861, GP-SSC; Seth Shaler Arnold, 25 Dec., 5 June 1863, Diary, VHS; Sarah Smith (Cox) Browne to Albert Gallatin Browne, [1863], BroFP-SL; Elizabeth Dwight Cabot to Mary Parkman, 20 Dec. 1863, CFP-SL; Caroline Gardiner Curtis, 17 June 1864, Diary, CFP3-MHS; Lilly Dana, 4 Aug. 1862, Diary, DFP-SL; see also Caroline Gardiner Curtis, 21 June 1864, Diary, CFP3-MHS. Attie, *Patriotic Toil.*

16. Zachariah Allen, 15, 22 July 1861, Diary, ZAP-RIHS; Fahs, *Imagined Civil War;* Zboray and Zboray, "Political News." Persis Sibley Andrews Black, 22 June 1862, 6 Sept. 1863, Diary, DFP-MHS; Charles M. Cobb, 18 Oct. 1861, 24 Feb., 19 Aug., 9 Nov. 1862, Journal, VHS. See also Ellen Wright to Martha Coffin Wright, 25 July 1861, GP-SSC; Sarah Smith (Cox) Browne, 20 Feb. 1862, Diary, BroFP-SL.
17. Persis Sibley Andrews Black, 11 May 1862, Diary, DFP-MHS. On related discussion, see Caroline Gardiner Curtis, 17 Apr. 1861, Diary, CFP3-MHS; Daniel F. Child, 2 Jan. 1863, Diary, DFCP-MHS; Elizabeth Dwight Cabot to Mary Parkman, 16 Aug. 1862, CFP-SL. News could generate a collective "excitement"; see Zachariah Allen, 1 Sept. 1862, Diary, ZAP-RIHS; Abby Clark Stimson, 3 Apr. 1865, Diary, DFP-RIHS. Caroline Gardiner Curtis, 23 Apr. 1861, Diary, CFP3-MHS; Elizabeth Dwight Cabot to Ellen Twisleton, 29 July 1862, CFP-SL; Kielbowicz, "Telegraph." See also Christopher Keith, 8 Nov. 1863, Diary, MMC-RIHS; Ellen Wright to Martha Coffin Wright, May 1861, GP-SSC. Elizabeth Dwight Cabot to Ellen Twisleton, 24 June [1861], CFP-SL. Sarah Smith (Cox) Browne, 12 Apr. 1865, Diary, BroFP-SL; Christopher Keith, 8 July 1864, Diary, MMC-RIHS; Charles M. Cobb, 24 Feb. 1862, Journal, VHS; Zachariah Allen, 11 Dec. 1862, Diary, ZAP-RIHS; Elizabeth Dwight Cabot to Edward Twisleton, 19 Aug. 1862, CFP-SL.
18. Sarah Smith (Cox) Browne to Albert Gallatin Browne, 15 Nov. 1863, BroFP-SL. Frank C. Morse to Ellen J. Morse, 9 Jan., 17 Apr. 1864, FCMP-MHS; Samuel Cabot Jr. to James Cabot, 3 Apr. [1862?], AFP-SL; Albert Gallatin Browne to Edward Cox Browne, 3 Dec. 1863, 19 Feb. 1864, and Edward Cox Browne to Albert Gallatin Browne, 28 Feb. 1864 (see also for maps), BroFP-SL; Albert Gallatin Browne to Alice Browne, 10 Oct. 1864, and Sarah Smith (Cox) Browne to Albert Gallatin Browne, 11 Dec. 1864, BroFP-SL, for exchange of journals; Sarah Smith (Cox) Browne to Albert Gallatin Browne, 29 Feb. 1864, BroFP-SL; see also Sarah Smith (Cox) Browne to Albert Gallatin Browne, 12 Jan. 1863, 11 Dec., 20 Jan., 15 Feb. 1864, BroFP-SL. On a father-to-be preparing for parenting, see Frank C. Morse, 17 Jan. 1863, Diary, and Frank C. Morse to Ellen J. Morse, 10 July 1864, 1 Jan. 1865, FCMP-MHS. Rose, *Victorian America,* chap. 4.
19. Albert Gallatin Browne to Edward Cox Browne, 30, 31 Oct., Dec. 1863, BroFP-SL. Ellen Wright to Martha Coffin Wright, 27 May 1861, GP-SSC.
20. Persis Sibley Andrews Black, 28 Apr. 1861, Diary, DFP-MHS. On the postbellum fate of several aspects of antebellum socioliterary experience, see Zboray and Zboray, *Literary Dollars,* 169–205.

Works Cited

Achenbaum, W. Andrew. *Old Age in the New Land: The American Experience Since 1790.* Baltimore: Johns Hopkins Univ. Press, 1978.

Alberigo, Giuseppe, Jean-Pierre Jossua, and Joseph A. Komonchak, eds. *The Reception of Vatican II.* Translated by Matthew J. O'Connell. Washington, D.C.: Catholic Univ. of America Press, 1987.

Allen, William. *An American Biographical and Historical Dictionary.* Boston: W. Hyde, 1832.

Allmendinger, David F. *Paupers and Scholars: The Transformation of Student Life in Nineteenth-Century New England.* New York: St. Martin's Press, 1975.

"The Amistad Captives." *Boston Courier,* 3 Sept. 1840.

Appadurai, Arjun, ed. *The Social Life of Things: Commodities in Cultural Perspective.* Cambridge: Cambridge Univ. Press, 1986.

Apperson, George Latimer. *The Social History of Smoking.* New York: Putnam, 1914.

Arksey, Laura, Nancy Pries, and Marcia Reed, eds. *American Diaries.* Vol. 1, *Diaries Written from 1492 to 1844.* Detroit: Gale Research, 1983.

Armstrong, Nancy, and Leonard Tennenhouse. *The Imaginary Puritan: Literature, Intellectual Labor, and the Origins of Personal Life.* Berkeley and Los Angeles: Univ. of California Press, 1992.

Arthur, Timothy Shay. "The Minister and the Merchant." In *The Tried and the Tempted.* Philadelphia: J. B. Lippincott, Grambo,1851.

Ashton, Dianne. *Rebecca Gratz: Women and Judaism in Antebellum America.* Detroit: Wayne State Univ. Press, 1997.

Assheton, J. T. *Historical Map of Palestine, or the Holy Land.* Boston: Wait and Ingraham, 1828.

Attie, Jeanie. *Patriotic Toil: Northern Women and the American Civil War.* Ithaca, N.Y.: Cornell Univ. Press, 1998.

Augst, Thomas. *The Clerk's Tale: Young Men and Moral Life in Nineteenth-Century America.* Chicago: Univ. of Chicago Press, 2003.

Avery, Dianne, and Alfred S. Konefsky. "The Daughters of Job: Property Rights and Women's Lives in Mid-Nineteenth-Century Massachusetts." *Law and History Review* 10 (1992): 323–57.

B., A. K. H. "Concerning Hurry and Leisure." *Littell's Living Age* 66 (29 Sept. 1860): 788–90.

Bahn, Eugene, and Margaret L. Bahn. *A History of Oral Interpretation.* Minneapolis: Burgess, 1970.

Bailyn, Bernard. *Education in the Forming of American Society: Needs and Opportunities for Study.* Chapel Hill: Univ. of North Carolina Press, 1960.

Ballou, Maturin Murray. *Fanny Campbell, the Female Pirate Captain; a Tale of the Revolution.* Boston: F. Gleason, 1845.

Barnes, James J. *Authors, Publishers, and Politicians: The Quest for an Anglo-American Copyright Agreement, 1815–1854.* Columbus: Ohio State Univ. Press, 1974.

Barnes, Mary Stephenson. *Long Distance Calling: A Record of Other World Communications Through Automatic Writing.* New York: William-Frederick Press, 1945.

Barnhurst, Kevin G., and John C. Nerone. *The Form of News: A History.* New York: Guilford Press, 2001.

Barthes, Roland. "The Death of the Author." In *Image, Music, Text,* by Roland Barthes, 142–48. Translated by Stephen Heath. London: Fontana, 1977.

———. "Written Clothing." In *Rethinking Popular Culture: Contemporary Perspectives in Cultural Studies,* edited by Chandra Mukerji and Michael Schudson, 424–45. Berkeley and Los Angeles: Univ. of California Press, 1991.

Baudrillard, Jean. *Symbolic Exchange and Death.* Translated by Iain Hamilton Grant. Thousand Oaks, Calif.: Sage, 1993.

Bauschinger, Sigrid. *The Trumpet of Reform: German Literature in Nineteenth-Century New England.* Translated by Thomas S. Hansen. Columbia, S.C.: Camden House, 1998.

Baym, Nina. *Novels, Readers, and Reviewers: Responses to Fiction in Antebellum America.* Ithaca, N.Y.: Cornell Univ. Press, 1984.

Beard, John Riley. *The Life of Toussaint L'Ouverture, the Negro Patriot of Hayti.* London: Ingram, Cooke, 1853.

Bedford, Gunning S. *Reports on the Artificial Anatomy of Dr. Auzoux.* New York: Vinten, 1840.

Benes, Peter, and Jane Montague Benes, eds. *Itinerancy in New England and New York.* Concord, Mass.: Boston Univ., 1986.

Benjamin, Walter. *The Arcades Project.* Translated by Howard Eiland and Kevin McLaughlin. Cambridge: Harvard Univ. Press, 1999.

———. "The Work of Art in the Age of Mechanical Reproduction." In *Illuminations,* edited by Hannah Arendt and translated by Harry Zohn, 217–51. New York: Schocken Books, 1968.

Bennett, John W. "Classical Anthropology." *American Anthropologist* 100 (1998): 951–56.

Works Cited

Berger, Arthur Asa. *Reading Matter: Multi-disciplinary Perspectives on Material Culture.* New Brunswick, N.J.: Transaction Publishers, 1992.

Berland, Kevin, Jan Kirsten Gilliam, and Kenneth A. Lockridge, eds. *The Commonplace Book of William Byrd II of Westover.* Chapel Hill: Univ. of North Carolina Press, 2001.

Berlin, James A. *Writing Instruction in Nineteenth-Century American Colleges.* Carbondale: Southern Illinois Univ. Press, 1984.

Berner, Richard C. *Archival Theory and Practice in the United States: A Historical Analysis.* Seattle: Univ. of Washington Press, 1983.

Bidwell, John. "The Size of the Sheet in America: Paper-Moulds Manufactured by N. & D. Sellers of Philadelphia." *Proceedings of the American Antiquarian Society* 87, pt. 2 (1977): 299–342.

Binford, Henry C. *The First Suburbs: Residential Communities on the Boston Periphery, 1815–1860.* Chicago: Univ. of Chicago Press, 1985.

Blecki, Catherine La Courreye, and Karin A. Wulf, eds. *Milcah Martha Moore's Book: A Commonplace Book from Revolutionary America.* University Park: Pennsylvania State Univ. Press, 1997.

Bledstein, Burton J. *The Culture of Professionalism: The Middle Class and the Development of Higher Education in America.* New York: W. W. Norton, 1976.

Bleich, David. *Readings and Feelings: An Introduction to Subjective Criticism.* Urbana, Ill.: National Council of Teachers of English, 1975.

Bloom, Lynn Z. "'I Write for Myself and Strangers': Private Diaries as Public Documents." In Bunkers and Huff, *Inscribing the Daily,* 23–37.

Blouin, Francis X. Jr. *The Boston Region 1810–1850.* Ann Arbor, Mich.: UMI Research Press, 1979.

Blumenthal, Henry. *American and French Culture, 1800–1900: Interchanges in Art, Science, Literature, and Society.* Baton Rouge: Louisiana State Univ. Press, 1975.

Bode, Carl. *American Lyceum: Town Meeting of the Mind.* New York: Oxford Univ. Press, 1956.

Bolster, W. Jeffrey. *Black Jacks: African American Seamen in the Age of Sail.* Cambridge: Harvard Univ. Press, 1997.

Booth, Wayne C. *The Company We Keep: An Ethics of Fiction.* Berkeley and Los Angeles: Univ. of California Press, 1988.

———. *The Rhetoric of Fiction.* Chicago: Univ. of Chicago Press, 1961.

Bottigheimer, Ruth B. *The Bible for Children: From the Age of Gutenberg to the Present.* New Haven, Conn.: Yale Univ. Press, 1996.

Bourdieu, Pierre. *Outline of a Theory of Practice.* Translated by Richard Nice. Cambridge: Cambridge Univ. Press, 1977.

Bourdieu, Pierre, and Jean-Claude Passeron. *Reproduction in Education, Society, and Culture.* Translated by Richard Nice. London: Sage, 1977.

Bowers, Brian. *Lengthening the Day: A History of Lighting Technology.* New York: Oxford Univ. Press, 1998.

Bowers, Fredson. *Principles of Bibliographical Description.* New York: Russell & Russell, 1949.

Bowyer, Mathew J. *They Carried the Mail: A Survey of Postal History and Hobbies.* Washington, D.C.: Robert B. Luce, 1972.

Boydston, Jeanne. *Home and Work: Housework, Wages, and the Ideology of Labor in the Early Republic.* New York: Oxford Univ. Press, 1990.

Boylan, Anne M. "Benevolence and Antislavery Activity Among African American Women in New York and Boston, 1820–1840." In Yellin and Van Horne, *Abolitionist Sisterhood,* 119–37.

———. *Sunday School: The Formation of an American Institution, 1790–1880.* New Haven, Conn.: Yale Univ. Press, 1988.

Boynton, Henry Walcott. *Annals of American Bookselling, 1638–1850.* New York: J. Wiley, 1932.

Brasher, Alan. "James Freeman Clarke's Journal Accounts of Ralph Waldo Emerson's Lectures." *Studies in the American Renaissance* 19 (1995): 83–100.

Braude, Ann. *Radical Spirits: Spiritualism and Women's Rights in Nineteenth-Century America.* Boston: Beacon Press, 1989.

Breen, T. H. "The Meanings of Things: Interpreting the Consumer Economy in the Eighteenth Century." In Brewer and Porter, *Consumption and the World of Goods,* 249–60.

Brekus, Catherine A. *Strangers and Pilgrims: Female Preaching in America.* Chapel Hill: Univ. of North Carolina Press, 1998.

Brewer, John, and Roy Porter, eds. *Consumption and the World of Goods.* London: Routledge, 1993.

Brooks, Marshall. *A Brief Illustrated History of the Bookshelf: With an Essay Which Pertains to the Subject.* Delhi, N.Y.: Birch Brook Press, 1998.

Brooks, Van Wyck. *The Flowering of New England, 1815–1865.* New York: E. P. Dutton, 1936.

Brown, Richard D. *Knowledge Is Power: The Diffusion of Information in Early America, 1700–1865.* New York: Oxford Univ. Press, 1989.

———. *The Strength of a People: The Idea of an Informed Citizenry in America, 1650–1870.* Chapel Hill: Univ. of North Carolina Press, 1996.

Brown, William Wells. *The Escape; or, A Leap for Freedom, a Drama in Five Acts.* Boston: R. F. Wallcut, 1858.

Bruford, Walter Horace. *The German Tradition of Self-Cultivation: Bildung from Humboldt to Thomas Mann.* London: Cambridge Univ. Press, 1975.

Buckingham, Joseph T. *Personal Memoirs and Recollections of Editorial Life.* 2 vols. Boston: Ticknor, Reed, and Fields, 1852.

Buckler, Patricia Prandini. "A Silent Woman Speaks: The Poetry in a Woman's Scrapbook of the 1840s." *Prospects* 16 (1991): 149–69.

Buckler, Patricia Prandini, and C. Kay Leeper. "An Antebellum Woman's Scrapbook as Autobiographical Composition." *Journal of American Culture* 14 (1991): 1–8.

Buell, Lawrence. "Introduction: In Pursuit of Ethics." *PMLA* 114 (1999): 7–19.

———. *New England Literary Culture from Revolution Through Renaissance.* Cambridge: Cambridge Univ. Press, 1986.

Bunkers, Suzanne L. *Diaries of Girls and Women: A Midwestern American Sampler.* Madison: Univ. of Wisconsin Press, 2001.

———. "Diaries: Public *and* Private Records of Women's Lives." *Legacy* 7 (1990): 17–26.

Bunkers, Suzanne L., and Cynthia Anne Huff, eds. *Inscribing the Daily: Critical Essays on Women's Diaries.* Amherst: Univ. of Massachusetts Press, 1996.

Burgum, Doug. "John Burgum (1826–1907)." In *John Burgum Historical Society,* chap. 3. At http://freepages.genealogy.rootsweb.com/~bfhs/chap3.html (accessed 27 Aug. 2004).

Burritt, Elihu. *The Learned Blacksmith: The Letters and Journals of Elihu Burritt.* Edited by Merle Curti. New York: Wilson-Erickson, 1937.

Burroughs, Catherine. "'Be Good!': Acting, Reader's Theater, and Oratory in Frances Anne Kemble's Writing." In *Romanticism and Woman Poets: Opening the Doors of Reception,* edited by Harriet Kramer Linkin and Stephen C. Behrendt, 125–43. Lexington: Univ. Press of Kentucky, 1999.

Bushman, Claudia L. *"A Good Poor Man's Wife": Being a Chronicle of Harriet Hanson Robinson and Her Family in Nineteenth-Century New England.* Hanover, N.H.: Univ. Press of New England, 1981.

Bushman, Richard L. *The Refinement of America: Persons, Houses, Cities.* New York: Knopf, 1992.

Butler, James Davie. "Commonplace Books: A Lecture." *Bibliotheca Sacra* 41 (July 1884): 478–505.

Calhoun, Daniel Hovey. *The Intelligence of a People.* Princeton, N.J.: Princeton Univ. Press, 1973.

Cameron, Kenneth Walter. *The Massachusetts Lyceum During the American Renaissance: Materials for the Study of the Oral Tradition in American Letters.* Hartford, Conn.: Transcendental Books, 1969.

Campbell, Colin. *The Romantic Ethic and the Spirit of Modern Consumerism.* Oxford: Blackwell, 1987.

———. "Understanding Traditional and Modern Patterns of Consumption in Eighteenth-Century England: A Character-Action Approach." In Brewer and Porter, *Consumption and the World of Goods,* 40–57.

Campbell, JoAnn. "'A Real Vexation': Student Writing in Mount Holyoke's Culture of Service, 1837–1865." *College English* 59 (1997): 767–88.

Campbell, Karlyn Kohrs. *Man Cannot Speak for Her.* Vol. 1, *A Critical Study of Early Feminist Rhetoric.* Westport, Conn.: Greenwood/Praeger, 1989.

Cannon, Carl L. *American Book Collectors and Collecting: From Colonial Times to the Present.* Westport, Conn.: Greenwood Press, 1969.

Capezzi, Rita A. "From Reading to Writing: American Domestic Advice Scrapbooks." Paper read at the annual meeting of the Conference on College Composition and Communication, Nashville, Tenn., 16–19 Mar. 1994. ERIC Document Reproduction Service, ED 373333.

Carey, James W. *Communication as Culture: Essays on Media and Society.* New York: Routledge, 1989.

Carvalho, David. *Forty Centuries of Ink.* 1904. Reprint, New York: Burt Franklin, 1971.

Cashin, Joan E., ed. *Our Common Affairs: Texts from Women in the Old South.* Baltimore: Johns Hopkins Univ. Press, 1996.

Casper, Scott E. *Constructing American Lives: Biography and Culture in Nineteenth-Century America.* Chapel Hill: Univ. of North Carolina Press, 1999.

Cavallo, Guglielmo, and Roger Chartier, eds. *A History of Reading in the West.* Translated by Lydia G. Cochrane. Amherst: Univ. of Massachusetts Press, 1999.

Cavell, Stanley. *Must We Mean What We Say? A Book of Essays.* New York: Scribner's, 1969.

Cayton, Mary Kupiec. *Emerson's Emergence: Self and Society in the Transformation of New England, 1800–1845.* Chapel Hill: Univ. of North Carolina Press, 1989.

———. "The Making of an American Prophet: Emerson, His Audiences, and the Rise of the Culture Industry in Nineteenth-Century America." *American Historical Review* 92 (1987): 597–620.

Certeau, Michel de. *The Practice of Everyday Life.* Translated by Steven Rendall. 2 vols. Berkeley and Los Angeles: Univ. of California Press, 1984.

Channing, William Ellery. *Self-culture: An Address Introductory to the Franklin Lectures.* Boston: Dutton and Wentworth, 1838.

Chartier, Roger, ed. *The Culture of Print: Power and the Uses of Print in Early Modern Europe.* Translated by Lydia G. Cochrane. Princeton, N.J.: Princeton Univ. Press, 1989.

Charvat, William. *Literary Publishing in America, 1790–1850.* Philadelphia: Univ. of Pennsylvania Press, 1959.

———. *The Profession of Authorship in America, 1800–1870: The Papers of William Charvat.* Edited by Matthew J. Bruccoli. Columbus: Ohio State Univ. Press, 1968.

Clark, Christopher. "Economics and Culture: Opening Up the Rural History of the Early American Northeast." *American Quarterly* 43 (1991): 279–301.

———. "The Household Economy, Market Exchange, and the Rise of Capitalism in the Connecticut Valley, 1800–1860." *Journal of Social History* 13 (1979): 169–90.

———. *The Roots of Rural Capitalism: Western Massachusetts, 1780–1860.* Ithaca, N.Y.: Cornell Univ. Press, 1990.

Clark, Clifford Edward Jr. *The American Family Home, 1800–1960.* Chapel Hill: Univ. of North Carolina Press, 1986.

Clifford, James, and George E. Marcus, eds. *Writing Culture: The Poetics and Politics of Ethnography.* Berkeley and Los Angeles: Univ. of California Press, 1986.

Clinton, Catherine. *Fanny Kemble's Civil Wars.* New York: Simon & Schuster, 2000.

Cmiel, Kenneth. *Democratic Eloquence: The Fight over Popular Speech in Nineteenth-Century America.* New York: William Morrow, 1990.

Cochem, Martin von. *The Life and Sufferings of Christ.* Philadelphia: T. K. and P. G. Collins, 1840.

Cohen, Daniel A. "Miss Reed and the Superiors: The Contradictions of Convent Life in Antebellum America." *Journal of Social History* 30 (1996): 149–84.

———. *Pillars of Salt, Monuments of Grace: New England Crime Literature and the Origins of American Popular Culture, 1674–1860.* New York: Oxford Univ. Press, 1993.

Cole, Phyllis. *Mary Moody Emerson and the Origins of Transcendentalism: A Family History.* New York: Oxford Univ. Press, 1998.

Comparato, Frank. *Books for the Millions: A History of the Men Whose Methods and Machines Packaged the Printed Word.* Harrisburg, Pa.: Stackpole, 1971.

———. *Chronicles of Genius and Folly: R. Hoe and Company and the Printing Press as a Service to Democracy.* Culver City, Calif.: Labyrinthos, 1979.

Conquergood, Dwight. "Rethinking Ethnography: Towards a Critical Cultural Politics." *Communications Monographs* 58 (1991): 179–94.

Cornelius, Janet Duitsman. *"When I Can Read My Title Clear": Literacy, Slavery, and Religion in the Antebellum South.* Columbia: Univ. of South Carolina Press, 1991.

Cott, Nancy F. *The Bonds of Womanhood: "Woman's Sphere" in New England, 1780–1835.* New Haven, Conn.: Yale Univ. Press, 1977.

Cottrol, Robert J., ed. *From African to Yankee: Narratives of Slavery and Freedom in Antebellum New England.* Armonk, N.Y.: M. E. Sharpe, 1998.

Coultrap-McQuin, Susan. *Doing Literary Business: American Women Writers in the Nineteenth Century.* Chapel Hill: Univ. of North Carolina Press, 1990.

Cowen, Wilson Walker, ed. *Melville's Marginalia.* 2 vols. New York: Garland, 1987.

Crain, Patricia. *The Story of A: The Alphabetization of America from The New England Primer to The Scarlet Letter.* Stanford, Calif.: Stanford Univ. Press, 2000.

Crane, Mary Thomas. *Framing Authority: Sayings, Self, and Society in Sixteenth-Century England.* Princeton, N.J.: Princeton Univ. Press, 1993.

Cremin, Lawrence. *American Education: The Colonial Experience, 1607–1783.* New York: Harper and Row, 1970.

———. *American Education: The National Experience, 1783–1876.* New York: Harper and Row, 1980.

Crowley, John E. "Artificial Illumination in Early America and the Definition of Domestic Space and Time." In *Travail et Loisir dans les Sociétés Pré-Industrielles,* edited by Barbara Karsky and Elise Marienstras, 59–67. Nancy, France: Presses Universitaires de Nancy, 1991.

Csikszentmihalyi, Mihaly. *Flow: The Psychology of Optimal Experience.* New York: Harper & Row, 1990.

Csikszentmihalyi, Mihaly, and Eugene Rochberg-Halton. *The Meaning of Things: Domestic Symbols and the Self.* Cambridge: Cambridge Univ. Press, 1981.

Cudahy, Brian J. *Cash, Tokens, and Transfers: A History of Urban Mass Transit in North America.* New York: Fordham Univ. Press, 1990.

Cullinan, Gerald. *The United States Postal Service.* New York: Praeger, 1968.

Culley, Margo, ed. *A Day at a Time: The Diary Literature of American Women from 1764 to the Present.* New York: Feminist Press at the City Univ. of New York, 1985.

Culver, Raymond Benjamin. *Horace Mann and Religion in the Massachusetts Public Schools.* New Haven, Conn.: Yale Univ. Press, 1929.

Curtis, Michael Kent. "The Curious History of Attempts to Suppress Antislavery Speech, Press, and Petition in 1835–1837." *Northwestern University Law Review* 89 (1995): 785–869.

Cutter, Barbara. *Domestic Devils, Battlefield Angels: The Radicalism of American Womanhood, 1830–1865.* DeKalb: Northern Illinois Univ. Press, 2003.

Dain, Phyllis, and John Y. Cole, eds. *Libraries and Scholarly Communication in the United States: The Historical Dimension.* New York: Greenwood Press, 1990.

Dall, Caroline W. H. *"Alongside": Being Notes Suggested by "A New England Boyhood" of Doctor Edward Everett Hale.* Boston: Privately printed, 1900.

Dana, Henry Swan. *History of Woodstock, Vermont.* Boston: Houghton Mifflin, 1889.

Daniels, George H. *American Science in the Age of Jackson.* New York: Columbia Univ. Press, 1968.

———, ed. *Nineteenth-Century American Science: A Reappraisal.* Evanston, Ill.: Northwestern Univ. Press, 1972.

Dauber, Kenneth. *The Idea of Authorship in America: Democratic Poetics from Franklin to Melville.* Madison: Univ. of Wisconsin Press, 1990.

Davidson, Cathy N., ed. *Reading in America: Literature and Social History.* Baltimore: Johns Hopkins Univ. Press, 1989.

———. *Revolution and the Word: The Rise of the Novel in America.* New York: Oxford Univ. Press, 1986.

Davis, David Brion, ed. *Ante-Bellum Reform.* New York: Harper & Row, 1967.

Davis, Keith F. "'A Terrible Distinctness': Photography of the Civil War Era." In *Photography in Nineteenth-Century America,* edited by Martha A. Sandweiss, 130–79. Fort Worth, Tex.: Amon Carter Museum, 1991.

De Bow, J. D. B. *Statistical View of the United States . . . , Being a Compendium of the Seventh Census.* Washington, D.C.: Beverly Tucker, 1854.

Decker, William Merrill. *Epistolary Practices: Letter Writing in America Before Telecommunications.* Chapel Hill: Univ. of North Carolina Press, 1998.

Deegan, Mary Jo. *American Ritual Dramas: Social Rules and Cultural Meanings.* New York: Greenwood Press, 1989.

Deese, Helen R., and Guy R. Woodall. "A Calendar of Lectures Presented by the Boston Society for the Diffusion of Useful Knowledge (1829–1847)." *Studies in the American Renaissance* 10 (1986): 17–68.

Denzin, Norman K., and Yvonna S. Lincoln, eds. *Handbook of Qualitative Research.* Thousand Oaks, Calif.: Sage, 1994.

Derrida, Jacques. *Dissemination.* Translated by Barbara Johnson. Chicago: Univ. of Chicago Press, 2000.

De Rosa, Deborah Carolina. "Into the Mouths of Babes: Nineteenth-Century Domestic Abolitionists' Literary Subversions." Ph.D. diss., Univ. of North Carolina, 1998.

Dibner, Martin. *Portrait of Paris Hill: A Landmark Maine Village.* Paris, Maine: Paris Hill Press, 1990.

Dickens, Charles. *A Christmas Carol in Prose, Being a Ghost Story of Christmas.* London: Chapman & Hall, 1843; New York: Harper & Brothers, 1844.

Dickerson, Donna Lee. *The Course of Tolerance: Freedom of the Press in Nineteenth-Century America.* Westport, Conn.: Greenwood Press, 1990.

Dickinson, Cindy. "Creating a World of Books, Friends, and Flowers: Gift Books and Inscriptions, 1825–1860." *Winterthur Portfolio* 31 (1996): 53–66.

Ditzion, Sidney Herbert. *Arsenals of a Democratic Culture: A Social History of the American Public Library Movement in New England and the Middle States from 1850–1900.* Chicago: American Library Association, 1947.

———. "Mechanics and Mercantile Libraries." *Library Quarterly* 10 (1940): 547–77.

Doane, Alger Nicolaus, and Carol Braun Pasternack, eds. *Vox Intexta: Orality and Textuality in the Middle Ages.* Madison: Univ. of Wisconsin Press, 1991.

Docherty, Linda J. "Women as Readers: Visual Interpretations." *Proceedings of the American Antiquarian Society* 107, pt. 2 (1998): 335–88.

Douglas, Ann. "Heaven Our Home: Consolation Literature in the Northern United States, 1830–1880." *American Quarterly* 26 (1974): 496–515.

Douglas, Jack D., ed. *Understanding Everyday Life: Toward the Reconstruction of Sociological Knowledge.* Chicago: Aldine, 1970.

Douglas, Mary, and Baron C. Isherwood. *The World of Goods: Towards an Anthropology of Consumption.* New York: Routledge, 1996.

Douglass, Frederick. *Vie de Frédéric Douglass esclave americain.* Translated by S. K. Parkes. Paris: Pagnerre, 1848.

Druett, Joan. "Those Female Journals." *Log of Mystic Seaport* 40 (1989): 115–25.

Dublin, Thomas. *Farm to Factory: Women's Letters, 1830–1860.* New York: Columbia Univ. Press, 1993.

———. *Transforming Women's Work: New England Lives in the Industrial Revolution.* Ithaca, N.Y.: Cornell Univ. Press, 1994.

Dudden, Faye. *Serving Women: Household Service in Nineteenth-Century America.* Middletown, Conn.: Wesleyan Univ. Press, 1983.

Durivage, Francis A. *Life Scenes: Sketched in Light and Shadow from the World Around Us.* Boston: Benjamin B. Mussey, 1853.

Dzwonkoski, Peter, ed. *American Literary Publishing Houses, 1638–1899.* 2 vols. Detroit: Gale Research, 1986.

Eckel, John C. *The First Editions of the Writings of Charles Dickens, Their Points and Values: A Bibliography.* New York: M. Inman, 1932.

Elbert, Monika M. "Striking a Historical Pose: Antebellum Tableaux Vivants, *Godey's* Illustrations, and Margaret Fuller's Heroines." *New England Quarterly* 75 (2002): 235–75.

Eldred, Janet Carey, and Peter Mortensen. *Imagining Rhetoric: Composing Women of the Early United States.* Pittsburgh: Univ. of Pittsburgh Press, 2002.

Eley, Geoff. "Labor History, Social History, 'Alltagsgeschichte': Experience, Culture, and the Politics of the Everyday—a New Direction for German Social History?" *Journal of Modern History* 61 (1989): 297–343.

Emerson, Ralph Waldo. *Essays: Second Series.* Boston: J. Munroe, 1844.

Engelsing, Rolf. *Analphabetentum und Lektüre: Zur Sozialgeschichte des Lesens in Deutschland Zwischen Feudaler und Industrieller Gesellschaft.* Stuttgart: Metzler, 1973.

———. *Der Bürger als Leser: Lesergeschichte in Deutschland, 1500–1800.* Stuttgart: Metzler, 1974.

English, Karen A. "'Genuine Transcripts of Private Experience': Margaret Fuller and Translation." *American Transcendental Quarterly* 15 (2001): 131–46.

Ezell, Margaret J. M, ed. *The Poems and Prose of Mary, Lady Chudleigh.* New York: Oxford Univ. Press, 1993.

———. *Social Authorship and the Advent of Print.* Baltimore: Johns Hopkins Univ. Press, 1999.

Fahs, Alice. *The Imagined Civil War: Popular Literature of the North and South, 1861–1865.* Chapel Hill: Univ. of North Carolina Press, 2001.

Faxon, Frederick Winthrop. *Literary Annuals and Gift Books: A Bibliography, 1823–1903.* 1912. Reprint, Pinner, Eng.: Private Libraries Association, 1973.

Fidler, Christine Ann. "'Young Limbs of the Law': Law Students, Legal Education, and the Occupational Culture of Attorneys, 1820–1860." Ph.D. diss., Univ. of California–Berkeley, 1996.

Fielding, Penny. *Writing and Orality: Nationality, Culture, and Nineteenth-Century Scottish Fiction.* Oxford: Clarendon, 1996.

Fields, Tim, Elan Zingman-Leith, and Susan Zingman-Leith. *The Secret Life of Victorian Houses.* Washington, D.C.: Elliott & Clark, 1993.

Fink, Steven. *Prophet in the Marketplace: Thoreau's Development as a Professional Writer.* Princeton, N.J.: Princeton Univ. Press, 1992.

Fink, Steven, and Susan S. Williams, eds. *Reciprocal Influences: Literary Production, Distribution, and Consumption in America.* Columbus: Ohio State Univ. Press, 1999.

Fischer, David Hackett. *Growing Old in America.* New York: Oxford Univ. Press, 1978.

Fish, Stanley. *Is There a Text in This Class? The Authority of Interpretive Communities.* Cambridge: Harvard Univ. Press, 1980.

———. *Surprised by Sin: The Reader in "Paradise Lost."* London: Macmillan, 1967.

Fishkin, Shelley Fisher. *From Fact to Fiction: Journalism and Imaginative Writing in America.* Baltimore: Johns Hopkins Univ. Press, 1985.

Florian, Mary-Lou E., and Lesley Manning. "The Ecology of the Fungal Fox Spots in a Book Published in 1854." *Restaurator* 20 (1999): 137–50.

Foley, Albert S. *Bishop Healy: Beloved Outcaste, the Story of a Great Priest Whose Life Has Become a Legend.* New York: Farrar, Straus, and Young, 1954.

Foley, Michael S. "A Mission Unfulfilled: The Post Office and the Distribution of Information in Rural New England, 1821–1835." *Journal of the Early Republic* 17 (1997): 611–50.

Ford, Jeanette White. *Archival Principles and Practice: A Guide for Archives Management.* Jefferson, N.C.: McFarland, 1990.

Formisano, Ronald P. "The Role of Women in the Dorr Rebellion." *Rhode Island History* 51 (1993): 88–104.

Forten, Charlotte. *The Journals of Charlotte Forten Grimké.* Edited by Brenda Stevenson. New York: Oxford Univ. Press, 1988.

Fowle, Priscilla Hawthorne. "Boston Daily Newspapers,1830–1850." Ph.D. diss., Radcliffe College, 1920.

Fowler, Dorothy Ganfield. *Unmailable: Congress and the Post Office.* Athens: Univ. of Georgia Press, 1977.

Fox, Adam. *Oral and Literate Culture in England, 1500–1700.* Oxford: Clarendon Press, 2000.

Foy, Jessica H., and Thomas J. Schlereth, eds. *American Home Life, 1880–1930: A Social History of Spaces and Services.* Knoxville: Univ. of Tennessee Press, 1992.

French, Hannah D. *Bookbinding in Early America: Seven Essays on Masters and Methods.* Worcester, Mass.: American Antiquarian Society, 1986.

Fried, Debra. "Valves of Attention: Quotation and Context in the Age of Emerson." Ph.D. diss., Yale Univ., 1983.

Fuhrer, Mary Babson. *Letters from the "Old Home Place": Anxieties and Aspirations in Rural New England, 1836–1843: From the White Family Collection at Old Sturbridge Village.* Boylston, Mass.: Boylston Historical Society, 1998.

Furman, Laura, and Elinore Standard, eds. *Bookworms: Great Writers and Readers Celebrate Reading.* New York: Carroll & Graf, 1997.

Garber, Marjorie. *Quotation Marks.* New York: Routledge, 2003.

Garcia, Hazel Dicken. *Journalistic Standards in Nineteenth-Century America.* Madison: Univ. of Wisconsin Press, 1989.

———. *To Western Woods: The Breckinridge Family Moves to Kentucky in 1793.* Rutherford, N.J.: Fairleigh Dickinson Univ. Press, 1991.

Garnett, Robert F. Jr. "Postmodernism and Theories of Value: New Grounds for Institutionalist/Marxist Dialogue?" *Journal of Economic Issues* 33 (1999): 817–34.

Garnham, Nicholas. "Political Economy and Cultural Studies: Reconciliation or Divorce?" *Critical Studies in Mass Communication* 12 (1995): 62–71.

Garvey, Ellen Gruber. *The Adman in the Parlor: Magazines and the Gendering of Consumer Culture, 1880s to 1910s.* New York: Oxford Univ. Press, 1996.

———. "Scissorizing and Scrapbooks: Nineteenth-Century Reading, Remaking, and Recirculating." In *New Media, 1740–1915,* edited by Lisa Gitelman and Geoffrey B. Pingree, 207–27. Cambridge, Mass.: MIT Press, 2003.

Gaskell, Philip. *A New Introduction to Bibliography.* New Castle, Del.: Oak Knoll, 1995.

Gaughan, Joseph P., and Louis A. Ferman. "Toward an Understanding of the Informal Economy." *Annals of the American Academy of Political and Social Science* 493 (1987): 15–25.

Gauld, Alan. *A History of Hypnotism.* Cambridge: Cambridge Univ. Press, 1992.

Geib, Susan. "'Changing Works': Agriculture and Society in Brookfield, Mass., 1785–1820." Ph.D. diss., Boston Univ., 1981.

Geison, Gerald L., ed. *Professions and Professional Ideologies in America.* Chapel Hill: Univ. of North Carolina Press, 1984.

Gere, Anne Ruggles. *Intimate Practices: Literacy and Cultural Work in U.S. Women's Clubs,* 1880–1920. Urbana: Univ. of Illinois Press, 1997.

Gilbar, Steven. *The Open Door: When Writers First Learned to Read.* Boston: D. R. Godine and Library of Congress, 1992.

Gilbert, Pamela K. "Ingestion, Contagion, Seduction: Victorian Metaphors of Reading." *Literature, Interpretation, Theory* 8 (1997): 83–104.

Gilmore, William J. "Elementary Literacy on the Eve of the Industrial Revolution: Trends in Rural New England, 1760–1830." *Proceedings of the American Antiquarian Society* 92, pt. 1 (1982): 87–178.

———. *Reading Becomes a Necessity of Life: Material and Cultural Life in Rural New England, 1780–1835.* Knoxville: Univ. of Tennessee Press, 1989.

Gilreath, James. "American Book Distribution." *Proceedings of the American Antiquarian Society* 95, pt. 2 (1985): 501–83.

Gilroy, Amanda, and W. M. Verhoeven, eds. *Epistolary Histories: Letters, Fiction, Culture.* Charlottesville: Univ. Press of Virginia, 2000.

Ginzburg, Carlo. *The Cheese and the Worms: The Cosmos of a Sixteenth-Century Miller.* Translated by John and Anne Tedeschi. Baltimore: Johns Hopkins Univ. Press, 1980.

Gleason, Cloye W. *Seven Lectures on the Philosophy of Life, and the Art of Preserving Health.* Columbus, Ohio: Scott & Bascom, 1852.

Gleason, Frederick. "A New Dress Throughout." *Flag of Our Union* 7, no. 24 (12 June 1852): 3.

Godelier, Maurice. *The Enigma of the Gift.* Translated by Nora Scott. Chicago: Univ. of Chicago Press, 1999.

Goffman, Erving. *The Presentation of Self in Everyday Life.* New York: Doubleday, 1959.

Golby, John M., and A. W. Purdue, eds. *The Making of Modern Christmas.* Athens: Univ. of Georgia Press, 1986.

Goldin, Claudia Dale. *Understanding the Gender Gap: An Economic History of American Women.* New York: Oxford Univ. Press, 1990.

Graff, Harvey J. *Labyrinths of Literacy: Reflections on Literacy Past and Present.* Pittsburgh: Univ. of Pittsburgh Press, 1995.

———. *The Legacies of Literacy: Continuities and Contradictions in Western Culture and Society.* Bloomington: Indiana Univ. Press, 1991.

———. *The Literacy Myth: Literacy and Social Structure in the Nineteenth-Century City.* New York: Academic Press, 1979.

Gramsci, Antonio. *Selections from the Prison Notebooks of Antonio Gramsci.* Edited and translated by Quintin Hoare and Geoffrey Nowell-Smith. New York: International Publishers, 1971.

Greenblatt, Stephen. *Shakespearean Negotiations: The Circulation of Social Energy in Renaissance England.* Berkeley and Los Angeles: Univ. of California Press, 1988.

———. "Towards a Poetics of Culture." In *The New Historicism,* edited by H. Aram Veeser, 1–14. New York: Routledge, 1989.

Grier, Katherine C. *Culture and Comfort: People, Parlors, and Upholstery,* 1850–1930. Rochester, N.Y.: Strong Museum, 1988.

———. "The Decline of the Memory Palace: The Parlor after 1890." In Foy and Schlereth, *American Home Life,* 51–63.

Griffin, Farah Jasmine, ed. *Beloved Sisters and Loving Friends: Letters from Rebecca Primus of Royal Oak, Maryland, and Addie Brown of Hartford, Connecticut, 1854–1868.* New York: Alfred A. Knopf, 1999.

Grimsted, David. *American Mobbing, 1828–1861: Toward Civil War.* New York: Oxford Univ. Press, 1998.

———. *Melodrama Unveiled: American Theater and Culture, 1800–1850.* Berkeley and Los Angeles: Univ. of California Press, 1987.

Gross, Robert A. "Much Instruction from Little Reading: Books and Libraries in Thoreau's Concord." *Proceedings of the American Antiquarian Society* 97, pt. 1 (1987): 129–88.

———. "Reconstructing Early American Libraries: Concord, Massachusetts, 1795–1850." *Proceedings of the American Antiquarian Society* 97, pt. 2 (1987): 331–451.

Grossberg, Michael. "Institutionalizing Masculinity: The Law as a Masculine Profession." In *Meanings for Manhood: Constructions of Masculinity in Victorian America,* edited by Mark C. Carnes and Clyde Griffen, 133–51. Chicago: Univ. of Chicago Press, 1990.

Groves, Jeffrey D. "Judging Literary Books by Their Covers: House Styles, Ticknor and Fields, and Literary Promotion." In *Reading Books: Essays on the Material Text and Literature in America,* edited by Michele Moylan and Lane Stiles, 75–100. Amherst: Univ. of Massachusetts Press, 1996.

Gundaker, Grey. *Signs of Diaspora/Diaspora of Signs: Literacies, Creolization, and Vernacular Practice in African America.* New York: Oxford Univ. Press, 1998.

Gutjahr, Paul C. *An American Bible: A History of the Good Book in the United States.* Stanford, Calif.: Stanford Univ. Press, 1999.

Haber, Samuel. *The Quest for Authority and Honor in the American Professions, 1750–1900.* Chicago: Univ. of Chicago Press, 1991.

Habermas, Jürgen. *The Structural Transformation of the Public Sphere: An Inquiry into a Category of Bourgeois Society.* Translated by Thomas Burger. Cambridge, Mass.: MIT Press, 1989.

Hackenberg, Michael R., ed. *Getting the Books Out: Papers of the Chicago Conference on the Book in 19th-Century America.* Washington, D.C.: Library of Congress, 1987.

Hale, Edward Everett. *A New England Boyhood.* New York: MSS Information, 1970.

Haliburton, Thomas Chandler. *The Clockmaker; or, The Sayings and Doings of Samuel Slick of Slickville.* Halifax: J. Howe, 1836.

Hall, David D. *Cultures of Print: Essays in the History of the Book.* Amherst: Univ. of Massachusetts Press, 1996.

Hall, Peter Dobkin. *The Organization of American Culture, 1700–1900: Private Institutions, Elites, and the Origins of American Nationality.* New York: New York Univ. Press, 1982.

Halloran, S. Michael. "From Rhetoric to Composition: The Teaching of Writing in America to 1900." In *A Short History of Writing Instruction from Ancient Greece to Twentieth-Century America,* edited by James Jerome Murphy, 213–46. Davis, Calif.: Hermagoras Press, 1990.

Halttunen, Karen. *Confidence Men and Painted Women: A Study of Middle-Class Culture in America, 1830–1870.* New Haven, Conn.: Yale Univ. Press, 1982.

Hamilton, Milton W. *The Country Printer, New York State, 1785–1830.* Port Washington, N.Y.: I. J. Friedman, 1964.

Hamilton, Sinclair. *Early American Book Illustrators and Wood Engravers.* 2 vols. Princeton, N.J.: Princeton Univ. Press, 1968.

Hampel, Robert L. *Temperance and Prohibition in Massachusetts, 1813–1852.* Ann Arbor, Mich.: UMI Research Press, 1982.

Hampsten, Elizabeth. *Read This Only to Yourself: The Private Writings of Midwestern Women, 1880–1910.* Bloomington: Indiana Univ. Press, 1982.

Handlin, Oscar. *Boston's Immigrants: A Study in Acculturation.* New York: Atheneum, 1941.

Haney, David P. "Aesthetics and Ethics in Gadamer, Levinas, and Romanticism: Problems of Phronesis and Techne." *PMLA* 114 (1999) : 32–45.

Hann, C. M., ed. *Property Relations: Renewing the Anthropological Tradition.* New York: Cambridge Univ. Press, 1998.

Hansen, Karen V. *A Very Social Time: Crafting Community in Antebellum New England.* Berkeley and Los Angeles: Univ. of California Press, 1994.

Hansen, Karen V., and Cameron L. Macdonald. "Surveying the Dead Informant: Quantitative Analysis and Historical Interpretation." *Qualitative Sociology* 18 (Summer 1995): 227–36.

Harris, Samuel. *Pernicious Fiction; or, The Tendencies and Results of Indiscriminate Novel Reading.* New York: American Female Guardian Society, 1853.

Harris, Samuel L., comp. *The Maine Register, and National Calendar, for the Year 1841.* Augusta, Maine: Daniel C. Stanwood; Portland, Maine: William Hyde, 1841.

Harris, Susan K. *The Courtship of Olivia Langdon and Mark Twain.* New York: Cambridge Univ. Press, 1985.

Haskell, Thomas L. "Capitalism and the Origins of the Humanitarian Sensibility." *American Historical Review* 90 (1985): 339–61.

Havelock, Eric A. *The Muse Learns to Write: Reflections on Orality and Literacy from Antiquity to the Present.* New Haven, Conn.: Yale Univ. Press, 1986.

Hayes, Kevin J. *A Colonial Woman's Bookshelf.* Knoxville: Univ. of Tennessee Press, 1996.

———. "Railway Reading." *Proceedings of the American Antiquarian Society* 106, pt. 2 (1997): 301–26.

Heininger, Mary Lynn Stevens. *At Home with a Book: Reading in America, 1840–1940.* Rochester, N.Y.: Margaret Woodbury Strong Museum, 1986.

Hellinga, Lotte. "The 'Marks in Books' Project of the Bibliographical Society (London)." *Papers of the Bibliographical Society of America* 91 (1997): 573–77.

Henkin, David M. *City Reading: Written Words and Public Spaces in Antebellum New York.* New York: Columbia Univ. Press, 1998.

Hewitt, John P. *Dilemmas of the American Self.* Philadelphia: Temple Univ. Press, 1989.

Hewitt, Nancy Ann. *Women's Activism and Social Change: Rochester, New York, 1822–1872.* Ithaca, N.Y.: Cornell Univ. Press, 1984.

Higginson, Thomas Wentworth. *Part of a Man's Life.* Boston: Houghton Mifflin, 1905.

Hindman, Sandra. *Printing the Written Word: The Social History of Books, c. 1450–1520.* Ithaca, N.Y.: Cornell Univ. Press, 1991.

Hobbs, Mary. *Early Seventeenth-Century Verse Miscellany Manuscripts.* Aldershot: Scolar Press, 1992.

Hodder, Ian, ed. *The Meanings of Things: Material Culture and Symbolic Expression.* London: Unwin Hyman, 1989.

Hoffert, Sylvia D. *Private Matters: American Attitudes Toward Childbearing and Infant Nurture in the Urban North, 1800–1860.* Urbana: Univ. of Illinois Press, 1989.

Holbrook, Stewart H. *The Yankee Exodus: An Account of Migration from New England.* Seattle: Univ. of Washington Press, 1968.

Holifield, E. Brooks. "On Teaching the History of Christianity: Traditions and Presuppositions." *Church History* 72 (2003): 237–50.

Holland, Norman N. *5 Readers Reading.* New Haven, Conn.: Yale Univ. Press, 1975.

Hook, Theodore Edward. *Sayings and Doings: A Series of Sketches from Life.* London: H. Colburn, 1824.

Horlick, Allan Stanley. *Country Boys and Merchant Princes: The Social Control of Young Men in New York.* Lewisburg, Pa.: Bucknell Univ. Press, 1975.

Horowitz, Daniel. *The Morality of Spending: Attitudes Toward the Consumer Society in America, 1875–1940.* Baltimore: Johns Hopkins Univ. Press, 1985.

Horton, James Oliver, and Lois E. Horton. *Black Bostonians: Family Life and Community Struggle in the Antebellum North.* New York: Holmes & Meier, 1999.

Hrkach, Jack. "Music, Drama, and Horsemanship! Hippodrama in the Circuses of Antebellum New York State." *Mid-Atlantic Almanac* 4 (1995): 43–53.

Huff, Cynthia A. "Reading as Re-Vision: Approaches to Reading Manuscript Diaries." *Biography* 23 (2000): 504–24.

Hunter, Dard. *Papermaking by Hand in America.* Chillicothe, Ohio: Mountain House Press, 1950.

Hunter, Jane H. "Inscribing the Self in the Heart of the Family: Diaries and Girlhood in Late Victorian America." *American Quarterly* 44 (1992): 51–81.

Hyde, Francis Edwin. *Cunard and the North Atlantic, 1840–1973: A History of Shipping and Financial Management.* Atlantic Highlands, N.J.: Humanities Press, 1975.

Hyde, Lewis. *The Gift: Imagination and the Erotic Life of Property.* New York: Vintage Books, 1983.

Inter-university Consortium for Political and Social Research. *Historical, Demographic, Economic, and Social Data: The United States, 1790–1970.* Ann Arbor, Mich.: Inter-university Consortium for Political and Social Research, c. 1970s, via http://fisher.lib.virginia.edu/census (last accessed 18 Sept. 2004).

Irons, Susan H. "Channing's Influence on Peabody: Self-Culture and the Danger of Egoism." *Studies in the American Renaissance* 16 (1992): 121–35.

Iser, Wolfgang. *The Fictive and the Imaginary: Charting Literary Anthropology.* Baltimore: Johns Hopkins Univ. Press, 1993.

———. *The Implied Reader: Patterns of Communication in Prose Fiction from Bunyan to Beckett.* Baltimore: Johns Hopkins Univ. Press, 1974.

———. *Prospecting: From Reader Response to Literary Anthropology.* Baltimore: Johns Hopkins Univ. Press, 1989.

Jabour, Anya. "Albums of Affection: Female Friendship and Coming of Age in Antebellum Virginia." *Virginia Magazine of History and Biography* 107 (1999): 125–58.

Jackson, Herbert G. *The Spirit Rappers.* Garden City, N.Y.: Doubleday, 1972.

Jackson, H. J. *Marginalia: Readers Writing in Books.* New Haven, Conn.: Yale Univ. Press, 2001.

Jackson, Leon. "The Reader Retailored: Thomas Carlyle, His American Audiences, and the Politics of Evidence." *Book History* 2 (1999): 146–72.

Jackson, Louise A. "Nineteenth-Century Elementary Composition Instruction." *Language Arts* 63 (1986): 601–6.

Jaffee, David. "Peddlers of Progress and the Transformation of the Rural North, 1760–1860." *Journal of American History* 78 (1991): 511–35.

Jauss, Hans-Robert. "Literary History as a Challenge to Literary Theory." Translated by Elizabeth Benzinger. *New Literary History* 2 (1970): 7–37.

———. "The Theory of Reception: A Retrospective of Its Unrecognized Prehistory." In *Literary Theory Today,* edited by Peter Collier and Helga Geyer-Ryan, 53–73. Ithaca, N.Y.: Cornell Univ. Press, 1990.

Jeffrey, Julie Roy. *The Great Silent Army of Abolitionism: Ordinary Women in the Anti-slavery Movement.* Chapel Hill: Univ. of North Carolina Press, 1998.

John, Richard R. *Spreading the News: The American Postal System from Franklin to Morse.* Cambridge: Harvard Univ. Press, 1995.

Johns, Adrian. *The Nature of the Book: Print and Knowledge in the Making.* Chicago: Univ. of Chicago Press, 1998.

Johnson, Clifton. *Old-Time Schools and School-Books.* New York: Dover, 1963.

Johnson, Nan. *Gender and Rhetorical Space in American Life, 1866–1919.* Carbondale: Southern Illinois Univ. Press, 2002.

———. "The Popularization of Nineteenth-Century Rhetoric: Elocution and the Private Learner." In *Oratorical Culture in Nineteenth-Century America: Transformations in the Theory and Practice of Rhetoric,* edited by Gregory Clark and S. Michael Halloran,139–57. Carbondale: Southern Illinois Univ. Press, 1993.

Jones, Justin. *The Belle of Boston: The Rival Students of Cambridge.* Boston: Frederick Gleason, 1844.

Kaestle, Carl F., and Maris Vinovskis. "From Apron Strings to ABCs: Parents, Children, and Schooling in Nineteenth-Century Massachusetts." In *Turning Points: Historical and Sociological Essays on the Family,* edited by John Demos and Sarane Spence Boocock, 39–80. Chicago: Univ. of Chicago Press, 1978.

Kagle, Steven E. *American Diary Literature, 1620–1799.* Boston: Twayne, 1979.

———. *Early Nineteenth-Century American Diary Literature.* Boston: Twayne, 1986.

———. *Late Nineteenth-Century American Diary Literature.* Boston: Twayne, 1988.

Kammen, Michael. *Mystic Chords of Memory: The Transformation of Tradition in American Culture.* New York: Knopf, 1991.

Kaplan, Catherine. "'He Summons Genius . . . to His Aid': Letters, Partisanship, and the Making of the Farmer's Weekly Museum, 1795–1800." *Journal of the Early Republic* 23 (2003): 545–71.

———. "'We Have Joys . . . They Do Not Know': Letters, Federalism, and Sentiment in the New Nation, 1790–1812." Ph.D. diss., Univ. of Michigan, 1998.

Kaser, David. *A Book for a Sixpence: The Circulating Library in America.* Pittsburgh: Beta Phi Mu, 1980.

———. *Books and Libraries in Camp and Battle: The Civil War Experience.* Westport, Conn.: Greenwood Press, 1984.

Katriel, Tamar, and Thomas Farrell. "Scrapbooks as Cultural Texts: An American Art of Memory." *Text and Performance Quarterly* 11 (1991): 1–17.

Katz, Jonathan Ned. "1837, Feb 2: Albert Dodd: Dear Beloved Trio." At http://www 2.outhistory.com/cgi-bin/iowa/events/event/16.html (accessed 6 Sept. 2004).

Kay, Richard. "The Intended Readers of Dante's *Monarchia.*" *Dante Studies* 110 (1992): 37–44.

Kellett, E. E. *Literary Quotation and Allusion.* Port Washington, N.Y.: Kennikat Press, 1933.

Kelley, Mary. "'A More Glorious Revolution': Women's Antebellum Reading Circles and the Pursuit of Public Influence." *New England Quarterly* 76 (2003): 163–96.

———. *Private Woman, Public Stage: Literary Domesticity in Nineteenth-Century America.* New York: Oxford Univ. Press, 1984.

———. "Reading Women/Women Reading: The Making of Learned Women in Antebellum America." *Journal of American History* 83 (1996): 401–24.

Kelly, Catherine E. *In the New England Fashion: Reshaping Women's Lives in the Nineteenth Century.* Ithaca, N.Y.: Cornell Univ. Press, 1999.

Kelly, Louis G. *The True Interpreter: A History of Translation Theory and Practice in the West.* New York: St. Martin's Press, 1979.

———. *Twenty-five Centuries of Language Teaching: An Inquiry into the Science, Art, and Development of Language Teaching Methodology, 500 B.C.–1969.* Rowley, Mass.: Newbury House, 1969.

Kemp, Wolfgang. *Der Betrachter ist im Bild: Kunstwissenschaft und Rezeptionästhetik.* Cologne: DuMont, 1985.

Kenny, Christine. "Memory, Truth, and Orality: The Lives of Northern Women Textile Workers." In *Women's Lives into Print: The Theory, Practice and Writing of Feminist Auto/Biography,* edited by Pauline Polkey, 34–43. New York: St. Martin's Press, 1999.

Kerber, Linda K. *No Constitutional Right to Be Ladies: Women and the Obligations of Citizenship.* New York: Hill and Wang, 1998.

Kett, Joseph. *The Pursuit of Knowledge Under Difficulties: From Self-Improvement to Adult Education in America, 1750–1990.* Stanford, Calif.: Stanford Univ. Press, 1994.

Kielbowicz, Richard B. *News in the Mail: The Press, Post Office, and Public Information.* New York: Greenwood Press, 1989.

———. "The Telegraph, Censorship, and Politics at the Outset of the Civil War." *Civil War History* 40 (1994): 95–118.

Kimberling, C. Ronald. *Kenneth Burke's Dramatism and Popular Arts.* Bowling Green: Bowling Green State Univ. Press, 1982.

Knoles, Thomas, and Lucia Zaucha Knoles. "'In Usum Pupillorum': Student-Transcribed Texts at Harvard College Before 1740." *Proceedings of the American Antiquarian Society* 109, pt. 2 (1999): 333–414.

Kohn, Abraham. "A Jewish Peddler's Diary." Edited and translated by Abram Vossen Goodman. In Marcus, *Critical Studies* 1:45–73.

Kopytoff, Igor. "The Cultural Biography of Things: Commoditization as Process." In Appadurai, *Social Life,* 77–90.

Kruger, Linda. "Home Libraries: Special Spaces, Reading Places." In Foy and Schlereth, *American Home Life,* 94–119.

Lagemann, Ellen Condliffe. "From Discipline-Based to Problem-Centered Learning." In *Education and Democracy: Re-imagining Liberal Learning in America,* edited by Robert Orrill, 21–43. New York: College Entrance Examination Board, 1997.

Lamb, Martha J. "Formative Influences." *Forum Magazine* 40 (Mar. 1891): 49–58.

Landroth, Roger B. "The History and Development of Pitmanic Shorthand in the United States: 1843–1976." Ph.D. diss., New York Univ., 1977.

Lane, Roger. *Policing the City: Boston, 1822–1885.* Cambridge: Harvard Univ. Press, 1967.

Lapsansky, Phillip. "Graphic Discord: Abolitionist and Antiabolitionist Images." In Yellin and Van Horne, *Abolitionist Sisterhood,* 201–30.

Larcom, Lucy. "Among the Lowell Mill-Girls: A Reminiscence." *Atlantic Monthly* 48 (Nov. 1881): 593–612.

Larkin, Jack. *The Reshaping of Everyday Life, 1790–1840.* New York: Harper & Row, 1988.

Laurie, Bruce. *Artisans into Workers: Labor in Nineteenth-Century America.* New York: Hill and Wang, 1989.

Lawes, Carolyn J. *Women and Reform in a New England Community, 1815–1860.* Lexington: Univ. Press of Kentucky, 2000.

Laws and Regulations for the Government of the Post Office Department. Washington, D.C.: C. Alexander, 1852.

Lechner, Joan Marie. *Renaissance Concepts of the Commonplaces: An Historical Investigation.* New York: Pageant Press, 1962.

Lefebvre, Henri. *Critique de la Vie Quotidienne.* Paris: Grasset, 1947.

Lefevere, André. "Introduction: Comparative Literature and Translation." *Comparative Literature* 47 (1995): 1–10.

———. "Translation: Its Genealogy in the West." In *Translation, History and Culture,* edited by Susan Bassnett and André Lefevere, 14–28. London: Pinter Publishers, 1990.

Lehmann-Haupt, Hellmut, Lawrence C. Wroth, and Rollo G. Silver. *The Book in America: A History of the Making and Selling of Books in the United States.* New York: Bowker, 1951.

Lehuu, Isabelle. *Carnival on the Page: Popular Print Media in Antebellum America.* Chapel Hill: Univ. of North Carolina Press, 2000.

Leighton, Lauren G. *Two Worlds, One Art: Literary Translation in Russia and America.* DeKalb: Northern Illinois Univ. Press, 1991.

Leonard, Thomas C. *News for All: America's Coming-of-Age with the Press.* New York: Oxford Univ. Press, 1995.

Leopold, Allison Kyle. *Allison Kyle Leopold's Victorian Keepsake: Select Expressions of Affectionate Regard from the Romantic Nineteenth Century.* New York: Doubleday, 1991.

Lerner, Gerda. *The Grimké Sisters from South Carolina: Rebels Against Slavery.* Boston: Houghton Mifflin, 1967.

Levine, Lawrence W. *Highbrow/Lowbrow: The Emergence of Cultural Hierarchy in America.* Cambridge: Harvard Univ. Press, 1988.

Lewis, R. M. "Tableaux Vivants, Parlor Theatricals in Victorian America." *Revue Française d'Études Americaines* 36 (1988): 280–91.

Lewton, Frederick Lewis. *The Servant in the House: A Brief History of the Sewing Machine.* Washington, D.C.: Smithsonian Institution, 1930.

Lincoln, Yvonna S., and Egon G. Guba. *Naturalistic Inquiry.* Beverly Hills, Calif.: Sage, 1985.

Lipsett, Linda Otto. *Remember Me: Women and Their Friendship Quilts.* Lincolnwood, Ill.: Quilt Digest Press, 1985.

Lockridge, Kenneth A. *Literacy in Colonial New England: An Enquiry into the Social Context of Literacy in the Early Modern West.* New York: Norton, 1974.

———. *On the Sources of Patriarchal Rage: The Commonplace Books of William Byrd and Thomas Jefferson and the Gendering of Power in the Eighteenth Century.* New York: New York Univ. Press, 1992.

Long, Elizabeth. *Book Clubs: Women and the Uses of Reading in Everyday Life.* Chicago: Univ. of Chicago Press, 2003.

———. "Textual Interpretation as Collective Action." In *The Ethnography of Reading,* edited by Jonathan Boyarin, 180–211. Berkeley and Los Angeles: Univ. of California Press, 1993.

Longfellow, Henry Wadsworth. *Song of Hiawatha.* Boston: Ticknor and Fields, 1855.

Lord, Albert Bates. *The Singer of Tales.* Cambridge: Harvard Univ. Press, 1960.

Lovejoy, Arthur O. *The Great Chain of Being: A Study of the History of an Idea.* Cambridge: Harvard Univ. Press, 1936.

Loving, Jerome. *Lost in the Customhouse: Authorship in the American Renaissance.* Iowa City: Univ. of Iowa Press, 1993.

Low, Harriett. *Lights and Shadows of a Macao Life: The Journal of Harriett Low, Travelling Spinster.* Edited by Nan Powell Hodges and Arthur William Hummel. 2 vols. Woodinville, Wash.: History Bank, 2002.

Lüdtke, Alf, ed. *The History of Everyday Life: Reconstructing Historical Experiences and Ways of Life.* Translated by William Templer. Princeton, N.J.: Princeton Univ. Press, 1995.

Lystra, Karen. *Searching the Heart: Women, Men, and Romantic Love in Nineteenth-Century America.* New York: Oxford Univ. Press, 1989.

Machor, James L. "Fiction and Informed Reading in Early Nineteenth-Century America." *Nineteenth-Century Literature* 47 (1992): 320–48.

———, ed. *Readers in History: Nineteenth-Century American Literature and the Contexts of Response.* Baltimore: Johns Hopkins Univ. Press, 1993.

Machor, James L., and Philip Goldstein, eds. *Reception Study: From Literary Theory to Cultural Studies.* New York: Routledge, 2001.

Madden, Etta M. *Bodies of Life: Shaker Literature and Literacies.* Westport, Conn.: Greenwood Press, 1998.

Maffesoli, Michel. *Ordinary Knowledge: An Introduction to Interpretative Sociology.* Translated by David Macey. Cambridge: Blackwell, 1996.

Mailloux, Steven. "Cultural Rhetorical Studies: Eating Books in Nineteenth-Century America." In *Reconceptualizing American Literary/Cultural Studies: Rhetoric, History, and*

Politics in the Humanities, edited by William E. Cain, 21–33. New York: Garland, 1996.

———. *Interpretive Conventions: The Reader in the Study of American Fiction.* Ithaca, N.Y.: Cornell Univ. Press, 1982.

———. *Reception Histories: Rhetoric, Pragmatism, and American Cultural Politics.* Ithaca, N.Y.: Cornell Univ. Press, 1998.

———. "The Rhetorical Use and Abuse of Fiction: Eating Books in Late Nineteenth-Century America." *Boundary 2* 17 (1990): 133–57.

Marcus, Jacob R., comp. *Critical Studies in American Jewish History: Selected Articles from American Jewish Archives.* 3 vols. Cincinnati: American Jewish Archives, 1971.

Martin, Theodora Penny. *The Sound of Our Own Voices: Women's Study Clubs, 1860–1910.* Boston: Beacon Press, 1987.

Masini, Mario. *La Lectio Divina: An Ancient Prayer that Is Ever New.* New York: Alba House, 1998.

Mason, Caroline A. Briggs. "The Soldier's Dream of Home." *National Anti-Slavery Standard* 23 (14 Feb. 1863): [4].

Matthews, William, comp. *American Diaries: An Annotated Bibliography of American Diaries Written Prior to the Year 1861.* Berkeley and Los Angeles: Univ. of California Press, 1945.

Mattingly, Carol. *Appropriate(ing) Dress: Women's Rhetorical Style in Nineteenth-Century America.* Carbondale: Southern Illinois Univ. Press, 2002.

Mauss, Marcel. *The Gift: Forms and Functions of Exchange in Archaic Societies.* Translated by Ian Cunnison. New York: Norton, 1967.

McCarthy, Molly. "'A Page, a Day': A History of the Daily Diary in America." Ph.D. diss., Brandeis Univ., 2004.

———. "A Pocketful of Days: Pocket Diaries and Daily Record Keeping among Nineteenth-Century New England Women." *New England Quarterly* 73 (2000): 274–96.

McCaughey-Silvia, Regina C. "Lectures and Discussion Questions of the Franklin Lyceum: A Guide to Attitudes and Ideas in Nineteenth-Century Providence." Ph.D. diss., Univ. of Rhode Island, 1991.

McCusker, John J. *How Much Is That in Real Money? A Historical Price Index for Use as a Deflator of Money Values in the Economy of the United States.* Worcester, Mass.: American Antiquarian Society, 1992.

McGaw, Judith A. *Most Wonderful Machine: Mechanization and Social Change in Berkshire Paper Making, 1801–1885.* Princeton, N.J.: Princeton Univ. Press, 1987.

McGillivray, Murray. *Memorization in the Transmission of the Middle English Romances.* New York: Garland, 1990.

McGovern, James R. *Yankee Family.* New Orleans: Polyanthos, 1975.

McHenry, Elizabeth. *Forgotten Readers: Recovering the Lost History of African American Literary Societies.* Durham, N.C.: Duke Univ. Press, 2002.

McKendrick, Neil, John Brewer, and J. H. Plumb, eds. *The Birth of a Consumer Society: The Commercialization of Eighteenth-Century England.* Bloomington: Indiana Univ. Press, 1982.

McKenzie, D. F. *Bibliography and the Sociology of Texts.* Cambridge: Cambridge Univ. Press, 1999.

McMurry, Sally. "Who Read the Agricultural Journals? Evidence from Chenango County, New York, 1839–1865." *Agricultural History* 63 (1989): 1–18.

McMurtrie, Douglas C. *Printers' Marks and Their Significance.* Chicago: Eyncourt Press, 1930.

McNeil, W. K. "From Advice to Laments: New York Autograph Album Verse, 1820–1850." *New York Folklore Quarterly* 25 (1969): 175–94.

McNeill, William H. "Diffusion in History. " In *The Transfer and Transformation of Ideas and Material Culture,* edited by Peter J. Hugill and D. Bruce Dickson, 75–90. College Station: Texas A&M Univ. Press, 1988.

McPherson, James M. "'Spend Much Time in Reading the Daily Papers': The Press and Army Morale in the Civil War." *Atlanta History* 42 (1998): 7–18.

Middleton, Alicia Hopton, comp. *Life in Carolina and New England during the Nineteenth Century.* Bristol, R.I.: D. B. Updike, 1929.

Milan, Sarah. "Refracting the Gaslier: Understanding Victorian Responses to Domestic Gas Lighting." In *Domestic Space: Reading the Nineteenth-Century Interior,* edited by Inga Bryden and Janet Floyd, 84–102. Manchester: Manchester Univ. Press, 1999.

Miles, Pliny. *American Phreno-Mnemotechny, Theoretical and Practical.* 2 vols. New York: W. Taylor, 1846.

Miller, Perry. *The Life of the Mind in America: From the Revolution to the Civil War.* New York: Harcourt, Brace & World, 1965.

Miller, Susan. *Assuming the Positions: Cultural Pedagogy and the Politics of Commonplace Writing.* Pittsburgh: Univ. of Pittsburgh Press, 1998.

Miner, Earl. "Literary Diaries and the Boundaries of Literature." In *Yearbook of Comparative and General Literature* 21 (1972): 46–51.

Monaghan, E. Jennifer. *A Common Heritage: Noah Webster's Blue-Back Speller.* Hamden, Conn.: Archon, 1983.

———. "Family Literacy in Early 18th-Century Boston: Cotton Mather and His Children." *Reading Research Quarterly* 26 (1991): 342–70.

———. "'She Loved to Read in Good Books': Literacy and the Indians of Martha's Vineyard, 1643–1725." *History of Education Quarterly* 30 (1990): 492–521.

Moran, Gerald F., and Maris Vinovskis. "The Great Care of Godly Parents: Early Childhood in Puritan New England." In *Religion, Family, and the Life Course: Explorations in the Social History of Early America,* edited by Gerald F. Moran and Maris Vinovskis, 109–39. Ann Arbor: Univ. of Michigan Press, 1992.

Morrow, Honoré W. *Tiger! Tiger! The Life Story of John B. Gough.* New York: W. Morrow, 1930.

Moss, Ann. *Printed Commonplace-Books and the Structuring of Renaissance Thought.* New York: Oxford Univ. Press, 1996.

Motz, Marilyn Ferris. "Folk Expression of Time and Place: 19th-Century Midwestern Rural Diaries." *Journal of American Folklore* 100 (1987): 131–47.

———. "The Private Alibi: Literacy and Community in the Diaries of Two Nineteenth-Century American Women." In Bunkers and Huff, *Inscribing the Daily,* 189–206.

———. *True Sisterhood: Michigan Women and Their Kin, 1820–1920.* Albany: State Univ. of New York Press, 1983.

Mulford, Carla, ed. *Only for the Eye of a Friend: The Poems of Annis Boudinot Stockton.* Charlottesville: Univ. Press of Virginia, 1995.

Mumey, Nolie. *A Study of Rare Books, with Special Reference to Colophones Press Devices. . . .* Denver: Clason, 1930.

Murphy, Patrick D. "Doing Audience Ethnography: A Narrative Account of Establishing Ethnographic Identity and Locating Interpretive Communities in Fieldwork." *Qualitative Inquiry* 5 (1999): 479–504.

Murphy, Teresa Anne. *Ten Hours' Labor: Religion, Reform, and Gender in Early New England.* Ithaca, N.Y.: Cornell Univ. Press, 1992.

Neal, Arthur G. *National Trauma and Collective Memory: Major Events in the American Century.* Armonk, N.Y.: M. E. Sharpe, 1998.

Nebel, Cecile. *The Dark Side of Creativity: Blocks, Unfinished Works and the Urge to Destroy.* Troy, N.Y.: Whitston, 1988.

Neuburg, Victor E. "Chapbooks in America: Reconstructing the Popular Reading of Early America." In Davidson, *Reading in America,* 81–113.

"Neurology." *United States Democratic Review* 12 (Jan. 1843): 79–93.

Newbury, Michael. *Figuring Authorship in Antebellum America.* Stanford, Calif.: Stanford Univ. Press, 1997.

"A New Fashion for Valentines." *Godey's Lady's Book* 38 (Feb. 1849): 73.

Nichols, Elisabeth B. "'Blunted Hearts': Female Readers and Printed Authority in the Early Republic." In Ryan and Thomas, *Reading Acts,* 1–28.

Nicolaisen, W. F. H., ed. *Oral Tradition in the Middle Ages.* Binghamton, N.Y.: Medieval and Renaissance Texts and Studies, 1995.

Nissenbaum, Stephen. *The Battle for Christmas.* New York: Alfred A. Knopf, 1996.

Nord, David Paul. *Communities of Journalism: A History of American Newspapers and Their Readers.* Urbana: Univ. of Illinois Press, 2001.

———. "The Evangelical Origins of Mass Media in America, 1815–1835." *Journalism Monographs* 88 (1984): 1–30.

———. "Systematic Benevolence: Religious Publishing and the Marketplace in Early Nineteenth-Century America." In Sweet, *Communication and Change,* 239–69.

Noyes, George Wallingford, ed. *John Humphrey Noyes: The Putney Community.* Oneida, N.Y.: privately printed, 1931.

Nylander, Jane C. *Our Own Snug Fireside: Images of the New England Home, 1760–1860.* New York: Knopf, 1993.

Ockenga, Starr. *On Women and Friendship: A Collection of Victorian Keepsakes and Traditions.* New York: Stewart, Tabori, and Chang, 1993.

Ogden, Sherelyn, ed. *Preservation of Library and Archival Materials: A Manual.* Andover, Mass.: Northeast Document Conservation Center, 1999.

Ong, Walter. *Orality and Literacy: The Technologizing of the Word.* London: Routledge, 1982.

Ono, Kazuto. "Concord Lyceum." *Studies in Languages and Cultures* 7 (1996): 13–24.

Packard, Vance. *The Waste Makers.* New York: D. McKay, 1960.

Paine, Ralph D. *The Old Merchant Marine: A Chronicle of American Ships and Sailors.* New Haven: Yale Univ. Press, 1921.

Painter, Nell Irvin. "Representing Truth: Sojourner Truth's Knowing and Becoming Known." *Journal of American History* 81 (1994): 461–92.

Parker, Theodore. *A Discourse Occasioned by the Death of Daniel Webster.* Boston: Benjamin B. Mussey, 1853.

Paterson, Stephanie Diane. "Embodied Narratives: Ways of Reading Student Literacy Histories." Ph.D. diss., Univ. of New Hampshire, 2001.

Pattie, Frank A. *Mesmer and Animal Magnetism: A Chapter in the History of Medicine.* Hamilton, N.Y.: Edmonston, 1994.

Pawley, Christine. *Reading on the Middle Border: The Culture of Print in Late Nineteenth-Century Osage, Iowa.* Amherst: Univ. of Massachusetts Press, 2001.

Pearson, David. *Provenance Research in Book History: A Handbook.* London: British Library, 1994.

Pease, Jane H., and William Henry Pease. *Ladies, Women, and Wenches: Choice and Constraint in Antebellum Charleston and Boston.* Chapel Hill: Univ. of North Carolina Press, 1990.

Perry, Lewis. *Boats Against the Current: American Culture Between Revolution and Modernity, 1820–1860.* New York: Oxford Univ. Press, 1993.

Persy de Metz, N. *Elementary Treatise on the Forms of Cannon and Various Systems of ARTILLERY . . . !* West Point, N.Y.: United States Military Academy, 1832.

Peters, Harry Twyford. *America on Stone: The Other Printmakers to the American People. . . .* Garden City, N.Y.: Doubleday, 1931.

Peters, John Durham. *Speaking into the Air: A History of the Idea of Communication.* Chicago: Univ. of Chicago Press, 1999.

Petroski, Henry. *Book on the Bookshelf.* New York: Knopf, 1999.

Phelps, C. Deirdre. "Printing, Publishing, and Bookselling in Salem, Massachusetts, 1825–1900." *Essex Institute Historical Collections* 124 (1988): 227–64.

Pierce, Sally, and Catharina Slautterback. *Boston Lithography, 1825–1880.* Boston: Boston Athenaeum, 1991.

Pierce, Sally, Catharina Slautterback, and Georgia Brady Barnhill, eds. *Early American Lithography: Images to 1830.* Boston: Boston Athenaeum, 1997.

Pilkington, James Penn. *The Methodist Publishing House: A History.* Nashville: Abingdon Press, 1968.

Pochmann, Henry A. *German Culture in America: Philosophical and Literary Influences, 1600–1900.* Madison: Univ. of Wisconsin Press, 1957.

Polly, Gregory Paul. "Private and Public Letters: Epistolary Negotiations in the Early Republic." Ph.D. diss., Harvard Univ., 1997.

Porter, Carolyn. *Seeing and Being: The Plight of the Participant Observer in Emerson, James, Adams, and Faulkner.* Middletown, Conn.: Wesleyan Univ. Press, 1981.

Pred, Allan. *Making Histories and Constructing Human Geographies: The Local Transformation of Practice, Power Relations, and Consciousness.* Boulder, Colo.: Westview Press, 1990.

———. *Urban Growth and City Systems in the United States, 1840–1860.* Cambridge: Harvard Univ. Press, 1980.

———. *Urban Growth and the Circulation of Information: The United States as a System of Cities, 1790–1840.* Cambridge: Harvard Univ. Press, 1973.

Purple, Samuel S. *Observations on Some of the Remedial Properties of Simaba Cedron and On Its Employment in Intermittent Fever.* New York: Samuel S. and W. Wood, 1854.

Putnam, John Jay. *The Petersham Lyceum, 1833–1848.* Worcester, Mass.: Blanchard Press, 1902.

Putnam, Lillian R. "Beginning Reading Methods: A Review of the Past." In *Exploring Literacy: Nineteenth Yearbook: A Peer Reviewed Publication of the College Reading Association,* edited by Wayne M. Linek and Elizabeth G. Sturtevant, 51–55. Platteville, Wisc.: College Reading Association, 1997.

Rabinowitz, Richard. *The Spiritual Self in Everyday Life: The Transformation of Personal Religious Experience in Nineteenth-Century New England.* Boston: Northeastern Univ. Press, 1989.

Radner, Joan Newlon. "Performing the Paper: Handwritten Newspapers and Village Life in Postbellum Maine." *Northeast Folklore* 35 (2000): 363–82.

Radway, Janice A. "Reading Is Not Eating: Mass-Produced Literature and the Theoretical, Methodological, and Political Consequences of a Metaphor." *Book Research Quarterly* 2 (1986): 7–29.

———. *Reading the Romance: Women, Patriarchy, and Popular Literature.* Chapel Hill: Univ. of North Carolina Press, 1984.

Railton, Stephen. *Authorship and Audience: Literary Performance in the American Renaissance.* Princeton, N.J.: Princeton Univ. Press, 1991.

Rancière, Jacques. *Ignorant Schoolmaster: Five Lessons in Intellectual Emancipation.* Translated by Kristin Ross. Stanford, Calif.: Stanford Univ. Press, 1991.

Ray, Angela G. "Pupils, Spectators, Citizens: Representations of U.S. Public Culture in the Nineteenth-Century Lyceum." Ph.D. diss., Univ. of Minnesota, 2001.

Reed, Rebecca Theresa. *Six Months in a Convent; or, The Narrative of Rebecca Theresa Reed.* Boston: Russell, Odiorne & Metcalf; New York: Leavitt, Lord, 1835.

Reiff, Daniel D. *Houses from Books: Treatises, Pattern Books, and Catalogs in American Architecture, 1738–1950: A History and Guide.* University Park: Pennsylvania State Univ. Press, 2001.

Reinhold, Meyer. *Classica Americana: The Greek and Roman Heritage in the United States.* Detroit: Wayne State Univ. Press, 1984.

Rener, Frederick M. *Interpretatio: Language and Translation from Cicero to Tytler.* Amsterdam: Rodopi, 1989.

Restad, Penne L. *Christmas in America: A History.* New York: Oxford Univ. Press, 1995.

Reynolds, David S. *Beneath the American Renaissance: The Subversive Imagination in the Age of Emerson and Melville.* New York: Knopf, 1989.

———. *Faith in Fiction: The Emergence of Religious Literature in America.* Cambridge: Harvard Univ. Press, 1981.

Rice, Grantland S. *The Transformation of Authorship in America.* Chicago: Univ. of Chicago Press, 1997.

Ring, Betty. *Let Virtue Be a Guide to Thee: Needlework in the Education of Rhode Island Women, 1730–1830.* Providence: Rhode Island Historical Society, 1983.

Roberts, Nancy L. "'Ten Thousand Tongues' Speaking for Peace: Purposes and Strategies of the Nineteenth-Century Peace Advocacy Press." *Journalism History* 21 (1995): 16–28.

Robinson, Douglas. *Western Translation Theory, from Herodotus to Nietzsche.* 2d ed. Manchester: St. Jerome, 2002.

Roe, Mary F., and Carol Vukelich. "Literacy Histories: Categories of Influence." *Reading Research and Instruction* 37 (1998): 281–95.

Rohrbach, Peter T. *American Issue: The U.S. Postage Stamp, 1842–1869.* Washington, D.C.: Smithsonian Institution Press, 1984.

Rose, Anne C. *Victorian America and the Civil War.* New York: Cambridge Univ. Press, 1992.

Rose, Jonathan. *The Intellectual Life of the British Working Classes.* New Haven, Conn.: Yale Univ. Press, 2001.

Rosenthal, William J. *Spectacles and Other Vision Aids: A History and Guide to Collecting.* San Francisco: Norman, 1996.

Rothermel, Beth Ann. "A Sphere of Noble Action: Gender, Rhetoric, and Influence at a Nineteenth-Century Massachusetts State Normal School." *Rhetoric Society Quarterly* 33 (2003): 35–64.

Rothman, Ellen K. *Hands and Hearts: A History of Courtship in America.* New York: Basic Books, 1984.

Rothman, Sheila M. *Living in the Shadow of Death: Tuberculosis and the Social Experience of Illness in America.* New York: Basic Books, 1994.

Rowell, George. "A Lyceum Sketchbook." *Nineteenth Century Theatre Research* 6 (1978): 1–23.

Rubin, Joan Shelley. "'They Flash Upon That Inward Eye': Poetry Recitation and American Readers." *Proceedings of the American Antiquarian Society* 106, pt. 2 (1997): 273–300.

Rudé, George F. E. *The Crowd in the French Revolution.* Oxford: Clarendon Press, 1959.

Ruoff, A. LaVonne Brown, and Jerry Washington Ward, eds. *Redefining American Literary History.* New York: Modern Language Association of America, 1990.

Rush, Nixon Orwin. *The History of College Libraries in Maine.* Worcester, Mass.: Clark Univ. Library, 1946.

Ryan, Barbara, and Amy M. Thomas, eds. *Reading Acts: U.S. Readers' Interactions with Literature, 1800–1950.* Knoxville: Univ. of Tennessee Press, 2002.

Ryan, Mary P. *Civic Wars: Democracy and Public Life in the American City during the Nineteenth Century.* Berkeley and Los Angeles: Univ. of California Press, 1997.

———. *Cradle of the Middle Class: The Family in Oneida County, New York, 1790–1865.* New York: Cambridge Univ. Press, 1981.

———. *The Empire of the Mother: American Writing About Domesticity, 1830–1860.* New York: Haworth, 1982.

Salado, Régis. "Lecteurs empiriques et 'lecteur idéal': Contribution aux études de réception." In *Le Comparatisme aujourd'hui,* edited by Sylvie Ballestra-Puech and Jean-Marc Moura, 65–80. Villeneuve d'Ascq, France: Université Charles de Gaulle, 1999.

Salvatori, Mariolina Rizzi, ed. *Pedagogy: Disturbing History, 1819–1929.* Pittsburgh: Univ. of Pittsburgh Press, 1996.

Saum, Lewis O. *The Popular Mood of Pre–Civil War America.* Westport, Conn.: Greenwood Press, 1980.

Savage, William S. *Controversy over the Distribution of Abolition Literature, 1830–1860.* New York: Negro Universities Press, 1968.

Scannell, Paddy, Philip Schlesinger, and Colin Sparks, eds. *Culture and Power: A Media, Culture and Society Reader.* London: Sage, 1992.

Schama, Simon. *Dead Certainties: (Unwarranted Speculations).* New York: Alfred A. Knopf, 1991.

Schantz, Mark S. "Religious Tracts, Evangelical Reform, and the Market Revolution in Antebellum America." *Journal of the Early Republic* 17 (1997): 425–66.

Schechter, Abraham A. *Basic Book Repair Methods.* Englewood, Colo.: Libraries Unlimited, 1999.

Schick, Frank Leopold. *The Paperbound Book in America: The History of Paperbacks and Their European Background.* New York: R. R. Bowker, 1958.

Schivelbusch, Wolfgang. *Disenchanted Night: The Industrialization of Light in the Nineteenth-Century.* Translated by Angela Davies. Berkeley: Univ. of California Press, 1988.

Schlissel, Lillian. *Women's Diaries of the Westward Journey.* New York: Schocken Books, 1982.

Schmidt, Leigh Eric. *Consumer Rites: The Buying and Selling of American Holidays.* Princeton, N.J.: Princeton Univ. Press, 1995.

———. "The Fashioning of a Modern Holiday: St. Valentine's Day, 1840–1870." *Winterthur Portfolio* 28 (1993): 209–45.

———. "Practices of Exchange: From Market Culture to Gift Economy in the Interpretation of American Religion." In *Lived Religion in America: Toward a History of Practice,* edited by David D. Hall, 69–91. Princeton, N.J.: Princeton Univ. Press, 1997.

Schob, David E. *Hired Hands and Plowboys: Farm Labor in the Midwest, 1815–60.* Urbana: Univ. of Illinois Press, 1975.

Scholten, Catherine M. *Childbearing in American Society, 1650–1850.* New York: New York Univ. Press, 1985.

Schrift, Alan D., ed. *The Logic of the Gift: Toward an Ethic of Generosity.* New York: Routledge, 1997.

Schulte, Rainer, and John Biguenet, eds. *Theories of Translation: An Anthology of Essays from Dryden to Derrida.* Chicago: Univ. of Chicago Press, 1992.

Schultz, Heidi Maria. "Southern Women Learn to Write, 1830–1860." Ph.D. diss., Univ. of North Carolina at Chapel Hill, 1997.

Schultz, Lucille M. *The Young Composers: Composition's Beginnings in Nineteenth-Century Schools.* Carbondale: Southern Illinois Univ. Press, 1999.

Scott, Alison M. "'These Notions I Imbibed from Writers': The Reading Life of Mary Ann Wodrow Archibald (1762–1841)." Ph.D. diss., Boston Univ., 1995.

———. "'This Cultivated Mind': Reading and Identity in the Nineteenth-Century Reader." In Ryan and Thomas, *Reading Acts,* 29–52.

Scott, Donald M. "Itinerant Lecturers and Lecturing in New England, 1800–1850." In Benes and Benes, *Itinerancy,* 65–75.

———. "The Popular Lecture and the Creation of a Public in Mid-Nineteenth-Century America." *Journal of American History* 66 (1980): 791–809.

Scott, Paula A. *Growing Old in the Early Republic: Spiritual, Social, and Economic Issues, 1790–1830.* New York: Garland, 1997.

———. "'Tis Not the Spring of Life with Me': Aged Women in Their Diaries and Letters, 1790–1830." *Connecticut History* 36 (1995): 12–30.

Shalhope, Robert E. *A Tale of New England: The Diary of Hiram Harwood, Vermont Farmer, 1810–1837.* Baltimore: Johns Hopkins Univ. Press, 2003.

Shera, Jesse Hauk. *Foundations of the Public Library: The Origins of the Public Library Movement in New England, 1629–1855.* Hamden, Conn.: Shoe String Press, 1965.

Sherman, Stuart C. *The Voice of the Whaleman, with an Account of the Nicholson Whaling Collection.* Providence, R.I.: Providence Public Library, 1965.

Shields, David S. *Civil Tongues and Polite Letters in British America.* Chapel Hill: Univ. of North Carolina Press, 1997.

———. "A History of Personal Diary Writing in New England, 1620–1745." Ph.D. diss., Univ. of Chicago, 1982.

Sicherman, Barbara. "Reading and Ambition: M. Carey Thomas and Female Heroism." *American Quarterly* 45 (1993): 73–103.

———. "Reading and Middle-Class Identity in Victorian America: Cultural Consumption, Conspicuous and Otherwise." In Ryan and Thomas, *Reading Acts,* 137–60.

———. "Sense and Sensibility: A Case of Study of Women's Reading in Late-Victorian America." In Davidson, *Reading in America,* 201–26.

Silber, Nina, and Mary Beth Sievens, eds. *Yankee Correspondence: Civil War Letters between New England Soldiers and the Home Front.* Charlottesville: Univ. Press of Virginia, 1996.

Silver, Rollo G. *The American Printer, 1787–1825.* Charlottesville: Bibliographical Society of the Univ. of Virginia, 1967.

———. *Typefounding in America, 1787–1825.* Charlottesville: Univ. Press of Virginia, 1965.

Skallerup, Harry R. *Books Afloat and Ashore: A History of Books, Libraries, and Reading During the Age of Sail.* Hamden, Conn.: Archon Books, 1974.

Smith, Deborah A. "Consuming Passions: Scrapbooks and American Play." *Ephemera Journal* 6 (1993): 63–76.

Smith, Florence C. "Introducing Parlor Theatricals into the American Home." *Performing Arts Resources* 14 (1989): 1–11.

Smith, Steven E., Catherine A. Hastedt, and Donald H. Dyal, eds. *American Book and Magazine Illustrators to 1920.* Detroit: Gale Research, 1998.

Sohn, Katherine K. "Gettin' Above Their Raisin's: Content Analysis of Literacy Narratives." Paper read at the annual meeting of the Conference on College Composition and Communication, Chicago, 1–4 Apr. 1998. ERIC Document Reproduction Service, ED420867.

Sokefeld, Martin. "Debating Self, Identity, and Culture in Anthropology." *Current Anthropology* 40 (1999): 417–47.

Soltow, Lee, and Edward Stevens. *The Rise of Literacy and the Common School in the United States: A Socioeconomic Analysis to 1870.* Chicago: Univ. of Chicago Press, 1981.

Sorby, Angela. "Learning by Heart: Poetry, Pedagogy, and Daily Life in America, 1855–1915." Ph.D. diss., Univ. of Chicago, 1996.

Spawn, Willman. *Bookbinding in America, 1680–1910: From the Collection of Frederick E. Maser.* Bryn Mawr, Pa.: Bryn Mawr College Library, 1983.

Spawn, Willman, and Thomas E. Kinsella. *It's the Ticket: Nineteenth-Century Bookbinding in the British Isles and the United States. . . .* Bryn Mawr, Pa.: Bryn Mawr College Library, 1998.

Spencer, Truman Joseph. *The History of Amateur Journalism.* New York: Fossils, 1957.

Springer, Haskell S., ed. *America and the Sea: A Literary History.* Athens: Univ. of Georgia Press, 1995.

Stabile, Susan M. *Memory's Daughters: The Material Culture of Remembrance in Eighteenth-Century America.* Ithaca, N.Y.: Cornell Univ. Press, 2004.

Staff, Frank. *The Valentine and Its Origins.* New York: Praeger, 1969.

Stainton, Anne L. "A Halifax Sailor's Taste in Poetry: Charles J. Da Freytas's Log and Commonplace-Book, 1841–1852." *Nova Scotia Historical Review* 15 (1995): 60–92.

Stapp, Carol Buchalter. *Afro-Americans in Antebellum Boston: An Analysis of Probate Records.* New York: Garland, 1993.

Starobin, Robert S., ed. *Blacks in Bondage: Letters of American Slaves.* New York: New Viewpoints, 1974.

Stearns, Samuel Horatio. *Life and Select Discourses.* Boston: Josiah A. Stearns, 1838.

Stephens, John S. *Incidents of Travel in Egypt, Arabia Petraea, and the Holy Land.* 2d ed. 2 vols. New York: Harper & Brothers, 1837.

Stern, Madeleine B. *Antiquarian Bookselling in the United States: A History from the Origins to the 1940s.* Westport, Conn.: Greenwood Press, 1985.

———. *Books and Book People in 19th-Century America.* New York: R. R. Bowker, 1978.

———. *Imprints on History: Book Publishers and American Frontiers.* Bloomington: Indiana Univ. Press, 1956.

———, ed. *Publishers for Mass Entertainment in Nineteenth-Century America.* Boston: G. K. Hall, 1980.

Stevenson, Louise L. *The Victorian Homefront: American Thought and Culture, 1860–1880.* New York: Twayne, 1991.

Stewart, Alex. *The Ethnographer's Method.* Thousand Oaks, Calif.: Sage, 1998.

Stewart, David M. "Cultural Work, City Crime, Reading, Pleasure." *American Literary History* 9 (1997): 676–701.

———. "Reading American Sensationalism: Print, Pleasure, and the Disorder of Books, 1830–1870." Ph.D. diss., Univ. of Chicago, 1997.

Stierle, Karlheinz. "Studium: Perspectives on Institutionalized Modes of Reading." *New Literary History* 22 (1991): 115–27.

Stiverson, Gregory A., and Cynthia Zignego Stiverson. *Books Both Useful and Entertaining: A Study of Book Purchases and Reading Habits of Virginians in the Mid-Eighteenth Century.* Williamsburg, Va.: Colonial Williamsburg Foundation, 1977.

Stoddard, Roger. *Marks in Books, Illustrated and Explained.* Cambridge: Houghton Library, Harvard Univ., 1985.

———. *"Put a Resolute Hart to a Steep Hill": William Gowans, Antiquary and Bookseller.* New York: Book Arts Press, 1990.

Stoneman, Patsy. *Brontë Transformations: The Cultural Dissemination of Jane Eyre and Wuthering Heights.* New York: Prentice Hall, 1996.

Stowe, Harriet Beecher. *The Christian Slave: A Drama Founded on a Portion of Uncle Tom's Cabin.* Boston: Phillips, Sampson, 1855.

Stuart, Moses. *A Grammar of the Hebrew Language.* Andover, Mass.: Flagg & Gould, 1828.

Suleiman, Susan R. "Varieties of Audience-Oriented Criticism." In *The Reader in the Text: Essays on Audience and Interpretation,* edited by Susan R. Suleiman and Inge Crosman, 3–45. Princeton, N.J.: Princeton Univ. Press, 1980.

Sutherland, Daniel E. *Americans and Their Servants: Domestic Service in the United States from 1800 to 1920.* Baton Rouge: Louisiana State Univ. Press, 1981.

Svenbro, Jesper. *Phrasikleia: An Anthropology of Reading in Ancient Greece.* Translated by Janet Lloyd. Ithaca, N.Y.: Cornell Univ. Press, 1993.

Sweet, Leonard I., ed. *Communication and Change in American Religious History.* Grand Rapids, Mich.: William B. Eerdmans, 1993.

Sweeting, Adam W. *Reading Houses and Building Books: Andrew Jackson Downing and the Architecture of Popular Antebellum Literature, 1835–1855.* Hanover, N.H.: Univ. Press of New England, 1996.

Talarico, Ross. *Spreading the Word: Poetry and the Survival of Community in America.* Durham, N.C.: Duke Univ. Press, 1995.

Tanselle, G. Thomas. *Guide to the Study of United States Imprints.* 2 vols. Cambridge: Harvard Univ. Press, 1971.

———. *Literature and Artifacts.* Charlottesville: Bibliographical Society of the Univ. of Virginia, 1998.

Tatham, David. *The Lure of the Striped Pig: The Illustration of Popular Music in America, 1820–1870.* Barre, Mass.: Imprint Society, 1973.

Tchen, John Kuo Wei. *New York Before Chinatown: Orientalism and the Shaping of American Culture, 1776–1882.* Baltimore: Johns Hopkins Univ. Press, 1999.

Tebbel, John. *A History of Book Publishing in the United States.* Vol. 1, *The Creation of an Industry: 1630–1865.* New York: R. R. Bowker, 1972.

Temin, Peter. "The Industrialization of New England, 1830–1880." In *Engines of Enterprise: An Economic History of New England,* edited by Peter Temin, 109–52. Cambridge: Harvard Univ. Press, 2000.

Thomas, Amy M. "Reading the Silences: Documenting the History of American Tract Society Readers in the Antebellum South." In Ryan and Thomas, *Reading Acts,* 107–36.

Thompson, Lawrance. "The Printing and Publishing Activities of the American Tract Society from 1825 to 1850." *Papers of the Bibliographical Society of America* 35 (1941): 81–114.

Thompson, Ralph. *American Literary Annuals and Gift Books, 1825–1865.* New York: H. W. Wilson, 1936.

Thornton, Tamara Plakins. *Handwriting in America: A Cultural History.* New Haven, Conn.: Yale Univ. Press, 1996.

Tilley, Christopher Y. *Material Culture and Text: The Art of Ambiguity.* London: Routledge, 1991.

———, ed. *Reading Material Culture: Structuralism, Hermeneutics, and Post-Structuralism.* Oxford: Blackwell, 1990.

Todd, Emily B. "Antebellum Libraries in Richmond and New Orleans and the Search for the Practices and Preferences of 'Real Readers.'" *American Studies* 42 (2001): 195–209.

Tomlinson, William, and Richard Masters. *Bookcloth, 1823–1980.* Stockport, Eng.: D. Tomlinson, 1997.

Tompkins, Jane P. "The Reader in History: The Changing Shape of Literary Response." In Tompkins, *Reader-Response Criticism,* 201–32.

———, ed. *Reader-Response Criticism: From Formalism to Post-Structuralism.* Baltimore: Johns Hopkins Univ. Press, 1980.

Trachtenberg, Alan. *Reading American Photographs: Images as History, Mathew Brady to Walker Evans.* New York: Hill and Wang, 1989.

"The Tree of Knowledge." *Harper's New Monthly Magazine* 7 (Aug. 1853): 362–71.

Trotter, David. *Circulation: Defoe, Dickens and the Economies of the Novel.* Basingstoke: Macmillan, 1988.

Tryon, Warren S. *Parnassus Corner: A Life of James T. Fields, Publisher to the Victorians.* Boston: Houghton Mifflin, 1963.

Tryon, Warren S., and William Charvat, eds. *The Cost Books of Ticknor and Fields: And Their Predecessors, 1832–1858.* New York: Bibliographical Society of America, 1949.

Ulrich, Laurel Thatcher. *The Age of Homespun: Objects and Stories in the Creation of an American Myth.* New York: Knopf, 2001.

———. *A Midwife's Tale: The Life of Martha Ballard Based on Her Diary, 1785–1812.* New York: Knopf, 1990.

Upton, Dell. "Ethnicity, Authenticity, and Invented Traditions." *Historical Archaeology* 30 (1996): 1–7.

U.S. Bureau of the Census. *Historical Statistics of the United States, Colonial Times to 1970.* Washington, D.C.: GPO, 1975.

U.S. Post Office Department. *United States Domestic Postage Rates, 1789 to 1956.* Washington, D.C.: GPO, 1956.

Veblen, Thorstein. *Theory of the Leisure Class.* 1899. Reprint, Fairfield, N.J.: A. M. Kelly, 1991.

Vickery, Amanda. "Women and the World of Goods: A Lancashire Consumer and Her Possessions." In Brewer and Porter, *Consumption and the World of Goods,* 274–301.

Waits, William Burnell. *The Modern Christmas in America: A Cultural History of Gift Giving.* New York: New York Univ. Press, 1993.

Warner, Sam Bass. *Streetcar Suburbs: The Process of Growth in Boston, 1870–1900.* Cambridge: Harvard Univ. Press, 1978.

Watts, George B. "The Teaching of French in the United States: A History." *French Review* 37 (1963): 3–165.

Watts, Isaac. *The Improvement of the Mind; or, A Supplement to the Art of Logick. . . .* London: James Brackstone, 1741. Reprint, Boston: J. Loring, 1833.

Webster, Noah. *The Elementary Spelling Book; Being an Improvement on the American Spelling Book.* New York: G. F. Cooledge & Brother, 1850.

Weiner, Annette B. *Inalienable Possessions: The Paradox of Keeping-While-Giving.* Berkeley and Los Angeles: Univ. of California Press, 1992.

Weisberg, Barbara. *Talking to the Dead: Kate and Maggie Fox and the Rise of Spiritualism.* San Francisco: HarperCollins, 2004.

Weiss, Harry B. *American Letter-writers, 1698–1943.* New York: New York Public Library, 1945.

Weitenkampf, Frank. *American Graphic Art.* New York: H. Holt, 1912.

Wells, James M. "Book Typography in the United States of America." In *Book Typography in Europe and the United States of America, 1815–1965,* edited by Kenneth Day, 325–70. London: Benn, 1966.

Welter, Rush. *The Mind of America, 1820–1860.* New York: Columbia Univ. Press, 1975.

Whitehill, Walter Muir. *Boston Public Library: A Centennial History.* Cambridge: Harvard Univ. Press, 1956.

Wiley, Bell Irvin. *The Life of Billy Yank: The Common Soldier of the Union.* Indianapolis: Bobbs-Merrill, 1952.

Wilk, Richard R. *The Household Economy: Reconsidering the Domestic Mode of Production.* Boulder, Colo.: Westview Press, 1989.

Williams, Gary. *Hungry Heart: The Literary Emergence of Julia Ward Howe.* Amherst: Univ. of Massachusetts Press, 1999.

Willis, William. *The History of Portland, from 1632 to 1864.* 2d rev. ed. Portland, Maine: Bailey & Noyes, 1865.

Wilson, Douglas L., ed. *Jefferson's Literary Commonplace Book.* Princeton, N.J.: Princeton Univ. Press, 1989.

Windhover, Ruth. "Literature in the Nineteenth Century." *English Journal* 68 (1979): 28–33.

Wink, Amy L. *She Left Nothing in Particular: The Autobiographical Legacy of Nineteenth-Century Women's Diaries.* Knoxville: Univ. of Tennessee Press, 2001.

Winterer, Caroline. *The Culture of Classicism: Ancient Greece and Rome in American Intellectual Life, 1780–1910.* Baltimore: Johns Hopkins Univ. Press, 2002.

———. "Victorian Antigone: Classicism and Women's Education in America, 1840–1900." *American Quarterly* 53 (2001): 70–93.

Wise, Isaac Mayer. "The World of My Books." Edited and translated by Albert H. Friedlander. In Marcus, *Critical Studies* 1:144–85.

Wolf, Edwin. *From Gothic Windows to Peacocks: American Embossed Leather Bindings, 1825–1855.* Philadelphia: Library Company of Philadelphia, 1990.

Wood, Marcus. *Blind Memory: Visual Representations of Slavery in England and America.* New York: Routledge, 2000.

Wosh, Peter J. *Spreading the Word: The Bible Business in Nineteenth-Century America.* Ithaca, N.Y.: Cornell Univ. Press, 1994.

Wright, Conrad Edick. *The Transformation of Charity in Postrevolutionary New England.* Boston: Northeastern Univ. Press, 1992.

Wright, Richardson Little. *Hawkers and Walkers in Early America: Strolling Peddlers, Preachers, Lawyers, Doctors, Players, and Others from the Beginning to the Civil War.* New York: F. Ungar, 1965.

Wright, William Winfield. "Extra-Institutional Sites of Composition Instruction in the Nineteenth Century." Ph.D. diss., Univ. of Arizona, 1994.

Wyss, Hilary E. *Writing Indians: Literacy, Christianity, and Native Community in Early America.* Amherst: Univ. of Massachusetts Press, 2000.

Yates, Frances Amelia. *The Art of Memory.* London: Routledge, 1966.

Yellin, Jean Fagan, and John C. Van Horne, eds. *The Abolitionist Sisterhood: Women's Political Culture in Antebellum America.* Ithaca, N.Y.: Cornell Univ. Press, 1994.

Zboray, Ronald J. *A Fictive People: Antebellum Economic Development and the American Reading Public.* New York: Oxford Univ. Press, 1993.

———. "Technology and the Character of Community Life in Antebellum America: The Role of Story Papers." In *Sweet, Communication and Change,* 185–215.

Zboray, Ronald J., and Mary Saracino Zboray. "Books, Reading, and the World of Goods in Antebellum New England." *American Quarterly* 48 (Dec. 1996): 587–622.

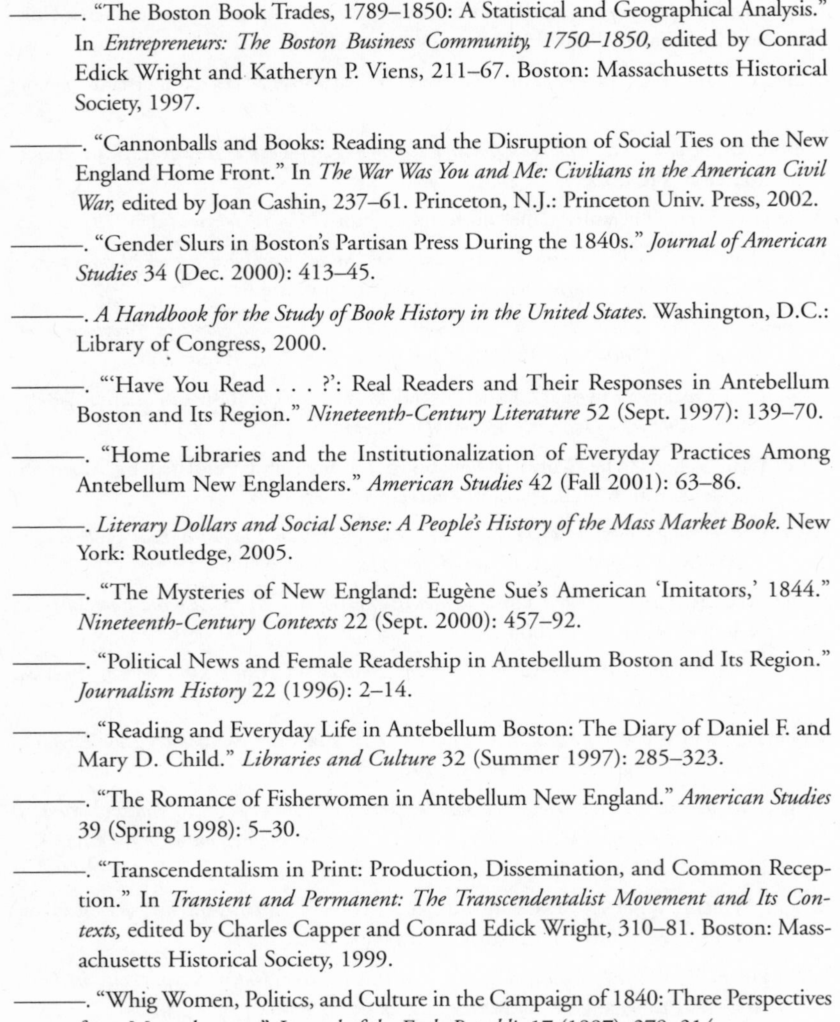

———. "The Boston Book Trades, 1789–1850: A Statistical and Geographical Analysis." In *Entrepreneurs: The Boston Business Community, 1750–1850,* edited by Conrad Edick Wright and Katheryn P. Viens, 211–67. Boston: Massachusetts Historical Society, 1997.

———. "Cannonballs and Books: Reading and the Disruption of Social Ties on the New England Home Front." In *The War Was You and Me: Civilians in the American Civil War,* edited by Joan Cashin, 237–61. Princeton, N.J.: Princeton Univ. Press, 2002.

———. "Gender Slurs in Boston's Partisan Press During the 1840s." *Journal of American Studies* 34 (Dec. 2000): 413–45.

———. *A Handbook for the Study of Book History in the United States.* Washington, D.C.: Library of Congress, 2000.

———. "'Have You Read . . . ?': Real Readers and Their Responses in Antebellum Boston and Its Region." *Nineteenth-Century Literature* 52 (Sept. 1997): 139–70.

———. "Home Libraries and the Institutionalization of Everyday Practices Among Antebellum New Englanders." *American Studies* 42 (Fall 2001): 63–86.

———. *Literary Dollars and Social Sense: A People's History of the Mass Market Book.* New York: Routledge, 2005.

———. "The Mysteries of New England: Eugène Sue's American 'Imitators,' 1844." *Nineteenth-Century Contexts* 22 (Sept. 2000): 457–92.

———. "Political News and Female Readership in Antebellum Boston and Its Region." *Journalism History* 22 (1996): 2–14.

———. "Reading and Everyday Life in Antebellum Boston: The Diary of Daniel F. and Mary D. Child." *Libraries and Culture* 32 (Summer 1997): 285–323.

———. "The Romance of Fisherwomen in Antebellum New England." *American Studies* 39 (Spring 1998): 5–30.

———. "Transcendentalism in Print: Production, Dissemination, and Common Reception." In *Transient and Permanent: The Transcendentalist Movement and Its Contexts,* edited by Charles Capper and Conrad Edick Wright, 310–81. Boston: Massachusetts Historical Society, 1999.

———. "Whig Women, Politics, and Culture in the Campaign of 1840: Three Perspectives from Massachusetts." *Journal of the Early Republic* 17 (1997): 279–314.

Index

Page numbers in **boldface** refer to illustrations.